Ius Comparatum – Global Studies in Comparative Law

Volume 52

As globalization proceeds, the significance of the comparative approach in legal scholarship increases. The IACL / AIDC with almost 800 members is the major universal organization promoting comparative research in law and organizing congresses with hundreds of participants in all parts of the world. The results of those congresses should be disseminated and be available for legal scholars in a single book series which would make both the Academy and its contribution to comparative law more visible. The series aims to publish the scholarship emerging from the congresses of IACL / AIDC, including: 1. of the General Congresses of Comparative Law, which take place every 4 years (Brisbane 2002; Utrecht 2006, Washington 2010, Vienna 2014, Fukuoka 2018 etc.) and which generate (a) one volume of General Reports edited by the local organizers of the Congress; (b) up to 30 volumes of selected thematic reports dealing with the topics of the single sections of the congress and containing the General Report as well as the National Reports of that section; these volumes would be edited by the General Reporters of the respective sections; 2. the volumes containing selected contributions to the smaller (2-3 days) thematic congresses which take place between the International Congresses (Mexico 2008; Taipei 2012; Montevideo 2016 etc.); these congresses have a general theme such as "Codification" or "The Enforcement of Law" and will be edited by the local organizers of the respective Congress. All publications may contain contributions in English and French, the official languages of the Academy.

More information about this series at http://www.springer.com/series/11943

Académie Internationale de Droit Comparé
International Academy of Comparative Law

Mads Andenas • Jeremy Perelman •
Christian Scharling
Editors

The Fight Against Poverty and the Right to Development

Springer

Editors
Mads Andenas
University of Oslo
Oslo, Norway

Jeremy Perelman
Sciences Po
Paris, France

Christian Scharling
Sciences Po
Paris, France

ISSN 2214-6881 ISSN 2214-689X (electronic)
Ius Comparatum – Global Studies in Comparative Law
ISBN 978-3-030-57323-2 ISBN 978-3-030-57324-9 (eBook)
https://doi.org/10.1007/978-3-030-57324-9

This Springer imprint is published by the registered company Springer Nature Switzerland AG.
The registered company address is: Gewerbestrasse 11, 6330 Cham, Switzerland

Preface

The fight against poverty has made it back to the core of development thinking and policy-making since the turn of the century. Although limited to certain areas and arenas, a movement of 'making poverty history' has taken ground in popular consciousness and generated a range of initiatives, from anti-globalization social movements, to televised charities and to high-profile, multi-billion dollar philanthropy.

Within the discipline of law, and while it has been argued that law and in particular the history and structure of international law have and continue to contribute to the patterns of poverty, the fight against poverty is primarily embedded in economic, social and cultural rights (ESCRs) and the debates that surround them. ESCRs are protected under various international and regional treaties, as well as in national constitutions. The Universal Declaration of Human Rights (UDHR) of 1948 provides a range of poverty-related economic and social rights. The International Covenant on Economic, Social and Cultural Rights of 1966 is the most comprehensive treaty that provides protection of these rights at the international level.

Different legal approaches to poverty are taken in domestic constitutions and legislation. Some constitutions recognize the right to an adequate standard of living, and rights to work, health, education, housing and water that may contribute to the fight against poverty.

The Right to Development (RtD) was introduced in various international instruments of the 1970s and 1980s and was then reaffirmed by the 1993 Vienna Declaration and Programme of Action. An open-ended Intergovernmental Working Group on the Right to Development recently held its twentieth session, and the United Nations (UN) Human Rights Council appointed a Special Rapporteur on the Right to Development in 2016. The very concept of the RtD remains, however, controversial. One discussion relates to whether the RtD is a right for a group of people or an individual right, or both. The way in which the RtD is included in the mandate of several UN bodies varies and does not resolve the issue.

The position of some States, such as the United States, is in opposition or is reluctant to recognize development as an international human right. At the same time, some of these opposing States have development programmes with striking similarities to the substance of the RtD.

The current volume scrutinizes these contentions and controversies while also more broadly investigating the legal framework around the fight against poverty. While research already exists on the legal framework around the fight against poverty and specifically the RtD, this volume is unique in comparatively examining the legal state of play in Europe, North and Latin America, Asia and Africa. Furthermore, the broad nature of the volume provides a range of interesting analyses and new perspectives. Ultimately, this volume tries to explore commonalities and differences between various jurisdictions to further investigate law and its potential role in the fight against poverty.

The volume consists of one general report, as well as eleven national reports. Olivier De Schutter, professor and UN Special Rapporteur on Extreme Poverty and Human Rights, also provided a thematic report on the international dimension of the RtD. The general report and the individual reports were prepared ahead of the 20th Congress of the International Academy of Comparative Law in Fukuoka, Japan, from 22 to 28 July 2018. The questionnaire prepared by general rapporteurs and editors, Mads Andenas and Jeremy Perelman, is included at the end of this volume.

At this stage, we want to thank Christian Scharling without whom this volume would not have been published. He has provided assistance and very full drafts at the highest level throughout the process leading up to the Congress and the publication of this volume. It has been a great pleasure to work with so many great authorities in this field of law who from various jurisdictions have contributed. Special thanks go to Professor Diego P. Fernàndez Arroyo whose support as the Secretary General of the International Academy of Comparative Law has been constant and generous, as well as for his assistance in including this volume in the *Ius Comparatum* series.

Last but not least, we, the editors, express our gratitude to Anja Trautmann, Abdus Salam Mazumder and Kay Stoll at Springer and Sabarigirinathan Thanikachalam (Sabari) and Krithika Shivakumar at SPi Global for their patience and warm encouragement in completing this volume.

Oslo, Norway — Mads Andenas QC
Paris, France — Jeremy Perelman
Paris, France — Christian Scharling

Contents

Contributors

Mads Andenas QC University of Oslo, Oslo, Norway

Raymond A. Atuguba University of Ghana, Faculty of Law, Accra, Ghana

Laura Betancur-Restrepo Universidad de los Andes, Faculty of Law, Bogotá, Colombia

Veronika Bílková Department of International Law, Charles University in Prague, Faculty of Law, Prague, Czech Republic

Aristoteles Constantinides University of Cyprus, Nicosia, Cyprus

Fons Coomans UNESCO Chair in Human Rights and Peace, Maastricht Centre for Human Rights, Maastricht University, Maastricht, The Netherlands

Olivier De Schutter Centre for Philosophy of Law (CPDR), Institute for Interdisciplinary Research in Legal Sciences (JUR-I), University of Louvain (UCL), Ottignies-Louvain-la-Neuve, Belgium
International Panel of Experts on Sustainable Food Systems, Brussels, Belgium
UN Committee on Economic, Social and Cultural Rights, Thematic Report, Geneva, Switzerland

Jörg Fedtke University of Passau, Faculty of Law, Passau, Germany

Lauro Gama Jr Private International Law and International Arbitration, PUC-Rio, Rio de Janeiro, Brazil

Lorenzo Gradoni Max Planck Institute Luxembourg for Procedural Law, Luxembourg, Luxembourg

Katarzyna Łasak Faculty of Law and Administration, Uniwersytet Gdański, Gdańsk, Poland

Li-Ju Lee CYCU, Taoyuan, Taiwan

Luca Pasquet Max Planck Institute Luxembourg for Procedural Law, Luxembourg, Luxembourg

Jeremy Perelman Sciences Po, Paris, France

Christian Scharling Sciences Po, Paris, France

Stefanie Schmahl International Law and European Law, Universität Würzburg, Würzburg, Germany

Pavel Šturma Department of International Law, Charles University in Prague, Faculty of Law, Prague, Czech Republic

Peggy ter Vrugt Maastricht Centre for Human Rights, Maastricht University, Maastricht, The Netherlands

Chapter 1
The Fight Against Poverty and the Right to Development: General Report

Mads Andenas, Jeremy Perelman, and Christian Scharling

Abstract This general report conducts a comparative study from two analytical points of view. First, it accounts for the legal dimensions of the fight against poverty and the Right to Development (RtD) as seen from domestic law. It examines the domestic legal tools such as constitutional law, which contribute to the fight against poverty and the RtD. Second, the general report accounts for the domestic contributions to the international legal framework. The report also examines crosscutting themes in relation to the fight against poverty and the RtD. The general report is based on several national reports and one thematic report, which are included as part of the overall volume.

Abbreviations

CPRs	Civil and Political Rights
ESCRs	Economic, Social and Cultural Rights
EU	European Union
ICESCR	The International Covenant on Economic, Social and Cultural Rights of 1966
MDGs	Millennium Development Goals
NGOs	Non-Governmental Organisations

The authors would like to express their gratitude to Professor Malcom Langford, Oslo, and Professor Tomaso Ferrando, Antwerpen, for useful comments on earlier drafts of this general report.

M. Andenas
University of Oslo, Oslo, Norway
e-mail: mads.andenas@jus.uio.no

J. Perelman · C. Scharling (✉)
Sciences Po, Paris, France
e-mail: jeremy.perelman@sciencespo.fr; christian.scharling@sciencespo.fr

M. Andenas et al. (eds.), *The Fight Against Poverty and the Right to Development*, Ius Comparatum - Global Studies in Comparative Law 52,
https://doi.org/10.1007/978-3-030-57324-9_1

RtD	Right to Development
SDGs	Sustainable Development Goals
UN	United Nations

Introduction

The fight against poverty[1] and the RtD are not constrained to one policy arena or one field of inquiry.

Following a long period during which most actors in the development field construed poverty alleviation as a component of development, or poverty itself as an unfortunate by-product of the development process understood as economic growth, the fight against poverty has emerged at the centre stage of development debates since the turn of the century. A number of initiatives, ranging from social movements to religious and philanthropic initiatives, found some echo in policy-making initiatives.[2]

In the policy-making arena, the international community celebrated the millennium with the adoption of the Millennium Development Goals (MDGs),[3] first of which was the reduction of the proportion of people living in extreme income poverty by half by the year 2015. More recently, in 2015, the United Nations General

[1]The concept and measure of poverty have generated a wide range of debates, in fields including moral and political philosophy, social theory, public and social policy, and development economics. In the latter field, an important distinction is made between absolute poverty (measured in terms of income below fixed income poverty lines) and relative poverty (measured in comparison with other segments of a population), as well as between unidimensional (focusing primarily on income and access to economic resources) and multidimensional approaches (see *e.g.* United Nations Development Program Human Development Index Multidimensional Poverty Index, which measures income as well as basic needs to measure extreme poverty). Among conceptual proponents of the latter, broader approach to poverty, one can point to Amartya Sen's approach to poverty as capability deprivation (see notably Sen 1999). Sen's celebrated approach suggests that poverty is not just a lack of income, but a deprivation of all freedoms that would allow for an individual to flourish and live a life he or she has reason to value (*i.e.* encompassing income but access to other components of "human development" more broadly understood such as literacy, food, drinking water, as well as employment and the ability to participate politically in decision-making processes). Also notable among the multidimensional approaches to poverty is former United Nations Independent Expert on Extreme Poverty Arjun Sengupta's concept of poverty as including a combination of income poverty, human development poverty and social exclusion (entailing the systematic exclusion from opportunities or benefits of development), see Sengupta (2010), pp. 85–89.

[2]For a historical analysis, suggesting that the reasons for a shift towards a focus on poverty as a central goal of development policy-making are numerous and complex, and include the fact that it allowed to overcome disagreement between U.N. agencies and International Financial Institutions such as the World Bank and the International Monetary Fund over neoliberal development "Washington Consensus" policies as a means towards development, see Fukuda-Parr (2017).

[3]The Millennium Declaration was adopted in 2000, which in 2001 gave birth to the MDGs. The United Nations General Assembly formally endorsed the MDGs in 2005. For a thorough analysis, see Fukuda-Parr (2017).

Assembly adopted the Sustainable Development Goals (SDGs), the first target of which now calls for the complete eradication of extreme poverty by 2030. A variety of other aid commitments and debt cancellation initiatives have been announced and celebrated, including the IMF and the World Bank's 1996 Highly Indebted Poor Countries (HPIC) initiative, supplemented in 2010 by the Multilateral Debt Relief Initiative, or the three United International Conferences on Financing for Development which took place in 2002, 2008 and 2015.

In the academic field, post-Cold War works on the 'End of History'[4] gave place to calls for the 'End of Poverty',[5] and questions about the social consequences of Washington Consensus policies of the 1980s and 1990s were raised in terms of poverty and inequality around the world. Proposals by Nobel Prize laureate Amartya Sen that both development and poverty be conceived and evaluated in broader terms than economic growth and income-based poverty, including a set of interdependent 'freedoms' related to both ESCRs as well as CPRs, were among the factors that gave rise to conceptual and methodological debates around new, competing sets of indicators of development. They also played a part, among other factors such as the aftermath of the Rwanda genocide,[6] in leading the United Nations to endorse in 1997 human rights-based approaches to development and the fight against poverty, which aimed to mainstream human rights concerns in policy-making processes. In the meantime, while spectacular progress in "lifting millions out of poverty" has been observed, primarily reflecting China and to a slightly lesser extent India and Latin America's progress in fighting absolute income poverty, an increasingly authoritative set of data suggests that the world's poor have become, and keep becoming, relatively poorer.[7] In the field of moral and political philosophy, scholars such as Thomas Pogge have called for freedom from poverty to be conceived as a human right, and for the recognition of rich countries' collective responsibility in violating the human rights of the world's poor.[8]

How did this all translate in law? In the field of international human rights law, the fight against poverty is closely associated with its underlying determinants, defined in human rights terms.[9] As an example, the absence of the capability to live a healthy

[4]Fukuyama (1992).

[5]Sachs (2005).

[6]For an early analysis of the mainstreaming of human rights in development discourse, see Uvin (2004).

[7]See *e.g.* Cornia (2004) and Milanovic (2016).

[8]Pogge (2002). For a useful discussion, see Langford (2017), pp. 258–298.

[9]The UN Committee on Economic, Social and Cultural Rights defined poverty in 2001 as "*a human condition characterized by the sustained or chronic deprivation of the resources, capabilities, choices, security and power necessary for the enjoyment of an adequate standard of living and other civil, cultural, economic, political and social rights*", in terms that echo Amartya Sen's vision of human rights as interdependent determinants of poverty. The Office of the UN High Commissioner for Human Rights added that poverty-related deprivations are deprivations that are related to the lack of income or access to other productive or economic resources "*not every case of a low level of well-being can be regarded as poverty (. . .) for poverty to exist, a lack of command over*

life, while always a case of a low level of well-being, can only be recognized as poverty if the ill health is caused by lack of access to basic health-care resources. Furthermore, from a positivist perspective, it will be considered a human rights violation if a breach of a state's obligation to respect, protect or fulfil a specific right (by commission or omission) can be identified in the causal chain leading to ill health.

While strong arguments can and have been made about the link between violations of civil and political rights (CPR) and poverty, either as a cause or a consequence of poverty,[10] the fight against poverty is mostly linked with ESCRs. Drawing on the increasingly sophisticated interpretative body of international human rights law on ESCR, such as the notion of minimum core obligations,[11] the obligation of non-retrogression[12] and the obligation of non-discrimination[13] in the fight against poverty, actors such as the United Nations Special Rapporteur on Extreme Poverty and Human Rights were able to make inroads in the international policy-making arena. The Rapporteur, whose mandate was created in 1998, led the U.N. Human Rights Council to adopt in 2012 the wide-ranging Guiding Principles on Extreme Poverty and Human Rights.[14] And the current holder of the mandate, former Chairman of the U.N. Committee on Economic, Social and Cultural Rights Philip Alston, has acquired an important and highly influential media presence in denouncing extreme poverty in human rights terms.[15] In parallel, efforts by human rights lawyers and scholars led to the adoption in 2011 by the Commission of Jurists of the Maastricht Principles on the Extra-Territorial Obligations of States in the area of Economic, Social and Cultural Rights, a set of disputed but increasingly influential doctrinal interpretations of ESCRs.

In parallel to this range of legal institutions and frameworks around which the fight against poverty can be and is often addressed, the concept of the RtD has proved to be resilient, despite its troubled history. The articulation of the RtD, one among other similar proposals to recognize a third generation of collective human rights in the 1970s and 1980s, occurred in the context of a newly configured

---

economic resources must play a role in the causal chain leading to a low level of well-being" (2004).

[10]See *e.g.* Dos Costa (2008).

[11]For a thorough analysis and discussion, see Young (2008).

[12]United Nations Committee on Economic, Social and Cultural Rights General Comment 3, *The Nature of States parties obligations (Art. 2, par. 1)*, 14 December 1990.

[13]United Nations Committee on Economic, Social and Cultural Rights General Comment 20, *Non-discrimination in economic, social and cultural rights* (*art. 2, para. 2, of the International Covenant on Economic, Social and Cultural Rights)*, 2 July 2009.

[14]United Nations Human Rights Council Resolution 21/11, 27 September 2012.

[15]See *e.g.* Carrington, "Climate apartheid: UN expert says human rights may not survive. Right to life is likely to be undermined alongside the rule of law, special rapporteur says", *The Guardian,* 25 June, 2019; Booth & Butler, "UK austerity has inflicted 'great misery' on citizens, UN says. Poverty envoy says callous policies driven by political desire for social re-engineering", *The Guardian,* 16 November 2019.

international stage, and of a specific political agenda. Following the decolonization wave of the 1950–1960s, several influential Third World countries leaders sought to use the entry *en masse* of newly independent countries in United Nations institutions, as well as South-South political alliances such as the Less Developed Countries and the Non-Aligned Movements to frame and claim what emerged as a set of demands for a "New International Economic Order" (NIEO). Linking political liberation and self-determination with economic emancipation based on the sovereign use of natural resources, the NIEO aimed to reconfigure the North-South power structure inherited from colonization and the Bretton-Woods system by writing a new set of rules for the globalized economy. Among the concepts associated with this political moment, a highly disputed proposition was the enshrinement, arguably as a legal version of the political and economic claims attributed to the NIEO, of a collective right to development in the international legal framework.

Originally articulated by Senegalese jurist Keba M'Baye[16] who based it directly on the 1945 UN Charter and the 1948 UDHR, the RtD is often considered as an African contribution to the international human rights legal framework. The RtD first crystallized in its legal form in the UN Commission on Human Rights in 1977.[17] It was then enshrined in Article 22 of the African Charter on Human and People's Rights 1981, which suggests that,

> (1) All peoples shall have the right to their economic, social and cultural development with due regard to their freedom and identity and in the equal enjoyment of the common heritage of mankind. (2) States shall have the duty, individually or collectively, to ensure the exercise of the right to development.[18]

After a decade of lengthy debates, the U.N General Assembly adopted the 1986 Declaration on a Right to Development,[19] which, while marked by North-South political controversy since its adoption, remains an oft cited reference in UN documents,[20] and the object of continuing work by human rights scholars and experts.[21] The Preamble of the Declaration states that,

---

[16]See M'baye (1972). See broader context and discussion in Yusuf (2014, 2016).

[17]UN Commission on Human Rights Res. 4 (XXXIII) (Feb 21, 1977).

[18]African Charter on Human and Peoples' Rights, OAU Doc. CAB/LEG/67/3 (Jun. 27, 1981), art. 22.

[19]Declaration on the Right to Development, UN GA Res. 41/128, U.N. Doc. A/Res/41/128 (Dec. 4, 1986).

[20]The Right to Development was reaffirmed as a "universal and inalienable right and an integral part of fundamental human rights" in the Vienna Declaration and Programme of Action, adopted at the World Conference on Human Rights in 1993 (Vienna Declaration and Programme of Action, UN Doc. A/CONF. 157/23, Jul. 12, 1993, Part I, par. 10).

[21]The Right to Development has survived institutionally, notably through the appointment in 1998 by the UN Commission on Human Rights of Indian economist Arjun Sengupta as the Independent Expert on the Right to Development, the establishment (UN Commission on Human Rights resolution 1998/72) of the open-ended Working Group on the Right to Development (renewed in 2007), and the creation in 2004 of a high-level task force on the implementation of the right to development. See overview at the OHCR home pages, http://www.ohchr.org/EN/Issues/

> . . .development is a comprehensive economic, social, cultural and political process, which aims at the constant improvement of the well-being of the entire population and of all individuals on the basis of their active, free and meaningful participation in development and in the fair distribution of benefits resulting therefrom.[22]

The controversies around the RtD focus on several issues.[23] One relates to whether the RtD is linked to the right to self-determination and can be qualified as jus cogens. Another dispute, which led some countries including the United States to reject the recognition of the RtD, relates to the perception that it will be used as an excuse for governments in developing countries to justify 'repressive' human rights policies, and the main worry has been for the protection of property rights and contractual relationships. A related dispute, of a doctrinal nature, concerns whether the holders of the RtD are people, individuals or States—and whether it is a group right of peoples, an individual right, or both. Scholarly debates have pitted arguments about the related indeterminacy and unenforceability of this right, against proponents of the RtD as a synthetic, "umbrella" right with both individual and collective dimensions or, going further, as a normative framework for global North-South redistribution.

Beyond ESCRs and the debates around the RtD, several related key contemporary themes, issues or debates can be considered to be relevant in the context of the fight against poverty. They include the issue of trade and human rights; the emerging field of human rights and investment, and the broader focus on business and human rights; questions related to human rights and the financing of development; the effects of foreign debt and other related international financial obligations of States on both development and the fight against poverty; the impact of the global financial crisis on human rights; the relationship between human rights and climate change; and indicators and the right to development.

It is important to underline how various ESCRs, the RtD and the fight against poverty are inextricably linked for the purpose of this general report. Thus, norms, expressions and various rights will be referenced and used interchangeably in the general report as well as in the national and thematic reports.

The general report conducts a comparative legal analysis based on several reports prepared by national and thematic rapporteurs.[24] It is divided into three main parts,

---

Development/Pages/Introduction.aspx [visited: 20.02.2020] and the Report of the Working Group on the Right to Development on its seventeenth session (Geneva, 25 April–3 May 2016).

[22]Declaration on the Right to Development, UN GA Res. 41/128, U.N. Doc. A/Res/41/128 (Dec. 4, 1986).

[23]Scholarly debates about and around the RtD have carried on long after 1986, and include critiques by prominent human rights scholars (*e.g.* Alston 2005, p. 755) as well as critical voices from the Global North (e.g. see Clapham and Marks 2005) or the Global South (*e.g.* Shivji 1989; Ibhawoh 2011), p. 76. For a useful analysis, see *also* Marks (2010).

[24]In total twelve reports prepared by sixteen rapporteurs. See above an overview of the contributors to this volume. In addition, Geneviève Dufour and David Pavot also provided a national report for Canada, but it is not published. Moreover, we have ourselves contributed from the contexts of France and Norway and have used input from our session at the 20th Congress of the International Academy of Comparative Law. In this regard, we would like to thank all participants at the session

which were identified in a questionnaire prepared in 2017.[25] In general, the questionnaire assisted in guiding the work of the national and thematic rapporteurs.

The first part deals with domestic law, including rights and concomitant remedies available to individuals under the RtD and the fight against poverty. Thus, this section contributes to a comparative analysis of domestic law and its relationship to international law obligations.

The second part focuses on the domestic contributions to the fight against poverty and the RtD at the international level. This will typically be through the development aid programmes of individual countries or through other means of international cooperation. Contributions by any single State will not, on their own, generate new norms of international law. However, they may assist in the clarification of other sources of international law and in the development of customary law. The use of 'progressive realization' as a standard for ESCRs in the UN conventions makes the interaction between domestic and international law particularly interesting. As such, this standard is one mechanism for determining the stages of realisation. Looking at different domestic jurisdictions provide a comparative framework and assist in establishing what the substantive rights and effective remedies mean.

The third part focuses on some of the crosscutting themes: Post-conflict contexts, international trade law and investment law as well as business and human rights. These themes were identified in the national and thematic reports, as well as during the session on the fight against poverty and the RtD at the 20th Congress of the International Academy of Comparative Law in Fukuoka Japan on 24 July 2018.

Before going to the first part of the general report, we want to note some of the shortfalls of the general report. For example, having only one national report from the regions of Africa, Latin America and Asia is not enough to make a full analysis of the state-of-play in relation to the fight against poverty and the RtD worldwide. Still, the perspectives from each of the national reports are important and they assist in the comparative legal analysis of the fight against poverty and the RtD both domestically and at the international stage. We return to the gaps of the general report in our final conclusion.

Domestic Law and Remedies

General Remarks

This part of the general report addresses the fight against poverty and the RtD within a domestic context. The focus is on the legal nature of the instruments and the

and especially our moderator Lauro Gama Jr., who also provided valuable input from the context in Brazil.

[25] The questionnaire prepared for the 20th Congress of the International Academy of Comparative Law is included in annex at the end of this chapter.

judicial remedies available to individuals. For example, to what extent constitutional ESCRs protection is justiciable to individuals versus if such constitutional protection is rather to guide overall State policy.

By comparing various jurisdictions and their domestic reality, the idea is to find similarities and differences between them, which can help inform the current legal framework for the fight against poverty and the RtD at domestic level.

Relationship to International Law

In the following section we will compare ESCRs with other international obligations in how such rights and obligations are transposed into domestic law. Secondly, we will explore some of the key international legal instruments in the fight against poverty and to what extent they are implemented by States. To this end, we focus on the States accounted for in the national reports.

How Are ESCR in International Law Transposed Into Domestic Law?

For this section, we imagined that there could have been a difference in the transposition of ESCRs versus other international obligations. Such differences could have been to apply extraterritorial effects to the legislation enacted so that for example multinational companies cannot escape domestic labour legislation by moving production abroad. Although not necessarily tied to transposing ESCRs obligations, France has recently done so with its vigilance law.[26] Moreover, another trend could have been generally looser justiciable frameworks for ESCRs, *i.e.* viewing the transposition of ESCRs as guidelines as opposed to implementing them and giving them justiciable effect.

From the national reports submitted, there has been little evidence to suggest such differences. Three national reports specifically mentioned that there exists no difference in the implementation of ESCRs compared to other international obligations.[27] However, even though the national reports of this general report largely did not deal with or did not find such differences, several previous studies have found interesting examples of it.[28] We may add the stages of the ICESCR implementation in Norway to illustrate different approaches. After ratification the implementation was supposed to take place in legislation and administrative practice. In 1994 a new article 110 c was introduced in the Norwegian Constitution incorporating Norway's international human rights. In 1999 a human rights act was adopted, expressly incorporating

[26] See section 3.4 for more information.

[27] Germany, Poland, Czechia.

[28] For a survey of a broader sample of countries, see Jung et al. (2014), pp. 1043–1094. See *also* Nolan et al. (2009).

among other human rights conventions the ICESCR by including it as a schedule to the act and providing that its provisions should prevail in case of conflict with other legislation. In 2014 new constitutional provisions about children's rights, the right to education and minimum subsistence were added to the provisions about the right to work (from the 1950s) and workers' codetermination (from the 1970s). On the other hand, Norway has not signed the ICESCR Optional Protocol, so individuals are left without any right of complaint to the treaty body.

The national report of the United States, did account for the lack of transposition of ESCRs, as for example the signing of the ICESCR has never led to ratification. The reason for this lack of transposition of ESCRs in the United States should be found in its political landscape.[29]

Another interesting perspective was brought in by the Colombian rapporteur, which accounted for the interaction between international and national legal frameworks in Colombia. Inspired in part by French constitutionalism, Colombia has since the mid-1990s used a concept, which allows international norms that are not directly mentioned in the constitution to still have the same effect and hierarchy.[30] Having the same hierarchy, has led the Colombian Constitutional Court to recognize the observations made by international monitoring bodies of ESCRs as relevant interpretive criteria of the Colombian constitutional ESCRs framework.[31] Similarly, Ghana's Supreme Court, which is also the Constitutional Court, has found the international right to work applicable within Ghana's legal order, despite the right is not explicitly provided for in Ghanaian law.[32]

To briefly summarize, it seems that for the national reports ESCRs are generally implemented the same way as for example CPRs and other international obligations, however, some jurisdictions provided interesting examples of how ESCRs may be less or more expansively applied as according to the national contexts. It is important to underline that even though the national reports of the general report did not find such differences, there are much work to suggest that there does indeed exist such differences in the implementation of ESCRs and CPRs.

[29]See in this volume Fedtke, Poverty and the Right to Development in the United States of America, section 2.

[30]See in this volume Betancur-Restrepo, the Colombian Legal Framework for Social Rights and the Challenges of a Post-Conflict Society, section 4.1.

[31]See in this volume Betancur-Restrepo, the Colombian Legal Framework for Social Rights and the Challenges of a Post-Conflict Society, section 4.1.

[32]See in this volume Atuguba, the Fight against Poverty and the Right to Development: The Ghana National Chapter, section 1.1.

Table 1.1 Implementation overview of key instruments in selected jurisdictions

States	ICESCR	ICESCR Optional Protocol	RtD Declaration 1986	Vienna Dec. and Programme of Action
Canada	Ratified/Adopted	No Action/Opposed	Ratified/Adopted	Ratified/Adopted
Colombia	Ratified/Adopted	No Action/Opposed	Ratified/Adopted	Ratified/Adopted
Cyprus	Ratified/Adopted	No Action/Opposed	Ratified/Adopted	Ratified/Adopted
Czech Republic	Ratified/Adopted	No Action/Opposed	Ratified/Adopted	Ratified/Adopted
France	Ratified/Adopted	Ratified/Adopted	Ratified/Adopted	Ratified/Adopted
Germany[a]	Ratified/Adopted	No Action/Opposed	Ratified/Adopted / Signed/Abstained	Ratified/Adopted
Ghana	Ratified/Adopted	Signed/Abstained	Ratified/Adopted	Ratified/Adopted
Italy	Ratified/Adopted	Ratified/Adopted	Ratified/Adopted	Ratified/Adopted
Netherlands	Ratified/Adopted	Signed/Abstained	Ratified/Adopted	Ratified/Adopted
Norway	Ratified/Adopted	No Action/Opposed	Ratified/Adopted	Ratified/Adopted
Poland	Ratified/Adopted	No Action/Opposed	Ratified/Adopted	Ratified/Adopted
Taiwan[b]	Ratified/Adopted	Not Applicable	Not Applicable	Not Applicable
United States	Signed/Abstained	No Action/Opposed	No Action/Opposed	Ratified/Adopted

[a]As the RtD was adopted before German reunification, the two German States at the time voted separately. [b]Taiwan is not able to become part of these instruments or vote in UN General Assemblies but have chosen to ratify the ICESCR regardless in 2009.

Colour explanation

Ratified/Adopted	No Action/Opposed	Signed/Abstained	Not Applicable

Overview of Ratification of Key Legal Instruments

In Table 1.1, we have highlighted the state of implementation of some key instruments in the fight against poverty and the RtD by the jurisdictions examined. Many online webpages may provide a more complete overview worldwide.[33]

[33]See for example, https://www.ohchr.org/EN/ProfessionalInterest/Pages/UniversalHumanRightsInstruments.aspx [visited: 20.02.2020].

Constitutional Protection

In this section we will explore to what extent constitutions recognise the right to an adequate standard of living and further what value, if any, constitutions give to rights relating to work, health, education, housing and water. Notably, we will also examine if these rights are justiciable or what other status they qualify to (*e.g.* "guiding principles of state policy").

How and to What Extent Constitutions Include ESCRs

Most jurisdictions considered in the general report included some reference to ESCRs and more specifically the right to an adequate standard of living in their constitutions.[34]

The jurisdiction, which utilised and referenced ESCRs the most in its constitution, was Colombia. The Colombian constitution describes Colombia as a 'Social Rule of Law'.[35] This has been interpreted by the Colombian Constitutional Court as a form government, which aims to achieve social justice and human dignity, ultimately suppressing social inequality. This position of the Court is further reflected in the extensive catalogue of rights protected by the constitution, which includes the State's duty to protect marginalized groups and especially those people who, "*due to their economic, physical and mental condition, are in a circumstance of obvious weakness*[.]"[36] The constitution also specifically accounts for rights to social security, education and health.[37] Specifically on the right to an adequate standard of living, the Constitutional Court has itself built this concept from a holistic interpretation of the constitution, including from the international obligations of Colombia both regionally (inter-American) and globally.[38]

Further to Colombia, six jurisdictions all accounted some level of reference and protection of ESCRs.[39] Out of these six, two of them specifically provided for the right to an adequate standard of living, namely Cyprus and Taiwan.

[34]Colombia, Cyprus, Czechia, Ghana, Italy, Poland, Taiwan.

[35]Constitution of Colombia, Article 1.

[36]See in this volume Betancur-Restrepo, the Colombian Legal Framework for Social Rights and the Challenges of a Post-Conflict Society, section 3.

[37]See in this volume Betancur-Restrepo, the Colombian Legal Framework for Social Rights and the Challenges of a Post-Conflict Society, section 3.

[38]See in this volume Betancur-Restrepo, the Colombian Legal Framework for Social Rights and the Challenges of a Post-Conflict Society, section 3.2.

[39]Cyprus, Czechia, Ghana, Italy, Poland, Taiwan. Also, France provides for ESCRs in paragraph 11 of the Preamble to the Constitution of 1946, see Roman (2012), p. 367.

In Cyprus, the constitution recognizes the 'right to a decent existence', an equivalent to the right of an adequate standard of living. Interestingly, it is argued that this right further protects other ESCRs in the Cypriot constitution, including rights to health, housing and water, which are otherwise not mentioned.[40] The Supreme Court of Cyprus has further provided that said constitutional provision (Article 9) places ESCRs on an equal footing with CPRs.[41]

Likewise, in Taiwan the 'right to existence', a rather broad and vague claim, is commonly understood as 'the right to an adequate standard of living'. The right is not understood as a fixed standard, rather it is conceived to reflect and accommodate an individual's and their family's actual needs and conditions. In other words, in Taiwan's constitution the right to an adequate standard of living is to be decided on a 'case-by-case' basis.[42]

Three jurisdictions in this general report had no direct constitutional reference to ESCRs. These three were Canada, Germany and the United States.

In Canada, while no formal recognition of ESCRs in the constitution exists, implicitly some rights mentioned in the Canadian Charter can only be ensured if an adequate standard of living is maintained. For example, the right to life and the right to dignity.[43] Furthermore, the Supreme Court of Canada has refused to rule out an interpretation of the Canadian Charter that would also protect ESCRs, specifically those included in various international covenants.[44]

In Germany, similarly there is no direct constitutional reference to ESCRs at the federal level. However, some German States provide this individually.[45] The reason for excluding specific references in the federal German constitution is historical. The Weimar constitution (the constitution governing Germany from 1919 to 1933) included ESCRs provisions, however, these rights remained unenforced. Therefore, the German founders of Germany's current constitution decided against their inclusion.[46] Still, the current constitution provides that Germany is a democratic and

[40]See in this volume Constantinides, the Legal and Policy Framework of Cyprus for the Fight Against Poverty at the Domestic and International Levels, section 2.2.

[41]See in this volume Constantinides, the Legal and Policy Framework of Cyprus for the Fight Against Poverty at the Domestic and International Levels, section 2.2.

[42]See in this volume Lee, the Fight against Poverty and the Right to Development in Taiwan, section 2.1.

[43]Article 1 & 4, Charter of fundamental freedoms and rights, Canada report, p. 7.

[44]Dufour & Pavot, Canada national report (2018) (unpublished), p. 8.

[45]See in this volume Schmahl, the Fight against Poverty and the Right to Development in the German Legal Order, section 2.1.

[46]See in this volume Schmahl, the Fight against Poverty and the Right to Development in the German Legal Order, section 2.1.

social federal state.[47] The social State principle is thus a constitutional obligation to continuously work towards the realization of social statehood and poverty eradication.[48] This principle is further part of the eternity guarantee, which means that it is not open to any constitutional amendment.[49]

Finally, the United States constitution does not recognize ESCRs at a general level. However, similarly to Germany, individual States do provide expressly for ESCRs in their constitutions. As examples, the State constitutions of New York and Alabama provide for protection equivalent to the right of an adequate standard of living.[50] And the right to education has been litigated in all US states, without exception. With these observations, some commonalities and differences can be drawn from the national reports. There seems to be a trend towards more recent constitutions including ESCRs.[51] Reasons for this may include the progressive recognition of ESCR as indivisible from and interdependent with CPR, in part due to the end of the Cold War, but also due to progress made in doctrinal interpretations of the nature and content of ESCR obligations.[52] Other reasons include constitutional changes that take place after important political and/or economic transitions, as was the case for the jurisdictions in this report that provide for ESCRs.[53]

Finally, the three jurisdictions, which did not directly and expressly include ESCRs,[54] are all federal States. The reason for not including ESCRs could be historical, like in the case of Germany and the United States. However, it could also be afforded to the power division/level of autonomy between the federal level and State level, which is also showcased by the examples of Germany and the United States.

The Justiciability of the Constitutional Rights Framework

We return to the constitutional situation in Canada, Germany and the United States which do not provide for ESCRs in their respective constitutions. However, there are still some nuances to this response.

---

47 Article 20(1), German Basic Law.

48 For an example of emerging social rights jurisprudence on this issue in Germany, see Bittner (2011), p. 1941.

49 See in this volume Schmahl, the Fight against Poverty and the Right to Development in the German Legal Order, section 2.1.

50 See in this volume Fedtke, Poverty and the Right to Development in the United States of America, section 2.1.

51 See for example the constitutions of Colombia, Cyprus, Ghana, Czechia and Poland.

52 For an analysis in this sense, see *e.g.* De Schutter (2010).

53 Colombia, Cyprus, Czechia, Ghana, Poland and Taiwan.

54 Canada, Germany, United States.

In Germany, its form of government has reference to the fight against poverty, namely the social state principle. Still, the principle is an objective and thus subject to what is financially and organizationally possible for the State. This implies that only the full replacement of social legislation would be undoubtedly unconstitutional.[55]

In the United States, the constitution similarly does not recognize justiciable ESCRs. This has been confirmed by the United States Supreme Court stating that the constitution contains no affirmative state obligation to care for the poor.[56] However, individual states have made constitutional ESCRs justiciable. As an example, the right to education has been litigated successfully: not only in the context of equal access but also with respect to adequate substantive levels of education. Another example is the right to housing, which in New York has provided individual entitlements, such as the right to emergency shelter for homeless persons.[57]

On the other end, Colombia and its justiciable constitutional rights framework has been viewed as Colombia's contribution to human rights in the American region.[58] Regarding the rights' framework justiciability, the Colombian constitution includes the possibility of claiming before judges, with a preferential procedure, the immediate protection of fundamental rights through the filing of the '*Acción de Tutela*' (*i.e.* a petition procedure which allows individuals to seek protection of fundamental human rights before any judge).[59] In relation to ESCRs, the Constitutional Court seemed first to specify that ESCRs were not justiciable through a '*Tutela*' as they depended on the means of the State.[60] However, in 2012 the Constitutional Court modified its position and affirmed that all rights are connected to each other and all are related to human dignity. During this year, the Court recognized the possibility that ESCR were justiciable through a '*Tutela*'. Also, on several occasions the Court has affirmed that the purpose of ESCRs is to fight poverty, which is the responsibility of the State and that its authorities must therefore take effective actions in this

---

[55]See in this volume Schmahl, the Fight against Poverty and the Right to Development in the German Legal Order, section 2.1.

[56]See in this volume Fedtke, Poverty and the Right to Development in the United States of America, section 2.2.

[57]See in this volume Fedtke, Poverty and the Right to Development in the United States of America, section 2.3.

[58]See in this volume Betancur-Restrepo, the Colombian Legal Framework for Social Rights and the Challenges of a Post-Conflict Society, section 3.2.

[59]Colombia Constitution, Article 86.

[60]See in this volume Betancur-Restrepo, the Colombian Legal Framework for Social Rights and the Challenges of a Post-Conflict Society, section 3.

regard.[61] Specifically, on Colombia's right to an adequate standard of living:[62] this right can be claimed by means of '*Tutela*'. Furthermore, the right is exclusive to the poor and a judge can make a ruling based on equity, which is otherwise not possible for several other ESCRs. Lastly, the right bearer is not only the State but also private actors.[63]

Like Colombia, Ghana's constitutional rights framework is justiciable. The High Court is given jurisdiction in human rights matters.[64] However, even though in principle individuals should be able to claim their rights, "*the challenge lies in the fact that victims of such violations have both the duty and burden to activate the legal process*[.]"[65] The traditional court system prevents poor segments of society from asserting their rights as the procedure is cumbersome and expensive. As an example, the Supreme Court is only located in the national capital; the Court of Appeal in a few major cities; and the High Courts are mostly found in regional capitals or other big towns. If you come from outside these cities, the costs to litigate are obvious.[66] However, there are other ways to lodge human rights complaints, for example the Commission for Human Rights and Administrative Justice.

Some jurisdictions only provide justiciability for some ESCRs, while others only provide justiciability indirectly through implementing laws of constitutional obligations.[67]

Poland is one of these jurisdictions, where ESCRs fall into two categories in terms of their justiciability. The first group encompasses ESCRs that may be pursued directly in reliance upon the constitution (and if applicable based on statutory law). The second group contains such ESCRs that may be exercised within statutorily prescribed limits and pursuant to relevant statutory law, not the constitution.[68] As such, the constitution for some ESCRs only lays the foundation of systems of laws, with ordinary statutes specifying their regime.[69] An example is the administration of social security, which is done by statute and may not be claimed through the

[61] See in this volume Betancur-Restrepo, the Colombian Legal Framework for Social Rights and the Challenges of a Post-Conflict Society, section 3.

[62] See in this volume Betancur-Restrepo, the Colombian Legal Framework for Social Rights and the Challenges of a Post-Conflict Society, section 3.1.

[63] See in this volume Betancur-Restrepo, the Colombian Legal Framework for Social Rights and the Challenges of a Post-Conflict Society, section 3.2.

[64] See in this volume Atuguba, the Fight against Poverty and the Right to Development: The Ghana National Chapter, section 2.1.

[65] See in this volume Atuguba, the Fight against Poverty and the Right to Development: The Ghana National Chapter, section 3.1.

[66] See in this volume Atuguba, the Fight against Poverty and the Right to Development: The Ghana National Chapter, section 3.2.

[67] Cyprus, Czechia, Poland, Taiwan.

[68] See in this volume Łasak, the Fight Against Poverty and the Right to Development in Poland, section 2.2.

[69] See in this volume Łasak, the Fight Against Poverty and the Right to Development in Poland, section 2.4.

constitution. For ESCRs that may be pursued through constitutional complaint, the prescribed judicial procedure must be exhausted first.[70] This include statutory laws incorporating constitutional obligations.[71]

Similarly, in Taiwan, ESCRs are divided into two categories, one being justiciable and one not. For example, the right to an adequate standard of living, the right to work and the right to education are all subject to judicial review.[72] These are understood as fundamental rights clauses and are thus justiciable. However, some rights listed in a separate chapter in the constitution are known as fundamental national policies. These do not allow individuals to bring claims against the State. Still, they are constitutional obligations and thus taken seriously by the Grand Justices of Judicial Yuan (the equivalent to a constitutional court).[73] An example is the constitutional obligation to establish a system of universal health care and medical insurance. The promise was fulfilled in 1994 by statute, then in 1999 the Grand Justices issued an interpretation, calling the law a "*realization of the said provisions of the Constitution*[.]"[74] The justices also advised that "*to those who cannot afford to pay the premium, the state shall give appropriate assistance and relief, in order to fulfil the Constitution's mandate of promoting national health insurance, protecting the dependent, the disabled and the financially disadvantaged.*"[75]

In the Czech Republic, ESCRs are justiciable in principle, but they may only be claimed within the confines of the laws implementing them. Whereas CPRs have an absolute nature, ESCRs are predominantly relative, which means that their development depends on the situation of the national economy and the State's general ability to fulfil its constitutional obligations.[76]

Likewise, in Cyprus, ESCRs are not directly justiciable but must be seen in relation to the laws implementing the constitutional obligation. This is exemplified by the Cypriot equivalent to the right to an adequate standard of living.[77] The State is bound to at some point enact a framework for the realisation of the right. Thus, the Courts can only assess the State's actions after their materialisation and not before

---

[70] See in this volume Łasak, the Fight Against Poverty and the Right to Development in Poland, section 2.4.

[71] See in this volume Łasak, the Fight Against Poverty and the Right to Development in Poland, section 2.4.

[72] See in this volume Lee, the Fight against Poverty and the Right to Development in Taiwan, section 2.1.

[73] See in this volume Lee, the Fight against Poverty and the Right to Development in Taiwan, section 2.1.

[74] See in this volume Lee, the Fight against Poverty and the Right to Development in Taiwan, section 2.1.

[75] See in this volume Lee, the Fight against Poverty and the Right to Development in Taiwan, section 2.1.

[76] See in this volume Šturma & Bílková, the Fight against Poverty and the Right to Development in the Czech Republic, section 1.2.

[77] Cypriot constitution, Article 9.

the State takes steps to fulfil its obligations. The Supreme Court has further stated that it views the right to an adequate standard of living in two parts, "*the first casts a general duty on the State to maintain minimum standards of existence and social security for everyone. The second imposes a specific duty to establish a system of social security for the protection of the weakest elements of society, the poor and the workers. The general duty, that is to say, one owed to everyone, is absolute in the sense that the State is enjoined to safeguard minimum standards for a decent existence for everyone. This is compatible with the ideal of a human society that places man [sic] in the epicentre of social action. The specific duties are relative, in the sense that social security for the poor and the workers must be compatible with and proportionate to the means of the State.*"[78] As such, the Cypriot constitution's ESCRs to some degree rely on the means of the State. Interestingly, it is not just those means presently available to the State, but those means that could be raised by appropriate legislation.[79]

To sum up, only two jurisdictions[80] provided for direct justiciability on a constitutional basis, while most jurisdictions had some level of justiciability either limited to a few ESCRs or through implementing laws.

In this regard, justiciability of ESCRs may not always be a successful way to measure the fight against poverty. During the Congress of the International Academy of Comparative Law, various examples were mentioned, which puts the justiciability of ESCRs into question. In both Brazil and Colombia, some justiciable constitutional ESCRs were not implemented, therefore many individuals started to claim their rights in court. This may seem positive at first, however, because of the many cases, the Brazilian and Colombian governments had to allocate large funds to the court systems to ensure access. These resources could potentially have been directed to the implementation of ESCRs instead. Said examples are not included to undermine the potential value of the justiciability of ESCRs, however, they bring an interesting perspective to the debate.

Remedies and Relationship to International Review Mechanism

In this section, we will explore more broadly the remedies available to individuals to protect rights, which are related to the fight against poverty. Moreover, we will look at how these remedies are connected to regional and/or international review mechanisms.

---

[78]See in this volume Constantinides, the Legal and Policy Framework of Cyprus for the Fight Against Poverty at the Domestic and International Levels, section 2.2.

[79]See in this volume Constantinides, the Legal and Policy Framework of Cyprus for the Fight Against Poverty at the Domestic and International Levels, section 2.2.

[80]Colombia, Ghana.

Secondly, we will examine if there is any legislation or case law on limiting social rights to their core. Moreover, is there any domestic parallel to the international law characterisation of ESCRs as subject to "progressive realization" or that takes into account the economic capacity of the domestic authorities?

Remedies Available in the Fight Against Poverty

National Remedies More Broadly

Besides constitutional protections and remedies, there are several other mechanisms available at the domestic level that are not necessarily constitutionally based.

As already accounted for, the German constitution does not reference ESCRs or make such rights enforceable. However, Germany's form of government—the social state principle—have in the past decades been given legal effect. Thus, the principle finds legislative concretization not only in social assistance and social insurance statutory laws, but also in seizure law, employment protection law and tax law.[81] Statutory laws are—unlike the constitutional social state principle—justiciable and legally enforceable. Furthermore, legal aid is available for those who cannot afford legal action, if the remedy in question has a reasonable chance of success in court.[82]

Similarly, in Canada there is generally not a constitutional framework to make ESCRs justiciable. The ICESCR should accommodate this, however, Canadian courts have preferred confined interpretations of the Canadian human rights charter, specifying that ESCRs are beyond their reach.[83] Canadian provinces, however, does have legislation to combat social exclusion, which is justiciable like in Germany.[84] This is also the case in the Czech Republic. However, social rights are in fact justiciable in principle, but they may only be claimed within the confines of the laws implementing the constitutional obligations. As in Germany and Canada, claimants must therefore rather rely on statutory laws than the constitution itself. In general, ESCRs in the Czech Republic remain to form a referential framework for the Constitutional Court.[85]

Some national reports also referenced administrative appeals systems, which for example are relevant in cases of arbitrary decisions to social aid or other public

---

[81] See in this volume Schmahl, the Fight against Poverty and the Right to Development in the German Legal Order, section 2.2.

[82] See in this volume Schmahl, the Fight against Poverty and the Right to Development in the German Legal Order, section 2.3.

[83] Dufour & Pavot, Canada national report (2018) (unpublished), p. 10.

[84] Dufour & Pavot, Canada national report (2018) (unpublished), p. 11.

[85] See in this volume Constantinides, the Legal and Policy Framework of Cyprus for the Fight Against Poverty at the Domestic and International Levels, section 2.5.

benefits.[86] Furthermore, also the Ombudsman function was highlighted in the justiciability of ESCRs within the domestic legal order.[87]

Connections with Regional and International Review Mechanisms

In relation to domestic remedies and their connections to regional and international review mechanisms.

First, within Europe both the EU and the Council of Europe provide for ESCRs instruments. This was highlighted in the German national report. Germany is part of the European Social Charter ('ESC'), which is a Council of Europe instrument. The ESC was not intended to lay down subjective or even individually enforceable rights. The limited level of control and enforceability of the rights laid down in the ESC is justified by its dependence on economic, financial and general conditions of the State concerned. Similarly, for the EU Charter of Fundamental Rights there is agreement that ESCRs are not extensively justiciable but allow the EU member States a wide margin of appreciation.[88] Therefore, the European ESCRs instruments do not amount to subjectively enforceable claims in the German legal order, except in cases where the social minimum standard is at stake.[89] Moreover, the recommendations of international review bodies have some domestic impact in Germany. For example, Germany gets criticism on the conditions for asylum seeking children and regarding the lack of free education at state universities.[90] However, while CPRs regularly gain immediate applicability in the German legal order, the direct applicability of ESCRs is not given on a regular basis, since the latter are subject to sufficient economic resources.[91]

In comparison to Germany, Italy has accepted the various international review mechanism's competences to examine individual claims.[92] Much of the monitoring to which Italy has been subjected in recent years focuses on the domestic dimension

[86]One such example is Cyprus, which provides for administrative appeal (*i.e.* the public administration is given a chance to rectify individual decisions). A recourse to the Cyprus Administrative Court is the only judicial venue available in the Cypriot legal order for challenging decisions of the State in connection to social benefits.

[87]See in this volume Constantinides, the Legal and Policy Framework of Cyprus for the Fight Against Poverty at the Domestic and International Levels, section 2.2 and Łasak, the Fight Against Poverty and the Right to Development in Poland, section 2.3.

[88]See in this volume Schmahl, the Fight against Poverty and the Right to Development in the German Legal Order, section 2.4.

[89]See in this volume Schmahl, the Fight against Poverty and the Right to Development in the German Legal Order, section 2.4.

[90]See in this volume Schmahl, the Fight against Poverty and the Right to Development in the German Legal Order, section 2.4.

[91]See in this volume Schmahl, the Fight against Poverty and the Right to Development in the German Legal Order, section 2.4.

[92]See in this volume Gradoni & Pasquet, Failing to protect basic human rights: the fight against poverty and the right to development in Italy's legal practice, section 3.

of the fight against poverty and the measures Italy took, or failed to take, to shield people under its jurisdiction from the effects of the global economic crisis.[93] Still, even though individuals are able to complain directly to international review mechanisms, it does not seem that the legal reality in relation to ESCRs is much different from Germany. Finally, references to international standards are relatively rare in Italy's domestic jurisprudence. One reason for this is that the Constitution protects economic and social rights in terms as broad and radical as to make the act of referring to international sources redundant in most cases.[94]

Secondly, going outside of Europe. In the United States, the link between national and international review mechanisms is not present, due to its historical and cultural roots. However, regional and international ESCRs instruments are used as arguments to move state courts toward more progressive readings.[95]

In Ghana, the State is subject to various international review mechanisms. However, in comparing Ghana's mechanism for enforcing ESCRs to international review mechanisms, one may hold the view that Ghana's mechanisms are more direct and stringent than international review mechanisms. Whereas Ghana has both constitutional and other modes by which ESCRs are enforced, with these modes open to a wide array of individuals and organizations, international review mechanisms draw mainly from reports on the progress of States in enforcing human rights. Still, because of the international review mechanisms, and the reporting mechanisms, they are a further opportunity for Ghana and other States to realize and enforce ESCRs.[96] Ghana's Constitutional Court has further referred to international ESCRs to fill a lacuna on the right to work in Ghana. Thereby implying that where a fundamental human right has not been explicitly stated in the Constitution of Ghana, reference can be made to that right by referring to provisions of international human rights instruments, *i.e.* to fill a gap in Ghanaian law.[97]

How Does National Systems Value ESCRs

If the ESCRs framework is not justiciable or only to a certain extent, it becomes interesting to examine what value then is given to ESCRs.

---

[93] See in this volume Gradoni & Pasquet, Failing to protect basic human rights: the fight against poverty and the right to development in Italy's legal practice, section 3.

[94] See in this volume Gradoni & Pasquet, Failing to protect basic human rights: the fight against poverty and the right to development in Italy's legal practice, section 2.

[95] See in this volume Fedtke, Poverty and the Right to Development in the United States of America, section 2.4.

[96] See in this volume Atuguba, the Fight against Poverty and the Right to Development: The Ghana National Chapter, section 4.0.

[97] See in this volume Atuguba, the Fight against Poverty and the Right to Development: The Ghana National Chapter, section 1.1.

In Cyprus, as already put forward the right to a decent existence does not give rise to justiciable rights. Instead the right to a decent existence and other ESCRs are rather guiding principles of State policy.[98]

Similarly, in Germany the social State principle is a mere state objective and thus subject to what is financially and organizationally possible to the State. This means that only the full replacement of social legislation would be unconstitutional.[99] Interestingly in Germany, ESCRs and the social state principle has been interpreted by the Federal Constitutional Court to include not only the economic-social but also the mental-psychological situation of people.[100]

Also, in the Czech Republic, the Constitutional Court has emphasized that social rights depend mainly on the economic situation of the State.[101]

Finally, the courts in the United States have generally seen limited government resources as a reason to limit judicial intervention in cases involving socio-economic claims. Further, the courts have not established a link between potentially growing public budgets and a corresponding realization of socio-economic entitlements.[102]

In fact, not only does national systems link the ability to realize ESCRs, also international monitory bodies do as much. For example, the UN Committee on Economic, Social and Cultural Rights has noted that the efforts of certain developing countries to comply with their international ESCRs obligations are impeded if they for example are highly indebted.[103] Moreover, it can be difficult for international review bodies and State courts to decide on specific levels of social protection schemes. This is seen in France and Norway, where the judiciaries recognizes the international ESCRs obligations, however, exercises its control of the social security system poorly.[104] The two main notions as to the justiciability of ESCRs in France, is first that such rights are in principle justiciable and secondly that the awarding of for example social security should be done in line with non-discrimination and equality objectives.[105] This is broadly the position also in Norway.

[98]See in this volume Constantinides, the Legal and Policy Framework of Cyprus for the Fight Against Poverty at the Domestic and International Levels, section 4.

[99]See in this volume Schmahl, the Fight against Poverty and the Right to Development in the German Legal Order, section 2.1.

[100]See in this volume Schmahl, the Fight against Poverty and the Right to Development in the German Legal Order, section 2.2.

[101]See in this volume Šturma & Bílková, the Fight against Poverty and the Right to Development in the Czech Republic, section 1.3.

[102]See in this volume Fedtke, Poverty and the Right to Development in the United States of America, section 2.5.

[103]See in this volume De Schutter, the International Dimensions of the Right to Development: Enabling Poverty-Reduction in Domestic Legal Orders by a Reformed International Legal Order, section 5.1.

[104]Roman (2012), p. 364.

[105]Roman (2012), p. 365.

Domestic Law Contributions in an International Context

General Remarks

This part of the general report addresses the domestic contribution to the fight against poverty and the RtD at the international level.

It has become a 'hot topic' to explore States' international responsibilities in relation to the RtD and to combat poverty more broadly. An example is the 2017 report of the Inter-American Commission on Human Rights focussing on poverty and human rights in the Americas.[106] For this specific part of the report, we were pleased to have Olivier De Schutter submit a thematic report to further qualify our findings. The report seeks to clarify the duties that are imposed on States by the Declaration on the Right to Development and the normative instruments in which the Declaration is grounded. Whereas the national reports focussed on specific jurisdictions, the thematic report of De Schutter rather accounted for several multilateral agreements and other relevant practice on the fight against poverty and the RtD.[107]

Domestic Constitutional or Legal Innovations

In this section we will explore domestic contributions to the fight against poverty and the right to development in an international context. For example, such domestic contribution could be a constitutional obligation to further the international legal order or as a developed country employ a comprehensive development programme.

Domestic Constitutional Contributions in an International Context

First, looking at some of the jurisdictions which did not have any constitutional contribution to the fight against poverty and the RtD in an international context.

In Germany, there are no provisions for a strict commitment to development aid or transnational poverty reduction. Neither can there be found a duty to combat poverty worldwide.[108] Furthermore, the RtD is not known to the German legal order. Development is not recognized as a subjective international human right. Hence, Germany's development program is not designed in accordance with the RtD.[109]

---

[106] IACHR, *Report on Poverty and Human Rights in the Americas*, 2017, p. 9.

[107] See in this volume De Schutter, the International Dimensions of the Right to Development: Enabling Poverty-Reduction in Domestic Legal Orders by a Reformed International Legal Order.

[108] See in this volume Schmahl, the Fight against Poverty and the Right to Development in the German Legal Order, section 3.1.

[109] See in this volume Schmahl, the Fight against Poverty and the Right to Development in the German Legal Order, section 3.1.

Similarly, in Canada, the United States and Cyprus, there is not any constitutional basis for a contribution to the fight against poverty and the RtD in an international context.[110] In the Czech Republic there is a provision entailing that the Czech Republic has to abide by its international obligations, however, it is not specific to the fight against poverty or the RtD and therefore the provision is not considered to refer to these.[111] The general Norwegian constitutional provision on human rights obliges the state authorities 'to respect and enforce' other human rights obligations in the Constitution itself and in the conventions Norway is bound by. That will mean that Norway is bound by international law on the right of development including the RtD, to the extent there were any duties to contribute outside the domestic jurisdiction.

At the other end of the spectrum, both Ghana and the Netherlands have a constitutional basis for the RtD and the fight against poverty in an international context.[112]

In the Netherlands, Article 90 of the Constitution provides for the constitutional duty to promote the development of the international legal order.[113] The government has noted that this provision should also promote the realisation of human rights, in the broadest sense of the word, which includes both CPRs and ESCRs.[114] Because of the broad wording of the provision, also the RtD forms part of it.[115] However, even though the government has recognised that CPRs and ESCRs are of equal importance, both in foreign and domestic policy ESCRs have received less attention and their legal status has been questioned.[116] This is for example visible in the Dutch foreign human rights policy in the area of development cooperation and assistance, where the RtD as a human right of a holistic nature has been absent. The government has expressly provided that because there is no agreement of the content of the RtD, it is necessary to do so first, before applying the concept in practice.[117]

[110] See in this volume Constantinides, the Legal and Policy Framework of Cyprus for the Fight Against Poverty at the Domestic and International Levels, section 3, Fedtke, Poverty and the Right to Development in the United States of America, section 2.6 and Dufour & Pavot, Canada national report (2018) (unpublished) p. 10.

[111] See in this volume Šturma & Bílková, the Fight against Poverty and the Right to Development in the Czech Republic, section 1.2.

[112] See in this volume Atuguba, the Fight against Poverty and the Right to Development: The Ghana National Chapter, section 2.1 and Coomans & ter Vrugt, The Netherlands and the Right to Development, section 2.

[113] See in this volume Coomans & ter Vrugt, The Netherlands and the Right to Development, section 2.

[114] See in this volume Coomans & ter Vrugt, The Netherlands and the Right to Development, section 2.

[115] See in this volume Coomans & ter Vrugt, The Netherlands and the Right to Development, section 2.

[116] See in this volume Coomans & ter Vrugt, The Netherlands and the Right to Development, section 2.

[117] See in this volume Coomans & ter Vrugt, The Netherlands and the Right to Development, section 2.

To sum up, there are few express constitutional provisions placing a duty on the state in question to make contributions to the fight against poverty in an international context. There seems to be limited basis within the jurisdictions examined in this general report to say that there is a general constitutional basis for the fight against poverty in an international context. Even for a jurisdiction like the Netherlands, the national report is pointing out that having a provision to promote the development of the international legal order does not necessarily apply to the RtD. The relationship between different fields of international law and their base in treaties and custom, domestic constitutional law and the possible emergence of legal principles of international law is an area which deserves further study.

Mechanisms of a Legal or Wider Regulatory Nature Contributing Internationally

The most common for the jurisdictions examined was that the developed countries had a development aid program targeted developing countries, which thus contributes to the fight against poverty and the RtD in an international context.

An example is Cyprus. Now, Cyprus is one country post World War II that has gone from an aid recipient State to an aid donor State. Since 1994, Cyprus started a technical assistance scheme for foreign countries, where they offered scholarships for third-country nationals within areas of Cypriot expertise.[118] Then, since its 2004 accession to the EU, its development programme got aligned with that of the EU.[119] Similarly, other EU jurisdictions follow EU policies and programmes and have both bilateral and multilateral development programmes.[120]

Still there seems to be scepticism from developed countries on the third generation of human rights. Some of the reasons for such scepticism were explained in the German national report. The underlying issue is the vagueness of the third generation of human rights' content.[121] Furthermore, the realization of these rights requires concerted efforts on the part not only of States or the international community, but also of societies, peoples, NGO's and individuals. Therefore, it becomes harder to monitor progress and define responsibilities.[122]

[118] See in this volume Constantinides, the Legal and Policy Framework of Cyprus for the Fight Against Poverty at the Domestic and International Levels, section 3.1.

[119] See in this volume Constantinides, the Legal and Policy Framework of Cyprus for the Fight Against Poverty at the Domestic and International Levels, section 3.1.

[120] See in this volume Schmahl, the Fight against Poverty and the Right to Development in the German Legal Order, section 3.1 and Šturma & Bílková, the Fight against Poverty and the Right to Development in the Czech Republic, section 2.1.

[121] See in this volume Schmahl, the Fight against Poverty and the Right to Development in the German Legal Order, section 4.

[122] See in this volume Schmahl, the Fight against Poverty and the Right to Development in the German Legal Order, section 4.

Specifically on the RtD, a country like Cyprus has traditionally been supportive of the concept in international fora, not least because of its prominent role in the Non-Aligned Movement until the movements decline in the 1990s. Since its EU accession, however, Cyprus has followed the EU policy on these issues.[123]

Different from Cyprus and the NIEO movement, the United States was the only State directly opposing the RtD Declaration at the time of its adoption.[124] However, a rough comparison between the Declaration and what is perhaps the closest US equivalent, the Millennium Challenge Account, show that both recognise a duty of developed nations to share their wealth by committing substantial resources to the task.[125] This approach give some common ground on the understanding of the RtD.

Moreover, in De Schutter's thematic report, he found that States have a global obligation derived from the RtD to conclude new agreements (bilateral, regional or multilateral) in order to address issues of a transnational nature that call for collective action by States.[126] De Schutter suggested that this was a procedural obligation, thus a requirement to enter into good faith negotiations, and not necessarily to conclude actual agreements. Many types of agreements can be envisaged; one could be bilateral and multilateral development programmes, as is evidenced by all developed jurisdictions examined having a development cooperation programme.[127] This is also supported in the 1993 Vienna Declaration and Programme of Action.[128] For example, Article 4 of the Vienna Programme of Action, which stipulates a duty of all States,

> ...to take steps, individually and collectively, to formulate international development policies with a view to facilitating the full realization of the [RtD] [with] sustained action [being] required to promote more rapid development of developing countries.[129]

De Schutter further outlines that the international dimension of the RtD entails that States implement, in good faith, decisions and recommendations emanating from international organizations of which the State is a member, to the extent that

[123]See in this volume Constantinides, the Legal and Policy Framework of Cyprus for the Fight Against Poverty at the Domestic and International Levels, section 4.

[124]See in this volume Fedtke, Poverty and the Right to Development in the United States of America, section 2.6.

[125]See in this volume Fedtke, Poverty and the Right to Development in the United States of America, section 2.6.

[126]See in this volume De Schutter, the International Dimensions of the Right to Development: Enabling Poverty-Reduction in Domestic Legal Orders by a Reformed International Legal Order, section 4.2.

[127]Canada, United States, Germany, Czechia, Cyprus, Netherlands, Poland, Italy.

[128]World Conference on Human Rights on 25 June 1993 and endorsed by General Assembly resolution 48/121 of 20 December 1993, para. 10.

[129]See in this volume De Schutter, the International Dimensions of the Right to Development: Enabling Poverty-Reduction in Domestic Legal Orders by a Reformed International Legal Order, section 3.1.

they contribute to the realization of the RtD. This goes beyond the duty to comply with treaties that the State is a party to.[130]

None of the national reports included references to domestic legal obligations with the general effect that recommendations and decisions of international organizations should be implemented, however, this could be an interesting approach for further research. The interplay between domestic law and international law in the formation of custom and general principles on, or with an impact on, the RtD may become increasingly important. Global action, building on domestic processes, is the outcome of the interplay between complex processes of a formal and informal character. The "soft law" nature of many instruments does not prevent them from producing legal effects. The cooperation between states is becoming more durable and international organisations serve as platforms and independent agents in the way in which they give effect to the wills of their member states. The distinction is not clear between practices and policies that are not legally binding and legal obligations with multi-layered implementation depending on the contributions of different states and organisations. Informal policy instruments may use the forms and words of treaties; and formal treaties may use general and open substantive norms, with varying (or no) provision for implementation and enforcement. The sum of international treaties, state practice, the role of international organisations and domestic processes and their interaction requires further attention. The dynamic processes are reaching a transformational stage where international law may bind states in ways which may make the RtD a clearer legal obligation.

Policy Monitoring and/or Accountability Mechanisms

As was identified in the previous section, the development aid programmes of developed States are considered a contribution to the fight against poverty in a global context. In this part we will explore further the *extent* to which the development programmes contribute to the RtD and the fight against poverty. This includes looking to policy monitoring and accountability mechanisms.

[130]See in this volume De Schutter, the International Dimensions of the Right to Development: Enabling Poverty-Reduction in Domestic Legal Orders by a Reformed International Legal Order, section 4.2.

Relationship Between Development Programmes and the RtD

The Presence of RtD, the SDGs and Other Development Related Policies

Only Canada of the jurisdictions examined had its development programme built accordingly to the RtD and as such Canada mainly focuses on poverty reduction.[131] The other jurisdictions examined did not explicitly provide reference to the RtD, but rather for example to the SDGs framework.

One such jurisdiction is Cyprus. Its prime focus has been the realization of the MDGs and later the SDGs through its development programme.[132] For example, a relevant line of ministries has been assigned as coordinators for the implementation of each one of the 17 SDGs. The Ministry of Labour, Welfare and Social Insurance is the coordinator of SDG 1.[133] Also, Germany applies the SDGs in its development programmes, which cooperates with a total of 85 countries.[134] Germany is further committed to food security and rural development, thus in effect contributing to the fight against poverty.[135] The same is true for the Czech Republic and Italy, where the eradication of poverty are part of their development programmes.[136]

Finally, the Netherlands has been consistently committed to the MDGs/SDGs, however, there has been a lot of lip-service rather than actual action. One of the underlying objectives for its development programme is as such to counter irregular migration flows to Europe out of self-interest.[137] Still the Netherlands' development cooperation policy and programs mainly focus on the poorest and most vulnerable groups.[138]

When it comes to the United States, the government was happy to see the strong recognition of extreme poverty eradication in the SDGs.[139] However, with the

[131] Dufour & Pavot, Canada national report (2018) (unpublished), p. 11.

[132] See in this volume Constantinides, the Legal and Policy Framework of Cyprus for the Fight Against Poverty at the Domestic and International Levels, section 3.2.

[133] See in this volume Constantinides, the Legal and Policy Framework of Cyprus for the Fight Against Poverty at the Domestic and International Levels, section 3.4.

[134] See in this volume Schmahl, the Fight against Poverty and the Right to Development in the German Legal Order, section 3.1.

[135] See in this volume Schmahl, the Fight against Poverty and the Right to Development in the German Legal Order, section 3.1.

[136] See in this volume Šturma & Bílková, the Fight against Poverty and the Right to Development in the Czech Republic, section 2.1 and Gradoni & Pasquet, Failing to protect basic human rights: the fight against poverty and the right to development in Italy's legal practice, section 4.

[137] See in this volume Coomans & ter Vrugt, The Netherlands and the Right to Development, section 3.2.

[138] See in this volume Coomans & ter Vrugt, The Netherlands and the Right to Development, section 3.3.

[139] See in this volume Fedtke, Poverty and the Right to Development in the United States of America, section 2.8.

Trump administration in the White House, focus on eradicating extreme poverty and contributing to the SDGs may be not be followed in practice.[140]

In general, it seems that all jurisdictions examined reference the SDGs in their development cooperation, however, there may be issues regarding to what extend this leads to different action.

Funding Levels for Development Programmes

In connection to the RtD, the question of the level of the development aid, which developed countries have committed to setting at 0.7 percent of their GNI,[141] naturally arises. The notion of 0.7% has many opponents, and the commitment is honoured more in breach than in the observance.[142] The most vocal opponent of the target is the United States.[143] The United States views its development programme as part of its foreign policy, and more specifically, as an integral component of national security considerations. The United States further stipulates that the provision of development aid remain a sovereign political decision of donor countries rather than a binding obligation under international law.[144]

Several European countries tend to follow the target of 0.7% and are thus currently reaching that level or working towards it.[145] Sweden and Norway have periodically exceeded their higher target of 1.0%. The financial crisis in 2008 had impacts on the levels of development aid, but no developed country decided to abolish its development programme completely. Moreover, since the recovery from the crisis, several countries have begun to raise their funding for development aid again. One such example is Italy; during the economic crisis funding was cut for its development programme, but in 2013 the Italian government pledged to increase the programme again, exceeding the country's 2008-level.[146]

[140]See in this volume Fedtke, Poverty and the Right to Development in the United States of America, section 2.10.

[141]See in this volume De Schutter, the International Dimensions of the Right to Development: Enabling Poverty-Reduction in Domestic Legal Orders by a Reformed International Legal Order, section 5.3.

[142]See in this volume De Schutter, the International Dimensions of the Right to Development: Enabling Poverty-Reduction in Domestic Legal Orders by a Reformed International Legal Order, section 5.3.

[143]See in this volume Fedtke, Poverty and the Right to Development in the United States of America, section 2.6.

[144]See in this volume Fedtke, Poverty and the Right to Development in the United States of America, section 2.6.

[145]Italy, Netherlands, Czechia.

[146]See in this volume Gradoni & Pasquet, Failing to protect basic human rights: the fight against poverty and the right to development in Italy's legal practice, section 3.

Likewise, in 2016 the Netherlands reached below the 0.7% threshold at 0.65. However, in the 2018-budget the Netherlands committed itself to raising its level again by 2021 to 0.7%.

Some international norms can be drawn from various developed countries practices with regards to the commitment of development aid. Even though the financial crisis could have been used as a scapegoat to substantially lower or completely abolish development programmes, developed countries still retained their development programmes.[147] Since the crisis several countries have further gone to increase their levels of aid working towards the 0.7% threshold or at least exceeding their pre-crisis levels.[148] Although a country like the United States maintains that development aid is a sovereign decision of donor countries, several developed countries having a development programme seem to pursue their development programme at least in part because of, and with express reliance on, international legal norms.[149]

It is not only the level of development aid that is interesting in relation to the fight against poverty and the RtD more specifically. Also, the content of the development programmes is important. In this regard, the rise in development aid post the financial crisis—at least in European jurisdictions—seem not to be directly benefitting developing countries. In fact, often no extra funding is in reality made available for the poorest people in the world, the raise in aid only restores previous budget cuts and spending. Furthermore, large parts of the development programmes are effectively not spent in developing countries, but within the developed countries themselves due to the recent migration and refugee crisis. Such tendency was observed in the Netherlands, Italy, the Czech Republic and Norway.[150] Even in Germany the highest priority in the development policy is currently coping with the high number of refugees received.[151] In fact, one estimate for the year 2015 provided that 17% of the aid from EU countries did not reflect a real transfer of resources to developing countries, because it was directed to *e.g.* refugee spending.[152]

A similar criticism is made by De Schutter, as he accounts for the OECD's way to calculate development assistance. For example, expenses such as temporary assistance to refugees (up to 12 months) is reportable as development aid, and all costs associated with eventual repatriation to the developing country of origin are also reportable. Of course, how development aid is calculated has major impacts on how

[147]United States, Netherlands, Italy, Cyprus, Germany, Czechia.

[148]Netherlands, Italy.

[149]Netherlands, Italy.

[150]See in this volume Gradoni & Pasquet, Failing to protect basic human rights: the fight against poverty and the right to development in Italy's legal practice, section 4, Šturma & Bílková, the Fight against Poverty and the Right to Development in the Czech Republic, section 2.1 and Coomans & ter Vrugt, The Netherlands and the Right to Development, section 3.8.

[151]See in this volume Schmahl, the Fight against Poverty and the Right to Development in the German Legal Order, section 3.1.

[152]See in this volume De Schutter, the International Dimensions of the Right to Development: Enabling Poverty-Reduction in Domestic Legal Orders by a Reformed International Legal Order, section 5.3.

the 0.7% of GNI is assessed. Therefore, De Schutter calls for not only looking at the percentage of development aid, but also the effectiveness of aid: whether aid is predictable over a number of years and untied, thus allowing receiving countries to plan long-term strategies and ensure national ownership.[153]

Accountability and Monitoring Mechanisms for Development Programmes

In this section, we will explore accountability and monitoring mechanisms, including how individuals and NGOs can intervene in the design, implementation and follow-up to development programmes.

Most jurisdictions had their development programmes monitored by parliament, for example through the yearly budget approval.[154] Some jurisdictions went further:

Starting with Canada, scrutiny on its development programme is likewise done annually by the Canadian parliament.[155] In addition, the competent minister consults with regional governments, international agencies and Canadian civil society organisations at least once every two years and takes their views and recommendations into consideration.[156]

In the Czech Republic, starting from 2009 the government created a new council for foreign development cooperation, which is responsible for ensuring interministerial cooperation of the development agenda. The 15-member council represents various ministries and other public bodies and as well representatives from the business sector and civil society. There is also a particular scheme for businesses in the development aid programme, which includes co-funding for projects with foreign companies. Civil society further provides expertise, for example when sending experts to target countries.[157]

In Ghana, although not a developed country, citizens, civil society organisations, private enterprises and development partners can still monitor policy, programmes', plans' or various projects' implementation and demand accountability from relevant duty bearers.[158] In addition, a civil society platform on SDGs has been established to

---

153 See in this volume De Schutter, the International Dimensions of the Right to Development: Enabling Poverty-Reduction in Domestic Legal Orders by a Reformed International Legal Order, section 5.3.

154 See in this volume Schmahl, the Fight against Poverty and the Right to Development in the German Legal Order, section 3.1.

155 Dufour & Pavot, Canada national report (2018) (unpublished), p. 11.

156 Dufour & Pavot, Canada national report (2018) (unpublished), p. 11.

157 See in this volume Šturma & Bílková, the Fight against Poverty and the Right to Development in the Czech Republic, section 2.2.

158 See in this volume Atuguba, the Fight against Poverty and the Right to Development: The Ghana National Chapter, section 5.1.2, 5.1.3, and 5.1.4.

promote collaboration among CSOs as well as foster effective partnerships with the government and the private sector.[159]

The United States stood out as a jurisdiction where individuals and NGOs had very little ways to engage in development cooperation and antipoverty policies overall.[160]

Unilateral/Bilateral Initiatives or Agreements

This part is included to look broader than just countries' development programmes and thus explore if there are other measures adopted unilaterally or bilaterally of a voluntary or binding nature related to the fight against poverty. The examples chosen below are thus very diverse and ranges widely. The purpose of this part is to provide inspiration for other initiatives which could contribute to coherence in the fight against poverty and the RtD.

In Ghana, the country's statistical service has set up a SDGs unit which is mandated to collate reliable and accurate data for tracking the SDGs indicators.[161] Furthermore, the National Development Plan of Ghana outlines the development roadmap of Ghana and is intended to be the means by which the national agenda of development is achieved. This plan provides a holistic picture of the nation's vision, from which all policies are drawn. Thus, it is from this plan that the extent of Ghana's intention to implement the RtD may be derived.[162]

In the Netherlands, the Court of Audit reports frequently about the efficiency and effectiveness of the Dutch foreign and development cooperation policy, including the progress made in the realisation of the SDGs. Recently, the body advised the Dutch government to better clarify what the government's concrete policy plans are to fulfil its commitments towards the realisation of the SDGs.[163]

In Taiwan, NGOs have since Taiwan's democratization in the 1990s played an important role in social policy making more broadly. Concretely, many law reforms are initiated by NGOs. During law drafting periods, both the legislature and administration would hold formal public hearings or informal seminars for gathering ideas, comments or suggestions from the civil society. NGOs are often invited or are welcome to attend to those hearings and seminars. In terms of anti-poverty and the

---

[159] See in this volume Atuguba, the Fight against Poverty and the Right to Development: The Ghana National Chapter, section 5.1.3.

[160] See in this volume Fedtke, Poverty and the Right to Development in the United States of America, section 2.6.

[161] See in this volume Atuguba, the Fight against Poverty and the Right to Development: The Ghana National Chapter, section 5.1.3.

[162] See in this volume Atuguba, the Fight against Poverty and the Right to Development: The Ghana National Chapter, section 5.1.1.

[163] See in this volume Coomans & ter Vrugt, The Netherlands and the Right to Development, section 3.7.

RtD, many Taiwanese NGOs with different focuses and concerns, including child welfare groups, women's groups, people with disabilities, housing rights groups, labour rights groups and other activist groups for economic and social equality, have contributed greatly in pushing through law reforms, providing essential information and policy suggestions, and establishing empowerment programs.[164]

Another example is seen in France, where a newer law on the "duty of vigilance for parent and instructing companies" have created much debate. The law gives extraterritorial effects, prompting companies with a presence in France to be liable for its activities abroad.[165] As the law wants to combat human rights abuses, the law can be seen as a way to further the RtD. This is supported in De Schutter's thematic report, where he writes that measures adopted unilaterally by one State can have impacts on the realization of the RtD.[166]

De Schutter also mentions other ways for States to take unilateral measures in the realization of the RtD. For example, when it comes to how States act in international organisations, they can incur responsibility under international law. As De Schutter writes,

> ...where a State seeks to avoid compliance with an international obligation by transferring powers to an international organisation and allowing it to take measures that run counter to such international obligations, it engages its responsibility under international law.[167]

This way to perceive how States could take 'wrong' decisions in international organisations is one way, but another could be that States could actively advance the realization of the RtD within international organisations.

Finally, as suggested by De Schutter in his report, States can further work towards the realization of the RtD by engaging in debt reduction for developing countries and work towards eliminating tax evasion.[168]

---

[164] See in this volume Lee, the Fight against Poverty and the Right to Development in Taiwan, section 2.2 and section 3.

[165] Brabant and Savourey (2017).

[166] See in this volume De Schutter, the International Dimensions of the Right to Development: Enabling Poverty-Reduction in Domestic Legal Orders by a Reformed International Legal Order, section 3.1.

[167] See in this volume De Schutter, the International Dimensions of the Right to Development: Enabling Poverty-Reduction in Domestic Legal Orders by a Reformed International Legal Order, section 2.3.

[168] See in this volume De Schutter, the International Dimensions of the Right to Development: Enabling Poverty-Reduction in Domestic Legal Orders by a Reformed International Legal Order, section 5.

Crosscutting Contemporary Themes

General Remarks

As mentioned in the introduction to the general report many crosscutting themes could be relevant in relation to the fight against poverty and the RtD, for example questions related to human rights and the financing of development; the effects of foreign debt and other related international financial obligations of States on both development and the fight against poverty; the impact of the global financial crisis on human rights and; the relationship between human rights and climate change. However, the general report will solely deal with and thus limit itself to the crosscutting themes identified over the course of writing this report.

In this regard, three overall crosscutting themes came up. These themes include the fight against poverty and the RtD in relation to post-conflict contexts, international trade and investment law and finally the new evolving area of business and human rights.

The Fight Against Poverty and the RtD in Post-Conflict Societies

The national report of Colombia put into perspective how legal frameworks for the fight against poverty and the RtD has the danger of being read as if their evolution and interpretation would be alien to the political decisions of their actors. In this context, the Colombian national rapporteur broad the peace agreement with the FARC guerrillas into the discussion. Concretely, how the peace agreement –which got Colombia to enter a post-conflict phase—can potentially enable social change.

As a background, in November 2016, after more than 50 years of internal armed conflict, the Colombian government signed a peace agreement with the FARC guerrillas. Even if the significant levels of violence have not been overcome, the Colombian Government considers that the post-conflict and peace-building phase have started.[169]

The economic consequences for a country in armed conflict is obvious. For example, Colombia had to allocate large economic resources to combat the guerrilla groups, resources that could otherwise have improved industry, infrastructure, rural development, etc. Moreover, the end of the conflict is an opportunity to attract higher amounts of foreign investment.[170] To this extent, the Colombian government has previously stated that the armed conflict impacted its ability to satisfy social

[169]See in this volume Betancur-Restrepo, the Colombian Legal Framework for Social Rights and the Challenges of a Post-Conflict Society, section 5.

[170]See in this volume Betancur-Restrepo, the Colombian Legal Framework for Social Rights and the Challenges of a Post-Conflict Society, section 5.

needs.[171] Such line of argument is consistent with other national reports suggesting that the protection of the ESCRs depend on the amount of economic resources available.[172] However, such connection raises many questions, as put by the national rapporteur,

> What exactly would make that in time of peace social needs will be guaranteed? Is it only a matter of economic resources that explains poverty and the violation of social rights in Colombia? The consequences that the armed conflict has had on inequality and the lack of an adequate standard of living for a large part of the population, are essentially due to a lack of economic resources, or are there other structural causes that need to be tackled?[173]

As put by the national rapporteur—without denying the relationship between the armed conflict and Colombia's economic resources—also a State's will to fulfill its ESCRs obligations must be accounted for. For example, Colombia maintains a budget limitation as an excuse for not fulfilling its social obligations, while demonstrating constant economic growth and presenting itself as one of the most robust economies in the Latin American region.[174]

This shows that the increase in economic resources does not guarantee on its own a greater compliance with ESCRs or the RtD. Such translation requires also political will. In the best case, Colombia is close to put aside the discourse of the armed conflict as an explanation of all the harms that affects it. However, after the armed conflict there will always be other discourses available that can help present the decisions made as external situations that objectively limit resources.[175] Currently, this could be the Venezuelan refugee crisis.[176]

As a country entering a post-conflict phase like Colombia demonstrates external circumstances may only be used to a certain degree to explain why ESCRs and the RtD are not ensured. In the end, also the political will of a country is essential to realize the RtD and the fight against poverty.

The Fight Against Poverty and the RtD in International Trade and Investment Law

During the workshop session at the 20th Congress of the International Academy of Comparative Law, we discussed how the fight against poverty and the RtD are

---

[171] See in this volume Betancur-Restrepo, the Colombian Legal Framework for Social Rights and the Challenges of a Post-Conflict Society, section 5.

[172] Germany, United States, Taiwan.

[173] See in this volume Betancur-Restrepo, the Colombian Legal Framework for Social Rights and the Challenges of a Post-Conflict Society, section 5.

[174] See in this volume Betancur-Restrepo, the Colombian Legal Framework for Social Rights and the Challenges of a Post-Conflict Society, section 5.

[175] See in this volume Betancur-Restrepo, the Colombian Legal Framework for Social Rights and the Challenges of a Post-Conflict Society, section 5.

[176] https://www.nationalgeographic.com/photography/proof/2018/06/refugees-venezuela-colombia-election-crisis-simon-bolivar-culture/ [visited: 20.02.2020].

broadly relevant in various fields of public international law. Take for example the principle of common but differentiated responsibilities and respective capabilities. This principle originally emerged in international economic law to justify positive discrimination in favour of developing countries: as an illustration the Second UNCTAD conference, convened in 1968, expressed itself in favour of giving preferential treatment solely to developing countries.[177] Moreover, it is interesting how the fields of international trade law and international investment law have incorporated elements of the RtD and the fight against poverty, as also noted by De Schutter in his thematic report.[178]

Human rights treaty bodies have also insisted that the negotiation and conclusion of trade and investment agreements should be preceded by human rights impact assessments. Moreover, the UN Committee on Economic, Social and Cultural Rights have recommended that trade and investment agreements include a specific provision about the primacy of human rights obligations.[179] De Schutter in his report also envisages how trade and investment agreements could make a positive contribution to the realization of the RtD.[180]

As international trade law and international investment law have evolved separately,[181] we will deal with these areas in two parts below.

International Trade Law

Today, international trade law is mainly governed by the World Trade Organization, as its agreement(s) covers about 164 States and 98% of world trade.[182]

The WTO's legal framework is composed of several agreements that together compose one single agreement—the Marrakesh Agreement[183]—which besides Annex 4 has to be accepted by members as a single undertaking. Although the WTO is thought to only deal with trade matters, there are many examples of

---

[177]See in this volume De Schutter, the International Dimensions of the Right to Development: Enabling Poverty-Reduction in Domestic Legal Orders by a Reformed International Legal Order, section 4.2.

[178]See in this volume De Schutter, the International Dimensions of the Right to Development: Enabling Poverty-Reduction in Domestic Legal Orders by a Reformed International Legal Order, section 5.5.

[179]See in this volume De Schutter, the International Dimensions of the Right to Development: Enabling Poverty-Reduction in Domestic Legal Orders by a Reformed International Legal Order, section 5.4 and section 5.5.

[180]See in this volume De Schutter, the International Dimensions of the Right to Development: Enabling Poverty-Reduction in Domestic Legal Orders by a Reformed International Legal Order, section 5.4 and section 5.5.

[181]For an account of how international trade law and international investment law have evolved, see *e.g.* Kurtz (2016).

[182]WTO website, https://www.wto.org/english/thewto_e/thewto_e.htm [visited: 20.02.2020].

[183]It is also referred to as the WTO Agreement and the WTO Institutional Agreement.

non-trade values within its legal system. For at start, the preamble of the Marrakesh Agreement takes into account,

> . . .allowing for the optimal use of the world's resources in accordance with the objective of sustainable development, seeking both to protect and preserve the environment and to enhance the means for doing so in a manner consistent with their respective needs and concerns at different levels of economic development.[184]

Another example is Article XX of the GATT, which contains a closed set of admissible justifications to otherwise prohibited measures, including environmental and social concerns.[185] In his thematic report, De Schutter argues that the clause could justify the reliance on environmental conditions or labour rights considerations to restrict market access of certain products.[186]

In this regard, De Schutter argues that the RtD as a framework could serve as a useful tool, especially if combined with a reference to the common but differentiated responsibilities and respective capabilities of different States. However, De Schutter also acknowledges that trade policy measures made to protect the environment and labour rights should be designed in a way that encourages countries to move in the right direction rather than be a sanctioning mechanism.[187]

Finally, De Schutter argues that as the WTO legal framework already provides for non-trade values it is possible to advance the international dimension of the RtD and fight against poverty within the system. As such he finds that,

> [t]rade can be a tool for development, provided countries use the flexibilities allowed under the multilateral trade regime, and provided they remain guided, in their reliance on such flexibilities, by the universally agreed human rights norms.[188]

International Investment Law

International investment law is heavily associated with international trade law, however, has mostly been kept as a separate field. An important difference from international trade law is the dispute settlement mechanism. Whereas, WTO law and international trade law issues have traditionally been settled by State-to-State mechanisms, international investment law has given the foreign investor the opportunity to file a complaint directly against the host State.

---

184 Marrakesh Agreement, Preamble.

185 See for example Article XX(g), GATT.

186 See in this volume De Schutter, the International Dimensions of the Right to Development: Enabling Poverty-Reduction in Domestic Legal Orders by a Reformed International Legal Order, section 5.4.

187 See in this volume De Schutter, the International Dimensions of the Right to Development: Enabling Poverty-Reduction in Domestic Legal Orders by a Reformed International Legal Order, section 5.4.

188 See in this volume De Schutter, the International Dimensions of the Right to Development: Enabling Poverty-Reduction in Domestic Legal Orders by a Reformed International Legal Order, section 5.4.

From the outset, it is thus interesting to note that international human rights claim mechanisms share procedural similarities with international investment law. Both fields allow a non-State actor to bring a claim against a State for a violation of an international obligation in a forum outside the domestic legal system.[189] As such, human rights law and investment law are widening public international law to more than just inter-State relations.

However, even though the two systems share procedural similarities, international investment treaties include almost no references to ESCRs, sustainable development, the fight against poverty or the RtD. Moreover, because of the investment regime's current structure some say it has stronger legal protection than that of human rights: forcing States to prioritize foreign investors over their own citizens.[190]

Under the current investment treaty regime, arbitral tribunals are not inclined to consider such difficulties for the State, as the system is balanced in favour of the investor.[191] To this extent, although not necessarily just because of human rights concerns, several States are terminating their investment treaties and/or removing the possibility for arbitration.[192] As an example, the European Union is looking to make an investment treaty, which would abolish the arbitration mechanism and also implement EU human rights jurisprudence.[193]

Furthermore, new-generation bilateral and multilateral investment treaties are including more ways for States to defend themselves against investor claims; for example, by excluding former investment protections or by legitimatizing traditional wrongdoings if the State have pursued human rights considerations. This approach, *i.e.* changing the substantive content of the investment regime, seem to be the current way forward.[194] From a legal viewpoint this seems as a promising avenue to regulate investment, as it changes the black letter of the treaties, which shall be given legal effect by arbitral tribunals or by whatever other dispute settlement mechanism established in the treaty.

Recently, this change in investment treaties has been driven by African countries, in what has been deemed the Africanization of international investment law.[195] The Pan-African Investment Code ("PAIC"), although not adopted as a binding instrument,[196] is highly innovate and showcases the potential future of investment treaties.[197] As such, the PAIC adopts human rights approaches in the treaty, while

[189]Khalfan (2011), p. 70.

[190]Sornarajah (2013), pp. 493–495.

[191]Muir Watt (2012), p. 2.

[192]Sornarajah (2013), p. 484.

[193]Sornarajah (2013), p. 476.

[194]Muir Watt (2012), p. 5.

[195]Mbengue and Scacherer (2018).

[196]Mbengue and Scacherer (2018).

[197]Mbengue and Scacherer (2018), pp. 447–448.

also omitting or curtailing several former investment protections. It even excludes several types of investment from treaty protection.[198]

In his thematic report, Olivier De Schutter confirms this trend in international investment law and proposes that the RtD should serve as a framework for arbitral tribunals to take into account human rights concerns.[199]

The Fight Against Poverty and the RtD in Business and Human Rights

The area of business and human rights has the potential to also contribute to the fight against poverty and the RtD, as a globalized world demands transnational solutions, when multinational companies operate abroad. For example, such need for transnational solutions was seen with the horrifying Rana Plaza collapse in 2013 killing more than 1000 factory workers in Bangladesh. A transnational solution was needed, as it can be difficult for individual States, specifically least developed countries, to prosecute multinationals for their actions.

In the example of the Rana Plaza collapse, a voluntary mechanism was implemented. Concretely, the textile industry, the trade unions and the International Labour Organization went together trying to ensure that such tragedy would not repeat itself.[200] Effectively, they made an agreement ("the Accord"): The Accord provides basic safety standards for the factories and involvement measures for the employees.[201] If the subsidiaries of the signatory companies do not comply with the Accord, then the mother company (the international investor) can ultimately face arbitration proceedings.[202]

Even though the Accord is voluntary in nature, more than two million factory workers are now covered by the Accord, which is over half of Bangladesh's workers in the textile industry.[203] Furthermore, the Accord foresees that the Bangladesh government eventually take over the responsibility of the Accord.[204]

The traction that the field of business and human rights currently has stems in some measure from the UN Human Rights Council unanimously endorsing the UN

[198] Mbengue and Scacherer (2018).

[199] See in this volume De Schutter, the International Dimensions of the Right to Development: Enabling Poverty-Reduction in Domestic Legal Orders by a Reformed International Legal Order, section 5.5.

[200] Accord, Introduction to the Accord on Fire and Building Safety in Bangladesh, Brochure, 2015, p. 3.

[201] Accord, Introduction to the Accord on Fire and Building Safety in Bangladesh, Brochure, 2015, p. 3.

[202] 2018 Accord on Fire and Building Safety in Bangladesh, Scope, p. 2.

[203] Accord, Introduction to the Accord on Fire and Building Safety in Bangladesh, Brochure, 2015, p. 6.

[204] 2018 Accord on Fire and Building Safety in Bangladesh, Termination of the Agreement, p. 8.

Guiding Principles on Business and Human Rights in 2011.[205] Many initiatives in addition to the Rana Plaza Accord have built on the UN Guiding Principles; as an example, the International Bar Association in 2016 adopted a guide on business and human rights directed at business lawyers.[206] The guide sets out how lawyers, when advising their clients, have a key role and responsibility in transmitting the principles found in the UN Guiding Principles.[207]

There is a range of other international instruments with an impact on the field. Corruption and money laundering are among the fields in which the international community has agreed on an international treaty regime in order to promote goals including the RtD. The rules include wide ranging duties on authorities, companies and individuals with home and host country authorities agreeing to administrative and criminal enforcement. International organisations and less permanent forms of cooperation contribute with monitoring and advice, in particular on money laundering. In the wider field of corporate liability most instruments share a "soft law" nature with the UN Guiding Principles. This does not prevent them from producing legal effects. The relationship between companies and the two principal sources of international law, treaty law and customary international law, is important. But there are clear shortcomings of treaties and custom in this field, but general principles of law are tools for the interpretation of state human rights obligations concerning corporate activities, and as a legal basis to develop corporate obligations.

Business and human rights were also mentioned in the national report of the Netherlands. Here, the Netherlands has begun to play the role of facilitator with a view to stimulating non-State actors, especially the corporate sector, to take responsibility for the achievement of fair labour conditions, sustainable production cycles and strengthening the rule of law.[208]

The business and human rights area is still emerging. For example, the United Nations High Commissioner for Human Rights have submitted reports on improving accountability and access to remedy for victims of business-related human rights abuse.[209] The interaction of international and domestic law may give rise to general principles of law. Among the questions for future exploration is the role of principles in interpreting the existing human rights obligations vis-à-vis corporate activities, the role of principles in developing obligations for corporations, and the existence, in international law, of a principle on corporate liability relevant to the protection of human rights. Principles of law, as an interpretative tool and as a source of obligations, provide for a complementary source of a high gap-filling potential in closing

---

[205]United Nations, Guiding Principles on Business and Human Rights, HR/PUB/11/04, 2011, New York and Geneva.

[206]IBA, "*Practical Guide on Business and Human Rights for Business Lawyers*", 2016, p. 7.

[207]IBA, "*Practical Guide on Business and Human Rights for Business Lawyers*", 2016, p. 7.

[208]See in this volume Coomans & ter Vrugt, The Netherlands and the Right to Development, section 5.

[209]See in this volume De Schutter, the International Dimensions of the Right to Development: Enabling Poverty-Reduction in Domestic Legal Orders by a Reformed International Legal Order, section 5.5.

the 'accountability gap' of companies in international law. In particular, the principles of abuse of rights, due diligence and good faith may have a role to play.

Concluding Remarks and Future Developments

It is an uneasy task to conclude on the above general comparative overview. We wanted the general report to reflect the diverse responses of national rapporteurs and the brought nature of the field. Although the questionnaire attached in annex assisted in delineating the subject, we deliberately encouraged national rapporteurs to think outside the box and prepare their reports in their own style. This approach provided many diverse examples on the contributions to the fight against poverty and the RtD specifically—such examples are referenced throughout the general report.

In this regard, it is important to underline the lack of Global South representation in the general report. This gap is even more apparent given the nature of the subject. The thematic report of Olivier De Schutter did balance such gap within the international dimension of the RtD, providing many examples from the Global South. However, we stress the need for future comparative studies of a similar kind, where the datasets are more heavily coming from the Global South as the outcomes and examples may differentiate substantially from the ones in this general report.

Still, the general report gives interesting perspectives of the current state-of-play for the fight against poverty and the RtD in the twenty-first century. We encourage readers to go through both the general report and individual reports, as the individual reports will be able to further qualify the findings of the general report and thus provide the reader with interesting new angles.

Starting with the domestic context, we primarily looked at whether principles from the RtD and the fight against poverty have translated into constitutional obligations or other domestic obligations for States. On a constitutional basis, there were some interesting commonalities: We notice that typically newer constitutions in unitary States would include obligations deriving from the fight against poverty, for example through justiciability of the right to an adequate standard of living. Also, the national reports provided some interesting examples on how State courts considers the justiciability of ESCRs. In general, State courts and international review monitoring mechanisms will pay attention to a State's economic ability to fulfil ESCRs obligations.

Going to the international context and how domestic contributions can further the fight against poverty and the RtD more specifically. Here, we had the thematic report of Olivier De Schutter qualify the findings from the national reports. Interestingly, the thematic report confirmed several propositions. For example, several national reports described how States had not abolished their development programmes during and after the 2008 economic crisis, in fact some developed States have started or have plans to surpass their pre-2008 development aid levels. Although this seem positive at first for the fight against poverty and enshrining RtD obligations, several reports also concluded that the reason for engaging in development policy was accorded to national agendas. As an example, several States wanted to lower the incentives for unskilled migration coming from developing countries. Consequently, development programmes are directed to further anti-terror and anti-immigration policies instead of directly contributing to the fight against poverty and the RtD more specifically. Moreover, some national reports described how otherwise important international processes—such as the SDG's—was used to cover up national agendas instead of truly delivering on RtD obligations. Indeed, all these tendencies were confirmed in the thematic report of Olivier De Schutter.

In addition, the perspectives from several crosscutting themes assist in broadening the debate around the fight against poverty and the RtD to more than traditional public international law issues. For example, the field of business and human rights which *inter alia* examines the potential to hold multinational companies responsible for breach of ESCRs, where nation States have otherwise often failed to provide remedies for victims of abuse. The interaction with other principles of law are important and is in need of further exploration. The RtD should be seen in broader terms than just obligations in relation to individuals and States. To this extent, the RtD can assist in greater coherence across international legal regimes.

Finally, we want to highlight the limits of the law, and some of the national rapporteurs and discussants highlighted the possibility that law may not be the right tool to address the challenges associated with the fight against poverty and the RtD. This was mentioned by several national rapporteurs and during the on-site discussion, which took place in the margins of the 20th Congress of the International Academy of Comparative Law. For example, there were critical voices raised about the possible 'justiciability' of ESCRs: One recurring argument is that a court process can drain economic resources, which could otherwise have been directed to fulfil ESCRs obligations. Moreover, legal action can take years to materialize, as the court systems are traditionally cumbersome. A starving person deprived of the right to an adequate standard of living will not be able to eat immediately by lodging a complaint. This highlights the limits of legal solutions in the fight against poverty and in the realization of the RtD.

However, rights without legal remedies may not be very effective. It is the interaction of rights in the domestic legal order and litigation that make these a reality. Domestic litigation and international litigation as well as access to other bodies such as UN treaty bodies and their individual complaints mechanism have similar functions, and may also develop and clarify how domestic law and international law interact in providing rights and remedies for the individual.

To this extent, litigation serves more than just individual justice in a specific case. Litigation can be a way in which the extent of a right is determined. Standards used in domestic law and international conventions, such as 'progressive realization', require review, and courts and international review mechanisms are increasingly taking such task upon them.

The interplay between domestic law and international law in the formation of custom and general principles on, or with an impact on, the RtD or poverty may become increasingly important. Global action, building on domestic processes, is the outcome of the interplay between complex processes of a formal and informal character. This applies with no less force in many domestic jurisdictions, gradually taking account of international economic rights and their consequences the nation State and its duties to counter poverty effects. The development cooperation between States is becoming more durable and international organisations serve as platforms and independent agents in the way in which they give effect to the wills of their member States. The distinction is not clear between practices and policies that are not legally binding and legal obligations with multi-layered implementation depending on the contributions of different States and organisations. Informal policy instruments may use the forms and words of treaties; and formal treaties may use general and open substantive norms, with varying (or no) provision for implementation and enforcement. The sum of international treaties, state practice, the role of international organisations and domestic processes and their interaction requires further attention. The RtD is increasingly based on the right to self-determination as a peremptory norm (*jus cogens*). The dynamic processes are reaching a transformational stage where international law may bind states in ways which may make the RtD a clearer legal obligation. Other economic and social rights that in general are subject to progressive realization are clarified in these dynamic processes with core rights that may constitute peremptory norms, for instance not to be subject to extreme poverty.

The reports that follow below provide a rich mine for anyone interested in these very fundamental and important issues. Comparative law is not law in the sense of a legal system that on its own provides binding norms or provides for their enforcement. Nevertheless, it assists both domestic law and international law in different ways, including in the determination of what domestic law or international law, or their interaction, mean. There may also be formal mechanisms for taking account of comparative law in the determination of the law that binds and is enforceable through court remedies. Contributions by single states will not, on their own, generate new norms of international law. Still, they may assist in the clarification of other sources of international law, and in the development of customary law and general principles of law. The use of 'progressive realization' as a standard for economic and social rights in the UN conventions, makes the interaction between domestic and international law particularly interesting. That interaction is one mechanism for determining the stages of this progressive realisation. Looking at different domestic jurisdictions provide comparators and assists in establishing what the substantive rights and effective remedies mean.

Legal Documents

UN Commission on Human Rights Res. 4 (XXXIII) (Feb 21, 1977).

African Charter on Human and Peoples' Rights, OAU Doc. CAB/LEG/67/3 (Jun. 27, 1981), art. 22

Declaration on the Right to Development, UN GA Res. 41/128, U.N. Doc. A/Res/41/128 (Dec. 4, 1986).

Vienna Declaration and Programme of Action, adopted at the World Conference on Human Rights in 1993 (Vienna Declaration and Programme of Action, UN Doc. A/CONF. 157/23, Jul. 12, 1993, Part I, par. 10)
UN Commission on Human Rights resolution 1998/72
Declaration on the Right to Development, UN GA Res. 41/128, U.N. Doc. A/Res/41/128 (Dec. 4, 1986)
Constitution of Colombia
German Basic Law
World Conference on Human Rights on 25 June 1993 and endorsed by General Assembly resolution 48/121 of 20 December 1993
WTO Agreement and the WTO Institutional Agreement
Accord, Introduction to the Accord on Fire and Building Safety in Bangladesh, Brochure, 2015
2018 Accord on Fire and Building Safety in Bangladesh
United Nations, Guiding Principles on Business and Human Rights, HR/PUB/11/04, 2011, New York and Geneva
International Bar Association, "*Practical Guide on Business and Human Rights for Business Lawyers*", 2016

Miscellaneous

Geneviève Dufour and David Pavot, reply to the Questionnaire on the Fight Against Poverty and the Right to Development for the 20th General Congress of the International Academy of Comparative Law, Canada national report, 2018 (unpublished).
Report of the Working Group on the Right to Development on its seventeenth session (Geneva, 25 April – 3 May 2016)
Inter-American Commission on Human Rights, *Report on Poverty and Human Rights in the Americas*, 2017

Websites

https://www.ohchr.org/EN/ProfessionalInterest/Pages/UniversalHumanRightsInstruments.aspx [visited: 20.02.2020].
https://www.nationalgeographic.com/photography/proof/2018/06/refugees-venezuela-colombia-election-crisis-simon-bolivar-culture/ [visited: 20.02.2020]
WTO website, https://www.wto.org/english/thewto_e/thewto_e.htm [visited: 20.02.2020]
http://www.ohchr.org/EN/Issues/Development/Pages/Introduction.aspx [visited: 20.02.2020]

News Articles

Damian Carrington, "Climate apartheid: UN expert says human rights may not survive. Right to life is likely to be undermined alongside the rule of law, special rapporteur says", *The Guardian,* 25 June, 2019

Robert Booth & Patrick Butler, "UK austerity has inflicted 'great misery' on citizens, UN says. Poverty envoy says callous policies driven by political desire for social re-engineering", *The Guardian,* 16 November 2019

References

Books and Journal Articles

Alston P (2005) Ships passing in the night: the current state of the human rights and development debate seen through the lens of the millennium development goals. Human Rights Q, 27

Bittner C (2011) Human Dignity as a Matter of Legislative Consistency in an Ideal World: The Fundamental Right to Guarantee a Subsistence Minimum in the German Federal Constitutional Court's Judgment of 9 February 2010" Special Section: The Hartz IV Case and the German Sozialstaat: Casenote. German Law J 12

Brabant S, Savourey E (2017) Loi relative au devoir de vigilance, des sanctions pour prévenir et réparer ? Revue Internationale de la Compliance et de l'Éthique des Affaires

Clapham A, Marks S (2005) Human rights. Lexicon, Oxford

Cornia GA (2004) Inequality, growth and poverty: an overview of changes over the last two decades. In: Cornia GA (ed) Inequality, growth and poverty in an era of liberalization and globalization. Oxford University Press

de Schutter O (2010) International human rights law: cases, materials, commentary, 1st edn. Cambridge University Press

Dos Costa F (2008) Poverty and human rights: from rhetoric to legal obligations a critical account of conceptual frameworks. Sur Revista Internacional de Direitos Humanos 5(9)

Fukuda-Parr S (2017) Millennium development goals: ideas, interests and influence. Routledge

Fukuyama F (1992) The end of history and the last man. Free Press

Ibhawoh B (2011) The right to development: the politics and polemics of power and resistance. Human Rights Q 33(1)

Jung C, Hirschl R, Rosevear E (2014) Economic and social rights in national constitutions. Am J Comp Law 62(4)

Khalfan A (2011) International investment law and human rights, preface. Kluwer Law International, Chapter 4

Kurtz J (2016) The WTO and international investment law. Cambridge University Press

M'baye K (1972) Le Droit du Développement comme un Droit de l'Homme. Revue des Droits de l'Homme 5:503

Marks SP (2010) Obligations to implement the right to development: philosophical, political, and legal rationales. In: Marks SP, Andreassen B (eds) Development as a human right, 2nd edn. Intersentia

Mbengue MM, Scacherer S (2018) The Africanization of international investment law: the Pan-African investment code and the reform of the international investment regime. Brill Nijhoff

Milanovic B (2016) Global inequality: a new approach for the age of globalization. Harvard University Press
Muir Watt H (2012) The contested legitimacy of investment arbitration and the human rights ordeal
Nolan A, Porter B, Lanford M (2009) The justiciability of social and economic rights: an updated appraisal. CHRGJ Working Paper No. 15
Pogge T (2002) World poverty and human rights: cosmopolitan responsibilities and reform, polity, 2002. For a useful discussion, see Malcom Langford, "Socio-Economic Rights". In: Maliks R, Schaffer J (eds) Moral and political conceptions of human rights: implications for theory and practice. Cambridge University Press, 2017
Roman D (2012) La justiciabilité DES DROITS SOCIAUX: vecturs et résistances
Sachs J (2005) The end of poverty: economic possibilities of our time. Penguin
Sen A (1999) Development as freedom. Oxford University Press
Sengupta A (2010) Human rights and extreme poverty. Econ Polit Week 45(17), April 24–30
Shivji IG (1989) The concept of human rights in Africa. Codesria
Sornarajah M (2013) The case against a regime on international investment law. Oxford University Press
Uvin P (2004) Human rights and development. Kumarian Press
Young K (2008) The minimum core of economic and social rights: a concept in search of content. Yale J Int Law 33(1)
Yusuf AA (2014) Pan-Africanism and International Law
Yusuf AA (2016) Diversity of legal traditions and international law. Cambridge Int Law J 24:681

Chapter 2
The Colombian Legal Framework for Social Rights and the Challenges of a Post-conflict Society

Laura Betancur-Restrepo

Abstract This national report on Colombia focus on the most relevant aspects of how social rights and the fight against poverty are addressed and protected in the Inter-American Human Rights System and in the Colombian constitutional law. It also tackles the main legal tools in the interaction between international and domestic law. The discussion on social rights at the inter-American and constitutional level takes place within the context of the right to a dignified life, the fight against poverty and the satisfaction of an adequate minimum standard of living. Additionally, at a domestic level, the report shows that the Colombian Constitutional Court has been an essential actor in guaranteeing the social rights charter included in the 1991 Constitution and in creating a privileged protection framework for the most vulnerable communities. Lastly, the report makes some remarks on these issues regarding the current situation of Colombia and its transition from an internal armed conflict to a post-conflict scenario, discussing how the peace agreement can potentially enable social change. This last part suggests that besides the relationship between the armed conflict and Colombia's economic resources, to achieve greater compliance with social rights requires also political will.

Introduction

The anxiety for development has always been present in the history of Colombia since its independence, as in other countries that have experienced decolonization followed by a process of integration and acceptance in an international society led by

I would like to thank Laura Arboleda and Juliana Barberena for invaluable research assistance. Mistakes that remain are my own.

L. Betancur-Restrepo (✉)
Universidad de los Andes, Faculty of Law, Bogotá, Colombia
e-mail: l.betancur52@uniandes.edu.co

M. Andenas et al. (eds.), *The Fight Against Poverty and the Right to Development*, Ius Comparatum - Global Studies in Comparative Law 52,
https://doi.org/10.1007/978-3-030-57324-9_2

those who colonized them.[1] This, together with the long internal armed conflict that has lashed the country for more than 50 years, have made the different issues related to development and poverty a part of the historical concerns of Colombian governments. Such issues have found different manifestations within their international and national legal framework. Many times, the different models of development implemented in Colombia have closely followed the models preferred internationally.[2] This is done probably with the hope that, if Colombia follows those international models, it will be able to get rid of the labels that classify it as a country that is some steps behind the group of States to which Colombia aspires to belong.[3]

If we examine the legal frameworks applicable to Colombia, we can attest that the international legal framework of which Colombia is currently part is very extensive. Colombia has traditionally been very active internationally, is part of multiple international organizations[4] and commercial alliances (including several free trade agreements)[5] and has ratified different international treaties and supported other initiatives related to the multiple dimensions of human rights, the fight against poverty and development.[6] At the domestic level, the protection of social rights is considered one of the pillars (and novelties) of the new Colombian constitutionalism

[1]There is plenty of literature on the relationship between the process of colonization and decolonization and the legal and political consequences assumed by the new States in order to be accepted on equal terms by the rest of the international society. See for example: Wilder (2014), p. 241; Anghie (2004); Eslava (2019).

[2]See: Alviar (2016a, b) and Eslava (2019).

[3]In recent decades, these labels have gone from "underdeveloped" or "developing country" to a "state with an emerging economy." Recently, this last label has been accompanied by the classification as one of the most inequitable States in the world. In the latest update of the Gini Index made in December 2015, the World Bank (WB) ranked Colombia as the second most unequal country in Latin America and the seventh globally, with an index of 51.1. In addition, if Colombia's income (considered by the WB as medium-high income) is taken into account, it is considered the most unequal in the region. See World Bank (2017) and BBC (2016).

[4]Colombia is a member of the United Nations (UN), the Organization of American States (OAS), part of the WB, the International Monetary Fund (IMF), the Inter-American Development Bank (IDB), the International Labor Organization (ILO), the World Trade Organization (WTO), the Andean Community of Nations (ACN), among others.

[5]For example: Pacific Alliance (2011), ACN Agreement (Act. No. 8, 1973), Free Trade Agreement (FTA) between Chile and Colombia (Act No. 1189, 2008), FTA between Mexico and Colombia (Act No. 172, 1994), FTA between the United States of America and Colombia (Act No. 1143, 2007), FTA between the European Union and Colombia (Act. No. 1669, 2013) or FTA between Canada and Colombia (Act no. 1363, 2009).

[6]For instance, Colombia is part of different ILO agreements (C002 (1919) ratified by Colombia on 1933, C003 (1919) ratified by Colombia on 1933, C008 (1920) ratified by Colombia on 1933, C012 (1921) ratified by Colombia on 1933, C017 (1925) ratified by Colombia on 1933, C095 (1949) ratified by Colombia on 1963, C099 (1951) ratified by Colombia on 1969, C189 (2011) ratified by Colombia on 2014, C100 (1951) ratified by Colombia on 1963); the International Covenant on Civil and Political Rights (1966), ratified by Colombia on 1969; the International Covenant on Economic, Social and Cultural Rights (1966), ratified by Colombia on 1969; the American Convention On Human Rights (ACHR) (1969) ratified by Colombia on 1972; the Universal Declaration of Human Rights (UDHR) (1948) signed by Colombia on 1948, the Declaration on the Right to Development

that emerged from the 1991 Constitution. In addition, topics such as development and the eradication of poverty have been incorporated into numerous legislations and public policies and are part of the action of multiple state agencies.

In this regard, the invitation to be a rapporteur for Colombia on issues of social rights, development and poverty is an immense task that can be approached from multiple angles. I have decided to choose some specific aspects that allow comparisons with other cases, considering that one of the main objectives of this series of studies seeks to present different national scenarios to facilitate a comparative study between the protection provided by the social rights and the fight against poverty as well as the interaction between the domestic and the international legal frameworks in that regard. Therefore, I decided to narrow the legal frameworks to the Inter-American Human Rights System (IAHRS) and constitutional law, and also to lay out some important challenges for the post-conflict context in which Colombia is. In order to do that, I will start describing the most relevant aspects of how social rights are addressed and protected in the IAHRS (section 'The Protection of Social Rights in the Inter-American Human Rights System (IAHRS)') and in the Colombian constitutional law (section 'Colombian Constitutional Framework'). Subsequently, I will highlight some of the legal tools most used in the interaction between international and domestic law (section 'Legal Tools for Interaction Between International and National Legal Frameworks'). Lastly, I will make some final remarks on these issues regarding the current situation of Colombia and its transition from an internal armed conflict to a post-conflict scenario (section 'Final Remarks: Challenges for Peace, Development and Poverty in the Discourse of Post-conflict Colombia').

Before continuing, I am aware of the restrictions involved in the selection of the legal frameworks chosen for this study, which must be interpreted within the limits and biases that they contain. On the one hand, the international presented here focuses on the IAHRS because I wanted to include a regional perspective that complements the perspective that other studies collected in this book will surely make of the universal system, and to highlight some peculiarities that this system has for Colombia. This, in no way, seeks to diminish the importance of the relationship between Colombian domestic law and universal international law. Quite the opposite: Colombia, being a State that traditionally wants to present itself as collaborative internationally, is part of most of international treaties, organizations or conferences and this, logically, includes the universal international system.

On the other hand, the selection of the constitutional legal framework seems interesting to me because the constitutional judge has probably been the most progressive state actor regarding the interpretation of the scope and level of protection that should be given to social rights, the role of the State, its duties against poverty and its obligations of guaranteeing a decent standard of living. However, at

(1986), voted in favor by Colombia on the United Nations General Assembly (A/RES/41/128) and the Rio Declaration on Environment and Development (1992) signed in 2011, among others.

the same time, it must be borne in mind that their work only represents a fraction of the legal operators in Colombia working on development and poverty.[7]

Lastly, the final notes related to the current situation in Colombia may seem detached from the other two sections that follow more closely the questionnaire given by the editors of this comparative study. However, I did not want to miss the opportunity to raise some of the challenges that the social rights and the fight against poverty have at this stage of the Colombian transition from armed conflict to peace. In that section, I just want to outline some remarks that arise in this post-conflict stage and that will undoubtedly play an important role in the way Colombia is going to decide how it will build peace faced with traditionally unprotected populations whose rights have been historically violated.

The Protection of Social Rights in the Inter-American Human Rights System (IAHRS)

Colombia, in addition to being a member of the OAS,[8] has recognized the competence of the two main organs that comprise the IAHRS: the Inter-American Commission on Human Rights (IACHR)[9] and the Inter-American Court of Human Rights (IACourtHR).[10] According to this, an individual who considers his rights violated by the Colombian State can go to the IACHR, which can decide to take the case before the IACourtHR. Colombia participates actively before the different instances of the IAHRS and its cases (contentious or not) have been the subject of multiple reports, observations and judgments.[11]

The protection of social rights is regulated in different inter-American treaties. The OAS Charter (1967) states in Article 2 that one of the essential purposes of the Organization is "To promote, by cooperative action, [the] economic, social, and cultural development" of its Member States (Article 2§f) and "to eradicate extreme poverty, which constitutes an obstacle to the full democratic development of peoples of the hemisphere" (Article 2§g). Article 3 identifies the elimination of extreme

[7]For a study that compares the role of the constitutional judge with other state entities, specifically in matters of economic development and the right to property, see: Alviar (2016a, b).

[8]The OAS was created in 1948 at the same time that the American Declaration of the Rights and Duties of Man was signed in Bogota.

[9]Organ in charge of monitoring of the human rights situation in the Member States and of receiving and processing individual petitions that denounce the breach of state obligations. A matter before the IACHR may end in a friendly settlement, in a report or in the case's referral to the IACourtHR.

[10]Autonomous judicial institution whose purpose is the application of the *corpus iuris* of the system. The Court can exercise adjudicatory and advisory jurisdiction. Colombia accepted its jurisdiction in 1985.

[11]"Colombia is the second country in the region with the most cases before the Inter-American Human Rights System, which includes the Commission and the Court." El Colombiano (2018) (own translation).

poverty as "an essential part of the promotion and consolidation of representative democracy and is the common and shared responsibility of the American States" and Article 34 reiterates the common objective of combating critical poverty and provides that Member States agree to devote their maximum efforts to the achievement of a series of basic goals.[12]

In addition to these general references, these rights are regulated by other treaties on human rights that are part of the basic instruments comprising the *corpus iuris* of the IAHRS,[13] mainly the American Convention on Human Rights (hereinafter ACHR, also called the Pact of San José de Costa Rica)[14] and the Additional Protocol to the American Convention on Economic, Social and Cultural Rights (also called Protocol of San Salvador).[15] Both treaties were strongly influenced by the content and the division of rights of the International Covenant on Civil and Political Rights and the International Covenant on Economic, Social and Cultural Rights. But despite this general division, the ACHR mentions the protection of Economic, Social and Cultural Rights (ESCR) and the Protocol of San Salvador emphasizes the indivisibility and interdependence of all human rights.[16]

Regarding the protection of ESCR, the Protocol of San Salvador specify that the States' obligation is to the "extent allowed by their available resources" and "taking into account their degree of development," similarly the ACHR says that the guarantee and protection measures must be taken "progressively."[17] That is the

[12]The goals mentioned include: modernization of rural life, proper nutrition, urban conditions for healthy, productive and full life, fair wages, acceptable working conditions, eradication of illiteracy, adequate housing, among others.

[13]Several human rights' treaties are part of the *corpus iuris* of the IAHRS and most of them are ratified by Colombia. See for example: Inter-American Convention to Prevent and Punish Torture (1999), Protocol of San Salvador (1997), Inter-American Convention on the Prevention, Punishment and Eradication of Violence Against Women "Convention of Belem Do Para" (1997), Inter-American Convention on the Forced Disappearance of Persons (2005), Inter-American Convention on the Elimination of All Forms of Discrimination against Person with Disabilities (2004).

[14]Ratified by Colombia in 1973.

[15]Ratified by Colombia in 1997.

[16]Protocol of San Salvador (1997), Preamble: "Considering the close relationship that exists between economic, social and cultural rights, and civil and political rights, in that the different categories of rights constitute an indivisible whole based on the recognition of the dignity of the human person, for which reason both require permanent protection and promotion if they are to be fully realized, and the violation of some rights in favor of the realization of others can never be justified." See Salvioli (2004, p. 12) on how the IACHR and IACourtHR have emphasized this indivisibility and interdependence of human rights.

[17]Protocol of San Salvador (1997) Article 1: "The States Parties to this Additional Protocol to the American Convention on Human Rights undertake to adopt the necessary measures, both domestically and through international cooperation, especially economic and technical, to the extent allowed by their available resources, and taking into account their degree of development, for the purpose of achieving progressively and pursuant to their internal legislations, the full observance of the rights recognized in this Protocol."

ACHR (1969) Chapter III: Economic, Social, and Cultural Rights, Article 26: Progressive Development "The States Parties undertake to adopt measures, both internally and through treaties comprise a difference between the protection that must be provided to civil and political rights (even if the resources are scarce) and the protection that States must provide in matters of ESCR. States are required to make an *effort* to comply with ESCR, but only as far as resources and degree of development allow them to. Within the margins of this limitation of state obligations, the IACHR has considered that Colombia, precisely because it has shown an accelerated economic development in recent years, should be able to more adequately guarantee social rights, including the right to a dignified life and the reduction of inequality and extreme poverty in the country. Instead, it has found that this economic development does not result in a better quality of life or a better distribution of resources among its population (particularly the most vulnerable ones due to race, gender, sexual orientation and poverty.)[18]

Another debate widely discussed regards the justiciability of the ESCR and the limits of its protection. Without going into details of this widely studied topic,[19] today it is possible to affirm that the IACHR, in its reports and recommendations, addresses the issue of social rights in conjunction with that of civil and political rights. Similarly, the IACourtHR has included in many of its judgments specific references to the ESCR and has gone from a timid application of the reference made by the ACHR of the ESCR, to a protection by connection with other civil and political rights and, finally, to a more direct application of the Protocol of San Salvador.[20]

In addition to this incorporation made of the ESCR in the general practice of the IACHR and the IACourtHR, it is worth noting that, since 2001, the IACHR began to refer specifically to the situation of poverty and extreme poverty as part of its study on the situation of human rights in the countries of the American region. For the IACHR, poverty constitutes "a generalized violation of all human rights, both civil and political as well as social, economic and cultural."[21] The interest in this topic resulted in the publication of the first report on the subject of poverty and human

---

international cooperation, especially those of an economic and technical nature, with a view to achieving progressively, by legislation or other appropriate means, the full realization of the rights implicit in the economic, social, educational, scientific, and cultural standards set forth in the Charter of the Organization of American States as amended by the Protocol of Buenos Aires".

[18] IACHR (2013) §596, §610.

[19] This debate has also taken place at the UN and at the domestic level, as we will see below on the discussion before de Colombian Constitutional Court. On the different topics addressed by the IACHR, see Salvioli (2004). On the justiciability before the IACourtHR see Instituto Interamericano de Derechos Humanos (IIDH) (2009) & Parra Vera (2011).

[20] "In this regard, the Court deems it is appropriate to recall the interdependence that exists between civil and political rights and economic, social and cultural rights, since they should be fully understood as human rights, without any rank and enforceable in all the cases before competent authorities," IACourtHR (2009), §101. In this case, the Court refers to European case law and observations of the UN ESCR Committee to reaffirm the application of the principles of progressiveness and non-regression in the protection of ESCR (see §102, 103).

[21] IACHR (2017) §1, quoting IACHR, Third Report on the Situation of Human Rights in Paraguay, March 2001, §5 (consulted in Spanish, all quotes are my own translation).

rights in the region in 2017.[22] In this report it was stated that in the American region, during the last decade, important advances were achieved in the area of social, economic, cultural and environmental rights, which allowed large sectors of the population to escape poverty and extreme poverty. However, the report also stated that the situation of poverty and extreme poverty persists in some of the OAS Member States and, as a result, there are serious obstacles to the effective enjoyment of human rights. In the case of Colombia, special mention is made about the particularly vulnerable situation of Afro population (and within this population, to even more unprotected sectors such as children, women and communities affected by violence).[23]

According to this report, the case law of the IACourtHR has addressed issues related to poverty and extreme poverty in relation to several human rights protected by inter-American treaties and taking into consideration contributions from the universal system. For the IACHR, this reflects that the organs of the IAHRS consider human rights treaties as "life instruments the interpretation of which must accompany the evolution of times and current life conditions."[24] According to this, despite the fact that the IACHR considers that the jurisprudence of people living in poverty is still in development, it affirms that this situation "results in specific state obligations."[25] Thus, the Court has determined that there is room for international responsibility of a State when it does not adopt necessary measures that allow people, groups and communities living in poverty and extreme poverty to have access to the minimum conditions that provide the possibility of having a dignified life.[26]

Regarding this, the Court has said that the situation of poverty, exclusion and marginalization can cause violations of human rights[27] or be an aggravating circumstance for human rights violations.[28] Likewise, the IACourtHR has found that poverty is a factor of social violence and exclusion of progress.[29] The Court has also referred to the concept of a dignified life within the obligations imposed by Article 4 of the ACHR that protects the right to life, and has established that "the fundamental right to life includes, not only the right of every human being not to be deprived of his life arbitrarily, but also the right that he will not be prevented from

---

[22]Ibid.

[23]Ibid. §379, 381, 386, 387, 389.

[24]Ibid, §142.

[25]Ibid, §143.

[26]Ibid, §205.

[27]IACourtHR (2006b) §117.

[28]IACourtHR (2006a) §181.

[29]In a case involving minors in a situation of poverty, the Court said: "the State did not provide [. . .] an environment that would protect them from violence and abuse, nor did it allow them access to basic services and goods, in such a way that said absence without doubt deprived the minors of their possibility to emancipate, develop, and become adults that could determine their own future". The Court also stressed the State's obligation to "ensure the protection of children and youngsters affected by poverty and socially alienated and, especially, to avoid their social stigmatization as criminals." IACourtHR (2006b) §116–117.

having access to the conditions that guarantee a dignified existence."[30] As part of the right to a dignified life, the Court has referred to specific conditions and demands of the State related to the special affectations of the right to health and, intimately related to it, the right to food and access to clean water, which have an impact on the basic conditions for the exercise of other human rights.[31] Many other rights, such as housing rights, have been indirectly protected when associated with the right to a dignified life (related actions).[32]

This legal framework of the IAHRS may be applied in Colombia at several levels. Firstly, the organs of the system can assess the compliance with Colombia's international obligations. This not only includes human rights' treaty law, but also IACourtHR case law.[33] Secondly, as I will explain later, the main human rights treaties of the IAHRS ratified by Colombia have constitutional status.

Colombian Constitutional Framework

One of the greatest innovations that the Colombian Constitution of 1991 introduced was the broad charter of constitutional rights and the way of making them enforceable, as well as their relation to the self-denomination of Colombia as a Social Rule of Law (*Estado Social de Derecho*), as stipulated by Article 1 of the Constitution. The Constitutional Court (court created by the 1991 Constitution and in charge of its interpretation) has interpreted the concept of Social Rule of Law as a "form of state organization aimed at achieving social justice and human dignity."[34] The court has said that in this type of State, "the social assumptions of the same freedom for all must be created, by suppressing social inequality."[35] The relationship of the Social

[30]IACourtHR (1999) §144, 191.

[31]IACourtHR (2005) §161 y 162. It also determined that "together with the lack of lands, the life of the members of the Sawhoyamaxa Community is characterized by unemployment, illiteracy, morbidity rates caused by evitable illnesses, malnutrition, precarious conditions in their dwelling places and environment, limitations to access and use health services and drinking water, as well as marginalization due to economic, geographic and cultural causes" IACourtHR (2006a) §168. See also Request for interpretation of the Judgment on Merits, Reparations and Costs of February 6, 2006.

[32]"In the current state of inter-American jurisprudence, the right to housing has been indirectly protected, by connection essentially, through the rights to life (Article 4) and right to a private property (Article 21). This in scenarios such as the minimum standard for indigenous peoples' living conditions, forced displacement, massacres, irruption without judicial order and destruction of property." IACourtHR (2016) §40–41.

[33]As I will explain later, in the "conventionality control tool", the IACourtHR has included its decisions as part of the *corpus iuris* with which all States Parties must comply, so they must adapt their legislation accordingly.

[34]Colombian Constitutional Court (2001) (own translation).

[35]Colombian Constitutional Court (1995b) (own translation).

Rule of Law, human dignity[36] and the desire to suppress social inequality is reflected in the extensive catalog of rights protected at the constitutional level, which includes several rights considered as social rights.

The way in which the rights were included in the Constitution reproduced the classic international division between civil and political rights and the ESCR. Therefore, Title II of the Constitution on "Rights, Guarantees and Duties" has a list of "fundamental rights" (chapter 1) and another list of "social, economic and cultural rights" (chapter 2).[37] Despite this division, several rights that we can call *social* are found in the two lists. Thus, within chapter 1, it is included peace as a right and a duty (Article 22), the right to work under decent and fair conditions (Article 25) or the right to create trade unions (Article 39). Additionally, it is said that "The State shall promote the conditions for equality to be real and effective and shall adopt measures in favour of discriminated or marginalized groups" (Article 13§2, own translation) and "The State shall protect especially those people who, due to their economic, physical or mental condition, are in a circumstance of obvious weakness, and shall punish the abuses or mistreatments committed against them" (Article 13§3, own translation). In the list of chapter 2 we find, among others, the right to social security (Article 48); the right to health and environmental sanitation as state public services (Article 49); the right to a decent life (Article 51); several minimum principles that must be part of the labour code (Article 53);[38] the right to collective bargaining to regulate labour relations (Article 55); the right to strike (Article 56); and education both as a right and a public service (Article 67).

In addition to that extensive list of rights explicitly included therein, the 1991 Constitution established that the chart of fundamental rights is an open chart, susceptible to be enriched with other rights. The main ways to enrich this list, to which I will refer later, are through the *constitutional block* (*bloque de constitucionalidad*) and through the *innominate or non enumerated rights* (*derechos innominados*).

Regarding enforceability, the Constitution of 1991 in Article 86 includes the possibility of claiming before judges, with a preferential procedure, the immediate protection of fundamental rights through the filing of the *Acción de Tutela* (a petition procedure which allows individuals to seek protection of fundamental human rights

---

[36]Human dignity has had a broad development in case law of the Constitutional Court. The Court has considered it the foundation of the Social Rule of Law and has said that the fulfillment of other rights is required to guarantee the minimum material conditions necessary to live with dignity. But it has also considered it an autonomous right that can be demanded without being contingent upon other rights. For the different nuances and levels of protection of human dignity in the case law of the Constitutional Court, see, among others: Restrepo Saldarriaga (2008), pp. 266–270; Martínez and Marín (2015), pp. 14–15.

[37]It is worth noting that, additionally, chapter 3 of that same title includes a series of rights called "collective and environmental" to which I will not refer in this text but that are in many ways related to other social rights.

[38]Among which is the equality of opportunities, the minimum wage, the inalienability of the minimum benefits, among others.

before any judge). Likewise, the Constitutional Court was entrusted with the task of reviewing the decisions of the lower-level judges. Additionally, Article 241 of the Constitution included within the functions of the Constitutional Court the power to decide on the public actions of unconstitutionality that any citizen may bring against any law that allegedly contravenes the Constitution (judicial review).

While reviewing the *Tutelas*, the Court determined from its beginnings, on the one hand, which were the rights that could be enforced by means of this legal action and, on the other hand, the nature of the different types of rights that the new Constitution included. Additionally, also while reviewing the *Tutelas* and by exercising judicial review of the laws, the Court has had the opportunity to widely develop the scope of the constitutional block and the innominate rights (including some related to social rights and vulnerable populations). This has meant that, through the case law of the Constitutional Court, the way in which social rights are protected in Colombia has been modified in a short period of time and in an important way. It has also led to a more fluid relationship between the international obligations and the internal enforceability of those obligations.

Protection of Social Rights by the Constitutional Court

During its early years, the Constitutional Court discussed whether or not social rights were equivalent to individual fundamental rights and whether they should be protected in an analogous manner (via *Tutela*). Several of the discussions and changes included in the case law of this Court have been similar to those that have been made at the international level, and have had an important influence on the type of constitutional protection that has been gradually granted to them and on the concrete and flexible application that today tends to be guaranteed.

In its first rulings, the Constitutional Court has clearly stated that guaranteeing the social rights depends on the available resources,[39] a situation that limited the action of the judge and what he or she ordered the State. In this sense, the traditional vision of international law was applied "to define social rights in relation to the scarcity of resources, something that [did] not happen with civil and political rights."[40]

In addition, the Court has discussed whether or not social rights were comparable to individual fundamental rights and whether they should be protected similarly. Considerations on this aspect have also been analogous to those that have been made at the international level, but it is noteworthy that the changes in the decisions of the Court have led to the concrete application of these rights, especially through the use of the *Tutela* (although also through judicial review).

In the first years of operation, the Constitutional Court considered that the ESCR (or rights of the second generation) were not of a fundamental nature, but were

[39]Colombian Constitutional Court (1997a).

[40]Lemaitre (2005), pp. 10–11 (own translation).

derechos prestacionales (welfare rights) and therefore could not be demanded by means of the *Tutela.* The Court stated that their development corresponded to the legislator and to the administration for being considered rights related to welfare benefits.[41] This led to the fact that the Constitutional Court, in multiple rulings during the 1990s, welcomed "the theoretical distinction between civil and political rights, on the one hand, and social, economic and cultural rights, on the other. The first ones were recognized for being fundamental rights susceptible of being protected directly via *Tutela*. The second ones were seen as welfare rights which require, therefore, a legislative or administrative action in order for them to be effectively enforced."[42]

Despite this distinction between rights, the Court began to admit the extension of protection to ESCR through the criterion of *related actions* (*conexidad*). Using this criterion the plaintiff proves that it is necessary the protection of an ESCR to obtain the protection of another right (this one considered a fundamental right), which allows the enforceability of the ESCR through a *Tutela*. "Under this parameter, ESCR were protected in very specific cases, such as the typical right to health and its direct relation to life; on the other hand, housing, when the prohibition of discrimination is violated; and in any case, when the violation of an ESCR endangers a first generation right."[43]

In 2007, the Court modified its position and affirmed that the criterion of related actions was "artificial" since all rights are connected to each other and all are related

[41]This can be reflected in several *Tutela* rulings. For example, in Judgment T-423 (Colombian Constitutional Court, 1992a), the right to decent housing is analyzed and the Court concludes that "it is a welfare right that must be promoted by the State, in accordance with the law, to be lent directly by this or through associative entities equally regulated by law. So it is not a "fundamental right" on which the *Tutela* considered here may fit" (own translation). Judgment T-495 (Colombian Constitutional Court, 1995a) deals with the right to decent housing where it is concluded that "it is a right of assistance nature that requires prior legal development and that must be provided directly by the administration or by the associative entities that intend to benefit from the programs and subsidies (...) Therefore, this right of social content does not give the person a subjective right to demand its full satisfaction immediately and directly from the State, since it is required to comply with legal-material conditions that make it possible" (own translation). In Judgment T-586 (Colombian Constitutional Court, 1999b) the right to social security is analyzed under the concept of payment for family allowance where the Court determines that "As such it is a social and economic right, not fundamental in principle. The case law of the Court has repeatedly affirmed that the economic, social and cultural rights, also called second generation rights, within which we find those included in the concept of social security, are not fundamental, since they do not impinge on the human condition. They do not have direct efficacy or immediate application, understood as the possibility of being claimed directly by the person obliged to recognize them, without a prior law establishing conditions for their exercise. They are, likewise, rights of progressive development, which means that the State has the obligation to extend the coverage of the service provision since they involve the measure of the greater economic and social development that the nation reaches" (own translation).

[42]Colombian Constitutional Court (2011b) (own translation).

[43]Martínez (2014), p. 24 (own translation).

to human dignity.[44] This led to rights that previously required the related actions criterion to have preferential protection, were now declared as fundamental.[45] This also led to its provision being ordered from the State budget in order to guarantee the effective enjoyment of the right.[46]

In 2008, the Court refers to the *prestacional* (welfare) character that was assigned to the ESCR and declares that this is not a characteristic that should belong only to the rights classified as ESCR. The Court reformulates its previous position saying that "the condition of *prestacional* does not belong to the 'rights' category, but to the 'facet of a right'" and that "every right has *prestacional* facets and facets that are *no prestacionales.*"[47] This allows the Court to affirm that all rights (social or not) that include obligations of *prestacional* aspect have particular complexities that cause their compliance to be *progressive*.[48] In this sense,

> progressivity justifies the impossibility of judicially demanding, in individual and concrete cases, the immediate fulfilment of all obligations deriving from the scope of protection of a constitutional right. However, the State is not granted permission to stop adopting appropriate and necessary measures to meet the obligations in question in a progressive manner.[49]

In 2011, the Court reiterated this position on the importance of the progressive fulfilment of the *prestacional* facets of rights, but is increasingly willing to erase the limits of traditional classifications between types of rights affirming that:

> One thing is the fundamentality of rights and another -very different- the ability to make effective, in practice, such rights or the ways used for that purpose. In a scenario like the Colombian characterized by the scarcity of resources, by virtue of the application of the principles of equity, solidarity, subsidiarity and efficiency, it is up to the State and the individuals acting on its behalf to design strategies with the purpose of conferring primacy on the guarantee of effectiveness of the rights of the most needy people because, in general, they lack the indispensable means to make viable the carrying out of their own life projects in conditions of dignity.
>
> In the case of the fundamental right to health, for example, the Constitutional Court has stressed on multiple occasions that this is not a right the protection of which can be requested prima facie through a *Tutela*. Its '*prestacional*' connotation obliges the State to rationalize

[44]Colombian Constitutional Court (2007).

[45]Colombian Constitutional Court (2008b).

[46]The Court (2008b) declared the possibility of filing protective actions to defend and guarantee the right to health, in Judgment C-376 of 2010 to guarantee the right to education and in Judgment T-544 of 2009 the right to access public services and housing, against State actions.

[47]Colombian Constitutional Court (2008b) (own translation).

[48]The Constitutional Court has taken the principle of "progressivity" from the international case law and doctrine. This principle is generally applied together with the principle of "non-regression," also of international inspiration. For the Court, a measure is considered regressive: "(1) when it reduces or limits the substantive scope of protection of the respective right, (2) when it substantially increases the requirements required to access the respective right; (3) when the public resources destined to the satisfaction of the right diminish or deviate significantly." Colombian Constitutional Court (2008a) (own translation).

[49]Ibid.

the allocation of sufficient investment so that its guarantee has an integral scope, as opposed to the need for support that also has the guarantee of other rights within a context of scarce resources.[50]

This classification of rights between those that could be claimed through a *Tutela* and those that could not, finally changed completely in 2012. During this year, the Court recognized the possibility that ESCR were enforceable through a *Tutela* without resorting to the related actions criterion.[51] In this ruling, it was recognized that "constitutional case law has been moving away, increasingly clearly, from the initial decisions that cataloged the protection of the economic, social and cultural rights involved in a *Tutela* as something exceptional due to the non-fundamental nature of the prerogatives that make up that category."[52] Thus, at present there is a greater possibility of requiring a *Tutela* to protect an ESCR, since the reason for accepting such protection no longer falls in the classification of rights, but in the constitutional relevance of the case and the need to resort to that legal action in order to enforce the right.

It is also worth noting that, for the Court, the protection of the ESCR is closely linked to the fight against poverty. The Court has considered that poverty undermines the validity of fundamental rights and the Social Rule of Law and that it must be combated through legislative and macroeconomic policies, measures that in addition to the Court's action require direct and immediate state intervention. The Court has emphasized that the actions of the State should be focused on people who, due to their economic, physical or mental condition, find themselves in circumstances of manifest weakness to improve their situation and that they can carry out any life project they wish,[53] and the authorities have the "obligation to design and execute public policies that allow achieving real and effective equality."[54]

In sum, the Constitutional Court has expanded and made more flexible the protection of the ESCR and the legal mechanisms to make them enforceable. On several occasions, the Court has affirmed that the guarantee of the ESCR is a measure to fight poverty, which is the responsibility of the State and that its authorities must take effective actions in this regard. One of the most significant

---

[50]Colombian Constitutional Court (2011c) (own translation). The same year the Court said: "all fundamental constitutional rights -regardless of whether they are civil, political, economic, social, cultural, environmental - have a *prestacional* nuance, and therefore their practical implementation will always depend on a greater or lesser budgetary expenditure. As a result, depriving the *prestacional* rights -such as the right to health, education, housing, access to drinking water among others- of their fundamental rights nature is not only confusing but contradictory, because if this thesis is adopted, one could not preach the fundamentality of rights, not even of the right to life". Colombian Constitutional Court (2011b) (own translation).

[51]Colombian Constitutional Court (2011c).

[52]Colombian Constitutional Court (2011b) (own translation).

[53]Colombian Constitutional Court (2014b).

[54]Colombian Constitutional Court (2013a) (own translation). In this same decision it is explained that the measures taken to eradicate poverty cannot be regressive, and cannot aggravate further the situation of marginalization of the most vulnerable population.

case law developments in the fight against poverty has been through the *right to the minimum standard of living (derecho al mínimo vital).*

Constitutional Right to the Minimum Standard of Living

Article 94 of the Colombian Constitution contains what has been called the clause of innominate rights (*derechos innominados*), since it stipulates that "the enunciation of the rights and guarantees contained in the Constitution and in the international conventions in force, should not be understood as a denial of others that, being inherent to the human person, do not appear expressly in them." One of the most important developments that the Constitutional Court has made from that clause is the construction in Colombia of the *right to the minimum standard of living (derecho al mínimo vital*) which seeks to "protect people from irreparable damage caused by the lack of attention to a social right."[55]

The Court has built this concept from a holistic interpretation of the Constitution,[56] including the international obligations of Colombia and the development that has been done on this issue at a universal and inter-American level. In this sense, the Court has said that "just as there is an essential content of civil and political rights, the international doctrine considers that there is an essential content of economic and social rights, which is materialized in the minimum rights of subsistence for all, regardless of the level of economic development."[57] This has led to the fact that the constitutional case law has estimated that there is a violation of international obligations of States when the right to the minimum standard of living is not guaranteed.

From its first rulings, the Court explained that the right to the minimum standard of living results from the principles of the Social Rule of Law, such as human dignity and solidarity, and that it is additionally related to the rights to life, integrity and equality.[58] It was later determined that this right

> constitutes the portion of the income of the worker or pensioner that is destined to the financing of their basic needs, such as food, housing, clothing, access to home public utilities, recreation, health care, prerogatives whose ownership is essential to achieve the right to human dignity, a fundamental value of the Colombian legal system.[59]

To fill this right with content, the Court has referred to international instruments. Thus, in Judgment T-199 of 2016, the Court quotes Article 25 of the Universal Declaration of Human Rights, Articles 7 and 11 of the International Covenant on Economic, Social and Cultural Rights and Article 7 of the Protocol of San Salvador.

---

[55] Arango and Lemaitre (2003), p. 23 (own translation).

[56] Arango (2001), p. 188.

[57] Colombian Constitutional Court (1997b) (own translation).

[58] Colombian Constitutional Court (1992b).

[59] Colombian Constitutional Court (1999a) (own translation).

The Court says that certain specific characteristics of the right to the minimum standard of living result from these international norms, namely: "(i) it is the basic access of decent conditions of existence for the development of the individual, (ii) it depends of its particular situation and (iii) it is an indeterminate concept the concretion of which depends on the particular circumstances of each case, so it requires a qualitative and a case-by-case analysis."[60]

This right, which can be claimed by means of *Tutela* as any other fundamental right protected at the constitutional level, has within its characteristics that it is available only to poor claimants and that the judge can make a ruling based on equity. The *Tutela* for the right to the minimum standard of living gives the judge a wide discretionary power: its classification depends on each case and, additionally, the protection of a minimum standard of life fits with respect to actions or omissions of the State but also of private actors.[61]

Some scholars have stressed that the protection and characteristics of this right, can be seen as contributions of Colombian constitutionalism in the field of human rights in societies with "structural situations of inequality,"[62] as an innovative way of distributing "access to justice service to benefit the poor"[63] and, in general, as a contribution of Colombian case law to the American region.[64]

In this regard, Julieta Lemaitre emphasizes its importance to deal with basic injustices contained in the law, either because of the alleged neutrality of the law (which actually favours the powerful and harms the poor) or because of the difficulties the poor have to access the basic procedures of ordinary justice (due to costs or other obstacles associated with the procedures). In this sense, within the limited scope of the judicial system in the fight against poverty, Lemaitre emphasizes the design of strategies specifically aimed for the vulnerable and disadvantaged population,[65] such as the right to a minimum standard of living. This right allows for "a special procedure, accessible, fast and effective, where the judge must rule with criteria of real equity and not of formal equality,"[66] based on the lack of resources to survive and the consequences for the plaintiff.

The protection through a *Tutela* of the right to the minimum standard of living, despite the limitations and contradictions of a concept built in case law,[67] has

---

[60]Colombian Constitutional Court (2016) (own translation).

[61]Colombian Constitutional Court (2013b).

[62]Arango R, quoted by Lemaitre (2005), p. 3, footnote 9.

[63]Lemaitre (2005), p. 3.

[64]Oberarzbacher Dávila (2011), pp. 363–400.

[65]Lemaitre explains how other reforms to justice in Colombia have benefited the poor only in an incidental way or have not helped to modify the unequal structure of the system. This has happened in reforms that see problems of access to justice as harmful to the market or with reforms that seek to give access to free legal services to the poor, without modifying structural inequalities. Lemaitre (2005), pp. 8–12.

[66]Ibid, p. 18.

[67]See Oberarzbacher Dávila (2011).

allowed to give substance and real judicial protection to social rights with emphasis on the situation of vulnerability that poverty brings.

Pluralist Notion of Development in the Colombian Constitutional Court Case Law

Before continuing with the emphasis given to this report on the legal framework for the protection of social rights and the fight against poverty, I would like to make some brief comments on the pluralistic notion of development in the Colombian Constitutional Court case law.

Another innovation brought by the 1991 Colombian Constitution is the case law that describes Colombia as a pluralistic society and therefore the protection and respect that the indigenous communities and their legal system deserve. I am not going to expand on the scope of this statement,[68] but I would simply like to point out that, in the interests of this pluralism, the Court has considered that it must be accepted that different understandings on development coexist in Colombia and that those different views must be protected and guaranteed.

This refers specifically to the understandings that indigenous communities have regarding *development* and *progress*. It is accepted that this understandings might differ from what the majority of the society recognizes as "general interest" and that, in order to guarantee the customs and views of the world of the indigenous communities, it is required to include their own view on development and their life project.[69] This has meant, for example, that when reviewing the constitutionality of environmental licenses for activities that affect the territory of indigenous communities (such as, mining exploitation or construction of roads and power plants), the Court has ordered that, in addition to the environmental aspects, the impact of those activities on the communities and on their views of development and progress must also be taken into account.[70]

---

[68]On this subject see, among others: Ariza (2009), Yrigoyen Fajardo (2011) and Sánchez Botero (2005).

[69]It stated that: "The modern "Western" understanding should not be arbitrarily imposed on the views of societies that preceded us and that surely understand better what 'well-being' is: for them, it means 'equilibrium.' These peoples who many called primitives lived in harmony with nature for thousands of years until the arrival of our technified modern society" Colombian Constitutional Court (2011a) (own translation). See also, Colombian Constitutional Court (2012a).

[70]In this sense, the Court has said: "it is plausible to reply that the debate on "development" or "progress" in the territories of ethnic communities must be analysed in the light of the development or progress of the peoples involved. In other words, due to the recognition of the worldview or mere view of the ethnic peoples against what is usually called, in abstract terms, the "general interest." For this reason, for the Court, it becomes indispensable to balance the recognition of the "other" and of the "other" different views of the ethnic groups that are part of the otherness and plurality of a Nation as a whole, who face the concept of development, as the Colombian nation.

In sum, the Constitutional Court has admitted that indigenous communities might have a different conception of development than the "majority" or "modern" part of the society and that this diversity of visions must have a place and protection in a pluralistic society. However, this does not imply that the Court criticizes the prevailing development model, the concepts of "western" or "modern society", nor that the Court proposes an alternative model of development.[71]

Legal Tools for Interaction Between International and National Legal Frameworks

As with the case of the right to the minimum standard of living, the Constitutional Court has constantly resorted to international texts to determine the scope and application of social rights and to define the meaning of the international norms that bind Colombia. However, this constant use of international law does not mean that the relationship between international and domestic legal frameworks is harmonious or free from difficulties, since the Court's use and reference of international texts has not always been clear and has often demonstrated profound ignorance of the basic characteristics of international laws.[72]

Next, I will briefly refer to two of the tools of interaction between international and domestic law commonly used by the Constitutional Court and its relationship with the protection of social rights: the *constitutional block* and the *conventionality control.*

According to studies, it is necessary that the State in an articulated manner guarantees and encourages the real and effective application of the fundamental right to prior consultation of ethnic communities. The tools that underlie the consultation, allow to reach an intermediate point of intercultural dialogue in which people exercise their right to autonomy with their own life plans against economic models based on market economy or similar." Colombian Constitutional Court (2011a) (own translation).

[71]For example, the Constitutional Court has said that "the protection of economic freedoms and rights, among them, free initiative, freedom of enterprise, competitiveness, and sustainable development, constitute an articulating principle of the constitutional economic order, since the Constitution entrusts to the State the development of economic life and within it offers a leading role to companies and the freedoms of particular economic rights. All this as an identity sign of an economic market system, intervened in any case, with greater or lesser margins of regulation according to the type of economic activity, but instituted from the Constitution as an essential piece of growth and as a guarantee of social goods." Colombian Constitutional Court (2012b) (own translation).

[72]On this subject, it is revealing the recent study published by Acosta López et al. (2017a) dedicated to studying the relationship between international law and Colombian law by the Constitutional Court and the contradictions, ambiguities and consequences that this entails.

Constitutional Block

The concept of constitutional block was brought from French constitutionalism and began to be used in Colombia in the mid 1990's.[73] This concept means that some international norms that are not specifically incorporated in the Constitution can have the same effect and rank, in the domestic legal framework, as any other constitutional norm. The main article from which the constitutional block concept was derived in Colombia is Article 93 of the Constitution, which says that "International treaties and conventions ratified by Congress -which recognize human rights and prohibit their limitation in states of exception- prevail in the internal order"[74] and that "The rights and duties included in this Charter shall be interpreted in accordance with the international treaties on human rights ratified by Colombia."

The first question that arises from Article 93 is to know specifically which treaties can be part of the constitutional block, and which cannot. Sometimes, the Court has explicitly determined that certain human rights treaties must be considered part of the constitutional block and therefore have the same normative hierarchy as the constitutional text. However, at other times, the Court has quoted numerous international treaties to support its decision, without specifically saying whether it considers them part of the block or in what way it is using them. In fact, most of the time that the Court uses texts of international origin, it does so without specifying the place they have in the domestic order and constantly confusing sources and their degree of obligatory nature.

This chaotic use of international texts by the Court has had several changes and, undoubtedly, there have been recent efforts to make a clearer and more refined use of international instruments.[75] Thus, in its beginnings, the Court even said that soft law documents were part of the constitutional block, which not only gave them domestic legal effects but also did it at the level of constitutional norms.[76] However, in recent years the Court has made an effort to use more rigorously the term constitutional block and to clarify, for example, that the texts considered in international law as soft law can be used internally as a parameter of interpretation (or "relevant hermeneutic criterion") in order to define the meaning of the norm that is binding, but not as part of the block itself.[77]

[73]About the evolution and the use of the constitutional block in Colombia, see: Ramelli (2015) and Uprimny (2005).

[74]Additionally, Article 214§2 of the Colombian Constitution, when regulating states of exception, affirms that "in all cases the rules of international humanitarian law will be respected." The Court has considered that all international humanitarian law is also part of the constitutional block.

[75]However, diversity and lack of clarity are still present. See Acosta López et al. (2017b).

[76]About the use of soft law: Camacho Rojas et al. (2017), pp. 404–409.

[77]See fragments of rulings that directly mention treaties such as the International Covenant on Economic Social and Cultural Rights, the ACHR, the Protocol of San Salvador and observations of committees such as the Committees of Economic, Social and Cultural Rights and the Human Rights Committee, to guide the interpretation of the scope of said norms and their application in the

In any case, despite the confusions that still persist, there is clarity on some issues. The Court has explicitly pointed out that several treaties that refer to the protection of social rights (i.e. the International Covenant on Economic Social and Cultural Rights, the ACHR and the Protocol of San Salvador) are part of the constitutional block and that the observations made by the committees or commissions authorized to interpret those treaties must be understood as relevant interpretive criteria.

That said, the case of the conventions of the International Labour Organization (ILO) deserves a separate mention, because Article 53 of the Constitution makes special reference to them and states that "International labour Conventions duly ratified, are part of the internal legislation." This wording leaves several doubts because, on the one hand, it does not say whether they should be interpreted as part of the block and, on the other hand, not all ILO conventions refer to rights the limitation of which are prohibited in states of exception, as established by Article 93. After several different pronouncements in which the Court seemed to consider indiscriminately that all the ILO Conventions were part of the block,[78] in 2009 the Court indicated that the only ILO conventions that are part of the block are the ones that this court, after examining them explicitly, considers appropriate. In 2014 it also clarified that only those ILO conventions that refer to the protection of human rights can be part of the block.[79]

Despite the lack of clarity that persists as to what constitutes the constitutional block, this tool has undoubtedly invigorated the articulation between international obligations and the domestic protection of social rights. The block has also served as a vehicle to include in its case law discussions carried-out internationally and that have often served as a parameter of interpretation for the constitutional judge.

Conventionality Control

The tool of the constitutional block already allows a constitutional application of numerous international standards and we have already said that the main treaties of the IAHRS are part of the block; however, there is an additional tool that seeks to guarantee the harmonization of inter-American norms and domestic regulations, called *conventionality control*.

Colombian legal system, in: Martínez and Marín (2015), pp. 15–17. See also: Camacho Rojas et al. (2017), pp. 400–401.

[78]In the case of the ILO, the Court had also affirmed the mandatory nature of the recommendations of the ILO committee, but later corrected that they are hermeneutical criteria and not part of the block. See Camacho Rojas et al. (2017), p. 406.

[79]Colombian Constitutional Court (2014a).

The conventionality control is a tool developed by the IACourtHR based on the joint reading of Articles 1.1,[80] 2[81] and 29[82] of the ACHR. It seeks to increase the level of compliance with inter-American norms by verifying the conformity of domestic law.[83] Initially the conventionality control was made with reference only to the obligations contained in the ACHR, but nowadays it has extended to all the treaties dealing with Human Rights of the IAHRS, but also the interpretations made by the IACourtHR in its judgments.[84] This control can be carried out by the IACourtHR itself or by state agents, including constitutional judges, and may result in modification, interpretation or expulsion of domestic laws by virtue of international obligations.[85]

However, unlike the broad development and explicit use of this concept by the IACourtHR, the Colombian Constitutional Court has been more reluctant to refer, specifically, to this control and to develop it. Probably because there are already other tools in Colombia that allow harmonizing the inter-American *corpus iuris* and the domestic legislation, the Court most of the time uses the inter-American norm, without explicitly mentioning the conventionality control.[86] In any case, used

[80]"Article 1. Obligation to Respect Rights: 1. The States Parties to this Convention undertake to respect the rights and freedoms recognized herein and to ensure to all persons subject to their jurisdiction the free and full exercise of those rights and freedoms, without any discrimination for reasons of race, colour, sex, language, religion, political or other opinion, national or social origin, economic status, birth, or any other social condition."

[81]"Article 2. Domestic Legal Effects: Where the exercise of any of the rights or freedoms referred to in Article 1 is not already ensured by legislative or other provisions, the States Parties undertake to adopt, in accordance with their constitutional processes and the provisions of this Convention, such legislative or other measures as may be necessary to give effect to those rights or freedoms."

[82]"Article 29. Restrictions Regarding Interpretation: No provision of this Convention shall be interpreted as: a) Permitting any State Party, group, or person to suppress the enjoyment or exercise of the rights and freedoms recognized in this Convention or to restrict them to a greater extent than is provided for herein. b) Restricting the enjoyment or exercise of any right or freedom recognized by virtue of the laws of any State Party or by virtue of another convention to which one of the said states is a party. c) Precluding other rights or guarantees that are inherent in the human personality or derived from representative democracy as a form of government. d) Excluding or limiting the effect that the American Declaration of the Rights and Duties of Man and other international acts of the same nature may have."

[83]See Acosta Alvarado (2015); Rivas Ramírez (2017), pp. 661–680; IACourtHR (2017).

[84]"The inter-American *corpus iuris*, not only recognizes the norms and principles contained and recognized in the inter-American instruments, but also includes the judgments of the Inter-American Court of Human Rights as an expression of the interpretations made by it." Rivas Ramírez (2017), p. 668 (own translation).

[85]The conventionality control may result in removing laws from the domestic legal system that are contrary to the treaties (by legislative or judicial means), the interpretation of the internal norms in a harmonic manner with the inter-American obligations, or the adjustment of the actions of the state organizations against the international obligations, among others. See IACourtHR (2017), p. 3.

[86]See the detailed study by Rivas Ramírez (2017) of this control. It shows how, in only 7 times, the Court effectively refers to the term conventionality control, that most of the time the term is developed by dissenting opinions of judges, but that despite this, the Court generally acts by applying the control, without saying it explicitly.

implicitly or explicitly, the conventionality control is another tool for harmonization of international standards at the domestic level that covers different rights protected by the IAHRS on which, as we saw earlier, has shown a recent interest in the protection of social rights and has considered that full compliance with the obligations of the States is to directly address the eradication of poverty.

Final Remarks: Challenges for Peace, Development and Poverty in the Discourse of Post-conflict Colombia

In order to allow a comparative study, this text has focused on offering a general description of the inter-American and constitutional legal frameworks applied in Colombia regarding the protection of social rights, the fight against poverty, the remedies available and the interaction between the international and national mechanisms. I have pointed out that similar discussions have taken place in the Constitutional Court of Colombia and the organs of the IAHRS on the appropriate way to protect social rights and its relevance with the fight against poverty.

The discussion on social rights at the inter-American and constitutional level has taken place within the context of the right to a dignified life and, subsequently, to the fight against poverty and the satisfaction of the need to have an adequate minimum standard of living. Additionally, at a domestic level, I have shown that the Constitutional Court has been an essential actor in guaranteeing the social rights charter included in the 1991 Constitution and, in particular, in creating a privileged protection framework for the most vulnerable communities through the right to the minimum standard of living. Also, the protection of indigenous communities has led to the conception of a pluralistic view of development that, although it does not criticize the development model of Colombia, allows it to coexist with other alternative views -particularly when these are likely to affect the indigenous communities. Lastly, I have explained that courts have used tools such as the constitutional block and the conventionality control to favoured a more fluid dialogue between the international and the internal protection frameworks.

The descriptive presentation of these legal frameworks has the danger of being read as if their evolution and interpretation would have occurred in a way that was alien to the political decisions of its actors, only determined by the existing legal instruments or the economic resources available. This obviously is not the case and I want to end this text by suggesting some discussions related to the period of transition to peace in which Colombia finds itself and that explicitly will test the need for political will to make profound social changes.

In November 2016, after more than 50 years of internal armed conflict and about 5 years of negotiations, the Colombian government signed a final peace agreement with the FARC-EP guerrillas (*Fuerzas Armadas Revolucionarias de Colombia, Ejército del Pueblo*), which was then the largest guerrilla in the country. Additionally, from July 2017 until July 2018, there were intermittent negotiations with the

ELN (*Ejército de Liberación Nacional*) the main guerrilla that persists active today in the Colombian conflict.[87] Even if the situation of violence is far from being overcome,[88] undoubtedly things changed enormously with the demobilization of the FARC, and, although for some it is hasty, the former Colombian Government considered that the post-conflict and peace-building stage had already begun.

The harmful effects for the country's economy have often been pointed out, among the multiple disastrous consequences that the armed conflict has brought for Colombia and its inhabitants.[89] On many occasions it has been shown that Colombia has had to allocate innumerable economic resources to combat militarily the armed groups,[90] resources that otherwise could have been destined to satisfy other needs of its population, to improve industry, infrastructure, rural development, etc. It has also been said that with the end of the conflict, there would be more confidence and foreign investment and there would be more economic and social dividends, there would be less destruction of material goods and human capital and greater social cohesion.[91]

---

[87]At the time of finalizing this report, the second presidential term of Juan Manuel Santos was ending. In this sense, this report focuses on the development and peace policies that were in force during the Santos government (2010–2014, 2014–2018). However, it is important to note that as of August 7, 2018, Iván Duque assumed the presidency of Colombia (2018–2022). This has brought numerous political changes, especially in relation to peace. For instance, from the beginning of his mandate, the negotiation table with the ELN were suspended, and finally ended in January 2019 after a car bomb attack carried out by this guerrilla. His Government has received numerous criticisms (internally and internationally) for the lack of support for the implementation of the Peace Agreement achieved with the FARC guerrilla and some members of his government and political party even deny that there was an armed conflict in Colombia (and consider that the violent acts of the guerrillas are terrorist acts of drug trafficking groups). Nevertheless, Duque affirms, at least formally, that his Government is complying with the peace agreement.

[88]El Espectador (2017).

[89]The economic costs of the conflict and its relation to the obvious inequality of the country have been supported by several studies. Among them stands out the study edited by Arias et al. (2014), economists from Universidad de los Andes, in which they show what the economic costs of the conflict have been. They analyse different sectors of the economy that have been affected, the consequences in human capital of the residents in conflict zones and propose scenarios to be strengthen during the post-conflict. Similarly, there is a study called "¿What will Colombia win with peace?" made by the UNDP and the Center of Resources for the Conflict Analysis (Cerac) (2014). In the presentation of this study, the United Nations coordinator in Colombia Fabrizio Hochschild, said that "Peace brings economic benefits and helps better address the country's structural problems such as inequality, the marginalization of certain regions or legislative weaknesses" (own translation). In the study, the following benefits to peace are predicted: the growth of the economy will accelerate; national income and average per capita income will increase; the distribution of income and land ownership will improve; untapped productive resources will be incorporated into the economy; there will be a better and more inclusive financial system; it will accelerate the reduction of poverty and improve the quality of life; there will be more efficiency in security spending, among others.

[90]It has been calculated that Colombia is, after Brazil, the State of the region that invests most in national defence. It is estimated that Colombia allocates 22 million US dollars in national defence and that an important part of this could be destined to other needs. Revista Semana (2012a).

[91]OECD (2017), p. 19.

Following this line of thought, the Colombian government has said: "nothing would contribute more to the satisfaction of the economic, social and cultural rights of the populations most affected by the armed conflict than its termination."[92] In other words, it is alleged that the conflict has affected the economy and this could explain the impossibility of satisfying social needs in many cases. Argument that is consistent with the traditional interpretation that the protection of the ESCR depends on the amount of resources available.

However, even accepting a close relationship among all these factors (i.e. violence, peace, economy, resources, social rights, vulnerability and poverty), many questions remain: What exactly would make that in time of peace social needs will be guaranteed? Is it only a matter of economic resources that explains poverty and the violation of social rights in Colombia? The consequences that the armed conflict has had on inequality and the lack of an adequate standard of living for a large part of the population, are essentially due to a lack of economic resources, or are there other structural causes that need to be tackle?

One can believe that the peace negotiations were an ideal opportunity to address this type of questions in order to achieve radical structural reforms to counteract some of the inequality in Colombia. But at the same time, during those long and very polarized negotiations, many accused the process of wanting to be an illegal constitutional reform in which Colombia, following the examples of Cuba or Venezuela, was going to replace its economic model with one related to the socialist tendencies of the guerrilla.[93]

At the end, the point of negotiations most akin to these issues occurred during the discussion around the situation of the countryside. As a result, the first chapter of the final peace agreement is called "Towards a New Colombian countryside: comprehensive rural reform"[94] and its purpose was described by the Office of the High Peace Commissioner as follows:

> This agreement lays the foundations for the transformation of the countryside and creates the standard well-being and good life for the rural population. It seeks the eradication of extreme rural poverty and the 50% reduction of poverty in the countryside within 10 years, the promotion of equality, the closing of the gap between the countryside and the city, the reactivation of the countryside and, especially, the development of peasant, family and community agriculture.[95]

The peace agreement makes, in this chapter, a diagnosis of the precarious conditions of life in the countryside and includes important reform proposals that

---

[92]Observations of Colombia on the Draft Report of the Inter-American Commission on Human Rights. Note S-GAIID-13-048140, of December 2, 2013, paragraph 342, quoted in: IACHR (2013).

[93]Álvaro Uribe, former President of Colombia and highly popular, was one of the main opponents of the peace negotiations and said about the agreement: "Here there is no peace agreement, here there is a claudication before a *narco-chavista* agenda that I believe is extremely serious for democracy, let's start because in the 297 pages of the agreement it was foreseen that they would replace the Constitution." Revista Semana (2016) (own translation).

[94]Colombian Government & FARC (2016) (own translation).

[95]Colombian High Commissioner for Peace (n.d.).

are today key challenges of implementation of the whole accord.[96] However, the peace agreement does not challenge Colombia's development model nor does it propose structural reforms that reorient it.[97]

This is consistent with the statement made several times by former President Juan Manuel Santos, who said that Colombia's economic model was not being discussed in the peace negotiations.[98] Indeed, the agreement was negotiated within the development framework established by the Government's National Development Plan (NDP). The NDP is a document that serves as a policy framework for each government at the beginning of its mandate and that materializes in a law. The NDP serves as a basis and provides the strategic guidelines of public policies formulated by the President of the Republic and, among other things, "points out the long-term national goals and objectives, the goals and priorities of the State action in the medium term and the general strategies and orientations of economic, social and environmental policy that will be adopted by the government."[99]

Specifically, the two NDPs of the Santos administrations[100] made direct mention of the search for peace and propose it as a key goal of the plan.[101] In this sense, the first chapter of the NDP of 2014–2018 was called "Colombia en Paz" and included 3 objectives that were:

> Objective 1. Strengthen the peace building process and guarantee its sustainability to allow the country and its citizens to reach their full potential as a nation;
>
> Objective 2. Integrate the territory and its communities to contribute to the closing of population and social gaps, promoting connectivity for productive inclusion and access to public goods, social services and information; and
>
> Objective 3. Reduce social and territorial inequalities between urban and rural areas, through the integral development of the countryside as a guarantee for equal opportunities.

---

[96]For example: it contains the creation of a land fund for landless peasants or for people with insufficient land. There is a massive property formalization plan for those who have land but no titles. They will update and modernize the rural cadastre, will create an agrarian jurisdiction to resolve conflicts around land, and will stimulate peasant productivity, technical assistance, social security guarantees for rural workers, access to credit, etc. Colombia Government & FARC (2016).

[97]In this sense, see the careful reading made by Amaya Castro and Olarte Olarte (2017) on how the agreement only reiterates what was established in the 1991 Constitution and was already widely recognized by the Constitutional Court. For an analysis that compares the views on development of the FARC and the government see also: Alviar (2016a, b).

[98]"We are not going to negotiate or talk about fundamental aspects of national life, such as the Constitution itself, the development model, the concept of private property, that is not in dispute and will not be discussed." Quote of President Juan Manuel Santos in: Revista Semana (2012b) (own translation).

[99]See the Colombian National Planning Department website (n.d.) (own translation). The NDP is regulated in the Political Constitution of Colombia of 1991 in its article 339.

[100]President Juan Manuel Santos has governed for two terms therefore he has implemented two NDPs, one from 2010 to 2014 and another from 2014 to 2018.

[101]In Duque's NDP (which entered into force on May 2019) peace is no longer a central theme of the plan, it is briefly addressed as a cross-cutting issue and focused on aspects of legality and security. Colombia (2018).

But, despite this, the development goals of those NDP followed international standards that were not discussed (much less criticized) in light of the needs of the context and the challenges that the implementation of the peace agreement would bring. Santos' NDPs focused on meeting the Sustainable Development Goals and the Post-2015 Development Agenda of the United Nations, all this aligned with the goal of joining the Organization for Economic Cooperation and Development (OECD).[102] It was also stated that the peace agreement would adopt the goals and policies set by the NDP.[103]

The discourse of the Santos' government presented the process of joining OECD as a great achievement for Colombia[104] and believed that the end of the conflict would undoubtedly clear up several of the irregularities that have prevented the country from growing economically. Of course, it was made clear that these changes won't happen overnight, but the difficult path was presented as transitional and dependent on a hard but temporary juncture, where there had been no room for criticism or rethinking of the model that has been adopted.

In other words, the model and goals of the NDP were not seen as a problem, nor should they be discussed even in the peculiar post-conflict situation. The conditions produced by the conflict, identified as affecting development and limiting Colombia's economic resources, were seen as anomalies that prevent compliance and need to be correct.[105]

Without denying the relationship between the armed conflict and Colombia's economic resources what I would like to observe is that the discourse that emphasizes the State's will to fulfil its social obligations but its inability to do so due to the high costs of the armed conflict is at least incomplete. In fact, a double discourse that Colombia maintains of the budget limitation as an excuse for not fulfilling its social

---

[102]Colombia joined the OECD on May 2018. See, OECD (2018).

[103]"To materialize the eventual peace agreements as the construction of the foundations for a sustainable peace, will be supported on the policies and strategies that this National Development Plan proposes to the country for the coming years, which will imply, of course, efforts not only from the State but from all Colombians." Colombia NDP (2014), p. 25 (own translation).

[104]In this sense, the 2010–2014 NDP (2010) said: "We have started the process to enter the OECD; something unthinkable just a few years ago." Additionally, the Colombian Embassy in France in the process of admission to the OECD said: "Colombia [is] an example in planning for the Sustainable Development Goals. This strategy is part of the NDP 2014 - 2018 "Todos por un nuevo país" that was conceived to align with the OECD standards and the goals proposed by the Agenda 2030." OECD-Bureau of Relations (2016) (own translation).

[105]Although I affirm that in the NDP of Santos the concept of development is not criticized or evaluated according to the context of conflict or post-conflict, it is always considered as an important element of the peace agreement and its implementation. This does not happen in the NDP presented by President Duque. In Duque's NDP the concept of development does not show major differences with respect to Santos NDP: it is reaffirmed the interest of "advancing in the fulfilment of the 17 Sustainable Development Goals (SDG) and in its accordance with the good practices of the Organization for Economic Cooperation and Development (OECD)". It indicates as main goals "to reduce poverty and inequality and advance in equity." But now development is not addressed with the goals of building peace in mind or related to the peace agreement. Colombian National Planning Department website (2018) (own translation), Colombia (2018).

obligations, while demonstrating constant economic growth and presenting itself as one of the most robust economies in the region, has already been detected as inconsistent. In this regard, the IACHR in its latest report on the situation of human rights in Colombia said the following:

> §595. The Commission notes that in Colombia, the context of prolonged internal armed conflicts exist alongside a situation of sustained economic growth, which has led to an unequal distribution of wealth, ranking Colombia as the "country with the second worst income distribution" in 2011, according to data from the Economic Commission for Latin America and the Caribbean (ECLAC).
>
> §596. In this connection, the Commission has noted that although Colombia has experienced solid economic development in recent years, not all Colombians have experienced concomitant improvement in their lives. In particular, vulnerable groups continue to face obstacles to the full enjoyment of the civil, political, economic, social, and cultural rights.
>
> §610. The Commission notes that Colombia's economic growth has not resulted in a balanced distribution of resources and that there are still parts of the country with major deficiencies in terms of infrastructure, presence of state institutions, access to basic services, and enjoyment of ESCR. These deficiencies are more acute where populations that have traditionally suffered discrimination or that live in poverty or extreme poverty are concerned. According to the information received, in some cases their situation has actually worsened with the implementation of large-scale economic projects, which affect their way of life and income generating activities; and the profits generated by those projects do not directly benefit those groups.
>
> §611. The Commission notes that, despite the many programs and actions implemented, the country shows high levels of poverty and extreme poverty, as well as deficiencies in accessing and enjoyment of rights such as food, health, housing and employment, deficiencies that are close but not exclusively linked to the armed conflict.[106]

This shows that the increase in economic resources does not guarantee on its own a greater compliance with social rights or a better fight against poverty. It requires also political will. In the best case, Colombia is close to put aside the discourse of the armed conflict as an explanation of all the harms that afflict it. However, after the armed conflict there will always be other discourses available that can help present the decisions made as external situations that objectively limit the available resources.[107]

The political will required may include to critically rethink what type of development should be implemented, rethink the mechanisms used in the fight of poverty

[106] IACHR (2013) §595, 596, 610, 611. In its annual report of 2018, the Commission follows-up the recommendations made in 2013 to Colombia and reiterates that despite some efforts: "in Colombia 1% of the population accounts for 20% of all income in the Country" and "that according to some studies by the Organization for Economic Cooperation and Development (OECD), Colombia is the most unequal country in Latin America as a result of the high income concentration, evident in a significant gap in income distribution, as well as low rates of access to good-quality jobs". IACHR (2018) §156, 157.

[107] This is the case nowadays with the discourses of the renewed fight against drug trafficking or the migration crisis from Venezuela (see: The Guardian 2017; El Tiempo 2018). Or even more unpredictable (and worrisome) is the discourse of some people in the political party of President Duque, who deny the existence of the armed conflict and, therefore, the need to address issues such as peace and post-conflict (see: Revista Semana 2019; El Espectador 2020).

and inequality, redefine economic priorities, question how these aspects can facilitate or hinder the construction of a society in peace, among many others. So far, the peace negotiations have not been the scenario to do so, but the stage of implementation of the peace agreement might offer a new opportunity.

References

Acosta Alvarado PA (2015) Diálogo judicial y constitucionalismo multinivel, el caso interamericano. Universidad Externado de Colombia, Bogotá

Acosta López JI, Acosta Alvarado PA, Rivas Ramírez D (eds) (2017a) De anacronismos y vaticinios: diagnóstico sobre las relaciones entre el derecho internacional y el derecho interno en Latinoamérica. Universidad de la Sabana, Universidad Externado de Colombia, Sociedad Latinoamericana de Derecho Internacional, Bogotá

Acosta López JI, Acosta Alvarado PA, Rivas Ramírez D (2017b) Conclusiones generales del proyecto de investigación. In: Acosta et al (eds) De anacronismos y vaticinios: diagnóstico sobre las relaciones entre el derecho internacional y el derecho interno en Latinoamérica. Universidad de la Sabana, Universidad Externado de Colombia, Sociedad Latinoamericana de Derecho Internacional, Bogotá, pp 705–716

Additional Protocol to the American Convention on Economic, Social and Cultural Rights (Protocol of San Salvador) (1997). Available at: http://www.oas.org/juridico/english/treaties/a-52.html. Accessed 10 Feb 2020

Alviar H (2016a) Rethinking law and development in Colombia: how a dynamic approach could overcome the chasm between law and ideas of economic development. Law Dev Rev 9 (2):411–435

Alviar H (2016b) ¿Perspectivas encontradas? ¿Nuevas soluciones? In: Alviar H, Jaramillo Sierra IC (eds) Perspectivas Jurídicas para la Paz. Ediciones Uniandes, Bogotá, pp 11–40

Amaya Castro JM, Olarte Olarte MC (2017) ¿Desarrollo vs Reforma Rural Integral en el Acuerdo de la Habana?. Proyecto Paz. Universidad de los Andes 10:1–11

American Convention on Human Rights (1969). Available at: https://www.cidh.oas.org/basicos/english/basic3.american%20convention.htm. Accessed 10 Feb 2020

American Declaration of the Rights and Duties of Man (1948). Available at: https://www.cidh.oas.org/Basicos/English/Basic2.american%20Declaration.htm. Accessed 10 Feb 2020

Anghie A (2004) Imperialism, sovereignty and the making of international law. Cambridge University Press, Cambridge, New York

Arango R (2001) La justiciabilidad de los derechos sociales fundamentales. Revista de Derecho Público-Universidad de los Andes 12:185–212

Arango R, Lemaitre J (2003) Jurisprudencia constitucional sobre el derecho al mínimo vital: estudio de caso: despido injusto de mujer embarazada. CIJUS-Universidad de los Andes, Bogotá

Arias MA, Camacho A, Ibáñez AM, Mejía D, Rodríguez C (eds) (2014) Costos económicos y sociales del conflicto en Colombia ¿Cómo construir un posconflicto sostenible? Universidad de los Andes, Facultad de Economía-CEDE, Ediciones Uniandes, Bogotá

Ariza L (2009) Derecho, saber e identidad indígena. Universidad de los Andes - Siglo del Hombre, Bogotá

BBC, What are the 6 most unequal countries in Latin America?, March 9, 2016., available at: http://www.bbc.com/mundo/noticias/2016/03/160308_america_latina_economia_desigualdad_ab. Accessed 10 Feb 2020

Camacho Rojas LC, Castellanos Obando NI, Ocampo Rueda MH (2017) El derecho internacional de los derechos humanos en el ordenamiento jurídico colombiano. In: Acosta et al (eds) De anacronismos y vaticinios: diagnóstico sobre las relaciones entre el derecho internacional y el derecho interno en Latinoamérica. Universidad de la Sabana, Universidad Externado de Colombia, Sociedad Latinoamericana de Derecho Internacional, Bogotá, pp 404–409

Colombia (1991) Constitución Política. Available at: http://wsp.presidencia.gov.co/Normativa/Documents/Constitucion-Politica-Colombia.pdf. Accessed 10 Feb 2020

Colombia (2010) NDP 2010-2014. Prosperidad para todos. Available at: https://www.dnp.gov.co/Plan-Nacional-de-Desarrollo/PND-2010-2014/Paginas/Plan-Nacional-De-2010-2014.aspx. Accessed 10 Feb 2020

Colombia (2014) NDP 2014-2018. Todos por un Nuevo País. Available at: https://colaboracion.dnp.gov.co/CDT/PND/PND%202014-2018%20Tomo%201%20internet.pdf. Accessed 10 Feb 2020

Colombia (2018) NDP 2018-2022. Pacto por Colombia, pacto por la equidad. Available at: https://colaboracion.dnp.gov.co/CDT/Prensa/PND-Pacto-por-Colombia-pacto-por-la-equidad-2018-2022.pdf. Accessed 12 Feb 2020

Colombian Constitutional Court (1992a) Judgment T-423

Colombian Constitutional Court (1992b) Judgment, T-426, 1992

Colombian Constitutional Court (1995a) Judgment T-495

Colombian Constitutional Court (1995b) Judgment C-566

Colombian Constitutional Court (1997a) Judgment SU-111

Colombian Constitutional Court (1997b) Judgment, C-251

Colombian Constitutional Court (1999a) Judgment, SU-995

Colombian Constitutional Court (1999b) Judgment T-586

Colombian Constitutional Court (2001) Judgment C-1064

Colombian Constitutional Court (2007) Judgment T-016

Colombian Constitutional Court (2008a) Judgment C-507

Colombian Constitutional Court (2008b) Judgment T-760

Colombian Constitutional Court (2009) Judgment T-544

Colombian Constitutional Court (2010) Judgment C-376

Colombian Constitutional Court (2011a) Judgment, T-129

Colombian Constitutional Court (2011b) Judgment T-160

Colombian Constitutional Court (2011c) Judgment, T-530

Colombian Constitutional Court (2012a) Judgment, T-348

Colombian Constitutional Court (2012b) Judgment, C-644

Colombian Constitutional Court (2013a) Judgment, T-385

Colombian Constitutional Court (2013b) Judgment, T-736

Colombian Constitutional Court (2014a) Judgment, SU-555

Colombian Constitutional Court (2014b) Judgment, C-389

Colombian Constitutional Court (2016) Judgment, T-199

Colombian Government, FARC (2016) Punto 1: Hacia un Nuevo Campo Colombiano: Reforma Rural Integral. In: Acuerdo Final para la Terminación del Conflicto y la Construcción de una Paz Estable y Duradera. Available at: http://www.altocomisionadoparalapaz.gov.co/procesos-y-conversaciones/Paginas/Texto-completo-del-Acuerdo-Final-para-la-Terminacion-del-conflicto.aspx. Accessed 10 Feb 2020

Colombian High Commissioner for Peace (n.d.) Information from the website: http://www.altocomisionadoparalapaz.gov.co/Documents/informes-especiales/abc-del-proceso-de-paz/politica-de-desarrollo-agrario-integral.html. Accessed 10 Feb 2020

Colombian National Planning Department (2018) Gobierno Nacional revela las bases del Plan Nacional de Desarrollo 2018-2022. Available at: https://www.dnp.gov.co/Paginas/En-el-marco-de-la-celebraci%C3%B3n-de-los-60-a%C3%B1os-del-DNP,-el-presidente-Duque-propone-a-los-colombianos-un-pacto-por-la-legalid.aspx. Accessed 10 Feb 2020

Colombian National Planning Department (n.d.) ¿Qué es el Plan Nacional de Desarrollo? Available at: https://www.dnp.gov.co/Plan-Nacional-de-Desarrollo/Paginas/Qu-es-el-PND.aspx. Accessed 10 Feb 2020

El Colombiano (2018) Colombia y su tensa relación con la CIDH. Medellín. 23 February. Available at: http://www.elcolombiano.com/colombia/colombia-y-su-tensa-relacion-con-la-cidh-YE8237706. Accessed 10 Feb 2020

El Espectador (2017) ¿Qué explica el cambio de violencia en Colombia después de la guerra? 24 September. Available at: https://colombia2020.elespectador.com/pais/que-explica-el-cambio-de-violencia-en-colombia-despues-de-la-guerra. Accessed 10 Feb 2020

El Espectador (2020) El concejal que quiere eliminar el término "conflicto armado" 7 Febrary. Available at: https://www.elespectador.com/noticias/nacional/el-concejal-que-quiere-eliminar-el-termino-conflicto-armado-articulo-903521. Accessed 12 Feb 2020

El Tiempo (2018) Con los venezolanos, Colombia vive la más grave crisis migratoria. 3 February. Available at: http://www.eltiempo.com/politica/gobierno/migracion-de-venezolanos-a-colombia-es-la-mas-grave-crisis-migratoria-del-pais-178596. Accessed 10 Feb 2020

Eslava L (2019) The developmental state: independency, dependency and the history of the south. In: von Bernstorff J, Dann P (eds) The battle for international law: south-north perspectives on the decolonization era. Oxford University Press, Oxford

IACHR (2013) Truth, justice and reparation: Fourth report on human rights situation in Colombia, OAS/Ser.L/V/II., Doc. 49/13, 31 December. Available at: http://www.oas.org/en/iachr/reports/pdfs/Colombia-Truth-Justice-Reparation.pdf. Accessed 10 Feb 2020

IACHR (2017) Report on Poverty and Human Rights, OEA/Ser.L/V/II. Doc.147, 7 September

IACHR (2018) Annual Report. Chapter V: Follow-up to Recommendations Made by the IACHR in its Country or Thematic Reports. Colombia. Available at: http://www.oas.org/en/iachr/docs/annual/2018/TOC.asp. Accessed 12 Feb 2020

IACourtHR (1999) Case of the "Street Children" (Villagrán Morales et al.) V. Guatemala. Judgment of November 19 (Merits, Reparations and Costs)

IACourtHR (2005) Case Yakye Axa Indigenous Community v. Paraguay. Judgment of June 17 (Meritrs, Reparations and Costs)

IACourtHR (2006a) Case Comunidad Sawhoyamaxa v. Paraguay. Judgment of March 29 (Merits, Reparations and Costs)

IACourtHR (2006b) Case Servellón García et al. v. Honduras. Judgment of September 21. (Merits, Reparations and Costs)

IACourtHR (2009) Case Acevedo Buendía et al. ("Discharged and Retired Employees of the Comptroller") v. Perú. Judgment of July 1, 2009 (preliminary objection, merits, reparations and costs)

IACourtHR (2016) Opinion: Judge Eduardo Ferrer Mac-Gregor Poisot. Case of Yarce et al. v. Colombia. Judgment of November 22 (Preliminary Objection, Merits, Reparations and Costs)

IACourtHR (2017) Cuadernillo de jurisprudencia de la Corte Interamericana de Derechos Humanos, N° 7: Control de Convencionalidad, breve introducción al control de convencionalidad. Available at: http://www.corteidh.or.cr/sitios/libros/todos/docs/cuadernillo7.pdf. Accessed 10 Feb 2020

IIDH (2009) La justicia directa de los derechos económicos, sociales y culturales, San José de Costa Rica

ILO Domestic Workers Convention (C189) (2011). Available at: https://www.ilo.org/dyn/normlex/en/f?p=NORMLEXPUB:12100:0::NO::P12100_INSTRUMENT_ID:2551460. Accessed 10 Feb 2020

ILO Equal Remuneration Convention (C100) (1951). Available at: https://www.ilo.org/dyn/normlex/en/f?p=NORMLEXPUB:12100:0::NO::P12100_ILO_CODE:C100. Accessed 10 Feb 2020

ILO Maternity Protection Convention (C003) (1919). Available at: https://www.ilo.org/dyn/normlex/en/f?p=NORMLEXPUB:12100:0::NO::P12100_ILO_CODE:C003. Accessed 10 Feb 2020

ILO Minimum Wage Fixing Machinery (Agriculture) Convention (C099) (1951). Available at: https://www.ilo.org/dyn/normlex/en/f?p=NORMLEXPUB:12100:::NO:12100:P12100_ILO_CODE:C099:NO. Accessed 22 Jan 2019

ILO Protection of Wages Convention (C095) (1949). Available at: https://www.ilo.org/dyn/normlex/en/f?p=1000:11300:0::NO:11300:P11300_INSTRUMENT_ID:312240. Accessed 10 Feb 2020

ILO Unemployment Convention (C002) (1919). Available at: https://www.ilo.org/dyn/normlex/en/f?p=NORMLEXPUB:12100:0::NO::P12100_ILO_CODE:C002. Accessed 22 Jan 2019

ILO Unemployment Indemnity (Shipwreck) Convention (C008) (1920). Available at: https://www.ilo.org/dyn/normlex/en/f?p=NORMLEXPUB:12100:0::NO::P12100_ILO_CODE:C008. Accessed 10 Feb 2020

ILO Workmen's Compensation (Accidents) Convention (C017) (1925). Available at: https://www.ilo.org/dyn/normlex/en/f?p=NORMLEXPUB:12100:0::NO::P12100_ILO_CODE:C017. Accessed 10 Feb 2020

ILO Workmen's Compensation (Agriculture) Convention (C012) (1921). Available at: https://www.ilo.org/dyn/normlex/en/f?p=NORMLEXPUB:12100:0::NO::P12100_ILO_CODE:C012. Accessed 10 Feb 2020

Inter-American Convention on the Elimination of All Forms of Discrimination against Person with Disabilities (2004). Available at: http://www.oas.org/juridico/english/treaties/a-65.html. Accessed 10 Feb 2020

Inter-American Convention on the Forced Disappearance of Persons (2005). Available at: http://www.oas.org/juridico/english/treaties/a-60.html. Accessed 10 Feb 2020

Inter-American Convention on the Prevention, Punishment and Eradication of Violence Against Women "Convention of Belem Do Para" (1997). Available at: http://www.oas.org/juridico/english/treaties/a-61.html. Accessed 10 Feb 2020

Inter-American Convention to Prevent And Punish Torture (1999). Available at: http://www.oas.org/juridico/english/treaties/a-51.html. Accessed 10 Feb 2020

International Covenant on Civil and Political Rights (1966). Available at: https://www.ohchr.org/en/professionalinterest/pages/ccpr.aspx. Accessed 10 Feb 2020

International Covenant on Economic, Social and Cultural Rights (1966). Available at: https://www.ohchr.org/en/professionalinterest/pages/cescr.aspx. Accessed 10 Feb 2020

Lemaitre J (2005) El Coronel sí tiene quien le escriba: la tutela por mínimo vital en Colombia. SELA (Seminario en Latinoamérica de Teoría Constitucional y Política) Papers 43:10–11. Available at: http://digitalcommons.law.yale.edu/yls_sela/43. Accessed 10 Feb 2020

Martínez HD (2014) Protección Constitucional de los Derechos Sociales. Implementación de Instrumentos Internacionales en las Decisiones de la Corte Constitucional. Estudios de Derechos LXXIN(158):21–40

Martínez HD, Marín JC (2015) Protección de los derechos económicos, sociales y culturales en el ordenamiento jurídico colombiano –el papel de los jueces. Justicia Juris 11(1):13–25

Oberarzbacher Dávila FE (2011) La justiciabilidad y el mínimo vital de los DESC: teoría y práctica en Colombia. Revista Facultad de Derecho y Ciencias Políticas 41(115):363–400

OECD (2017) Economic studies: Colombia. May, p 19. Available at: http://www.oecd.org/economy/surveys/Colombia-2017-OECD-economic-survey-overview.pdf?TSPD_101_R0=f64bb7f7d884f3ce83282e201807a67ai10000000000000000808137b5ffff00000000000000000000000000005a9f0f140088b2032f. Accessed 10 Feb 2020

OECD (2018) OECD countries agree to invite Colombia as 37th member. 25 May. Available at: http://www.oecd.org/newsroom/oecd-countries-agree-to-invite-colombia-as-37th-member.htm. Accessed 10 Feb 2020

OECD-Bureau of Relations (2016) Informe de la OCDE sobre el mercado laboral colombiano. Newsletter No. 18 Embassy of Colombia in France. January 18

Parra Vera O (2011) Justiciabilidad de los derechos económicos, sociales y culturales ante el sistema interamericano. Comisión Mexicana de Derechos Humanos, México

Ramelli A (2015) Relaciones entre el derecho internacional y el derecho interno. In: Urueña R (ed) Derecho Internacional. Poder y límites del derecho en la sociedad global. Ediciones Uniandes -Universidad de los Andes, Bogotá, pp 511–531

Restrepo Saldarriaga E (2008) Los significados del derecho a la vida. In: Alviar H et al (eds) Manual de constitución y democracia. Universidad de los Andes, Bogotá, pp 259–277

Revista Semana (2012a) Colombia, el segundo país suramericano que más gasta en armament. 5 November. Available at: http://www.semana.com/nacion/articulo/colombia-segundo-pais-suramericano-mas-gasta-armamento/257797-3. Accessed 10 Feb 2020

Revista Semana (2012b) Santos: "El modelo económico y político no está en discusión con las FARC". 16 November. Available at: https://www.semana.com/nacion/articulo/santos-el-modelo-economico-politico-no-esta-discusion-farc/267919-3. Accessed 10 Feb 2020

Revista Semana (2016) "Cuando veo todo esto de Venezuela, digo: para allá vamos": Uribe. 24 October. Available at: http://www.semana.com/nacion/articulo/alvaro-uribe-asegura-que-acuerdos-con-las-farc-podrian-convertir-a-colombia-en-venezuela/500056. Accessed 10 Feb 2020

Revista Semana (2019) Pese a la polémica, Gobierno nombra a Darío Acevedo en la dirección del Centro de Memoria. 19 February. Available at: https://www.semana.com/nacion/articulo/gobierno-nombro-a-dario-acevedo-en-la-direccion-del-centro-de-memoria-historica/601972. Accessed 12 Feb 2020

Rivas Ramírez D (2017) El (des)control de convencionalidad en las sentencias de la Corte Constitucional colombiana. In: López A et al (eds) De anacronismos y vaticinios: diagnóstico sobre las relaciones entre el derecho internacional y el derecho interno en Latinoamérica. Universidad de la Sabana, Universidad Externado de Colombia, Sociedad Latinoamericana de Derecho Internacional, Bogotá, pp 661–680

Salvioli F (2004) La protección de los derechos económicos, sociales y culturales en el sistema interamericano de derechos humanos. Revista IIDH. San José de Costa Rica 39:101–167

Sánchez Botero E (2005) Reflexiones en torno de la jurisdicción especial indígena en Colombia. Revista IIDH. San José de Costa Rica 41:225–250

The Guardian (2017) Colombia's coca production soars to highest level in two decades, US says. 14 March. Available on: https://www.theguardian.com/world/2017/mar/14/colombia-coca-cocaine-us-drugs. Accessed 10 Feb 2020

UN, General Assembly (1948) Universal Declaration of Human Rights (Resolution 217 A). Available at: http://www.un.org/en/universal-declaration-human-rights/. Accessed 10 Feb 2020

UN, General Assembly (1986) Declaration on the Right to Development (A/RES/41/128). Available at: https://www.un.org/ga/search/view_doc.asp?symbol=A/RES/41/128. Accessed 10 Feb 2020

UNESCO (1992) Rio Declaration on Environment and Development. Available at: http://www.unesco.org/education/pdf/RIO_E.PDF. Accessed 10 Feb 2020

UNPD-CERAC (2014) ¿Qué ganará Colombia con la paz? Study and presentation of Hochschild. Available at: http://www.co.undp.org/content/colombia/es/home/presscenter/articles/2014/06/10/-qu-ganar-colombia-con-la-paz-.html. Accessed 10 Feb 2020

Uprimny R (2005) El bloque de constitucionalidad en Colombia. Un análisis jurisprudencial y un ensayo de sistematización doctrinal. In: Compilación de jurisprudencia y doctrina nacional e internacional, Dejusticia. Bogotá, pp 1–35. Available at: https://www.dejusticia.org/el-bloque-de-constitucionalidad-en-colombia-un-analisis-jurisprudencial-y-un-ensayo-de-sistematizacion-doctrinal/. Accessed 10 Feb 2020

Wilder G (2014) Freedom time: negritude, decolonization, and the future of the world. Duke University Press, Durham

World Bank (2017) Database on the Gini index. Available at: https://datos.bancomundial.org/indicador/SI.POV.GINI?view=map. Accessed 10 Feb 2020
Yrigoyen Fajardo RZ (2011) El horizonte del constitucionalismo pluralista: del multiculturalismo a la descolonización. In: Rodríguez C (ed) El derecho en América Latina. Un mapa para el pensamiento jurídico del siglo XXI. Siglo veintiuno ed. Buenos Aires, pp 139–159

Chapter 3
The Legal and Policy Framework of Cyprus for the Fight Against Poverty at the Domestic and International Levels

Aristoteles Constantinides

Abstract The legal framework of Cyprus for the domestic fight against poverty is premised on the constitutional right to a decent existence, an equivalent to the right to an adequate standard of living. This right is not directly justiciable but the courts can assess the legislation which the State is bound to enact for its realisation. The Guaranteed Minimum Income scheme was introduced in 2014 in the aftermath of the financial crisis that severely hit Cyprus, to guarantee minimum living standards for the neediest. At the international level, Cyprus has gone from aid recipient to donor, primarily due to its EU accession in 2004. Its aid programme was established by executive decision in 2005 but, despite a promising start channelling aid to sectors directly related to the MDGs, it fell victim to the financial crisis, which saw the relevant aid agency suspending its operations and Cyprus' ODA plummeting from 0.23% of GNI in 2010 to 0.09% in 2015. Yet, the aid programme was not discontinued and Cyprus has renewed its strong political commitment for the implementation of the SDGs and participates in relevant initiatives.

Introduction

The Republic of Cyprus is an island state in the Eastern Mediterranean.[1] Cyprus was a former colony of the United Kingdom and gained its independence on 16 August 1960. Since 1 May 2004, Cyprus is a member of the European Union (EU) and joined the Eurozone on 1 January 2008. Cyprus is not a member of the Organization

[1]Cyprus is de facto divided since 1974 when Turkey invaded the island and occupied almost 37% of its territory. The present chapter covers the legal and policy framework in the areas of Cyprus under the control of the Government of the Republic of Cyprus.

A. Constantinides (✉)
University of Cyprus, Nicosia, Cyprus
e-mail: ariscons@ucy.ac.cy

M. Andenas et al. (eds.), *The Fight Against Poverty and the Right to Development*, Ius Comparatum - Global Studies in Comparative Law 52,
https://doi.org/10.1007/978-3-030-57324-9_3

for Economic Cooperation and Development (OECD) and its Development Assistance Committee (DAC).

Cyprus was considered to have, for more than three decades, a welfare state system with a relatively dense social safety net,[2] in the sense that it provided numerous social benefits and allowances for vulnerable groups. However, the global financial crisis did not leave Cyprus and its social model unharmed. Cyprus faced an unprecedented economic crisis that reached its peak in 2013, when its banking sector collapsed. The crisis created significant domestic challenges in terms of poverty, social exclusion and unemployment. Poverty figures for the period 2014–2015 deteriorated, the labour market conditions worsened and the income of the population decreased.[3] In 2013, Cyprus adopted an Economic Adjustment Programme which aimed, *inter alia*, at reforming social benefit schemes to use resources more efficiently and to ensure a balance between welfare assistance and incentives to take up work. Yet, Cyprus managed to exit the Programme in March 2016 without a successor arrangement; economic growth has resumed since 2015 and unemployment is in decline.[4]

Cyprus has supported international development mainly through public funding contributions disseminated through CyprusAid, in alignment with the EU policy. CyprusAid functions within the framework of a policy-making mechanism that was put in place with a view to steering Cyprus' Official Development Assistance (ODA). Cyprus ODA was channelled to sectors directly related to the Millennium Development Goals (MDGs), such as social and services sectors (healthcare, education, development of human capital, etc), infrastructure development (construction of bridges, public works, health infrastructure, etc) and environment (climate change adaptation, environmental sustainability, etc). However, the 2013 financial crisis caused a considerable setback to those activities, as attention focused to crisis management at the domestic level rather than international development cooperation. Consequently, Cyprus' economic contribution to development cooperation was considerably reduced.

Nevertheless, Cyprus continued to support the needs of the world's poor in international fora (UN and EU) and was actively involved in the process of adopting the Sustainable Development Goals (SDGs) and their targets.

---

[2]Christou et al. (2016), pp. 79–80.

[3]For analytical figures, see Ministry of Foreign Affairs (2017), p. 15.

[4]Ibid.

Addressing Poverty in Cyprus: The Legal Framework

Human Rights Treaties in the Domestic Legal Order

In general, there is a hierarchy of sources of law in the domestic legal order of Cyprus, as the rules of law form a pyramid.[5] At the top lies the *acquis communautaire*, as per the fifth amendment of the 1960 Constitution of Cyprus which gave precedence to EU law.[6] At the second tier lies the Constitution, as per Article 179(1) which declares the Constitution (subject to EU law) as the "supreme law of the Republic". This provision has been characterized as "the cardinal and all pervasive norm of the Constitution; the bedrock of constitutional order".[7] Therefore, no law or decision may be repugnant to, or inconsistent with, any provision of the Constitution.[8]

At the third tier are international treaties, conventions and agreements that have been ratified in accordance with the required internal procedures, as per Article 169 of the Constitution. Particularly, Article 169(3) provides that as from their publication in the Official Gazette of the Republic, such international instruments have superior force to any municipal law. Treaty obligations are transposed into the Cypriot domestic order in accordance with that provision; there is no distinct procedure for incorporating human rights treaties.

The Constitution is however silent on the status of international customary law within the Cypriot legal order and the courts have not taken a (clear) stand on the issue.[9] The most plausible approach could be that of the UK courts, according to which customary international law is incorporated into the legal system with no superior status to ordinary legislation.[10] However, unlike the UK, Cyprus does have a written constitution that provides for the (superior) place of international (treaty) law in the domestic legal order, which could arguably cast doubt on the propriety of following the British approach on this issue.

Cyprus is party to a large number of treaties safeguarding human rights, including socioeconomic rights, such as the European Convention on Human Rights (ECHR) and its additional Protocols,[11] the International Covenant on Civil and Political Rights (ICCPR), the International Covenant on Economic, Social and Cultural

---

[5]Markides (2006). See also, *Malachtou v. Armefti* (1987) 1 CLR 207, 217.

[6]Law relating to the Fifth Amendment of the Constitution (Law 127(I) of 2006).

[7]Pikis (2006), p. 9.

[8]See *Stylianou v. The Police* (1962) CLR 152; *Petrides v. The Greek Communal Chamber* (1963) 2 CLR 417.

[9]Constantinides (2015), pp. 236–238.

[10]Polyviou (2015), p. 152.

[11]The European Convention for the Protection of Human Rights (Ratification) Law (Law 39 of 1962), which ratified the ECHR and Protocol No. 1. Cyprus has ratified all additional protocols, with the exception of Protocol No. 16, which it has not signed yet.

Rights (ICESCR),[12] the European Social Charter (ESC),[13] the International Convention on the Elimination of All Forms of Racial Discrimination,[14] the Convention on the Elimination of All Forms of Discrimination against Women,[15] the Convention on the Rights of the Child[16] and the Convention on the Rights of Persons with Disabilities.[17]

In regard to the European Social Charter, the Republic of Cyprus has accepted the Additional Protocol providing for a system of collective complaints, but has yet to make a declaration enabling national non-governmental organisations to submit collective complaints.[18] Two collective complaints have been filed against Cyprus thus far; the first one, alleging the lack of explicit prohibition of all corporal punishment of children in the family, schools and other settings, was eventually struck out from the list of complaints;[19] and the second one, alleging failure to observe the principle of equal pay for women and men for equal, similar or comparable work, was found admissible and was pending before the European Committee of Social Rights at the time of writing.[20] Moreover, Cyprus is not a party to the Optional Protocol to the ICESCR, thus the Committee on Economic, Social and Cultural Rights (CESCR) cannot consider individual communications concerning violations of the ICESCR against Cyprus.

Constitutional Provisions

Following the example of many post-war constitutions, the 1960 Constitution of Cyprus adopts a holistic approach and guarantees not only civil and political rights,

---

[12] Both ICCPR and ICESCR were ratified via the International Covenants (Economic, Social and Cultural and Civil and Political Rights) (Ratification) Law (Law 14 of 1969).

[13] The European Social Charter Ratification Law (Law 64 of 1967), which was then replaced by the Revised European Social Charter (Ratification) Law (Law 27(III) of 2000). Cyprus has also ratified the Protocol amending the European Social Charter, with the European Social Charter (Amending Protocol) (Ratification) Law (Law 10(III) of 1993).

[14] The Convention on the Elimination of All Forms of Racial Discrimination (Ratification) Law (Law 12 of 1967).

[15] The Convention on the Elimination of All Forms of Discrimination against Women (Ratification) Law (Law 78 of 1985).

[16] The Convention on the Rights of the Child (Ratification) Law (Law 243 of 1990).

[17] The Convention on the Rights of Persons with Disabilities (Ratification) Law (Law 8(III) of 2011).

[18] The Additional Protocol to the European Social Charter Providing for a System of Collective Complaints, with the Additional Protocol of the European Social Charter for the Submission of Collective Complaints (Ratification) Law (Law 9(III) of 1996).

[19] *Association for the Protection of All Children (APPROACH) Ltd v. Cyprus* (Complaint No. 97/2013), Decision of 12 May 2014.

[20] *University Women of Europe (UWE) v. Cyprus* (Complaint No. 127/2016), Decision on admissibility of 4 July 2017.

but also social, economic and cultural rights.[21] In particular, Part II of the Constitution (Articles 6 to 35), entitled "Fundamental Right and Liberties", is dedicated to the protection of human rights,[22] and is substantially based on Articles 2 to 14 of the ECHR and its First Protocol, which served as the prototypes for drafting the relevant constitutional provisions.[23] In addition to these provisions, and after a proposal by Professor Marcel Bridel of the University of Lausanne at the Joint Constitutional Committee, social and economic rights were also included in the Constitution.[24] There is no mention of the right to development, which only appeared as a concept in the mid 1960s,[25] that is, several years after the adoption of the Cyprus Constitution.

The Right to a Decent Existence

Article 9 of the Constitution recognizes the 'right to a decent existence' (which can also be translated from Greek as the right to a 'decent living'), which resembles the internationally guaranteed right to an adequate standard of living, and states that "[e]very person has the right to a decent existence and to social security. A law shall provide for the protection of the workers, assistance to the poor and for a system of social insurance". This right is afforded to 'every person' and does not make a distinction between nationals/EU citizens and non-nationals.

The Constitution does not elaborate on the definition of 'decent existence' (or decent living).[26] According to Tornaritis, Article 9 establishes the state's obligation "to create and maintain such conditions of living, of work and of health as to enable every person to enjoy a standard of living adequate for the health and well-being of himself and his family".[27] It is also argued that Article 9 has an umbrella effect and further protects the rights to health, housing and water, which are essential for safeguarding a person's decent living,[28] but are not enshrined in the Constitution. Interestingly, in *Community of Pyrga and ors v Republic and ors*, Article 9, in conjunction with the right to life under Article 7 of the Constitution, was also related

[21] *Dinos Kontos v. Republic (Permits Authority)* (1974) 3 CLR 112; *Apostolou and others v. Republic* (1984) 3 CLR 509; *Georghios Hadjisavva v. Republic (Council of Ministers)* (1972) 3 CLR 174.

[22] Regarding the history, nature and peculiarities of the Constitution of Cyprus, see generally Tornaritis (1980).

[23] Report of Cyprus under Art. 40 of the International Covenant on Civil and Political Rights to the Human Rights Committee, UN Doc. CCPR/C/1/Add. 6, 6 April 1977; *Christou v. Christou* (1964) CLR 336, at 346. See also, Article 5 of the Treaty concerning the Establishment of the Republic of Cyprus between the United Kingdom Greece, Turkey and Cyprus, Cmnd 1252; UNTS vol. 382, 16 August 1960.

[24] Tornaritis (1968).

[25] Constantinides (2014), p. 946.

[26] Loizou (2001), p. 50.

[27] Tornaritis (1968), p. 546.

[28] For a detailed analysis of Article 9, see Kombos (2016), pp. 62–66.

to the right of individuals and groups (albeit through municipal local authorities) to bring a claim for the protection of the environment to the extent that their health was affected by executive decisions leading to harmful activities to the natural environment in which they live.[29]

In *Apostolides a.o. v. the Republic*, a case concerning the right to social security, the Supreme Court held that "Article 9 has the effect of placing social rights on an equal footing with political rights"[30] (presumably denoting both civil and political rights). Earlier on, in *Papafilippou v. Republic*, the Supreme Constitutional Court had accepted that "[t]he appropriate organs of the Republic are certainly bound by the second sentence of Article 9 of the Constitution to enact within a reasonable time a law as provided in that sentence".[31] The Courts can however only assess the state's actions after their materialisation and not before the state takes any steps to fulfil its obligations under Article 9.[32] In this sense, Article 9 does not establish an actionable right for the provision of benefits that would bring about an adequate standard of decent living.[33]

Moreover, in *Apostolides a.o. v. the Republic*, the Supreme Court held that Article 9 embodies a constitutional directive for the state to safeguard the fundamental human right to social security, in order to fence an individual from the hazards of poverty and social insecurity that reduce his ability to participate and contribute to the social aims.[34] The Supreme Court further stated that:

> Article 9 may be divided into two parts:
>
> The first casts a general duty on the State to maintain minimum standards of existence and social security for everyone. The second imposes a specific duty to establish a system of social security for the protection of the weakest elements of society, the poor and the workers. The general duty, that is to say, one owed to everyone, is absolute in the sense that the State is enjoined to safeguard minimum standards for a decent existence for everyone. This is compatible with the ideal of a human society that places man [sic] in the epicentre of social action. The specific duties are relative, in the sense that social security for the poor and the workers must be compatible with and proportionate to the means of the State. Arguably, the means of the State in this area are not those presently available, but those that could be raised by appropriate legislation.[35]

[29]See *Community of Pyrga through the President of the Community and the local authority of Pyrga and ors v Republic of Cyprus through the Council of Ministers and ors*, Interim decision, Case no 671/1991, ILDC 1790 (CY 1991), (1991) CLR 3498, 7th November 1991, Supreme Court [Sup Ct], para. 17. See also *the Republic v. Board of Improvement Geriou* (1998) 3 CLR 210.

[30]*Apostolides a.o. v. the Republic* (1982) 3 CLR 928, 932; *Economides v. Director of Social Insurance* (1989) 2 CLR 235.

[31](1961) 1 RSCC 62.

[32]See also, *Pelidi a.o. v. the Republic*, Recourse Nos. 1650/1999 and 789/2000, 15 June 2001; *Hadjisavvas v. Republic*, Case No. 396/2005, 31 July 2006; *Kaoulas v. Republic*, Case No. 407/2009, 18 March 2011.

[33]Paraskeva (2015), pp. 116–117.

[34]*Apostolides a.o. v. the Republic* (1982) 3 CLR 928. See also *Katsaras a.o. v. the Republic* (1973) 3 CLR 145.

[35]*Apostolides a.o. v. the Republic* (1982) 3 CLR 928.

Other Socioeconomic Rights

Article 20 of the Constitution enshrines the right to education. Paragraph 3 provides for compulsory elementary education, thus establishing a relevant duty upon individuals until the age of fifteen.[36] In line with Article 13 paragraph 2 of the ICESCR, primary and secondary education is compulsory and free in public schools.[37] Furthermore, Article 25 of the Constitution protects the right to work and provides that "[e]very person has the right to practice any profession or to carry on any occupation, trade or business".

All rights enshrined in Part II of the Constitution create substantive obligations on the state, as per Article 35 of the Constitution, which provides that "[t]he legislative, executive and judicial authorities of the Republic shall be bound to secure, within the limits of their respective competence, the efficient application of the provisions of this Part".

Finally, it should be noted that the constitutionally protected human rights (civil, political, social, economic) are only subject to such limitations as expressly permitted by the Constitution and in accordance with its conditions.[38] The Supreme Court has also reiterated that the core of fundamental human rights cannot be negated.[39] Thus, any law found to affect and neutralize the core of any constitutionally protected right or freedom will be declared by the courts as unconstitutional.[40]

Legislation on Guaranteed Minimum Income

The House of Representatives has enacted numerous laws to fulfil its constitutional obligations under Article 9 of the Constitution such as the 2010 Social Insurance

---

[36]See also the Primary and Secondary Education (Compulsory Attendance and Provision of Free Education) Law (Law No. 24(I) of 1993) and The Primary and Secondary Education (Compulsory Attendance and Provision of Free Education) (Amendment) Law (Law No. 220(I) of 2004).

[37]Article 20(2) of the Constitution provides that primary education shall be free. However, the House of Representatives has extended the right to free education to secondary education as well, as per Article 3 of the Primary and Secondary Education (Compulsory Attendance and Provision of Free Education) Law, as amended.

[38]See *Police v. Ekdotiki Eteria* (1982) 2 CLR 63; *Police v. Georghiades* (1983) 2 CLR 33; *Pingouras v. Police* (1987) 2 CLR 18.

[39]See *The Ship "Panagia Myrtidiotissa v. Sidiropoulos a.o.* (1998) 1 CLR 1000; *Foinikaridou v. Odysseos* (2001) 1 CLR 1744.

[40]See *Sigma Radio TV Ltd v. Radio and Television Authority* (2004]) 4 CLR 1; *Georgiou v. Police* (1999) 2 CLR 616; *Police v. Liveras*, 3 RSCC 65; *Nicosia Police v. Georghiou a.o.*, 4 RSCC 36; *District Officer Nicosia a.o. v. Michael*, 4 RSCC 126; *Kontos v. Republic* (1974) 3 CLR 112; *Marabou Floating Restaurant Ltd v. Republic* (1973) 3 CLR 397; *Meridien Trading v. Minister of Commerce* (1987) 3 CLR 1930; *Pettemerides v. Republic* (1988) 3 CLR 1880.

Law,[41] the 2001 General System of Health Law,[42] the 1995 Provision of Social Pension Law,[43] the 2006 Public Assistance and Services Law,[44] the 2002 Child's Benefits Law,[45] the 2015 State Student Welfare Law,[46] etc. It is noteworthy that since 2014 social assistance in Cyprus is regulated through the minimum income support system provided by the Guaranteed Minimum Income (GMI) Scheme, introduced via the Guaranteed Minimum Income and Social Benefits Law.[47] These laws are significant for safeguarding and implementing Article 9 as well as fighting poverty in Cyprus. Indeed, the GMI scheme figures prominently in the 2017 voluntary national review on implementation of Agenda 2030 of Cyprus as the main instrument adopted with a view to achieving SDG 1 to end poverty.[48]

More specifically, as explained in the 2017 national review, "the GMI provides for basic needs based on a minimum consumption basket and covers also other needs, such as housing (rent or mortgage interest), municipality taxes and extraordinary needs, as well as child care needs and long-term care. The GMI is also provided to families which were not receiving any income support benefits in the past as it incorporates a new eligible group, the working poor, and consolidates low-income pensioners".[49] The GMI scheme is arguably the most important social reform in recent years that was enacted to remedy shortcomings faced in the administration of benefits, eliminate duplicate benefits and provide better support to groups exposed to the risk of poverty (including the working poor that were not recipients of any other income support benefit in the past), especially on the verge of the economic crisis that severely affected Cyprus and its people.[50] According to the explanatory statement of the Attorney-General introducing the GMI Act to the House of Representatives, the aim of the scheme is to "secure for every person or family a minimum standard of living on the basis of criteria relating to income, immovable property and financial data, the composition of the family, housing needs

[41]Social Insurance Law of 2010 (Law 59(I) of 2010), as amended. Part III (Articles 21–45) of the Social Insurance Law provides for: (a) periodical benefits, such as maternity allowance, sickness benefit, unemployment benefit, disability pension, statutory/old-age pension, widow's/widower's pension, orphan's benefit, missing person's allowance and paternity allowance, and (b) for lump-sum benefits, such as marriage grant (which was abolished in 2012), maternity grant and funeral grant. Part IV (Articles 46–66) further provide for employment injury benefits, which include temporary incapacity (injury benefit), disability benefit and death benefit.

[42]Law 89(I) of 2001.

[43]Law 25(I) of 1995, as amended. The social pension is also available to recipients of statutory pension, whenever the latter is considered very low, in accordance with Article (3)(1)(c) and 4(1) of the Provision of Social Pension Law of 1995, as amended.

[44]Law 95(I) of 2006.

[45]Law 167(1) of 2002, as amended.

[46]Law 203(I) of 2015.

[47]Law 109 (I) of 2014, as amended.

[48]Ministry of Foreign Affairs (2017), pp. 15–16.

[49]Ibid, at p. 16.

[50]See International Monetary Fund (2013a), para. 15; Koutsampelas (2016), pp. 3–4.

and any specialized needs, as well as the creation of structures that will be able to support in the best possible way the families and persons who are in need of such support".[51] It then states that the proposed legislation "provides an ultimate safety net to all those who have a real need and guarantees the fundamental human right of every citizen to an adequate standard of living securing a minimum income to every person or family that does not have adequate living resources".[52]

Yet, despite its promising potential and the apparently benign intentions, it seems that the GMI scheme has failed to fully rise to expectations. In its Concluding Observations on Cyprus of 2016, the UN Committee on Economic, Social and Cultural Rights, which monitors the implementation of the ICESCR, expressed concern at, *inter alia*, "[t]he insufficient level of the benefit, which does not guarantee an adequate standard of living to beneficiaries and their families", and "[t]he exclusion of beneficiaries of the existing public assistance programmes, who may not qualify for the guaranteed minimum income, although they are still in need of social assistance".[53] The Committee recommended the increase and periodical review of the GMI account and adequate protection for those who do not qualify for the guaranteed minimum income but remain in need of social assistance.[54]

The Committee also recommended that Cyprus

> take fully into account its obligations under the Covenant and ensure the full enjoyment of the rights enshrined therein in the implementation of the 2030 Agenda for Sustainable Development at the national level, with international assistance and cooperation when needed. Achievement of the Sustainable Development Goals would be significantly facilitated by the State party establishing independent mechanisms to monitor progress and treating beneficiaries of public programmes as rights holders who can claim entitlements. Implementing the Goals on the basis of the principle of participation, accountability and non-discrimination would ensure that no one is left behind.[55]

In addition to legislation enacted by the House of Representatives, there are also numerous social benefits allocated by the Council of Ministers through executive orders in an effort to combat the high rates of poverty and risk of social exclusion of certain vulnerable social groups (e.g. elderly, single-parent families, etc). Such benefits include the scheme for supporting pensioners' households with low income, the so-called 'Easter allowance', the 'Christmas allowance', the mother allowance, etc.

Implementation and administration of the abovementioned benefits is entrusted to the Ministry of Labour, Welfare and Social Insurance, through various departments.[56] Applications for receiving such benefits are examined by the Director or

---

[51]Official Gazette of the Republic, No. 4146, 23 July 2014, at 1036.

[52]Ibid.

[53]Committee on Economic, Social and Cultural Rights (2016), para. 29.

[54]Ibid, para. 30.

[55]Ibid, para. 47.

[56]Such departments under the control and supervision of the Ministry of Labour, Welfare and Social Insurance include: the Social Insurance Services (implementing the governmental policy, schemes and measures in the field of social insurance, identifying social and economic needs that can be

other officers of the relevant Department of the Ministry of Labour, Welfare and Social Insurance, who may approve in whole or in part, or may reject the application.

The Impact of the Financial Crisis

In the aftermath of the severe global financial crisis of 2008, the first signs of recession were detected in the Cypriot banking system in 2009. By 2011, Cyprus was cut off from international capital markets and the banking sector collapsed, *inter alia*, due to its exposure to the Greek sovereign debt. On 25 March 2013, the Government reached an agreement with the Eurogroup on the key elements necessary for a future Economic Adjustment Programme (EAP).[57]

The Eurogroup agreed to an unprecedented agreement to provide €10 billion to Cyprus in the form of a 'bail-in' (i.e. using own means).[58] Cyprus agreed to resolve Laiki Bank, the country's second largest bank, levying all uninsured deposits[59] and levying 47.5% of uninsured deposits in the Bank of Cyprus. Put differently, uninsured depositors in Laiki Bank lost all their deposits and uninsured depositors in the Bank of Cyprus lost almost half of their deposits. Furthermore, Cyprus was subject to strict conditionality pursuant to the EAP, which required many reforms, including the reform of the welfare system in a way that would 'streamline' the broad range of benefits provided, while aiming at protecting the most vulnerable and disadvantaged.[60]

The financial crisis led to considerable increase in unemployment and in the percentage of people at risk of poverty and social exclusion.[61] More specifically, the percentage of people at risk of poverty and social exclusion increased from 23.3% in 2008 to 24.6% in 2011, to 27.1% in 2012, 27.8% in 2013, 27.4% in 2014, 28.9% in 2015 and dropped to 27.7% in 2016.[62] Significant cuts were introduced in almost all

confronted with social security, making payments for the majority of benefits and pensions), the Social Welfare Services (safeguarding social cohesion and social solidarity, providing social protection, achieving social inclusion and combating poverty and social exclusion), the Department for Social Inclusion of Persons with Disabilities (improving the quality of life of persons with disabilities, creating new prospects for their social inclusion through the design, coordination and implementation of reforming policies and providing social benefits to persons with disabilities), the Welfare Benefits Administration Service (implementing the guaranteed minimum income and administering various social schemes).

[57]On 30 April 2013, the House of Representatives endorsed the Programme, which was detailed in the MoU on Specific Economic Policy Conditionality, with the Financial Assistance Facility Agreement (Ratifying) Law (Law 1(III) of 2013).

[58]The Loan Agreement for the financial assistance package towards Cyprus amounted to €10 billion, with the ESM providing up to €9 billion and the IMF contributing around €1 billion.

[59]An uninsured deposit is the deposit which is larger than €100,000.

[60]International Monetary Fund (2013b).

[61]Trimikliniotis (2012).

[62]By comparison, in 2015 the EU risk-of-poverty or social exclusion rate was 23.7%.

social benefits, as observed in a report by the Statistical Service of the Ministry of Finance, regarding social protection expenditures (including old age, sickness, disability, unemployment and housing benefits).[63] According to the said report, expenditures for social protection for the year 2014 amounted to €4.036,9 million, in comparison to €4.381,6 million in 2013.[64] This was the first reduction in the total social protection expenditure since 2000.[65]

Undoubtedly, the financial crisis had a negative impact in the Cypriot society. Legislation was amended to introduce reforms in social benefit schemes, as per the EAP, with a view to using the resources more efficiently and to ensuring a balance between welfare assistance and incentives to take up work. Most of these reforms concerned the introduction of a series of stricter criteria for becoming a recipient of social benefits.[66] The constitutionality of these reforms has by and large not been discussed in terms of a possible violation of Article 9 of the Constitution, or in connection to the fight against poverty or the right to development.[67]

The impact of austerity measures on socioeconomic rights did not skip the attention of the CESCR, which noted with concern "the continuing significant decrease in public spending, particularly in the areas of social protection, housing, health and education, under fiscal consolidation measures", the "disproportionately adverse impact on the enjoyment of economic, social and cultural rights by disadvantaged and marginalized individuals and groups";[68] and that "more than a quarter of the population (27.4%) is at risk of poverty [. . .] and does not enjoy an adequate standard of living".[69]

---

[63] Statistical Service, Ministry of Finance (2017).

[64] Ibid, at p. 15.

[65] Ibid.

[66] See for instance, the Social Insurance (Amending) Law (Law 193(I) of 2012); the Social Insurance (Amending) Law (Law 106(I) of 2014); the State Medical Institutions and Services General (Amending) Regulations 2013 (Regulation 143 of 2013); the Special Contribution for Officials, Employees and Pensioners of the Public Sector and Wider Public Sector (Amending) Law (Law 184(I) of 2012).

[67] There is however case law relating to the financial crisis and its impact on the right to property (Article 23 of the Constitution); see, *Georgios Charalambous a.o. v. Ministry of Finance a.o,* Joined cases Nos. 1480/2011, 1481/2011, 1482/2011, 1483/2011, 1484/2011, 1591/2011, 1625/2011, 11 June 2014; *Maria Koutselini-Ioannidou a.o. v. the Republic a.o,* Joined cases nos. 740/11, 891/11, 892/11, 893/11, 927/11, 928/11, 930/11, 931/11, 960/11, 963/11, 964/11, 966/11, 996/11, 997/11, 998/11, 999/11, 1028/11, 1029/11, 1031/11, 1032/11, 1033/11, 1034/11, 1035/11, 1036/11, 1040/11, 1048/11, 1051/11, 1087/11, 1150/11, 1163/11, 1186/11, 1187/11, 1191/11, 1205/11, 1206/11, 1276/11, 1287/11, 1310/11, 1364/11, 1540/11, 1612/11, 1681/11, 1710/11, 114/12, 556/12, 563/12, 564/12, 587/12, 7 October 2014; *Myrto Christodoulou a.o. v. Central Bank of Cyprus a.o* (2013) 3 CLR 427; *Vias Demetriou a.o. v. Central Bank of Cyprus a.o.*, joined cases Nos. 1034/2013, 1102/13, 2799/13, 3932/13, 4717/13, 4965/13, 5064/13, 5173/13, 5318/13, 5479/13, 5496/13, 5523/13, 5554/13, 5566/13, 5584/13, 5588/13, 5900/13, 5903/13, 5951/13, 5960/13, 5961/13, 5966/13, 5968/13, 6117/13, 6125/13, 6134/13, 6141/13, 6179/13, 6183/13, 6184/13, 6195/13, 6246/13, 6266/13 και 6272/13, 9 October 2014.

[68] Committee on Economic, Social and Cultural Rights (2016), para. 11.

[69] Ibid, para. 35.

Domestic Review Mechanisms and Remedies

Administrative Appeal

Most laws on social benefits include provisions that enable the applicant to bring an administrative appeal against the department's decision, either to the same body that took the contested decision or to a hierarchically superior authority or to an organ with monitoring powers.[70] Through this non-judicial process, individuals seek redress and the administration is given an opportunity to remedy any errors in its decision. Thus, applicants may file a written complaint with the competent organ or authority within a specific period prescribed in the relevant statute.

Recourse to the Administrative Court

A recourse to the Administrative Court is the only judicial venue currently available in the Cypriot legal order for challenging decisions of the state in connection to social benefits.[71] More specifically, Article 146 of the Constitution, as amended,[72] provides that the Administrative Court has "exclusive jurisdiction to decide in the first instance on a recourse made to it on a complaint that a decision, an act or omission of any organ, authority or person, exercising any executive or administrative authority is contrary to any of the provisions of this Constitution or of any law or is made in excess or in abuse of powers vested in such organ or authority or person". Upon such recourse, the Administrative Court has the authority to: (a) confirm, either in whole or in part, such administrative decision or act or omission, (b) declare, either in whole or in part, such decision or act to be null and void and of no effect whatsoever, or (c) declare that such omission, either in whole or in part, ought not to have been made and that whatever has been omitted should have been performed.[73]

As a result, an aggrieved individual, whose application for social benefits has been rejected or partially approved, may challenge the decision of the administration before the Administrative Court.[74] However, the Administrative Court can either

---

[70]See for instance, Article 83 of the Social Insurance Law, Article 15 of the State Student Welfare Law, Article 11 of the Child's Benefits Law.

[71]See *Pancyprian Organization of Large Families a.o. v. Attorney-General*, App. No. 6914/2012, 22 March 2017; *Eirini Patsalosavvi-Leontiou v. The Republic* (1997) 3 CLR 70 and *Electricity Authority of Cyprus v. Filiastidi* (2003) 3 CLR 342, where the Plenary of the Supreme Court reaffirmed that the proper procedure for challenging decisions related to social benefits is through filing a recourse to the Supreme Court acting as Administrative Court.

[72]Law relating to the Eighth Amendment of the Constitution, (Law 130(I) of 2015).

[73]Article 146(4)(a), (b) and (c) of the Constitution of Cyprus.

[74]See for instance, *Georgiou v. the Republic,* Case No. 990/2015, 17/1/2018; *Daphne Kakoulli v. Ministry of Labour, Welfare and Social Insurance (Department of Social Services)*, App. No. 426/2015, 31 December 2015; *Andri Andreou v. Ministry of Labour, Welfare and Social Insurance*

reject the application and uphold the decision of the administration or it may declare the decision as null and void. It does not have the authority to amend the decision. Finally, when filing a recourse against an administrative decision, pursuant to Article 146 of the Constitution, a petitioner may also challenge, incidentally, the constitutionality of a legislative provision.

Complaint to the Commissioner for Administration and Human Rights (Ombudsman)

The 1991 Commissioner for Administration Law introduced the institution of the ombudsman in the Cypriot legal order with the aim of safeguarding the rule of law and human rights.[75] The Commissioner for Administration and Human Rights is appointed by the President of the Republic at the suggestion of the Council of Ministers and with the agreement of the majority of the House of Representatives.[76] The Ombudsman has the power to investigate complaints against any public authority or officer for actions that violate human rights, or are in breach of the laws or regulations of proper administration and correct behaviour towards individuals.[77] In July 2015, the Office of the Ombudsman submitted an application for accreditation as National Human Rights Institution (NHRI) under the Paris Principles to the Subcommittee on Accreditation of the UN International Coordinating Committee of National Institutions for the Promotion and Protection of Human Rights. The Office has been accredited with B Status (i.e. not fully in compliance with the Paris Principles). This was a matter of concern to the CESCR, which recommended that Cyprus take "all measures necessary to ensure that the Office of the Commissioner for Administration and Human Rights is fully compliant with the Paris Principles".[78]

The Ombudsman may initiate an investigation after the submission of a complaint by an individual who is directly and personally affected by the contested action. An investigation may also commence by an order of the Council of Ministers or the Ombudsman may take up investigations *proprio motu* on matters of general interest. The complaints lodged are categorized and assigned to the six sectors within the office of the Commissioner, one of which is the health, social protection and relations between the state and the citizen sector.

If the complaint is well-founded, the Ombudsman draws up a report or issues conclusions, decisions or suggestions that aim at resolving the issue and avoiding

---

(Social Welfare Services), App. No. 5894/2013, 11 September 2014; *Andreas Christou a.o. v. The Republic*, App. No. 346/2011, 4 October 2012: *Suzana Demourtsidou v. The Republic*, App. No. 5808/2013, 10 February 2016; *Giorgos Charalambous v. The Republic*, App. No. 6462/2013, 20 December 2015.

[75]Commissioner for Administration Law (Law 3 of 1991).

[76]Ibid, Article 3(1).

[77]Ibid, Article 5.

[78]Committee on Economic, Social and Cultural Rights (2016), para. 8.

similar issues in the future. If the complainant has suffered any harm or injustice, the Ombudsman submits a recommendation to the competent authority for reparation of the harm or injustice, and may further determine the time within which the harm or injustice must be remedied.

The Ombudsman's findings (either in the form of reports, suggestions, decisions or conclusions) are not legally binding. However, in case the relevant executive or administrative authority or organ does not implement those suggestions, recommendations or decisions and the reasons given by the authority or organ are not sufficiently justified, the Ombudsman may submit the result of their consultations to the Council of Ministers and the House of Representatives, and may publicize the authority/organ's refusal or failure to comply.

The Contribution of Cyprus to International Development Cooperation

The Constitution of Cyprus provides no basis for contributing to the fight against poverty and the realization of the right to development on the international level. This has not prevented Cyprus from contributing to international development cooperation, especially since its accession to the EU in 2004, when it officially joined the efforts of the international community and the EU in the fight against poverty.

From Aid Recipient to Aid Donor

Cyprus was not always a donor country. Since 1963 Cyprus has received loans from the World Bank for various projects such as power projects,[79] dams[80] etc. Since the 1974 Turkish invasion, Cyprus has also received technical assistance by international organisations such as the UN, the Commonwealth Fund for Technical Cooperation, and by states on a bilateral basis (Greece, United States of America, etc.).[81] Two decades later, in 1994, Cyprus launched the "Technical Assistance Scheme for Foreign Countries", which offered foreign nationals training scholarships in various Cypriot tertiary academic institutions. The areas of studies offered were tourism, management and forestry, where Cyprus had developed expertise, and which could provide third nationals technical skills, which they could take back to their home

[79]See Legal ISC Files (1963) and World Bank (1969).

[80]World Bank (1979).

[81]CyprusAid (2005), p. 2.

countries and enhance the local development process.[82] From 1994 to 2004, Cyprus offered 1155 scholarships to nationals of third countries.[83]

Since its 2004 accession to the EU, Cyprus' development cooperation policy has been aligned with that of the EU. In 2005, by executive order, the Council of Ministers of Cyprus established CyprusAid as the development cooperation agency of the Republic with a view to fulfilling the obligations of Cyprus under EU's development policy. The implementation of CyprusAid has been entrusted with the Ministry of Foreign Affairs, which is responsible for both the setting and the implementation of Cyprus' Official Development Assistance policy.[84] CyprusAid functions within the framework of a policy making mechanism that was put in place to steer Cyprus' Official Development Assistance.

Cyprus aids through traditional methods (i.e. financial contributions to the EU and other international organisations, emergency response and humanitarian assistance as well as technical assistance) and through new means of assistance delivery (i.e. delegated cooperation). Technical assistance has taken the form of scholarships and was provided on bilateral basis through diplomatic (official) channels. The countries that participated in the technical assistance programme include Armenia, Bangladesh, Bosnia and Herzegovina, China, Cuba, East Timor, Georgia, Gambia, Iran, Kazakhstan, Kenya, Kyrgyzstan, Moldova, Pakistan, Seychelles, Sudan, Sri Lanka, Tajikistan and Uzbekistan.

Cyprus also implemented development assistance projects in partner states through Delegated Cooperation/Silent Partnerships in cooperation with other EU member state development agencies and international organisations. These partnerships were usually undertaken in the form of memoranda of understanding (MoUs) and subsidiary agreements, and enabled Cyprus to gradually build up its aid delivery know-how. Cyprus financed development assistance projects in so-called 'priority countries' (Autonomous Palestinian Territories, Bosnia-Herzegovina, Egypt, Lebanon, Lesotho, Mali and Yemen) as well as in 'non-priority countries' (Afghanistan, Caribbean countries, Guinea, Malawi and Nepal).

CyprusAid: Contribution to the Realization of the Millennium Development Goals

The establishment of CyprusAid was also connected with the realization of the MDGs, taking into consideration the funding priorities of CyprusAid's policy framework and focus on social and economic development. The implementation

---

[82] Webster (2013).

[83] Ministry of Foreign Affairs (2007).

[84] See Decision by the Council of Ministers, No. 75.141, dated 24/5/2013.

of the MDGs was proclaimed a foreign policy priority.[85] The Official Development Assistance of Cyprus was channelled to sectors directly related to the MDGs, such as social and services sectors (healthcare, education, tourism, development of human capital, etc.), infrastructure development (construction of bridges, public works, health infrastructure, etc.) and the environment (climate change adaptation, environmental sustainability, etc.).

In connection to the promotion of sustainable development, Cyprus focused on providing recipient countries with the means (human resources, infrastructure or structural changes) to eventually become self-sufficient in their quest for attaining higher standards of living.[86] It prioritized projects promoting the recipients' capacity for self-sustainment rather than money allocations. More specifically, Cyprus has implemented development projects in developing countries in cooperation with other EU member state development agencies and international organizations that effectively contribute to all MDGs. Such projects include:[87]

- The Early Childhood Education Enhancement Project in Egypt, in partnership with the United Nations World Food Programme (UNWFP). Cyprus contributed $1,000,000 to this project which aimed, *inter alia*, at increasing attendance of girls in schools by providing food to families with a girl in primary education;
- The Protracted Relief Operation for Non-Refugee Palestinians Project in the Autonomous Palestinian Territories with the UNWFP. Cyprus contributed $350,000 for the provision of food to vulnerable groups including children and pregnant women. Similarly, Cyprus has implemented several other projects in partnership with the UNWFP in the Autonomous Palestinian Territories such as the Emergency Food Assistance for Operation Lifeline Gaza Project ($200,000) and the Targeted Assistance for Relief, Support to Productive Activities and Skills Development for Vulnerable Non-Refugee Palestinians Project (€230,000);
- The Improving Trade of Animals and Products in Bosnia and Herzegovina Project, in collaboration with the Government of Sweden, with the goal of speeding up food export and import (€850,000);
- The Good Governance for Enhanced Post-War Reconstruction Project in Southern Lebanon, with the United Nations Human Settlements Programme (UN-HABITAT), aimed at enhancing the administrative capacity of local government to manage immediate reconstruction plans and long-term sustainable development (€522,000);
- The "Improving teaching and learning practices in Lebanon through introducing active learning and gender sensitive approaches" project, in partnership with UNESCO, for the improvement of teaching and learning practices in schools across Lebanon (€14,663);

[85] See for instance, several statements made by the former President of the Republic [Ministry of Foreign Affairs (2008); Ministry of Foreign Affairs (2009)].

[86] CyprusAid (2005), p. 4.

[87] Antoniou (2013), pp. 30–34; Agrotis (2013), pp. 3–4.

- The Programme for the Construction of Crossing-over Works in Koulikoro region (Mali), in partnership with the Government of Belgium, where Cyprus contributed €400,000 for the construction of four bridges to facilitate access to the villages of the area;
- The provision of rations of wheat and vegetable oil throughout the school year 2007–2008 to families with girls attending elementary education in Ammran, Yemen, in the framework of the UNWFP Country Programme for Yemen, for the total amount of €170,000 (which covered around 2788 girls in 67 schools).

CyprusAid in the Aftermath of the Financial Crisis

CyprusAid was created by executive order in 2005 and, as a result, it lacks a legislative basis and framework; it could be revoked, discontinued, or amended at any time by another executive order. In 2013, due to the economic crisis, the development cooperation policy remained at the same level, while the undertaking of new projects and technical assistance was frozen.[88] Since 2013, CyprusAid has suspended its operations, and the implementation of Official Development Assistance, including the relevant budget, resources and staff, have been assigned to the Ministry of Foreign Affairs.

The priorities of the state were the recovery of confidence in the Cypriot economy and its banking system, fiscal consolidation, reduction of unemployment rates, rather than foreign development aid. This is evident in the downward trend of the Official Development Assistance as share of the gross national income (GNI), in the outbreak of the first signs of recession in 2011. Particularly, in 2006 the Official Development Assistance amounted to 0.15% of the GNI, in 2007 and 2008 to 0.17%, in 2009 to 0.20%, in 2010 to 0.23%, in 2011 to 0.16%, in 2012 to 0.12%, in 2013 to 0.10% and in 2014 and 2015 to 0.09%.[89]

Nonetheless, according to the 2017 national review of the 2030 Agenda:

> Cyprus continues to fulfill its contractual obligations concerning the European Development Policy, as well as towards international organizations such as WFP, FAO, UNIDO, UNDP, UNHCR etc. Small steps are being made towards reactivation of bilateral development programs, such as the formulation of a scholarship programme, while full blown development cooperation planning will be hopefully reactivated in the near future. In 2015, the Cypriot ODA contribution amounted to 0.09% GNP [...] Although economic contributions have been reduced, Cyprus continues to be active in multilateral fora, such as the EU and the UN, in supporting the needs of the worlds' poorer, with an increased focus on Least Developed Countries, Africa and countries coming out of conflict. Similarly, Cyprus supports small island developing states (SIDS) that need enhanced support to meet the challenge of climate change to which they are most vulnerable.[90]

---

[88] Ministry of Foreign Affairs (2017), p. 9.

[89] Eurostat (2018).

[90] Ministry of Foreign Affairs (2017), p. 9.

Interestingly (or perhaps surprisingly), the low level of Cyprus' contribution of ODA was not addressed in the CESCR Concluding Observations on Cyprus of 2016.

Cyprus and the 2030 Agenda for Sustainable Development

Cyprus strongly supported the process leading to the post-2015 sustainable development agenda,[91] and recognised the need for the international community to recommit to a new concrete agenda aimed at poverty eradication, inclusive economic and social development, environmental sustainability and peace and security for all, backed with solid commitments within the future development framework. In his address at the UN Summit for the adoption of the post-2015 development agenda, the President of the Republic characterized the 2030 Agenda ("Transforming our world: the 2030 Agenda for Sustainable Development") as "a monumental achievement of the international community", a universal agenda which is "a truly ambitious and inclusive one, with poverty eradication and sustainable development at its heart" and the renewal of the "commitment to complete the job of the unfinished [MDGs]".[92]

The institutional mechanism for the implementation of Agenda 2030 falls under the coordination of the Ministry of Foreign Affairs and comprises mainly Ministries and governmental services. A relevant line Ministry has been assigned as coordinator for the implementation of each of the 17 SDGs; for instance, the Ministry of Labour, Welfare and Social Insurance is the coordinator of SDG 1, the Ministry of Education and Culture is the coordinator of SDG 4, the Ministry of Agriculture, Rural Development and Environment is the coordinator of SDG 14, etc.

In December 2016, Cyprus indicated its support for the global fight against poverty by pledging €5.32 million to the International Development Association (IDA18 Replenishment). The funding will enable the International Development Association to help fight climate change, promote gender equality, build stronger institutions, create jobs and transform economies in the world's poorest countries.

The Role of Civil Society and the Private Sector

The government has developed cooperation with civil society organizations aiming at raising local citizens' awareness concerning the SDGs by having an active role in the drafting, communication and implementation of relevant initiatives. In this respect, in May 2017, the Ministry of Foreign Affairs and the Ministry of Education

[91]Themistokleous et al. (2017).

[92]Permanent Mission of the Republic of Cyprus to the United Nations (2015).

and Culture conducted a public internet survey on 'Sustainable Development Goals: Review of progress and determination of priorities of the Republic of Cyprus' with a view to including the results in the Review on the implementation of the 2030 Agenda in Cyprus, which was presented at the High-Level Political Forum on Sustainable Development in July 2017.

Despite their active role and the political support by the government (especially the Ministry of Foreign Affairs and the Ministry of Education and Culture), civil society organisations did not have the necessary funding to promote many such initiatives nor sufficient capacity and understanding to link their activities with the SDGs.[93] Since 2017, Cypriot civil society organisations have been awarded with EU projects specifically targeting the promotion of awareness on the SDGs.[94] Moreover, civil society organisations act as multipliers through a pool of experts who may contribute considerably both by promoting the SDGs at the general public and by training other operators to increase the capacity of civil society.[95]

Furthermore, Cyprus has recognized that the private sector is a key source for solutions that can effectively address sustainability issues. Corporate Social Responsibility is seen as a key tool through which the private sector can become more responsible towards both the society and the environment.[96] As of 2012, the government has reinforced its efforts to promote business responsibility and sustainability, mainly through awareness actions falling under the National Action Plan for Corporate Social Responsibility for 2013–2015. It has further developed various tools and initiatives that help companies adopt Corporate Social Responsibility practices which can directly or indirectly contribute to the achievement of most of the SDGs.

Concluding Remarks

Cyprus is among those states that turned from aid recipient to donor, primarily due to its EU accession in 2004 and its ensuing commitments to development contribution through Official Development Assistance under the EU development cooperation framework. Its aid programme and the relevant (CyprusAid) Agency did not have a legislative basis but was established by executive decision in 2005. As a result, despite a rather promising start in the aftermath of EU accession, there was no institutional/legislative 'safety net' to sustain CyprusAid when the Cyprus economy was severely hit by the global financial crisis, leading to the virtual collapse of its banking system and the conclusion of a Memorandum of Understanding on Specific

[93] Ministry of Foreign Affairs (2017), p. 12.

[94] Ibid, Annex 2, 'Civil Society's action towards achieving the Sustainable Development Goals in Cyprus', pp. 72–73.

[95] Ibid, at p. 73.

[96] Ibid, at p. 13.

Economic Policy Conditionality with EC/ECB/IMF in 2013. The Agency has suspended its operations since 2013 and Cyprus' ODA figures have plummeted (from 0.23% of GNI in 2010 to 0.09% in 2015). Yet, throughout this period, Cyprus has officially expressed its constant political commitment to the fight against poverty in the international plane through its participation in relevant initiatives.

In the domestic sphere, priority was understandably given to overcoming short and medium-term financial, fiscal and structural challenges and to stabilizing and reactivating the economy without losing sight of the needs of the most vulnerable. In this respect, the GMI scheme was introduced as the principal measure to achieve SDG1 to end poverty and also implement the constitutional obligation to realise the right to decent existence (or decent living) in accordance with Article 9 of the 1960 Constitution. Interestingly, this provision was enshrined prior to the adoption of the 1966 ICESCR. It has not been interpreted as giving rise to justiciable rights but rather as a guiding principle to state policy. Not all internationally recognized social rights are however enshrined in the Constitution. Most importantly, there is no constitutional protection of the right to health. There is also no mention of the right to development either in the Constitution or in domestic legislation and political debates although Cyprus has been traditionally supportive of the right to development in international fora, not least because of its prominent role in the Non-Aligned Movement until the Movement's decline in the 1990s. Since its EU accession in 2004, Cyprus has followed the EU policy on relevant issues. Yet, despite the generous rhetoric and good intentions, its ODA as share of GNI has been disappointingly low. Non-membership in the OECD and DAC and the financial crisis can no longer be an excuse.

References

Agrotis S (2013) How can Cyprus Aid contribute to the achievement of the Millennium Development Goals?. http://www.ngo-sc.org/Portals/0/pdf/How%20does%20CyprusAid%20contribute%20to%20the%20achievement%20of%20the%20MDGs%20FINAL.pdf. Accessed 24 Jan 2019

Antoniou M (2013) The millennium development goals: education for peace and development. NGO Support Centre, Nicosia

Christou O, Ioannou C, Shekeris A (2016) The cypriot welfare state at a time of crisis. In: Schubert K, de Villota P, Kuhlmann J (eds) Challenges to European welfare systems. Springer, Berlin, pp 79–104

Committee on Economic, Social and Cultural Rights (2016) Concluding observations on the sixth periodic report of Cyprus, E/C.12/CYP/CO/6, 28 October 2016

Constantinides A (2014) Human right to development. In: Mihr A, Gibney M (eds) The SAGE handbook of human rights. SAGE Publications, London, pp 941–958

Constantinides A (2015) The status of international law in the Cypriot legal order. In: Samara-Krispi A (ed) Essays of law and international relations in memory of Professor Elias Krispis (Αίνος Μνήμης Καθηγητού Ηλία Κρίσπη: Συμβολές στην Επιστήμη του Δικαίου και των Διεθνών Σχέσεων). Sakkoulas, Athens-Thessaloniki, pp 229–240

CyprusAid (2005) Medium Term Strategy for Official Development Assistance 2006–2010. http://www.cyprusaid.gov.cy/planning/cyprusaid.nsf/all/

ACD30B2200A98B00C2257A0600337FEC/$file/%CE%9CEDIUM%20TERM%20STRATEGY.pdf?openelement. Accessed 24 Jan 2019

Eurostat (2018) Official development assistance as share of gross national income (source: OECD). <https://ec.europa.eu/eurostat/tgm/table.do?tab=table&init=1&language=en&pcode=sdg_17_10&plugin=1>. Accessed 24 Jan 2019

International Monetary Fund (2013a) Cyprus Letter of Intent to the International Monetary Fund, 29 August 2013, https://www.imf.org/external/np/loi/2013/cyp/082913.pdf. Accessed 24 Jan 2019

International Monetary Fund (2013b) Letter of Intent of the government of Cyprus, which describes the policies that Cyprus intends to implement in the context of its request for financial support from the IMF. https://www.imf.org/external/np/loi/2013/cyp/042913.pdf. Accessed 24 Jan 2019

Kombos C (2016) Social rights in the Republic of Cyprus. In: Wojtyczek K (ed) Social and economic rights as fundamental rights. Eleven, The Hague, pp 57–86

Koutsampelas C (2016) The Cypriot GMI scheme and comparisons with other European countries. Cyprus Econ Policy Rev 10(1):3–26

Legal ISC Files (1963) Cyprus - Power Project: Loan 0335 - Loan Agreement - Conformed (English). World Bank, Washington, DC

Loizou AN (2001) The Constitution of the Republic of Cyprus (Σύνταγμα Κυπριακής Δημοκρατίας). Nicosia

Markides A (2006) The Republic of Cyprus. In: Kortmann C, Fleuren J, Voermans W (eds) Constitutional law of 10 EU Member States: the 2004 enlargement. Kluwer, Deventer, pp I.3–I.77

Ministry of Foreign Affairs (2007) Speech by Ambassador Alexandros N. Zenon, during an event for the organization of the European Development Days, (in Greek). http://www.mfa.gov.cy/mfa/mfa2016.nsf/All/785C73D865C73663C2257FAA003153A7?OpenDocument. Accessed 24 Jan 2019

Ministry of Foreign Affairs (2008) Statement by the President of the Republic Mr Demetris Christofias to the General Debate of the 63rd Session of the General Assembly of the United Nations, 24 September 2008, (in Greek). http://www.mfa.gov.cy/mfa/mfa2016.nsf/All/2D06151B110CC8F1C2257FA0004582A0?OpenDocument&print. Accessed 24 Jan 2019

Ministry of Foreign Affairs (2009) The President of the Republic received the credentials of the new Ambassador of Mali, 02/11/2009 (in Greek). http://www.mfa.gov.cy/mfa/mfa2016.nsf/All/3EC443F9FDC002F4C2257FA000458E86?OpenDocument&print. Accessed 24 Jan 2019

Ministry of Foreign Affairs (2017) Review on the Implementation of the 2030 Agenda in Cyprus. https://sustainabledevelopment.un.org/content/documents/15886Cyprus.pdf. Accessed 24 Jan 2019

Paraskeva C (2015) Cypriot constitutional law: fundamental rights and freedoms (Κυπριακό Συνταγματικό Δίκαιο: Θεμελιώδη Δικαιώματα και Ελευθερίες). Nomiki Vivliothiki, Athens

Permanent Mission of the Republic of Cyprus to the United Nations (2015) Address by President Anastasiades at the UN Summit for the Adoption of the post-2015 Development Agenda. https://sustainabledevelopment.un.org/content/documents/20508cyprus.pdf. Accessed 24 Jan 2019

Pikis GM (2006) Constitutionalism – Human Rights – Separation of Powers: the Cyprus Precedent. Martinus Nijhoff, Leiden-Boston

Polyviou PG (2015) Cyprus: a study in the theory structure and method of the legal system of the Republic of Cyprus. Chryssafinis & Polyviou, Nicosia

Statistical Service, Ministry of Finance (2017) Social Protection in Cyprus: Revenue and Expenditure 2014, General Social Statistics, Series III, Report No. 11. http://www.mof.gov.cy/mof/cystat/statistics.nsf/All/093F9B160BCB4842C2257833002D024B/$file/SOCIAL_PROTECTION-2014-280217.pdf?OpenElement. Accessed 24 Jan 2019

Themistokleous S, Anastasiou I, Vrasidas C (2017) Cyprus: Fit to deliver on the 2030 Agenda for Sustainable Development? Social Watch Report. http://www.socialwatch.org/node/17714. Accessed 24 Jan 2019

Tornaritis C (1968) The social and economic rights under the Law of the Republic of Cyprus. In: Mélanges Marcel Bridel: Recueil de travaux publiés par la Faculté de droit. Lausanne, Imprimeries réunies, pp 533–556

Tornaritis C (1980) Cyprus and its constitutional and other problems. Nicosia

Trimikliniotis N (2012) Social and Employment Situation in Cyprus. European Parliament, Directorate General for Internal Policies, Policy Department A: Economic and Scientific Policy. https://ec.europa.eu/social/BlobServlet?docId=9595&langId=en. Accessed 24 Jan 2019

Webster C (2013) Human Rights and Development Assistance/Co-operation: Consideration for the Republic of Cyprus. http://www.ngo-sc.org/Portals/0/pdf/Human%20Rights%20and%20Development%20Assistance%20Co-operation%20-%20FINAL.pdf. Accessed 24 Jan 2019

World Bank (1969) Cyprus - Third Power Project (English), Public utilities projects, no. PU 25. World Bank, Washington, DC

World Bank (1979) Cyprus - Vasilikos - Pendaskinos Water Resources Development Project (English). World Bank, Washington, DC

Chapter 4
The Fight Against Poverty and the Right to Development in the Czech Republic

Pavel Šturma and Veronika Bílková

Abstract The contribution (national report) briefly describes the fight against poverty and the right to development form the perspective of the Czech Republic. The first part provides a survey of Czech international treaty obligations and the constitutional and legal framework in the field of social rights. The second part deals with the Czech contributions to the fight against poverty and the right to development in the international context. Development cooperation makes an integral part of the Czech foreign policy. The Czech Republic has general commitments stemming from its membership in the UN and the EU. It should strive to increase the resources allocated to development assistance to 0.7% of its GNI but the achievement of this goal does not seem realistic in the nearest future.

Domestic Law and Remedies

The Czech Republic a democratic State based on the rule of law and respect of human rights and freedoms.[1] Although it is not put expressly into its Constitution, unlike the modern post-WWII constitutions of some other European States, the Czech Republic can be also called a "social State". This qualification however is not self-evident and can only be drawn from the analysis of its international law obligations, constitutional standards of human rights and case-law of the Constitutional Court of the Czech Republic.

[1]See Art. 1, Constitution of the Czech Republic, Act No. 1/1993 Coll.

P. Šturma · V. Bílková (✉)
Department of International Law, Faculty of Law, Charles University, Prague, Czech Republic
e-mail: sturma@prf.cuni.cz; bilkova@prf.cuni.cz

M. Andenas et al. (eds.), *The Fight Against Poverty and the Right to Development*, Ius Comparatum - Global Studies in Comparative Law 52,
https://doi.org/10.1007/978-3-030-57324-9_4

Relationship to International Law

Many international obligations in the field of human rights are not of recent vintage. The respective international instruments have been ratified already by Czechoslovakia and became binding on the Czech Republic, as a matter of State succession in respect of international treaties, after 1993. This is not only the case of the International Covenant on Economic, Social and Cultural Rights (1966)[2] but also of many International Labour Organization (ILO) Conventions. In addition, some ILO Conventions were ratified before 1993 but published only after the dissolution of Czechoslovakia. Among the high number of such conventions, we will mention just few of those dealing with fundamental rights and freedoms as well as those related to the minimum wages and social security.

Of the human rights instruments, the Czech Republic has ratified the ILO Conventions No. 11 (freedom of association),[3] No. 29 (forced labour),[4] No. 87 (freedom of association),[5] No. 98 (right to organization and collective bargaining),[6] No. 100 (equality in remuneration),[7] No. 105 (abolition of forced labour),[8] No. 111 (discrimination in employment),[9] No. 135 (representatives of workers),[10] No. 144 (tripartite consultations),[11] and No. 182 (the worst forms of child labour).[12]

When it comes to other ILO Conventions, the Czech Republic has ratified *inter alia* the Conventions Nos. 26, 95 and 99 (minimum wages, their protection)[13] and Nos. 102, 128 and 130 (social security, health care and assistance),[14] not to mention a number of older conventions from the pre-WWII period.

On the regional level, the Czech Republic is party to the European Social Charter (1961) and some of the protocols thereto.[15] However, the process of ratification of this treaty was relatively slow and burdened by the reluctance of conservative Governments and the majority in Parliament throughout the 1990s. The reasons behind this reluctance were similar to debates on the constitutional status of

[2]Published under No. 120/1976 Coll.

[3]Published under No. 98/1924 Coll.

[4]Published under No. 506/1990 Coll.

[5]Published under No. 489/1990 Coll.

[6]Published under No. 470/1990 Coll.

[7]Published under No. 450/1990 Coll.

[8]Published under No. 231/1998 Coll.

[9]Published under No. 465/1990 Coll.

[10]Published under No. 108/2001 Coll.of Int. Treaties.

[11]Published under No. 109/2001 Coll.of Int. Treaties

[12]Published under No. 90/2002 Coll.of Int. Treaties.

[13]Published respectively under No. 439/1990, No. 411/1991, No. 470/1990 Coll.

[14]Published respectively under No. 461/1991, No. 416/1991, No. 537/1990 Coll.

[15]See the original ESC (1961), published under No. 14/2000 Coll.of Int. Treaties; Additional protocol (1988), No. 15/2000 Coll.of Int. Treaties.

economic and social rights which were taking place at the same period. The Czech Republic has not ratified the Revised European Social Charter adopted in 1996.

Constitutional Protection

In spite of the long history of legal and/or constitutional protection of social rights in Czechoslovakia and its predecessors (Austro-Hungarian monarchy) dating back to the end of the nineteenth century,[16] the growing recognition and development of those rights only started, similarly as in other countries, in the post-WWII period. However, this development was heavily influenced by a regime change in 1948. For the first time, social rights were elevated to the constitutional level in the Constitution of May 1948, in Articles 26 to 29.[17] Although this constitutional act was prepared before the takeover of power by the communist party, its content and interpretation bears on the new regime's political preferences. This holds true even more for the Czechoslovak Constitution of 1960 and for its chapter Two.[18]

Therefore, there is discontinuity rather than continuity in the constitutional guarantees of human rights, including social rights, after the restoration of democratic regime (s.-c. Velvet Revolution) in Czechoslovakia. Pending drafting a new federal constitution (never adopted due to the dissolution of Czechoslovakia in the end of 1992), the new Charter of Fundamental Rights and Freedoms was promulgated by the Constitutional Act No. 23/1991. Later, after the creation of the independent Czech Republic, the content of the Charter was not directly incorporated into the text of the Czech Constitution of 1993. However, the Charter was promulgated again, in the act of the Czech Parliament, and it forms a part of the Czech Republic's constitutional order, i.e. the constitution *largo sensu*.

The Charter of Fundamental Rights and Freedoms is a complex document which builds on the modern constitutional bills of rights and international human rights treaties. Social rights are included, together with economic and cultural rights, in Chapter Four of the Charter. This chapter includes a standard catalogue of economic, social and cultural rights (see below).

The above mentioned debates on social rights after 1990 were influenced by several factors. In addition to the political will to set a clear distinction from the attitude under the communist regime, preferring social rights against civil and political rights, it is also the view that social rights belong to the rights of the so called second generation. It implies that they require certain positive measures for their fulfilment.

The Charter reflects those facts, as it provides in Article 41 that those rights are not unqualified or absolute. Although they are justiciable in principle, they may be

[16]See Acts No. 1/1888 and 33/1888.

[17]Constitutional Act No. 150/1948 Coll.

[18]Constitutional Act No. 100/1960 Coll.

claimed only within the confines of the laws implementing these provisions.[19] This limitation applies to most but not all aspects of economic and social rights.

The differentiation of human rights was clearly spelled out already in the Explanatory Report to the Charter of Fundamental Rights and Freedoms (of 8 January 1991). Whereas rights and freedoms regulated in the previous chapters have an absolute nature and as such are protected by the Constitution, the rights in Chapter Four are predominantly relative, which means that their development depends on the state of national economy and mainly on its material outcomes.[20]

However, it is important to point out that the legislator does not have an unfettered right to limit, on the basis of implementing laws, economic and social rights. According to Article 41 para. 4, "*when employing the provisions concerning limitations upon fundamental rights and freedoms, the essence and significance of these rights and freedoms must be preserved*".

Neither Chapter Four of the Charter, nor any other constitutional provision recognize *expressis verbis* a general right to an adequate standard of living. However, the right is included, though in a weaker form, in other social rights guaranteed by the Charter.

First, Article 26 provides for the right to work. Under its para. 1, *"/e/verybody has the right to the free choice of her profession and the training for that profession, as well as the right to engage in enterprise and pursue other economic activity"*. In addition, this article sets that everybody has the right to acquire the means of his/her livelihood by work. Obviously, the Czech constitutional and legal order gives priority to work, a full employment and a possibility to ensure an adequate standard of living by work. Nevertheless, the same provision also sets that *"the State shall provide an adequate level of material security to those citizens who are unable, through no fault of their own, to exercise this right; conditions shall be provided for by law"* (para. 3).

This is one of the articles on social rights which include qualifications and refer to the need of implementing legislation. First, Article 26 makes it clear that conditions and limitations may be set by law upon the right to engage in certain professions and activities (para. 2). Second, law may provide for different rules for aliens (para. 4). Finally, the condition of law is expressly provided within the realm of Art. 26 para. 3. One of the related laws is Act on Employment.[21]

The corollary of the right to work is the right to fair remuneration in Article 28. The brief provision sets that employees have the right to fair remuneration for their work as well as the right to satisfactory work conditions. Again, this article is qualified by reference to detailed provisions to be set by law. The key domestic

[19]"(1) The rights listed in Article 26, Article 27 para. 4, Articles 28 to 31, Article 32 paras. 1 and 3, Article 33, and Article 35 of this Charter may be claimed only within the confines of the laws implementing these provisions."

[20]Explanatory Note to the Constitutional Law No 23/1991.

[21]Act No. 435/2004 Coll., as amended by later laws.

legislation on fair remuneration rests with the Labour Code, Part 6.[22] Remuneration (salary) and work conditions are regulated by this Code unless special laws provide otherwise. Such special laws include the Act on Pay and remuneration in public budgetary organizations,[23] Act on Pay and some other entitlements of public prosecutors,[24] or Act on Pay and other entitlements related to the exercise of function of public officials, judges and members of the European Parliament.[25]

With respect to the right to fair remuneration, the Czech Government has the power to regulate the minimum salary by its regulations.[26] In order to make the right to fair remuneration effective, the Parliament also passed the Act on the protection of employees in case of insolvency of the employer.[27] The receivables of employees not honored by the employer may be compensated under certain conditions by the Labour Office of the Czech Republic.

Another important constitutional right contributing to the fight against poverty is the right to social security (Article 30). This right includes two different aspects. First, citizens have the right to adequate material security in old age and during periods of work incapacity, as well as in the case of the loss of their provider. Second, everyone who suffers from material need has the right to such assistance as is necessary to ensure him/her a basic living standard. As usual for other social rights, detailed provisions shall be set by law (para. 3).

The first paragraph of Article 30 is implemented by a number of laws, as it includes several important legal issues. One of them is the right to adequate social security in old age which is guaranteed by the Act on social (pension) insurance[28] and some related laws.[29] This right belongs to the rights of citizens. The pension insurance is comprehensive and includes the following benefits: old-age pension, invalidity pension, widow's and widower's pension and orphan's pension. Payment of premiums is mandatory under the law.

Next, the right to social security also includes the right to adequate material security during periods of work incapacity. Again, two situations have to be distinguished. First, the case of permanent incapacity gives rise to payments from the system of pension insurance, in form of full or partial invalidity (disablement) pension.[30] Second, in case of temporary work incapacity the insured persons are entitled to payments from sickness insurance. This is governed by the Act on

[22] Act No. 262/2006 Coll., as amended by later laws.

[23] Act No. 143/1992 Coll., as amended by later laws.

[24] Act No. 201/1997 Coll., as amended by later laws.

[25] Act No. 236/1995 Coll., as amended by later laws.

[26] Regulation No. 567/2006 Coll., as amended by later regulations.

[27] Act No. 118/2000 Coll., as amended.

[28] Act No. 155/1995 Coll., as amended by later laws.

[29] See acts No. 582/1991 Coll., on Organisation of Social Security, as amended, and No. 589/1992 Coll., on Premiums for Social Security and Contribution to the State Policy of Employment, as amended.

[30] See Act No. 155/1995 Coll., as amended by later laws.

sickness insurance.[31] The aim of sickness insurance is to provide financial support when a person loses his or her earnings due to illness or maternity leave. Participation in sickness insurance by employee is mandatory, while participation in this insurance by self-employed persons is voluntary. Under sickness insurance no difference is made in terms of whether an employee is a citizen of the Czech Republic or of another country. All kinds of insurance are run by the Czech Social Security Administration, a public authority which falls under the Czech Ministry of Labour and Social Affairs.

The second paragraph of Article 30 aims at another, quite different problem of persons in material need. The right to assistance in material need is implemented by several laws, namely the Act on State social assistance,[32] Act on benefits to disabled persons,[33] and Act on assistance in material need.[34] The concept of State social assistance includes many welfare benefits typical for modern social States, including subsidies to child, social subsidy, subsidy to housing, subsidy to transportation. Those benefits are paid to a large number of beneficiaries who may or may not be in a situation of poverty. On balance, the concept of assistance in material need is related to a living minimum and a subsistence minimum, it is a tool how to ensure not necessarily adequate but at least basic living standards of people facing to danger of poverty.

Concerning other social rights, the right to health and the right to education should be mentioned. The first one is proclaimed in Article 31 of the Charter. Everyone has the right to the protection of his/her health. Quite importantly, this article also sets that *"citizens shall have the right, on the basis of public insurance, to free medical care and to medical aids under conditions provided for by law."* The right to free medical care is reserved to citizens.

This right is implemented by several laws, in particular the Act on public health insurance,[35] Act on premiums to general (national) health insurance,[36] and Act on Medical services.[37]

The general (national) health insurance is mandatory for both employees and self-employed persons. It is one of the important achievements of the welfare state and the struggle against poverty. At the same time, however, it is also an object of political disputes as to the limited resources to health insurance, their rational distribution and use, as well as the issue of contributions by citizens within and outside the system of public insurance.

The implementation of so-called regulatory health fees by the conservative Government in 2007 gave rise to the constitutional complaint. The plenary judgment

[31] Act No. 187/2006 Coll., on Sickness Insurance.

[32] Act No. 117/1995 Coll., on State Social Assistance, as amended.

[33] Act No. 329/2011 Coll., on granting benefits to disabled persons.

[34] Act No. 111/2006 Coll., on Assistance in Material Need, as amended.

[35] Act No. 48/1997 Coll., on Public Health Insurance, as amended.

[36] Act No. 592/1992 Coll., as amended.

[37] Act No. 372/2011 Coll., on Medical Services.

of the Czech Constitutional Court No. 1/08 of 23 September 2008 is probably one of the most important, though controversial, decisions on social rights.

National (Constitutional) Remedies

Any human rights, whether protected by the constitutional Charter or by international conventions binding on the Czech Republic, are under the judicial protection. The most important and last resort remedy (on national level) is a complaint to the Constitutional Court. The Czech Constitutional Court has very broad powers to provide interpretation and protection of human rights.

However, the Constitutional Court subscribed to the differentiation of fundamental (hard core) rights and social rights. When it comes to the latter, it was able to apply a self-restraint on the review of constitutionality of acts of Parliaments challenged on the basis of alleged violation of constitutionally guaranteed rights.

In its plenary judgment No. 1/08, on the constitutionality of regulatory fees in the public health care system, the Constitutional Court dealt with one section of the challenged Act on stabilization of public budgets which had introduced those fees. The majority of constitutional judges refused to declare the law unconstitutional. For this purpose, they applied, instead of the usual test of proportionality, the so-called rational-basis test.

It also refers to its previous plenary judgment No. 2/08, where it emphasizes that social rights *"depend mainly on the economic situation of a State. The level of their provision reflects not only economic and social development of the State but also a relation between State and citizen, based on a mutual responsibility and recognition of the principle of solidarity".*

Consequently, the Constitutional Court set up a four-step test how to review the constitutionality of an act implementing social rights guaranteed by the Constitution:

(1) determination of the meaning and substance of a social right, i.e. its essential content. This core of the right in the present case arises from Article 31 and Article 4(4) of the Charter.
(2) assessment whether the act interferes with the very existence of the social right or its essential content. If not, then
(3) evaluation if the legislation aims at a legitimate goal, i.e. it is not an arbitrary restriction of the overall standard of fundamental rights. And finally,
(4) consideration of the question whether the legislative means employed to its achievement is rational, although not necessarily the best, the most appropriate, the most effective or the wisest one.[38]

To conclude, it seems that, in spite of certain overestimation of social rights in the period before 1990 and underestimation in the following period, social rights are

[38] Constitutional Court, Judgment No. Pl. 1/08, of 20 May 2008, para. 103.

protected by constitutional and statutory law. Though they are justiciable in principle, they may be claimed only within the confines of the laws implementing the provisions of the constitutional Charter of Fundamental Rights and Freedoms. Nevertheless, they remain to form, together with international human rights conventions ratified by the Czech Republic, a basic referential framework for the Constitutional Court.

Domestic Law Contributions to the Fight Against Poverty and the Right to Development in an International Context

Domestic Legal Framework Applicable to the Fight Against Poverty and the Right to Development

Apart from a general provision confirming that *"the Czech Republic honours the commitments stemming for it from international law"* (Article 1(2) of the Constitution of the Czech Republic), there is no legal basis for contributing to the fight against poverty and the right to development in an international context enshrined in the Constitution of the Czech Republic. The Charter of Fundamental Rights and Freedoms, which makes part of the constitutional order, contains quite an extensive list of social and economic rights. These rights however apply solely within the jurisdiction of the Czech Republic and they do not encompass the rights of the third generation, such as the right to development.

That nonetheless does not mean that the Czech Republic is not committed to contribute to the fight against poverty and the right to development in the international context.[39] Development cooperation makes an integral part of the Czech foreign policy. Since 2015, when a new ***Concept of the Foreign Policy of the Czech Republic***[40] was adopted, development cooperation has been ranked under two out of the three main pillars of the Czech foreign policy (see Fig. 4.1)—Pillar 2. Prosperity and Sustainable Development, and Pillar 3. Human Dignity and Human Rights. It is also closely linked to Pillar 1. Security.

The second pillar (Prosperity and Sustainable Development) seeks to *"improve the material conditions and quality of life enjoyed by Czech citizens"* and to *"contribute to rising global prosperity, leading to an improved worldwide security situation"* (Point 4.2). The Czech Republic acknowledges that as a high-income economy, it has an obligation to contribute to the reduction of global inequalities. It pledges to take active steps to contribute to the pursuit of Sustainable Development Goals and to meet its EU commitments so that the EU could reach its collective target of 0.7% of gross national income spending on development cooperation. The

---

[39]See also Horký and Lightfoot (2013).

[40]Concept of the Czech Republic's Foreign Policy, 13 July 2015, available online at http://www.mzv.cz/jnp/en/foreign_relations/policy_planning/concept_of_the_czech_republic_s_foreign.html.

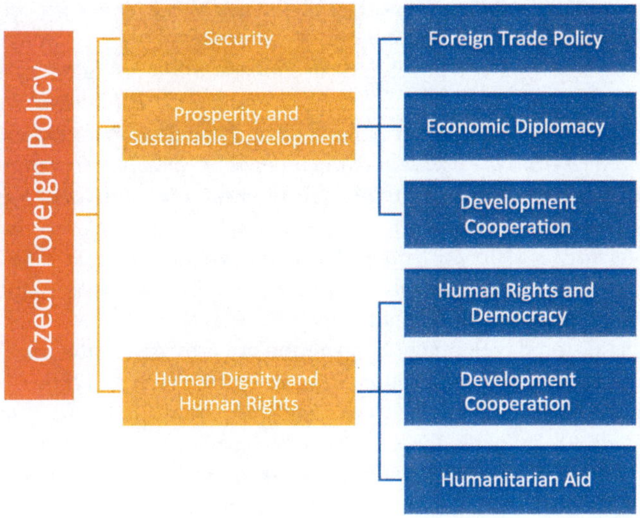

Fig. 4.1 Scheme of the Czech foreign policy

Czech Republic hopes to accomplish these goals in cooperation with other countries as well as with the private sector.

The third pillar (Human Dignity and Human Rights) strives to *"promote global efforts to safeguard a dignified life"* (Point 4.3). It uses three main instruments to achieve this aim—the promotion of human rights and democracy, development cooperation, and humanitarian aid. Development cooperation thus pursues a twofold aim of helping achieve global prosperity (under Pillar 2) and of contributing to the advocacy of human dignity (under Pillar 3).

The section relating to the first pillar (Security) mentions development cooperation only briefly, ranking it among the tools that could help prevent security threats and radicalisation of people in countries with undignified living conditions. In reality, however, this dimension has played an important role in the Czech foreign policy, especially since the inception of the current migration crisis. A substantive part of the resources newly allocated to the development cooperation in 2015–2017 has been used to support initiatives linked to migration (conditions in refugee camps, fostering of the asylum systems in transit countries, etc.).

The eradication of poverty is mentioned twice in the Concept. With respect to Pillar 2, the Concept states that *"the Czech Republic's development cooperation will contribute, in particular, to the eradication of poverty and to the establishment of stable communities in less developed parts of the world by means of sustainable socio-economic development, while respecting the development goals and needs of partner countries involved in the programme and project planning at the level of central and local government as well as non-governmental actors"* (Point 4.2). With respect to Pillar 3, the Concept notes that *"/c/ommitments to eradicate poverty and combat inequalities, as part and parcel of sustainable development, spearhead the pursuit of human dignity"* (Point 4.3).

The legal framework for development cooperation is provided by the ***Act No. 161/2010 Coll.,*** *on Development Cooperation and Humanitarian Aid, and Amending Related Laws.* The act defines development cooperation as *"the set of activities financed from the national budget aimed at contributing to the eradication of poverty in the context of sustainable development, including the fulfilment of the Millennium Development Goals, to economic and social development, to environmental protection, and to the promotion of democracy, human rights and good governance in developing countries"* (Article 2(a)). The Act also establishes a new institution, the Czech Development Agency (CDA).

Further details on development cooperation are provided in the policy document entitled the *Development Cooperation Strategy of the Czech Republic* (DCS). So far, two DCS have been adopted, one covering the period 2010–2017, the other the period 2018–2030. In 2013, the Czech Government also approved a shorter-term *Strategy of Multilateral Development Cooperation of the Czech Republic 2013–2017.* The DCS 2018–2030 builds on the Agenda 2030 and on the Sustainable Development Goals. It identifies five main sectoral priorities on which the Czech Republic wants to focus in the upcoming 13 years. Those are: good governance, sustainable treatment of natural resources, economic transformation and development, agriculture and the development of countryside, and inclusive social development. The priorities are virtually identical to those identified in the DCS 2010–2017.

Development cooperation takes place either through multilateral fora, mainly the EU, the UN and other international organizations, or through bilateral cooperation, especially that with priority and specific countries.[41] These countries, for the period starting from 2018, were identified by the Czech Government in July 2016. The priority countries encompass Bosnia and Hercegovina, Cambodia, Ethiopia, Georgia, Moldova and Zambia. The specific countries are Afghanistan, Palestine, Ukraine and Syria. Unlike the priority countries, which should remain stable for the whole period 2018–2030, the specific countries may be changed depending on the situation in the target countries and on foreign policy interests of the Czech Republic. The selection of the countries is again largely identical to that under the DCS 2010–2017, though three countries (Kosovo, Mongolia and Serbia) have been removed. Development cooperation uses various tools, such as direct financial help, provision of scholarships, sending of experts, or funding of common projects.

Development cooperation is one of the areas of the Czech foreign policy. The fight against poverty, however, is also a question of domestic policy. Despite the fact that the Czech Republic is the country with the lowest poverty level in the European Union, with less than 10% of the inhabitants living on or below the verge of income poverty, the fight against poverty is still considered as an important issue in the country. To set the ground for dealing with this issue, the Ministry of Labour and Social Affairs has adopted, and regularly updated, several instruments dealing with

[41] See also Horký-Hlucháň (2015), pp. 338–364.

various aspects of the fight against poverty (National Action Plan for the Social Inclusion, Strategy for Social Inclusion 2014–2020, Concept Aimed at Solving the Problem of Homelessness before 2020 etc.). There is also a document entitled the *National Plan for the Fight Against Poverty*,[42] which however simply provides an overview of the available instruments.

Policy Monitoring and Accountability Mechanisms

The main body responsible for the implementation of Czech development cooperation is the *Ministry of Foreign Affairs* (MFA). The MFA assumes the general coordination of the area, concludes international agreements related to it, and allocates resources for bilateral projects and multilateral initiatives. Within the MFA, a special Department for Development Cooperation and Humanitarian Assistance (Odbor rozvojové spolupráce a humanitární pomoci) exists to deal with the agenda. In 2009, the Czech Government created a new Council for Foreign Development Cooperation (Rada pro zahraniční rozvojovou spolupráci) which is responsible for ensuring inter-ministerial cooperation of the development agenda. The Council has 15 members representing various ministries and other public bodies, and associate members representing the Czech Development Agency, private (business) sector and civil society.

Czech development cooperation is administered by the *Czech Development Agency* (Česká rozvojová agentura, CDA). The CDA is a government administrative unit funded from the budget of the Ministry of Foreign Affairs (MFA). It is responsible both for the provision of development cooperation and for the implementation of humanitarian aid projects. The CDA replaced an older institution of the same name, which had been established in 2008 by an administrative act of the MFA. The resources allocated to development cooperation have increased from 1 billion CZK in 2001 (0.047% GDP) to 6.38 billion CZK in 2016 (0.143% of the GDP). The increase is largely due to the commitments stemming from the membership in the European Union. These commitments have also pushed the Czech Republic to restructure its development programmes. Most significantly, the share of the bilateral cooperation has dropped from almost 60% of the total expenditure in 2004 to some 22% in 2016, to the benefit of the multilateral cooperation (carried out, in most cases, through the EU). Even with the recent increase, the Czech Republic fails to honour the commitment for developed countries to allocate 0.7% of its GNI to development cooperation, agreed in the 1970s within the UN.

The Czech model of the development cooperation is not radically different from that used in other EU countries. One characteristic feature, nonetheless, is the

[42]Národní akční plán boje proti chudobě, available in Czech at https://ipodpora.odbory.info/soubory/dms/wysiwyg_uploads/75085b71d75f30d0/uploads/Narodni-plan-boje-proti-chudobe.pdf.

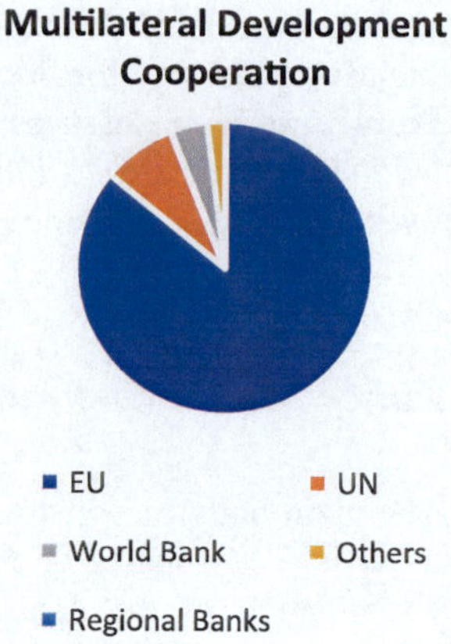

Fig. 4.2 Multilateral development cooperation (Source: Development Cooperation of the Czech Republic 2015, *Factsheet,* Ministry of Foreign Affairs, 2016, http://www.czechaid.cz/wp-content/uploads/2016/10/Factsheet_ZRS_CR_ENG_2015.pdf)

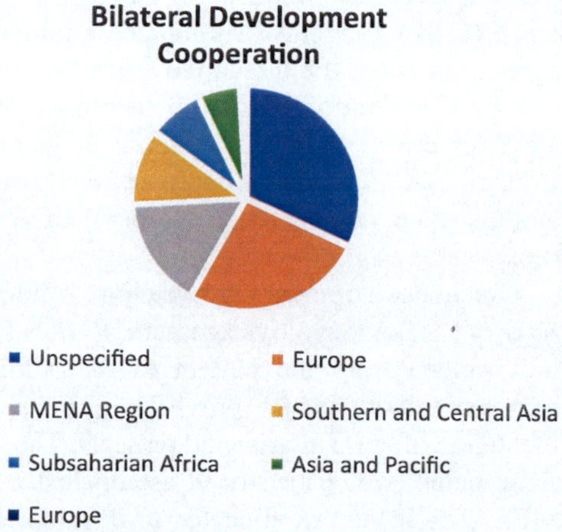

Fig. 4.3 Bilateral development cooperation (Source: Development Cooperation of the Czech Republic 2015, *Factsheet,* Ministry of Foreign Affairs, 2016, http://www.czechaid.cz/wp-content/uploads/2016/10/Factsheet_ZRS_CR_ENG_2015.pdf)

emphasis placed on the cooperation with, and involvement of, civil society and private sector. This is particularly visible in the area of bilateral cooperation, which takes place through tenders, grants or other programmes open for non-state actors (Figs. 4.2 and 4.3).

Private sector is the main addressee of the so-called *B2B* (Business to Business)[43] *Programme*, which aims at bringing together business actors from the Czech Republic and from the third countries. It offers up to 90% co-financing, thus reducing the risks of entering the development market for Czech business actors. The programme unfolds in three main phases: (a) the preparation phase, when a feasibility study is prepared to assess the risks in the target country, a partner is found in this country and a business plan is drafted; (b) the implementation phase, when the

[43]For more details, see online at http://www.czechaid.cz/en/get-involved/private-sector/.

cooperation takes place; and (c) the evaluation phase, when the results of the cooperation are assessed. The main indicators used in the assessment are the number of newly created jobs, the involvement of local producers in value chains, the transfer of know-how and technology, the sustainability of the partnership and the financial efficiency. For 2017, 20 million CZK was allocated to the programme, marking an increase by one fourth from the previous year. The business actors involved in development cooperation have their platform entitled the *Platform of Businessmen for International Development Cooperation* (Platforma podnikatelů pro zahraniční rozvojovou spolupráci).[44]

Civil society has a dual role in the Czech development cooperation. First, non-governmental organizations take an active part in this cooperation, for instance by sending experts to the target countries. Secondly, they monitor the implementation of this area of the Czech foreign policy. Similarly as business actors, civil society also has at its disposal a specific platform, entitled the *Czech Forum for Development Cooperation* (České forum pro rozvojovou spolupráci, FORS). It is an association of over 30 non-governmental organizations and other civil society entities, which was established in 2002 and seeks to coordinate the activities of its members. FORS regularly assesses the efficiency of the Czech development cooperation and puts forward proposals aimed at bringing the concrete steps taken in this area in line with the international obligations of the Czech Republic.[45] FORS and its individual members take part in designing development policy through their formal participation in the Council for Foreign Development Cooperation and also through their public activities (press releases, newsletters, publications, campaigns, etc.).

The assessment of the various projects and programmes of development cooperation takes place at the level of the MFA—the desk officer for the evaluation within the Department of Development Cooperation and Humanitarian Assistance has a crucial role here. This system was assessed by the OECD Development Assistance Committee and found in compliance with the OECD standards.[46] There is no special accountability mechanism established in the area of development cooperation. The standard political and legal tools (political control of State activities, prosecution for misuse of public resources, etc.) can be used. With the exception of FORS, Czech civil society and the public do not however pay too much attention to this area of public policy.

Unilateral/Bilateral Initiatives or Agreements

The Czech Republic has general commitments stemming from its membership in the UN and the EU. It should strive to increase the resources allocated to development

[44] For the website in Czech, see https://www.ppzrs.org/.

[45] For the website in Czech, see http://www.fors.cz/.

[46] OECD (2016), pp. 101–104 (Czech Republic).

assistance to 0.7% of its GNI but the achievement of this goal does not seem realistic in the nearest future. The Czech Republic is also bound by various bilateral agreements concluded both with the priority and specific countries, and with actors from the third countries. Most of the agreements of the former type are rather general in nature. Some of them date several decades back, to the period of the (socialist) Czechoslovakia—this is for instance the case of the 1977 *Agreement with Ethiopia on Scientific-Technical Cooperation.*[47] Concrete parameters of the bilateral development cooperation are, nonetheless, usually set in policy documents adopted within the Czech Republic.[48] The latter agreements usually set details of specific cooperation initiatives. The agreements have standard contents and they do not foresee any original legal mechanisms that could serve as an inspiration for other countries.

References

Horký O, Lightfoot S (eds) (2013) From Aid Recipients to Aid Donors. Development Policies of Central and Eastern European States. Routledge, London

Horký-Hlucháň O (2015) Development Dimension of Czech Foreign Policy. In: Kořan M (ed) Czech Foreign Policy in 2013: Analysis. Institute of International Relations, Prague, pp 338–364

Národní akční plán boje proti chudobě (National Action Plan of the Struggle against Poverty), adopted by the Czech Government. Available in Czech at: https://ipodpora.odbory.info/soubory/dms/wysiwyg_uploads/75085b71d75f30d0/uploads/Narodni-plan-boje-proti-chudobe.pdf

OECD (2016) Evaluation Systems in Development Cooperation: 2016 Review

[47]The Decree 68/1977 Coll., on the Agreement between the Government of the Czechoslovak Socialist Republic and the Temporary Military Government of the Socialist Ethiopia on Scientific-Technical Cooperation.

[48]See, for instance, the Programme of the Development Cooperation with Ethiopia for 2012–2017

Chapter 5
The Fight Against Poverty and the Right to Development in the German Legal Order

Stefanie Schmahl

Abstract This national report deals with to the fight against poverty and the right to development in the German legal order. The first part of the report examines domestic law at the constitutional and the statutory levels and accounts for the legal remedies within the national context. In a second section, the report analyzes the contributions of the German legal system to the fight against poverty in an international context, including Germany's participation in the association and development aid policy of the European Union.

Introduction

Germany is an economically prosperous country. After the end of World War II, when the country was not only morally and ethically but also economically in ruins, a veritable economic miracle (*Wirtschaftswunder*) took place in the "old" Federal Republic of Germany in a relatively short time-period. This was partly due to the serious, even iron will of the Germans to rebuild the country in the post-war period. But, there is no doubt that without the support of the Western-Allied Powers, especially without the Marshall Plan aid,[1] the upswing could not have been accomplished.

This contribution was first published in: Martin Schmidt-Kessel (ed), German National Reports on the 20th International Congress of Comparative Law, Mohr Siebeck, Tübingen 2018, pp. 483–509. The author thanks the publisher Mohr Siebeck for the approval of a second publication with Springer. The manuscript was last updated in 2018.

[1]The European Recovery Programme (so-called Marshall Plan) was inspired by the US Secretary of State, *George C. Marshall*, who suggested that the USA should give financial and economic aid to

S. Schmahl (✉)
Julius-Maximilians-Universität Würzburg, Lehrstuhl für deutsches und ausländisches öffentliches Recht, Völkerrecht und Europarecht, Würzburg, Germany
e-mail: schmahl@jura.uni-wuerzburg.de

M. Andenas et al. (eds.), *The Fight Against Poverty and the Right to Development*, Ius Comparatum - Global Studies in Comparative Law 52,
https://doi.org/10.1007/978-3-030-57324-9_5

Germany, reunited on 3 October 1990, has also succeeded in remaining at the top of the world economic order despite numerous hurdles[2] due to the unification of diametrically opposed political, social and economic systems of the former two German states.[3] This success, too, can be attributed to a variety of reasons. Certainly, the Germans themselves have a considerable share of this success. But the former European Economic Community and the later European Union have also significant merits of the economic prosperity of today's Federal Republic of Germany.[4]

Despite this finding, there was and still is economic poverty in Germany. This poverty, of course, is far from being comparable to the extreme poverty faced by some other states in the world. There are no slums or districts without proper dwelling, electricity and water supply in Germany. Rather, since 1949, Germany has explicitly oriented itself to the principles of the social market economy, not only trusting the free forces of the market and the competitive power, but to a certain extent also stipulating elements of solidarity and making social redistribution of goods in favour of those who are in need.[5] In this way, a minimum standard of living and subsistence conditions is guaranteed for all citizens and legal residents.[6] Therefore, economic poverty in Germany usually means no absolute poverty. Nevertheless, there is a significant proportion of people living in relative poverty. Relative poverty is to be understood as a lack of means and possibilities to live and shape life as it is usually possible in German society on the basis of the historically achieved prosperity level. This is shown by the Federal Government's Fifth Poverty and Wealth Report of 2017.[7] Ten years after the onset of the financial and economic crisis, Germany's economy continues to be, in sum, very solid. Unbroken economic growth, the highest number of employees and the lowest unemployment rate since the German unification and rising real wages are the expression of this economic stability.[8] But there are also people who are exposed to material deprivation, threatened by social exclusion or are considered at risk of poverty. These include, for instance, long-term unemployed persons, persons in precarious employment and single parents with their children.[9] In addition, the group of refugees seeking

---

the European countries within the framework of a coordinated programme that the Europeans would draw up themselves. For a fuller account see Hogan (1987), *passim.*

[2]In the 1990s, unemployment and social deprivation following Germany's reunification hit particularly Eastern Germany, see Lembke (2018), p. 57.

[3]See, for instance, the memories of former Chancellor *Helmut Kohl* on this topic: Kohl (2009), *passim.*

[4]See Schmahl (2012), pp. 1 et seq.

[5]See Hofmann (2018), Art. 20 mn 27. Already in the 1880s, imperial Chancellor *Otto von Bismarck* introduced the first health, injury and pension insurance schemes and was thus a pioneer of creating a modern welfare state.

[6]See Federal Constitutional Court (*Bundesverfassungsgericht*), BVerfGE 82, 60 (80); 137, 34 (72).

[7]Federal Ministry of Labour and Social Affairs (2017), p. 8.

[8]Federal Ministry of Labour and Social Affairs (2017), p. 5.

[9]Federal Ministry of Labour and Social Affairs (2017), pp. 5, 9 et seq.; 25 et seq.

protection or asylum in Germany since 2015 has, *inter alia*, raised the question of how to integrate them in the German social welfare systems.[10]

All in all, the question of how the struggle against (relative) poverty is or should be answered in legal terms remains on the top of issues to be tackled with in the domestic context. In addition, due to the recent large immigration movements to Germany, there are also more and more voices calling for a reduction in the causes of flight.[11] There is no doubt that (civil) wars, natural disasters and poverty are among the most crucial factors for fleeing one's home countries and for global migration.[12] Thus, the fight against (mostly absolute) poverty in an international context and the corresponding development policy of the Federal Republic of Germany are both becoming increasingly important in the current political discourse.

German Domestic Law and Legal Remedies in the Domestic Context

Constitutional Law

The German federal constitution, i.e. the Basic Law (*Grundgesetz*), does not expressly recognize the right to an adequate standard of living or to social development. The same is true for other social and economic rights such as the rights to work, health, housing and water. Contrary to what is provided for in the constitutions of several German federal states (*Länder*),[13] the founders of the Basic Law have decided against a broad, explicit standardization of fundamental social rights.[14] This happened on the one hand with regard to the Weimar Constitution and its social rights provisions, which remained unfulfilled promises.[15] On the other hand, the provisional nature of the Basic Law was regarded as allowing further economic and social developments in the future.[16] The founders of the Basic Law could therefore only agree on the definition of the principle of social welfare. According to Article 20 (1) of the Basic Law, the Federal Republic of Germany is a democratic and social federal state. According to Article 28 (1) 1 of the Basic Law, it is a social state governed by the rule of law. The social state principle is thus a constitutional

---

[10]Federal Ministry of Labour and Social Affairs (2017), p. 6.

[11]See, e.g., Federal Ministry for Economic Cooperation and Development (2017a), p. 14, with further references.

[12]See, e.g., Kälin (2017), pp. 207 et seq.

[13]See, e.g., Articles 106 and 166 of the Constitution of Bavaria; Articles 45, 47, and 48 of the Constitution of Brandenburg, and Article 28 of the Constitution of Hesse.

[14]For more details on the historical background see Stern (1984), p. 879; and Enders (2005), pp. 9 et seq.

[15]See Murswiek (2011), § 192 mn 50.

[16]Papier (2006), § 30 mn 13.

obligation to continuously work towards the realization of social statehood and poverty eradication. Or in other words: the Basic Law is directed to the establishment of social justice and security; the liberal and democratic constitutional state is complemented by the right to equality and the fight against social ills and outrages.[17] Because of its importance, the social state principle enshrined in Article 20 (1) forms even part of the eternity guarantee of Article 79 (3) of the Basic Law which means that it is not open to any constitutional amendment.[18]

However, the normative quality of the social state principle lags behind the constitutional principles of democracy, the rule of law, and federal statehood, which are equally stipulated in Article 20 (1) of the Basic Law. Different to these constitutional principles, the social state principle is a mere state objective and thus subject to the financially and organizationally possible.[19] Only the core of the welfare state, i.e. the guarantee of a basic standard of social security, is constitutionally established. This means that only the full replacement of social legislation would be undoubtedly unconstitutional.[20] By contrast, the social standard achieved so far is not unchangeable. If the limits of financial affordability are reached, even social protection already granted can be withdrawn up to the core of the social state principle without infringing the Basic Law.[21]

Moreover, since the social state principle is not constitutionally enshrined as a fundamental subjective right, it can only have a direct effect in exceptional cases.[22] Only a few fundamental rights of the Basic Law are interpretable as social rights, such as the protection of marriage and family,[23] freedom of association,[24] protection of life and physical integrity,[25] and respect for human dignity.[26] These fundamental rights, which have been originally conceived as liberal defenses against state interference, can additionally be understood in their function as state's duties to protect and to fulfil social rights.[27] However, in order to identify a violation of the state's obligation to protect or fulfil a specific fundamental right by omission, it is necessary to strike a careful and proper balance between social rights on the one hand and public interests and freedoms of third parties on the other.[28] Redistribution on the basis of the social state principle can only be justified to the extent that it is

[17] See Sommermann (2010), Art. 20 (1) mns 128 et seq.

[18] Clearly BVerfGE 84, 90 (121); 94, 49 (103).

[19] See Zacher (2004), § 28 mn 54.

[20] See Grzeszick (2013), Art. 20 mn 26; Sommermann (2010), Art. 20 (1) mn 122.

[21] BVerfGE 77, 340 (344); further see Grzeszick (2013), Art. 20 mns 23 et seq.; Hofmann (2018), Art. 20 mn 29.

[22] BVerfGE 27, 253 (283); 82, 60 (80); 110, 412 (445); see also Murswiek (2011), § 192 mn 58.

[23] See Art. 6 (1) of the Basic Law.

[24] See Art. 9 (1) and Art. 9 (3) of the Basic Law.

[25] See Art. 2 (2) of the Basic law.

[26] See Art. 1 (1) of the Basic Law.

[27] See Stern (1984), pp. 706 et seq.; Papier (2006), § 30 mns 13, 18 et seq.

[28] BVerfGE 134, 204 (223); see also Hofmann (2018), Art. 20 mn 28.

permissible in the light of all other constitutional legal premises, in particular the protection of private property.[29] The Basic Law does not legitimize a centrally controlled supply to people in need but only argues for a liberal welfare state.[30] Claims to state benefits do therefore not arise from the principle of social state as such. At best, they can be deduced from the right to equality and the principle of equal opportunities enshrined in Article 3 (1) of the Basic Law.[31] Yet, also the principle of equal opportunities, read in connection with the social state principle, must not lead to a leveling down of the individual's development potential.[32] Only in that regard can social statehood justify constitutionally the protection of jobs and the fight against unemployment.[33] The welfare state requirement does not authorize any social legal design or social law enforcement that would dissolve the state's obligation to respect the freedoms of third parties.

On the other hand, the social state principle, especially when linked to the fundamental rights of the Basic Law, does not constitute a mere obligation that is only bound by a progressive realization in the distant future.[34] Social and economic rights as well as fundamental rights to social participation are always tied to the prohibition of insufficient means (*Untermaßverbot*).[35] The state cannot escape its obligation to protect and fulfil a specific social or economic right, but is instead required to demonstrate that the realization of the minimum core standard of living is guaranteed for everyone. Therefore, constitutional jurisprudence increasingly emphasizes the protection of the weaker by the state or third parties, as far as need is concerned.[36] Such a protection legitimizes social protection systems, such as social pension, accident insurance, and long-term care insurance. However, it does not fundamentally relieve the citizen of private risk taking.

Only the inviolability of human dignity as enshrined in Article 1 (1) of the Basic Law has led to a subjective legal right to social minimum standards at the constitutional level.[37] The case law of the Federal Constitutional Court has deduced the subsistence minimum of welfare ("*Hartz IV*")-recipients and of asylum seekers from the social state principle in connection with human dignity. In its "*Hartz IV*"-judgement of 2010, the Federal Constitutional Court ruled that the determination of the regular benefits for adults and children under the Social Security Code II

[29]For more details see Enders (2005), pp. 35 et seq.

[30]See Sommermann (2010), Art. 20 (1) mns 107 et seq.; Jarass (2016a), Art. 20 mn 159.

[31]See, e.g., BVerfGE 9, 124 (130 f.); 10, 264 (270); 22, 83 (86); 35, 348 (354 f.); 78, 104 (117 f.); 117, 173 (187).

[32]BVerfGE 33, 303 (333).

[33]BVerfGE 100, 271 (284); 103, 293 (307).

[34]Sommermann (2010), Art. 20 (1) mn 130.

[35]For more detail see Isensee (2011), § 191 mn 303.

[36]BVerfGE 26, 16 (37); 35, 202 (236); 45, 376 (387 f.); 89, 214 (232); 103, 197 (221). Critical assessment by Sachs (2018), Art. 20 mn 46.

[37]See BVerfGE 40, 121 (133); 43, 13 (19); 99, 216 (233); 125, 175 (222); 132, 134 (159); 137, 34 (72).

(entitled "basic security for jobseekers") did not fulfil the constitutional right to ensure a decent subsistence level.[38] It pointed out that the Basic Law does not permit an exact quantification of the scope of these subsistence services, but gives the legislator a leeway of action.[39] In terms of the subsistence level, however, the legislator must be guided by the economic development of the German polity and society as a whole. In particular, the Court found that the rule set to secure the existential minimum needs of children had to be recalculated.[40] The right of children to social participation within the meaning of Article 1 (1), read in conjunction with Article 20 (1) of the Basic Law, extends not only to the physical, but also to the socio-cultural existence, which includes school education and health care.[41]

Also, the benefits under the (former) Asylum Seekers Benefits Act of 1993[42] did not withstand a constitutional review. These benefits were considerably, about 30%, among the basic security benefits granted by the Social Security Code II and were determined on the basis of blanket estimates for both adults and children.[43] Furthermore, the determination of lump-sum discounts for children was calculated in relation to the needs of an adult, although children are no "small adults".[44] Against this background, it is not surprising that the asylum seekers benefits of legal residents were declared unconstitutional by the Federal Constitutional Court in a decision of 2012.[45] The Court even considered the amount of cash benefits under the 1993 Asylum Seekers Benefits Act to be obviously insufficient.[46] Although the objective of asylum law is to reduce migration incentives emanating from the social assistance systems in Germany,[47] immigration policy control mechanisms may not be used to deny a decent demand of human needs. In fact, the absoluteness of human dignity laid down in Article 1 (1) of the Basic Law must not be relativized for reasons of immigration policy.[48] This is especially true when it comes to the needs of children and adolescents.[49] The right to minimum subsistence results from human dignity and is cogent constitutional law.[50]

---

[38]BVerfGE 125, 175 (227).

[39]BVerfGE 134, 1 (16); Höfling (2018), Art. 1 mn 32; Herdegen (2009), Art. 1 mn 78.

[40]BVerfGE 125, 175 (257 et seq.).

[41]BVerfGE 125, 175 (213).

[42]*Asylbewerberleistungsgesetz*, Federal Law Gazette (*Bundesgesetzblatt*), BGBl. 1993 I p. 1074. In the meantime, the Act has been amended several times, lastly by BGBl. 2017 I p. 2541.

[43]See Mahler and Follmar-Otto (2011), pp. 380 et seq.; Janda (2013), pp. 175 et seq.

[44]Schmahl (2017a), Art. 26 mn. 8.

[45]BVerfGE 132, 134 (166).

[46]BVerfGE 132, 134 (166 et seq.).

[47]See Official Record of the Federal Parliament (*Bundestags-Drucksache*), BT-Drucks. 12/4451, pp. 1, 5 and BT-Drucks. 18/6185, p. 1.

[48]BVerfGE 132, 134 (173).

[49]Janda (2013), p. 177; see also, with a more critical view, Rothkegel (2012), p. 360.

[50]See Kirchhof (2015), p. 4.

It follows from the two decisions of the Federal Constitutional Court that the principle of social state in connection with the absolute duty of all state authorities to respect human dignity can actually lead to a definitive commitment of the legislator. The humane subsistence minimum of the individual is not at the free hands of the legislature; it rather has the compulsive task to specify the necessary expenditures and must perform this task in a transparent and appropriate procedure.[51] In addition, the legislator must align the subsistence minimum according to the actual need, i.e. in timely and realistically accurate recording of the social reality in Germany and not by referring to the existence level in other countries.[52] In other words, Article 1 (1), in conjunction with the social state principle pursuant to Article 20 (1) of the Basic Law, implies a subjective fundamental right to a decent minimum of subsistence.[53] Only the determination of the necessary amount and the required extent of the social benefits are at the sole discretion of the legislator, who must, however, carry out the calculations in a realistic and appropriate manner. The fact that the determination of the specific amount of social benefits is reserved for the legislature follows from the principle of separation of powers. It is not up to the courts to determine the amount and the conditions for social assistance required in each individual case.[54] The judgement of the Federal Constitutional Court on the "*Hartz IV*"-benefits, in which concrete sums have partly been fixed, has therefore been criticized in legal literature.[55]

While the federal legislature has implemented the legal requirements of the "*Hartz IV*"-decision of 2010 without significant delays in the Standard Needs Assessment Act,[56] in view of the Federal Constitutional Court's ruling on the Asylum Seekers Benefits Act of 2012, a compromise was reached only after lengthy debates in December 2014. With effect from 1 March 2015, the amended version of the Asylum Seekers Benefits Act[57] establishes a new level of benefits which is fundamentally based on social assistance in accordance with the Social Security Code II and specifically determines the benefit payments for children and adolescents according to their needs. However, as a result of the high numbers of refugees who have entered Germany since the autumn of 2015, benefits have primarily been converted into contributions-in-kind or vouchers.[58] In addition, a new provision has recently been introduced in the Asylum Seekers Benefits Act (Article 1a),[59]

---

[51] BVerfGE 125, 175 (222 et seq.).

[52] BVerfGE 125, 175 (222); 132, 134 (160 f.).

[53] BVerfGE 125, 175 (222 et seq.); 132, 34 (159 et seq.); 137, 34 (72).

[54] See, e.g., Federal Administrative Court *(Bundesverwaltungsgericht)*, BVerwGE 150, 44 (53); Windthorst (2017), Art. 20 mns 262a, b.

[55] See Nolte (2013), pp. 245 et seq. See also Voßkuhle (2011), pp. 181 et seq.

[56] *Regelbedarfsermittlungsgesetz*, BGBl. 2011 I p. 453. Critical view by Lenze (2011), pp. 1104 et seq.; and by Lembke (2018), p. 65.

[57] See BGBl. 2014 I p. 2187.

[58] See BGBl. 2015 I p. 1722.

[59] See BGBl. 2016 I p. 1824; see also BGBl. 2016 I p. 1939.

according to which the entitlement to benefits for persons who are not recognized as asylum seekers has been reduced to securing the physical subsistence minimum only.[60] This new rule does not run counter the Federal Constitutional Court's view, since the ruling of 2012 referred primarily to cases in which a legal stay preceded.[61] However, it remains doubtful whether the reduction of minimum healthcare, maintained by the amended Asylum Seekers Benefits Act of 2015, is compatible with the constitutional right to minimum subsistence.[62]

Statutory Laws

As has been demonstrated, the constitutional social state principle can hardly—or only very exceptionally—be condensed to definite individual fundamental rights because of its high indeterminacy and lack of guidelines.[63] It is thus primarily a matter for the legislature to realize and maintain a just social order.[64] In past decades, numerous laws have been passed that fill the social state principle with life. Thus, the principle of social state finds legislative concretization not only in social assistance and social insurance statutory laws, but also in seizure law, employment protection legislation and tax law.[65]

A particularly succinct expression of the social state principle is the legal system of social insurance against the vicissitudes of life. It contains both insurance and social welfare components. Essential elements of social insurance statutory laws are pension insurance as well as survivor's pension,[66] health insurance,[67] accident insurance,[68] unemployment insurance[69] and long-term care insurance.[70] However, a constitutional guarantee of the existing system of social security and its fundamental organizational principles cannot be inferred from the Basic Law.[71] Moreover, one should be aware that the principle of compulsory insurance is in constant conflict with the freedom and autonomy of personal life.[72] In addition, the efficiency of some

---

[60] For more detail see Dietz (2015), pp. 728 et seq.

[61] Concurring view by Kluth (2015), p. 341. Critical assessment by Groß (2014), p. 1221.

[62] See, e.g., Rixen (2015), pp. 1642 et seq.

[63] BVerfGE 1, 97 (105); 27, 253 (283); 65, 182 (193); 71, 66 (80); 82, 60 (80); 110, 412 (445); see also Leisner (2018), Art. 20 mn 21.

[64] BVerfGE 94, 241 (263); 102, 258 (298). Further see Eichenhofer (2012), pp. 140 et seq.

[65] See Leisner (2018), Art. 20 mn 24a.

[66] BVerfGE 28, 234 (348 et seq.); 68, 193 (209).

[67] BVerfGE 68, 193 (209); 124, 25 (37).

[68] BVerfGE 45, 376 (387).

[69] BVerfGE 51, 115 (121); 53, 313 (326 et seq.).

[70] BVerfGE 103, 197 (221).

[71] See the references cited in note 21.

[72] BVerfGE 59, 172 (213); see also Hofmann (2018), Art. 20 mn 29.

social systems, such as the statutory health and pension insurance, is under increasing political pressure. In view of demographic changes in the German society, models for a so-called general civil insurance are recently being discussed.[73]

Regardless of social security, caring for the needy, i.e. for persons who are hindered in their personal or social development, is one of the natural obligations of a social welfare state.[74] The cause of poverty and need may be financial distress, physical or mental illness,[75] severe disability,[76] long-term care,[77] personal weakness or criminal guilt, incompetence or social disadvantage,[78] or any other circumstance, such as unemployment.[79] There must be social assistance that ensures the minimum conditions for a decent existence. According to the social state principle, the state is obliged to secure these minimum conditions for the penniless citizen.[80] The insurmountable prerequisite for this, however, is a real indigence or poverty. The liberal welfare state must not refrain from encouraging the individual to become aware of the indispensability of self-responsibility, and it has to determine the neediness in each individual case.

Caring for the needy includes, as mentioned, social assistance to fellow citizens who are hindered in their personal and social development due to physical or mental handicaps or personal weakness or (criminal) guilt. The state community must therefore secure the minimum conditions for a dignified existence and provide adequate care, which is reflected in long-term care insurance, for example.[81] The demand for re-socialization of (former) prisoners is also an expression of the social state principle.[82] Furthermore, the social state conception of the Federal Constitutional Court includes not only the economic-social but also the mental-psychological situation of people. In the professional world, the provisions of the Staff Representation Act in labour statutory laws[83] and the concern for training and education count therefore among these elements of the social state principle.[84] Likewise, the establishment and administration of guardianship[85] and the granting of legal aid count eventually to its essential components.[86]

---

[73]Critical assessment by Depenheuer (2014), pp. 201 et seq.; see also *Sodan* (2004), pp. 217 et seq., both with further references.

[74]BVerfGE 100, 271 (284).

[75]BVerfGE 113, 88 (108 et seq.); 115, 25 (43).

[76]BVerfGE 44, 353 (375).

[77]BVerfGE 103, 197 (221).

[78]BVerfGE 35, 202 (235 et seq.).

[79]BVerfGE 43, 213 (226 et seq.); 100, 271 (284); 116, 202 (223).

[80]BVerfGE 40, 121 (133); 82, 60 (80); 100, 271 (286); 113, 88 (108 et seq.).

[81]BVerfGE 103, 197 (221).

[82]BVerfGE 35, 202 (235); see also Jarass (2016a), Art. 20 mn 72a.

[83]*Personalvertretungsgesetz*, BGBl. 1974 I p. 693, last amended by BGBl. 2017 I p. 2581.

[84]BVerfGE 33, 303 (331). Further see Robbers (2009), Art. 20 mn 1539.

[85]BVerfGE 54, 268 (268 et seq.).

[86]BVerfGE 81, 347 (356).

Legal Remedies in the "Broader" Domestic Context

As stated, the legislature is constitutionally obliged to guarantee economic, social, and cultural rights to maintain the minimum standard of living for everyone. These rights are more than just guiding principles of state policy. Rather, they are usually designed as individual rights at the statutory-law level. Thus, they are—unlike the constitutional social state principle—fully justiciable and legally enforceable. For this purpose, various legal remedies before different courts are available; jurisdiction in social matters plays, of course, a prominent role in this respect. Furthermore, legal aid is available for the poor if the legal remedy in question has a reasonable chance of success in court.[87] The Basic Law requires an assessment of the overall situation of the well-to-do and the impoverished plaintiff in order to realize legal protection.[88] Less wealthy or poor people shall not face a disproportionate difficulty in pursuing legal action in comparison to the average.

After exhaustion of the legal remedies before the ordinary courts, the individual concerned is authorized to lodge a constitutional complaint on the grounds that a concrete fundamental right to social participation has arbitrarily not been granted or that the subsistence level flowing from human dignity has not been secured. Since no individual claims arise from the social state principle alone, the Federal Constitutional Court does not accept a constitutional complaint based solely on the violation of the social state principle.[89] However, concrete individual rights can be derived from the state's duty to ensure and fulfil fundamental rights in conjunction with the social state principle.[90]

If a constitutional complaint is unsuccessful, the person concerned may even subsequently bring an individual complaint to the European Court of Human Rights (ECtHR). The European Convention on Human Rights (ECHR)[91] does not lay down any claim to certain social benefits of the state.[92] Rather, it is up to contracting states to decide on the design of their national social security systems.[93] Nevertheless, in individual cases, the Court takes on the duty to provide state-funded financial services to avert poverty that threatens the existence of a person. In doing so, the Court either resorts to the positive obligation of the states following from the prohibition of inhumane treatment (Article 3 ECHR) or uses the prohibition of discrimination (Article 14 ECHR) when an applicant is refused of social benefits

[87]See BVerfGE 122, 39 (49); Hofmann (2018), Art. 20 mn 33.

[88]See BVerfGE 9, 124 (130 et seq.); 81, 347 (356); 117, 163 (183).

[89]See, with regard to Article 20 (1) of the Basic Law in general, BVerfGE 6, 376 (385).

[90]Jarass (2016a), Art. 20 mn 167.

[91]ETS No.005; BGBl. 1953 II p. 578.

[92]See ECtHR, Decision of 28 October 1999, Application No. 40772/98, *Pancenko*, § 2; see also ECtHR, Decision of 15 March 2001, Application N. 30517/96, *Aunola*; Decision of 22 November 2005, Application No. 58830/00, *Sarmina and Sarmin*.

[93]Tomuschat (2007), pp. 859 et seq.

and legal aid by the state authorities in an arbitrary way.[94] Of course, the physical and financial benefits under the ECHR are always merely a matter of establishing a minimum standard.[95] Nevertheless, a ruling by the European Court of Human Rights, which is binding not only under international law[96] but also in the German domestic law context,[97] may in individual cases even lead to a compensation payment to the successful complainant.[98]

International Law Mechanisms Relevant to Germany

Yet, Germany is not only a party to the European Convention on Human Rights, but also a member of the European Social Charter (ESC),[99] which, unlike the ECHR, has been deliberately created as an instrument for the protection of economic, social, and cultural rights in Europe.[100] According to the preamble of the ESC, the contracting state parties pursue the objective of improving the standard of living of their population in urban and rural areas. The Charter, in accordance with its Article 20, gives the Contracting States the option of accepting five out of a catalogue of seven rights as binding ("à la carte approach").[101] However, it was not intended to lay down subjective or even individually enforceable rights.[102] On the contrary, the founders of the ESC deliberately avoided setting up an individual complaint procedure similar to that of Article 34 ECHR; instead they limited themselves to the creation of a periodic reporting system and a collective complaint mechanism.[103]

[94]See ECtHR, Judgement of 9 October 1979, Application No. 6289/73, *Airey*, § 26; Judgement of 10 May 2001, Application No. 29392/95, *Z.*, §§ 69 et seq.; Judgement of 15 February 2005, Application No. 68416/01, *Steel and Morris*, §§ 59 et seq.; Judgement of 6 July 2005, Application No. 65731/91, *Stec*, §§ 50 et seq. On this topic see also Sudre (2003), pp. 766 et seq.; Grabenwarter (2006), p. 91; Schmahl and Winkler (2010), pp. 422 et seq.

[95]See Meyer-Ladewig and Renger (2017), Art. 53 mn 1.

[96]See Article 46 ECHR.

[97]See Article 59 (2) 1 of the Basic Law as well as BVerfGE 111, 307 (319, 323); 128, 326 (367 et seq.); 131, 268 (296); 133, 59 (84); 134, 33 (59 et seq.).

[98]See Art. 41 ECHR.

[99]Of 18 October 1961 (entered into force on 26 February 1965); ETS No. 35; BGBl. 1964 II p. 1262. Changes in substance have been introduced by the revised European Social Charter, signed on 3 May 1996 (CETS No. 163). However, the Federal Republic of Germany has not ratified this (revised) instrument in order to maintain its sovereign leeway of action, see Giegerich (2008), pp. 21 et seq.

[100]The historical development, the regulatory structure, the elements of substance and the monitoring system of the ESC of 1961 and its revision in 1996 are analyzed in detail by Dörr (2017), pp. 507 et seq.

[101]Dörr (2017), mn 23.17.

[102]See Pellonpää (1994), p. 857.

[103]For more detail see, e.g., Harris and Darcy (2001), pp. 293 et seq.; De Schutter (2012), pp. 468 et seq.

This limited level of control and enforceability of the rights laid down in the European Social Charter is justified by its dependence on economic, financial and general conditions of the society concerned.[104]

The same applies to the EU Charter of Fundamental Rights,[105] which is binding for the EU member states and thus also for Germany. Although Title IV "Solidarity" (Articles 27 et seq.) of the EU Charter is particularly devoted to social and economic rights, there is agreement that these rights are not extensively justiciable, but allow the contracting states a wide margin of appreciation.[106] Also the citizenship of the European Union is only based on a limited degree of financial solidarity between the nationals of different EU member states.[107] The European Commission's recent "Europe 2020" paper does not change that fact. It introduced new features to the European system of combating poverty and social exclusion in order to aim at Europe becoming a smart, sustainable, inclusive economy delivering high levels of employment, productivity and social cohesion, thus setting out a vision of Europe's social market economy for the twenty-first century.[108] This strategy combines social inclusion with cohesion in order to equip individuals with the ability to anticipate and manage change of the labour market, discover new opportunities and improve their competitiveness.[109] The relevant guidelines at European level are, however, effective only if implemented in national law, whereby the member States are given a substantial leeway.[110] Nevertheless, the rights laid down in Articles 27 et seq. of the EU Charter are predominantly designed as individual rights. The subsistence minimum and elementary survival conditions must be guaranteed to everyone. Like in the German legal order, here, too, it is a question of ensuring a minimum social standard that covers the basic needs of every human being as an expression of the inviolability of human dignity.[111]

Beyond the regional level, the Federal Republic of Germany is also bound by various universal human rights treaties that have been drafted within the framework of the United Nations. This applies, for instance, to the International Covenant on Civil and Political Rights (ICCPR),[112] which, like the ECHR, recognizes a ban on inhumane treatment, from which a claim can be drawn to secure the minimum standard of humane living conditions. Particularly important, however, are the

---

[104]See Neubeck (2002), pp. 166 et seq.

[105]Of 12 December 2007 (firstly proclaimed on 7 December 2000), OJ 2007, C 303/1; BGBl. 2009 II p. 1223.

[106]See Jarass (2016b), Art. 34 mn 2; Rudolf (2014), Art. 34 mn 14.—As to the tedious development of social and solidarity rights in the European Union see Giegerich (2008), pp. 22 et seq.

[107]See, e.g., Guibboni (2018), pp. 273 et seq.; Schmahl and Jung (2016), pp. 1272 et seq.

[108]European Commission, Communication from the Commission 'Europe 2020: A strategy for smart, sustainable and inclusive growth', COM(2010) 2020 final, 3 March 2010, p. 5.

[109]See Peña-Casas (2011), p. 162.

[110]Peña-Casas (2011), p. 160.

[111]See Rudolf (2014), Art. 34 mn 20; Kingreen (2016), Art. 34 mns 4, 15.

[112]Of 19 December 1966 (entered into force on 23 March 1976), 999 UNTS 171, BGBl. 1973 II p. 1553.

International Covenant on Economic, Social and Cultural Rights (ICESCR)[113] and other special human rights conventions dedicated to the rights of women,[114] children[115] and persons with disabilities.[116] All these specific human rights conventions, to which Germany is a contracting party, guarantee key economic, social, and cultural rights, such as the right to work, the right to a decent standard of living, the right to social security, education and the highest attainable standard of health.[117] Although the relevant treaty texts regularly set social and economic rights under the proviso of progressive realization or sufficient financial resources,[118] the expert committees, which monitor state compliance with the human rights conventions, are now increasingly making it clear that the contracting states cannot escape their duty to protect and to fulfil by relying on flimsy arguments.[119] Every economic, social, and cultural right has an inviolable core content that must be realized immediately;[120] and the majority of the obligations of states under the ICESCR are perceived as a combination of "obligations of conduct" and "obligations of result".[121] Germany, too, gets occasionally into the crossfire of criticism, for example with regard to social rights of asylum seeking childrens[122] or with regard to the right of free education at state universities pursuant to Article 13 (2) lit. c ICESCR.[123]

Nevertheless, the overall actual impact of these human rights conventions on the national legal order and in particular on the social state principle remains in Germany rather low.[124] There are a number of reasons for this: Firstly, human rights conventions, like all international treaties that Germany has ratified, only have the rank of an ordinary federal statute (see Article 59 (2) 1 of the Basic Law). Thus, they cannot supersede constitutional requirements, including the social state principle of the

[113]Of 19 December 1966 (entered into force on 3 January 1976), 993 UNTS 3; BGBl. 1973 II p. 1570.

[114]Convention on the Elimination of All Forms of Discrimination against Women (CEDAW), entered into force on 3 September 1981; BGBl. 1985 II p. 647.

[115]Convention on the Rights of the Child (CRC), entered into force on 2 September 1990; BGBl. 1992 II p. 990.

[116]Convention on the Rights of Persons with Disabilities (CRPD), entered into force on 3 May 2008; BGBl. 2008 II p. 1419.

[117]See, for instance, Articles 6, 8, 9, 12 and 13 ICESCR.

[118]See, e.g., Article 2 (1) ICESCR, Article 4 CRC, Article 4 (2) CRPD. Slightly different scope: Article 3 CEDAW.

[119]For more detail on the views adopted by the Committee on Economic, Social and Cultural Rights in this respect, see Riedel (2008), pp. 80 et seq.; Baderin and McCorquodale (2010), pp. 360 et seq.

[120]See Müller (2009), p. 581.

[121]Baderin and McCorquodale (2010), pp. 355 et seq.

[122]Committee of the Rights of the Child, Concluding Observations: Germany, CRC/C/DEU/CO/3-4, 2014, para. 56b; see also Schmahl (2017a), Art. 24 mn 27.

[123]For a fuller account see, e.g., Riedel and Söllner (2006), pp. 270 et seq.; Lorenzmeier (2006), pp. 59 et seq.

[124]See Grewe (2012), pp. 400 et seq.

Basic Law.[125] Accordingly, the rights enshrined in the ICESCR, as well as those guaranteed by other human rights conventions, are not constitutionally anchored.

Secondly, the overwhelming opinion in literature and jurisprudence assumed for a long time that the economic, social, and cultural rights guaranteed in the international treaties had no or only limited effect in Germany. The rights enshrined in the ICESCR were, for instance, considered as a minor category of rights, even only as objective and non-justiciable rights.[126] Today, the views and judicial findings have changed to a considerable extent. At least, the subjective character of economic, social, and cultural rights is not fundamentally called into question anymore.[127] These so-called second generation or second dimension rights[128] are by no means "second-rate";[129] the indivisibility of human rights, as promulgated in the 1993 Vienna Declaration and Program of Action,[130] is universally recognized and has a firm foothold in Germany as well. However, while the classical human rights of the first dimension regularly gain even immediate applicability in the German legal order, the direct effectiveness of social rights is regularly not given, since the latter are subject to the reservation of sufficient resources. The social and economic obligations under international law that are stipulated in human rights conventions leave the states mostly with significant margin of appreciation.[131]

Lastly, the very special mandate and practical output of the monitoring bodies on the economic, social, and cultural rights are not always unassailable. There is at least a risk that their perspectives become too one-sided and conflicting human rights and freedoms of third parties will not be sufficiently observed. In any case, the idea of absolute protection against discrimination, which the UN Committee on the Rights of Persons with Disabilities advocates on several occasions,[132] tends to overlook the necessity of a practical concordance between different human rights concerns and between the various functions and dimensions of human rights.[133]

Therefore, the social rights enshrined in international human rights conventions do not amount to subjectively enforceable claims in the German legal order, except

[125] BVerfGE 74, 358 (370); 111, 307 (317, 329); 128, 326 (365, 370). For more detail see Schmahl (2017b), pp. 818 et seq.

[126] See the description of former views by Grewe (2012), p. 398; and Buergenthal (2017), pp. 296 et seq., both with further references.

[127] See Riedel (2008), pp. 75 et seq. Further see the in-depth analysis by Trilsch (2012), pp. 436 et seq.

[128] As to the terms of "generations" and "dimensions" see Riedel (1989), pp. 9 et seq.

[129] Grewe (2012), p. 414; see also Vöneky (2014), p. 69.

[130] UN General Assembly, Vienna Declaration and Programme of Action, 12 July 1993, UN Doc. A/CONF.157/23, para 2. See also UN General Assembly, World Summit Outcome, Resolution 60/1, 16 September 2005, para 121.

[131] See Marauhn (2004), pp. 275 et seq.

[132] See, e.g., Committee on the Rights of Persons with Disabilities, Concluding observations on the initial report of Germany, UN-Doc. CRPD/C/DEU/CO/1, of 13 May 2015, paras 37 et seq., in particular para 38b.

[133] See Uerpmann-Wittzack (2016), pp. 200 et seq.; Schmahl (2017c), pp. 88 et seq.

in cases where the social minimum standard is at stake. The rights guaranteed by the ICESCR do generally not justify, with few exceptions, full subjective rights even after their transposition into national law; what is indispensable is a domestic legislative act that establishes subjective rights.[134] An obligation to constitutionalize social human rights cannot be deduced from international law.[135] It is therefore compatible with international law that a constitution—like the Basic Law—anchors the social state principle only as a state objective. On the other hand, the Basic Law consciously establishes an "open statehood"[136] and is designed in a friendly attitude toward international law.[137] On the basis of the constitutional principle of the international law-friendliness of the Basic Law, the social state principle might well be interpreted in conformity with international law prerequisites. Yet, social rights do not have to be implemented in a constitution; it suffices that they are stipulated in statutory laws.[138]

A different question is whether transnationally active corporations or business enterprises should be bound by human rights social standards in order to combat poverty effectively. This question is intensively investigated in various reports of the Special Representative of the UN Secretary General on the issue of human rights and transnational corporations which finally resulted in the adoption of the non-binding "Ruggie Principles".[139] However, a direct obligation of transnational corporations to respect human rights can be found neither in the Basic Law nor in human rights treaties. The international obligation to prevent human rights abuses is first and foremost an obligation to prevent human rights violations by state organs.[140] In addition, states have a duty to take preventive action against violations of human rights within their jurisdiction by non-state actors. A state must therefore also regulate and control companies that operate in or from its territory.[141] In contrast, companies can only be said to have a non-legal, ethical responsibility to respect human rights.[142] For reasons of private autonomy and freedom, companies are not directly committed to human rights treaties; they may at most voluntarily bind

[134]See Murswiek (2011), § 192 mn 49.

[135]Concurring opinion by Grewe (2012), p. 413; and Vöneky (2014), p. 70. Similarly, with regard to the right to the highest attainable standard of health, Kaltenborn and Tröppner (2017), pp. 747 et seq.

[136]The term "*Offene Staatlichkeit*" was first used by Vogel (1964), p. 42.

[137]See BVerfGE 111, 307 (318 et seq.); 112, 1 (25 et seq.); 128, 326 (268 et seq.).

[138]Rightly so Murswiek (2011), § 192 mns 68 et seq.

[139]See the Reports of the Special Representative of the Secretary General of the United Nations, *John Ruggie*, on the Issue Human Rights and Transnational Corporations and Other Business Enterprises, of 7 April 2008, UN Doc. A/HRC/8/5; of 22 April 2009, UN Doc. A/HRC/11/13; of 9 April 2010, UN Doc. A/HRC/14/27. On the basis of these reports, the UN Human Rights Council adopted the Guiding Principles on Business and Human Rights, of 21 March 2011, UN Doc. A/HRC/17/31. See also Higham (2013), pp. 333 et seq.; Wallace (2015), pp. 233 et seq.

[140]See Weissbrodt (2013), p. 728.

[141]See McCorquodale (2012), pp. 458 et seq.

[142]McCorquodale (2012), p. 465.

themselves on human rights.[143] Strengthening national compliance mechanisms is, hence, desirable to prevent companies from outsourcing their production to third countries with low or even non-existing social standards.

Contributions of the German Legal Order to the Fight Against Poverty and the Right to Development in an International Context

A different picture has to be painted with regard to the German contributions to the fight against poverty in an international context.

Domestic Law

Even though the Federal Republic of Germany has been involved in development cooperation since its founding,[144] there is no provision in the Basic Law which strives for a strict commitment to development aid or transnational poverty reduction. Neither can a duty to combat poverty worldwide be taken from the fundamental rights of the Basic Law,[145] nor may an extra-territorial application of the social state principle be applied.[146]

The social state principle in Article 20 (1) of the Basic Law is expressly tailored as a state objective closely linked to the Federal Republic of Germany, since Germany is referred to in this provision as a "democratic and social federal state". According to Article 1 (3) of the Basic Law, the fundamental rights set out in the German Constitution shall bind the legislature, the executive and the judiciary as directly applicable law. This binding includes basically the entire sphere of influence or power of German public authorities,[147] even if the interference takes place abroad or has an impact there.[148] Thus foreigners abroad can also invoke fundamental rights in their function as defense rights against interference by German state organs. However, in the case of social and economic rights or fundamental rights to social participation, the relationship with German public authorities must be thoroughly scrutinized. Social and economic rights or other participation rights are only

[143] Vöneky (2014), p. 78.

[144] An overview can be found on the website of the Federal Ministry for Economic Cooperation and Development, see http://www.bmz.de/de/ministerium/geschichte/index.html.

[145] See Dann (2013), § 249 mns 43 et seq.

[146] Because of its vagueness, the social state principle regularly does not create a right to gain specific benefits even within the Federal Republic of Germany, see BVerfGE 110, 412 (445).

[147] See Höfling (2018), Art. 1 mn 86.

[148] See, e.g., BVerfGE 6, 290 (295); 57, 9 (23). Further see Badura (2006), § 47 mns 13 et seq.

applicable if there is a genuine connection to German territory or sovereignty. Therefore, an obligation to fight extra-territorial poverty is highly exceptional and may be considered only in cases where the core of human dignity is systematically and seriously infringed. For the rest, however, there is no constitutional duty to fight poverty on a global level.

Also, a global right to development is not known to the German legal order. Development is not recognized as a subjective international human right. Rather, the right to development is an objective recognized under customary law, which, however, does not provide for concrete obligations to provide a specific amount of development aid.[149] Therefore, Germany has no legal development program that is similar to the international right to development model as conceived by the (legally non-binding) 1986 UN Declaration on the Right of Development.[150] However, the German Government is—as its previous and current engagement shows—well aware of the recognition of rich countries' political and moral responsibilities in helping underdeveloped states to develop. For this reason, both bilateral and multilateral development policies have been included in the federal budget, which is passed annually by the Federal Parliament, the *Bundestag*. For 2017, the budget of the Federal Ministry for Economic Cooperation and Development is estimated at 8.541 billion euros. 4.124 billion euros will be invested in bilateral cooperation, 1.667 billion euros in multilateral cooperation and 822 million euros in the European Development Fund. The rest is earmarked for special initiatives, cooperation with non-governmental organizations, and civil society.[151]

As part of bilateral and multilateral development cooperation, the Federal Ministry for Economic Cooperation and Development cooperates with a total of 85 different countries. Applying the—legally non-binding—UN Agenda 2030 for sustainable development and its 17 sustainable development goals,[152] the Federal Republic of Germany's involvement in development cooperation focuses on climate policy and the promotion of sustainable economic development of the value added chain, for example in the textiles sector.[153] In addition, the Federal Government is committed to food security and rural development, above all in Africa.[154] Because the main cause of hunger is poverty, fighting hunger is always regarded as poverty alleviation. Moreover, hunger is particularly a rural phenomenon, which is why any

---

[149] See Barral (2012), pp. 385 et seq.

[150] UN General Assembly, Declaration on the Right to Development (4 December 1986), UN Doc. A/RES/41/128.

[151] As to the figures mentioned, see Federal Ministry for Economic Cooperation and Development (2017b), p. 2.

[152] See UN General Assembly, Transforming our World: The 2030 Agenda for Sustainable Development (25 September 2015), UN Doc. A/RES/70/1.

[153] See Federal Ministry for Economic Cooperation and Development (2017c), pp. 14 et seq.; see also Federal Ministry for Economic Cooperation and Development (2017b), p. 4.

[154] Federal Ministry for Economic Cooperation and Development (2017d) pp. 24 et seq.; see also Federal Ministry for Economic Cooperation and Development (2017b), p. 6.

sustainable development must start there.[155] The highest priority in the development policy of Germany, however, is coping with the high number of refugees which Germany has been receiving since autumn 2015. In addition to the budget for development aid, around 9 billion euros have been spent since 2015 on reducing the causes of flight over the long term.[156]

European Union Law

The Federal Republic of Germany is also involved in the association and development aid policy of the European Union. This includes, firstly, the constitutional association of the overseas countries and territories under Articles 198 et seq. TFEU and, secondly, the contractual development association with the African, Caribbean and Pacific (ACP) states pursuant to Article 217 TFEU, which for a long time was shaped by the Treaties of Yaoundé and Lomé and is today expressed in the 2000 Cotonou Partnership Agreement.[157]

Both forms of association serve primarily development-policy objectives, with the overseas territories enjoying a certain degree of privilege for historical reasons over the ACP states which have been independent since the decolonization phase.[158] However, as former colonies, the ACP countries enjoy a special status in EU development policy through the Cotonou Partnership Agreement, which has been signed in 2000 for the duration of 20 years between the European Union and 79 ACP states.[159] The development cooperation with other developing countries is governed by Articles 208 et seq. TFEU and covers various states from Asia and Latin America.[160] In addition, there are several association agreements with the southern and south-eastern Mediterranean coastal states, which also have a clear development

---

[155]Federal Ministry for Economic Cooperation and Development (2015a), p. 6.

[156]See Federal Ministry for Economic Cooperation and Development (2017b), p. 4.

[157]The Cotonou Partnership Agreement is reprinted in OJ 2000, L 317/3. As to the development of the contractual development association with the ACP states see, e.g., Vöneky and Beylage-Haarmann (2015), Art. 217 mns 113 et seq.

[158]See Resolution 2013/I/755/EU, OJ 2013, L 344/1.—The EU states first excluded the overseas territories, which were under the territorial sovereignty of their mother states, from the scope of the European treaties by means of a '*réserve coloniale*' (see Article 52 (2) TEU in conjunction with Article 255 (2) TFEU) and then selectively reintroduced them to the Union through the special regime under Article 198 et seq. TFEU. The constitutional association thus creates not only privileges, but also distance, because EU membership is not wanted, see Schmalenbach (2014), § 6 mn 3.

[159]See Bungenberg (2015), Art. 217 mn 130. For more detail see Arts (2003), pp. 95 et seq.

[160]See Streinz and Kruis (2018), Art. 208 mn 3.

policy focus and were concluded in the context of a Euro-Mediterranean partnership, which was launched in 1995.[161]

All the association agreements under Article 217 TFEU although they are, without exception, concluded as mixed agreements,[162] form an integral part of EU law and are considered by the European Court of Justice (ECJ) as one single entity.[163] They stand in the hierarchical rank between EU primary and secondary law.[164] Thus integrated into the EU legal order, they must be measured against EU primary law,[165] while being given priority not only to EU secondary legislation[166] but also to the national legal systems of the EU member states.[167] Together with its member states, the European Union provides around 75 billion euros in development aid, reaching more than 140 states.[168]

Overall, the European Union has a long-standing record of involvement in development cooperation. From the 1957 Treaty of Rome, which established the European Economic Community, to the present day, the modalities, main features and priorities of EU policies and specific activities have changed significantly.[169] Since the policy of association agreements was originally aimed at allowing the former colonies and territories of the member states to participate in the construction of Europe and its economic development, today it is more akin to classical development cooperation under Article 208 TFEU.[170] The emphasis is on the fight against poverty, which is reflected in Article 208 (1) 2 TFEU.[171] Thereby, the concept of poverty is to be interpreted in line with the general objective of the external action of the Union laid down in Article 21 (2) lit. d TEU.[172] Hence, poverty is defined not only as a mere lack of income and financial resources, but also as a deficit of basic skills such as lack of access to education, health services, natural resources or political participation.[173]

[161]The Euro-Mediterranean partnership was promulgated by the European Commission, see COM (2008) 319 final. Further see Khan (2017), Art. 208 mn 9.

[162]See Schmalenbach (2016), Art. 217 mn 15.

[163]See ECJ, Case 181/73, *Haegeman*, ECR 1974, 449, §§ 2, 6; Case 12/85, *Demirel*, ECR 1987, 3747 (3752 et seq.).

[164]See Terhechte (2012), Art. 216 mn 20.

[165]See ECJ, Joint Cases C-402/05 P and C-415/05 P, *Kadi et al.*, ECR 2008, I-6351, § 308.

[166]See ECJ, Case C-308/06, *Intertanko*, ECR 2008, I-4057, § 42; Case C-228/06, *Soysal*, ECR 2009, I-1031, § 59.

[167]See Hummer (2018), Art. 216 mn 19.

[168]See European Commission, press release of 11 April 2017; see also OECD, DAC Peer Review 2017 of the European Community, p. 23.

[169]See Arts (2008), pp. 217 et seq.

[170]Benedek (2012), Art. 208 mns 10 et seq.

[171]For more detail, see COM(2010) 758 final (16 December 2010).

[172]See Streinz and Kruis (2018), Art. 208 mn 16.

[173]Schmalenbach (2016), Art. 208 mn 8.

Accordingly, the European Union continuously participates in the development of countries in need, with financial, technical and humanitarian assistance,[174] the latter especially in the form of food aid.[175] The financial and technical aid provided for includes also trade policy measures. For example, the Union has created a general preference system for all developing countries.[176] Further tariff exemptions are provided as incentives for sustainable development and good governance.[177] For the least developed countries, tariffs are even fully suspended for all goods except arms.[178] Furthermore, both association policy and development cooperation more and more incorporate social, cultural, and environmental objectives.[179] Democratic approaches and human rights policy are also increasingly used as instruments of political control.[180] Many development agreements are even subject to explicit human rights conditionality.[181] As they form an integral part of the agreements, these human rights clauses enable the Union to terminate or suspend the treaty in accordance with Article 60 of the 1969 Vienna Convention on the Law of Treaties.[182] Last but not least, in the context of development cooperation, the Union also takes action to prevent and resolve conflicts, as peace and security are undoubtedly a necessary condition for development and the fight against poverty.[183]

In sum, the today's development policy of the European Union stands in line with the signs of the times. It has emerged from the post-colonial interests of some member states and continues to be particularly committed to the overseas territories and the ACP countries. However, EU development policy has been globalizing in recent years, especially through development cooperation, and addresses today the needs of all developing countries.[184] Special efforts apply to the least developed countries.[185] This is also clear from the recent strategy papers of the European

---

[174]Zimmermann (2015), Art. 208 mns 50 et seq.

[175]For more detail, see COM(2010) 127 final (31 March 2010).

[176]See Article 6 of EC Regulation No. 732/2008, OJ 2008, L 211/1, revised by EU Regulation No. 1236/2009, OJ 2009, L 332/28. For more details see Zimmermann (2015), Art. 208 mns 37 et seq.

[177]See, in particular, Articles 7 to 10 of EC Regulation No. 732/08, OJ 2008, L 211/1. For a fuller account see Kuon (2010), *passim*.

[178]See Articles 11 to 14 of EC Regulation No. 732/08, OJ 2008 L 211/1 (so-called "Everything but Arms" initiative). For more detail see Bartels (2007), pp. 743 et seq.

[179]See Zimmermann (2015), Art. 208 mn 78; see also COM(2000) 264 final.

[180]See Benedek (2012), Art. 208 mn 52. For a fuller account see Lerch (2004), *passim.*

[181]See Bartels (2007), pp. 738 et seq. This practice of human rights conditionality has been accepted by the European Court of Justice, see ECJ, Case C-268/94, *Portugal/Council of the European Union*, ECR 1996, I-6177, §§ 23 et seq.

[182]See Streinz and Kruis (2018), Art. 208 mn 23, with further references.

[183]For a fuller account see Schmalenbach (2016), Art. 208 mns 10 et seq. See also EU Regulation No. 230/2014, OJ 2014, L 77/1.

[184]See Oppermann et al. (2016), § 41 mn 59.

[185]See, for instance, Articles 11 to 14 of EC Regulation No. 732/08, OJ 2008, L 211/1.

Commission.[186] The European Union, in compliance with the 17 sustainable development goals and its 169 sub-goals of the UN Agenda 2030 for Sustainable Development, has lately adopted a strategy to secure sustainable development in Europe and worldwide.[187] One focus is the sustainability target No. 6 'water', i.e. the "availability and sustainable management of water and sanitation for all" which stands in line with the stipulations of Articles 11 and 12 ICESCR.[188] This means that the European Union's development aid policy undoubtedly serves to combat poverty globally,[189] even though it still privileges certain regions of the world, and even though there are no concrete obligations which emanate from the association treaties in terms of type, extent and amount for the aid delivered.

Conclusion

Regardless of the original distinction between civil and political rights on the one hand and economic, social, and cultural rights on the other, all human rights, of whatever category or dimension, have in common the goal of enabling the individual to lead a dignified existence in freedom. However, living in hunger, homelessness and without adequate medical care is not considered a decent humane living, even if civil and political rights are fully guaranteed.[190] The mental-spiritual and intellectual-political existence of human beings cannot be separated from their physical needs.[191] Effective protection of civil and political rights requires the guarantee of a minimum standard of economic, social, and cultural rights.[192] These second dimension rights not only serve to establish social justice and equality, but are also meant to be a means of securing individual freedom.[193] The originally intended rigid separation between the different human rights dimensions can therefore no longer be maintained to this extent today. Rather, at the latest since the Vienna Declaration and the Program of Action of the UN World Conference on Human Rights of 1993,[194] the indivisibility, the mutual dependence and the close contextual

[186] See, e.g., COM(2010) 2020 final; COM(2010) 758 final; COM(2013) 39 final.

[187] See COM (2011) 637 final. Currently, a revised strategy in view of the UN sustainable development goals is being developed at EU level, see Laskowski (2017), pp. 65 et seq.

[188] See Committee on Economic, Social and Cultural Rights, General Comment No. 15 (2002), The Right to Water, UN Doc. CESCR.E/C.12/2002/11. Critical assessment by Klein (2015a), p. 183.

[189] Gómez Urquijo (2017), pp. 49 et seq.

[190] See Riedel (2005), p. 121.

[191] Rightly so Tomuschat (2009), p. 140; Cremer (2008), pp. 44 et seq.

[192] This view is shared by the German Government see Federal Ministry for Economic Cooperation and Development (2015b), p. 4.

[193] Langford (2009), pp. 3 et seq.

[194] See note 130.

relationship between the various dimensions and categories of human rights must be assumed.[195]

Also, the German legal system, which formerly used to make a strict distinction between the various dimensions of human rights, has in the course of time opened up to the idea of the indivisibility and complementarity of human rights. Although this does not mean that all categories and dimensions of human rights are aligned and equalized in terms of content and effect, there is nevertheless a certain level of justiciability of the so-called second dimension rights, particularly on the level of statutory laws which often have direct effects. On the constitutional level, by contrast, the situation remains different. While classical civil liberties continue to play a prominent role in the German legal order by obliging the state to abstain from conduct violating these rights ("duty to respect"), social and economic rights usually only contain an obligation for the state to ensure and fulfil a minimal level of material existence to its citizens ("duty to ensure and fulfil").[196] Thus, these rights do not drop behind the first dimension rights in their meaning and importance, but they do indeed so in their power of enforcement, since they are subject to the general reservation of what is financially and organizationally possible.[197] As a rule, second dimension rights merely establish "obligations of conduct". Therefore, judicial procedures before international bodies or constitutional courts are generally not well suited for the specific vindication of economic, social, and cultural rights as "obligations of result". At least, it is hard to see how a judicial body could adjudicate concrete claims for the grant of social benefits on the sole basis of second dimension rights or of the social state principle without having to rely on (domestic) legislative acts.[198] Only as far as minimum core obligations are concerned, the economic, social, and cultural rights can become directly operative on the international and the constitutional levels. If however, social welfare benefits are introduced under a general scheme, they should accrue to everyone under the principle of non-discrimination, and encroachments can indeed be sanctioned by judicial means.[199]

By contrast, the third dimension of human rights—especially the right to development, to a habitable environment and participation in the common heritage of mankind which were developed theoretically by *Karel Vasak* in his inaugural lecture at the International Human Rights Institute in Strasbourg in 1979[200]—are still not recognized in the German legal system. The reason for this is that both legal object and functionality of these solidarity rights are considered with skepticism, because of the vagueness of their content.[201] Not only on the national but also on the

---

[195]Schmahl and Winkler (2010), p. 411.

[196]BVerfGE 137, 34 (72); see also Rudolf (2014), Vorbem. zu Titel IV, mn 38.

[197]See Trilsch (2012), pp. 23 et seq., with further references.

[198]Tomuschat (2014), p. 148.

[199]See Kradolfer (2012), pp. 255 et seq.

[200]Vasak (1979), *passim*. For more detail see Alston (1982), pp. 307 et seq.

[201]See Partsch (1986), pp. 153 et seq.; Partsch (1987), pp. 25 et seq.; Tomuschat (1985), pp. 568 et seq. Different accentuation by Wolfrum (2013), pp. 410 et seq.

international level, there is even uncertainty about who can be the beneficiary of these solidarity rights. Sometimes collective entities such as nations or populations are discussed as beneficiaries.[202] Sometimes individuals, in addition to collective entities, are seen as being able to be holders of these rights.[203] The scope of parties subject to duties is also not easily identifiable. It is unclear, for instance, whether states have duties towards their citizens, or whether merely economically "stronger" states should have obligations towards "weaker" states.[204] Furthermore, in many cases, the realization of these third dimension rights depends on factors such as natural disasters which, as a rule, extend beyond the scope of influence of the states.[205] Taken as a whole, third dimension rights are therefore not be regarded as genuinely enforceable rights but rather as "agreed objectives which the international community has pledged to pursue".[206] Nevertheless, they play a supporting role in the fight against global poverty which is not insignificant. The recognition of collective rights as policy benchmarks does strengthen the protection of fundamental human rights and the right to minimum existence afforded to the individual under the first and second dimension rights.[207] However, the realization of the third dimension right to development requires concerted efforts on the part not only of states or the international community, but also of societies, peoples, non-governmental organizations and individuals.[208]

Finally, the following consideration should also be taken into account: The argument of the birth right lottery rightly says that it is a mere coincidence where and when someone is born.[209] The connection between birth and assignment of a political affiliation is thus an arbitrary one. Yet, this does not mean that the recognition of the birth right lottery would be able to establish a new kind of distributional justice on the global scale or to transform the (international) right to development into a directly applicable, full right. The lottery argument plays a central role in the justice theory of *John Rawls*.[210] There, however, it is from the outset related to a limited community. Only within this community is the distribution of natural gifts, talents and assets considered to be accidental and therefore morally arbitrary.[211] The extension of the distribution problem to the global community of

[202]See, e.g., UN General Assembly, Declaration on the Right of Peoples to Peace, Resolution 39/11, 12 November 1984.

[203]See, e.g., UN General Assembly, Declaration on the Right to Development, Resolution 41/128, 4 December 1986. See also, more recently, UN General Assembly, Resolution 67/171, 20 December 2012.

[204]See Tomuschat (2014), pp. 152 et seq.; Baderin and McCorquodale (2010), p. 357.

[205]Schmahl (2016), p. 5.

[206]Tomuschat (2014), p. 154. See also Waldron (1993), p. 342.

[207]See Wellman (2000), pp. 642 et seq.

[208]Wolfrum (2013), p. 410.

[209]See Shachar (2009), *passim*.

[210]Rawls (1979), pp. 94 and 122.

[211]See Rawls (2002), p. 43.

states was not the subject of *Rawls*' reflections.[212] Rather, nation-state communities have not lost their legitimacy even in the age of globalization. Although the Agenda 2030 recurs to a somewhat "global public interest",[213] current international law remains genuinely intergovernmental in character and continues to depend on the existence and the political will of nation states. As part of humanity, human communities owe each other mutual help on the basis of moral values. However, directly enforceable legal claims under international law do not inevitably follow from this ethical value-oriented attitude.[214] Rather, international human rights are created through treaty and international customary law and build on state consensus. Therefore, they remain primarily committed to their legal roots and legal existence and not so much to their moral foundation.

References

Alston P (1982) A third generation of solidarity rights: progressive development or obfuscation of international human rights law? Netherlands Int Law Rev 29:307–322

Arts K (2003) ACP-EU relations in a new era: The Cotonou Agreement. Common Market Law Rev 40:95–116

Arts K (2008) The European Communities' contribution to the fight against poverty in developing countries: normative and real? German Yearb Int Law 51:217–250

Baderin M, McCorquodale R (2010) Poverty and the international covenant on economic, social and cultural rights. In: Van Bueren G (ed) Freedom from poverty as a human right. UNESCO, Paris, pp 345–368

Badura P (2006) Der räumliche Geltungsbereich der Grundrechte. In: Merten D, Papier H-J (eds) Handbuch der Grundrechte, § 47, vol II

Barral V (2012) Sustainable development in international law: nature and operation of an evolutive legal norm. Eur J Int Law 23:377–400

Bartels L (2007) The trade and development policy of the European Union. Eur J Int Law 18:715–756

Baumann M-O (2017) Reformdruck durch die 2030-Agenda. Vereinte Nationen:104–109

Benedek W (2012) Commentary on Article 208 TFEU. In: Grabitz E, Hilf M, Nettesheim M (eds) Das Recht der Europäischen Union, Kommentar, Art. 208. CH Beck, München

Buergenthal T (2017) Human rights: from San Francisco to The Hague. Heidelberg J Int Law 77:289–304

Bungenberg M (2015) Commentary on Article 217 TFEU. In: von der Groeben H, Schwarze J, Hatje A (eds) Europäisches Unionsrecht, Kommentar, Art. 217, 7th edn. Nomos, Baden-Baden

Cremer H-J (2008) Wirtschaftliche, soziale und kulturelle Rechte – eine sinnvolle Normenkategorie? In: Giegerich T, Zimmermann A (eds) Wirtschaftliche, soziale und kulturelle Rechte im globalen Zeitalter. Duncker & Humblot, pp 35–70

Dann P (2013) Entwicklungszusammenarbeit. In: Isensee J, Kirchhof P (eds) Handbuch des Staatsrechts, § 249, vol XI, 3rd edn. CF Müller, Heidelberg

De Schutter O (2012) The European Social Charter. In: Krause C, Scheinin M (eds) International protection of human rights. A textbook, 2nd edn. Åbo Akademi University, Turku, pp 468 et seq

[212]See Funke (2017), pp. 536 et seq.

[213]For more detail see Baumann (2017), pp. 104 et seq.

[214]See Klein (2017), pp. 304 et seq. See also Klein (2015b), pp. 7 et seq.

Depenheuer O (2014) Auf dem Wege zu einer Totalisierung des sozialen Sicherheitsdenkens. Neue Zeitschrift für Sozialrecht:201–206

Dietz A (2015) Leistungsbeschränkungen nach § 1a AsylbLG für Asylbewerber aus sicheren Herkunftsstaaten. Die Öffentliche Verwaltung:727–734

Dörr O (2017) European Social Charter. In: Schmahl S, Breuer M (eds) The Council of Europe. Its law and policies, Chapter 23. Oxford University Press

Eichenhofer E (2012) Der soziale Rechtsstaat – ein Staat sozialer Rechte? In: Haerendel U (ed) Gerechtigkeit im Sozialstaat. Nomos, Baden-Baden, pp 139–152

Enders C (2005) Sozialstaatlichkeit im Spannungsfeld von Eigenverantwortung und Fürsorge. Veröffentlichungen der Vereinigung der Deutschen Staatsrechtslehrer 64:7–52

Federal Ministry for Economic Cooperation and Development (*Bundesministerium für wirtschaftliche Zusammenarbeit und Entwicklung*) (2015a) Eine Welt ohne Hunger ist möglich: Lösungsansätze der deutschen Entwicklungspolitik, December 2015, Berlin

Federal Ministry for Economic Cooperation and Development (*Bundesministerium für wirtschaftliche Zusammenarbeit und Entwicklung*) (2015b) BMZ-Bildungsstrategie: Gerechte Chancen auf hochwertige Bildung schaffen, July 2015, Berlin

Federal Ministry for Economic Cooperation and Development (*Bundesministerium für wirtschaftliche Zusammenarbeit und Entwicklung*) (2017a) Perspektiven für Flüchtlinge schaffen, March 2017, Berlin

Federal Ministry for Economic Cooperation and Development (*Bundesministerium für wirtschaftliche Zusammenarbeit und Entwicklung*) (2017b) Deutsche Entwicklungszusammenarbeit wirkt: Beispiele im Überblick, January 2017, Berlin

Federal Ministry for Economic Cooperation and Development (*Bundesministerium für wirtschaftliche Zusammenarbeit und Entwicklung*) (2017c) Der Zukunftsvertrag für die Welt: Die Agenda 2030 für nachhaltige Entwicklung, March 2017, Berlin

Federal Ministry for Economic Cooperation and Development (*Bundesministerium für wirtschaftliche Zusammenarbeit und Entwicklung*) (2017d) Afrika und Europa: Neue Partnerschaft für Entwicklung, Frieden und Zukunft, January 2017, Berlin

Federal Ministry of Labour and Social Affairs (*Bundesministerium für Arbeit und Soziales*) (2017) Lebenslagen in Deutschland. Der Fünfte Armuts- und Reichtumsbericht der Bundesregierung, April 2017, Berlin

Funke A (2017) Das Flüchtlingsrecht zwischen Menschenrecht. Hilfspflicht und Verantwortung. JuristenZeitung:533–542

Giegerich T (2008) Steuern Völker- und Europarecht die Globalisierung "im Geiste der Brüderlichkeit"? – Einführender Überblick. In: Giegerich T, Zimmermann A (eds) Wirtschaftliche, soziale und kulturelle Rechte im globalen Zeitalter. Duncker & Humblot, Berlin, pp 7–34

Gómez Urquijo LG (2017) The Europeanisation of policy to address poverty under the new economic governance: the contribution of the European Semester. J Poverty Social Justice 25:49–64

Grabenwarter C (2006) Sozialstandards in der Europäischen Menschenrechtskonvention. In: Becker U et al (eds) Die Implementierung internationaler Sozialstandards. Nomos, Baden-Baden, pp 83–121

Grewe C (2012) Wirtschaftliche, soziale und kulturelle Rechte: Menschen- oder auch Grundrecht? In: Hestermeyer H et al (eds) Coexistence, cooperation and solidarity. Liber Amicorum Rüdiger Wolfrum, vol I. Brill, Nijhoff, Leiden, pp 397–415

Groß T (2014) Integration durch Rechtsgleichheit. Deutsches Verwaltungsblatt 129:1217–1222

Grzeszick B (2013) Commentary on Article 20 Grundgesetz. In: Maunz T, Dürig G (eds) Grundgesetz, Kommentar, Loseblattsammlung, Art. 20. CH Beck, München

Guibboni S (2018) Free movement of persons and transnational solidarity in the European Union: a melancholic eulogy. In: Matteucci S, Halliday S (eds) Social rights in Europe in an age of austerity. Routledge, London, pp 273–290

Harris D, Darcy J (2001) The European Social Charter, 2nd edn. Ardsley, New York

Herdegen M (2009) Commentary on Article 1 Grundgesetz. In: Maunz T, Dürig G (eds) Grundgesetz, Kommentar, Loseblattsammlung, Art. 1. CH Beck, München
Higham I (2013) 'Re-righting Business'. John Ruggie and the struggle to develop international human rights norms for transnational firms. Hum Rights Q 35:333–364
Höfling W (2018) Commentary on Article 1 Grundgesetz. In: Sachs M (ed) Grundgesetz, Kommentar, Art. 1, 8th edn, CH Beck, München. 1
Hofmann H (2018) Commentary on Article 20 Grundgesetz. In: Schmidt-Bleibtreu B, Hofmann H, Henneke H-G (eds) Grundgesetz, Kommentar, Art. 20, 14th edn. Heymanns, Köln
Hogan M (1987) The Marshall Plan: America, Britain and the reconstruction of Western Europe (1947–1952). Cambridge University Press
Hummer W (2018) Commentary on Article 216 TFEU. In: Vedder C, Heintschel von Heinegg W (eds) Europäisches Unionsrecht, Kommentar, Art. 216, 2nd edn, Nomos, Baden-Baden
Isensee J (2011) Das Grundrecht als Abwehrrecht und als staatliche Schutzpflicht. In: Isensee J, Kirchhof P (eds) Handbuch des Staatsrechts, § 191, vol IX, 3rd edn. CF Müller, Heidelberg
Janda C (2013) Quo vadis, AsylbLG? Zeitschrift für Ausländerrecht und Ausländerpolitik:175–182
Jarass HD (2016a) Commentary on Article 20 Grundgesetz. In: Jarass HD, Pieroth B (eds) Grundgesetz, Kommentar, Art. 20, 14th edn. CH Beck, München
Jarass HD (2016b) Commentary on Article 34 EU Charter of Fundamental Rights. In: Jarass HD (ed) Charta der Grundrechte der Europäischen Union, Kommentar, Art. 34, 3rd edn. CH Beck, München
Kälin W (2017) Klimaflüchtlinge oder Katastrophenvertriebene? Vereinte Nationen 2017:207–212
Kaltenborn M, Tröppner D (2017) Globales Gesundheitsrecht. JuristenZeitung:745–754
Khan D-E (2017) Commentary on Article 208 TFEU. In: Geiger R, Khan D-E, Kotzur M (eds) EUV/AEUV, Kommentar, Art. 208, 6th edn. CH Beck, München
Kingreen T (2016) Commentary on Article 34 EU Charter of Fundamental Rights. In: Calliess C, Ruffert M (eds) Das Verfassungsrecht der Europäischen Union mit Europäischer Grundrechtecharta, Kommentar, Art. 34, 5th edn. CH Beck, München
Kirchhof F (2015) Die Entwicklung des Sozialverfassungsrechts. Neue Zeitschrift für Sozialrecht:1–8
Klein E (2015a) Die internationale Dimension des demographischen Wandels. In: Calliess C (ed) Herausforderungen and Staat und Verfassung. Liber Amicorum Torsten Stein. Nomos, Baden-Baden, pp 176–195
Klein E (2015b) The importance and challenges of value-based legal orders. Intercultural Hum Rights Law Rev 20:1–23
Klein E (2017) Zum (völker-)rechtlichen Unter- und Hintergrund von Menschenrechtsverträgen: Gibt es ein menschenrechtliches corpus iuris? Archiv des Völkerrechts 55:303–323
Kluth W (2015) Das Asylverfahrensbeschleunigungsgesetz. Zeitschrift für Ausländerrecht und Ausländerpolitik:337–343
Kohl H (2009) Vom Mauerfall zur Wiedervereinigung. Meine Erinnerungen, Knaur, München
Kradolfer M (2012) Verpflichtungsgrad sozialer Menschenrechte. Archiv des Völkerrechts 50:255–284
Kuon D (2010) Good governance im europäischen Entwicklungsrecht. Nomos, Baden-Baden
Langford M (2009) The justiciability of social rights: from practice to theory. In: Langford M (ed) Social rights jurisprudence. Cambridge University Press, pp 3–45
Laskowski S (2017) Nachhaltige Wasserwirtschaft zwischen UN-Agenda 2030 und CETA. Zeitschrift für Umweltrecht:65–66
Leisner WG (2018) Commentary on Article 20 Grundgesetz. In: Sodan H (ed) Grundgesetz, Kommentar, Art. 20, 4th edn. CH Beck, München
Lembke U (2018) European case studies: Germany. In: Matteucci S, Halliday S (eds) Social rights in Europe in an age of austerity. Routledge, London, pp 54–79
Lenze A (2011) Sind die neuen Hartz-IV-Sätze verfassungskonform? Neue Zeitschrift für Verwaltungsrecht:1104–1108

Lerch M (2004) Menschenrechte und europäische Außenpolitik. Verlag für Sozialwissenschaften, Wiesbaden
Lorenzmeier S (2006) Völkerrechtswidrigkeit der Einführung von Studienbeiträgen und deren Auswirkung auf die deutsche Rechtsordnung. Neue Zeitschrift für Verwaltungsrecht:759–762
Mahler C, Follmar-Otto P (2011) Asylbewerberleistungsgesetz auf dem menschenrechtlichen Prüfstand. Zeitschrift für Ausländerrecht und Ausländerpolitik:378–383
Marauhn T (2004) Social rights beyond the tradition welfare state: international instruments and the concept of individual entitlements. In: Benvenisti E, Nolte G (eds) The welfare state, globalization, and international law. Springer, Heidelberg, pp 275–319
McCorquodale R (2012) International human rights law and transnational corporations: responsibilities and cooperation? In: Hestermeyer H et al (eds) Coexistence, cooperation and solidarity. Liber Amicorum Rüdiger Wolfrum, vol I. Brill, Nijhoff, Leiden, pp 453–475
Meyer-Ladewig J, Renger D (2017) Commentary on Article 53 ECHR. In: Meyer-Ladewig J et al (eds) Europäische Menschenrechtskonvention, Kommentar, Art. 53, 4th edn. Nomos, Baden-Baden
Müller A (2009) Limitations to and derogations from economic, social and cultural rights. Hum Rights Law Rev 9:557–601
Murswiek C (2011) Grundrechte als Teilhaberechte. In: Isensee J, Kirchhof P (eds) Handbuch des Staatsrechts, § 192, vol IX, 3rd edn. CF Müller, Heidelberg
Neubeck X (2002) Die Europäische Sozialcharta und ihre Protokolle. Peter Lang, Frankfurt
Nolte J (2013) Rationale Rechtsfindung im Sozialrecht: Die vom Bundesverfassungsgericht aufgestellten Anforderungen an die Bestimmung des Existenzminimums im Lichte neuerer sozialgerichtlicher Rechtsprechung. Der Staat 52:245–265
Oppermann T, Classen CD, Nettesheim M (2016) Europarecht, 7th edn. CH Beck, München
Papier H-J (2006) Grundrechte und Sozialstaatsbestimmung. In: Merten D, Papier H-J (eds) Handbuch der Grundrechte, § 30, vol II. CF Müller, Heidelberg
Partsch KJ (1986) Menschenrechte und "Rechte der Völker": Eine Standortbestimmung. Vereinte Nationen 34:153–160
Partsch KJ (1987) The enforcement of human rights and peoples' rights. In: Bernhardt R, Jolowicz J-A (eds) International enforcement of human rights. Springer, Heidelberg, pp 25–29
Pellonpää M (1994) Economic, social and cultural rights. In: Macdonald RS, Matscher F, Petzold H (eds) The European system for the protection of human rights. Nijhoff, Dordrecht, pp 855–874
Peña-Casas R (2011) Europe 2020 and the fight against poverty and social exclusion: fooled into marriage? Soc Dev Eur Union:159–185
Rawls J (1979) Eine Theorie der Gerechtigkeit. Akademie Verlag, Berlin
Rawls J (2002) Das Recht der Völker. De Gruyter, Berlin
Riedel E (1989) Menschenrechte der dritten Dimension. Europäische Grundrechte Zeitschrift 16:9–21
Riedel E (2005) International law shaping constitutional law: realization of economic, social and cultural rights. In: Riedel E (ed) Constitutionalism – old concepts, new worlds. Berliner Wissenschaftsverlag, Berlin, pp 105–121
Riedel E (2008) Zur Durchsetzung wirtschaftlicher, sozialer und kultureller Rechte im Völkerrecht. In: Giegerich T, Zimmermann A (eds) Wirtschaftliche, soziale und kulturelle Rechte im globalen Zeitalter. Duncker & Humblot, Berlin, pp 71–93
Riedel E, Söllner S (2006) Studiengebühren im Lichte des UN-Sozialpakts. JuristenZeitung:270–277
Rixen S (2015) Zwischen Hilfe, Abschreckung und Pragmatismus: Gesundheitsrecht der Flüchtlingskrise. Neue Zeitschrift für Verwaltungsrecht:1640–1644
Robbers G (2009) Commentary on Article 20 Grundgesetz. In: Kahl W, Waldhoff C, Walter C (eds) Bonner Kommentar zum Grundgesetz, Art. 20. CF Müller, Heidelberg
Rothkegel R (2012) Das Gericht wird's richten – das AsylbLG-Urteil des Bundesverfassungsgerichts und seine Ausstrahlungswirkungen. Zeitschrift für Ausländerrecht und Ausländerpolitik:357–369

Rudolf B (2014) Commentary on Article 34 EU Charter of Fundamental Rights. In: Meyer J (ed) Charta der Grundrechte der EU, Kommentar, Art. 34, 4th edn. Nomos, Baden-Baden
Sachs M (2018) Commentary on Article 20 Grundgesetz. In: Sachs M (ed) Grundgesetz, Kommentar, Art. 20, 8th edn. CH Beck, München
Schmahl S (2012) Deutschland und die europäische Integration – Grund und Grenzen der verfassungsrechtlichen Regelung unionsbezogener Fragen. Bayerische Verwaltungsblätter:1–8
Schmahl S (2016) Reflections on the categorization of international human rights. In: Ziebertz H-G, Ballin EH (eds) Freedom of religion in the 21st century. Brill, Leiden, pp 1–25
Schmahl S (2017a) Kinderrechtskonvention mit Zusatzprotokollen, Kommentar, 2nd edn. Nomos, Baden-Baden
Schmahl S (2017b) Meaning and effects of the European Convention on Human Rights and of the judgements of the European Court of Human Rights in Germany. J Siberian Federal Univ Hum Soc Sci 6:818–825
Schmahl S (2017c) Stellung und Rolle der UN-Behindertenrechtskonvention im Gefüge des universellen Menschenrechtsschutzsystems. In: Diekmann A et al (eds) Betreuungsrecht im internationalen Kontext: Aktuelle Aspekte in Deutschland – Betrifft: Betreuung, vol 15. Bochum, pp 82–89
Schmahl S, Jung F (2016) Die Unionsbürgerschaft: Ein komplexes Rechtsinstitut mit weitreichenden Folgen. Juristische Ausbildung:1272–1284
Schmahl S, Winkler T (2010) Schutz vor Armut in der EMRK? Archiv des Völkerrechts 48:405–430
Schmalenbach K (2014) Assoziierung und Erweiterung. In: von Arnauld A (ed) Europäische Außenbeziehungen, Enzyklopädie Europarecht, § 6, vol X. Nomos, Baden-Baden
Schmalenbach K (2016) Commentary on Articles 208 and 2017 TFEU. In: Calliess C, Ruffert M (eds) Das Verfassungsrecht der Europäischen Union mit Europäischer Grundrechtecharta, Kommentar, Art. 208, Art. 217, 5th edn. CH Beck, München
Shachar A (2009) The birthright lottery. Citizenship and global inequality. Harvard University Press
Sodan H (2004) Die "*Bürgerversicherung*" als Bürgerzwangsversicherung. Zeitschrift für Rechtspolitik:217–221
Sommermann K-P (2010) Commentary on Article 20 Grundgesetz. In: von Mangoldt H, Klein F, Starck C (eds) Grundgesetz, Kommentar, Art. 20, 6th edn. CH Beck, München
Stern K (1984) Staatsrecht, vol I. CH Beck, München
Streinz R, Kruis T (2018) Commentary on Article 208 TFEU. In: Streinz R (ed) EUV/AEUV, Kommentar, Art. 208, 3rd edn. CH Beck, München
Sudre F (2003) La protection des droits sociaux par la Cour européenne des Droits de l'Homme: un exercice de 'jurisprudence fiction' ? Revue trimestrielle des droits de l'homme:755–779
Terhechte JP (2012) Commentary on Article 216 TFEU. In: Schwarze J (ed) EU-Kommentar, Art. 216, 3rd edn. Nomos, Baden-Baden
Tomuschat C (1985) Human rights in a world-wide framework. Heidelberg J Int Law 45:547–584
Tomuschat C (2007) Social rights under the European Convention on Human Rights. In: Breitenmoser S et al (eds) Human rights, democracy and the rule of law. Liber Amicorum Luzius Wildhaber, NP Engel, Kehl, pp 837–864
Tomuschat C (2009) Die Einheit von liberalen Freiheitsrechten und sozialen Rechten. In: Gander H-H (ed) Menschenrechte: Philosophische und juristische Positionen. Alber, Freiburg, pp 140–165
Tomuschat C (2014) Human rights: between idealism and realism, 3rd edn. Oxford University Press
Trilsch M (2012) Die Justiziabilität wirtschaftlicher, sozialer und kultureller Rechte im innerstaatlichen Recht. Springer, Heidelberg
Uerpmann-Wittzack R (2016) Die UN-Behindertenrechtskonvention in der Praxis des Ausschusses für die Rechte von Menschen mit Behinderungen. Archiv des Völkerrechts 54:181–212
Vasak K (1979) For the third generation of human rights: the rights of *solidarity*. Inaugural Lecture to the Tenth Study Session of the International Institute of Human Rights, Strasbourg, 2–27 July

Vogel K (1964) Die Verfassungsentscheidung des Grundgesetzes für die internationale Zusammenarbeit. Mohr Siebeck, Tübingen

Vöneky S (2014) Der Einfluss völkerrechtlicher Rahmenbedingungen auf die Entwicklung sozialer staatlicher Strukturen. In: Stürner R, Bruns A (eds) Globalisierung und Sozialstaatsprinzip. Mohr Siebeck, Tübingen, pp 63–81

Vöneky S, Beylage-Haarmann B (2015) Commentary on Article 217 TFEU. In: Grabitz E, Hilf M, Nettesheim M (eds) Das Recht der Europäischen Union, Kommentar, Art. 217. CH Beck, München

Voßkuhle A (2011) Der Sozialstaat in der Rechtsprechung des Bundesverfassungsgerichts. Die Sozialgerichtsbarkeit:181–186

Waldron J (1993) Liberal rights. Collected papers 1981–1991. Cambridge University Press

Wallace D (2015) Human rights and business: a policy oriented perspective. Brill, Leiden

Weissbrodt D (2013) Roles and responsibilities of non-state actors. In: Shelton D (ed) The Oxford handbook of international human rights law. Oxford University Press, pp 719–736

Wellman C (2000) Solidarity, the individual, and human rights. Hum Rights Q 22:639–657

Windthorst K (2017) Commentary on Article 20 Grundgesetz. In: Gröpl C, Windthorst K, von Coelln C (eds) Grundgesetz, Studienkommentar, Art. 20, 3rd edn. CH Beck, München

Wolfrum R (2013) Solidarity. In: Shelton D (ed) The Oxford handbook of international human rights law. Oxford University Press, pp 401–419

Zacher HF (2004) Das soziale Staatsziel. In: Isensee J, Kirchhof P (eds) Handbuch des Staatsrechts, § 28, vol II, 3rd edn. CF Müller, Heidelberg

Zimmermann A (2015) Commentary on Article 208 TFEU. In: von der Groeben H, Schwarze J, Hatje A (eds) Europäisches Unionsrecht, Kommentar, Art. 208, 7th edn. Nomos, Baden-Baden

Chapter 6
The Fight Against Poverty and the Right to Development: The Ghana National Chapter

Raymond A. Atuguba

Abstract Development has no end; the journey to that place of sublime comfort exists in perpetuity; and with this in mind, the world must remain ever resilient in our march towards development, as we strategically pull down the walls of engrained and radical poverty. This paper investigates Ghana's outlook on development and the fight against poverty, through the lenses of the Constitution, Statutory Laws, International Law applicable in Ghana, National Policies, Government Institutions, Case Law and Development Programmes; highlighting the areas of significant improvement and marking out the ailing parts that need pruning.

The opener to this Chapter takes an in-depth view into the bond between Ghana's municipal law and the law of nations (international law) and discerns ways by which Ghana's law unites with conventions, treaties, principles, customs and usages of public international law, which contribute immensely to the expansion of the pathways to development; at the same time exploring a wealth of multilateral treaties signed or ratified by Ghana at the sub-regional, regional, and global levels. It proceeds to discuss the local measures and mechanisms to attain enhanced development in Ghana, especially, the role of judicial and quasi-judicial bodies in promoting the right to development through adjudication and enforcement of human rights claims. However, the argument is made that the rights which usually come to the fore are civil and political; with a dearth of judicial activism in advancing purely economic, social and cultural rights. The paper also brings to light, Ghana's methodological approach towards the realization of the Sustainable Development Goals (SDGs) and various bilateral deals with foreign countries to further her developmental interests.

I thank Phoebe Washington-Nortey, Lorenda Parker, and Kobby Afari Yeboah for research and editorial assistance in the course of writing this article.

R. A. Atuguba (✉)
University of Ghana School of Law, Legon, Accra, Ghana

M. Andenas et al. (eds.), *The Fight Against Poverty and the Right to Development*, Ius Comparatum - Global Studies in Comparative Law 52,
https://doi.org/10.1007/978-3-030-57324-9_6

Relationship Between Ghanaian Domestic Law and International law

How Social Rights in International Law are Transposed into Domestic Law with Other International Law Obligations

The 1992 Constitution of Ghana is "the supreme law of Ghana and any other law found to be inconsistent with any provision of this Constitution shall, to the extent of the inconsistency, be void".[1] The Constitution provides in its Article 11, the Sources of Law in Ghana. These are: the Constitution itself; enactments made by or under the authority of Parliament; any Orders, Rules and Regulations made by any person or authority under a power conferred by the Constitution; the existing law—a reference to rules of law applicable in Ghana before the coming into force of the 1992 Constitution in January 1993 and not inconsistent with that Constitution; and the common law,[2] in that order. According to the Constitution, the common law encapsulates the Customary Law, a reference to the rules of law which by custom are applicable to particular communities in Ghana.[3]

The Constitution does not, in the fore, include International Law as part of the laws of Ghana. Therefore, to be part of the laws of Ghana, International Law must be located in one or more of the sources of law listed above. This is the typical dualist scenario, where International Law commitments need to be positively incorporated into domestic law in order to be effective in a State. This is contradistinguished from monism, where international law commitments are almost automatically translated into domestic law and directly enforceable.[4]

---

[1]See: Article 1 (2) of the 1992 Constitution of Ghana which states: "This Constitution shall be the supreme law of Ghana and any other law found to be inconsistent with any provision of this Constitution shall, to the extent of the inconsistency, be void."

[2]Under Article 11 (2) of the 1992 Constitution of Ghana, it is provided: "The common law of Ghana shall comprise the rules of law generally known as the common law, the rules generally known as the doctrines of equity and the rules of customary law including those determined by the Superior Court of Judicature."

[3]See also: Article 272 which states: "The National House of Chiefs shall; (b) undertake the progressive study, interpretation and codification of customary law with a view to evolving, in appropriate cases, a unified system of rules of customary law, and compiling the customary laws and lines of succession applicable to each stool or skin." The Courts Act 1993, (Act 459), section 55 (2) provides that "If there is doubt as to the existence or content of a rule of customary law relevant in any proceedings before a court, the court may adjourn the proceedings to enable an inquiry to be made under subsection (3) of this section after the court has considered submissions made by or on behalf of the parties and after the court has considered reported cases, textbooks and other sources that may be appropriate to the proceedings". Section 55(3) of Act 459 provides that "the inquiry shall be held as part of the proceedings in such manner as the court considers expedient, and the provisions of this Act relating to the attendance and testimony of witnesses shall apply with such modifications as may appear to the court to be necessary".

[4]Shaw (2003), pp. 121–124; Brownlie (2003), pp. 31–33.

Flowing from this, I identify seven (7) ways by which the array of international rules, practices and conventions may crystallize to form a part of Ghana's domestic law. These modes are:

1. Ratification by Parliament of an International Treaty or Convention through the mechanism of an Act of Parliament;
2. Ratification by Parliament of an International Treaty or Convention through the mechanism of a Resolution of Parliament;
3. Where the provisions of Ghana's Constitution or other laws of Ghana coincide with principles of International Law;
4. Incorporation of International Law by reference to constitutional provisions;
5. Incorporation of International Law by way of interpretation and exposition of particular provisions of Ghana's laws;
6. Where there is a lacuna or unclarity in Ghana law respecting a particular issue and government officials or judges resort to International Law principles to fill that void; and
7. Incorporation by reference to Customary International Law through the medium of the common law.

Traditionally, International Law in the form of treaties and conventions, are made part of Ghana law by Parliament passing them into law. In practice, this is done by passing an Act of Parliament and annexing the Treaty or Convention as a Schedule to the Act.[5] This is in accordance with Article 75 of Ghana's Constitution, which provides that the President may execute or cause to be executed treaties, agreements or conventions in the name of Ghana, and these shall be subject to ratification by an Act of Parliament or a Resolution of Parliament.

Under Article 106 of the Ghana Constitution, ratification by Act of Parliament gives such an international agreement the force of law. It acquires the same status as any other Act of Parliament and is subject only to the Constitution. It also has the potential to override any prior Act that is inconsistent with it. Examples of ratification by this mode are the African and UN Refugee Conventions[6] which find expression by way of domestication in Ghana's Refugee Act (PNDCL 305) of 1992.

The Ghana Constitution provides another method by which Parliament may ratify international treaties and conventions. This other method, also contained in article 75, is by "a Resolution of Parliament supported by the votes of more than one-half of all the members of Parliament".[7] Ghana's Supreme Court has recently held in a line

---

[5]The United Nations Convention on the Recognition and Enforcement of Foreign Arbitral Awards (New York, 1958) is annexed to the Alternative Dispute Resolution (ADR) Act of Ghana, 2010 (Act 798) as Schedule One.

[6]AU Convention Governing Specific Aspects of Refugee Problems in Africa (1969); the UN Convention Relating to the Status of Refugees (1951); and the UN Protocol Relating to the Status of Refugees (1967).

[7]This is laid down in article 75(2)(b) of the Constitution, 1992. It states that: a treaty, agreement or convention executed by or under the authority of the President shall be subject to ratification by a resolution supported by the votes of more than one-half of all members of Parliament.

of cases, that this second method of ratifying international treaties and conventions does not have the effect of incorporating them into the domestic laws of Ghana, in the manner and with the effect the first method does. A Resolution by Parliament does not give the International Agreement the force of Law in Ghana. It only signifies that Ghana is bound internationally by the Agreement. Thus, a Resolution of Parliament cannot override other Acts of Parliament or Regulations made under Acts of Parliament.

In the case of *Republic v. High Court (Commercial Division), Accra; Ex parte Attorney General (NML Capital and Republic of Argentina–Interested Parties),*[8] the effect of ratification by a Resolution of Parliament was explained by Justice Date-Bah in the Supreme Court when he said:

> . . .treaties, even when the particular treaty has been ratified by Parliament, do not alter municipal law until they are incorporated into Ghanaian law by appropriate legislation. This position of the law is usually referred to as reflecting the "dualist" school of thought, as distinct from the monist approach followed by some other States. . . . The mere fact that a treaty has been ratified by Parliament through one of the two modes indicated above does not, of itself, mean that it is incorporated into Ghanaian law. A treaty may come into force and regulate the rights and obligations of the State on the international plane, without changing rights and obligations under municipal law. Where the mode of ratification adopted is through an Act of Parliament, that Act may incorporate the treaty, by appropriate language, into the municipal law of Ghana. . . . The need for the legislative incorporation of treaty provisions into municipal law before domestic courts can apply those provisions is reflective of the dualist stance of Commonwealth common law courts and backed by a long string of authorities. . . . From the above, the court confirmed the dualist nature of Ghana's legal system and emphasized that, until a treaty is incorporated under the municipal law of Ghana by the appropriate language by an Act of Parliament, its ratification at the international level only regulates the rights and obligations of the State on the international plane, without changing rights and obligations under the municipal law.

On the same subject of ratification or approval by Parliament short of legislative action, Atuguba JSC, also in Ghana's Supreme Court, said in *John Ndebugre v Attorney General,*[9] that ". . .It must be emphasized that when parliamentary approval is given under article 268(1) the agreement in question remains an executive act and not the act of the legislature. . ." which therefore strips it of power to override a Statute.

It is worthy of mention that apart from the constitutional safeguards that entrench the dualist reception of international law in Ghanaian jurisprudence, an Inter-Ministerial Committee on 5th February 2008 brought forth the "The Republic of Ghana TREATY MANUAL"[10] which specifies the guidelines for the domestic ratification of treaties/agreements/conventions under the dualist approach and for

---

[8]The Republic v High Court (Commercial Division), Accra, *Ex parte* Attorney-General, NML Capital Ltd. 1st Interested Party; Republic of Argentina, 2nd Interested Party (Supreme Court Decision-Suit No. J5/10/2013).

[9]John Ndebugre v Attorney-General (Supreme Court Decision-Suit No. J1/5/2013).

[10]Republic of Ghana Treaty Manual. United Nations Organization (Legal). Available at: http://legal.un.org/avl/documents/scans/GhanaTreatyManual2009.pdf?teil=II&j.

the transformation of treaties into national legislation. By all indications, Ghana is an intentionally dualist State. However, this does not mean that International Law cannot apply in Ghana outside intentional legislation of same into domestic law. Both Articles 40[11] and 73[12] of the Ghana Constitution require the government to fulfil her international legal obligations even when these are not domesticated. This point was emphasised by the Ghana Supreme Court in *New Patriotic Party v. Inspector-General of Police*[13] where Justice Archer profoundly stated: "I do not think that the fact that Ghana has not passed specific legislation to give effect to the charter [African Charter on Human and Peoples' Rights], means the charter cannot be relied upon." For Justice Archer, it is enough (for their application) that such instruments are in consonance with the provisions of the 1992 Constitution of Ghana.

There are, therefore, other ways by which International Law finds expression in Ghana law and we will identify these presently. Aside the two modes contained in article 75 and discussed above, a third is where the Constitution and laws of Ghana, by their clear words coincide with the provisions of International Law. For example, our Constitution and laws do not condone genocide,[14] a crime that is also proscribed by International Law.

The fourth scenario is where our laws incorporate International Law by reference. For example, Article 33(5) of the Ghana Constitution provides that: the rights, duties, declarations and guarantees relating to the fundamental human rights and freedoms specifically mentioned in Chapter 12 of the 1992 Constitution of Ghana, shall not be regarded as excluding others not specifically mentioned which are considered to be inherent in a democracy and intended to secure the freedom and dignity of man.[15] This means that all the body of International Human Rights Law, which meets the constitutional standards just articulated, are incorporated into Ghana law by virtue of that provision. Again, in the case of *New Patriotic Party v. Inspector General of Police*,[16] Justice Hayfron-Benjamin affirmed that Article 33(5) exists to accommodate rights not specified in the Constitution. This case dealt with an alleged breach of Article 21 of the 1992 Constitution of Ghana, which enshrines freedom of

---

[11]Article 40 provides: "...In its dealings with other nations, the Government shall...(c) promote respect for international law, treaty obligations and the settlement of international disputes by peaceful means; (d) adhere to the principles enshrined in or as the case may be, the aims and ideals of- i) the Charter of the United Nations; ii) the Charter of the Organisation of African Unity; iii) the Commonwealth; iv) the Treaty of the Economic Community of West African States; and v) any other international organisation of which Ghana is a member."

[12]Article 73 provides that, "The Government of Ghana shall conduct its international affairs in consonance with the accepted principles of public international law and diplomacy in a manner consistent with the national interest of Ghana."

[13]New Patriotic Party v. Inspector-General of Police [1993–94] 2 GLR 459.

[14]Section 49A of the Criminal and Other Offences Act, 1960 (Act 29) of Ghana says: "(1) Whoever commits genocide shall on conviction be sentenced to death."

[15]See: Article 33 (5) of the 1992 Constitution of Ghana.

[16]New Patriotic Party v Inspector General of Police [1993–94] 2 GLR 459 p. 505.

speech, expression, assembly and of movement. The Plaintiffs in this case sought a declaration that Ghana's Public Order Law[17] was unconstitutional to the extent that it required the procuration of a permit or licence in order to proceed with a public demonstration. Justice Hayfron-Benjamin in delivering his judgment, said as follows:

> It is interesting to note that article 33(5) of the Constitution, 1992 extends the scope of human rights enjoyment when it says that the rights mentioned in chapter 5 '. . .shall not be regarded as excluding others not specifically mentioned which are considered to be inherent in a democracy and intended to secure the freedom and dignity of man.' I have no doubt in my mind that the framers of the Constitution, 1992 intended that the citizens of this country should enjoy the fullest measure of responsible human and civil rights. Therefore, any law which seeks to abridge these freedoms and rights must be struck down as unconstitutional. The requirement of a permit or licence is one such abridgement of the constitutional right.

Again, articles 73 and 40 of the Constitution provide that the Government of Ghana shall conduct her international affairs in consonance with the accepted principles of public international law and diplomacy in a manner consistent with the national interest of Ghana; and that, in its dealings with other nations, the Government shall promote and protect the interests of Ghana; seek the establishment of a just and equitable international economic and social order; promote respect for international law, treaty obligations and the settlement of international disputes by peaceful means; and adhere to the principles enshrined in or as the case may be, the aims and ideals of: the Charter of the United Nations; the Charter of the African Union; the Commonwealth; the Treaty of the Economic Community of West African States; and any other international organisation of which Ghana is a member.

Flowing from the above, it is possible for Ghanaian officials and judges to incorporate the provisions of International Law to the laws of Ghana despite the missing ingredient of parliamentary ratification by Act of Parliament, so as to ensure that Ghana meets her international obligations as stated in the Constitution.[18] This is what happened in the case of *Tsatsu Tsikata v. The Republic*,[19] where Justice Atuguba speaking in the Supreme Court held that:

> It is clear that if Ghanaians are to be free from the effects of decisions such as the infamous case of Re Akoto,[20] when an opportunity of upholding fundamental human rights was

[17]Public Order Decree 1972 (NRCD 68). This has been repealed by the Public Order Act of 1994 (Act 491).

[18]In the Commissioner, CHRAJ, Grace Fosu & Thelma Hammond v. Ghana National Fire Service & Attorney General (Suit No. HR 0063/2017), the trial High Court judge applied the Convention on the Elimination of all Forms of Discrimination against Women (CEDAW) and the International Covenant on Civil and Political Rights (ICCPR) in arriving at a decision, though those conventions have not been ratified by way of Act of parliament.

[19]Tsikata v. Republic Criminal Appeal (J3/3/2010) [2011] GHASC 3 (19 January 2011) [online] Available at: https://ghalii.org/gh/judgment/supreme-court/2011/3.

[20]Re: Akoto and 7 Others, [1961] GLR 523.

> allowed to slip away from the Supreme Court, the courts of today should strive to uphold these rights whenever a construction in that regard is possible. The attitude of the 1992 Constitution towards international law and its proper application is clearly stated in article 40 of the constitution in Chapter 6, The Directive Principles of State Policy... But the core principle is in article 73[21]....

The fifth scenario for its application is where International Law is incorporated into Ghana law by way of interpretation and exposition of particular provisions of our laws. For example, in the case of *Gladys Mensah v Stephen Mensah*,[22] which dealt with the devolution of marital properties upon divorce, the Supreme Court referred to the provisions of the Universal Declaration of Human Rights, and the Convention on the Elimination of all forms of Discrimination Against Women (CEDAW), which latter Convention has not been domesticated into Ghanaian law by legislation, to elucidate and extend the relevant elements in Ghana's constitution on non-discrimination against women.[23] Justice Jones Dotse stated that:

> It is to be understood that discrimination and violence against women differ from country to country and each situation has to be considered on a case by case basis. In our Ghanaian context, we have referred to the provisions of article 33 (5) of the Constitution...Article (1) of the Universal Declaration of Human Rights provides as follows:
>
> **'All human beings are born free and equal in dignity and rights.** They are endowed with reason and conscience, and should act towards one another in a spirit of brotherhood.'"
>
> Article 12 (1) and (2) of the Constitution 1992 give the scope and content of the Fundamental Human Rights and Freedoms which the individual is entitled to enjoy. As a matter of fact, even though the Universal Declaration of Human Rights is not a binding treaty, its principles and underpinning philosophy have been incorporated into national constitutions and referred to by several national courts. This is the context into which our national Constitution 1992 has to be understood in relation to this principle of Jurisprudence of Equality. Ghana is also a signatory to the Convention on the Elimination of all forms of Discrimination Against Women (CEDAW)...Furthermore, article 5 of CEDAW adds a key concept to international equal protection analysis; the need to eradicate customary and all other practices which are based on the idea of the inferiority or the superiority of the sexes or on stereotyped roles for men and women. He therefore held that, "On the basis of the above conventions and treaties and drawing a linkage between them and the Constitution 1992, it is our considered view that the time has indeed come for the integration of this principle of 'Jurisprudence of Equality' into our rules of interpretation such that meaning will be given to the contents of the Constitution 1992, especially on the devolution of property to spouses after divorce".

In doing this, the Ghana Supreme Court remained faithful to the Interpretation Act of that country which provides as follows: "Where a Court is concerned with ascertaining the meaning of an enactment, the Court may consider a relevant treaty,

[21]Republic of Ghana Treaty Manual. United Nations Organization (Legal). Available at: http://legal.un.org/avl/documents/scans/GhanaTreatyManual2009.pdf?teil=II&j.

[22]Gladys Mensah v. Stephen Mensah [2012] 1 SCGLR 300.

[23]This provision (Article 22(3) of the 1992 Constitution) states that: "With a view to achieving the full realization of the rights referred to...(a) spouses shall have equal access to property jointly acquired during marriage; (b) assets which are jointly acquired during marriage shall be distributed equitably between the spouses upon dissolution of the marriage."

agreement, convention or any other international instrument which has been ratified by Parliament or is referred to in the enactment of which copies have been presented to Parliament or where the Government is a signatory to the treaty or the other international agreement; and the *travaux preparatoires* or preparatory work relating to the treaty or the agreement. . ."[24] Although the provision does not appear to have been very carefully drafted, it is clear that the legislature intended to allow Ghana's judges to utilize a broad range of international law instruments as aids to the interpretation of domestic legislation even where the President has merely signed the international instrument.

Ghana's Supreme Court is consistently extending the inculcation of international law principles to treaties that obviously fall outside Ghana's regional circumference. Such is evidenced in the 2018 Supreme Court decision of *Republic v Eugene Baffoe-Bonnie & Others*,[25] where Adinyirah JSC (delivering judgment on behalf of the court) referred to Article 6 of the European Convention for the Protection of Human Rights and Fundamental Freedom which stresses on rudimentary principle of adequacy for preparation in a fair trial, in interpreting the full range of Article 19 (2) (e) and (g) of the 1992 Constitution of Ghana.

The sixth way by which International Law can become law in Ghana is where there is a lacuna or unclarity in Ghana law respecting a particular issue and government officials or judges resort to International Law principles to fill that void. In *Ghana Lotto Operators Association v. National Lottery Authority*,[26] the Supreme Court referred to the International Convention on Economic, Social and Cultural Rights to fill a lacuna on the Right to Work in Ghana. In that case, Justice Date-Bah stated first of all that, *"the plaintiffs are not altogether explicit about how Act 722*[27] *violates Article 33(5). Clarity requires that the plaintiffs specify what rights of theirs have been infringed by Act 722 and which are not mentioned in Chapter 5 of the Constitution, but which should nevertheless be regarded as fundamental human rights or freedoms. Evidence of such rights can be obtained either from the provisions of international human rights instruments (and practice under them) or from the national human rights legislation and practice of other states"*. Therefore, the Supreme Court implied that where a Fundamental Human Right or elements of it are not clear in the Constitution of Ghana, reference may be made to international conventions, and practice under those conventions, for clarity and supplementation. The Supreme Court then proceeded to draw on the provisions of the international Human Rights Instruments on the Right to Work, stating that the right to work is "*an important human right which is inherent in a democracy*" but is not explicitly provided for

[24] Section 10 (1) (c) of the 2009 Interpretation Act of Ghana (Act 792). The inelegant phraseology is the drafter's.

[25] The Republic v Eugene Baffoe-Bonnie and 4 others (Supreme Court Decision-Suit No. J1/06/2018).

[26] Ghana Lotto Operators Association v. National Lottery Authority [2007–2008] SCGLR 1088.

[27] The National Lotto Act, 2006, (Act 722).

in Ghanaian Law. In this, the Supreme Court emphasized the fourth method for the application of International Law in Ghana discussed above. Moving on, and particularly on the sixth method now under discussion, the Supreme Court held in this case that "the right to work may be a human right that international human right instruments recognize" and proceeded to draw elements of that right from "Article 6 of the International Covenant on Economic, Social and Cultural Rights, 1966...".[28]

The seventh source for the application of international law in Ghana is by reference to Customary International Law[29] principles through the medium of the Common Law. It is conceivable that the Common Law of Ghana, as a Source of Law, includes Customary International Law.[30] Nevertheless, in the *Republic v. High Court; Ex parte Attorney General* case,[31] Justice Date-Bah clarified this contention when he explained that:

> Ghanaian law on this basic question is no different from the usual position of Commonwealth common law jurisdictions. It is that customary international law is part of Ghanaian law; incorporated by the weight of common law case law...In Chung Chi Cheung v The King [1939] AC 160, the Judicial Committee of the Privy Council, speaking through Lord Atkin, stated this common law position as follows (at p. 168): 'The courts acknowledge the existence of a body of rules which nations accept among themselves. On any judicial issue they seek to ascertain what the relevant rule is, and, having found it, they will treat it as incorporated into the domestic law, so far as it is not inconsistent with rules enacted by statutes or finally declared by their tribunals.

There are, therefore, at least seven (7) ways of incorporating International Law into Ghana's domestic legal regime, as discussed above. In summary, where Ghana signs, ratifies, and then incorporates an International Instrument into her domestic law by legislation, she is bound by it internationally and domestically. Where she only signs or ratifies, but has not incorporated an Instrument into her domestic laws in this way, she is bound by it only at the international level, but not domestically. In this scenario, her obligation with respect to that instrument is to desist from conduct that defeats the purpose and objectives of the Instrument.[32]

---

[28]Ghana Lotto Operators Association v. National Lottery Authority [2007–2008] SCGLR 1088.

[29]The concept of customary international law entails two elements, namely State Practice and *Opinio Juris*. State practice is how states behave in practice that forms the basis of customary law. Evidence of what a state does can be obtained from numerous sources. Examples include, a government's administrative acts, legislation, decisions of courts and activities on the international stage, for example, treaty-making. *Opinio Juris* is a belief that a state activity is legally obligatory, and this forms the factor which turns the usage into a custom and renders it part of the rules of international law.

[30]See: Article 11(1)(e) and (3) of the 1992 Constitution of Ghana.

[31]The Republic v. High Court (Commercial Division), Accra, Ex Parte Attorney-General, NML Capital Ltd. 1st Interested Party; Republic of Argentina, 2nd Interested Party (Suit No.J5/10/2013).

[32]Affirmed by Article 18 of the Vienna Convention on the Law of Treaties. See Atuguba (2005), p. 19.

In addition, norms and principles of customary international law and principles of *jus cogens*[33] will bind Ghana since these principles are said to be non-derogable, whether or not Ghana formally incorporates them into domestic law.[34] Customary International Law and *jus cogens* are also part of the law of Ghana by virtue of the incorporation of the Common Law, which includes Customary International Law, into the laws of Ghana by Article 11 of the Constitution.

Also, norms and principles contained in International Instruments may nonetheless bind Ghana if they already form part of the domestic laws of Ghana; or where judges, by processes of interpretation, using domestic constitutional and legislative entry points, make International Law part of domestic law.

International or Regional Instruments Ratified by Ghana

Ghana after independence, has signed, and in some cases ratified on the international plane, the major international and regional treaties geared towards the protection and promotion of Human Rights. At the same time, the government has taken steps to review, repeal, and amend relevant parts of certain laws and enacted new ones to conform to the country's Constitution or its international commitments. At the international level, Ghana has signed (S) and/or ratified (R)[35] a cornucopia of conventions, treaties, agreements and protocols.[36] A host of international, regional and sub-regional treaties signed and/or ratified by Ghana is attached to this paper as an Appendix.

These international, regional and sub-regional agreements have political or socio-economic implications which Ghana believes are in line with her foreign policy, and are also crucial in advancing her national development. On the international scene, some of the most recent treaty ratifications include the Arms Trade Treaty of 2013

[33] *Jus cogens,* also known as peremptory norms, refers to certain fundamental principles of International Law which no international legal personality or State is permitted to set aside, violate or derogate from. *Jus cogens* has been captured under Article 53 of the Vienna Convention on the Law of Treaties (VCLT) concluded at Vienna on 23 May 1969 as follows: "A treaty is void if, at the time of its conclusion, it conflicts with a peremptory norm of general international law. For the purposes of the present Convention, a peremptory norm of general international law is a norm accepted and recognized by the international community of States as a whole as a norm from which no derogation is permitted and which can be modified only by a subsequent norm of general international law having the same character." (Article 53 is Captioned: TREATIES CONFLICTING WITH A PEREMPTORY NORM OF GENERAL INTERNATIONAL LAW ("JUS COGENS")). Examples of *jus cogens* norms include prohibitions against genocide, human trafficking and crimes against humanity.

[34] See Atuguba (2005), p. 14.

[35] University of Minnesota Database: [online] Available at: http://hrlibrary.umn.edu/research/ratification-ghana.html.

[36] Find list of regional and international instruments attached as Appendix, with Tables 6.1, 6.2, 6.3 and 6.4.

which was ratified by Ghana in 2015.[37] The Arms Trade Treaty (ATT) is an international treaty that regulates the international trade in conventional arms and seeks to prevent and eradicate illicit trade and diversion of conventional arms by establishing international standards governing arms transfers.[38] There is also the Paris Agreement of 2015, ratified just a year after its adoption in 2016. Its central aim is to strengthen the global response to the threat of climate change by keeping a global temperature rise this century well below 2 °C above pre-industrial levels and to pursue efforts to limit the temperature increase even further to 1.5 °C.[39]

Ghana has taken steps to meet the international labour standards designed by the International Labour Organization by signing or ratifying a total of 51 conventions, including all 8 of their Fundamental Conventions.[40] Continentally, Ghana has also demonstrated its resolve to combine forces with African Countries to foster development through African unity by ratifying instruments of the African Union, including being the first African country, together with Kenya, to ratify the Africa Continental Free Trade Agreement of 2018. Ghana has also demonstrated a commitment to sub-regional peace, security, stability, harmony and economic development through its membership of the Economic Community of West Africa States (ECOWAS) and the signing of its accompanying treaties.[41]

Despite the bold attempts made by Ghana to express her commitment towards international agreements by intimating consent through ratification, the country's parliamentary base has not been forthcoming in enacting Acts of Parliament that would fully incorporate the majority of treaties and conventions into national laws.

Constitutional Protection of the Right to an Adequate Standard of Living: The Right to Development and the Fight Against Poverty in the Ghanaian Context

Ghana recognizes the right to an adequate standard of living for her citizens. The 1992 Constitution provides that "the State shall, in particular, take all necessary steps to establish a sound and healthy economy whose underlying principles shall include the recognition that the most secure democracy is the one that assures the basic

[37] Refer to Appendix.

[38] Arms Trade Treaty (ATT); see https://thearmstradetreaty.org.

[39] UNFCC website: https://unfccc.int/process-and-meetings/the-paris-agreement/the-paris-agreement.

[40] International Labour Organization, *Ratifications for Ghana.* Available at: https://www.ilo.org/dyn/normlex/en/f?p=NORMLEXPUB:11200:0::NO::P11200_COUNTRY_ID:103231.

[41] Economic Community of West African States, 2013. Status of Ratification of the ECOWAS Revised Treaty, Protocols and Conventions as at 10th July, 2013. Available at: http://ecowasmigration.ug.edu.gh/wp-content/uploads/2015/04/ECOWAS-2013-Status-of-Ratification-of-ECOWAS-Revised-Treaty-and-protocols-as-at-10-July-2013.pdf.

necessities of life for its people as a fundamental duty."[42] In addition, "the State shall afford equality of economic opportunity to all citizens; and, in particular, the State shall take all necessary steps so as to ensure the full integration of women into the mainstream of the economic development of Ghana. The State shall also guarantee the ownership of property and the right of inheritance and shall safeguard the health, safety and welfare of all persons in employment, and shall establish the basis for the full deployment of the creative potential of all Ghanaians".[43] Further to this, article 37 (6) (a) provides that the State "shall ensure that [social security] contributory schemes are instituted and maintained that will guarantee economic security for self-employed and other citizens of Ghana." Even a cursory observation of these provisions shows that Ghana is intentional in ensuring a proper standard of living for its citizenry. There is no doubt that these measures are geared towards a fight against poverty of any form.

The Ghana Constitution enjoins the Executive, Legislature and the Judiciary; all organs of government and all legal persons, to respect and uphold all the fundamental Human Rights and freedoms contained in the Constitution.[44] The Constitution further provides that every person is entitled to these rights and freedoms,[45] and designates the High Court as Ghana's Human Rights Court.[46] Thus, the Constitution makes substantial effort to protect the rights and freedoms of the people of Ghana.

Although a broad range of rights with the capacity to concretize the Right to Development are contained in Ghana's Constitution, their realization, in accordance with the tenets of the 1986 Declaration of the Right to Development, is not a one-way street. The Right to Development (RTD) encompasses all Human Rights–civil, political, economic, social and cultural,[47] and so the protection of these rights in various forms under the Constitution of Ghana would equal the protection of the RTD. In the 2004 Right to Development Report: Ghana Country Study,[48] it was noted that "the measure of collective and individual wellbeing today is woven around basic human needs of health, education and food." It further explained that "since the launching of the Ghana Human Development Report (GHDR) in 1998, health, education and food have been the main indices used in ascertaining the level of human development."[49] This move to firmly capture economic and social rights in the calculus for Human Development and the Right to Development has been long in coming, and we welcome it.

---

[42] Article 36(2)(e) the 1992 Constitution of Ghana.

[43] Article 36(6), (7) and (10) of the 1992 Constitution.

[44] Article 12(1) of the 1992 Constitution of Ghana.

[45] Article 12(2) of the 1992 Constitution of Ghana.

[46] Article 33(1) and 140(2) of the 1992 Constitution of Ghana.

[47] United Nations Human Rights Office of the High Commissioner, *The Right to Development at Glance*, *http://www.un.org/en/events/righttodevelopment/pdf/rtd_at_a_glance.pdf*.

[48] Bortei-Doku Aryeetey et al. (2014), p. 38.

[49] *Ibid.*

Under the 1992 Constitution of Ghana, an entire chapter has been dedicated to the issue of Fundamental Human Rights and Freedoms.[50] They include political and civil rights; and economic, social and cultural rights. Chapter 6 of the 1992 Constitution, dedicated to the "Directive Principles of State Policy" (guidelines and roadmaps to streamline executive policy-making), hosts the third-generation rights—a conglomeration of collective political, civil, economic, social and cultural rights and the Right to Development.

Political and civil rights in CHAPTER 5 of the 1992 Constitution include the following:

- Protection of the right to life in Article 13;
- The right to personal liberty in Article 14;
- Respect for human dignity in Article 15;
- Protection from slavery and forced labour in Article 16;
- Equality and freedom from discrimination in Article 17;
- Protection of privacy of home and other property in Article 18;
- The right to a fair trial in Article 19;
- Protection from deprivation of property in Article 20; and
- General fundamental freedoms such as the right to: freedom of speech and expression; freedom of thought, conscience and belief; freedom to practice religion and freedom of assembly, in Article 21.

The provisions on economic, social and cultural rights in Chapter 5 of the 1992 Constitution include:

- Property rights of spouses (Article 22);
- Economic rights—which include the right to work under satisfactory, safe and healthy conditions (Article 24);
- Educational rights (Article 25);
- Cultural rights (Article 26);
- Women's rights (Article 27);
- Children's rights (Article 28);
- Rights of persons with disability (Article 29) and
- Rights of the sick (Article 30).

[50]Chapter 5 of the 1992 Constitution of Ghana.

Remedies and their Relationship to International Review Mechanisms

There are different mechanisms for the enforcement of human rights claims in Ghana. The 2004 Right to Development (RTD) Report: Ghana Country Study[51] describes various legislative and institutional processes aimed at promoting and protecting Human Rights in Ghana. Chief amongst these are the courts of law, the Commission on Human Rights and Administrative Justice and others Specified Institutions.[52]

The Courts of Law

In Ghana, justice emanates from the people and is administered in the name of the Republic by an independent Judiciary, subject only to the Constitution.[53] Furthermore, under Article 125 (2) of the Constitution, citizens may exercise popular participation in the administration of justice through the institutions of public and customary tribunals and the jury and assessor systems.

Although the Constitution prescribes the High Court as the Human Rights Court for persons seeking redress for human rights violations, in some instances, the Supreme Court may hear human rights cases at first instance. For instance, the Supreme Court may determine a human right claim where the matter concerned involves a right exercisable by all persons in Ghana (a public right) as was held in the Ghanaian case of *Adjei Ampofo v. Accra Metropolitan Authority*.[54]

The Human Rights enforcement jurisdiction of Ghana's High Court has been utilized very productively. In the recent case of *Martin Kpebu v. Attorney General*[55] for instance, the Applicant filed an application for judicial review at the High Court. By the application he sought an order of mandamus "to compel the State through the Attorney General to implement Section 8(3) of the Domestic Violence Act, 2007 (Act 732) which mandates the State to provide free medical care to victims of domestic violence..." The case was duly recognized as a Human Rights action. The court held that the application had merit in fact and in law and ought to be granted.

Very early on, and immediately after the coming into force of Ghana's 1992 Constitution, it was the Supreme Court which set the stage for the High Court to

[51] Bortei-Doku Aryeetey et al. (2014).

[52] These include the National Media Commission (NMC), the National Commission for Civic Education (NCCE) and the National Commission on Women and Development (NCWD), which is now part of the Ministry for Gender, Children and Social Protection.

[53] Article 125(1) of the 1992 Constitution of Ghana.

[54] Adjei Ampofo v. Accra Metropolitan Assembly [2007–2008] 1 SCGLR 611.

[55] Martin Kpebu v. Attorney General (Suit No. HR/0088/2-16).

actively assume its role as the Human Rights Court in the seminal case of *Abel Edusei v. Attorney General & Another.*[56] Here, Hayfron-Benjamin JSC observed that:

> [...] It is not for nothing that chapter 5 is captioned FUNDAMENTAL HUMAN RIGHTS AND FREEDOMS. A broad and liberal interpretation of its articles will ensure that we appreciate the correct intentions of the framers of the constitution. Their intention was that we should have freedom and have it abundantly...[57] (original emphasis).

The Supreme Court continued to support the High Court in guarding fundamental human rights and freedoms. As noted earlier, in *New Patriotic Party v. Inspector-General of Police*,[58] right after the coming into force of the current Constitution of Ghana, her Supreme Court declared that under that Constitution, no police permit was to be taken, in order to organize a demonstration. This decision led to the repeal of the Public Order Decrees[59] and their replacement with the less restrictive Public Order Act of 1994.[60]

A distinct characteristic of these human rights inclined cases is that, majority of them are linked to legal remedies for a claim on civil and political rights. Litigious claims on economic, social or cultural rights which are equally guaranteed by 1992 Constitution are seldom adjudicated upon in court. Even the *CIBA* case,[61] which originated from issues relating to economic enterprise, was decided on the political and civil rights issue of freedom of association. Whilst there may be evidence that such economically motivated rights of persons may be violated, perhaps, the challenge lies in the fact that victims of such violations have both the duty and burden to activate the legal process. It appears that whilst the rights and freedoms of vulnerable groups in Ghana are affected by the violations of economic, social and cultural rights, this same caliber of citizens neither possess the assertiveness nor have the resources to engineer the legal process to effectively address these escalating violations.

Another identifiable feature of these cases is that they show continuity with a particular political constitutional trend in Ghana which is suggestive of one tone—that the "politics of Human Rights" is legendary in Ghana.[62] The cases of *Re Okine*,[63]

---

[56]Abel Edusei v. Attorney-General & Another [1996–97] S.C.G.L.R 1.

[57]*Ibid.* at p. 32.

[58]New Patriotic Party v. Inspector-General of Police [1993–94] 2 GLR 459.

[59]NRCD 68 and PNDCL 48.

[60]Act 491. This Act does not require a permit as a condition for such events, but a notification to the police of the event.

[61]New Patriotic Party v Attorney-General (CIBA case) (1996–97) SC GLR 729.

[62]Kunbor (2001).

[63][1959] GLR 1. This case was about the rights of persons detained under the Preventive Detention Act (PDA) of 1958 (Act No 17). The detainees applied for a writ of Habeas Corpus before the court, but this was denied on the basis that the court was barred from enquiring into those matters of which the Governor-General had indicated that he was 'satisfied' that the detention was within the remits of the PDA.

Re Akoto,[64] *Kwakye v. Attorney General,*[65] *Tuffour v. Attorney General,*[66] *Edusei v. A-G,*[67] *New Patriotic Party v. Attorney-General (31st December Case),*[68] and the *New Patriotic Party v Attorney-General (CIBA case)*[69] are ground-breaking judicial opinions that are illustrative of the insistence of the courts to strictly marry human rights with political and civil petitions, whilst pushing economic and social rights claims to the backburner.

So long as the ordinary Ghanaian views expressions of Human Rights contained in the 1992 Constitution as proclamations without the legal bite, they would remain oblivious to their right to pursue Human Rights litigation. As rightly noted by one intelligent observer, Human Rights will continue to be viewed as "... a blue print for a just society; but one with vacant spaces, disallowing at the outset the pre-conditions for exercising the right to be human".[70]

Although the Supreme Court in *New Patriotic Party v Attorney-General (31st December case)*[71] had definitively pronounced that the Chapter dedicated to Directive Principles of State Policy, which hosts collective socio-economic rights was

---

[64][1961] GLR 523. This case was also about the rights of persons detained under the Preventive Detention Act (PDA) of 1958. The detainees applied for a writ of Habeas Corpus before the court, but it was refused on grounds that the Act had vested plenary discretion in the Governor-General which cannot be called in question by the court.

[65][1981] GLR 944.This case involved the purported trial and conviction of the plaintiff in absentia under the military regime of the Armed Forces Revolutionary Council (AFRC). The plaintiff questioned the legality of his purported trial at the Supreme Court under the 1979 republican democratic dispensation. The court was of the view that there was a judicial action taken by the special court under the AFRC regime, and therefore upheld the conviction.

[66][1980] GLR 637. This case was about whether or not Justice Apaloo was deemed the Chief Justice under the newly established 1979 Constitution. The plaintiff in the matter was not Justice Apaloo, but an ordinary citizen, who challenged the vetting and rejection of Justice Apaloo by the Parliament. The court ruled in favour of the plaintiff and held that Justice Apaloo was deemed CJ after the coming into force of the 1979 Constitution.

[67][1996–97] SCGLR 1. This case involved a citizen whose passport was impounded by the government of Ghana and he applied to the Supreme Court for redress. The case was struck out at the Supreme Court on grounds that the Supreme Court was not the appropriate forum at first instance for human rights proceedings.

[68][1993–94] 2 GLR 35. This case involved whether or not the government at the time could celebrate the 31st December 1981 Coup d'état with public funds. The Supreme Court of Ghana held that it was unconstitutional for the Coup d'état to be celebrated with public funds.

[69][1996–97] SC GLR 729. In this case, the plaintiff, a political party registered as a body corporate, invoked the original jurisdiction of the Supreme Court for a declaration that: (1) the Council of Indigenous Business Associations Law, 1993 (PNDCL 312) was inconsistent with and in contravention of articles 21(1)(e), 35(1) and 37(2)(a) and (3) of the 1992 Constitution of Ghana, and consequently void. The court held that the plaintiff as a legal person had capacity under article 2 (1) of the Constitution, 1992 to bring the action. The court also held that the directive principles of state policy were not by themselves legally enforceable by any court unless read in conjunction with other enforceable provisions. There court went on to assert the constitutional principle of freedom of association.

[70]Baxi (1994), pp. 1 and 2.

[71]New Patriotic Party v Attorney-General (31st December case) [1993–94] 2 GLR 35.

justiciable because the Constitution itself is a justiciable document, the Supreme Court, three years after this ground-breaking opinion, gently clawed back this declaration through *New Patriotic Party v Attorney-General (CIBA case).*[72] The Supreme held that the economic and social rights in the Directive Principles of State Policy were goals for governmental and legislative programmes and acted as a guide to judicial interpretation, and were not of and by themselves legally enforceable by any court. Further, that, to pass the test of justiciability, the principles had to be read in conjunction with Chapter 5 of the 1992 Constitution which contained the fundamental human rights. Despite this controversy, in 2008, the Supreme Court in *Ghana Lotto Operators Association & Others v National Lotteries Authority*[73] found a middle-ground to settle this legal impasse. The court was fully convinced that the ESCRs in Chapter 6 of the Constitution were entirely justiciable unless there were strong indications contrary to this basic position in the text or context of the Constitution. In other words, the Directive Principles of State Policy were *prima facie*, justiciable.

Two years down the line, in *Federation of Youth Associations of Ghana v. Public Universities of Ghana* (No 2),[74] the Supreme Court again, coiled into its shell when it applied article 38 of the Directive Principles of State Policy purely as a guide in interpreting article 25(1) (c) enshrined in the Human Rights Chapter of the Constitution. This case was in respect of whether the Ghanaian fee-paying policy of Public Universities contravened article 25(1) (c) of the 1992 Constitution, which guarantees the right to access higher education. The Supreme Court, unmoved to order government to commit resources to achieve the progressive development of this right, hid behind the cloak of lack of resources and held that the government could not sustain the provision of bursaries for all qualified students.

In 2014, the Supreme Court was seized with yet another opportunity to hold the government accountable for the implementation of socio-economic policies through the weapon of the Directive Principles of State Policy. In *Progressive Peoples' Party v Attorney General,*[75] the plaintiff's case was that, the government had failed to bring to reality the effect of articles 25(1) (a) and 38(2) of the Constitution which placed a duty on the administration to ensure that 'free compulsory universal basic education' was a basic right enjoyed by all, 10 years after the promulgation of the Constitution. Unsurprisingly, the Court shirked its constitutional duty and was of the view that the matter was not one which invoked the original jurisdiction of the court to interpret or enforce the Constitution. The excuse was that the provision in question had already been interpreted by the court in the *Fedyag case.*[76]

---

[72]New Patriotic Party v Attorney-General (CIBA case) [1996–97] SC GLR 729.

[73]Ghana Lotto Operators Association and Others v National Lotteries Authority [2007–2008] 2 SCGLR 1088.

[74]Federation of Youth Associations of Ghana v. Public Universities of Ghana (No 2) [2011] 2 SCGLR 1081.

[75]Supreme Court of Ghana, Suit No J1/8/2014; judgment delivered on 28 July 2015.

[76]See Nyinevi (2017), p. 155.

ESCRs require capital input and it seems the courts are unwilling to subject government to this task as they will prefer to take a political stance on the implementation of these rights. Nonetheless, even if the courts are hesitant in advocating for a complete and direct justiciability of ESCRs, it is incontrovertible that the courts retain an essential role in enforcing these rights. The system of judicial precedent has been given legitimacy in terms of binding decisions of the Superior Courts of Judicature.[77] To drill Human Rights deep into the conscience, psyche, and resulting practices of the nation, therefore, there must be enough judicial precedent at the highest level of the court system on Human Rights issues-civil, political, economic, social, cultural, developmental.

As another intelligent observer has noted, the realization of human rights through lawyering may be expressed in at least three ways: a contest of litigation, a public conversation or lawyering together towards social change.[78] The initial part is in respect of the usual form of adversarial contest in our courts; the second is in reference to the scenario where legal action is commenced with the secondary aim of drawing the public's attention to the issues at stake; and the third is the means by which both lawyers and non-lawyers come together to reflect on injustices of their immediate world and strategize on the actions to embark on in generating solutions to tackle them.[79] It is clear that the role of the judiciary in addressing and enforcing Human Rights cannot be downplayed, as new generation lawyers utilize the courts actually, instrumentally or even opportunistically to realise human rights and broader social justice goals.

The Commission on Human Rights and Administrative Justice (CHRAJ)

Aside the regular courts, an important feature of Ghana's Constitution is the provision for a human rights commission.[80] Conceptually, the commission has three types of mandates: a human rights mandate; an administrative justice mandate; and an anti-corruption mandate.[81] It is arguable that all these three are really human rights mandates. The functions of the commission may be categorised under three broad heads: the investigation of complaints of violations of Human Rights, injustice, corruption, abuse of power and unfair treatment; the enforcement of its decisions

[77]See Articles 129 (3), 136 (5) and 141. Also see Bimpong-Buta (1983–86), pp. 129–151 for a detailed discussion on judicial precedent in Ghana.

[78]White (1988).

[79]*Ibid.*

[80]Established under article 216 of the 1992 Constitution of Ghana.

[81]See section 7 of the Commission on Human Rights and Administrative Justice Act, 1993 (Act 456).

before the courts of law; and the education of the public on the Fundamental Human Rights provisions in the 1992 Constitution.[82]

Salient features of the legal framework governing the Commission's activities include: the power to investigate complaints concerning practices and actions by persons, private enterprises and other institutions where such complaints allege violations of fundamental Human Rights under the Constitution;[83] the mandate to establish regional, district and other lower structures of the Commission that will facilitate its operations;[84] and the provision for either written or verbal complaints as sufficient to invoke the Commission's jurisdiction.[85]

The commission is also mandated to take appropriate action to remedy, correct and reverse instances of human rights violations through means which are fair, proper and effective.[86] Such means include: negotiation and compromise between the parties concerned; causing the complaint and its finding on it to be reported to the superior of an offending person; bringing proceedings in a competent court for a remedy to secure the termination of the offending action or conduct, or the abandonment or alteration of the offending procedures; and bringing proceedings to restrain the enforcement of such legislation or regulation by challenging its validity if the offending action or conduct is sought to be justified by subordinate legislation or regulation which is unreasonable or otherwise *ultra vires*.[87]

It must be pointed out that according to the provisions in Article 219 (2) of the 1992 Constitution, the Commission shall not investigate a matter which is pending before a court or judicial tribunal; or a matter involving the relations or dealings between the Government and any other Government or an international organization; or a matter relating to the exercise of the prerogative of mercy.

From the above analyses there are two important features of the Commission that have the potential to address the Human Rights of vulnerable segments of the Ghanaian society. These are the informal procedure of lodging complaints before the Commission and the decentralization of her operations to the regions, districts and possibly to lower levels.

An aspect of the English-received court system that prevents poorer segments of the society from asserting their rights relates to cumbersome, unintelligible, and expensive procedures. Meanwhile, only the Superior Courts in Ghana have an express human rights jurisdiction.[88] Physically, the Supreme Court is located only in the National Capital; the Court of Appeal in a few major cities, and the High Court is mostly found in regional capitals and other big towns. The financial implications for potential Human Rights litigants coming from outside these areas are obvious.

---

[82]Constitutional Instrument number 17, (C. I. 17).

[83]Section 7 (1) of Act 456.

[84]*Ibid.*, section 10.

[85]See sections 12–16 and 18 of Act 456 and C. I. 17 generally.

[86]See article 218(d) of the 1992 Constitution of Ghana.

[87]*Ibid.*

[88]See article 140 (2) of the 1992 Constitution.

By establishing District offices, the commission holds the potential of taking human rights enforcement opportunities, capacities and capabilities closer to the doorsteps of ordinary Ghanaian.

The commission has been operational since 1993. Over this period (1993 to 2018) it has received a total number of 256,049 complaints, and managed to resolve 252,992 of these.[89] Within the period of 2010–2018, the Commission was able to classify 88,684 complaints under her Human Rights Mandate, 4864 under her Administrative Justice Mandate and 433 under her Anti-Corruption Mandate.[90] As argued earlier, it is possible to see all these three mandates as human rights mandates, since administrative injustice and corruption are also human rights abuses.

The 2013 Annual Report of the CHRAJ,[91] which is the most recent of its annual reports, summarizes key programmes initiated and undertaken by the Commission to achieve its fundamental objectives. They include: the disposal of 10,219 cases; 3382 public education activities nationwide; and nationwide monitoring of the State of Human Rights covering 294 Basic Schools, 211 Health Facilities, 215 Communities, 497 Police Stations, and 34 Prison Facilities.[92]

The review of its performance for the year 2013, highlights the following:

1. Promotion of the Human Rights mandate through the development of the National Human Rights Action Plan (NAHRAP) by organizing meetings for the Working Group comprising the Commission and experts to review the NAHRAP baseline report;[93]
2. Monitoring of 294 public basic schools which revealed that Government's Capitation Grant generally led to an increase in enrolment of pupils;[94]
3. Monitoring of health institutions in both the public and private sectors and assessment of education on maternal health, the National Health Insurance Scheme (NHIS) and the rights of people living with HIV/AIDS;[95]
4. Monitoring twenty-two (22) orphanages across the country to assess their compliance with laid down international and national standards;[96] and
5. Public Education and Outreach by way of commemoration of UN Day in Support of Victims of Torture and the UN Human Rights Day, after which it issued a report on its annual State of Human Rights monitoring exercise, which covered

[89]Overview of Case Statistics Since Inception of CHAJ: 1993–2018. (On file with CHRAJ and author).

[90]Overview of Case Statistics Since Inception of CHAJ: 1993–2018. Classification of Complaints Received According to Human Rights, Administrative Justice and Corruption. (On file with CHRAJ and author).

[91]Commission on Human Rights and Administrative Justice, Twentieth Annual Report (2013). Available at https://chraj.gov.gh/wp-content/uploads/2019/04/2013-Annual-Report.pdf.

[92]*Ibid.* at p. 11.

[93]*Ibid.* at p. 19.

[94]*Ibid,* p. 20.

[95]*Ibid,* p. 20.

[96]*Ibid.* at p. 21.

economic, social and cultural rights and made recommendations. The Commission continued with its Annual Human Rights lecture aimed at addressing the elimination of the worst forms of child labour.[97]

An important dimension of the report of the Commission is the fact that it devotes enough space to evaluating the Human Rights situation in Ghana and strides being made towards the protection and promotion of Human Rights in the country.

How the Commission's Human Rights and Administrative Justice Mandate Contributes Towards the Enforcement of Economic and Social Rights

In exercise of its administrative justice mandate and in fulfilment of the economic and social rights of complainants, the Commission conducts investigations into complaints of persons, whether natural or artificial, against agencies or departments of government or private enterprises, for acts which could be construed as willful abuse of power, unfair treatment or discrimination.

The following are concluded cases which demonstrate the Commission's mandate in the pursuit of human rights and administrative justice for all and sundry. These cases depict CHRAJ's distinct contribution towards the enforcement of economic and social rights, and the vast progress made ahead of the Human Rights Court in securing the realization of the right to development in Ghana. For a fact, it can be confidently stated that the Commission has become the hub for redress of socio-economic human rights grievances of victims who bear the brunt of deprivation of their right to development.

Arbitrariness of an Authority's Decision in Releasing an Employee: Simpson Anim Boateng v Local Government Service, Case Number: CHRAJ/194/2016

The Complainant was a Director of the Accra Metropolitan Assembly (AMA) Public Health Department who was relieved of his position due to alleged misconduct. This was done without him being privy to the hearing regarding the allegations, which could have exonerated him.

Two letters are of concern in this complaint. The first letter was addressed to the complainant, and signed by Chief Director for the Local Government Service Secretariat, informing the Complainant of the decision taken. The AMA was afterwards directed by the first letter to release the Complainant to the Ghana Health Service (GHS) pending investigations. The basis for investigations was quoted,

[97] *Ibid.* at p. 23.

> Attention of the Local Government Secretariat was being drawn to activities of the Complainant in his capacity as the Director of the Metropolitan Public Health Department of the AMA.

The second letter was signed by the then Metropolitan Director of Budget of the AMA on behalf of the Chief Executive Officer and addressed to the Complainant, informing him of his release to the Ghana Health Service based on allegations in the first letter. In response to the complaint, the Respondent argued that the position of the Director of the Metropolitan Public Health Department was an established position in the Local Government Service for persons duly appointed by the Head of the Civil Service and for that reason, since the Complainant was not a member of the Local Government Service, he was not qualified for that position.

From the record of proceedings, the Respondent had failed on two occasions, to provide substantive justifications for why the Complainant was denied a right to fair hearing pending his release. In arriving at its decision, the Commission considered two key issues:

1. Whether or not the Complainant was denied the opportunity to be heard?
2. Whether or not the Complainant is entitled to any remedy?

The final decision was that:

> In view of the arbitrariness and unfairness of the Respondent's decision, the Commission decided that the government pays Mr. Simpson, all entitlements/benefits, including monetary allowances that he would have received as Director of Public Health of the Accra Metropolitan Assembly from the date of his release.

Unfair Treatment in Job Promotion and Work Transfers: George Mensah v Ghana Cocoa Board (GCB), Case Number: CHRAJ/61/2016

Mr. Mensah alleged that GCB was perpetually promoting his peers ahead of him, despite having requisite qualifications for immediate promotion. He also explained that he had been a victim of arbitrary transfers.

The Complainant claimed that while acting as a whistleblower under the Whistleblowers Act, 2006 (Act 720) in June 2008 concerning mismanagement by the Respondent institution for the Commission on Human Rights and Administrative Justice (CHRAJ) and the Economic and Organised Crime Organisation (EOCO), the Respondent became aware of the Complainant's identity, further stymieing his promotional efforts. The Complainant further alleged that he used to receive 60 l of fuel. However, when he was transferred to Cocoa Clinic and subsequently to Cocoa Health Extension Division, he was given 40 l of fuel a week, even though the letter transferring him stated his Conditions of Service will not be varied.

The Respondent, denied the Complainant's claims stating that, regarding arbitrary transfers, the Complainant's claim of being transferred twice within a period of two (2) years was not true and that the Complainant's last transfer occurred on 18th February, 2016 when he was transferred from Cocoa Clinic to Cocoa Health and Extensive Division (CHED).

The Respondent argued that the Complainant's allegation of discrimination regarding his promotion was also not true. The Respondent contended that the Complainant was in the position of Audit Officer from 1998 to October, 2003. He was promoted on 15 October 2003 as Senior Audit Officer till October, 2008. The Complainant was further promoted in January 2009 as Principal Audit Officer and subsequently promoted in 2012 to Deputy Audit Manager. The Respondent explained that its Scheme of Service on promotions provides that "to be eligible for promotion to any grade, one should have done a minimum of 3 years satisfactory service on his or her current grade". Furthermore, promotion is dependent on a combination of factors such as availability of vacancies, proven competencies, length of service and additional qualification commensurate with the position.

On fuel allocation, the Respondent stated that the Complainant's allegation could not be sustained because fuel allocation to managers at Ghana Cocoa Board was 40 and not 60 l as alleged.

The Commission made these findings:

1. *The Respondent acted well within its Scheme of Service by promoting the Complainant after three years upon attaining his professional qualification, which does not amount to discrimination against the Complainant.*
2. *The Respondent has discretion under Section 1.6.1 of its Scheme of Service to waive the minimum period of three years when it comes to promotions.*
3. *The Complainant is not entitled to eight (8) months' Salary arrears as alleged because his promotion letter clearly took effect from 12th June, 2012.*
4. *The Complainant's fuel allocation of 60 l a week was reduced to 40 l a week when he was transferred from Cocoa Marketing Board to Cocoa Clinic.*
5. *The Respondent having transferred the Complainant three times within the period of two years acted unfairly and therefore abused its power regarding transfer of its staff.*
6. *The deduction of rent from the Complainant's salary is justified because the Complainant is not the only person whose salary is being deducted for rent. The Respondent's Policy Guideline on rent is clear that staff provided with accommodation should pay economic rent. On the basis of this, the payment of rent by the Complainant is lawful.*

However, its final ruling was that,

1. *The Respondent should, in accordance with Article 296 of the Constitution, prescribe guidelines on how employees are promoted in situations whereby the Respondent decides to waive the minimum requirement of three years as stated under Section 1.6.1 of its Scheme of Service.*
2. *The Complainant is entitled to the payment of fuel allocation of 60 l a week. Therefore, the difference of 20 l of fuel a week since January 2015, which was not paid should be converted to monetary terms and paid to the Complainant at the current price of fuel.*

3. *Since the transfer of the Complainant is unfair and not justified, his transfer should be reversed and the Complainant should be recalled to Cocoa Clinic, where he was initially transferred to before the other transfers took place.*

Unfair Treatment in the Payment of Gratuities: Prof. A. K. Addae v Controller and Accountant General's Department, Case Number: CHRAJ/2010/HQ/02287

The Complainant (Professor Addae), alleged that his full pension (under CAP 30) was being withheld by the Respondent. The Controller and Accountant General's Department (CAGD) said this was due to the professor not working the sufficient amount of years, which, according to its guidelines, amounts to 10 *'continuous years of service'*. The Complainant petitioned the Commission for the computation of his years of service at the Ghana Atomic Energy Commission (GAEC) under the CAP 30 Pension Ordinance.

Being convinced that his years of service at the GAEC cannot guarantee him full pension under the CAP 30 Pension, the Complainant proposed to the Commission that his years of service with the Ministry of Fuel and Power (MFP) be added to that of GAEC to enable him meet the minimum qualifying years of service for full pension under the CAP 30 Pension Ordinance.

The Commission ruled that the Respondent should pay gratuity to the Complainant in accordance with Section 5 (1) of Part Two of the Pensions Act, 1950 (CAP 30), which provides that

> Every officer, otherwise qualified for a pension, who has not completed the minimum period of qualification for a pension, may be granted on retirement a gratuity not exceeding five times the annual amount of the pension which, if there had been no qualifying period, might have been granted to him under regulation 4.

Unfair Dismissal and Sexual Harassment: Tettey v. Novor

The complainant was an employee of an airline operating domestic flights within Ghana. The respondent was owner and Managing Director of the Airline. The complainant was dismissed without explanation. In her petition to the Commission, she alleged that the respondent had sexually harassed her because she rebuffed his sexual advances. During the hearing of the case, she testified to several occasions the respondent had subjected her to unwelcome verbal remarks and physical contact of a sexual nature. The Commission found that the petitioner was discriminated against by the respondent contrary to Articles 17 (1), (2) and (3), and 33 (5) of the 1992 Constitution. Also, that his conduct constituted sexual harassment, sex discrimination and unwarranted reprisals.

Deprivation of Means of Livelihood of Pregnant and Nursing Mothers: Case Number CHRAJ/561/93

The petitioner in this case was a pregnant lady who received a letter from her employers declaring her redundant from her employment. She contested the position indicating that under Section 43 of the Labour Decree (NLCD 157) she ought not to be so declared given her pregnancy. The Commission, in upholding her contention, declared that her redundancy breached Article 27 of the 1992 Constitution; which provides that special care shall be accorded mothers during reasonable periods before and after childbirth. It held further that during such periods, mothers are to be given paid-leave.

Central to the Commission's reasoning in these cases is its sensitivity to the human condition, gender and the social context in which the Human Rights provisions have to be rightly posited. A former Commissioner is noted to have stated that:

> The myth that economic, social and cultural rights are not important as civil and political rights has been laid to rest. Efforts should be made to give them the same legal recognition. Pursuit of civil and political rights does not justify violation of economic, social and cultural rights.[98]

With no intention to undermine the incredible work of the Commission in the context of the right to development, it is still noticeable that the bulk of cases decided by her are more or less intrinsically linked to, and tied with, political and civil rights. Regardless, and as compared to the hesitance of the law courts in pushing for the enforceability of ESCRs, Ghana's Commission on Human Rights has been extremely instrumental in seeking, attempting and striving to uphold the economic claims of its complainants.

National Media Commission

The regular courts and the human rights commission have an express human rights mandate and have the power to take on human rights cases, decide on them, and enforce their decisions. There is also the National Media Commission (NMC),[99] established by the Constitution and an Act of Parliament[100] with a human rights decision-making and enforcement mandate to the extent that media freedom is considered a human right. The Constitution provides for freedom and independence of the media,[101] prohibits censorship of the media and dispenses with the need for a license to establish or operate a newspaper, journal or other mass media. It also

[98] Short (1997), p. 99.

[99] Established under article 166 of the 1992 Constitution of Ghana.

[100] National Media Commission Act, 1993 (Act 449).

[101] See Article 162 of the 1992 Constitution of Ghana.

provides for the setting up of the NMC, which among other functions is to: promote and ensure the freedom and independence of the media for mass communication or information; and insulate the state media from governmental control.

In furtherance of the above constitutional provisions, the National Media Commission Act of 1993 was passed, and included in the mandate of the NMC the following: to take all appropriate measures to ensure high journalistic standards in the mass media, including investigations, mediation and settlement of complaints made against or by the press or other media[102] and for the setting up of a Complaints Settlement Committee to hear petitions brought to the Commission by aggrieved parties.[103]

For instance, in a 1998 case, the National Media Commission determined a complaint lodged by one Mr. J.K.L. Nkansah against the Ghanaian Chronicle for a publication against him which turned out to be untrue.[104] The Commission therefore directed that: the Ghanaian Chronicle should retract the story and apologise unconditionally to Mr. Nkansah; that the Ghanaian Chronicle should also send a personal written apology to Mr. Nkansah; that the retraction and apology should be published in two continuous issues of the newspaper and given enough prominence; and that the directives should be carried out within 14 days of the statement.[105]

A remedy of a similar nature was sought by Mr. Ebo Quansah in 2011, when he lodged a complained against Multimedia Group Limited and ASEMPA FM.[106] The gravamen of the complaint was that ASEMPA FM in October 2010 broadcast a recording of a private conversation between him and his friend. The solicitors and representatives of Multi-Media Group Limited admitted that ASEMPA FM had acted unprofessionally and rendered an unqualified apology to the complaint.[107] By so doing, the NMC had concretized a just precedent for the endorsement of the Right to Privacy, which must be balanced against the public interest.[108] The Management of ASEMPA FM fulfilled its pledge in February 25, 2011, reaffirming its

[102]Section 2(1)(b) of National Media Commission Act, 1993 (Act 449).

[103]The National Media Commission (Complaints Settlement Procedure) Regulations, 1994 (LI 1587).

[104]The National Media Commission, "Complaint Settlement". Available at: https://www.ghanaweb.com/GhanaHomePage/NewsArchive/Complaint-Settlement-23722.

[105]*Ibid.*

[106]Decisions of the Complaints Settlement Mechanism of the National Media Commission (2011). On file with the National Media Commission and author.

[107]*Ibid.*

[108]This assertion was affirmed by the Supreme Court in Raphael Cubagee v Michael Yeboah & Others (Supreme Court, Suit No. J6/04/2017) where Pwamang JSC, delivering judgment on behalf of the Supreme Court, admitted that Ghana's laws undertake a balancing exercise by balancing the rights of the ordinary citizen and that of the public interest, in respect of admission of illegally obtained evidence which impinges on the right to privacy guaranteed in Article 18(2) of the 1992 Constitution of Ghana.

apology and promising to recommit itself to the highest standard of editorial discretion.[109]

In 2014, the current President of Ghana, Nana Addo Dankwa Akufo-Addo, before his ascension to the presidency, utilized the complaints settlement mechanism of the NMC[110] in pursuing a remedy garbed in "defamation"—a civil claim concerning an allegation of disparagement of one's character, usually adjudicated upon by the courts of law. His case was that, the publications of the Daily Post, the Ghanaian Lens, the Enquirer, the Informer and the Al-Hajj newspapers were "offensive and derogatory", stating: "the substance of the stories complained of, are in all essentials utterly false, a product of the imagination of the publishers of the newspapers specified above". The Complaints Settlement Committee, exercising its powers under LI 1587[111] to adjudicate on complaints before it, examined the content of the said publications against the ethics of journalism and ruled that the mentioned newspapers had no justification for publishing these allegations without adducing verifiable evidence. The NMC directed the newspapers to retract and apologize to the complainant.

In reinforcing its human rights mandate to protect the reputation of others, the NMC on 26th April 2019 also directed that Efo Korsi Senyo, Editor of the Awake Newspaper, to apologize to the Registrar-General, Mrs. Jemima Mamaa Oware, for publishing unsubstantiated allegations against her in print and online editions of his newspaper and on social media platforms.[112]

In an unconventional complaint brought before the NMC in 2017, the Commission imprinted its role in maintaining high standards in broadcasting whilst upholding the social right to decency.[113] This was done in pursuance of a complaint filed by Mr. James Oberko and Mr. Tommy Annan Forson against the television stations XYZ TV, Thunder TV and Ice TV, for airing of pornographic materials which sinned against the letter and spirit of Section 7(e) of the NMC Broadcasting Guidelines that prohibits TV stations from transmitting actual sexual intercourse to their viewers.[114] The Commission examined the complaint and concluded that the content complained about did not meet the standards of decency required by the Broadcasting Standards.

---

[109]Decisions of the Complaints Settlement Mechanism of the National Media Commission (2011). (On file with the National Media Commission and author).

[110]Findings and Rulings of NMC Settlement Committee: Nana Akufo-Addo vrs Daily Post, Ghanaian Lens, The Enquirer, Informer and Al Hajj Newspapers (On file with the National Media Commission and author).

[111]National Media Commission (Complaints Settlement Procedure) Regulations 1994 (LI 1587).

[112]NMC DIRECTS AWAKE NEWSPAPER TO APOLOGISE TO REGISTRAR-GENERAL (PRESS RELEASE, 2019). Registrar-General v Emmanuel Efo Korsi Senyo, Awake Newspaper. (On file with author).

[113]Givelber (1982), pp. 42–75.

[114]NMC Settles Complaint on Pornography. https://www.ghanaweb.com/GhanaHomePage/NewsArchive/GJA-expresses-concern-about-pornography-36473.

National Labour Commission

Again, there is the National Labour Commission (NLC).[115] To the extent that labour issues are human rights issues, the Labour Commission also possesses a human rights decision-making and enforcement mandate. In line with the powers of the Commission vested by section 139 (1) of the Labour Act, 2003 (Act 651) to settle industrial and labour disputes, a total of 718 complaints were filed with the Commission by individual workers, workers' organizations, trade unions and employers, as disclosed by its 2017 Annual Report.[116] The 2017 report details that, out of the 718 complaints filed that year, 232 complaints representing 32% were successfully settled.[117] In addition to the cases settled, 113 complaints were also resolved.[118] The statistics also show that, in relation to human rights claims, there were 251 complaints received on unfair termination, 76 on unpaid salaries and wages and 151 complaints in respect of poor conditions of service, maternity protection and leave entitlements.[119] To enforce the Commission's decisions, the Commission filed 19 applications in the High Court for the determination of cases where parties had failed to comply with the Commission's directives.[120] Gleaning from these statistics, it is evident that disputants in labour-management relations are gaining confidence in the human rights cloaked adjudicative role of the National Labour Commission[121] in advancing the socio-economic rights of workers.

Here are some case law reports on the labour rights resolved by the Commission:

In *Joshua Tetteh Asare v U. S. Embassy*,[122] the complainant filed a complaint at the NLC against the U. S. Embassy for unfair termination in 2016. The Complainant, who had been employed as a Procurement Clerk by the Respondent, contended that insofar as he was ignorant of the allegations which grounded his termination, it was unfair. The Commission upon a careful examination of the complaint held that the Respondent had failed to give the Complainant an opportunity to be heard in accordance with the law of natural justice, and similarly, it failed to follow legal

[115]The National Labour Commission (NLC) is established under section 135 of the Labour Act (Act 651). Its functions are spelt out under section 138 of Act 651 and they include: facilitating the settlement of industrial disputes; investigating labour related complaints; and taking steps necessary to prevent labour disputes. By section 139(2) of Act 651, the Commission has powers of the High Court in respect of enforcing attendance of witnesses and examining them on oath; compelling the production of documents and issuing a commission to examine a witness abroad. The NLC Regulations (2006), (LI 1822) and the Labour Regulations (2007), (LI 1833) are the subsidiary legislation governing the operations of the NLC.

[116]National Labour Commission, Annual Report (January 1–December 2017). On file with NLC and author.

[117]*Ibid.* p. 19.

[118]*Ibid.* p. 19.

[119]*Ibid.* p. 20.

[120]*Ibid.* pp. 21–23.

[121]*Ibid.* p. 24.

[122]NLC/G 254/016/2017/35[s] (On file with NLC and author).

procedures to terminate the contract of the Complainant, thereby rendering the termination wrongful. The Commission, on 28th July 2017, ordered the Respondent to pay: one months' salary as payment in lieu of notice; outstanding leaves commuted to cash; and 6 month's salary as compensation for unfair termination, within 14 days upon receipt of the decision.

In a most recent decision, the Commission also settled another case of unfair termination in *Gilda Eyram Aku Bansah v Karpower Ghana Company Limited.*[123] The brief facts were that, the complainant had been engaged as a Field Auditor by the Respondent in 1999 until 2018, when her appointment was terminated on grounds of redundancy with 2 months' salary as severance pay. The Commission admitted that redundancy was a legitimate basis for termination under the Labour Act; nonetheless, it concluded that the termination was still unfair because the procedure for redundancy in law had not been complied with, and the amount for compensation (3 months' salary) had not been paid to her. The Respondent was ordered by the Commission to pay 6 months salary as compensation and the Ghana Cedi equivalent of USD 200 as "Handshake" (end of service benefit) pursuant to the Respondent's Employee's Handbook, less any payments that have been made in advance to the Complainant.

The Commission, also in 2019, upheld a claim by the Complainants in the *Ghana Mineworkers' Union (GGMU) v Shaanxi Mining Ghana Limited*[124] for failure on the part of the Respondent to implement financial and other provisions of a signed Collective Agreement (CA). The Respondents were directed by the Commission to comply with the ruling, and orders of the Commission made in 2017, and pay all salaries and other benefits to the affected workers.

The Commission further exercises its jurisdictional powers through the Alternative Dispute Resolution (ADR) mechanism, specifically mediation and arbitration. In *Ebenezer Opoku-Asomani v Energoprojekt Ghana Limited,*[125] after a voluntary submission of their dispute to mediation, a sole mediator was appointed to mediate in the complaint lodged by the complainant with the NLC for unfair termination of his appointment. In conclusion, the parties agreed that the Respondent pays compensation, which includes all entitlements due to the Complainant, as full and final settlement of the matter.

For the arbitration wing, the Commission in 2015 rendered a binding arbitration award in *Robert Gorden Allan Lindsey v Coastal Mining/Exploration Limited.*[126] The case for the complainant was that, upon acceptance of an employment offer as Mechanical Foreman, the terms of engagement spelt out in the correspondence between the parties included a monthly salary of USD 10,000 tax free; however,

[123]NLC/G 293/18/2019/79 (On file with NLC and author).

[124]NLC/G293/18/2019/79^{Z} (On file with NLC and author).

[125]Mediation Report: In the Matter Between Ebenezer Opoku-Asomani (Complainant) and Energoprojekt Ghana Limited (Respondent) (On file with NLC and author).

[126]Arbitration Award: In the matter of Voluntary Arbitration between Robert Gorden Allan Lindsey (Complainant) and Coastal Mining/Exploration Limited (Respondent) (On file with NLC and author).

the Respondent had refused to pay his salaries from July to September of that year. The sole arbitrator found in favour of the Complainant and after careful consideration, awarded him, amongst others, USD 30,000 representing the three months salary in arrears.

Electoral Commission and National Commission for Civic Education

The mandates of the Electoral Commission (EC) and the National Commission for Civic Education (NCCE) are a little different. Since the EC operationalises the human right to vote as contained in the Ghana constitution,[127] it may be considered to have a human rights mandate. In *Abu Ramadan & Evans Mensah v Electoral Commission & Attorney General*,[128] Chief Justice Wood affirmed the role of the Electoral Commission in actualizing the right to vote stated in Article 42 of the 1992 Constitution, by holding that the said provision reserves the right to vote in public elections and referenda **solely** in citizens of Ghana of eighteen years and above and of sound mind.

The human rights mandate of the NCCE is even more discreet, but nevertheless important. The NCCE can be said to address the human right "to know one's rights". The relevant functions of the NCCE in this regard include:[129]

- creating and sustaining within the society the awareness of the principles and objectives of the Constitution as the fundamental law of the people of Ghana; and
- formulating, implementing and overseeing programmes intended to inculcate in the citizens of Ghana awareness of their civic responsibilities and an appreciation of their rights and obligations as a free people.

The above key functions of the NCCE have a number of implications and potential for the full implementation of the Right to Development (RTD) in Ghana. The Human Rights provisions in the Constitution, including the Directive Principles of State Policy (DPSP), are important principles that all Ghanaians need to be aware of. Sustaining such awareness in Ghana creates useful spaces of hope for meaningful participation by Ghanaians in its development efforts. In the same vein, the formulation and implementation of programmes for awareness of civic responsibilities, obligations and Human Rights of the Ghanaian citizen, as a function of the NCCE, is a useful springboard for the implementation of the RTD in Ghana. The Declaration on the Right to Development emphatically places a responsibility on all

[127] The right of every citizen of Ghana who is 18 years or above and is of sound mind to vote in public elections or referenda, is guaranteed under Article 42 of the 1992 Constitution.

[128] Abu Ramadan & Evans v. Electoral Commission & Attorney General (J8/108/2016) [2016] GHASC 19 (05 July 2016).

[129] The functions of the NNCE are specified in Article 233 of the 1992 Constitution.

human beings individually and collectively to actively participate in the development process.[130] Such a responsibility may only be discharged meaningfully through sustained awareness on the development agenda and the role of beneficiaries in the process.

The NCCE law provides for the setting up of branches of the Commission in regional, districts and other lower structures as would facilitate its work.[131] The Independence of the Commission is guaranteed through security of tenure of the members of the Commission and the fact that the Commission is only subject to the Constitution and no other authority in the performance of its functions.[132]

The 2017 report of the Commission[133] summarizes the operations and activities of the various departments of the NCCE, geared towards the realization of its constitutional mandate. The current Chairperson, Josephine Nkrumah, indicated that, the year 2017 saw a total of 75,524 activities being organized across the country, reaching 5, 244, 379 Ghanaians directly in their communities, with thousands more reached through the Commission's media engagements.[134] As part of its activities, the Commission launched its 16th Annual Constitution Week and carried out the following activities in accordance with its constitutional duties:

- Dialogue with Security Agencies on the need to sustain and uphold the 1992 Constitution as a living document;
- Annual Citizenship Week for Basic and Junior High Schools across the country;
- A National Dialogue under the theme: "Restoring the Ghanaian Identity: Our values, Our Passion"; and
- The Electronic Constitution quiz competition for Senior High Schools across the country.[135]

The Commission also held the Project Citizen flagship programme which engages the youth in Senior High Schools in research, acquisition of knowledge, skills development and dispositions to influence public policy and to solve community problems.[136] Under the theme : "Child Marriage is a Human Rights Violation... Education is a Panacea to Human and National Development", the showcase sought to empower participants, especially girls and peer support groups on their civic rights and responsibility.[137]

---

[130] Article 2(2) of the 1986 UN Declaration on the Right to Development.

[131] See sections 4 and 16 of National Commission for Civic Education Act, 1993 (Act 452).

[132] See Article 234 of the 1992 Constitution and National Commission for Civic Education Act, 1993 (Act 452), section 3.

[133] National Commission for Civic Education, Twenty-Fourth Annual Report and Accounts, 2017 (published July, 2018), (on file with NCCE and author).

[134] *Ibid,* p. 7.

[135] *Ibid,* p. 8.

[136] *Ibid,* p. 32.

[137] *Ibid.*

A total of 30,337 community sensitisations, workshops and public engagements were conducted in 2017.[138] The primary aim of these programmes was to empower citizens by strengthening and advancing democracy and civil and public rights and responsibilities in Ghana. The engagements touched on areas such as: domestic violence, teenage pregnancy and homosexuality in Ghana; discrimination against Persons with Disability (PWDs); anti-mob action campaign; Rights of the Ghanaian Child, the Children's Act and Child Labour; and Gender Equality and Human rights in general.[139]

To curb the spate of illegal small-scale mining (*galamsey*) which has a snowball effect on increasing the poverty index in Ghana, the NCCE organized town hall meetings in six (6) selected districts where galamsey activities are endemic, to create awareness through public education campaigns about the destruction of farmlands and water bodies by *galamsey* activities.[140]

Ghana's Participation in the Fight Against Poverty and the Right to Development on the International Plane

There are also a variety of international "enforcement" mechanisms that Ghana subscribes to as a part of her general treaty obligations. For example, Ghana has signed on to the International Covenant on Economic, Social and Cultural Rights (ICESCR) and its optional protocol that overseas compliance with this treaty, using the mechanism of the Committee on Economic, Social and Cultural Rights (CESCR).[141] The CESCR requires Ghana to prepare reports every 5 years on the situation of economic, social and cultural (ESC) rights in the country. The CESCR examines the extent to which ESC rights are being achieved and releases concluding observations which highlight the progress made in fulfilling ESC Rights, difficulties in achieving these rights, areas of concern and recommendations for Ghana.[142]

Within the scope of the International Covenant on Civil and Political Rights (ICCPR) which Ghana ratified in the year 2000,[143] Ghana has voluntarily declared on the international front to protect and preserve basic human rights such as: the right

[138] *Ibid,* p. 60.

[139] *Ibid.*

[140] *Ibid,* p. 68.

[141] The Committee on Economic, Social and Cultural Rights is a body of 18 independent experts that monitors implementation of the ICESCR by its States parties. The Committee was established under ECOSOC Resolution 1985/17 to carry out the monitoring functions of the United Nations Economic and Social Council (ECOSOC): https://www.ohchr.org/EN/HRBodies/CESCR/pages/cescrindex.aspx.

[142] *Human Rights Enforcement Mechanisms of the United Nations:* https://www.escr-net.org/resources/human-rights-enforcement-mechanisms-united-nations [Accessed on: 23rd July, 2019].

[143] Stand Ghana, *Human Rights Instruments Ghana Ratified*. Available at: https://www.standghana.org/your-rights/human-rights-instruments-ghana-ratified/.

to life and human dignity;[144] equality before the law;[145] right to personal liberty,[146] amongst others, and to undertake administrative, judicial and legislative measures to protect the rights expressed in the treaty. The Human Rights Committee is the body of independent experts that monitors implementation of the ICCPR by its State parties. It requires State parties to submit reports on how the Convention is being implemented, initially one year after accession and then whenever the Committee requests (usually every 4 years). The Committee examines each report and addresses its concerns and recommendations to the State party in the form of "concluding observations".[147]

In respect of gender equality as a pathway towards development, in 1986, Ghana ratified the Convention on the Elimination of All Forms of Discrimination Against Women (CEDAW)[148] which enjoins states to prohibit discrimination against women and take appropriate measures, including legislative measures, to ensure the full development and advancement of women in all fields.[149] The Committee on the Elimination of Discrimination against Women (CEDAW) monitors the implementation of the convention. At each of its sessions, the Committee reviews national reports submitted by the States parties within one year of ratification and accession, and thereafter every 4 years. The Committee then makes recommendations on any issue affecting women to which it believes the State parties should devote more attention.[150]

Ghana is also a signatory to the Convention on the Rights of the Child (CRC), ratified in 1990. The main way the Convention is enforced is through ongoing monitoring by the independent team of experts called the UN Committee on the Rights of the Child. All states are obliged to submit reports on how the rights enshrined in the Convention are being implemented, initially 2 years after acceding to the Convention and every 5 years.[151] In reviewing the reports, the Committee provides implementation and improvement recommendations to each individual State and urges all levels of government to use the Convention as a guide in policy-making and legislation, to: develop a comprehensive national agenda; develop permanent bodies or mechanisms to promote coordination, monitoring and evaluation of activities throughout all sectors of government; and ensure that all legislation is fully compatible with the Convention and, if applicable, the

---

[144]Article 6 of the ICCPR.

[145]Article 3 & 14 of the ICCPR.

[146]Article 9 of the ICCPR.

[147]United Nations Human Rights, Office of the High Commissioner (OHCHR). Available at: https://www.ohchr.org/EN/HRBodies/CCPR/Pages/CCPRIndex.aspx.

[148]Int'l Fin. Corp (2007), p. 28.

[149]See: Article 2 and 3 of the CEDAW.

[150]The United Nations Committee on the Elimination of Discrimination against Women (CEDAW), an expert body established in 1982, is composed of 23 experts on women's issues from around the world. Available at: https://www.un.org/womenwatch/daw/cedaw/committee.htm.

[151]UN Committee on the Rights of Children.

Optional Protocols, by incorporating the provisions into domestic law or ensuring that they take precedence in cases of conflict with national legislation.[152]

Thus, aside the internal human rights enforcement mechanisms we have extensively discussed, Ghana is also bound by her responsibility to adhere to the review mechanisms associated with International Agreements. Generally, there is the responsibility to report on the progress of promoting Fundamental Human Rights that the State is obliged to observe, within a specified timeframe. Thus, these measures serve as further opportunities for realizing and enforcing Fundamental Human Rights.

In comparing Ghana's internal mechanism for enforcing Fundamental Human Rights to International Review mechanisms, one may hold the view that Ghana's mechanisms are more direct and stringent than international review mechanisms. Whereas Ghana has both constitutional and other modes by which Fundamental Human Rights are enforced, with these modes open to a wide array of individuals and organizations, international review mechanisms draw mainly from reports on the progress of States in enforcing Human Rights, with little by way of concrete human rights enforcement.

Notwithstanding that these international human rights instruments have not been ratified by Act of Parliament domestically, it does not detract from the fact that Ghana is still bound by them on the international plane.

Domestic Law Contributions to the Fight Against Poverty and the Right to Development

As already stated, the Human Rights provisions in Ghana's Constitution are important principles that are enforceable as the fundamental rights and freedoms of persons in Ghana. With regards to enforcing Human Rights by our courts however, there has been some hesitation in according economic, social, cultural and development rights the same status as civil and political rights. In *New Patriotic Party v. Attorney-General (CIBA Case)*,[153] Ghana's Supreme Court was of the view that the Directive Principles of State Policy in Ghana's Constitution, which contain what are generally called second and third generation rights, could not be enforceable in themselves, and could only be justiciable when read and applied in conjunction with any substantively guaranteed Human Rights and Freedoms set out in Chapter 5 of the Ghana Constitution-which contains mainly civil and political rights.

[152]United Nations, Children and Educational Fund (UNICEF), *Implementing and monitoring the Convention on the Rights of the Child: Turning child rights into action and results for children.* Available at: https://www.unicef.org/child-rights-convention/implementing-monitoring.

[153]New Patriotic Party v. Attorney-General (CIBA Case) [1997–98] 1 GLR 378.

In truth, there has been a long-standing debate over the appropriateness of making second and third generation rights justiciable.[154] However, some governments like Ghana have defied the logic of various objections and provided for such rights in their constitutions. Perhaps the rationale to some degree, is to demonstrate a commitment to social integration, solidarity and equality, and above all the yearning of the majority of the populations in the global south for development.[155] It also demonstrates a major concern for the protection of vulnerable groups, such as the poor.[156]

It did not take very long for Ghana's Supreme Court to see the light. Ten years after the decision just discussed, *Ghana Lotto Operators Association v National Lottery Authority*,[157] came to the rescue. The Supreme Court said:

> ...an issue is justiciable if it is capable of being settled by a court. Prima facie, one would have thought that everything in a Constitution should be justiciable. The Constitution is a legal document containing the most important rules on political governance. The courts have the responsibility of ensuring that these rules are complied with. To my mind, therefore, the starting point of analysis should be that all the provisions in the Constitution are justiciable, unless there are strong indications to the contrary in the text or context of the Constitution.

Thus, the fact that the Directive Principles of State Policy (DPSP) contained in chapter six of the 1992 Constitution are to "guide all citizens, Parliament, the President, the Judiciary, the Council of State, the Cabinet, political parties and other bodies and persons in applying or interpreting this Constitution or any other law and in taking and implementing any policy decisions, for the establishment of a just and free society"[158] and also, since "the President shall report to Parliament at least once a year all the steps taken to ensure the realization of the policy objectives contained in this Chapter and, in particular, the realization of basic human rights, a healthy economy, the right to work, the right to good health care and the right to education"[159] are provisions in the 1992 Constitution of Ghana, they become matters enforceable in the court of law. And by virtue of the fact that these rights, freedoms and state policy fall within the context of the right to development and the fight against poverty, Ghana is poised to support the global agenda to alleviate poverty and enforce the implementation of RTD principles.

---

[154]In the discourse of Human Rights, there is a marked schism between civil/political rights and socio-economic rights. The fundamental cause of this is justiciability. Even advanced democracies like Canada and the United States did not give the latter rights any constitutional protection. In some African countries like Botswana, Tunisia, Zimbabwe and Zambia, such rights are not provided for. Yet in other African countries they are explicitly provided for as justiciable rights. Ghana and South Africa are apt examples. Comparatively however, the socio-economic rights in Ghana are not as exhaustive as those in the South African Constitution. For instance, they do not include an explicit provision on the right to health.

[155]Atuguba (2013), pp. 109–116.

[156]Eide et al. (ed) (2001), p. 5.

[157]Ghana Lotto Operators Association v National Lottery Authority [2007–2008] SCGLR 1088.

[158]Article 34(1) of the 1992 Constitution of Ghana.

[159]Article 34(2) of the 1992 Constitution of Ghana.

Further, it must be noted that although it appears that socio-economic rights are entrenched in the 1992 Constitution of Ghana, these socio-economic rights stated in the Constitution are limited. They include the rights to: education; property rights; the rights of workers in employment; and the property rights of spouses. Other pertinent socio-economic rights such as the right to health care, water, food and adequate housing are not explicitly provided for. The Directive Principles of State Policy as already discussed contain more elaborate provisions on socio-economic rights than those provided for in chapter 5 of the 1992 Constitution of Ghana. Scholars however recommend that for a better and more just form of democracy, Civil and Political Rights must irrevocably be interconnected with Socio-Economic Rights.[160] To separate these sets of rights, and attach differential remedial content labels is to court a dubious structural imbalance in our conception of rights.[161] Ghana must aim at a comprehensive Human Rights regime that values life and the dignity of persons. Socio-Economic Rights are a prior commitment to such a regime and a foundation to the wellbeing of individuals. Civil and Political Rights are presumably lame without enforceable Socio-Economic Rights.[162]

Policy Monitoring and Accountability Mechanisms

The Relationship Between Ghana's International Development Programme and the International Right to Development Model

Policy monitoring in Ghana is done through the National Monitoring and Evaluation (M & E) framework and the Annual Progress Reports (APRs) prepared by Ministries, Departments and Agencies (MDAs) and Metropolitan, Municipal and District Assemblies (MMDAs). The Parliament of Ghana is also responsible for reviewing the APRs and ensuring that the MDAs account for their performance against the targets already outlined.

The National Development Planning Commission (NDPC), which is tasked with monitoring and evaluating the implementation of the Plan and submitting annual M&E reports to Parliament, also conducts assessments of selected policies.[163] Currently, the three policy objectives that are relevant to the work of the NDPC from the 2018–2021 National Medium-Term Development Policy Framework (NMTDDF), "Agenda for Jobs" are: ensuring improved fiscal performance and

---

[160] See Kooijman (1990), p. 320 (he saw the relevance of providing for these sets of socioeconomic rights and civil and political rights in equal proportions and advocated mutuality in their conception and enforcement).

[161] See Willes (2006–2007), p. 35.

[162] See Addo (1992), pp. 93–117.

[163] Article 86 and 87 of the 1992 Constitution of Ghana.

sustainability; improving decentralized planning; and enhancing capacity for policy formulation and coordination.[164]

The National Development Plan,[165] with its latest version being the 7-year Development Plan (Coordinated Programme of Economic and Social Development Policies) launched by the government in 2018, outlines the development roadmap of Ghana and is intended to be the means by which the national agenda of development is to be achieved by 2024. The 7-year plan is founded on five pillars of growth and development, namely revitalizing the economy; transforming agriculture and industry; revamping economic and social infrastructure; strengthening social protection and inclusion; and reforming delivery system of public services institutions.[166] Thus, it is from this plan that the extent of Ghana's current intention to implement the international Right to Development may be derived.

Policy Frameworks that Support the Realization of the Sustainable Development Goals (SDG)

At the 2012 United Nations Conference on Sustainable Development in Rio de Janeiro, the seeds for a globalized development-driven agenda for the next decade were sown. Three years later, these investments blossomed into the now globally recognized Sustainable Development Goals (SDGs), launched in 2015. The SDGs replaced the Millennium Development Goals (MDGs), its precursor initiative that began the global effort in 2000 to tackle the scourge of poverty.[167] For 15 years, the

---

[164]National Development Planning Commission, Medium Term Expenditure Framework (MTEF) for 2019–2022. Available at https://www.mofep.gov.gh/sites/default/files/pbb-estimates/2019/2019-PBB-NDPC.pdf.

[165]The National Development Plans for Ghana are traceable to the pre-independence era. They include: Guggisberg Plan: 1919–27; The 10-year development plan (condensed into 5 years): 1951–56; The consolidated development plan: 1957–59; The 5-year development plan: 1959–1964; The 7-year Development Plan: 1963/64–1969/70, which aimed at modernizing the economy of Ghana through industrialization; The 2-year Development Plan: 1967/68–1969/70; The 1-year development Plan: 1970–1971; The 5-year Development Plan: 1975/76–1979/80 Part 1; The 5-year Development Plan: 1975/76–1979/80 Part 2; The Economic Recovery Programme: 1984–86; The Ghana-Vision (2020) (1997–2020); The Ghana Poverty Reduction Strategy (GPRS I): 2003–2006; The Ghana Growth and Poverty Reduction Strategy (GPRS II): 2006–2009; The Better Ghana Agenda: 2010–2013; The 40-year National Development Plan: 2018–57; 7-year National Development Plan: 2018–2024

See: Tandoh-Offi (2013) (Serial Number 2), pp. 98–99. Also see Fosu and Aryeetey (2010), pp. 8, 27.

[166]President Akufo-Addo launches 7-year Co-ordinated Programme of Economic and Social Development Policies. Available at http://www.ghana.gov.gh/index.php/news/4560-president-launches-action-plan-to-combat-anti-microbial-resistance.

[167]United Nations Development Programme (UNDP). *Sustainable Development Goals, Background of the Goals.* Available at: *https://www.undp.org/content/undp/en/home/sustainable-development-goals/background.html.*

MDGs served as the building elements around which development-oriented strides were taken.

Ghana, determined to achieve the 8 goals laid down in the MDGS, set them out in strategy documents and implemented them through its public policy framework. According to the 2015 MDG Report of Ghana,[168] the operationalization of the MDGs was marked by Annual Progress Reports (APR) on the implementation of Ghana's medium-term development frameworks, namely, the Ghana Poverty Reduction Strategy I and II (GPRS I and GPRS II) and the Ghana Shared Growth and Development Agenda I and II (GSDA I and GSDA II).[169] The report further indicates that Goal 1 on Eradication of extreme poverty and hunger was largely achieved. Statistics backing this proclamation was that, the national poverty index which was 16.5% in 2006 had declined to 8.4 by 2013 (almost a reduction by half).[170]

Despite her commendable effort in attaining the MDGs, deep-seated poverty remains. By advent of the 17 Goals of the SDGs, Ghana is aligning its development priorities in collaboration with Civil Society Organizations (CSOs) and the private sector on achieving the SDGs jointly.[171] The SDGs are reflected in the President's Coordinated Programme of Economic and Social Development (2017–2024)[172] and Ghana's 2018 budget is also mapped to the SDGs.

In December 2017, Ghana's Minister for Planning, Professor Gyan-Baffour, stated that a Technical Committee set up by government for the implementation of the Sustainable Development Goals (SDGs) had already developed indicators for measuring Ghana's SDG performance. This, he pointed out, has been ratified by the respective Ministries, Departments and Agencies. He also mentioned the fact that the Government has aligned the SDGs and its targets with Ghana's national development priorities and aspirations.[173]

In respect of this, on 17th July 2019, Professor George Gyan-Baffour presented Ghana's first Voluntary National Review report on the implementation of the 2030 Agenda for Sustainable Development Goals at the 2019 High-Level Political Forum

---

[168] Ghana Millennium Development Goals: 2015 Report (2015), pp. 1–97. https://www.undp.org/content/dam/ghana/docs/Doc/Inclgro/UNDP_GH_2015%20Ghana%20MDGs%20Report.pdf.

[169] *Ibid,* p. 1.

[170] *Ibid,* p. 9.

[171] See: UNDP (2017) (pdf). *The Sustainable Development Goals (SDGs) in Ghana: Why they matter & How we can help*. Available at: https://www.undp.org/content/dam/unct/ghana/docs/SDGs/UNCT-GH-SDGs-in-Ghana-Avocacy-Messages-2017.pdf.

[172] See United Nations Sustainable Development Partnership (UNSDP) 2018–2022 Ghana: Between the Government of the Republic of Ghana and the United Nations in Ghana. https://www.undp.org/content/dam/unct/ghana/docs/Delivering%20as%20One/UNCT-GH-UNSDP-2018.pdf.

[173] Ghana's Progress Report on SDGs to be submitted to UN General Assembly: https://www.ghanaweb.com/GhanaHomePage/business/Ghana-s-progress-report-on-SDGs-to-be-submitted-to-UN-General-Assembly-607009.

(HLPF) at the United Nations.[174] The Minister revealed that Ghana had made progress on many SDG targets, adding that "overall, poverty had declined marginally from 24.2% in 2013 to 23.4% in 2017. He also mentioned that growth in GDP remained robust, accelerating to 8.1% in 2017, thus making Ghana the second fastest growing economy in Africa that year.

National Development Planning Commission (NDPC)

The National Development Planning Commission is the key agency for ensuring overall long-term sustainable development of Ghana.[175] In the execution of its mandate, the primary vehicles for implementing the SDGs in Ghana are the sector and district medium-term plans which are anchored on the decentralized planning system. The SDGs are therefore integrated into the National Development Policy Framework and the corresponding Results Framework.

To enhance cross-sectoral collaboration the following additional structures have been put in place:

- **High Level Ministerial Committee** with oversight responsibility for implementing the SDGs.
- **SDGs Implementation Coordination Committee** to provide strategic direction for implementation and coordination of SDGs activities both locally and internationally. This committee is made up of representatives from key government agencies, civil society organizations and the philanthropy platform.[176]
- **Technical Committee** to provide technical leadership for implementing, monitoring and reporting on SDGs-related interventions in all sectors. It is made up of representatives from all MDAs, civil society organizations and the private sector.

The Ghana Statistical Service has set up the SDGs Unit which is mandated to collate reliable and accurate data for tracking the SDGs indicators.[177] In addition to these, the Parliament of Ghana has declared strong support for SDG implementation.[178] Further, a Civil Society Platform on SDGs has been established to promote collaboration among CSOs as well as foster effective partnerships with Government

[174]Government of Ghana, *GHANA REPORTS ON PROGRESS OF IMPLEMENTATION OF SDGS AT 2019 HLPT*. Available at: http://www.ghana.gov.gh/index.php/media-center/news/5846-ghana-reports-on-progress-of-implementation-of-sdgs-at-2019-hlpf.

[175]National Development Planning Commission: http://www.ndpc.gov.gh [Accessed on: 31st March, 2018].

[176]Partnerships for the SDGs: https://sustainabledevelopment.un.org/partnership/?p=11224.

[177]Data Production for SDG Indicators in Ghana (March 2017) and Ghana's Data for Sustainable Development Roadmap (April 2017), statsghana.gov.gh [Accessed on: 23rd July, 2019].

[178]United Nations.org (March, 2017). "Overview of institutional arrangements for implementing the 2030 Agenda at national level" [online] Available at: https://sustainabledevelopment.un.org/content/documents/10735Updated_Issues_Brief_rev10_1_March_2017.pdf.

and the Private Sector.[179] There is also the SDGs Philanthropy platform which seeks to mobilize resources from both local and international philanthropy organizations for implementing the SDGs.[180]

Overall, the MDAs are to be responsible for implementing the Plans developed by the NDPC, whereas the NDPC is responsible for monitoring and evaluating the implementation of the Plans and submitting annual M&E reports to Parliament. By this mechanism, government is monitored to ensure that expenditure is effectively regulated so as to achieve the optimum results from the funds and other resources devoted to the realisation of the SDGs. Thus, through the implementation of the Coordinated Programme, the possibility of the SDGs being met is enhanced.

How Individuals or NGOs may Intervene in the Design of Development and Anti-Poverty Policy

Citizens, Civil Society Organizations (CSOs), private enterprises and development partners can, if they so desire, monitor policies, programmes, plans or projects implementation and demand accountability from relevant duty bearers. At almost every level of development, NGOs are at liberty to intervene in ensuring that the nation develops effectively. Under the 1992 Constitution, the Fundamental Human Rights are an entitlement for all persons in Ghana subject only to the respect for the rights and freedoms of others and for the public interest.[181] Thus individuals, agencies and companies are entitled to their rights and freedoms and they may seek redress in the High Court for an infringement of any right.[182]

Further, Article 2(2) of the 1992 Constitution provides the opportunity for anyone who alleges that either an enactment or anything contained in or done under the authority of that or any enactment; or any act or omission of any person is inconsistent with, or is in contravention of a provision of the Constitution, to bring an action in the Supreme Court for a declaration to that effect. Also, there have been instances were CSOs have taken up constitutional litigation in the public interest, as demonstrated in the consolidated cases of *Ahumah Ocansey v Electoral Commission*; *Centre for Human and Civil Liberties (CHURCIL) v. Attorney-General & Electoral Commission* (consolidated)[183] where the Supreme Court of Ghana ruled

[179]Media Foundation for West Africa, "Civil Society Set Up SDGs Platform in Ghana" [online] Available at: http://www.mfwa.org/country-highlights/civil-society-set-up-sdg-platform-in-ghana/.

[180]SDG Philanthropy Platform.org, "Engaging Philanthropy to Take Actions on the SDGs" [online] Available at: https://www.sdgphilanthropy.org/.

[181]Article 12(2) of the 1992 Constitution of Ghana.

[182]Article 33(1) and Article 140(2) of the 1992 Constitution of Ghana.

[183]Ahumah Ocansey v Electoral Commission; Centre for Human and Civil Liberties (CHURCIL) v. Attorney-General & Electoral Commission [2010] SCGLR 575.

that the right to vote was so fundamental that it extended to prisoners or persons incarcerated for various offences.

In addition to the various modes by which the 1992 Constitution creates an avenue for redress, individuals and NGOs may intervene right from the planning stages of various policies, such as the manifesto presentations of political parties vying for the seat of government, knowing that the manifestos of these parties drive their governmental agenda. By voicing their concerns at this stage, their interests are more likely to be considered as the voice of the people and will subsequently be given consideration. They can also intervene at the presentation of national development plans and at various government budget readings. These different avenues by which individuals and organizations may contribute must be taken advantage of in order to ensure that the design for development and the anti-poverty strategy is clearly marked out, rather than being given a cursory reference now and again. A study conducted by Abdul-Gafaru and Ruby Quantson[184] reveals that there have been apparent changes in the role of CSOs in policy dialogue.[185] The considerable improvement was attributable to the fact that CSOs were engaged in mitigating the negative impacts of public policies, and they were to a large extent objective on their views; additionally, their policy recommendations were based on practical experience in matters concerning poverty.[186] Furthermore, at the implementation and monitoring phases of various developmental and anti-poverty projects, agencies and individuals may intervene to facilitate the proper implementation of project goals.[187]

The National Development Planning (System) Act[188] was enacted to "provide for a National Development Planning System, define and regulate planning procedure and provide for related matters." This was to be a decentralised national planning system with the National Development Planning Commission as its national co-ordinating body.[189]

The National Development Planning (System) Regulations, 2016[190] defines the roles of various institutions in the NDPC Act, to ensure compliance with the planning requirement under the specific provisions in the Act. Thus, the "bottom up" mechanism of participation, where the various institutions address the specific tasks assigned to them in order to contribute to the larger goal of national development, is utilised here.

---

[184]Abdulai and Quantson (2008/2009), pp. 114–151.

[185]*Ibid.* at p. 136.

[186]*Ibid.* at p. 137.

[187]Ghana Developing Communities Association (GCDA) is an NGO working in Northern Ghana to eliminate poverty and empower communities. A number of their projects that are in line with the SDGs include the Kaya Girls Project and Empowerment for Life and Communities Fighting Hunger Project. https://www.gdcaghana.org/copy-of-empowerment-for-life.

[188]National Development Planning (System) Act of 1994 (Act 480).

[189]*Ibid.*, section 1(1).

[190]National Development Planning (System) Regulations, 2016 (L.I 2232).

A collaboration between the public and private sector can therefore be easily identified. Government creates systems and checks by which it would monitor the effective implementation of its anti-poverty and developmental projects through the NDPC, but at the same time individuals and NGOs can follow up and assess progress themselves. Under the immediate past government of Ghana under President John Mahama, an initiative was developed to restructure Government for greater efficiency. This initiative was a financial and technical assistance programme funded by the United Kingdom's Department for International Development (DFID). It was aimed at improving and strengthening the processes of policymaking, and also to help track the implementation of Presidential/Executive priority policy decisions taken by the Cabinet, as an activity of direct support to the Presidency. The initiative, known as the Reconstructing Government for Delivery—or DELIVER Programme, was mainly conceptualised to complement other interventions on policy and delivery, and not to replace them. This system of monitoring from the presidential level served as a self-check on the government itself.

Further to this initiative, the current President has appointed a Monitoring and Evaluation Minister. The Ministry was set up primarily to consolidate government's activities by ensuring appointees live up to set targets and culminate in the overall growth agenda. By this, a two-way monitoring and evaluation system can be expected, where government in itself is to be its own check in addition to the external monitors by way of individuals and organizations, not forgetting the media. The government therefore ensures that measures by which its policies may be assessed are provided, in addition to measures provided by CSOs and the private sector.

Bilateral and Multilateral Initiatives or Agreements

Whether or not Ghana has Adopted any Engagement of a Voluntary or Binding Nature Related to the Fight Against Poverty and/or the Right to Development?

Global partnerships in this present age are imperative to fast-track developmental initiatives of individual member states of the United Nations and to fill the loopholes created by stagnated development in Africa. It is pleasing to note that Ghana has made tremendous progress in its fight against poverty by aligning itself with other like-minded countries who share in the same vision of eliminating poverty and striving for development, globally. Through donor aid and the implementation of social schemes from Global Partnerships, Ghana remains a beneficiary of the Global Partnership agenda boldly imprinted as Goal 17 of the United Nations Sustainable Development Goals (SDGs).

Ghana has had bilateral and multilateral relations with several countries since independence. The country's largest donor is the Government of the United States of America represented by its Development Agency, USAID. Among other major partners are the Department for International Development (DFID), Danish International Development Agency (DANIDA), China International Development Cooperation Agency (CIDCA) and the Japan International Cooperation Agency (JICA).

By signing and ratifying various International Agreements, Ghana voluntarily engages to be bound by these multilateral agreements. In line with that, the State agrees to the presentation of reports in the periods stated in the agreements. For instance, and as already captured, pursuant to Articles 16 and 17 of the International Covenant on Economic, Social and Cultural Rights (ICESCR), Ghana is obliged to submit regular reports on how the Rights are being implemented.[191] States are to prepare reports every five years on the situation of Economic, Social and Cultural Rights in their country.

Specific Multilateral and Bilateral Agreements which Include Contributions to the Fight Against Poverty and/or International Development for a Fixed Period of Time

Multilateral Treaties

- Sustainable Development Goals: At the Millennium Development Summit Ghana was one of the 70 countries selected to be part of the Open Working Group (OWG) constituted to develop a post 2015 global development agenda known as the Sustainable Development Goals.[192] The SDGs are specifically aimed to meet urgent environmental, political and economic challenges in our world today, especially in the developing world. Top among these goals is the fight against poverty. The aim is to meet these goals by the year 2030.[193]
- Agenda 2063.[194] This is a strategic framework established by the African Union for the socio-economic transformation of the continent over the next 50 years. It builds on and seeks to accelerate the implementation of past and existing continental initiatives for growth and sustainable development. As a member of the African Union, Ghana is a party to the framework. Agenda 2063 has seven key African Aspirations,[195] which include:

  1. A Prosperous Africa, based on inclusive growth and sustainable development,

[191] COMMITTEE ON THE RIGHTS OF PERSONS WITH DISABILITIES—Article 36—Consideration of reports: http://www.ohchr.org/EN/HRBodies/CRPD/Pages/ConventionRightsPersonsWithDisabilities.aspx.

[192] THE SUSTAINABLE DEVELOPMENT GOALS (SDGS) www.ghana.gov.gh/index.php/media-center/press-release/1958-the-sustainable-development-goals-sdgs.

[193] SUSTAINABLE DEVELOPMENT GOALS: http://www.gh.undp.org/content/ghana/en/home/sustainable-development-goals.html.

[194] Agenda 2063: https://au.int/en/agenda2063.

[195] *Ibid.*

2. An Africa of good governance, democracy, respect for human rights, justice and the rule of law, and
3. An Africa whose development is people driven, relying on the potential offered by people, especially its women and youth and caring for children.

- More recently, Ghana[196] and other African countries signed the framework to establish the African Continental Free Trade Area (AfCFTA) during the 10th Ordinary Session of African Union Heads of State summit held in Kigali. This framework was the initiative of the African Union and "will be one of the world's largest free-trade areas in terms of the number of countries, covering more than 1.2 billion people and over $4 trillion in combined consumer and business spending if all 55 countries join".[197] Aims of the AfCFTA include harmonizing intra-African trade and contributing to sustainable economic development.

For the purposes of this paper, we will focus on five bilateral and grant agreements between Ghana and some of her major donors: Governments of the United States, the United Kingdom, Denmark, China and Japan.

United States

Ghana's relations with the United States Government has remained dynamic over the years. Ghana is a member of the African Growth and Opportunity Act, introduced to improve trade relations between the US and her partners in Sub-Saharan countries.[198] The US Agency for International Development (USAID) leads all development projects and programmes abroad. There are partnerships such as the International Military Education and Training programme (IMETP), African Contingency Operations Training and Assistance programme, International Visitor Leadership Programme, State Partnership Programme, the West African Trade and Investment Hub, and the Peace Corps.[199]

United Kingdom

Furthermore, Ghana's relationship with the United Kingdom (UK) continues to remain cordial since independence. The UK bilateral relations consists of five

[196] Forty-four countries sign historic African Union free trade agreement: http://www.africanews.com/2018/03/21/forty-four-countries-sign-historic-africa-union-free-trade-agreement//.

[197] Africa's big new free trade agreement, explained: https://www.washingtonpost.com/news/monkey-cage/wp/2018/03/29/the-countdown-to-the-african-continental-free-trade-area-starts-now/?utm_term=.6b0b54ab32af.

[198] See: "About AGOA" [online] Available at: https://agoa.info/about-agoa.html.

[199] US Department of State, Bureau of African Affairs, 2019. U.S. Relations with Ghana. https://www.state.gov/r/pa/ei/bgn/2860.htm.

principles: Developing Country Ownership; Participatory and Evidence-Based Policy-Making; Predictability; Harmonisation; and Transparency and Accountability.[200] This partnership allows the UK government, through its Department for International Development (DFID) to relieve Ghana of its aid funds dependency with a focus on trade and investment, fighting corruption in the public sector, and reduce gender disparities and inequality, so that the poor and vulnerable have better opportunities to sustain their future needs.

One of the agreements between the two countries is the PASS education programme or Girls' Participatory Approaches for Student Success in Ghana. Introduced in 2012, PASS is expected to benefit about 81,000 female students and 38 educational institutions. By doing this, the poverty and inequality gap between women and men would be bridged as women would be empowered and prepared for a competitive job market to earn incomes that would improve their living standards. An in-depth description of the PASS programme is contained in their 2018 Annual report. The programme is identified by the number: GB-1-202493.[201]

Through the UK Department for International Development (DFID) a series of other development-driven programmes with the United Kingdom have been implemented, and they include:

1. The Market Development in Northern Ghana (MADE, 2013–2020). The programme is intended to reduce poverty in Northern Ghana by empowering farmers and local entrepreneurs with the needed skills to enhance their businesses and quality of life. The programme is identified by the code: GB-1-201857.[202]
2. The Ghana Health Sector Support Programme (2012–2018). The primary focus of the Ghana Health Sector Support Programme is central to attaining targets on reducing child mortality, improve maternal health and combat HIV/AIDS and Tuberculosis. Under the SDGs, the programme is expected to achieve Goal number 3 (Improve Sustainable Health and Wellbeing). Trainings, financial support and medical equipment are supplied to the Ministry of Health to ensure that Ghanaians have access to at least their basic healthcare needs. The programme number is GB-1-203536.[203]
3. Africa Division Funding to the African Agriculture Company (AgDevCo). The programme is identified by the code: GB-1-204270. AgDevCo works to ensure food security, economic growth, job opportunities, income stability and a

[200] Department for International Development—DFID, Foreign and Commonwealth Office, HM Treasury (2015), *Partnerships for Poverty Reduction: Rethinking Conditionality.* A UK Policy Paper. https://assets.publishing.service.gov.uk/government/uploads/system/uploads/attachment_data/file/211182/partnerships-poverty-reduction.pdf.

[201] Department for International Development (DFID), Girls' Participatory Approaches for Student (G's PASS or G-PASS), 2012. https://devtracker.dfid.gov.uk/projects/GB-1-202493/documents.

[202] Department for International Development (DFID), Market Development in Northern Ghana (MADE). Retrieved from https://devtracker.dfid.gov.uk/projects/GB-1-201857/documents.

[203] Department for International Development (DFID), Ghana Health Sector Support Programme (2012–2018) https://devtracker.dfid.gov.uk/projects/GB-1-203536.

sustainable quality of life for its stakeholders.[204] The company focuses on early stage Small and Medium Enterprise in agribusiness in some eight sub-Saharan countries including Ghana.

4. Ghana Oil and Gas Inclusive Growth (GOGIG), 2014–2019. This programme is intended to regulate activities in the oil and gas sector, while providing training and capacity for CSOs, Parliament and other stakeholders to follow and monitor government's engagements in the sector for transparency and accountability reasons.[205]
5. Policy Research Fund (2014–2019). DFID's short-term policy research programmes are intended to provide reliable information on the department's engagements in health, agriculture, education, good governance, trade, social protection, energy, economics and innovation. The programme is coded: GB-1-204584.[206]

Denmark

In the immediate past, Denmark has shared four bilateral development agreements with Ghana, which are now aimed at helping Ghana transition from aid dependency to trade. These agreements are:[207]

1. Multi-Donor Budget Support from 2010–2014. Together with other international development partners, this support programme was designed to assist Ghana with the implementation and subsequent monitoring of the Medium-Term Development Policy Framework (MTDPF). The MTDPF was focused on economic growth and stability, helping Ghana achieve middle-income status, as well as meeting the demands and requirements of the Millennium Development Goals (MDG) by 2015.
2. Support to Private Sector Development (2010–2014). As part of Government of Ghana's (GoG's) private sector development strategy, the programme focused on business strategies that would encourage local and foreign investment, business advocacy, and training and capacity development of farmers and stakeholders in Ghana's agri-business.

[204]Africa Division Funding to the African Agriculture Company (AgDevCo), *Addendum to Business Case for Bridge Funding and Scale-Up Cost and Time Extensions* (01/2019). https://devtracker.dfid.gov.uk/projects/GB-1-204270/documents.

[205]Department for International Development (DFID), Annual Review—Summary Sheet (07/2018), *Ghana Oil and Gas for Inclusive Growth (GOGIG)*. Retrieved from https://devtracker.dfid.gov.uk/projects/GB-1-204330/documents.

[206]Department for International Development (DFID). Annual Review Summary Sheet, 2018. Policy Research Fund. Retrieved from https://devtracker.dfid.gov.uk/projects/GB-1-204584/documents.

[207]Ministry of Foreign Affairs of Denmark, Danida. Denmark—Ghana Partnership Policy 2014–2018. http://ghana.um.dk/en/danida-en.

3. Health Sector Programme Support Phase V (2012–2016). This programme targeted Ghana's attainment of MDGs 4 (Reduce Child Mortality) and 5 (Improve Maternal Health by 2015), and provided funding to health services and the Ministry of Health to ensure that the poor and vulnerable have access to decent healthcare and support.
4. The Right to Services and Good Governance Programme (2014–2018). This Programme was designed with the success of the Multi-Donor Budget Support and Support to Private Sector Development programmes in mind. It was expected that by 2018, Ghana's decentralization, human rights and good governance mechanisms would be strengthened enough to depend on itself over the course of time.

Denmark also has other current partnerships with Ghana including:

1. DANIDA Business Partnership,[208] which is aimed at helping Ghana to improve on economic growth to provide jobs and income enhancement opportunities. This strategy is critical for poverty reduction, reduced aid dependency and to help Ghana meet her SDG commitments on the international front.
2. DANIDA Business Finance[209] is designed to foster inclusive economic growth through sustainable measures, which would help Ghana meet her SDG targets. The partnership provides access to the Paris Club and also brings together Danish business mindsets and local enterprises to exchange knowledge and build a path that achieves the SDGs.
3. Building Stronger Universities Programme[210] is a research partnership between Danish universities and eleven DANIDA partners, including Ghana's elite Universities-University of Ghana, Legon, Accra, and the Kwame Nkrumah University of Science and Technology (K.N.U.S.T.), Kumasi.

China

Since 1960, Ghana's relationship with China has always been a springboard for promoting mutual economic activity. From the year 2000, trade and investment in Ghana has greatly increased. In 2010, Ghana signed a succession of multibillion-dollar deals with China to finance infrastructure projects and change its economy through an anticipated oil and gas-driven industry; the agreements accumulating to approximately US $13 billion in value.[211] As at 2011, the Ghana Investment Promotion Centre had acknowledged that China was on top of foreign direct

[208]Ministry of Foreign Affairs of Denmark. Danida Business Partnerships. http://kenya.um.dk/en/danida-en/menu-1/danida-business-partnerships/.

[209]Ministry of Foreign Affairs of Denmark. Financing for Development http://um.dk/en/danida-en/Sustainable%20Growth/financing-for-development/.

[210]Building Stronger Universities in Developing Countries. Retrieved http://bsuud.org.

[211]Sarpong (2015), p. 1440.

investment in Ghana, with a cumulative total of 23 new projects registered in the first quarter of that year.[212]

Recently, in 2018, Ghana and China signed eight (8) Co-operation Agreements and Memoranda of Understanding in different sectors of their respective economies.[213] The agreements are the "One belt one road Memorandum of Understanding", "Memorandum on Regional Aviation Co-operation", "Agreement for Co-operation in the peaceful use of nuclear energy", "Co-operation to carry out Maternal and Child Health Project", "Framework Agreement on Financing Insurance Co-operation" ($2 billion Sino-Hydro deal), "Economic co-operation on Phase 2 project of the University of Health and Allied Sciences, Ho", "Co-operation on the expansion of the Cape Coast Stadium", and "Co-operation on the supply of police vehicles to the Ghana Police Service."[214]

Again, in 2018, a new agreement under the Joint Commission on Economic, Trade and Technical Cooperation[215] was entered into between Ghana and China, and Ghana is expected to benefit from a US $60 billion Chinese Fund for Africa.[216] By the agreement, Ghana will receive financial support for development of the power, transport, telecommunications, education and municipal construction sectors of its economy.

China International Development Cooperation Agency (CIDCA) was a major contributor to the "Access to satellite TV for 10000 African villages" project in Ghana, which was completed in May 2019, and 300 remote villages in the Ghana have since bid farewell to a history of no satellite TV.[217]

Japan

As one of the leading pioneers of human security, the Government of Japan, through the Japan International Cooperation Agency (JICA), has worked tirelessly in Ghana in areas covering education, health, governance, transportation, natural resources and energy, private sector development, agriculture and rural development, natural and environmental conservation and food security. Japan has partnered with the

---

[212] *Ibid.* See Abstract of the paper.

[213] Government of Ghana, GHANA, CHINA SIGN COOPERATION AGREEMENTS. Available at: http://www.ghana.gov.gh/index.php/news/4959-ghana-china-sign-cooperation-agreements.

[214] *Ibid.*

[215] The Joint Commission on Economic, Trade and Technical Cooperation is a medium term Development Assistance Agreement, expected to be signed every four years between the two countries to ensure economic cooperation.

[216] Ghana Investment Promotion Centre, *Ghana to Benefit from US $60 Billion Chinese Fund for Africa…Signs New Agreement with China.* Available at: https://www.gipcghana.com/press-and-media/570-ghana-to-benefit-from-us-60-billion-chinese-fund-for-africa-signs-new-agreement-with-china.html.

[217] CIDCA, China-aided satellite TV project completed in Ghana. Available at: http://subsites.chinadaily.com.cn/cidca/2019-05/14/c_373099.htm.

Government of Ghana and the Carter Centre, a US NGO, to fight the spread of Dracunculiasis in the northern parts of the country. In the year 2004 for example, 135 million yen (about $1.2 million) was pumped into the Ghana Guinea Worm Eradication Programme to help eradicate the disease. To make this agenda sustainable, access to potable water free from the guinea worm larvae was promoted. This led to the construction of foot-operated water pumps and filtration systems for clean water harvest.[218] This innovation has been scaled to cover several regions in the country.[219]

JICA has also invested in the Ministry of Health's Community-Based Health Planning and Services (CHPS), which was carved out of successful research activity by the Navrongo Health Research Centre (NHRC) in 1990. The study was conducted with the objective of identifying and addressing gaps and inequities in health care delivery in the Kassena-Nankana District in the Upper East Region. The Ministry of Health requested for the final results and duplicated its findings to cover other remote districts in the country. The Ministry's nation-wide programme became the Community-Based Health Planning and Services (CHPS). CHPS provides essential health care services to vulnerable populations in all districts in the country. However, financial, logistical and technical constraints have slowed down its success rate.[220]

With JICA's expressed interest in poverty reduction and universal health coverage in the northern regions, some of these challenges have been bridged. Between 2006 and 2009, Community Health Officers (CHOs), volunteers, supervisors and leadership benefitted from training courses through this intervention. Additionally, an improved facilitative supervision system was established to lessen the disparities in health care delivery in these regions. This system works with the Community Health Action Plans (CHAPS), Emergency Transportation Systems (ETS), the Health Improvement Programme for Residents in the Upper West Region, and the Japan Overseas Corporation Volunteer Projects. Flowing from this Grant Agreement, 64 CHPS compounds were developed and equipment provided to 75 CHPS compounds to improve access to health facilities in Upper West Region.[221]

Furthermore, JICA, together with the Ministry of Education, and implemented by the Ghana Education Service and the Teacher Education Division, commenced operations on a Project for Strengthening the Capacity of In-Service Training (INSET) Management from 2009 to 2013. INSET is aimed at improving basic

---

[218] Japan International Cooperation Agency, 2015. News: Fight to Eradicate Guinea Worm Disease in Ghana. https://www.jica.go.jp/english/news/field/2015/150625_01.html.

[219] Japan International Cooperation Agency, 2015. News: Fight to Eradicate Guinea Worm Disease in Ghana. https://www.jica.go.jp/english/news/field/2015/150625_01.html.

[220] "Population Health Management: Ghana." Improvement Strategies. Primary Health Care Performance Initiative, 2018, https://improvingphc.org/ghana.

[221] Japan International Cooperation Agency, 22 March 2016. Press Release: Commissioning Ceremony of CHPS Compound and Equipment by the "Project for the Development of Community-based Health Planning and Service Infrastructure in the Upper West Region". https://www.jica.go.jp/ghana/english/office/topics/press_160322.html.

education through peer-to-peer teacher training especially in the fields of Mathematics and Science. The Project for Strengthening the Capacity of INSET Management is designed as a nationwide management system for a structured, quality improvement initiative for these two subjects.[222]

Conclusion and Recommendation

It is clear that achieving the Right to Development and eliminating poverty in Ghana is a constitutional injunction and a policy imperative. It is also palpable that many executive, legislative, judicial, administrative, and international cooperation efforts have been undertaken to realise these noble goals. I end this paper where I started, by reiterating that Development has no end; the journey to that place of sublime comfort exists in perpetuity; and with this in mind, the world must remain ever resilient in our march towards development, as we strategically pull down the walls of engrained and radical poverty. As Ghana's Constitution reminds us: *"the most secure democracy is the one that assures the basic necessities of life for its people as a fundamental duty."*[223]

[222]The Republic of Ghana, Japan International Cooperation Agency. Project to Support the Operationalisation of the In-Service Training Policy, 2006. https://www.jica.go.jp/project/ghana/0604654/pdf/GhanaINSET_Sourcebook2.pdf.

[223]Article 36(2)(e) the 1992 Constitution of Ghana.

Appendix[224]

Table 6.1 International Treaties, Conventions, Agreements and Protocols Ghana has signed or ratified, arranged in alphabetical order[a]

Name of instrument	Signature	Accession[b] (a) Acceptance[c] (b) Approval (b) Adoption[d] (c) Amended[e] (e) Ratification[f] (r) Succession[g] (d)
Additional Protocol to the Convention concerning Customs Facilities for Touring, relating to the Importation of Tourist Publicity Documents and Material, 1954.		16/06/1958 a
Agreement establishing the Common Fund for Commodities, 1980.	01/12/1982	19/01/1983 r
Agreement establishing the International Fund for Agricultural Development, 1976.	19/10/1977	05/12/1977 r
Agreement for Facilitating the International Circulation of Visual and Auditory Materials of an Educational, Scientific and Cultural Character, 1949.		22/03/1960 a
Agreement for the Suppression of the Circulation of Obscene Publications, 1949.	07/04/1958	
Agreement on the Importation of Educational, Scientific and Cultural Materials, 1950.		07/04/1958 d
Agreement on the Privileges and Immunities of the International Criminal Court, 2002.	12/09/2003	
Amendments to the Convention on the International Maritime Organisation, 1993.		01/07/1996 c
Arms Trade Treaty, 2013.	24/09/2013	22/12/2015 r
Basel Convention on the Control of Transboundary Movements of Hazardous Wastes and their Disposal, 1989.		30/05/2003 a
Basel Protocol on Liability and Compensation for Damage Resulting from Transboundary Movements of Hazardous Wastes and their Disposal, 1999.		09/06/2005 a
Cartagena Protocol on Biosafety to the Convention on Biological Diversity, 2000.		30/05/2003 a
Comprehensive Nuclear-Test-Ban Treaty, 1996.	03/10/1996	14/06/2011 r
Constitution of the United Nations Industrial Development Organisation, 1979.	09/04/1979	08/02/1972 r
Convention Concerning Customs Facilities for Touring, 1954.		16/06/1958 a

(continued)

[224]University of Minnesota Database: [online] Available at: http://hrlibrary.umn.edu/research/ratification-ghana.html.

Table 6.1 (continued)

Name of instrument	Signature	Accession[b] (a) Acceptance[c] (b) Approval (b) Adoption[d] (c) Amended[e] (e) Ratification[f] (r) Succession[g] (d)
Convention for Limiting the Manufacture and Regulating the Distribution of Narcotic Drugs. Geneva, 1931, and Lake Success, New York, 1946.		07/041958 r
Convention for the Protection of Producers of Phonograms against Unauthorised Duplication of their Phonograms, 1971.	04/11/2016	
Convention for the Suppression of the Circulation of, and Traffic in, Obscene Publications, 1947.		07/04/1958 r
Convention for the Suppression of the Traffic in Persons and of the Exploitation of the Prostitution of Others, 1950.	24/09/2003	
Convention on a Code of Conduct for Liner Conferences, 1974.	14/05/1975	24/06/1975
Convention on Biological Diversity. Rio de Janeiro, 1992.	12/06/1992	29/08/1994 r
Convention on Cluster Munitions, 2008.	03/12/2008	03/02/2011 r
Convention on Conditions for Registration of Ships, 1986.		29/08/1990 r
Convention on Contracts for the International Sale of Goods, 1980.	11/04/1980	
Convention on Fishing and Conservation of the Living Resources of the High Seas, 1958.	29/04/1958	
Convention on Psychotropic Substances, 1971.	21/02/1971	10/04/1990 r
Convention on the Continental Shelf, 1958.	29/04/1958	
Convention on the High Seas, 1958.	29/04/1958	
Convention on the International Maritime Organisation, 1948.		0607/1959 a
Convention on the Non-Applicability of Statutory Limitations to War Crimes and Crimes against Humanity, 1968.		07/09/2000 a
Convention on the Prevention and Punishment of Crimes against Internationally Protected Persons, including Diplomatic Agents, 1973.		25/04/1975 a
Convention on the Privileges and Immunities of the Specialised Agencies, 1947.		09/09/1958 a
Convention on the Privileges and Immunities of the United Nations, 1946.		05/08/1958 a
Convention on the prohibition of military or any other hostile use of environmental modification techniques, 1976.	21/03/1978	22/06/1978 r
Convention on the Prohibition of the Development, Production, Stockpiling and Use of Chemical Weapons and on their Destruction, 1992.	14/01/1993	09/07/1997 r
Convention on the Prohibition of the Use, Stockpiling, Production and Transfer of Anti-Personnel Mines and on their Destruction, 1997.	04/12/1997	30/06/2000 r

(continued)

Table 6.1 (continued)

Name of instrument	Signature	Accession[b] (a) Acceptance[c] (b) Approval (b) Adoption[d] (c) Amended[e] (e) Ratification[f] (r) Succession[g] (d)
Convention on the Recognition and Enforcement of Foreign Arbitral Awards, 1958.		09/04/1968 a
Convention on the Territorial Sea and the Contiguous Zone, 1958.	29/04/1958	
Customs Convention on the Temporary Importation of Private Road Vehicles, 1954.		16/08/1958 a
Final Protocol to the Convention for the Suppression of the Traffic in Persons and of the Exploitation of the Prostitution of Others, 1950.	24/09/2003	
International Cocoa Agreement, 2001.	17/06/2002	21/02/2003 r
International Cocoa Agreement, 2010.	19/09/2011	18/12/2012 r
International Convention Against the Taking of Hostages, 1979.		10/11/1987 a
International Convention for the Protection of All Persons from Enforced Disappearance, 2006.	06/02/2007	
International Convention for the Suppression of Acts of Nuclear Terrorism, 2005.	06/11/2006	
International Convention for the Suppression of Terrorist Bombings, 1997.		06/09/2002 a
International Convention for the Suppression of the Financing of Terrorism, 1999.	12/11/2001	06/09/2002 r
International Convention for the Suppression of the White Slave Traffic, 1949.		07/04/1958 r
International Convention to Facilitate the Importation of Commercial Samples and Advertising Material, 1952.		07/04/1958 d
International Opium Convention, 1946.		07/04/1958 e
International Tropical Timber Agreement, 1994.	12/07/1995	28/08/1995 r
International Tropical Timber Agreement, 2006.	07/10/2008	
Kyoto Protocol to the United Nations Framework Convention on Climate Change, 1997.		30/05/2003 a
Minamata Convention on Mercury, 2013.	24/09/2014	23/05/2017 r
Montreal Protocol on Substances that Deplete the Ozone Layer, 1987.	16/09/1987	14/07/1992 r
Nagoya Protocol on Access to Genetic Resources and the Fair and Equitable Sharing of Benefits Arising from their Utilisation to the Convention on Biological Diversity, 2010.	20/05/2011	
Optional Protocol concerning the Compulsory Settlement of Disputes, 1961.	18/04/1961	
Optional Protocol of Signature Concerning the Compulsory Settlement of Disputes, 1958. This name doesn't sound right	29/04/1958	

(continued)

Table 6.1 (continued)

Name of instrument	Signature	Accession[b] (a) Acceptance[c] (b) Approval (b) Adoption[d] (c) Amended[e] (e) Ratification[f] (r) Succession[g] (d)
Optional Protocol of Signature concerning the Compulsory Settlement of Disputes, 1958.	29/04/1958	
Optional Protocol to the Convention against Torture and Other Cruel, Inhuman or Degrading Treatment or Punishment, 2002.	06/11/2006	23/09/2016 r
Optional Protocol to the Convention on the Elimination of Discrimination against Women.	24/02/2000	3/02/2011 r
Optional Protocol to the Convention on the Rights of the Child on the involvement of children in armed conflict.[h]	24/09/2003	09/12/2014 r
Optional Protocol to the International Covenant on Civil and Political Right.	07/09/2000	07/09/2000 r
Optional Protocol to the Vienna Convention on Consular Relations concerning Acquisition of Nationality. Vienna, 1963.	24/04/1963	04/10/1963 r
Optional Protocol to the Vienna Convention on Consular Relations concerning the Compulsory Settlement of Disputes. Vienna, 1963.	24/04/1963	
Optional Protocol to the Vienna Convention on Diplomatic Relations, Concerning Acquisition of Nationality. Vienna, 1961.	18/04/1961	
Optional Protocol to the Vienna Convention on Diplomatic Relations, Concerning the Compulsory Settlement of Disputes. Vienna, 1961.	18/04/1961	
Paris Agreement. Paris, 2015.	22/04/2016	21/09/2016 r
Protocol against the Illicit Manufacturing of and Trafficking in Firearms, Their Parts and Components and Ammunition, supplementing the United Nations Convention against Transnational Organised Crime, 2001.	14/02/2014	
Protocol against the Smuggling of Migrants by Land, Sea and Air, supplementing the United Nations Convention against Transnational Organized Crime.		21/08/2012 a
Protocol against the Smuggling of Migrants by Land, Sea and Air, supplementing the United Nations Convention against Transnational Organized Crime, 2000.		21/09/2012 a
Protocol Amending the Single Convention on Narcotic Drugs, 1961; Geneva, 1972.	25/03/1972	
Protocol Bringing under International Control Drugs Outside the Scope of the Convention of 13 July 1931 for Limiting the Manufacture and Regulating the Distribution of Narcotic Drugs, as amended by the Protocol signed at Lake Success, New York, on 11 December 1946. Paris, 19 November 1948.		07/04/1958 r

(continued)

Table 6.1 (continued)

Name of instrument	Signature	Accession[b] (a) Acceptance[c] (b) Approval(b) Adoption[d] (c) Amended[e] (e) Ratification[f] (r) Succession[g] (d)
Protocol on the Privileges and Immunities of the International Seabed Authority, 1998.	12/01/1999	23/09/2016 r
Protocol Relating to the Status of Refugees.		30/10/1968 a
Protocol to Eliminate Illicit Trade in Tobacco Products, 2012.	24/09/2013	
Protocol to Prevent, Suppress and Punish Trafficking in Persons, Especially Women and Children, supplementing the United Nations Convention against Transnational Organised Crime Preamble.		21/06/2012 a
Protocol to Prevent, Suppress and Punish Trafficking in Persons, Especially Women and Children, supplementing the United Nations Convention against Transnational Organised Crime, 2000.		21/09/2012 a
Rome Statute of the International Criminal Court, 1998.	18/07/1998	20/12/1999 r
Rotterdam Convention on the Prior Informed Consent Procedure for Certain Hazardous Chemicals and Pesticides in International Trade, 1998.	11/09/1998	30/05/2003 r
Second Optional Protocol to the International Covenant on Civil and Political Rights, aiming at the abolition of the death penalty.	07/09/2000	07/09/2000 r
Signatory to the Constitution of the World Health Organisation	08/04/1957	
Single Convention on Narcotic Drugs, 1961, as Amended by the Protocol Amending the Single Convention on Narcotic Drugs, 1961. New York, 1975.		10/04/1990 a
Single Convention on Narcotic Drugs, 1961. 30/03/1961.		15/01/1964 r
Stockholm Convention on Persistent Organic Pollutants, 2001.	23/05/2001	30/05/2003 r
Supplementary Convention on the Abolition of Slavery, the Slave Trade, and Institutions and Practices Similar to Slavery, 1956.		03/05/1963 a
Tampere Convention on the Provision of Telecommunication Resources for Disaster Mitigation and Relief Operations, 1998.	18/06/1998	
The Convention Against Torture (CAT) and Other Cruel, Inhuman or Degrading Treatment or Punishment.	07/9/2000	07/09/2000 r
The Convention on the Elimination of all Forms of Discrimination against Women (CEDAW).	17/07/1980	02/01/1986 r
The Convention on the Prevention and Punishment of the Crime of Genocide.		24/12/1958 a
The Convention on the Rights of the Child (CRC).	29/01/1990	05/02/1990 r

(continued)

Table 6.1 (continued)

Name of instrument	Signature	Accession[b] (a) Acceptance[c] (b) Approval (b) Adoption[d] (c) Amended[e] (e) Ratification[f] (r) Succession[g] (d)
The International Convention on the Elimination of all Forms of Racial Discrimination (CERD).	08/09/1966	08/09/1966 r
The International Covenant on Civil and Political Rights (ICCPR).	07/09/2000	07/09/2000 r
The International Covenant on Economic, Social and Cultural Rights (ICESCR)	07/09/2000	07/09/2000 r
The Rome Statute on the International Criminal Court (ICC).	18/07/1998	20/12/1999 r
The UN Convention relating to the Status of Refugees.		18/03/1963 a
Treaty on the Prohibition of Nuclear Weapons, 2017.	20/09/2017	
United Nations Agreement to Establish the South Centre, 1994.	17/10/1994	
United Nations Convention against Corruption 27/06/2007.	09/12/2004	28/06/1962 r
United Nations Convention against Corruption, 2003.	09/12/2004	27/06/2007 r
United Nations Convention against Illicit Traffic in Narcotic Drugs and Psychotropic Substances, 1988.	20/12/1988	10/04/1990 r
United Nations Convention against Transnational Organized Crime.		21/08/2012 a
United Nations Convention on the Law of the Sea, 1982.	10/12/1982	07/06/1983 r
United Nations Framework Convention on Climate Change (UNFCCC or FCCC)	12/061992	06/09/1995 r
United Nations Framework Convention on Climate Change, 1992.	12/06/1992	06/09/1995 r
Vienna Convention for the Protection of the Ozone Layer, 1985.		24/07/1989 a
Vienna Convention on Consular Relations. Vienna, 1963.	24/04/1963	04/10/1963 r
Vienna Convention on Diplomatic Relations.	18/04/1961	28/06/1962
Vienna Convention on Diplomatic Relations. Vienna, 1961.	18/04/1961	28/06/1968 r
Vienna Convention on the Law of Treaties, 1969.	23/05/1969	
WHO Framework Convention on Tobacco Control, 2003.	20/06/2003	29/11/2004 r

[a]See Republic of Ghana Treaty Manual. Available at: http://legal.un.org/avl/documents/scans/GhanaTreatyManual2009.pdf?teil=II&j

[b]"Accession" is the act whereby a state accepts the offer or the opportunity to become a party to a treaty already negotiated and signed by other states. It has the same legal effect as ratification. Vienna Convention on the Law of Treaties, Vienna on 23 May 1969, United Nations, *Treaty Series*, Arts.2 (1) (b) and 15, vol. 1155, p. 331 available from http://legal.un.org/ilc/texts/instruments/english/conventions/1_1_1969.pdf

[c]The instruments of "acceptance" or "approval" of a treaty have the same legal effect as ratification and consequently express the consent of a state to be bound by a treaty. In the practice of certain states acceptance and approval have been used instead of ratification when, at a national level, constitutional law does not require the treaty to be ratified by the head of state. Vienna Convention

(continued)

on the Law of Treaties, Vienna on 23 May 1969, United Nations, *Treaty Series*, Arts.2 (1) (b) and 14 (2), vol. 1155, p. 331 available from http://legal.un.org/ilc/texts/instruments/english/conventions/1_1_1969.pdf

[d]"Adoption" is the formal act by which the form and content of a proposed treaty text are established. As a general rule, the adoption of the text of a treaty takes place through the expression of the consent of the states participating in the treaty-making process. Vienna Convention on the Law of Treaties, Vienna on 23 May 1969, United Nations, *Treaty Series*, Art. 9, vol. 1155, p. 331 available from http://legal.un.org/ilc/texts/instruments/english/conventions/1_1_1969.pdf

[e]The term "amendment" refers to the formal alteration of treaty provisions affecting all the parties to the particular agreement. Vienna Convention on the Law of Treaties, Vienna on 23 May 1969, United Nations, *Treaty Series*, Art. 40, vol. 1155, p. 331 available from http://legal.un.org/ilc/texts/instruments/english/conventions/1_1_1969.pdf

[f]Ratification defines the international act whereby a state indicates its consent to be bound to a treaty if the parties intended to show their consent by such an act. Vienna Convention on the Law of Treaties, Vienna on 23 May 1969, United Nations, *Treaty Series*, Arts.2 (1) (b), 14 (1) and 16, vol. 1155, p. 331 available from http://legal.un.org/ilc/texts/instruments/english/conventions/1_1_1969.pdf

[g]Vienna Convention on Succession of States in respect of Treaties, Vienna on 23 August 1978, United Nations, *Treaty Series*, Vol. 1946, p. 3 available from http://legal.un.org/ilc/texts/instruments/english/conventions/3_2_1978.pdf

[h]United Nations Treaty Collection: https://treaties.un.org/Pages/ViewDetails.aspx?src=IND&mtdsg_no=IV-11-b&chapter=4&lang=en

Table 6.2 International Labour Organization (ILO) conventions ratified by Ghana[a]

Name of instrument	Signature	Accession (a) Acceptance (b) Approval (b) Adoption (c) Amended (e) Ratification (r) Succession (d)
Abolition of Forced Labour Convention, 1957 (No. 105)	15/12/1958	
Abolition of Forced Labour Convention, 1957 (No. 105)	15/12/1958	
Discrimination (Employment and Occupation) Convention, 1958 (No. 111)	04/06/1961	
Employment Service Convention, 1948 (No. 88)	04/04/1961	
Equal Remuneration Convention, 1951 (No. 100)	14/05/1968	
Equality of Treatment (Accident Compensation) Convention, 1925 (No. 19)		
Equality of Treatment (Accident Compensation) Convention, 1925 (No. 19)	20/05/1957	
Fee-Charging Employment Agencies Convention (Revised), 1949 (No. 96)	21/08/1973	
Final Articles Revision Convention, 1961 (No. 116)	27/08/1963	
Forced Labour Convention, 1930 (No. 29)	20/05/1957	
Freedom of Association and Protection of the Right to Organise Convention, 1948 (No. 87)	02/06/1965	

(continued)

Table 6.2 (continued)

Name of instrument	Signature	Accession (a) Acceptance (b) Approval (b) Adoption (c) Amended (e) Ratification (r) Succession (d)
Guarding of Machinery Convention, 1963 (No. 119)	18/03/1965	
Hours of Work (Commerce and Offices) Convention, 1930 (No. 30)	19/06/1973	
Hours of Work (Industry) Convention, 1919 (No. 1)	19/06/1973	
Hygiene (Commerce and Offices) Convention, 1964 (No. 120)	21/11/1966	
Indigenous and Tribal Populations Convention, 1957 (No. 107)	15/12/1958	
Labour Administration Convention, 1978 (No. 150)	27/05/1986	
Labour Clauses (Public Contracts) Convention, 1949 (No. 94)	04/04/1961	
Labour Inspection Convention, 1947 (No. 81)	02/07/1959	
Labour Relations (Public Service) Convention, 1978 (No. 151)	27/05/1986	
Maternity Protection Convention (Revised), 1952 (No. 103)		
Maternity Protection Convention (Revised), 1952 (No. 103)	27/05/1986	
Minimum Age Convention, 1973 (No. 138)	06/06/2011	
Minimum Wage-Fixing Machinery Convention, 1928 (No. 26)	02/06/1959	
Night Work (Women) Convention (Revised), 1948 (No. 89)		
Night Work (Women) Convention (Revised), 1948 (No. 89)	02/07/1959	
Night Work of Young Persons (Industry) Convention (Revised), 1948 (No. 90)		
Night Work of Young Persons (Industry) Convention (Revised), 1948 (No. 90)	04/04/1961	
Nursing Personnel Convention, 1977 (No. 149)	27/05/1986	
Radiation Protection Convention, 1960 (No. 115)		
Radiation Protection Convention, 1960 (No. 115)	07/11/1961	
Recruiting of Indigenous Workers Convention, 1936 (No. 50)		
Right of Association (Agriculture) Convention, 1921 (No. 11)	14/03/1968	
Right to Organise and Collective Bargaining Convention, 1949 (No. 98)	02/06/1959	
Safety and Health in Agriculture Convention, 2001 (No. 184)	06/06/2011	
Seafarers' Identity Documents Convention, 1958 (No. 108)	19/02/1960	
Social Policy (Basic Aims and Standards) Convention, 1962 (No. 117)	18/06/1964	

(continued)

Table 6.2 (continued)

Name of instrument	Signature	Accession (a) Acceptance (b) Approval (b) Adoption (c) Amended (e) Ratification (r) Succession (d)
Tripartite Consultation (International Labour Standards) Convention, 1976 (No. 144)	06/06/2011	
Underground Work (Women) Convention, 1935 (No. 45)		
Underground Work (Women) Convention, 1935 (No. 45)	20/05/1957	
Weekly Rest (Commerce and Offices) Convention, 1957 (No. 106)	15/12/1958	
Weekly Rest (Industry) Convention, 1921 (No. 14)	19/06/1973	
Working Environment (Air Pollution, Noise and Vibration) Convention, 1977 (No. 148)	27/05/1986	
Worst Forms of Child Labour Convention, 1999 (No. 182)	13/06/2000	

[a]International Labour Organization, *Ratifications for Ghana.* Available at: https://www.ilo.org/dyn/normlex/en/f?p=NORMLEXPUB:11200:0::NO::P11200_COUNTRY_ID:103231

Table 6.3 Treaties, conventions and protocols of the African Union (organization of African unity) signed or ratified by Ghana[a]

Treaty title	Signature date	Ratification date	Deposit date
Additional Protocol to the OAU General Convention on Privileges and Immunities[b] – 0001			
African Charter on Human and Peoples Rights – 0002	03/07/2004	24/01/1989	0/03/1989
African Charter on the Rights and Welfare of the Child – 0003	18/08/1997	15/07/2005	15/07/2005
African Civil Aviation Commission Constitution (AFCAC) – 0004	17/01/1969	26/11/1970	10/12/1970
African Convention on the Conservation of Nature and Natural Resources – 0005	15/09/1968	17/05/1959	17/05/1969
African Maritime Transport Charter – 0006	02/07/2004	–	
African Rehabilitation Institute (ARI) – 0007	02/07/2004	–	
Bamako Convention on the Ban of the Import into Africa and the Control of Transboundary Movement and Management of Hazardous Waste within Africa – 0008	02/07/2004	–	
Constitution of the Association of African Trade – 0009	25/02/1974	12/08/1971	08/05/1978
Constitutive Act of the African Union – 0010	12/07/2000	12/08/1971	21/05/2001

(continued)

Table 6.3 (continued)

Treaty title	Signature date	Ratification date	Deposit date
Convention for the Elimination of Mercenarism in Africa – 0011	08/06/1978	20/07/1978	21/05/1978
Convention for the Establishment of the African Centre for Fertilizer Development – 0012	02/07/2001	–	
OAU Convention on the Prevention and Combating of Terrorism – 0013	14/07/1999	30/08/202	06/11/2002
Cultural Charter for Africa ([b]) – 0014		15/06/1977	28/07/1977
General Convention on the Privileges and Immunities of the OAU – 0015	25/10/1965	01/08/1968	01/08/1968
Inter-African Convention establishing an African Technical Co-operation programme – 0016	02/07/2004	–	
OAU Convention Governing the Specific aspects of refugee problems in Africa – 0017	10/09/1969	19/06/1975	18/08/1983
Phyto-sanitary Convention for Africa ([b]) – 0018	–	–	
Protocol relating to the establishment of the Peace and Security Council of the African Union – 0019	09/07/2002	04/07/2003	07/07/2003
Protocol to the African Charter on Human and People's Rights on the establishment of an African Court on Human and Peoples Right – 0020	09/06/1998	25/08/2004	16/08/2005
Protocol to the Treaty establishing the African Economic Community relating to the Pan African Parliament – 0021	20/09/2002	15/09/2003	04/02/2004

[a]Republic of Ghana Treaty Manual. United Nations Organization (Legal). p. 10. Available at http://legal.un.org/avl/documents/scans/GhanaTreatyManual2009.pdf?teil=II&j
[b]These treaties do not require signatures

Table 6.4 ECOWAS protocols, conventions and treaties signed and ratified by Ghana[a]

Protocols and conventions	Date of ratification
General Convention on Privileges and Immunities of the ECOWAS signed in Lagos on 22nd April, 1978	30/03/79
Protocol on Non-Aggression signed in Lagos on 22nd April, 1978	30/03/79
Protocol A/P1/5/79 relating to free movements of persons, residence and establishment signed in Dakar on 29th May, 1979	08/04/80
Supplementary Protocol A/SPI/5/79 amending the French text of the Protocol relating to the Definition of the concept of Products originating from Member States (Article 1) signed in Dakar on 29th May, 1979	02/04/85
Supplementary Protocol A/SP2/5/79 amending the definition of the concept of Products originating from Member States (Article 2) signed in Dakar on 29th May, 1979	02/04/85
Supplementary Protocol A/SP3/5/80 amending Article 8 of the French text of the Protocol relating to the Definition of Concept of originating Products from Member States (Treatment of Mixtures) signed in Freetown on 29th May, 1980	02/04/85

(continued)

Table 6.4 (continued)

Supplementary Protocol A/SPI/5/81 amending Article 2 of the Protocol relating to the Concept of Originating products (Handicraft Products) signed in Freetown on 29th May, 1981	02/04/85
Supplementary Protocol A/SP2/5/81 amending Article 4 of the ECOWAS Treaty relating to Community Institutions signed in Freetown 29th May, 1981	02/04/85
Protocol A/SP3/5/81 relating to Mutual Assistance on Defence signed in Freetown on 29th May, 1981	12/05/89
Protocol A/P1/5/82 on the establishment of an ECOWAS Brown Card relating to Motor Vehicle Third Party Liability Insurance, signed in Cotonou on 29th May, 1982	02/04/85
Convention A/P2/5/82 regulating Inter-State Road Transportation between ECOWAS Member States, signed in Cotonou on 29th May, 1992	02/04/85
Protocol A/P3/5/82 relating to the Definition of Community Citizen, signed in Cotonou on 29th May, 1982	02/03/85
Convention A/P4/5/82 relating to the Definition of Community Citizen, signed in Cotonou on 29th May, 1982	02/03/85
Convention A/P5/5/82 on Mutual Administrative Assistance in Customs Matters, signed in Cotonou on 29th May, 1982	02/04/85
Protocol A/P1/11/84 relating to the Community Enterprises signed in Lome, 23rd November, 1984	12/05/89
Supplementary Protocol A/SP1/11/84 amending Article 9 paragraph 1 (c) of the Treaty of the Economic Community of West African States signed in Lome, 23rd November, 1984	12/05/89
Convention A/P1/7/85 relating to the temporary importation of passenger vehicle into Member States signed in Lome, 23rd November, 1984	12/05/89
Supplementary Protocol A/SP1/7/85 relating to the Code of Conduct for the Implementation of the Protocol on Free Movement of Persons, the Right of Residence and establishment signed in Lome, 6th July, 1985	12/05/89
Supplementary Protocol A/SPI/7/86 on the Second Phase on Free	12/05/89
Movement of Persons (Right of Residence) signed in Abuja, 1st July, 1986	
A/PI/7/87 Cultural Framework Agreement for the ECOWAS signed in Abuja, 9th July, 1987	12/03/91
A/P2/7/87 Protocol on the Establishment of a West African Health Organisation signed in Abuja, 9th July, 1987	12/05/89
A/SPI/6/88 Supplementary Protocol amending Article 4 and 9 of the ECOWAS Treaty relating to the Institutions of the Community and its technical and specialised Commissions respectively signed in Lome, 25th June, 1988	12/05/89
A/SP2/6/88 Supplementary Protocol amending Article 53 of the ECOWAS Treaty on the Budget of the Community signed in Lome, 25th June, 1988	12/05/89
Supplementary Protocol A/SPI/6/89 amending and complementing the Provisions of Article 7 of the Protocol on Free Movement, Right of Residence and Establishment signed in Ouagadougou on 30th June, 1989	14/12/92
Supplementary Convention A/SPI/5/90 establishing a Community Guarantee Mechanism for Inter-State Road Transit of Goods. Signed in Banjul, 29th May, 1990	16/04/91
Supplementary Protocol A/SP2/5/90 on the Implementation of the Third Phase (Right of Establishment) of the Protocol on Free Movement of Persons, Right of Residence and Establishment signed in Banjul, 29th May, 1990	16/04/91

(continued)

Table 6.4 (continued)

Protocol A/PI/7/91 on the Community Court of Justice signed in Abuja on 6th July, 1991	07/12/92
Convention A/PI/7/92 on Mutual Assistance in Criminal Matters signed, in Dakar, on 29th July, 1992	07/12/92
Protocol A/PI/7/93 relating to the West African Monetary Agency signed in Cotonou, on 24th July, 1993	29/06/95
Supplementary Protocol A/SPI/7/93 amending Article 1 of the Protocol relating to the contributions by Member States to the Budgets of the Economic Community of West African States, signed in Cotonou on 24th July, 1993	29/06/95
Convention A/PI/8/94 on Extradition signed in Abuja on 6th August 1994	29/06/95
Protocol A/P2/8/94 relating to the Community Parliament	29/06/95
Protocol A/PI/7/96 on Conditions governing the application of the Community Levy	24/09/98
Protocol A/P2/7/96 establishing Value Added Tax in ECOWAS	28/10/98
Protocol A/PI/12/99 relating to the Mechanism for Conflict, Prevention, Management, Resolution, Peace-keeping and Security	24/01/05
Protocol A/PI/12/01 amending Articles 1, 3, 6 and 21 of the ECOWAS Revised Treaty	18/10/02
Protocol A/P2/12/01 relating to the ECOWAS Bank for Investment and Development (EBID)	18/10/02
Protocol A/P3/12/01 on the Fight Against Corruption	18/10/02
Supplementary Protocol A/SP.1/12/01 on Democracy and Good Governance Supplementary to the Protocol relating to the Mechanism for Conflict Prevention, Management, Resolution, Peacekeeping and Security	18/10/02
Supplementary Protocol A/SP.2/12/01 amending the Protocol on the establishment of an ECOWAS Brown Card relating to motor vehicle third party liability insurance	18/10/02
General Convention A/C.I/01/03 on the Recognition and Equivalence of Degrees, Diploma, Certificates and Other Qualifications in ECOWAS Member States	
Protocol A/P.1/01/03 relating to the Definition of the Concept of Products Originating from Member States of the Economic Community of West	24/01/05
African States (ECOWAS)	
Protocol A/P.2/01/03 Relating to the Application of ECOWAS Member States As a result of the Trade Liberalisation Scheme	24/01/05
Protocol A/P.3/01/03 on Education and Training	
Protocol A/P.4/01/03 on Energy	24/01/05
Supplementary Protocol A/SP.1/01/05 amending the Preamble and Articles 1, 2, 9, 22 and 30 of Protocol A/P.1/7/91 relating to the Community Court of Justice and Article 4 Paragraph 1 of the English version of the said Protocol	
Protocol A/P.1/01/06 Establishing an ECOWAS Criminal Intelligence and Investigation Bureau	
Supplementary Protocol A/SP.I/01/06 amending Articles VI-C, VI-L, IX-8, X1-2 and XII of Protocol A/P2/7/87 on the Establishment of the West African Health Organisation (WAHO)	
Supplementary Protocol A/SP.1/06/06 amending the Revised ECOWAS Treaty	

(continued)

Table 6.4 (continued)

Supplementary Protocol A/SP.2/06/06 amending Article 3 Paragraphs 1, 2 and 4, Article 4 Paragraphs 1, 3, and 7 and Article 7 Paragraph 3 of the Protocol on the Community Court of Justice	
Supplementary Protocol A/SP.3/06/06 amending Protocol A/P2/8/94 relating to the Community Parliament	
ECOWAS Convention on small arms and light weapons, their ammunition and other related materials	

[a]Republic of Ghana Treaty Manual. United Nations Organization (Legal). pp. 7–9. Available at http://legal.un.org/avl/documents/scans/GhanaTreatyManual2009.pdf?teil=II&j

References

Abdulai A-G, Quantson R (2008/2009) The changing role of CSOs in public policy making in Ghana. Ghana Soc Sci J 5 & 6(1 & 2)

Addo MK (1992) Justiciability re-examined. In: Beddard R, Hill DM (eds) Economic, social and cultural rights: progress and achievement. St. Martin's Press, New York, p 1992

Atuguba RA (2005) Human trafficking in Ghana: a review legislation. ILO, Geneva

Atuguba RA (2013) Equality, non-discrimination and fair distribution of the benefits of development. In: Realizing the right to development: essays in commemoration of 25 years of the United Nations Declaration on the Right to Development, New York and Geneva. United Nations Publication

Baxi U (1994) Inhuman wrongs and human rights: unconventional essays. Har-Anand Publications, pp 1 and 2

Bimpong-Buta SY (1983–86) Sources of law in Ghana. Rev Ghana Law 15:129–151

Bortei-Doku Aryeetey E et al (2014) The right to development report: Ghana country study (on file with author)

Brownlie I (2003) Principles of public international law, 6th edn. Oxford University Press

Eide A et al (eds) (2001) Economic, social and cultural rights. Martinus Nijhoff Publishers

Fosu AK, Aryeetey E (2010) Ghana's Post Independence Growth (1960–2000). Available at: https://www.researchgate.net/publication/288587408_Ghana's_post independence_economic_growth_1960-2000. Accessed 8 Aug 2019

Givelber D (1982) The right to minimum social decency and limits of evenhandedness: intentional infliction of emotional distress by outrageous conduct. 82(1):42–75. Available at: https://www.jstor.org/stable/1122238?seq=1#page_scan_tab_contents. Accessed 8 Aug 2019

Int'l Fin. Corp (2007) Gender and Economic Growth Assessment for Ghana (2007), 28

Kooijman (1990) Human rights – universal Panacea? – Some reflections on the so-called human rights of the third generation. Neth Int Law Rev:320

Kunbor B (2001) Epistolary jurisdiction of the Indian Courts and Fundamental Human Rights in Ghana's 1992 constitution: some jurisprudential lessons. Law Soc Justice Global Dev 2. http://elj.warwick.ac.uk/global/issue/2001-2/kunbor.html

Nyinevi CY (2017) Challenges to judicial enforcement of socio-economic rights in Africa: comparative lessons from Ghana and South Africa. In: Ghana @ 60: governance and human rights in twenty-fist century Africa. Pretoria University Law Press

Sarpong LA (2015) Ghana-China relations (figures of controversy), Conference: Advances in Economic and Business Management, New Delhi, vol 2(14), pp 1138–1142

Shaw MN (2003) International law, 5th edn. Cambridge University Press

Short EF (1997) Economic, social and cultural rights in the 1992 constitution- what legal consequences. In: Open fora on human rights issues in Ghana. KAF, Accra, p 99

Tandoh-Offi P (2013) Development planning in Ghana since 1992: implications for decentralization process. International Relations and Diplomacy 1(2):93–107
White LE (1988) Lessons from Driefontein on lawyering and power. Wis Law Rev:699
Willes E (2006–2007) Aspirational principles or enforceable rights: the future for socio-economic rights in national law. Am Univ Int Law Rev 22:35

Chapter 7
The Fight Against Poverty and the Right to Development in Italy

Lorenzo Gradoni and Luca Pasquet

Abstract The Chapter casts a glance at the fight against poverty and the right to development as they come into sight at the intersection between public international law and Italy's domestic and international legal practice. In public international law, "fight against poverty" is shorthand for a vast domain of political and diplomatic action as well as for an ill-defined bundle of economic and social rights, at the core of which lies the universal entitlement to an adequate standard of living, including adequate food, clothing and housing. Italy is a party to several treaties recognizing that right at the universal and regional levels and, as such, it is subject to various form of international oversight. As for the right to development, none of the treaties mentioning it binds Italy and Italian judicial and administrative authorities never took it into account for interpretative purposes. The Chapter argues that the right to development is decaying into a mere appendage of the 2030 Agenda for Sustainable Development and the Sustainable Development Goals (SDGs) it formulates, and that the latter, far from being the continuation of international law by other means, are expressive of a different kind of normativity, which ousts much more than it complements international law. The review mechanism put in place under the SDGs rests on a purely voluntary basis and, as Italy's recent experience shows, it allows little scope for criticism of national performances. After a preliminary discussion of Italy's compliance with the relevant rules and principles of international law via the ordinary operation of its own legal order, the Chapter contends that Italy's record before international monitoring bodies is as inglorious—especially for

This contribution is a modified version of an article first published under a partly different title in Annuario di dirtto comparato e di studi legislativi, vol IX, 2018, pp. 295–322.

L. Gradoni
Max Planck Institute Luxembourg for Procedural Law, Luxembourg, Luxembourg
e-mail: lorenzo.gradoni@mpi.lu

L. Pasquet (✉)
Utrecht University School of Law, Utrecht, The Netherlands
e-mail: l.pasquet@uu.nl

M. Andenas et al. (eds.), *The Fight Against Poverty and the Right to Development*, Ius Comparatum - Global Studies in Comparative Law 52,
https://doi.org/10.1007/978-3-030-57324-9_7

what was not done to cushion the economic and financial crisis—as the report it submitted under the 2030 Agenda is vainglorious, and likely to go unchallenged. In short, Italy's enthusiastic embrace of the 2030 Agenda hardly conceals its continuing debacle in the fight against poverty and in defence of basic social rights, both at home and internationally.

Introduction

The present Chapter casts a glance at the fight against poverty and the right to development as they come into sight at the intersection between public international law and Italy's domestic and international legal practice.

In public international law, "fight against poverty" is shorthand for a vast domain of political and diplomatic action as well as for an ill-defined bundle of economic and social rights, at the core of which lies the universal entitlement "to an adequate standard of living [. . .] including adequate food, clothing and housing", as expressed in Article 11(1) of the International Covenant on Economic, Social and Cultural Rights (ICESCR)[1] and foreshadowed in Article 25(1) of the Universal Declaration of Human Rights (UDHR).[2] Three other human rights treaties concluded under the auspices of the United Nations between 1979 and 2016—the Convention on the Elimination of All Forms of Discrimination against Women (CEDAW),[3] the Convention on the Rights of the Child,[4] and the Convention on the Rights of Persons with Disabilities (CRPD)[5]—expressly ascribes identical or similar entitlements to

---

[1]United Nations Treaty Series, vol. 993, p. 3 (conclusion: 16 December 1966; entry into force: 3 January 1976).

[2]According to Article 25(1) UDHR, "[e]veryone has the right to a standard of living adequate for the health and well-being of himself and of his family, including food, clothing, housing and medical care and necessary social services, and the right to security in the event of unemployment, sickness, disability, widowhood, old age or other lack of livelihood in circumstances beyond his control".

[3]United Nations Treaty Series, vol. 1249, p. 13 (conclusion: 18 December 1979; entry into force: 3 September 1981). Article 14 (2)(h) CEDAW sets forth the obligation to ensure to women in rural areas the right "to enjoy adequate living conditions, particularly in relation to housing, sanitation, electricity and water supply, transport and communications".

[4]United Nations Treaty Series, vol. 1577, p. 3 (conclusion: 20 November 1989; entry into force: 2 September 1990). Article 27 CRC recognizes the right of every child "to a standard of living adequate for the child's physical, mental, spiritual, moral and social development", while prescribing that State parties "take appropriate measures to assist parents and others responsible for the child to implement this right and [. . .] in case of need provide material assistance and support programmes, particularly with regard to nutrition, clothing and housing". Ratified by Italy on 5 September 1991.

[5]United Nations Treaty Series, vol. 2515, p. 3 (conclusion: 13 December 2006; entry into force: 3 May 2008). Following closely the formula of Article 11(1) ICESCR, Article 28 CRPD recognizes the right of persons with disabilities to "an adequate standard of living for themselves and their families, including adequate food, clothing and housing, and to the continuous improvement of living conditions".

vulnerable categories of persons. Italy is a party to all these conventions.[6] In addition, Italy is bound, at the regional level, by the European Social Charter (ESC), whose Article 30 recognizes a right to protection against poverty and social exclusion, a right that the contracting parties must implement through "measures within the framework of an overall and coordinated approach to promote the effective access of persons who live or risk living in a situation of social exclusion or poverty, as well as their families, to, in particular, employment, housing, training, education, culture and social and medical assistance".[7]

Apart form setting forth the right to an adequate standard of living, the ICESCR, almost in the same breath—at Article 11(2)—makes explicit what should be regarded as the innermost core of that right, that is, "the right of everyone to be free from hunger". Negotiated in the optimistic atmosphere brought about by two decades of sustained economic growth, the ICESCR goes so far (one is tempted to say "went") as recognizing, again in Article 11(1), "the right of everyone [. . .] to the continuous improvement of living conditions". This is the point at which, conceptually, second-generation human rights meld with the third-generation human right to development, as solemnly spelled out, first and foremost, in the Declaration on the Right to Development adopted by the United Nations General Assembly on 4 December 1986.[8] The Declaration is a late product of the 1970s ill-fated struggle for the realization of a New International Economic Order.[9] As such the Declaration, apart from reasserting existing social and economic rights, while adding an egalitarian twist to them ("fair distribution of income"),[10] laid much stress on the cooperative dimension of the striving towards the ambitious goals it was setting. Article 4 (1) is in this respect emblematic: "States have the duty to take steps, individually and collectively, to formulate international development policies with a view to facilitating the full realization of the right to development". Less ambitiously, yet clearly in the same vein, Article 11(2)(b) ICESCR provides (one is again tempted to use the past tense) that States "shall take, individually and through international co-operation, the measures, including specific programmes, which are needed [. . .] to ensure an equitable distribution of world food supplies in relation to need". Nothing of the sort has ever been done or attempted, not even in the much less

[6]Italy ratified the ICESCR on 15 September 1978, the CEDAW on 10 June 1985, the CRC on 5 September 1991, and the CRPD on 15 May 2009.

[7]European Treaty Series 163 (conclusion: 3 May 1996; entry into force: 1 July 1999). Italy ratified the ESC on 5 July 1999. The earlier version of the ESC (European Treaty Series 35, conclusion: 18 October 1961, entry into force: 26 February 1965, ratified by Italy on 22 October 1965) did not recognize a right to protection against poverty and social exclusion.

[8]UN Doc. No. A/RES/41/128 (1986).

[9]See, in particular, Article 3(3): "States have the duty to co-operate with each other in ensuring development and eliminating obstacles to development. States should realize their rights and fulfil their duties in such a manner as to promote a new international economic order based on sovereign equality, interdependence, mutual interest and co-operation among all States, as well as to encourage the observance and realization of human rights".

[10]See *ibid.*, Article 8(1).

advanced front on which the battle against hunger is fought.[11] More controversial today than it was at the time of its debut, the right to development still plods like a zombie from one diplomatic meeting to the next in New York and Geneva. The Working Group on the Right to Development is deadlocked.[12] The Human Rights Council (HRC) could not even appoint a special rapporteur on the topic (as it eventually did) without attracting a salvo of negative votes and abstentions.[13] Italy is currently not a member of the HRC but it would have in all likelihood abstained as several other EU members have done. The remarkably progressive Article 3 of the Italian Constitution, on which we will come back later, could well be seen as a national version of the right to development, if it did not lack the all-important international cooperation limb of the original. No treaty featuring the right to development binds Italy and, to our knowledge, Italian judicial and administrative authorities never took it into consideration for interpretative purposes.

Upon perusal of the most recent official documents, we came to the conclusion that, on the one hand, the right to development is being seamlessly merged into the pool of existing human rights, as a recent report of Zamir Akram, the Chair-Rapporteur of the Working Group, seems to imply: "[s]ince there can be no human rights without addressing human needs, the right to development, aimed at addressing human needs, is an integral part of all human rights".[14] On the other hand, and more importantly, the right to development is decaying into a mere appendage of the 2030 Agenda for Sustainable Development and the Sustainable Development Goals (SDGs) it formulates.[15] As to the latter—as well as to their predecessors, the Millennium Development Goals (MDGs)[16]—we believe that, far from representing the continuation of international law by other means, as it were, they are expressive of a totally different kind of normativity, which ousts much more than it complements international law.[17] One of its main features is the trust it places in the multitude's creativity while downplaying the institutions of the international

[11] See Gradoni (2015).

[12] See the Resolution adopted by the Human Rights Council on 29 September 2016, *The Right to Development*, UN Doc. No. A/HRC/RES/33/14 (2016), pp. 2–3.

[13] *Ibid.*, p. 6, para. 18. France and the United Kingdom voted against the Resolution. Albania, Belgium, Georgia, Germany, Latvia, the Netherlands, Portugal, Slovenia, South Korea, Switzerland, and the Former Yugoslav Republic of Macedonia abstained.

[14] *Standards for the Implementation of the Right to Development: Report of the Chair-Rapporteur of the Working Group on the Right to Development*, UN Doc. No. A/HRC/WG.2/17/2 (2016), p. 11, para. 44.

[15] See *Transforming Our World: the 2030 Agenda for Sustainable Development*, UN Doc. No. A/RES/70/1 (2015). Compare Report of the Working Group on the Right to Development on its 70th Session (Geneva, 25 April-3 May 2016), UN doc. A/HRC/33/45 (2016), p. 20, 74(d): "The Working Group, in its future deliberations, study the contributions made by States at the national, regional and international levels to the implementation of the right to development, in keeping with mechanisms relating to the Sustainable Development Goals".

[16] *United Nations Millennium Declaration*, UN doc. A/RES/55/2 (2000).

[17] Compare Alston (2005), p. 771.

community of States.[18] It is from the spontaneous interactions between individuals and social groups that the means to ensure the supply of essential global public goods should come.[19] The multitude should be energized, stimulated, and become more and more interconnected to form fluid alliances that define and redefine 'strategies' in the endless fight against poverty, while States act as if they were less and less burdened by legal constraints.

The SDGs, like the MDGs before them, entertain a complex relationship with international human rights law. Their stylistic pastiche integrates the idiom of human rights, but strips it of all legal niceties. At the same time, the withering away of inter-State cooperation in the pursuit of social justice, on whose ashes the MDGs/SDGs normative complex was built, also brought about, as an illusory compensation, the idea of far-reaching *individual* extraterritorial obligations of States. The Maastricht Principles on the Extraterritorial Obligations of States in the Area of Economic, Social and Cultural Rights, adopted on 28 September 2011 during a gathering of experts convened by Maastricht University and the International Commission of Jurists, proclaims that "[a] State has obligations to respect, protect and fulfil economic, social and cultural rights [in] situations over which State acts or omissions bring about foreseeable effects on the enjoyment of economic, social and cultural rights, whether within or outside its territory".[20] The brittle root of this understanding of economic, social and cultural rights lies in the circumstance that the scope of those rights, unlike that of first-generation rights under Article 2(1) of the International Covenant on Civil and Political Rights (ICCPR), is *not* territorially-bounded, according to the letter of Article 2(1) ICESCR.[21] However, as State practice overwhelmingly suggests, a jurisdictional limit was probably implied. To our knowledge, Italy did not endorse the Maastricht Principles in any form. Not human rights law proper, but human-rightist phantasmagorias like the Maastricht Principles are the SDGs' ideal companion.

As a party to the aforementioned human rights treaties, Italy is subject to various forms of international oversight. Living up to these procedural obligations may be burdensome. None of these procedures, however, may result in the adoption of a

[18]The following is a representative statement: "Children and young women and men are critical agents of change and will find in the new Goals a platform to channel their infinite capacities for activism into the creation of a better world" (*Transforming Our World: the 2030 Agenda for Sustainable Development*, cit., p. 12, para. 51).

[19]The 2030 Agenda defines itself as a "plan of action for people, planet and prosperity" (*ibid.*, p. 1, para. 1 of preamble). Compare Zaniboni (2017).

[20]http://www.etoconsortium.org/nc/en/main-navigation/library/maastricht-principles, para. 9(a). See also De Schutter et al. (2012) and Viterbo (2012).

[21]Compare Article 2(1) ICCPR, according to which each State must protect the rights of "all individuals within its territory and subject to its jurisdiction", with Article 2(1) ICESCR: "Each State Party to the present Covenant undertakes to take steps, individually and through international assistance and co-operation, especially economic and technical, to the maximum of its available resources, with a view to achieving progressively the full realization of the rights recognized in the present Covenant by all appropriate means, including particularly the adoption of legislative measures".

binding decision. A review mechanism was put in place under the SDGs, too, but it rests on a purely voluntary basis and—as Italy's recent experience shows—it allows little scope for criticism of national performances. As we will see in section "Italy Screened by International Monitoring Bodies", Italy's record before human rights bodies is as inglorious—especially for what was not done to cushion the economic downturn—as the report it submitted under the 2030 Agenda is vainglorious, and likely to go unchallenged or pass unnoticed, as we explain in section "Italy's Embrace of the 2030 Agenda for Sustainable Development". Section "The Impact of Public International Law in Domestic Law and Litigation as Concerns the Fight Against Poverty and the Right to Development" addresses the preliminary question of Italy's compliance with the relevant rules and principles of international law via the ordinary operation of its own legal order.

The Impact of Public International Law in Domestic Law and Litigation as Concerns the Fight Against Poverty and the Right to Development

Italy's Constitution connects to the sphere of public international law in sophisticated ways. Dubbed "permanent transformer" (*trasformatore permanente*), Article 10(1) provides for the automatic and continuous adjustment of domestic law to the "generally recognized norms of international law", a notion that encompasses all unwritten international law of a universal character.[22] Domestic acts found by the Constitutional Court to be in conflict with such law are declared invalid, unless the international norm in question turns out to be itself at variance with constitutional principles of a fundamental character.[23] To our knowledge, unwritten international law has up to now never been suggested as a source of basic economic and social rights in proceedings before Italian courts and tribunals. As regards treaties in force for Italy, a constitutional amendment enacted in late 2001 makes them prevail over conflicting legislative acts, without lifting them up to the level of the Constitution itself.[24] The domestic law status of treaties is therefore slightly inferior to that of

[22]An unofficial English translation of the Constitution of the Italian Republic is provided by the Parliamentary Information, Archives and Publications Office of the Senate Service for Official Reports and Communications. We stick to that text unless we say otherwise. Article 10(1) was translated as follows: "The Italian legal system conforms to the generally recognized principles of international law". Since an exclusive reference to "principles" is warranted neither by the letter ("*norme*") nor by the legislative history of the provision, we opted for a different rendering.

[23]See, e.g., Constitutional Court, Judgments 48/1979 of 18 June 1979 and 238/2014 of 22 October 2014.

[24]OJ No. 248 of 24 October 2001, p. 3. Article 117(1) of the Constitution, as amended, reads as follows: "Legislative powers shall be vested in the State and the Regions and exercised in compliance with the Constitution and with the constraints deriving from European Union law and international obligations" (translation slightly changed, see note 22 above). On the face of it, Article

unwritten international law, as treaties remain subject to the whole body of constitutional law, not only to its core principles.[25] A clash between treaties on economic and social rights and constitutional law is, however, highly unlikely, since the Constitution is all but inimical to those rights. To this we should add that, unlike the international law taken in by the "permanent transformer", treaties in force for Italy are not automatically incorporated into domestic law. Their assimilation requires, as a rule, an act of Parliament. Since, however, the Parliament customarily orders the incorporation of a treaty at the same time as it authorizes its ratification, and by the very same act, no real risk exists that the lack of automatic incorporation makes treaties in force for Italy domestically unenforceable.

Before the entry into force of the aforesaid constitutional amendment, treaties enjoyed the same legal status as the domestic act incorporating them. They were nonetheless, to the largest extent possible, granted precedence over legislative acts via the application of a legal hermeneutics known as "conforming interpretation" (*interpretazione conforme*), which requires that domestic law be read so as to keep it in line with Italy's international obligations. As a conflict-avoidance technique, conforming interpretation is still much in use today and is practiced not only to prevent collisions between international law and sub-constitutional domestic law but also to justify internationally-oriented readings of the Constitution itself, as we shall see in a moment.

The constitutionally-sanctioned supremacy of international law over domestic law should in principle ensure that Italy's lives up to its international obligations by the mere operation of its domestic legal order. Since, however, the realization of economic and social rights typically requires positive legislative and administrative action, an action that the judicial branch is not always in the position to impose to, or perform in lieu of, the Government or Parliament, it is by no means excluded that a gap opens up between domestic law and international human rights standards. And yet, references to such standards are relatively rare in the decisions of Italian courts and tribunals. One reason for this is that the Constitution protects economic and social rights in terms that are as broad and radical as to make the act of referring to international sources of obligation redundant in most cases. Article 3(2) of the Constitution spells out the Republic's duty "to remove those obstacles of an economic or social nature which constrain the freedom and equality of citizens, thereby impeding the full development of the human person and the effective participation of all workers in the political, economic and social organization of the country". It is hard to figure out what internationally-recognized social and economic right could *not* be drawn from this sweeping formula, or found in the relevant sections of the Constitutions' "bill of rights" (Articles 29–47). It should not come as a surprise,

---

117(1) would indistinctly apply to any rule of international law, irrespective of its source, but Article 10(1) takes precedence over it qua *lex specialis* as far as general international law is concerned.

[25] See Constitutional Court, Judgments 347 and 348/2007 of 24 October 2007; Judgment 49/2015 of 14 January 2015.

then, that appeals to international economic and social rights voiced before Italian courts seldom aim at contesting the validity of domestic acts allegedly providing inadequate protection. The remedy to such failures is more readily found in the Constitution.

Having reached a considerable level of specification, the panoply of international human rights instruments is more often conjured up to assist the interpretation of relevant constitutional provisions, including the resourceful Article 2, according to which "[t]he Republic recognises and guarantees the inviolable rights of the person, both as an individual and in the social groups where human personality is expressed". The Constitutional Court's case law exemplifies this trend. In a number of cases the Court, in reading out of the Constitution the right to adequate housing—a right of "primary importance in the life of individuals" that "must be adequately and effectively protected by the law"[26]—referred to Article 11 IESCR and Article 25 UDHR as auxiliary means of interpretation, and eventually subsumed such "fundamental human right" under Article 2 of the Constitution.[27] The Court likewise read Article 38(3) of the Constitution, according to which "[d]isabled persons are entitled to receive education and vocational training", in the light of the "clearer and more detailed" Article 15 of the European Social Charter.[28] The Court made a similar interpretative move when it relied on Article 8 of the same Charter to assert that minimum standards as to maternity leave are implied in Articles 31(2) and 37 (1) of the Constitution, respectively on the Republic's duty to protect "mothers, children and the young" and the rights of working women.[29] In a later case, and again to similar effects, the Court drew inspiration from Article 24 of the by then revised European Social Charter in delineating the constitutional guarantees to which workers are entitled in case of dismissal.[30]

The fact that the Constitution affords strong protection to economic and social rights, and does it through the aforementioned Article 3—whose emancipatory potential can be downplayed but hardly exhausted—also contributes to explaining why the Government shows no awareness of acting under some international obligation when implementing the so-called National Plan to Fight Poverty and Social Exclusion. Although "poverty" is not a word to be found in the Constitution, in approving the latest anti-poverty measure, known as Revenue for Inclusion ("Reddito di inclusione" or "REI"), the Parliament made exclusive reference to Article 3 of the Constitution and, on top of it, to unspecified principles enshrined in the EU Charter of Fundamental Rights.[31] Measures of this kind are rather

---

[26] Judgment No. 252/1983 of 15 July 1983, para. 4; Judgment No. 559/1989 of 20 December 1989, para. 3.

[27] Judgment No. 404/1988 of 7 April 1988, para. 3.

[28] Judgment No. 163/1983 of 2 June 1983, para. 6. The Court refers here to the 1961 ESC. See *supra* note 7.

[29] Judgment No. 86/1994 of 15 March 1994, para. 2.

[30] Judgment No. 46/2000 of 7 February 2000, paras. 3 and 5.

[31] See Law No. 33 of 15 March 2017, in OJ No. 70 of 24 March 2017, as implemented by Decree No. 147 of 15 September 2017, in OJ No. 240 of 13 October 2017.

showcased as proof of Italy's constant striving to live up to the 2030 Sustainable Development Agenda.[32]

National court cases where individuals sought to base their claims on Italy's international obligations are rare. Most of them concern the legality of measures taken against the unauthorized occupation of public housing by destitute individuals. In these cases, the claimants alleged that if evicted, they could not afford decent housing at market prices, a circumstance that in their view made the order to leave the premises incompatible with Article 11 ICESCR and Article 30 ESC.[33] In 2010 the Milan Regional Administrative Tribunal (TAR) partially granted the claim upon a reading of the Regional Regulation on the Allocation of Public Housing Benefits that takes into consideration Italy's international obligations, in particular under Article 11 ICESCR. According to the TAR, public authorities may not issue an eviction order without previously making sure, through a formal inquiry, that the occupant's socio-economic conditions are not such as to make his or her stay strictly necessary. The TAR also ruled that the occupant had a right to take part in the inquiry by filing written arguments and evidence. In the case at hand, the TAR annulled the eviction order because the local administration failed to perform the inquiry as prescribed.[34] In subsequent cases, the occupant's claims were rejected upon verification that the public authorities had effectively discharged the procedural obligation, regardless of the outcome of the inquiry.[35] In not a few instances, the TAR's holding was actually rejected as contrary to the "right to good administration", as spelled out in Article 41 of the EU Charter of Fundamental Rights, a right understood here as defeating any claim of economic necessity as extenuating circumstance in cases of illegal occupation of public property.[36] It should also be noted that the Milan TAR's approach to the relevance of international law in the definition of housing rights has not been consistent across the board. In a case concerning the eviction of caravans illegally installed on private land, the Tribunal ruled that since provisions like Article 11 ICESCR and Article 30 ESC do not confer individual rights—they just "set a goal and provide a basis for policy programmes"—evictions are allowed to proceed regardless of the availability of alternative housing solutions.[37]

---

[32]See *infra*, section "Italy's Embrace of the 2030 Agenda for Sustainable Development".

[33]Milan TAR, I Section, Judgment No. 7602 of 20 December 2010; III Section, Judgment No. 252 of 29 January 2013; I Section, Judgments No. 1030 of 22 April 2013, No. 1031 of 22 April 2013 and No. 908 of 7 April 2014; Rome TAR, III Section, Judgments No. 4696 of 23 March 2015 and No. 1430 of 27 January 2015; Campobasso TAR, I Section, Judgment No. 329 of 2 October 2017.

[34]Milan TAR, I Section, Judgment No. 7602 of 20 December 2010.

[35]Rome TAR, III Section, Judgment No. 1430 No. 27 January 2015.

[36]Milan TAR, III Section, Judgment No. 252 of 29 January 2013; Milan TAR, I Section, Judgments No. 1030 of 22 April 2013, No. 1031 of 22 April 2013 and No. 908 of 7 April 2014; Roma TAR Roma, III Section, Judgment No. 4696 of 23 March 2015.

[37]Milan TAR, IV Section, Judgment No. 1632 of 18 July 2017.

Another significant strand in the case law concerns the need to ensure that public tender offers are in line with the rules on minimum wages laid down in national collective labour agreements.[38] By way of example, the Bari TAR annulled a public procurement decision because the offer failed to provide assurances as to the minimum wage of 8 workers.[39] Even though rulings of this kind refer to national legislation as their main touchstone, international standards such as those expressed in Article 11 ICESCR are sometimes enlisted in support.[40] As the Bari TAR pointed out, the sanctity of minimum wages addresses the "basic need that the dignity and safety of workers be respected", as recognized by the ICESCR and the ESC alike.[41]

Relevant for our research is also the case law of ordinary courts concerning the issuance of residence permits for humanitarian reasons. Such permits are granted to individuals exposed to dangers against which Italy is bound to offer protection under its own Constition or international law.[42] In 2016, a Tribunal in Milan held that a Gambian citizen rightfully invoked humanitarian protection to escape extreme poverty, which is endemic in his country, as attested by the low average life expectancy of its people.[43] For the Tribunal, Gambia's economic situation, especially in the rural region the claimant came from, would have endangered his capacity to enjoy rights as fundamental and closely connected to the right to life as the rights to food and to health. The Tribunal expressly referred to Italy's obligations under Article 25 UDHR and Article 11 ICESCR, which in its view would not be adequately discharged if Italy failed to provide humanitarian protection to those escaping from socio-economic conditions that are "totally incompatible with the minimum standard of living and human dignity required by the aforesaid provisions". Although the claimant had entered Italy's territory illegally, he and his family were therefore entitled to stay as a consequence of Italy's duty to protect them against extreme poverty.[44] Later in the year, a Tribunal in Genoa ruled that a Senegalese citizen, unschooled and unemployed, and having fled his country when he was still a minor, was entitled to humanitarian protection because "if he returned to Senegal he would have lost his livelihood".[45] Following the same line or reasoning, a Tribunal in Rome held that a citizen of Guinea-Bissau had a right to a humanitarian residence permit since "upon returning to his country of origin, he

[38]Bari TAR, I Section, Judgment No. 1572 of 20 June 2007; Rome TAR, I Section, Judgment No. 11317 of 18 October 2004.

[39]Bari TAR, I Section, Judgment No. 1572 of 20 June 2007.

[40]See Article 1 of Law No. 327 of 7 November 2000, in OJ No. 265 of 13 November 2000, p. 4 ff.

[41]Bari TAR, I Section, Judgment No. 1572 of 20 June 2007, n. 1572; Rome TAR, I Section, Judgment No. 11317 of 18 October 2004.

[42]See Court of Cassation, *Akpasubi v. Ministry of Interior*, Order No. 22111 of 17 October 2014. See also Article 5(6) of Legislative Decree No. 286 of 25 July 1998, in OJ No. 191 of 18 August 1998, Supplement No. 139, p. 5 ff.

[43]Milan Tribunal, I Civil Section, Order of 31 March 2016.

[44]*Ibid.*, para 5. The Tribunal reiterated the same reasoning in a later case concerning another Gambian citizen. See Milan Tribunal, I Civil Section, Order of 7 October 2016.

[45]Genoa Tribunal, Order of 4 July 2016.

would be exposed to a situation of extreme vulnerability and would plunge into a situation of poverty he could in no way break out from, having no family support or resources of his own".[46] The case law is however far from consistent with regard to the conditions for granting humanitarian protection. The Court of Cassation has recently denied that poverty or bad health conditions may constitute in and of themselves sufficient grounds for granting a residence permit.[47] The Supreme Court held that socio-economic factors are relevant only if they exist as a consequence of a "serious violation of human rights suffered by the claimant in her country of origin, as per Articles 2, 3 and 4 of the European Convention on Human Rights",[48] thereby seemingly implying that humanitarian protection must be granted only in cases where there is a risk of serious violation of civil and political rights.

Italy Screened by International Monitoring Bodies

As a party to a number of human rights treaties, Italy is subject to various forms of international oversight, from the less demanding assessment of periodic compliance reports to potentially more intrusive procedures like the examination of individual or inter-State complaints or the conduct of an inquiry in cases where there are credible allegations of grave or systematic violations. Italy has the obligation to submit periodic reports, every 2 to 5 years, to the Committee on Economic, Social and Cultural Rights (CESCR),[49] the Committee on Elimination of All Forms of Discrimination Against Women,[50] the Committee on the Rights of the Child,[51] the Committee on the Rights of Persons with Disabilities,[52] and the European Committee of Social Rights (ECSR).[53] Italy also accepted the Committees' competence to

[46]Roma Tribunal, Order of 17 March 2016.

[47]Court of Cassation, IV Civil Section, *A.A.Q. v. Ministry of Interior*, Order No. 28015 of 23 November 2017.

[48]*Ibid.*

[49]Articles 16 and 17 ICESCR (report due every 5 years).

[50]Article 18 CEDAW (report due every 4 years).

[51]Article 44 CRC (report due every 5 years).

[52]Articles 35 and 36 CRPD (report due every 4 years).

[53]Under Article C of the ESC, Italy has the duty to submit a report to the ECSR every 2 years on the implementation of those provisions of Part II of the Charter it has accepted, that is, all provisions except Article 25 (see Declaration contained in a Note Verbale from Italy's Permanent Representation, handed to the Secretary General at the time of deposit of the instrument of ratification: "Italy does not consider itself bound by Article 25 – the right of workers to the protection of their claims in the event of the insolvency of their employer – of the Charter"). The aforementioned Article C incorporates by reference Articles 21 to 24 of the 1961 ESC, which then still govern the reporting procedure.

examine individual communications,[54] except in the case of ECSR, whose jurisdiction is confined to so-called collective complaints filed by listed categories of non-governmental organizations.[55] Italy generally recognizes the Committees' power to conduct inquiries,[56] with the conspicuous exception of the CESCR,[57] while the ECSR had no such power. As for the Committees' competence to receive inter-State complaints, Italy accepts that of Committee on the Rights of the Child,[58] but not that of the CESCR.[59] On top of all that, Italy, as any other State member of the United Nations, is subject to the so-called Universal Periodic Review (UPR), which takes place under the auspices of the UN Human Rights Council (HRC). Every four and a half years,[60] each State is called upon to present its human rights record, including in respect of "voluntary pledges and commitments", and to discuss it with all interested UN Members, also on the basis of information submitted by "other relevant stakeholder", like intergovernmental organizations and NGOs, as

[54] See Article 2 of the Optional Protocol to the International Covenant on Economic, Social and Cultural Rights (UN doc. A/RES/63/435 (2008)), adopted on 10 December 2008, entered into force on 5 May 2013, and ratified by Italy on 20 February 2015; Article 1 of the Optional Protocol to the Convention on the Elimination of All Forms of Discrimination against Women (United Nations Treaty Series, vol. 2131, p. 83 ff.), concluded on 6 October 1999, entered into force on 22 December 2000, and ratified by Italy on 22 September 2000; Article 5 of the Optional Protocol to the Convention on the Rights of the Child on a Communications Procedure (UN doc. A/RES/66/138 (2011)), adopted on 19 December 2011, entered into force on 14 April 2014, and ratified by Italy on 4 February 2016; Article 1 of the Optional Protocol to the Convention on the Rights of Persons with Disabilities (United Nations Treaty Series, vol. 2518, p. 283), adopted on 13 December 2006, entered into force on 3 May 2008, and ratified by Italy on 15 May 2009.

[55] On 3 November 1997 Italy ratified the Additional Protocol to the European Social Charter Providing for a System of Collective Complaints, concluded on 9 November 1995 and entered into force on 1 July 1998 (European Treaty Series No. 158). Under Article 1 of the Additional Protocol, the following organizations are entitled to submit collective complaints "(a) international organisations of employers and trade unions referred to in paragraph 2 of Article 27 of the Charter; (b) other international non-governmental organisations which have consultative status with the Council of Europe and have been put on a list established for this purpose by the Governmental Committee; (c) representative national organisations of employers and trade unions within the jurisdiction of the Contracting Party against which they have lodged a complaint". Under Article 2 of the same Protocol, a State party may bestow the right to lodge collective complaints on "other representative national non-governmental organisation within its jurisdiction which has particular competence in the matters governed by the Charter".

[56] See Article 8 of the Optional Protocol to the CEDAW; Article 13(1) of the Optional Protocol to the CRC on a Communications Procedure; Article 6 of the Optional Protocol to the Convention on the Rights of Persons with Disabilities.

[57] Italy could have decided to subject itself to such power under the opt-in clause of Article 11 of the Optional Protocol to the ICESCR.

[58] See Article 12 of the Optional Protocol to the Convention of the Rights of the Child on a Communications Procedure.

[59] Italy could have recognized the CESCR competence to receive and consider inter-state claims under the opt-in clause of Article 10 of the Optional Protocol to the ICESCR.

[60] See UN Human Rights Council, Resolution 16/21, *Review of the work and functioning of the Human Rights Council*, UN doc. A/HRC/RES/16/21 (2011), Annex, para. 3: "the periodicity of the review for the second and subsequent cycles will be of four and a half years".

selected by the Office of the UN High Commissioner for Human Rights.[61] Much of the monitoring to which Italy has been subjected in recent years focuses on the domestic dimension of the fight against poverty and the measures Italy took, or failed to take, to shield people under its jurisdiction from the effects of the global economic crisis.

In its Concluding Observations on Italy's seventh periodic report, the Committee on the Elimination of Discriminations Against Women expressed concern about the austerity measures taken to address the economic downturn.[62] The Committee stressed, in particular, that "low levels of social benefits and very strict eligibility criteria have resulted in a situation in which many women living in poverty, in particular single mothers, older women and those without previous employment, are excluded from social protection".[63] The Committee on the Rights of the Child likewise called attention on the weakness of Italy's response to the increasing incidence of poverty and social exclusion. While considering the report submitted by Italy in 2011, the Committee expressed deep concern "at the high number of children living in poverty in the State party and the disproportional concentration of child poverty in southern Italy".[64] It also pointed out that "the State party has the second-lowest employment rate among women in the European Union (below 50 per cent), in particular given that child poverty is closely linked with unemployment among women".[65] Italy was also blamed for the limited nature of the financial benefits granted in the years 2008–2009 to low-income families, the so-called Family Bonus (*Bonus famiglia*) and the Social Card, which in its view "only marginally reduced inequalities and poverty".[66]

Similar remarks appear in the Concluding Observations on the Initial Report of Italy formulated in 2016 by the Committee on the Rights of Persons with Disabilities. The Committee voiced its preoccupation regarding, in particular, "(a) regional variations of social protection mechanisms; (b) the lack of Minimum Standards of Social Assistance; (c) the high level of poverty among persons with disabilities and their families, in particular children with disabilities; and (d) the lack of assessment

[61] See the UN General Assembly, Resolution 60/251 establishing the Human Rights Council, UN doc. A/RES/60/251(2006), para. 5 (e); UN Human Rights Council, Resolution 5/1, *Institution-building of the United Nations Human Rights Council*, UN doc. A/HRC/RES/5/1 (2007); UN Human Rights Council, Resolution 16/21, cit.; UN Human Rights Council, Decision 17/119, *Follow-up to the Human Rights Council Resolution 16/21 With Regard to the Universal Periodic Review*, A/HRC/DEC/17/119 (2011).

[62] Committee on the Elimination of Discrimination against Women, *Concluding Observations on the Seventh Periodic Report of Italy*, UN doc. CEDAW/C/ITA/CO/7, 24 July 2017.

[63] *Ibid.*, p. 15, para 43.

[64] Committee on the Rights of the Child, *Consideration on Reports Submitted by States Parties Under Article 44 of the Convention*, UN doc. CRC/C/ITA/CO/3-4, 31 October 2011, p. 15, para 57.

[65] *Ibid.*

[66] *Ibid.*

of the adverse effect of austerity measures".[67] To this it added that "the policy framework for addressing child poverty for those with disabilities is inadequate and monitoring mechanisms absent".[68]

In 2015 the CESCR identified many of the same shortcomings in its Concluding Observations on Italy's fifth periodic report, an assessment that starts by noting "the increasing rate of poverty in recent years".[69] Having expressed concern about "the high rate of child poverty and the regional disparities in poverty prevalence as well as the increase in income inequality across the country", the Committee urged Italy "to step up its efforts to address poverty while paying particular attention to child poverty and poverty in the southern provinces".[70] As to the choice of measures to address the economic crisis, the Committee recommended the strengthening of "social and financial support for families in situations of vulnerability" and the development of "human rights-based poverty-reduction programmes, taking into consideration the Committee's statement on poverty and the International Covenant on Economic, Social and Cultural Rights".[71]

Italy's record before regional monitoring bodies is equally unfavourable. In 2017 the ECSR held that "the situation in Italy is not in conformity with Article 30 of the Charter on the ground that there is no adequate overall and coordinated approach to combating poverty and social exclusion".[72] This finding, contained in the Committee's conclusions on Italy's periodic report, replicates comments already put on record in 2009, 2013, and 2015.[73] In the Committee's view, then, Italy has been lacking a consistent strategy in the fight against poverty at least from the onset of the economic crisis. The Committee took cognizance of information provided by the Italian National Institute of Statistics (ISTAT) and Eurostat, according to which, between 2012 and 2014, the poverty incidence among persons under the age of 18 had increased by 1.5%, whereas "the poverty rate (after social transfer) for the age group 18–24 years is still pronounced in comparison to the overall rate, standing at

[67]Committee on the Rights of Persons with Disabilities, *Concluding Observations on the Initial Report of Italy*, UN doc. CRPD/C/ITA/CO/1, 6 October 2016, p. 9, para 71.

[68]*Ibid.* p. 3, para 17.

[69]Committee on Economic, Social and Cultural Rights, *Concluding Observations on the Fifth Periodic Report of Italy*, UN doc. E/C.12/ITA/CO/5, 28 October 2015, p. 7, para 38.

[70]*Ibid.*, para 39.

[71]*Ibid.* See also Committee on Economic, Social and Cultural Rights, *Substantive Issues Arising in the Implementation of the International Covenant on Economic, Social and Cultural Rights: Poverty and the International Covenant on Economic, Social and Cultural Rights: Poverty and the International Covenant on Economic, Social and Cultural Rights*, Statement adopted on 4 May 2001, UN doc. E/C.12/2001/10 (2001).

[72]European Committee on Social Rights, *Conclusions on the Report of Italy – Article 30*, doc. n. 2017/def/ITA/30/EN, 8 December 2017.

[73]European Committee on Social Rights, *Conclusions on the Report of Italy – Article 30*, doc. n. 2009/def/ITA/30/EN, 2 January 2010; European Committee on Social Rights, *Conclusions on the Report of Italy – Article 30*, doc. n. 2013/def/ITA/30/EN, 6 December 2013; European Committee on Social Rights, *Conclusions on the Report of Italy – Article 30*, UN Doc. No. 2015/def/ITA/30/EN, 4 December 2015.

26.1% in 2015 (up from 25% in 2013)". It was also pointed out that "the poverty rates in Italy remains very high and also rising if referring to the poverty rate after social transfers", for the impact of such transfers "is less in Italy than in the EU on average (a poverty reducing effect of 21.7% in Italy compared to EU average of 33.2%)". Even more alarmingly, the risk of poverty had been growing faster for children than for the population in general, in a country where one child out of three is already "at risk of poverty or social exclusion, which is among the highest rates in Europe". The Committee then noted that in spite of all this, Italy's report referred to measures taken in the fight against poverty "only summarily [. . .] and without any particular indication of how they add up to an overall and coordinated approach". In a situation calling for the adoption of "extraordinary measures", as the Committee conclusively characterized it, Italy failed to show to the Committee's satisfaction that "the budgetary resources allocated to combating poverty and exclusion are sufficient in view of the challenges as required by Article 30".

Issues concerning the external dimension of the fight against poverty came up only twice, most notably in the context of the Universal Periodic Review (UPR). The report submitted by Italy for the purposes of the UPR addressed the topic of development aid in an exculpatory tone:

> the context of the global financial and economic crisis, with the consequent need to contain public expenditure, has led to downsizing the funding of [Official Development Assistance (ODA)] in recent years. In 2008 Italian ODA reached 0.22% of GDP, fluctuating to 0.14% of GDP in 2012. In 2013 the Italian government committed itself to ensure a 10% increase of ODA, with the goal to gradually align our ODA to international standards. According to this commitment to growth, we expect to reach 0.28/0.31% of GDP in 2017.[74]

The Committee on the Rights of the Child had previously "encouraged Italy to strive to redress the fall in official development assistance and recover its growth path in order to meet the internationally agreed target of 0.7 per cent of gross national product by 2015".[75] As is known, the legal status of 0.7 target, which was first incorporated in UN General Assembly's resolution 2626 (XXV) of 24 October 1970,[76] remains somewhat uncertain, even though the alleged obligors seldom act or speak as if they were legally bound by it. Be that as it may, some potential obligees (Bangladesh, China, Sierra Leone, Tunisia) took the UPR as an occasion to press Italy to "implement its commitment to increase the ODA for developing countries, particularly least developed countries",[77] or to "increase overseas

[74]Italy, *National Report Submitted in Accordance with Paragraph 5 of the Annex to Human Rights Council Resolution*, UN Doc. No. 16/21, A/HRC/WG.6/20/ITA/1, 21 July 2014, pp. 18–19, para 88.

[75]*Compilation Prepared by the Office of the United Nationals High Commissioner for Human Rights in Accordance with Paragraph 15 (b) of the Annex to Human Rights Council Resolution 5/1 and Paragraph 5 of the Annex to Council Resolution 16/21 (Summary of UN Information)*, UN Doc. No. A/HRC/WG.6/20/ITA/2 (2014), p. 13, para 92.

[76]UN Doc. No. A/RES/25/2626, para. 43.

[77]Human Rights Council (HRC), Report of the Working Group on the Universal Periodic Review – Italy, UN Doc. No. A/HRC/28/4 (2014), para. 145.183 (China).

development assistance to aim at achieving the agreed target of 0.7 per cent of GDP",[78] or to "continue its efforts to reach quickly the international target of 0.7 per cent ODA",[79] or to "raise the level of ODA to 0.7 per cent of GDP".[80] As the next section will show, Italy is not going to live up to this commitment anytime soon.

Italy's Embrace of the 2030 Agenda for Sustainable Development

"We recognize that eradicating poverty in all its forms and dimensions, including extreme poverty, is the greatest global challenge and an indispensable requirement for sustainable development".[81] This is the opening salvo of the resolution by which the UN General Assembly solemnly adopted, on 25 September 2015, the document entitled "Transforming Our World: The 2030 Agenda for Sustainable Development". The document is essential reading for all those with an interest in the fight against poverty and the right to development, and a depressing one at that. Like its predecessor, the Millennium Declaration, the 2030 Agenda not only does not even faintly resemble a set of legal rules—a circumstance that should discourage any attempt to categorize it as "soft *law*"—it also crowds international law out by the sheer power of a throbbing managerial rhetoric infused with messianic zeal. As to the status of the benchmarks it sets, which are said to "come into effect on 1 January 2016",[82] the UN General Assembly made it clear that they are "aspirational and global, with each Government setting its own national targets guided by the global level of ambition but taking into account national circumstances".[83] It is, in other words, for each State to decide "how these aspirational and global targets should be incorporated into national planning processes, policies and strategies".[84]

The Sustainable Development Goals (SDGs) set by the 2030 Agenda form an overlong and convoluted pattern of wishes, pledges and benchmarks, so much so that the representative of Japan, speaking at the end of the drafting process, regretfully declared: "it is hard to say that we have agreed to a set of goals and targets that are concise, easy to communicate and tweetable".[85] Will it be nonetheless "world-transformative", as the resolution's title proclaims? In this respect it is worth noting

[78] *Ibid.*, para 145.184 (Sierra Leone).

[79] *Ibid.*, para 145.185 (Tunisia).

[80] *Ibid.*, para 145.186 (Bangladesh).

[81] *Transforming Our World: the 2030 Agenda for Sustainable Development*, UN Doc. No. A/RES/70/1 (2015), p. 1, para. 1 of preamble.

[82] *Ibid.*, p. 6, para. 21.

[83] *Ibid.*, p. 13, para. 55.

[84] *Ibid.*

[85] *Report of the Working Group on Sustainable Development Goals, Addendum: Further Explanations of Positions and Reservations on the Report*, UN Doc. No. A/68/970/Add.2 (2015), p. 2.

that the 2030 Agenda displays two features that were missing in the Millennium Declaration. First of all, while the latter were almost silent on the policies by which the goals themselves were to be pursued, the SDGs insists on "the means required for implementation of the Goals and targets".[86] Secondly, the SDGs come with a "systematic follow-up and review" mechanism, based on periodic but entirely voluntary national reporting and administered by the High-Level Political Forum on Sustainable Development (HLPF), which meets annually under the auspices of the UN Economic and Social Council and every 4 years, at the level of Heads of State and Government, under the auspices of the UN General Assembly.[87] Italy led with Brazil the consultations for the definition of the HLPF working methods and, as we shall see later in this section, already submitted its first report under the 2030 Agenda.

With regard to the means of implementation, it should be stressed, however, that the 2030 Agenda fell short of minimum expectations, as the Brazilian delegate to the Open Working Group (OWG) on SDGs, speaking also on behalf of Nicaragua, eloquently stated:

> We must express a feeling of deep frustration in respect of the means of implementation. We made good progress in formulating a new vision for development, but we failed to properly devise the means that will make it happen. In fact, there is a huge disparity between the level of ambition of the sustainable development goals and their respective, and missing, means of implementation. We have witnessed the deliberate watering down of the means of implementation to their minimum expression, right up to the end of the debates.[88]

Like Brazil, Italy was among the 30 members of the OWG set up within the UN General Assembly in late 2012, sharing the seat with Spain and Turkey.[89] Italy has not been a critical voice in the process that led to the adoption of the SDGs, whose overall logic it actually embraces with enthusiasm. "The three keywords that we propose for the Declaration are: Shared, Common and All", a delighted Italian delegate was heard saying in the lead-up to such adoption.[90] In 2016, during the G20 Meeting in Hangzhou, the Italian Government announced that "[i]n the spirit of the 2030, all Italian actors are mobilizing".[91] It also disclosed that the Chamber of Deputies had established a 2030 Agenda Committee and that a Working Group on Agenda 2030 had been set up within the National Council for Development Cooperation, a multi-stakeholder forum created by the Development Cooperation Act

[86] *Transforming Our World: the 2030 Agenda for Sustainable Development*, cit., p. 10, para. 41.

[87] *Ibid.*, pp. 11–12, paras. 47–48.

[88] *Report of the Working Group on Sustainable Development Goals, Addendum: Explanations of Positions and Reservations on the Report*, UN Doc. No. A/68/970/Add.1 (2014), p. 7.

[89] See, for the text of the decision and the list of the members of the Open Working Group, UN Doc. No. A/67/L.48/Rev.1 (2013).

[90] *Intergovernmental Negotiation on the Post-2015 Development Agenda, Open Discussion or Draft Declaration, Italy's Statement for General Discussion*, New York, 20 February 2015.

[91] *G20 Action Plan on the 2030 Agenda for Sustainable Development*, adopted in Hangzhou on 8 September 2016, p. 32.

2014,[92] to which a second multi-stakeholder platform, the Italian Alliance for Sustainable Development, was added.[93] Italy also joined "the Addis Tax Initiative (ATI) to improve domestic revenue mobilisation in partner countries and the Global Partnership for Sustainable Data [whose] goal is to strengthen the statistical capabilities on partner countries".[94] As for official development assistance (ODA), i.e. its *own* money and capabilities, Italy was more elusive: "The Italian government has also decided a substantial increase of ODA for the triennium 2016–2018".[95] We will come back to this in our assessment of Italy's initial report under the 2030 Agenda, a document whose reading requires some familiarity with the SDGs' complex architecture.

The SDGs are organized in a three-tier normative structure, going from the lofty regions of the 17 Goals, through a meandering set of 126 more specific Targets, to the (supposedly) down-to-earth dimension of the 43 Means of Implementation (MoI), which relate to Targets and Goals alike. In the SDGs grammar, simple numerals, from 1 through to 17, stand for the Goals. Composite numerals, like 1.1, 1.2, 2.1, etc., stand for the Targets and express their clustering around given Goals. The preamble to the Agenda deceptively advertises the existence of 169 Targets, a figure that actually includes the 43 MoI.[96] Under each Goal, the MoI are listed below the Targets and marked out by letters: 1.a, 1.b, 2.a, etc. An abridged reproduction of what may be called the "Goal 1 Cluster" shows what the SDGs three-tier structure looks like:

Goal 1. End poverty in all its forms everywhere

1.1 By 2030, eradicate extreme poverty for all people everywhere, currently measured as people living on less than $1.25 a day

1.2 By 2030, reduce at least by half the proportion of men, women and children of all ages living in poverty in all its dimensions according to national definitions

1.a Ensure significant mobilization of resources from a variety of sources, including through enhanced development cooperation, in order to provide adequate and predictable means or developing countries, in particular least developed countries, to implement programmes and policies to end poverty in all its dimensions

1.b Create sound policy frameworks at the national, regional and international levels, based on pro-poor and gender-sensitive development strategies, to support accelerated investment in poverty eradication actions.

---

[92] Law No. 125 of 11 August 2014, in OJ No. 199 of 28 August 2014.

[93] *G20 Action Plan on the 2030 Agenda for Sustainable Development*, cit., pp. 32–33.

[94] *Ibid.*, p. 33.

[95] *Ibid.*

[96] *Transforming Our World: the 2030 Agenda for Sustainable Development*, cit., p. 1, para. 3 of preamble.

As can be gleaned from the example, the MoI are tuned to such an airy pitch—they amount to a little more than a windy restatement of the Goal—that they hardly deserve the name. It should also be noted that Goal 17, under the caption "Strengthen the means of implementation and revitalize the Global Partnership for Sustainable Development", breaks down into 19 Targets but provides no section on MoI. This is due to the fact that Goal 17, in spite of its name, was itself understood as a set of MoI to foster the attainment of the other Goals. What this "instrumental Goal" seeks to capture is the cooperative dimension, both international and transnational, of the striving towards the SDGs. But the semantics of the SDGs is tricky. Under Goal 17 both Targets and MoI are listed in no discernible order. Item 17.3 ("Mobilize additional financial resources for developing countries from multiple sources"), would have elsewhere fallen under the category of the vaguely-stated MoI, whereas item 17.2 appears at first sight as a neatly-defined Target. It also happens to be one of the salient points of the entire 2030 Agenda, as it encapsulates a commitment that developed States had failed to make, or refused to confirm, when subscribing to the Millennium Declaration:

17.2 Developed countries to implement fully their official development assistance commitments, including the commitment by many developed countries to achieve the target of 0.7% of gross national income for official development assistance (ODA/GNI) to developing countries and 0.15 to 0.20% of ODA/GNI to least developed countries; ODA providers are encouraged to consider setting a target to provide at least 0.20% of ODA/GNI to least developed countries.

Now, this Target is also a MoI with respect to every other Goal, and a very important one at that.[97] We would be tempted to say that the time-frame for its realization should differ from that of the other Goals: 2030 could be too late for devising what is, in essence, a MoI and not a Target, although it is formally listed among the latter. While an argument could be made to the effect that MoI should be implemented immediately, the Addis Ababa Action Agenda, which the 2030 Agenda incorporates by reference, clearly implies that ODA targets are meant to be achieved, like every other goal, "within the time-frame of the post-2015 agenda",[98] a circumstance that countries like Italy will find reassuring.

In July 2017, Italy submitted to the HLPF a 97-page report detailing a "National Sustainable Development Strategy (NSDS)".[99] The NSDS fully reflects Italy's fondness for the SDGs, bringing the latter's penchant for military, sports or managerial argot to new extremes, while marginalizing the language of politics, law and

---

[97] *Initial Input of the Secretary-General to the Open Working Group on Sustainable Development Goals*, UN Doc. No. A/67/637 (2012), pp. 18–19, 22.

[98] *Addis Ababa Action Agenda of the Third International Conference on Financing for Development*, endorsed by the UN General Assembly in resolution 69/913 of 27 July 2015, UN Doc. No. A/RES/69/913 (2015), pp. 26–27, para. 51.

[99] *National Sustainable Development Strategy: National Voluntary Review (Italy)*, 2017, p. 8.

rights. Words like "strategy" or "strategic" meets the reader's eye with disturbing frequency, as where it is explained that the national strategy is "organized in five core areas", each of which "consists of a set of national strategic choices articulated in strategic national goals".[100] But Italy took the SDGs' principle of national ownership no less seriously, so much so that, instead of structuring the report along the lines of the delicately constructed list of Goals, Targets and MoI making up the 2030 Agenda, it reshuffled all the items in the list and laid them out in a five-dimensional framework of its own invention. But the SDGs' grand scheme was not completely lost sight of. The five poles around which Italy's strategy is said to revolve closely track the concepts showcased in the second section of the SDGs' preamble, also known as the five Ps, to wit: People, Planet, Prosperity, Peace and Partnership. The Italian edit of the SDGs comes, however, with its own jargon. The five Ps are designated as "Areas". Areas branch out into "Strategic Choices", which in turn split into "National Strategic Goals", a denomination that confusingly recalls the SDGs' top-echelon norms. As to the possible equivalences between the two vocabularies, the Italian government spared no effort to map them out. The outcome was, however, an overwhelmingly complex web of cross-references that mixes up what in the SDGs' terminology are Goals, Targets and MoI, or rather tries them in new and at times counterintuitive configurations. SDGs Goals are referenced at the levels of Areas and National Strategic Goals, but not at the meso-level of Strategic Choices. National Strategic Goals are in turn spelt out by importing Target and MoI coming from different Goals, without contributing any original content. Table 7.1 exemplifies this tiresome *modus operandi* as applied to the Area that most closely relates to the fight against poverty.

Since sets of quantitative indicators for each Goal are still in the making at the UN[101]—indicators make the fourth tier of the SDGs' edifice—the Italian Government was justified in thinking that the application of such indicators would have been premature at such an early stage of the review process.[102] It produced, instead, a rough qualitative estimate by placing, next to each Target and MoI, a tick-box whose colour signal the breadth of the gap between Italy's current situation and the goal set for 2030: "For each of them, the degree of consistency with the 2030 Agenda (high, medium, low) is highlighted with different grey shading, while key implementation tools are linked".[103] By the term "implementation tools", whose meaning is left unspecified, the drafters probably intended to refer to specific legislative or regulatory measures. If so, they forgot to "link" them, leaving the

[100]*Ibid.*

[101]See *The Sustainable Development Goals Report 2017*, p. 58; *Report of the Inter-agency and Expert Group on Sustainable Development Goals Indicators*, UN Doc. No. E/CN.3/2017/2 (2017).

[102]*National Sustainable Development Strategy: National Voluntary Review – Italy*, 2017, p. 5. See also *ibid.*, p. 4: "A future Plan of Action will be developed by the end of 2017 and will include numerical and quantitative targets at 2030, as well as monitoring and review mechanisms and analytical models capable of measuring the impacts of policies on the NSDS objectives". At the time of writing (early 2018) the Plan of Action had not been disclosed yet.

[103]*Ibid.*, p. 85.

Table 7.1 Conceptual correspondences between Italy's National Sustainable Development Strategy and the 2030 Sustainable Development Agenda

Italy's National Sustainable Development Strategy			2030 Sustainable Development Agenda	
Area	Strategic choice	National Strategic Goal	Goals	Targets & MoI
People	I. Fight poverty and social exclusion, eliminating territorial gaps	I.1 Reduce the intensity of poverty	1 · 5 · 10	1.1 · 1.2 · 1.b · 5.4 10.1 · 10.2
		I.2 Combat food and material deprivation	1 · 2 · 5 · 6	1.a · 2.1 · 5.1 · 6.2
		I.3 Reduce inadequate housing	1 · 5 · 6 · 7 · 11	1.4 · 5.a · 6.1 · 6.4 7.1 · 11.1
	II. Guarantee the conditions for the development of human potential	II.1 Reduce unemployment for the weakest segments of the population	2 · 4 · 5 · 8	2.3 · 4.4 · 4.6 · 5.5 5.a · 5.b · 5.c · 8.5
		II.2 Ensure the effectiveness of the social protection and security system	1 · 3 · 4 · 5 · 16	1.3 · 3.5 · 4.2 · 5.1 5.4 · 16.6
		II.3 Reduce the school drop-out rate and enhance the education system	4 · 5 · 8	4.1 · 4.2 · 4.5 · 4.7 4.a · 5.1 · 8.6 · 8.7 13.3
		II.4 Fight deviance through prevention and social integration of vulnerable individuals	3 · 10	3.5 · 10.2
	III. Promote health and welfare	III.1 Reduce population exposure to anthropogenic and environmental risks	1 · 2 · 3 · 6 10 · 11 · 13	1.5 · 2.4 · 3.9 · 6.3 11.5 · 11.6 · 13.1
		III.2 Promote healthy lifestyles and strengthen preventive healthcare systems	2 · 3 · 5 · 11	2.2 · 3.3 · 3.4 · 3.5 3.6 · 3.7

(continued)

Table 7.1 (continued)

Italy's National Sustainable Development Strategy			2030 Sustainable Development Agenda	
Area	Strategic choice	National Strategic Goal	Goals	Targets & MoI
				· 3.a · 5.6 11.2
		III.3 Guarantee access to effective healthcare services and reduce territorial gaps	3 · 5	3.1 · 3.2 · 3.8 · 3. c 5.3

reader clueless as to the means by which Italy might have reached the positions it claims to occupy as against each benchmark. A few generic and self-gratulatory references to the Jobs Act, an ultraliberal reform of labour law, and to the efficiency gains allegedly brought about by a "public administration reform" hardly make up for such reticence.[104] The drafters also forgot to point out in which direction one should read the three shades of grey expressing their qualitative assessment. Does dark grey mean success or failure? As Target 1.1 of the SDGs ("eradicate extreme poverty for all people everywhere [. . .] measured as people living on less than $1.25 a day") is matched to a dark grey tick-box, dark must stand for a positive outcome, if only because nowadays very few people experience such levels of hardship in a country like Italy. The act of painting Target 1.1 dark grey is actually more interesting for what it says about how the drafters read the term "everywhere". They meant everywhere *in Italy*, whereas Target 1.1, especially from the standpoint of a rich country, should rather be taken as referring to the world at large.

This brings us to what is, symptomatically, the shortest section of Italy's report, that on the Global Partnership for Sustainable Development—SDG 17, or the external dimension of the 2030 Agenda—where Italy's structural incapacity or unwillingness to live up to its commitments until the very *end* of the 2030 Agenda's lifecycle is tersely recognized: "ODA intermediate growth targets are set to achieve 0.3% of GDP in 2020 and 0.7% in 2030".[105] And not a word is spent on the minimum quota that, according to SDG 17, should go to least developing countries.

As for the domestic dimension of the fight against poverty, it will be recalled that Italy, under Target 1.2, pledged to reduce "at least by half the proportion of men, women and children of all ages living in poverty in all its dimensions according to national definitions". Italy's report boasts a dark grey tick-box for this Target, too. This, however, stands in stark contrast to what ISTAT, the National Institute of Statistics, disclosed in July 2017—the very same month Italy completed its report—about the *increasing* incidence of absolute poverty in Italy, measured according to

[104] *Ibid.*, pp. 19–20.
[105] *Ibid.*, p. 8.

national standards: from 7.6% of the population, in 2015, to 7.9% in 2016.[106] Although ISTAT itself warned that the registered increase should not be regarded as statistically significant, the available evidence does not support Italy's optimism and exposes the propagandistic character of its self-awarded medal.

The HLPF raised no objections. In the friendly atmosphere that envelops the 2030 Agenda's follow-up and review process, the national reports, including Italy's, were repeatedly praised for their "high quality" and as offering "an inspiring repertoire of country profiles in action".[107] As Italy itself had noted in the lead-up to the adoption of the 2030 Agenda, the review process "should not be used to rate the performance of countries".[108] Italy has actually used it to elaborately conceal its continuing debacle in the fight against poverty and in defence of basic social rights, both at home and internationally, as certified in particular by human rights bodies' monitoring activity.

References

Alston P (2005) Ships passing in the night: the current state of the human rights and development debate seen through the lens of the millennium development goals. Hum Rights Q 27:755–829

Gradoni L (2015) La spettacolarizzazione della lotta alla fame ovvero l'impotenza delle organizzazioni internazionali di fronte alla sfida della sicurezza alimentare mondiale. In: Vellano M (ed) Il futuro delle organizzazioni internazionali: prospettive giuridiche. Atti del XIX Convegno della Società italiana di Diritto internazionale (Courmayeur 26–28 giugno 2014). Editoriale Scientifica, Naples, pp 237–279

Schutter D et al (2012) Commentary to the Maastricht principles on extraterritorial obligations of states in the area of economic, social and cultural rights. Hum Rights Q 34:1084–1169

Viterbo A (2012) L'applicazione extraterritoriale del Patto internazionale sui diritti economici, sociali e culturali: i Principi di Maastricht del 2011. Diritti umani e diritto internazionale 5:210–216

Zaniboni E (2017) Le diseguaglianze economiche interne agli Stati nella prospettiva giuridica internazionale. In: D'Onghia M, Zaniboni E (eds) Tutela dei soggetti deboli e trasformazioni del lavoro tra diritti e libertà: prospettive nazionali e internazionali. Editoriale Scientifica, Naples, pp 135–186

[106] As reported in ISTAT, *La povertà in Italia: anno 2016*, 13 July 2017, p. 1.

[107] *Voluntary National Reviews 2017: Synthesis Report*, pp. ii, vi.

[108] *IGN 5th Session on Post-2015, Statement by Italy on Follow-up, Monitoring and Review*, New York, 18 May 2015.

Chapter 8
The Netherlands and the Right to Development

Fons Coomans and Peggy ter Vrugt

Abstract The report on The Netherlands discussed the right to development as a human rights norm and as a policy objective in the external policies of the Netherlands. It provides a description and critical analysis of recent Dutch human rights and development cooperation policies. It is concluded that the right to development as a human right does not play a self-standing role in Dutch human rights and development cooperation policy. More in general, economic, social and cultural rights are not seen as the normative framework for development cooperation and only play a marginal role in Dutch human rights foreign policy. Although some promising initiatives have been taken recently, development issues are treated as a policy matter and not grounded in human rights obligations of the Netherlands.

Introduction

The present report on The Netherlands will focus on both the right to development as a human rights norm and as a policy objective in the external policies of the Netherlands. Development issues belong to the mandate of the Minister of Foreign Trade and Development Cooperation, thus reflecting that the latter two domains are interrelated. This contribution will provide a description and critical analysis of recent Dutch human rights and development cooperation policies and follow the guidelines presented in the questionnaire to the authors. It will use primary sources

F. Coomans (✉)
UNESCO Chair in Human Rights and Peace, Maastricht Centre for Human Rights, Maastricht University, Maastricht, The Netherlands
e-mail: fons.coomans@maastrichtuniversity.nl

P. ter Vrugt
Maastricht Centre for Human Rights, Maastricht University, Maastricht, The Netherlands
e-mail: peggy.tervrugt@maastrichtuniversity.nl

M. Andenas et al. (eds.), *The Fight Against Poverty and the Right to Development*, Ius Comparatum - Global Studies in Comparative Law 52,
https://doi.org/10.1007/978-3-030-57324-9_8

and materials, mainly those issued by the Government. This report will not deal with domestic law and remedies available to individuals as tools for claiming economic, social and cultural human rights (hereafter ESC-rights) which can be used in the fight against poverty.[1]

Constitutional Basis for the Contribution to the Fight Against Poverty and the Right to Development in an International Context

Article 90 of the Netherlands Constitution provides for the constitutional duty to promote the development of the international legal order. Its full text reads as follows: 'The Government shall promote the development of the international legal order.'[2] Previously, this was officially translated as: 'The government shall promote the development of the *international rule of law'*. However, this was a mistranslation but this version of Article 90 of the Netherlands Constitution still circulates.[3] The legal history of this Article shows that its nature and meaning has changed from peaceful settlement of international disputes into a general provision on the duty to promote the development of the international legal order. Already in 1983, the government made it clear that the current wording of 'international legal order' has a wide scope and that it needs to be understood in the broad sense of an international legal order based on universally valid legal standards.[4] This means that this Article is not only the legal basis for concluding international and European treaties by the Dutch government, but also for using armed force to promote the development of the international legal order.[5] The government noted that this Article should also promote the realisation of human rights, in the broadest sense of the word, which includes both civil and political rights and economic, social and cultural rights.[6]

According to Besselink, there are three different 'layers' which can be distinguished in the legal history of Article 90 of the Netherlands Constitution. The first historical layer should be understood entirely in the context of war and peace and

[1]This subject has been dealt with extensively by Vlemminx in the 2014 report on The Netherlands. Vlemminx (2014).

[2]The official translation of the Constitution of the Kingdom of the Netherlands by the Ministry of Foreign Affairs can be found on: https://www.government.nl/documents/regulations/2012/10/18/the-constitution-of-the-kingdom-of-the-netherlands-2008.

[3]Besselink (2003), p. 90.

[4]*Kamerstukken* II 1979/80, 15 049 (R 1100), nr. 7, p. 5.

[5]This remains somewhat disturbing that the government has used this Article (especially concerning its wording 'promoting the development of the international legal order) as a legal basis to use armed forces to promote international legal order. Especially, since this Article originated from the preferred option of peaceful means over use of armed force. See more about this discussion: Besselink (2003), pp. 137–138.

[6]*Kamerstukken II* 1979/80, 15 049 (R 1100), nr. 7, p. 5.

embodied the duty to achieve peaceful dispute settlement.[7] During the constitutional amendments of 1953 the second layer was added, stating that 'the King promotes the development of the international legal order'.[8] This added layer broadened the meaning of the provision to also international cooperation and integration.[9] The constitutional revision of 1983 was influenced by the Cold War and tensions between the Western and Eastern Europe. This led to the third layer which aimed at an improvement in foreign relations focusing on issues of development and human rights.[10] The idea was that the amendment should express ideas and values of promoting the universal relations of human rights in the broadest sense, including ESC-rights, the promotion of 'the well-being of the world population and 'global solidarity' as expressed in a policy of development cooperation and promoting a New International Economic Order'.[11]

At first, during the constitutional revision of 1983 the Netherlands government proposed to remove Article 90 of the Constitution. According to the government, the provision would be superfluous because the Netherlands has a tradition to cooperate and to promote the international legal order and would also do so without such a constitutional duty.[12] However, Parliament disagreed[13] and introduced the explicit duty of care in the area of the international legal order.[14] This was a wise decision, because especially in light of current debates about refugee policy and providing development aid, this provision is highly relevant.

There are different opinions about the validity and efficiency of this Article. Some argue that by using the phrase 'promote', the nature of Article 90 of the Netherlands Constitution is dynamic and imposes a strong duty on the government. The Dutch government should not only respect and preserve the international legal order, but also strive to further 'development', with a view to change and improvement.[15] Others argue that Article 90 of the Netherlands Constitution is somewhat vague and that its original objective is difficult to determine and therefore it holds the danger of

[7]Besselink (2003), p. 102.

This first layer dates back to 1922 and in its later version it retained the element of the pursuit of peaceful means in case of international dispute. See: *Handelingen, Bijlagen* 2374, nr. 3, p. 3.

[8]Art. 58 Grondwet voor het Koninkrijk der Nederlanden (1953), Tweede Hoofdstuk, Van de Koning. Zesde afdeling, Van de macht des Konings. The translated text reads as follows: 'The King has the supreme authority over the conduct of foreign affairs. He promotes the development of the international legal order'.

[9]Besselink (2003), p. 103.

[10]Besselink (2003) p. 104.

[11]Parliamentary documents: *Naar een nieuwe Grondwet,* Vol. pp. 48–50, 63, 113, 127, 140, 172, 176. See also: Besselink (2003), p. 105.

[12]*Kamerstukken II* 1977/78, 15 049 (R 1100), nr. 3, p. 9.

[13]*Kamerstukken II* 1977/78, 15 049 (R 1100), nr. 6, p. 6.

[14]*Kamerstukken II* 1977/78, 15 049 (R 1100), nr. 7, p. 5 and *Kamerstukken II* 1977/78, 15 049 (R 1100), nr. 8.

[15]Vlemminx (2017), p. 18.

being too broad.[16] Lastly, it was argued that one could better conclude a treaty for promoting the international legal order, instead of codifying it into the Constitution.[17]

In our opinion, using the words ‘to promote’ means that Article 90 has a dynamic nature which means that the international legal order is not yet complete and that other rules can be added to it. The legal status of the right to development is soft law.[18] This term refers to a group of human rights which have been generally accepted by the world community and they have been reaffirmed in declarations and resolutions by many states. Nevertheless, they do not have any legally binding force in those countries. At the same time, soft law is often the first stage of becoming ‘hard’ law. Soft law invokes the responsibility of the international community and as such it falls under ‘the promotion of the international legal order’. This makes the right to development part of the international legal order which implies that the Netherlands government has the constitutional duty to promote the right to development.

Netherlands Policy Towards the Right to Development and the Fight Against Poverty

The Netherlands and the Notion of the Right to Development

Although the Netherlands Government has recognised that civil and political rights and ESC-rights are of equal importance both in foreign and domestic policy, ESC-rights have received less attention and their legal status has been questioned.[19] Furthermore, in Dutch human rights foreign policy and policies in the area of development cooperation and assistance the right to development as a human right of a holistic nature has been absent. Although the Netherlands voted in favour of the adoption of the Declaration on the Right to Development in 1986 by the UN General Assembly, the right to development is not recognized as a legal human right. Its legal nature is questioned. For example, in 2010, in a response to UN Human Rights Council resolution 15/25 on the right to development, the Government expressed the view:[20]

---

[16] *Handelingen I* 1952–1953, p. 469.

[17] Besselink (2003), p. 117.

[18] It is widely accepted that the right to development can be described as ‘soft law’, generally accepted but not legally binding. See for example: Kirchmeier (2006), p. 11; Arts and Tamo (2016), p. 224; De Feyter (2013).

[19] Reiding (2007), p. 18. See also: Baehr (2006), pp. 190–191.

[20] Submission in follow-up to HRC resolution 15/25, The Right to Development—The Netherlands, available at: http://www.ohchr.org/_layouts/15/WopiFrame.aspx?sourcedoc=/Documents/Issues/Development/Session12/Netherlands.pdf&action=default&DefaultItemOpen=1.

> that it is first necessary to reach agreement on the content of the right to development, before applying this concept in practice. Furthermore, (..), we consider that states have a primary responsibility towards the persons in their jurisdiction and still have a number of questions regarding states collective and individual responsibilities at the international level.
>
> With regard to the conclusions and recommendations, in particular regarding suggestions for further action, the Netherlands is of the opinion that many of the suggestions can be taken forward but that a step-by-step approach is necessary based on a logical sequence of the proposals for further action.
>
> The first step should be to gather comments of all relevant actors on the criteria, sub-criteria and indicators for the right to development. Consequently, these comments should be discussed with the support of experts with a view to reaching agreement on them.
>
> Once agreement is reached on the criteria and operational sub-criteria, a comprehensive and coherent set of standards could be developed for the operationalisation of the right in practice.
>
> Standards should be made operational in terms of benchmarks and indicators with regard to the obligations of states, which include the empowerment of individuals as active agents in the development process. This step of developing a set of standards could start with seeking information on existing types of instruments used in the UN to translate policy into action (e.g. guidelines, codes of conduct and practice notes).
>
> At the same time it could then be explored to what extent existing treaty regimes could accommodate right to development issues within their legal and institutional settings, to what extent the preparation of a template for reporting would be useful and whether it would be useful to include reporting on the right to development in the UPR process.
>
> As is well-known, the Netherlands is not in favour of a legally binding international instrument on the right to development. We think that the responsibility to create an enabling environment cannot be translated into binding obligations. Furthermore we hold the view that a legally binding instrument is not an appropriate instrument for moving the right to development from political commitment to development practice.

From this explanation the conclusion can be drawn that the right to development is seen as a political commitment which is in need of concrete standards for the practical operationalisation of the concept.

The Netherlands Development Cooperation Policy and the Role of Human Rights

Already in 2003 the Netherlands Advisory Council on International Affairs concluded that a human rights component in Dutch development cooperation policy did not exist, especially as part of assistance programs with countries in the South.[21] In the Council's view the value of the right to development lies in particular in the connecting function of this right: it connects and integrates the right to life, food,

[21] AIV Advies (2003), p. 41.

primary health care and participation in cultural and political life.[22] The Netherlands Inspectorate on Development Cooperation and Policy Evaluation of the Ministry of Foreign Affairs concluded that in the practice of Dutch human rights foreign policy the focus has been on civil and political rights. Development cooperation aims at realising social and economic rights, but this is not seen as a rights issue in policy and practice and the link with the normative human rights framework is missing.[23] In policy notes successive Governments have acknowledged the link between development, human rights, the rule of law and the achievement of the Millennium Development Goals, but this has largely remained lip-service short of programs for the implementation of ESC-rights and the role of The Netherlands as a donor country.[24] More recently, the Government was criticised by the UN Committee on Economic, Social and Cultural Rights for the lack of systematic human rights impact assessments of its international development and cooperation policy.[25] The new Netherlands Government which took office in October 2017 will focus its human rights foreign policy on human rights defenders and LGBT-rights. Development cooperation is aimed at tackling the root causes of poverty, migration, climate change, strengthening new economies in the South and promoting the rule of law within the framework of the Sustainable Development Goals. One of the underlying objectives is to counter irregular migration flows to Europe out of self-interest. From the perspective of poverty reduction, sexual and reproductive health and rights, food security and access to water will also remain spearheads of Dutch development cooperation policy.[26] It is submitted that this cannot be qualified as an approach inspired by human rights obligations. Also the Netherlands position does not seem to reflect familiarity with the recent emerging notion that in a globalized economy state and corporate activities abroad affecting ESC-rights may give rise to extraterritorial human rights obligations which may be closely related to the implementation of the right to development.[27]

---

[22]AIV Advies (2003), p. 21.

[23]Inspectie Ontwikkelingssamenwerking en Beleidsevaluatie (2006), pp. 3–4 and 41.

[24]Ministry of Foreign Affairs (2007), pp. 83–84; Ministry of Foreign Affairs (2013), pp. 35–36.

[25]UN Committee on Economic, Social and Cultural Rights, Concluding Observations on the sixth periodic report of the Netherlands, 6 July 2017, UN Doc. E/C.12/NLD/CO/6, para. 9.

[26]Government Coalition Agreement, *Confidence in the Future*, The Hague, 10 October 2017, pp. 48–49.

[27]See the Maastricht Principles on Extraterritorial Obligations of States in the Area of Economic, Social and Cultural Rights (2011), www.etoconsortium.org; UN Committee on Economic, Social and Cultural Rights, General Comment No. 24 on Economic, Social and Cultural Rights in the Context of Business Activities, Sect. III-C, UN Doc. E/C.12/GC/24 (2017).

Current Dutch Foreign and Development Cooperation Policy to Support the Realisation of the SDGs

There are several policy frameworks designed by the Netherlands government which support the realisation of the Sustainable Development Goals [hereafter: SDGs]. In the policy document 'A World to Gain' the Ministry of Foreign Affairs decided to change its approach due to the one-billion euro cuts in the development budget agreed upon in 2012 and the changing situation in the world. The Netherlands established four priorities which were given more attention in the Dutch policy concerning development, trade, aid and investments.[28] These are (i) women's rights and sexual and reproductive health and rights; (ii) water; (iii) food security; and (iv) security and the rule of law. There are also three cross-cutting themes: gender equality, private sector development and climate change.

The Netherlands' development cooperation policy and programs mainly focus on the poorest and most vulnerable groups. This is, among others, clear from the selection of the Netherlands' partner countries: 11 out of its 15 partner countries are Least Developed Countries.[29] Dutch development policy is based on three different relationships with countries. The aid provided and measures taken by the government depend on the kind of relationship it has with the country in question.

The first type of relationship encompasses the countries with an aid relationship with the Netherlands. These are low-income countries, fragile states and (post-) conflict countries, including Afghanistan, Burundi, Mali, Yemen, Rwanda, South Sudan and the Palestinian Territories. In these countries, combating poverty is the main focus of the Dutch policy and the Netherlands also focuses on the four above mentioned priorities.[30]

The second category, transitional relationships, focuses on low- and middle-income countries with burgeoning economies. In a transitional relationship, a combination of aid and trade will both benefit the developing country and the Netherlands. This category includes the following countries: Bangladesh, Benin, Ethiopia, Ghana, Indonesia, Kenya, Mozambique and Uganda. Next to a focus on the four priority areas, Dutch policy also aims at improving access to international and regional markets, supporting entrepreneurs and governments, promoting equal opportunities and stimulating corporate social responsibility.[31] The third category lists the countries with a trade relationship with the Netherlands. Here, the aim is to

---

[28]Ministry of Foreign Affairs of the Netherlands (2013), pp. 22 and 26. Available at: https://www.government.nl/documents/letters/2013/04/05/global-dividends-a-new-agenda-for-aid-trade-and-investment.

[29]Kingdom of the Netherlands, 'Report on the implementation of the Sustainable Development Goals', United Nations High-Level Political Forum on Sustainable Development, 2017, p. 18.

[30]Ministry of Foreign Affairs of the Netherlands (2013), pp. 34–40.

These are as mentioned above, women's rights and sexual and reproductive health and rights, water, food security and security and the rule of law.

[31]Ministry of Foreign Affairs of the Netherlands (2013), pp. 40–46.

promote trade and investment with activities which contribute to economic growth and development in the Netherlands.[32]

The above mentioned categories and countries are chosen based on criteria such as income levels and levels of poverty, ranking in UNDP's Human Development Index, the activities of other donors and the knowledge and expertise that the Netherlands has to offer. However, the historical relationship with the Netherlands and possible opportunities for the Dutch private sector are also taken into account when determining the possible partner countries.[33]

Although the eradication of extreme poverty is the first objective of 'A World to Gain' a focus on poverty reduction in Dutch instruments and policy is not always visible. It is not always clear how the four priorities are linked and actually contribute to the eradication of extreme poverty. In addition, a human rights framework is not used as main reference or frame for action and policy formulation. The integration of human rights is not used as a starting point with regard to the policy for its priorities on water and food security, nor are human rights identified as a cross-cutting issue. The Netherlands policy towards these priorities, and thus the realisation of SDG 1, are merely seen as important development goals instead of a human right to which every person is entitled. The Dutch policy in relationship to these goals is merely seen as important development objective instead of an issue of human rights implementation. It is problematic that the Dutch policy on these subjects seems to imply that development cooperation automatically implements ESC-rights because of its focus on poverty reduction. Furthermore, the right to development is completely ignored in the Dutch development policy. We therefore submit that instead a right-based approach which is based on the right to development is needed in the Netherlands policy on food security and water issues.[34]

The next key policy document 'the Inclusive Development Action Plan', is based on 'A World to Gain'. In this policy memorandum the Netherlands government has stated how it wants to contribute to the eradication of extreme poverty and sustainable development growth in developing countries. It is convinced that the realisation of SDG 1, i.e. to eliminate extreme poverty by 2030, is only achievable when inequality is tackled. Therefore, the Netherlands wants to stimulate sustainable and inclusive growth and development.[35] This is done by using the five different international strategies for inclusive development: creating jobs, equal opportunities through development of human and physical capital, combating discrimination and exclusion, redistribution by taxes and transfers.[36] These strategies are included in

---

[32]Ministry of Foreign Affairs of the Netherlands (2013), p. 47.

[33]Ministry of Foreign Affairs of the Netherlands (2013), p. 27.

[34]Uvin (2007), p. 600.

[35]Aid, Trade and Investments, *Kamerstukken II* 2015–2016, 33 625, nr. 182, pp. 4–6.

[36]Kingdom of the Netherlands, 'Report on the Implementation of the Sustainable Development Goals', United Nations High-Level Political Forum on Sustainable Development, 2017, p. 18.

It is now widely accepted that there is a broad consensus worldwide about a good approach to inclusive development and thus ending extreme poverty. For example, the World Bank Group and the International Monetary Fund mention its policy agenda for increasing the inclusiveness and

20 different actions which the Netherlands implemented in order to support the poorest and most marginalised groups. These 20 actions are based on two perspectives: work for women and young people and a stronger political dialogue with developing countries on inclusive growth and development.[37] €350 million from the foreign trade and development budget was allocated for this action plan.[38] The 'Inclusive Development Action Plan' seems to build on the "leaving no one behind" motto of the SDGs, however this policy document lacks measures to eradicate extreme poverty. Although it mentions and identifies several excluded groups which need special attention, it is unclear whether there is a poverty focus within these groups.

The 'She Decides' Initiative: Special Attention for Women's Rights and Sexual Reproductive and Health Rights

Although human rights are not prioritised in policy areas such as water and food security, this does not mean that the current development agenda does not integrate human rights at all. The priority area of women's rights and sexual reproductive and health rights (SRHR) strongly reflect a focus on human rights. This is well illustrated by the recent 'She Decides' initiative launched by the then Dutch Minister for Foreign Trade and Development Cooperation on 24 January 2017. This is an international initiative set up to raise financial and political support for sexual and reproductive health worldwide. She Decides is a response to the Global Gag Rule, a decision by the USA government to withdraw funding for foreign organisations if they offer women in developing countries access to, or information about, safe

---

sustainability of growth in developing countries which encompasses creating jobs, investing in human capital, using safety nets and green growth, see: The World Bank Group and the International Monetary Fund (2015), pp. 95–156.

The IMF mentions next to macroeconomic policy, also fair and efficient taxes and government expenditures for investments in education and financial inclusion, see: International Monetary Fund (2015), pp. 30–32.

The G-20 made country strategies with inclusive growth policies together with the World Bank which correspond to these strategies, see: United Nations Development Programme (2013), pp. 15–21.

The Asian Development Bank used a definition of inclusive growth based on three pillars in its Strategy 2020 namely: high and sustainable growth, by investing in human capital, more opportunities for the poor to participate in growth and safety nets to reduce extreme deprivation, see: Asian Development Bank (2014), p. 18 and 19. See also for example: CAFOD (2014), p. 7.

[37]Aid, Trade and Investments, *Kamerstukken II* 2015-2016, 33 625, nr. 182, p. 14.

[38]Kingdom of the Netherlands, 'Report on the Implementation of the Sustainable Development Goals', United Nations High-Level Political Forum on Sustainable Development, 2017, p. 18.

abortion.[39] This measure is especially detrimental to organisations dealing with all aspects of sexual and reproductive health and family planning. According to many organisations, this measure will increase the number of unintended pregnancies, (unsafe) abortions and maternal deaths.[40]

The aim of the She Decides initiative is that indispensable provisions and services for sexual health and family planning can continue to exist in developing countries. It includes sex education, birth control, obstetric care, HIV testing and treatment and safe abortion. She Decides not only calls upon governments and organisations to financially and politically support sexual health and family planning worldwide, also private organisations, companies and citizens can contribute. So far, the Dutch government has pledged €29 million for this fund and worldwide more than €260 million has been raised.[41]

She Decides is an initiative which fits perfectly into the Dutch priority on women's rights and SRHR and it touches directly on the realisation of SDGs 3 and 5.[42] It is very clear that the Dutch policy on this priority and She Decides is based on a human rights perspective. This is also noted by the former Minister of Foreign Trade and Development Ploumen who stated that 'we cannot let women and girls down. They should have the right to decide if they want to have children, when they want to have children, and with whom they want to have children'.[43] As mentioned above, this human rights emphasis is lacking on other Dutch priorities such as water and food security which are solely based on an aid perspective. Therefore the Dutch government should take its good practice on women's rights

[39]White House Presidential Memoranda, 'Presidential Memorandum Regarding the Mexico City Policy', issued on 23 January 2017 by President Donald J. Trump. Available at: https://www.whitehouse.gov/presidential-actions/presidential-memorandum-regarding-mexico-city-policy/.

[40]For example, PAI, a reproductive health NGO, noted that this measure will cost many around the world their lives, especially women, see: PAI, 'The Harmful Impact of the Global Gag Rule', 10 October 2017. Available at: https://pai.org/policy-briefs/harmful-impact-global-gag-rule/. The International Women's Health Coalition stated that this measure will increase maternal deaths by putting essential sexual and reproductive health care out of reach for far too many women, see: International Women's Health Coalition, 'Taking the Pulse of Trump's Deadly Global Gag Rule', News item of 6 November 2017. Available at: https://iwhc.org/2017/11/taking-the-pulse-of-trumps-deadly-global-gag-rule/. The same consequences of this measure were also stated by Human Rights Watch, see: Human Rights Watch, 'US: Trump Policy Harming Kenya, Uganda Health Services- expanding 'Mexico City' Policy causing cuts in HIV and reproductive care', News item of 26 October 2017. Available at: https://www.hrw.org/news/2017/10/26/us-trump-policy-harming-kenya-uganda-health-services.

[41]Rijksoverheid, 'Tussenstand She Decides: 260 miljoen euro', News item of 28 July 2017. Available at: https://www.rijksoverheid.nl/onderwerpen/she-decides/nieuws/2017/07/28/tussenstand-she-decides-260-miljoen-euro.

[42]SDG 3 encompasses the goal of the realisation of 'Good health and well-being', whereas SDG 5 aims at 'Gender equality'.

[43]Speech by the Minister for Foreign Trade and Development Cooperation Liliane Ploumen on She Decides and equal rights for girls and women, at George Washington University on 24 April 2017. Available at: https://www.government.nl/topics/she-decides/documents/speeches/2017/04/24/speech-minister-ploumen-on-she-decides.

and SRHR as example and implement and prioritise human rights also in its other key policy areas.

Dutch Private Sector Involvement and Development Cooperation

The cut in the budget mentioned above has also led to a shift in the Dutch approach to development cooperation and its funding, with less emphasis on general state budget contributions and more focus on private sector cooperation.[44] Social development is important from a human rights point of view but without economic development it is not sustainable.[45] This kind of economic development cannot be achieved without contributions from the private sector, and consequently the Dutch foreign policy focuses on human rights in relation to the private sector. Human rights issues are integrated increasingly into the Dutch private sector by encouraging international Corporate Social Responsibility [hereafter: CSR] or Responsible Business Conduct. Dutch companies are expected to comply with the OECD Guidelines on Multinational Companies and the UN Guiding Principles on Business and Human Rights as proposed by Professor John Ruggie and adopted by the UN Human Rights Council. Furthermore, companies are expected to act in compliance with the due diligence principle by taking measures to prevent abuses in their supply chains in relation to working conditions, child labour, the environment, corruption and human rights.[46]

A good example of the involvement of the Dutch private sector into development cooperation is the Dutch Good Growth Fund [hereafter: DGGF],[47] which helps financing entrepreneurs who want to trade with and invest in low- and middle-income countries.[48] It is a revolving fund of €750 million, meaning that resources are repaid and therefore can be used again. Next to the financial part, the Fund is also accompanied by supportive measures which include help in drafting a good business plan or technical assistance. This Fund is a cooperative agreement between the Netherlands Ministry of Economic Affairs, companies and civil society. There is also a clear link with human rights since all activities supported by this Fund must be

[44]Ministry of Foreign Affairs of the Netherlands (2013), p. 8.

[45]Ministry of Foreign Affairs of the Netherlands (2013), p. 17.

[46]Ministry of Foreign Affairs of the Netherlands (2013), pp. 45 and 46.

[47]Besluit van de Minister voor Buitenlandse Handel en Ontwikkelingssamenwerking van 10 juni 2014 tot vaststelling van beleidsregels voor het verstrekken van subsidie in het kader van onderdeel 1 van het Dutch Good Growth Fund, *Staatscourant* 2014, 16589.

[48]There are 66 low- and middle-income countries who are participating in the Dutch Good Growth Fund. The full country list can be found in the annex of the policy document of the Ministry of Foreign Affairs of the Netherlands (2013), p. 67.

in compliance with of the OECD Guidelines and the UN Guiding Principles.[49] With the establishment of the DGGF, the Dutch government did not only strengthen the role of the private sector in development cooperation, but also encouraged the use of CSR and investing in fragile states.

Since 2013 successive Governments have been active in stimulating, facilitating and persuading the business sector in adopting and implementing a policy of responsible conduct in its activities abroad.[50] This is in line with the UN Guiding Principles on Business and Human Rights. These initiatives are aimed at reaching voluntary agreements between stakeholders in a particular sector. Stakeholders include employers and their associations, trade unions, the government and civil society organisations. Although these initiatives are not aimed directly at fostering development, they should be seen through the lens of promoting economic growth by means of creating an enabling environment which tries to mitigate the negative consequences of economic globalisation especially in production and supply chains. The State has a role to play in facilitating such an enabling environment by helping in agreeing on voluntary standards for business activities. Usually human rights language, let alone the right to development as a human right, is not used or referred to, but related terms are, such as CSR and due diligence responsibilities for business partners. In this regard it is worth mentioning that the mandate of the Netherlands Minister for Development Cooperation includes Foreign Trade, thus linking the two areas.

The Netherlands government has taken the lead, together with like-minded states, to improve living and working conditions and rights at work in the textiles and garment industry in Asia through agreements between all stakeholders. An example is the Voluntary Agreement on Sustainable Garment and Textile which was concluded between Dutch trade unions, employer associations, civil society organisations and the Government in 2016.[51] An example of a commitment taken up by the Netherlands government is to conclude agreements with local or national authorities in the state where the garment production takes place about strengthening the labour inspection system and collaboration with private labour standards initiatives. Similar initiatives have been taken to make the palm oil production and supply value chain more sustainable with a view to giving effect to SDG 2, 8, 12 and 15.[52] In the same vein, the Netherlands has undertaken various actions to promote a so-called *living wage* for workers in the Asian textiles industry. It is well-known that there is a gap between actual wages in that sector and the wage that is required to enjoy an adequate standard of living for the worker and his/her family. Here the government

---

[49]Ministry of Foreign Affairs of the Netherlands (2013), p. 45.

[50]See for a short overview of developments, Mensenrechten in het buitenlands beleid, *Kamerstukken II* 2014–2015, 32735, no. 143, pp. 6–7.

[51]https://www.ser.nl/en/publications/publications/2016/agreement-sustainable-garment-textile.aspx, p. 31.

[52]Letter of 28 September 2017 from the Minister for Foreign Trade and Development Cooperation to the President of the House of Representatives on the Annual Report on Policy Coherence for Development, *Kamerstukken II* 2017–2018, 33625, no. 250, pp. 8–9.

has said that this is a human right issue, a condition for poverty reduction and an instrument against child labour. There is also a link with SDG 1 and 8.[53] The Netherlands government aims at achieving a living wage by facilitating platforms and conferences for discussion and agreements between the international stakeholders; supporting the social dialogue and strengthening labour inspection systems in Asian countries; stimulating voluntary agreements between stakeholders, such as fashion companies and importing firms, in The Netherlands.[54]

A final example relates to strengthening models for land governance based on the rule of law with a view to reducing cases of land grabbing in countries in the South. Again this is an issue which is very much related to human rights (right to food, housing, property, security of tenure, land rights) and indirectly to the right to development and poverty reduction.[55] However, the Government has not adopted a human rights-based approach to the problem. The goals underlying the Netherlands policy in strengthening land governance are:[56]

1. Improving knowledge about legislation and policy in land matters
2. Strengthening systems for land administration
3. Better use of land and more sustainable land governance
4. Reducing conflicts about land
5. Enlarging access to land for women

The role the Netherlands has assigned for itself is to facilitate a multi-stakeholder dialogue between governments, land registry offices, companies, civil society organisations, embassies, Dutch banks and investors (such as pension funds) aimed at reaching agreements in countries where Dutch actors operate. These agreements are voluntary in nature, however not free of obligations. The Netherlands also supports financially local land administration and registration and tenure systems.[57]

National Implementation Plan for the SDGs

In 2016 the Netherlands government adopted a plan for the implementation of the SDGs.[58] It is a pragmatic plan of implementation characterized by a bottom-up approach. It departs from existing institutions, policy initiatives and division of labour. According to the government, a separate specific sustainable development

[53]Mensenrechten in het buitenlands beleid, *Kamerstukken II* 2015–2016, 32735, no. 153, p. 1.

[54]Mensenrechten in het buitenlands beleid, *Kamerstukken II* 2015–2016, 32735, no. 153, p. 3.

[55]Note on Land Grabbing, *Kamerstukken II* 2012–2013, 26234, no. 136.

[56]Note on Land Governance, *Kamerstukken II* 2013–2014, 26234, no. 156, p. 2.

[57]Note on Land Governance, *Kamerstukken II* 2014–2015, 26234, no. 164.

[58]The Netherlands Develops in a Sustainable Way, Plan for the implementation of the SDGs, *Kamerstukken II* 2016-2017, 26485, no. 232.

strategy has no value added.[59] The government has made an inventory of policies at the international, national and local level for the current and future implementation measures of each SDG.[60] Domestic stakeholders play a role in giving effect to existing and new policy initiatives. These include the corporate sector, knowledge centres, local, provincial and central government authorities, the financial sector and civil society. However, it is not clear from the plan what exactly the role of these stakeholders is. They have participated in formulating recommendations for the implementation of the SDGs. The central government performs the key coordinating function for the implementation and will involve the other stakeholders in this process.[61] Partnerships between stakeholders have been established under the umbrella of the Global Goals Charter.[62] This is typical for the bottom-up implementation approach. Political accountability for the plan lies with governmental departments under the coordination of the Minister of Foreign Trade and Development Cooperation. No new accountability mechanisms have been created. The usual lines of accountability through Parliament apply.[63]

Mechanisms to Monitor the Realisation of the SDGs

Currently, there are two main bodies that are authorised to examine the Dutch foreign and development cooperation policy. The first body is the Policy and Operations Evaluation Department of the Ministry of Foreign Affairs [hereafter: IOB], which is responsible for investigating whether the Dutch foreign policy is efficient and effective. Although it is part of the Ministry of Foreign Affairs, it has a mandate from the House of Representatives and it operates independently as it makes its own decisions on what to evaluate. Its evaluations are not only used to enable the ministers to account to parliament for policy, but also to improve the Dutch foreign policy. All the evaluations done by the IOB are public and sent to the Dutch parliament.[64] The IOB evaluates on a broad range of topics in the field of development cooperation and other areas of foreign policy, which could include evaluating the realisation of the SDGs. However, there is no specific evaluation of

[59]Plan for the implementation of the SDGs, p. 3.

[60]Plan for the implementation of the SDGs, pp. 5–8.

[61]Plan for the implementation of the SDGs, p. 15.

[62]http://www.globalgoalscharter.org.

[63]Plan for the implementation of the SDGs, pp. 21–22.

[64]All information about the IBO can be found on its website: https://www.iob-evaluatie.nl/organisatie.

the realisation of the SDGs yet and the SDGs are only mentioned briefly in several evaluation reports.[65]

The second body, the Court of Audit, has the constitutional task of examining the spending of public funds and monitoring Dutch policy, also in the field of development cooperation and foreign policy.[66] Its legal status is a High Council of State which means that it is a national public body established to safeguard the democratic rule of law and that it is an independent body separated from the government and parliament. The Court of Audit reports frequently about the efficiency and effectiveness of the Dutch foreign and development cooperation policy, including progress made in the realisation of the SDGs. Recently, the Court of Audit advised the Dutch government to better clarify what the government's concrete policy plans are to fulfil its commitment towards the realisation of the SDGs.[67]

Next to two independent bodies which monitor Dutch foreign policy, there is also a monitoring tool called the Integral Assessment Framework [hereafter: IAF], which is a uniform assessment tool of policy. This tool assesses the current policy on a large number of aspects including its environmental, employment and business effects. However, the IAF does not examine a number of SDG aspects such as poverty reduction, inequality and food security. Therefore some members of the House of Representatives submitted a motion to establish a new monitoring tool, the so-called 'SDG-toets' (SDG review). This is a kind of test specifically designed for the SDGs which will examine whether every policy measure or regulation has a positive or negative effect on one or more SDG.[68] Recently, the former Minister for Development Cooperation informed the House of Representatives about the advantages and disadvantages of establishing this tool. As advantages she stated that all aspects of SDGs are then taken into account and that the 'SDG-toets' will be more focused on developing countries, whereas adding another monitoring tool could also lead to more complexity, duplication and contradictions.[69] It is now up to the new government to decide whether or not it wants to establish the 'SDG-toets'.

Analysis of the Netherlands Development Aid Policy

There have also been developments in the area of Official Development Assistance (ODA). First of all, the cuts in the budget for development aid by the Government which was in power between 2012 and 2017 have considerably influenced the new

[65]For example in: Inspectie Ontwikkelinssamenwerking en Beleidsevaluatie (2016), p. 62, where is stated that 'there is still a large gap between actual funding and funding needed to comply with the proposed SDG targets in most former partner countries'.

[66]Art. 76 of the Dutch Constitution and the Government Accounts Act 2001.

[67]Algemene Rekenkamer (2017), pp. 7 and 8.

[68]Motion by MPs Dijkgraaf and Karabulut, *Kamerstukken II* 2016–2017, 34 725 XVII, nr. 10.

[69]Buitenlandse Zaken, 'SDG-toets', *Kamerstukken II* 2016–2017, 26485, nr. 250, pp. 1–3.

Dutch approach towards development cooperation. In 2016, the Netherlands' ODA budget reached 0.65% of GNI, below the promised goal of 0.7%. In addition to this budget cut, all costs relating to the reception of asylum-seekers in The Netherlands were funded from this ODA budget. In 2017, the ODA budget has even more decreased compared to 2016. This is because part of the ODA budget for 2017 was already used in 2015.[70] The Advisory Council on International Affairs criticised that decision and emphasized the need for a substantial budget for development cooperation which should also include achieving the goals of the 2015 Paris Climate Change Agreement and tackling the causes of migration.[71] The UN Committee on Economic, Social and Cultural Rights was also critical about the budget reduction and called upon the government to progressively increase ODA to the 0.7% norm.[72]

In the coalition agreement for 2017–2021, the new government will increase the ODA budget by €180 million in 2019, rising to €331 euro in 2021. This means that the ODA budget will return to 0.7% of GNI. In addition, a total of €1 billion of extra funds for development cooperation will be added during this cabinet period.[73]

With these data, the new government announced that the development budget will increase 'substantially' in the coming years, while in reality it will remain unchanged. In 2018, the Netherlands has a total budget of €4.5 billion available for development cooperation. As mentioned above the current budget will decrease to €4.1 billion because part of the budget for 2017–2021 was already used in 2015 and 2016. This decline in budget is now restored by the coalition agreement by increasing the ODA budget and providing extra funds. However, in practice this means that no extra money is made available for the poorest people in the world.

Next to the fact that a substantial increase of the ODA budget will probably turn out to be an illusion, a large part of the future ODA budget will also be spent in the Netherlands itself. A considerable part of the ODA budget will be used to cover expenses for the reception and relief of refugees in the region (Northern Africa, Middle East). In 2015, 23% of the ODA-budget was used to cover the costs for the reception of asylum-seekers in the Netherlands. Another 8% was used that year as subsidies for Dutch companies.[74] Also during the coming years, a large part of the development budget will be spent in the Netherlands to cover asylum costs and the

---

[70] Organisation for Economic Co-operation and Development (2017a), p. 238.

[71] Advisory Council on International Affairs (2016), pp. 7–9.

[72] UN Committee on Economic, Social and Cultural Rights, Concluding Observations on the sixth periodic report of the Netherlands, 6 July 2017, UN Doc. E/C.12/NLD/CO/6, para. 10.

[73] Government Coalition Agreement 2017–2021, *Confidence in the Future*, The Hague, 10 October 2017, p. 48.

[74] Organisation for Economic Co-operation and Development (2017a), p. 238. See also: Oxfam Novib, 'Derde van Ontwikkelingsbudget blijft in Nederland: hulp aan allerarmsten ondermijnd door bedrijfssteun en asielkosten', News item of 13 April 2016. Available at: https://www.oxfamnovib.nl/persberichten/derde-van-ontwikkelingsbudget-blijft-in-nederland-hulp-aan-allerarmsten-ondermijnd-door-bedrijfssteun-en-asiel-kosten.

new climate action plan.[75] This means that a considerable part of the ODA budget is not spent in the poorest countries, but in the Netherlands itself.

Unilateral/Bilateral Initiatives or Agreements

The Netherlands engages in strengthening systems in developing countries through contributions to multilateral organisations and bilateral agreements. As mentioned above, the Netherlands has many bilateral relationships with other countries which reflect the long term goal of the Dutch policy: to establish with all these countries a trading partnership. Dutch foreign policy has established 15 focus countries, of which seven have entered an aid relationship with the Netherlands. Here the policy is more oriented towards combating poverty and the four priorities mentioned above. The remaining eight focus countries entered a transitional relationship with the Netherlands which entails a combination of aid, trade and investment.[76] In 2018, Lebanon, Jordan and Iraq will be added as focus countries.[77]

Problematic in these bilateral relationships and aid programmes is that the relationship is not based on the right to development or any other human right. The human rights framework and the needs and preferences of the focus countries are not used as a starting point for development cooperation, but some of the Dutch priorities are. If human rights become a frame of reference for development policy that should also entail that development policy no longer depends on specific interests of the donor countries, since human rights are beyond such interests.[78] Furthermore, budgets are more and more managed from the Netherlands, with limited possibilities for governments of the focus countries to give any input into decisions. This is in contrast with the Netherlands' leadership role in the Global Partnership for Development Effectiveness and the Busan Partnership which puts 'the ownership of development priorities with developing countries' at the forefront.[79]

[75]Dutch Coalition Agreement 2017–2021, p. 48.

[76]Ministry of Foreign Affairs of the Netherlands (2013), pp. 34–40 and 40–46.

[77]Government Coalition Agreement 2017–2021, p. 49.

[78]Hamm (2001), p. 1014.

[79]Art. 11 (a) of the Busan Partnership for Effective Development Co-operation, Fourth High Level Forum on Aid Effectiveness, Busan, Republic of Korea, 29-1 December 2011.

In 2015, the Netherlands was a co-chair of the Global Partnership for Effective Development Cooperation, together with Mexico and Malawi.

As for multilateral agreements: the Netherlands is funding a total of 43 institutions,[80] of which 31 receive core funding.[81] The Dutch multilateral financial resources for development aid support a wide range of development themes. Here, there is also a strong focus on its four policy priorities: the multilateral agencies that are central to these priorities received the most funding in 2015. These include the World Bank, the International Fund for Agricultural Development, the United Nations Development Fund, the United Nations Population Fund and the United Nations International Children's Emergency Fund. Although the Netherlands entered into many multilateral agreements, the overall funding for multilateral agencies has decreased over the years due to budget cuts: in 2011 32% of the total ODA budget was allocated to these agencies, whereas in 2015 this was 27%.[82]

Concluding Remarks

We conclude that the right to development as a human right does not play a self-standing role in Dutch human rights and development cooperation policy. More in general, ESC-rights are not seen as the normative framework for development cooperation and only play a marginal role in Dutch human rights foreign policy. Although some promising initiatives have been taken recently, development issues are treated as a policy matter and not grounded in human rights obligations of the Netherlands. What is missing is a real rights-based approach to development. Article 90 of the Constitution is not implemented in practice in the sense of promoting legal standards. It is clear that the Netherlands only adopted a human rights perspective with regard to women's rights and sexual reproductive and health rights. However, the integration of human rights in this area is not used as a starting point for policies on the Government's other priorities on water and food security, and thus the realisation of SDG 1. The Dutch policy towards these goals is merely seen as the achievement of important development goals instead of giving effect to human rights obligations. The Netherlands seems to imply that development cooperation automatically implements ESC-rights because it is focused on poverty reduction. Therefore, the Dutch government should use its policy on women's rights and sexual reproductive and health rights as an example and implement the same human rights framework with respect to all its other priorities. More recently the Netherlands has begun to play the role of a facilitator with a view to stimulating non-state actors,

[80] This includes for example the European Development Fund, OCHA, UNICEF, African Development Bank, World Food Programme, UNDP, UNFPA, UNESCO, UNAIDS, UN Women etc. See: Organisation for Economic Co-operation and Development (2017b), p. 49.

[81] A full list can be found in: Minister voor Buitenlandse Handel en Ontwikkelingssamenwerking, 'Kamerbrief over multilaterale scorekaarten', *Kamerstukken II* 33 625, nr. 17, 19 June 2015.

[82] Organisation for Economic Co-operation and Development (2017b), p. 49. See also: Aid (ODA) disbursement to countries and regions [DAC2a], database: available at: http://stats.oecd.org/Index.aspx?QueryId=42231&lang=en Accessed 5 Jan 2018.

especially the corporate sector, to take responsibility for the achievement of fair labour conditions, sustainable production cycles and strengthening the rule of law in land issues. In an indirect way this helps in promoting development, however the appreciation that development is a human rights obligation that should be translated in a rights-based approach is missing.

References

Advisory Council on International Affairs (2003) Een mensenrechtenbenadering van ontwikkelingssamenwerking, no. 30. The Hague. http://www.AIV-ADVIES.NL

Advisory Council on International Affairs (2016) The Future of ODA, no. 29. The Hague. http://www.AIV-ADVICE.NL

Algemene Rekenkamer (2017) Voorbereiding realisatie van de Sustainable Development Goals. The Hague. http://www.rekenkamer.nl

Arts K, Tamo A (2016) The right to development in international law: new momentum thirty years down the line? Neth Int Law Rev 63:221–249

Asian Development Bank (2014) ADB's Support for Inclusive Growth, Thematic Evaluation Study-Independent Evaluation

Baehr PR (2006) The Netherlands- A Walhalla of economic, social and cultural rights? In: Howard-Hausmann RE, Welch CE Jr (eds) Economic rights in Canada and the United States. University of Pennsylvania Press, Philadelphia

Besselink LFM (2003) The constitutional duty to promote the development of the international legal order: the significance and meaning of Article 90 of the Netherlands Constitution. Neth Yearb Int Law 34:89–138

CAFOD (2014) What is "inclusive growth"? CAFOD Discussion Paper

De Feyter K (2013) Towards a framework convention on the right to development. International Policy Analysis Friedrich-Ebert-Stiftung

Hamm BI (2001) A human rights approach to development. Human Rights Q 23:1005–1031

Inspectie Ontwikkelingssamenwerking en Beleidsevaluatie (2006) Evaluatie van het Nederlandse mensenrechtenbeleid in de externe betrekkingen, IOB Evaluation no. 302

Inspectie Ontwikkelinssamenwerking en Beleidsevaluatie (2016) The gaps left behind- an evaluation of the impact of ending aid, IOB Evaluation no. 415

International Monetary Fund (2015) Causes and Consequences of Income Inequality: A Global Perspective. IMF Staff Discussion Note

Kirchmeier F (2006) The right to development- where do we stand?, Occasional Paper Friedrich-Ebert-Stiftung, vol 23

Ministry of Foreign Affairs (2007) Human dignity for all – a human rights strategy for foreign policy. The Hague

Ministry of Foreign Affairs (2013) Justice and respect for all. The Hague

Ministry of Foreign Affairs of the Netherlands (2013) A world to gain: a New Agenda for aid, trade and investment. The Hague

Netherlands' Government and Parliamentary Documents (*Kamerstukken II* en *Handelingen*) available in Dutch at https://zoek.officielebekendmakingen.nl/zoeken/parlementaire_documenten

Organisation for Economic Co-operation and Development (2017a) Development Co-operation Report 2017- Data for development

Organisation for Economic Co-operation and Development (2017b) OECD Development Co-operation Peer Reviews-The Netherlands

Reiding H (2007) The Netherlands and the development of international human rights instruments. Intersentia, Antwerp

The World Bank Group and the International Monetary Fund (2015) Global Monitoring Report 2014-2015- Ending Poverty and Sharing Prosperity, A World Bank Group Flagship Report

United Nations Development Programme (2013) A Toolkit of Policy Options to Support Inclusive Green Growth-Submission to the G20 Development Working Group by the AfDB, the OECD, the UN and the World Bank

Uvin P (2007) From the right to development to the rights-based approach: how 'human rights' entered development. Dev Pract 17-4

Vlemminx FMC (2014) The Doctrine of dutch social and economic rights: how the Netherlands went the wrong way. Netherlands Reports to the Nineteenth International Congress of Comparative Law (unpublished paper; on file with the authors)

Vlemminx FMC (2017) Commentaar op artikel 90 van de Grondwet. In: Hirsch Ballin EMH, Leenknegt G (eds) Artikelsgewijs commentaar op de Grondwet. Nederland Rechtsstaat, Tilburg, https://www.nederlandrechtsstaat.nl/grondwet/artikel.html?artikel=90##artikel90

Chapter 9
The Fight Against Poverty and the Right to Development in Poland

Katarzyna Łasak

Abstract This chapter seeks to provide a comprehensive breakdown of issues pertinent to combating poverty in Poland. The report provides a brief historical profile of social rights development, the right to development in Poland, with a presentation of their current shape they assume in law and practice against the backdrop of their application as the tools to prevent, combat existent areas of poverty and to stimulate an improvement of everyday life conditions of the poorest, to invigorate economic growth, thereby exerting an influence on boosting the whole society living standards. Not only does the present report rely on the analysis of the acts of domestic law, but having regard for the international law standards that bind Poland, it does also attempt to canvass its actual implementation.

Introduction

The role, participation and contribution of Poland to initiatives on the protection of social rights[1] and the right to development have been primarily taking similar shape to that of other European countries welded and united together in and through inspirational thinking, religion, political concepts as well as economic doctrines, starting with the crystallization of Christian community in Europe, through the birth and entrenchment of national identity of individual European nations, establishment of bilateral and further on multilateral cooperation initiated in the area of social rights

[1]For the purposes of this study, I have adopted a broad understanding of the term 'social rights,' which corresponds to the principle that all human rights are universal, indivisible, interdependent and interrelated. The same also obviously applies to the right to development. Vienna Declaration and Programme of Action 1993, www.ohchr.org: (visited:10.02.2020), § 5.

K. Łasak (✉)
University of Gdańsk, Faculty of Law and Administration, Gdańsk, Poland
e-mail: k.lasak@prawo.ug.edu.pl

M. Andenas et al. (eds.), *The Fight Against Poverty and the Right to Development*, Ius Comparatum - Global Studies in Comparative Law 52,
https://doi.org/10.1007/978-3-030-57324-9_9

in 1907, setting up International Bureau of Public Hygiene[2] to giving rise to the political and economic subculture of a supranational community, which the European Union has become. It was in 1919 that the International Labour Organization pioneered a viable cooperation of a broader—than European—circle of nations in the field of social rights and the right to development, with Poland as one of its very first members.[3]

Poland has been currently working in a variety of common-type organizations, *inter alia* the United Nations Organization, United Nations Educational, Scientific and Cultural Organization or United Nations Development Programme, whose core focus falls on human rights protection, with social rights and the right to development. In this respect, Poland has been developing regional cooperation (e.g. within the Council of Europe[4]) and bilateral cooperation with the countries whose nationals pursue in the territory of Poland tasks vested in them by the country of their nationality (e.g. diplomatic functions), or their own professional or economic goals, thereby requiring adequate protection.[5]

The Republic of Poland is a country of democracy and the rule of law and as such it has been implementing the principles of social justice, ensuring freedoms, personal and citizens' rights, safety and security, and promoting environmental protection in reliance upon the principle of a sustainable development.[6] Since under the principle of the law of treaties one may not invoke internal law to justify the failure to perform international obligations,[7] Poland recourses to a palette of legislative, administrative and judicial measures flowing from both domestic and international law to pursue its own initiatives in the area of social rights and the right to development.

[2]See more: Iriye (2000).

[3]http://www.ilo.org/dyn/normlex/en/f?p=1000:11003:0::NO (visited:10.02.2020).

[4]E.g. Framework Convention for the Protection of National Minorities of 1995, European Treaty Series (ETS) No 157, https://www.coe.int/en/web/conventions/full-list/-/conventions/treaty/157 (visited:10.02.2020); J. of L. 2002, No 22, item 209, http://isap.sejm.gov.pl (visited:10.02.2020).

[5]E.g. The agreement between the government of the Republic of Poland and the government of the Republic of Eastern Uruguay on the promotion and mutual protection of investments [Umowa między Rządem Rzeczypospolitej Polskiej a Rządem Wschodniej Republiki Urugwaju w sprawie popierania i wzajemnej ochrony inwestycji) of 1991], J. of L. 1995, No 55, item 291, http://isap.sejm.gov.pl (visited:10.02.2020).

[6]Art. 2 and 5 of the Constitution of the Republic of Poland, J. of L. 1997, No 78, item 483 as amended, http://isap.sejm.gov.pl (visited:10.02.2020).

[7]*Mutatis mutandis*, Vienna Convention on the Law of Treaties 1969, https://treaties.un.org/Pages/showDetails.aspx?objid=080000028003902f&clang=_en Art. 27; J. of L. 1990, No 74, item 439, http://isap.sejm.gov.pl (visited:10.02.2020).

Domestic Law and Remedies

Relationship to International Law

The question of adequate relations between domestic and international law was expressly set forth in the Constitution of the Republic of Poland adopted by the National Assembly[8] on 2 April 1997.[9] The Constitution enshrines a general clause introducing a requirement for Poland to observe a binding international law.[10] The Constitution, statutes,[11] ratified international agreements and regulations[12] are the sources of the law in force in the Republic of Poland, with the Constitution as the supreme law in Poland. Each and every legislative act must be in compliance with the Constitution. A directive encompasses sources of international law that address human rights and facilitate combating poverty. A ratified international agreement upon its publication in the Journal of Laws of the Republic of Poland[13] becomes a part of domestic legal order and is directly applied unless its application is contingent on passing a law.

Determining mutual relation of an international agreement to domestic law acts, the Constitution establishes precedence a ratified agreement takes over the law by virtue of an authority stipulated in the law if such law is in collision or irreconcilable with the agreement.[14]

Amongst 5 categories of international agreements, for the ratification of which a prior consent stipulated in the law is required, there are agreements that govern civic freedoms, rights and duties laid down in the Constitution,[15] the ones that also secure fundamental individual economic, social and cultural needs, as well as such that concern its specifically defined duties towards others or society. Not only did the

[8]The constitutional law term applied to denote joint sessions of parliament houses: lower (the Sejm) and upper (the Senate) in the events laid down by the Constitution. See: e.g. Gierach (2015).

[9]See: Masternak-Kubiak (1997), p. 199.

[10]Art. 9, the Constitution.

[11]Art. 91 (1), the Constitution. The law is a national legislative act adopted by the parliament. In contrast to the Constitution, which can in reliance on the Polish constitutional tradition be defined also as the Basic Law, the other laws are referred to as ordinary laws, or most often just laws. Law must be compliant with the Constitution, and other legislation should not collide with ordinary laws. The law may govern any issue except for the unequivocally precluded ones. Some questions expressly require statutory regulation. Said issues pertain to freedoms, human and citizens' rights and duties, their type or kind notwithstanding. See: e.g. Art. 64 (3) Constitution, which provides that an ownership may be limited only statutorily and insofar as it does not infringe the substance of the property rights.

[12]Ordinances are issued by the institutions set forth in the Basic Law (e.g. the Council of Ministers) through a specific authority enshrined in the law and for its enforcement. See: Art. 92 (1), the Constitution.

[13]The main official gazette of the Republic of Poland.

[14]Art. 91 (2), the Constitution.

[15]Art. 89 (1), the Constitution.

authors of the Constitution make its substance mirror a current trend of the international law development, opening an opportunity to apply treaty standards to all the fields of international cooperation and its viable intensification also with regard to human rights, not precluding the ones falling under the second or the third generation categories, but what they also did was implying material regulatory barriers for the domestic legislator. The law function limitation is to be deemed an expression of a consequence or consistency in the approach to current international law evolution trends.[16]

The Constitution does not pertain to other international agreements than the ratified ones that Poland consented to be bound by. Thus, they are not perceived as commonly binding law. The Constitution is silent with regard to such sources of international law as international custom and general principles of law. Nonetheless, taking account of the stipulation on the observance of international law in whatever form it manifests itself, we may allow an assumption as to the openness of the Polish system of law to international law and, correspondingly, a necessity of its deference in the process of domestic law application and construction, with international custom and general principles of law not precluded. Polish courts apply the foregoing,[17] albeit rarely. It is worth noting that since they do not play a significant role in combating poverty and fighting for development in international law, their significance in Polish law remains correspondingly marginal.[18]

The Constitution fails to mention resolutions of international organizations in a catalogue of the sources of law. Poland belongs to a number of international organizations and exercises the duty to observe their both primary and secondary law. While the application of an international custom or a general principle of law

[16]Masternak-Kubiak (1997), p. 200.

[17]See: e.g. Regional Court in Warsaw, decision of 2015-10-28 on the purchase of an immovable by a foreigner, V Ca 4126/14, http://orzeczenia.ms.gov.pl (visited:10.02.2020); Regional Court in Warsaw, decision of 2016-11-09 on the admissibility of certain types of security of claims accruing from bank operations in a situation of an economic pressure or duress to debtors, XXVII Ca 3448/16, http://orzeczenia.ms.gov.pl (visited: 10.02.2020) 09.09.2017); Supreme Administrative Court, decision of 2017-07-18 on appeal to decision by the Head of the Treasure Administration Chamber in Wrocław on tax on inherited and donated apartment, II FSK 1682/15, http://orzeczenia.nsa.gov.pl (visited:10.02.2020).

[18]Even assuming that the ban on tortures or inhuman and humiliating treatment is recognised, with no reservations, as an international custom, the international courts (e.g. International Criminal Tribunal for the Former Yugoslavia, *Furundzija*, T-95-17/1-T, judgement of 10 December 1998, § 165, http://www.icty.org (visited:10.02.2020)), adopting such thesis, understood it as a rule of disallowing psychical and physical abuse in its classic terms, not as a failure to ensure a diet of an adequate calorific value. This is the direction that, for example, the case law of the European Court of Human Rights has been going with regard to prisoners (e.g. *Kadiķis v. Latvia* (no. 2), no. 62393/00, § 55, judgement of 4 May 2006, HUDOC (visited: 20.02.2020). In this respect, however, it is difficult to claim that there is an international custom of a substance that corresponds to the foregoing case-law tendency. It is even more difficult to defend a similar approach pertinent to a general principle of law. Genuine implications of said sources of international law might well be discussed in the context of combating poverty resultant from an ongoing armed conflict. Yet, this issue has been presumed to go beyond this research.

will primarily depend on the judge's knowledge and discretion, an international organization's resolution may occasionally necessitate more interference with the system of internal law.[19] Legislator decided therefore to at least partially regulate the underlying question by establishing that if it transpires from a ratified by the Republic of Poland agreement on the constitution of an international organization, its law shall be directly applicable with precedence where there is a collision with statutes.[20] The EU law is, nonetheless, the only one to satisfy the conditions so prescribed. Notwithstanding positive an approach of the Basic Law to the international law, which is also pertinent to the resolutions of the international organizations, it is necessary to examine their type so as to devise and assess steps to be taken. The problem assumes more weight from the perspective of the subject-matter of our research, the more so when numerous resolutions of the international organizations that concern themselves with the human rights with a right to development are of different status or legal nature, which requires a distinct behaviour of the state.[21]

Apart from an express determination of place for the ratified international agreements in a hierarchy of the sources of Polish law, formal guaranties have been devised to safeguard an overriding role of the Constitution. They allow the Constitutional Court to adjudicate on the constitutionality of all international agreements and on the compatibility of laws with ratified international agreements, for the ratification of which a statutory consent is required.[22] The Constitutional Court exercises power to oversee compliance of international agreements with the Constitution prior to ratification,[23] which is not only an express manifestation of the implementation of the *pacta sunt servanda* principle, but also a security measure adopted in an international legal environment. Furthermore, the Constitutional Court

[19]See more: Czapliński and Wyrozumska (2014), p. 674.

[20]Art. 91 (3), the Constitution.

[21]United Nations Security Council resolution imposing economic sanctions, which invariably impacts financial situation of the citizens of an affected country, necessitates issuance of acts of universally binding law. See: e.g. an already repealed "Regulation of 27 April 1999 by the Council of Ministers on the introduction of a ban on the export of oil and petroleum products from the Republic of Poland to the Federal Republic of Yugoslavia," J. of L. 1999 No. 39, item 386 as amended, http://isap.sejm.gov.pl (visited:10.02.2020). Resolutions of the International Labour Organization, in turn, which influence the economic, social and cultural situation of individuals or groups, sometimes are subject to procedures typical of international agreements. See: e.g. Protocol of 2014 to the Forced Labour Convention, 1930, where the parliament had to express consent for its ratification through legislative act and in compliance with the Constitution, J. of L. 2016, item 1942, http://isap.sejm.gov.pl (visited:10.02.2020). In the same vein, a type of EU secondary law act and its substance will carry a material significance to the actions the state will undertake to implement it into the system of Polish law. EU regulations are not incorporated except for specifically stipulated cases. Council Regulation (EEC) No. 3820/85 of 20 December 1985 on the harmonization of certain social legislation relating to road transport, Art. 17 (1) OJ L 370 of 31.12.1985, p. 1; EU Official Journal Special edition in Polish, Chapter 5, v. 1, p. 319) https://eur-lex.europa.eu/legal-content/EN/TXT/?uri=CELEX%3A31985R3820, (visited:10.02.2020). See more: Office of the Committee for European Integration (2009), pp. 40–44.

[22]Art. 188 (1–2), the Constitution.

[23]Art. 133 (2), the Constitution. See: Masternak-Kubiak (1997), p. 201.

holds a capacity to assess the compliance of domestic legislative acts drafted by the central public authorities with the ratified international agreements.[24]

The openness of the Polish constitutional system to an international law reflects itself also in having a direct recourse to the application of its regulations in specifically stipulated situations. To illustrate, it might be mentioned that in the event a foreigner seeks protection in the Republic of Poland from persecution or repression which undoubtedly adversely affect his financial status, he/she may be granted a refugee status pursuant to international agreements binding upon the Republic of Poland.[25]

Finally, the Constitution encompasses provisions that allow statutory limitation of some human and citizens' rights and freedoms provided that the conditions of international agreements, with Poland as their party, are met. The question at stake is highlighted by a freedom of employees and employers to associate and trade unions rights whose scope may be subject to only such statutory limitations which are permissible in accordance with international agreements to which the Republic of Poland is a party.[26]

Focusing on the implementation (formally ensuring application) of the most fundamental, from the perspective of the underlying research, source of international law—international agreements—which protect human rights, specifically social rights, and promote the right to development, we may presume in reliance on the Polish doctrine that what we observe here is nothing but a dual system that envisages transformation[27] or incorporation.[28] In the field under discussion, there is no differentiation whatsoever in respect of the status between the agreements on human rights or on combating poverty and other international agreements that require statutorily prescribed ratification through parliamentary consent.

On a formal note, the foregoing international agreements in the same manner as other sources of international law apply for the domestic law standards to be interpreted (indirect application), or for a specific legal situation to be determined (direct application). The application of an international law for the interpretation of a domestic law standard may take place only when there already exists a legal standard in Polish law. Such reference to international law does not serve any substitution, change or modification of a Polish legal standard. What it does is provide a direction to construe law in conformity with international law.[29]

---

[24] Art. 188 (3), the Constitution.

[25] Art. 56 (2), the Constitution.

[26] Art. 59 (4), the Constitution. See: Masternak-Kubiak (1997), pp. 202–203.

[27] Barcik and Srogosz (2014), pp. 29–30.

[28] Czapliński and Wyrozumska (2014), p. 506.

[29] See: e.g. Regional Court in Bielsko-Biała, judgement of 25.04.2017 on the right of an employee with the prosecutor's office in the capacity of a driver to overtime payment in the context of Art. 30 (2) of the Act of 16.09.1982 on the employees of public authorities, J. of L. 2014, item.1502, as amended; construed under Art. 4 (2) of the European Social Charter of 1961 (the Charter), VI Pa 91/16, http://orzeczenia.ms.gov.pl (visited: 13.02.2020); Appellate Court in Poznań, decision of 07. 11. 2013 on dismissal of appellant's motion for exemption from the court costs by virtue of Art.

International law is applied to determine a specific legal situation provided that there is no corresponding standard in Polish law or the existent standard is in conflict with an international law standard governing such situation. It must be underlined here that for this type of application the international law standard must be already applicable and effective in the system of Polish law, with its efficacy conditional upon the place it takes in the hierarchy of domestic law sources.[30]

Poland has been a party to numerous agreements that pertain to human rights protection or are more broadly oriented towards the enhancement of people's social and living conditions, as well as towards their development. Amongst the most representative agreements[31] concluded under the auspices of UN are: International Covenant on Economic, Social and Cultural Rights 1966 (ICESC),[32] International Covenant on Civil and Political Rights 1966 (ICCPR),[33] Convention on the Rights of Persons with Disabilities 2006 (CRPD);[34] of the Council of Europe: Convention for the Protection of Human Rights and Fundamental Freedoms 1950 (the European

102 (1) of the Act of 28 July 2005 on court costs in civil cases, J. of L. 2010, No. 90, item 594 as amended; construed under Art. 6 (1) Convention on the protection of human rights and fundamental freedoms of 1950, I ACz 1869/13, http://orzeczenia.ms.gov.pl (visited:10.02.2020); District Court in Olsztyn, decision of 18.01.2017 on the principles of deductions from wages by virtue of Art. 8–10 of the Convention of International Labour Organization No. 95 on the protection of wages, under Art. 87 (1) of the Act of 26 June 1974 – Labour Code, J. of L. 1974, No. 24, item 141; IV P 2/15, http://orzeczenia.ms.gov.pl (visited:11.02.2020).

[30]Appellate Court in Warsaw, judgement of 03.03.2010 on the violation of Art. 46 of the Convention for the protection of Human Rights and Fundamental Freedoms of 1950 (the Convention) and Art. 91 (1), Art. 9 of the Constitution, deriving from the fact that in its determination the first instance court had no regard to a binding judgement of the European Court of Human Rights of 19 June 2006 (*Hutten Czapska v. Poland*), as well as to a correlated legally protected claimant's expectation, which in consequence led to an oversight of the fact that a statutory incapacitation of the claimant to derive equitable benefit from her property breached Art. 1 of the Protocol to the Convention of 1952, which was unlawful and required imposing on the respondent a compensatory obligation towards the claimant, I ACa 1060/09, http://orzeczenia.ms.gov.pl (visited: 13.02.2020); Appellate Court in Warsaw, judgement of 2010-10-07 determining that Art. 3 of the Convention has priority over Art. 248 of the Code of Penal Procedure (C.P.P.); Act of 6 June 1997– Code of Penal Procedure, J. of L. 1997, No. 90, item 557 and since the substance of Art. 248 C.P.P. are irreconcilable with the substance of Art. 3 of the Convention, its violation amounts to unlawfulness of defendant's actions – the State Treasury (overcrowded prison cell), VI ACa 176/10, http://orzeczenia.ms.gov.pl (visited:13.02.2020).

[31]More information on: https://traktaty.msz.gov.pl/international-version.

[32]https://treaties.un.org/Pages/showDetails.aspx?objid=080000028002b6ed&clang=_en (visited:10.02.2020); J. of L. 1977, No. 38, item 169, http://isap.sejm.gov.pl (visited:10.02.2020).

[33]https://treaties.un.org/Pages/showDetails.aspx?objid=0800000280004bf5&clang=_en (visited:21.02.2020).

[34]https://treaties.un.org/Pages/showDetails.aspx?objid=080000028005883c&clang=_en (visited:10.02.2020); J. of L. 2012, item 1169, http://isap.sejm.gov.pl (visited:06.02.2020).

Convention)[35] and European Social Charter 1961 (the Charter);[36] and the acquis of the International Labour Organization: Social Security (Minimum Standards) Convention (the MSC), 1952 (No. 102),[37] Employment Policy Convention (the EPC), 1964 (No. 122)[38] or Human Resources Development Convention (the HRDC), 1975 (No. 142).[39]

As a party to the Treaty of Lisbon amending the Treaty on European Union and the Treaty establishing the European Community (the Treaty of Lisbon) Poland must also observe its provisions provided for under the Charter of Fundamental Rights of the European Union.[40]

Constitutional Protection

The Constitution categorizes rights and freedoms primarily with regard to the object of protection. It enumerates: (1) personal rights and freedoms;[41] (2) political rights and freedoms;[42] (3) economic, social and cultural rights and freedoms.[43]

---

[35]ETS No 005, https://www.coe.int/en/web/conventions/full-list/-/conventions/treaty/005; J. of L. 1993, No. 61, item 284, http://isap.sejm.gov.pl (visited:10.02.2020).

[36]ETS 035, https://www.coe.int/en/web/conventions/full-list/-/conventions/treaty/035 (visited: 21.02.2020); J. of L. 1999, No. 8, item 67 and J. of L. 2011, No. 168, item 1007, http://isap.sejm.gov.pl (visited:11.02.2020).

[37]http://www.ilo.org/dyn/normlex/en/f?p=normlexpub:12100:0::No:12100:p12100_instrument_id:312247:No (visited:18.02.2020); J. of L. 2005, No. 93, item 775, http://isap.sejm.gov.pl (visited:19.02.2020).

[38]http://www.ilo.org/dyn/normlex/en/f?p=normlexpub:12100:0::No:12100:p12100_instrument_id:312267:No (visited:12.02.2020); J. of L. 1967, No 8, item 31, http://isap.sejm.gov.pl (visited: 06.02.2020).

[39]http://www.ilo.org/dyn/normlex/en/f?p=normlexpub:12100:0::No:12100:p12100_instrument_id:312287:No (visited:10.02.2020) 21.09.2017); J. of L. 1979, No. 29, item 164, http://isap.sejm.gov.pl (visited:10.02.2020).

[40]http://eur-lex.europa.eu/legal-content/en/txt/?uri=celex%3a12007l%2ftxt (visited:14.02.2020); J. of L. 2009, No. 203, item 1569, http://isap.sejm.gov.pl (visited:12.02.2020).

[41]Art. 38–56, the Constitution. They catalogue e.g. *habeas corpus* guarantees (Art. 41), or freedom and privacy of communication (Art. 49).

[42]Art. 57–63, the Constitution. This group comprises e.g. freedom of peaceful assembly and participation in such assemblies (Art.57) and the freedom of association in trade unions, socio-occupational organizations of farmers, and in employers' organizations (Art.59).

[43]Art. 64–76, the Constitution. They are: right to ownership (Art. 64), freedom of work, right to remuneration, obligation to pursue policy of full employment (Art. 65), the right to work health and safety, to days free from work and to paid annual leaves (Art. 66), the right to social security (Art. 67), the right to health protection (Art. 68), the right of disabled persons to aid (Art. 69), the right to education (Art. 70), family protection (Art. 71), the child rights protection (Art. 72), the freedom of artistic creation and scientific research as well as dissemination of the fruits thereof, the freedom to teach and to enjoy the products of culture (Art. 73), ensuring ecological security of current and future generations (Art. 74), pursuing policies conducive to satisfying the housing needs of citizens

It has been observed that social rights in contrast to other rights and freedoms envisaged by the Constitution enable an individual to obtain subsistence means to meet basic living needs and conditions.[44] Such indication might intimate social rights in their narrow sense that encompass merely a social aspect, while it obviously correlates with an individual's economic activity, his /her cultural development and participation in the political life. It is right and advisable to perceive social rights in the Constitution through their relations with other human and citizens' rights[45] and through the prism of other constitutional regulations that may fashion their interpretation.[46]

The Constitution introduced a parallel qualitative differentiation of rights and freedoms, with the specific ones to be enjoyed accordingly by reason of either holding a status of a man/individual,[47] or a status of a citizen.[48] Some rights and freedoms accrue also to legal persons.[49]

It is essential how the Constitution factored in and profiled economic, social and cultural considerations. It seems indispensable to show that not only does it enumerate certain rights and freedoms of specific entities, but it also correlates them with the public duties. Alternative approach would suggest solely a facade nature of the constitutional regulation of social rights that would at most express political needs of the state.[50]

There does appear a problem in the manner (the nature) particular constitutional rights and freedoms are perceived in the Constitution. It envisages in the Art. 81 that rights (the concept of freedom was overlooked and seems to be implied through the substance of specific provisions) set forth under Art. 65 (4)[51] and (5),[52] Art. 66,[53]

(Art. 75), protection of consumers, customers, hirers or lessees against activities threatening their health, privacy and safety, as well as against dishonest market practices (Art. 76). As observed, the right to fair and adequate standard of living has not been expressly formulated in the Polish Constitution, albeit its elements might be detected/ implied in the structure of rights established by the substance of the Constitution.

[44]Czarny (2013), p. 112.

[45]E.g. construction of the right to access to public service (Art. 60) will affect the realisation of a freedom to choose and pursue profession and to choose place of work (Art.65).

[46]These would predominantly be the principles of a system laid down in Chapter I of the Constitution entitled *The Republic,* such as the once, for instance, denoted in Art. 20: The principles of social market economy and freedom of economic activity. See further: Oniszczuk (2005), pp. 35–37; Salitra (2003), Florek (1997), pp. 8–14.

[47]The right of a child to protection against violence, Art. 72 (1).

[48]E.g. The right to social security accrues only to Polish citizens, Art. 67.

[49]E.g. guarantees of autonomy to the institutions of higher education, Art. 70 (5).

[50]See: Oniszczuk (2005), pp. 38–41.

[51]Minimum wage for work or the manner such pay is assessed are governed statutorily.

[52]An obligation of public authorities to pursue a policy towards a full and productive employment through the realisation of programmes to combat unemployment, incl. organization and promotion of counselling, vocational training, public works and intervention works.

[53]An employee's right to statutory days free from work and paid annual leaves; maximum workload are prescribed statutorily, Art. 66 (1); An employee's right to statutory days free from work and paid annual leaves; maximum workload are prescribed statutorily, Art. 66 (2).

Art. 69,[54] Art. 71,[55] Art. 74,[56] Art. 75,[57] and Art. 76[58] may be pursued within the limits stipulated by law. Consequently, taking account of an application criterion laid down in Art. 81 (i.e. statutory protection guarantees), said social rights may fall into two groups. The first group encompasses social rights that may be pursued directly in reliance upon the Constitution (and additionally on the basis of other relevant laws).[59] The second group contains such social rights that may be exercised within statutorily prescribed limits and pursuant to relevant law, not the Constitution.[60] Every one of the adopted regulations is accompanied by a distinct range of the obligations imposed upon the state. Hence, the fact that the housing needs of the citizens found their place in the constitutional catalogue of economic, social and cultural rights and freedoms merely proves their social weight. They cannot be viewed as individual constitutional rights (and they are not linguistically condensed into a formula of a right), since there is no likelihood of their realisation,[61] which explains the way they were included in the Constitution. Nonetheless, the question of protection and access to the place of residence, types of use of residential premises, amount of rent, admissibility of eviction is far from neutral to either party in a legal relationship underlying housing needs satisfaction, with lease being a good case in point here. Correspondingly, legislator assumes that the protection of the rights of tenants is governed statutorily,[62] there being more such laws than one.[63]

---

[54]Disabled people are statutorily provided assistance by the public authorities in securing subsistence, vocational training and social communication.

[55]Directive for the state to have regard to family welfare in its social and economic policy. Families in difficult financial and social situation, specifically those with many children or single-parent families are entitled to special assistance from public authorities, Art. 71 (1). Prior to or upon childbirth, mother is entitled to a special assistance from public authorities to the extent specified by statute, Art. 71 (2).

[56]Directive for the public authorities to pursue a policy that would ensure ecological security to current and future generations, Art. 74 (1); a duty of public authorities to protect environment, Art. 74 (2); the right of every one to information on the environment quality and protection, Art. 74 (3); supporting by the public authorities activities of citizens to protect and improve the quality of environment, Art. 74 (4).

[57]Directive for the public authorities to pursue a policy conducive to satisfying housing needs of the citizens, in particular combating homelessness, promoting development of low-income housing and supporting activities aimed at the acquisition of a home by each citizen, Art. 75 (1); Protection of tenants' rights is set forth by statute, Art. 75 (2).

[58]Public authorities shall protect consumers, customers, hirers or lessees against activities threatening their health, privacy and safety, as well as against dishonest market practices. The scope of such protection is specified by statute, Art. 76.

[59]E.g. freedom to enjoy the products of culture, Art. 73, the Constitution.

[60]E.g. citizens' right to have his health protected, Art. 68 (1), the Constitution.

[61]Art. 75 (1), the Constitution.

[62]Art. 75 (2), the Constitution.

[63]E.g. Act of 21 June 2001 on the protection of tenants' rights, municipality housing stock and the Civil Code revision, J. of L. 2016, item 8, as amended; http://isap.sejm.gov.pl (visited:10.02.2020).

The problem of a diverse in nature enforcement of social rights manifests itself in the case-law of the Constitutional Court. Said case-law divides economic, social and cultural rights into two categories, namely such, which within the meaning of Art. 81 of the Constitution may be sought within statutory limits (for the most part constitutionally entrenched in the programmatic norms/standards) and others, to which limits set forth in Art. 81 do not apply. Binding legislator with the second type of constitutional guarantees that include a citizen's right to social security—its range and form statutorily prescribed—in the event of incapacity to work due to a disease or invalidity and reaching retirement age, has been recognised as the strongest right despite a recurrent specific statutory determination of the scope and substance of the rights subsumed under the same category.[64] Ultimately, it was ascertained that the limits and nature of recourse to statutory regulations cannot be identical with regard to both categories. While in respect of the rights and freedoms enumerated in Art. 81 the assessment of the scope and substance of the rights was left to legislator's discretion, with the second category—the substance of the rights in their material elements and their limits are directly shaped by the Constitution, close determination or the manner of deployment of the same guarantees being statutorily governed.[65]

The foregoing observations unveil a considerable problem pointing to the fact that social rights regulations are of diverse nature when it comes to an ordinary legislator's discretion. It also manifests itself in the manner the Constitution is construed on this score. Legislator formulates obligations for the public authority to pursue variety of initiatives, programmes and normative procedures in Chapter II (social, economic, cultural rights and freedoms). With regard to an ordinary legislator's discretion, said provisions of the Constitution differ in nature. Thus, Art. 65 (5),[66] Art. 68 (3),[67] (4),[68] (5),[69] Art. 69,[70] Art. 72 (1),[71] (2),[72] Art. 74 (1),[73] (2)[74]

[64]E.g. right to work health and safety, Art. 66 (1) of the Constitution.

[65]The Constitutional Court, decision of 8.05.2002 on the constitutionality of the principles of assessing owner's share in the premises separated from a joint immovable property and of the principles of establishing separate ownership of the premises. SK 22/99, http://ipo.trybunal.gov.pl (visited:21.02.2020).

[66]See footnote 46.

[67]The obligation of public authorities to ensure special health care to children, pregnant women, handicapped people and persons of advanced age.

[68]The obligation of public authorities to combat epidemic illness and prevent negative health consequences of the degradation of environment.

[69]Directive for public authorities to support the development of physical culture, particularly amongst children and young persons.

[70]Providing by the public authorities statutory aid to disabled persons to ensure their subsistence, adaptation to work and social communication.

[71]The right of a child deprived of a parental care to care and assistance provided by public authorities.

[72]The Republic of Poland ensures protection of the rights of a child. Everyone has the right to demand of the public authority bodies that they protect a child against violence, cruelty, exploitation and demoralization.

[73]See footnote 50.

[74]*Ibidem.*

and (4),[75] Art. 75 (1)[76] point at certain premises, directions or strategies of action. Nevertheless, what does not transpire from the above provisions is the obligation to pursue and realise said undertakings through the adoption of laws. Another approach is exhibited by Art. 66 (1),[77] Art. 67 (1)[78] and (2),[79] Art. 68 (2),[80] Art. 69,[81] Art. 71 (2),[82] Art. 76[83] where an ordinary legislator is compelled to pursue statutory work, albeit without specific instructions as to its nature.

Alternatively, not only is the obligation to pass law prescribed, but also the object and direction of an ordinary law enactment are stipulated at least to some extent in the Art. 64 (3),[84] Art. 65 (1),[85] (2),[86] (3),[87] (4),[88] Art. 66 (2),[89] Art. 70 (1),[90] (3),[91] and Art. 75 (2).[92] The question whether beneficiaries of the actions of public authorities mentioned in the above exemplary groups of situations are concurrently

[75] Supporting by public authorities activities of citizens to protect and improve the quality of environment.

[76] See footnote 51.

[77] See footnote 47.

[78] See footnote 49.

[79] The right of a citizen who is involuntarily without work and has no other means of support to social security with its scope and form set forth by statute.

[80] Citizens, irrespective of their financial situation, are ensured by public authorities equal access to health care services financed from public funds. The conditions for and the scope of services rendered are stipulated by statute.

[81] See footnote 48.

[82] A mother, before and after the childbirth, is entitled to a special assistance from public authorities, the scope of which is set forth statutorily.

[83] See footnote 52.

[84] The right of ownership may only be limited by a statute and only insofar as it does not violate the substance of such right.

[85] Everyone is ensured freedom to choose and pursue their profession and choose their place of work. Exceptions are specified by statute.

[86] An obligation to work may only be imposed by statute.

[87] Permanent employment of children under the age of 16 is prohibited. Types and form of admissible employment are laid down statutorily.

[88] Minimum wage for work or the manner it is calculated is set forth by statute.

[89] See footnote 47.

[90] Everyone has the right to education. Education to 18 years of age is compulsory. The manner school obligation is pursued is prescribed statutorily.

[91] Parents enjoy freedom to choose other than public schools for their children. Citizens and institutions exercise the right to establish primary, secondary schools, institutions of higher education, and institutions of development and education. The conditions for establishing and operating non-public schools, financial participation of public authorities in their financing, as well as the principles of educational supervision over schools and institutions of development and education are set forth by statute.

[92] Protection of the rights of tenants is prescribed statutorily.

the subjects of the right to demand concrete actions for their benefit and what legal forms this entails—requires careful and an in-depth analysis of a specific case.[93]

A catalogue of social rights in the Constitution, their type and content are an effect of a compromise typical of a law-making process. What is no less significant is a modus of its construction. It is the constitutional case-law that plays a paramount role in the foregoing area in a democratic rule of law. In reliance upon the Constitutional Court case-law analysis it might be assumed that apart from detailed regulations from Chapter II of the Constitution, social rights interpretation regime encompasses general principles of a Chapter II catalogue of rights and freedoms (dignity, equality, proportionality, limitation conditions), Chapter I constitutional regulations, and in particular the principles of rule of law and social justice, as well as law sources regulations.[94]

Remedies and Relationship to International Mechanism

I presume that it is primarily about measures of recourse to a competent public authority in the event of an infringement of the right and freedom established by a concrete international law act. Remedies envisaged in and sought in the practice of the Polish law application to human rights protection, irrespective of their generation and thus pertinent also to social rights, and even potentially, to the right to development, remain in close relationship with the relevant international law provisions. International law recognises the existence and effective functioning of domestic remedies as a formal aspect of the human rights protection. Hence, through an international supervision and proportionately to an assessed *status quo*, it has been prescribed and required for the same remedies, very often of a stipulated shape, albeit different name, to be implemented in the domestic law regimes and to be modified by determining various infringement categories. Specifically comprehensive in this regard is the case-law of the European Convention review authorities where reliance not only upon its Art. 6 or 13, but also a distinction between substantive and procedural aspects in almost all the remaining provisions frequently

[93]The Constitutional Court, decision of 2 July 2002 on the constitutionality of the provisions governing the principles to provide financial assistance solely to the full-time students, U 7/01, J. of L. 2002, No. 104, item 933, http://ipo.trybunal.gov.pl (visited:20.02.2020). An assessed in the case Art. 70 (4) of the Constitution places itself in the second raised by the Constitutional Court group of social rights present in the Constitution. The Constitution fails here to closely specify the standard the law, whose issuance this provision compels to, is to meet. In this respect, legislator enjoys a substantial discretion insofar as he makes law within the scope prescribed by this provision. For this reason, the Constitutional Court in (an invoked in the same case) decision on the constitutionality of provisions introducing payment for education in an institution of higher education, defined 'constitutional obligation under Art. 70 (4)' as a factor of 'establishing educational policy mechanisms,' and not as a source of an individual right, SK 18/99 of 08.11.2002, J. of L. 2000, No. 101, item 1091, http://ipo.trybunal.gov.pl (visited:10.02.2020).

[94]Oniszczuk (2005), p. 42. See also: idem, Oniszczuk (1993), Banaszak (2017).

results in finding a dual violation solely within the scope of one and the same provision.

The structure, understanding and pursuance of the European Convention stand out from other legal solutions, which does not necessarily amount to the resignation from the rights or freedoms, established in a similar mode in a given international agreement, nominally more expressly oriented towards protection in the area of combating poverty and promoting development. Said rights and freedoms may either undergo dilution through adopted regulations or become subject to interpretation by the review authorities.[95] With regard to the second type of approach, a given country's legal tradition and culture, not excluding Poland, will exert more influence on the shape of remedies indispensable to the protection of rights stipulated in an international agreement.

The Polish Constitution envisages that everyone shall have the right to compensation for any harm done to him by any action of an organ of public authority contrary to law.[96] The term *public authority* reflects Montesquieu's doctrine of the separation of powers.[97] Self-governments participate in exercising public authority.[98] Each and every party shall have the right to appeal against the judgements and decisions rendered in the first instance. Exceptions to this principle and the procedure of appeal is at all times to be specified by statue.[99] What is more, statutes shall not bar a recourse by any person to the courts in pursuit of claims alleging infringement of rights and freedoms.[100] Polish law distinguishes three main types of procedures, i.e. civil, penal and administrative. Sets of remedies established within their frameworks carry primary significance to the protection of social rights and combating poverty. Alongside classic types of procedures, there co-exists a panel of branching out incidental procedures with remedies resembling original mechanisms and assuming their specificity of procedure. Incidental procedures, which are of essence in the area under discussion, may be exemplified by fiscal penal procedures,[101] a priority in fighting tax crimes[102] or petty offense

[95]E.g. In the Charter, remedy (court proceedings) is present only in the substance of the right of migrant workers and their families to protection and assistance, Art. 19 (7), whereas in the MCS, if the claims are heard by the courts specifically established to determine social security cases, in which courts the persons represented are protected, the right to appeal shall not be provided, Art. 70 (3).

[96]Art. 77 (1), the Constitution.

[97]Art. 10 (1), the Constitution.

[98]Art. 16 (2), the Constitution.

[99]Art. 78, the Constitution.

[100]Art. 77 (2), the Constitution.

[101]Penal procedure is applicable here.

[102]E.g. tightening and sealing up VAT system through an effective combating of extortions in the year 2016 enabled Polish government to finance social programme '500 plus' in the year 2017, the idea of which further on in the underlying study, http://polskieradio.pl/130/5788/Artykul/1812386,Wyludzenia-VAT-Moglismy-miec-program-Rodzina-5000-Plus (visited: 28.02.2020).

proceedings[103] over cases set forth in Art. 8(e) of the Act of 10 October 2002 on a minimum wage for work.[104]

Civil procedure offers ordinary and extraordinary remedies.[105] An ordinary remedy is of suspensive nature, which means that such recourse measure suspends validity and finality of the rulings contested. Amongst ordinary remedies, we distinguish devolutive remedies, seeking of which results in referring the case to the court of higher instance, and non-devolutive remedies, whose application does not bring a similar effect. Here, appeal[106] and interlocutory appeal[107] typify such devolutive ordinary remedies. Ordinary remedies of non-devolutive nature comprise: objection to a judgement by default,[108] objection to the payment order in injunctive proceedings,[109] objection to the payment order in writ proceedings,[110] petition against the court executive officer's actions,[111] allegations in enforcement proceedings,[112] petition against court division officer's decision.[113] Alternatively, amongst extraordinary remedies there are: cassation,[114] application for reopening of proceedings,[115] plea of illegality of non-appealable ruling[116] and a motion to set aside a judgement of the conciliation court.[117] Further stages of division of appellate measures in civil proceedings pertain to the type of rulings and grounds for appeal, which is specifically provided for by the C.C.P. The abundant and immensely extensive group of appellate measures in Polish civil procedure delivers an essential tool for the protection against poverty and for an individual's development. For instance, it is in civil proceedings that a remarkable majority of cases derive from the range of labour law.[118]

[103] Art. 17 (2) of the Law of the Code of Procedure on petty offences of 24.08.2001, J. of L. 2001, No. 106, item 1148, as amended, http://isap.sejm.gov.pl (visited:19.02.2020).

[104] In the event an entrepreneur or a person acting on his or other organizational entity's behalf pays a mandate or the person rendering services for every hour of work performed or service rendered an amount lower than a standing hourly minimum wage, he shall be subject to a fine of PLN 1000 up to PLN 30,000, J. of L. of 2017, item 847.

[105] Such issues are provided for by the Law of the Code of Civil Procedure (C.C.P.) of 17.11.1964, J. of L. 1964, No. 43, item 296, as amended, http://isap.sejm.gov.pl (visited:10.02.2020). See more e.g. Fik et al. (2013), Wiśniewski (2016).

[106] Art. 361–391, C.C.P.

[107] Art. 394 –397, C.C.P.

[108] Art. 344–349, C.C.P.

[109] Art. 493–497, C.C.P.

[110] Art. 497.1–505, C.C.P.

[111] Art. 767–67.3, C.C.P.

[112] Art. 1027, C.C.P.

[113] Art. 398.22–398.23, C.C.P.

[114] Art. 398.1–398.21, C.C.P.

[115] Art. 399–416.1, C.C.P.

[116] Art. 424.1–424.12, C.C.P.

[117] Art. 1209–1211, C.C.P.

[118] Art. 477–477.7a, C.C.P.

As with civil procedure, penal procedure offers identical classification foundations for suspensive and devolutive and, consequently, ordinary and extraordinary remedies.[119] Subsequent categories depend also on analogous criteria. A group of remedies in penal procedure is equally substantial and a similar terminology applies. Thus, ordinary remedies comprise: an interlocutory appeal,[120] appeal,[121] an objection to penal order,[122] an objection to a judgement by default,[123] motion for a fine discharge,[124] quasi objection-motion for the reinstatement of the time-limits,[125] appeal against the ruling of a presiding judge,[126] appeal to court against a decision of the Petty Offences Board.[127] Extraordinary remedies are as follows: cassation,[128] appeal against the appellate court's decision,[129] application for reopening of proceedings,[130] motion to set aside rulings against persons persecuted and repressed for their activity towards an independent existence of Poland.[131] Remedies in penal procedure may play a paramount role in the protection from poverty and development opportunity deprivation. Alternatively, an arbitrary and unreasonable sentencing may adversely affect financial situation or business activity of the convicted and their families. In Poland, by virtue of its historical specificity, a good case in point might be persons persecuted and repressed for their opposition activity and political views. Sentenced to many years of imprisonment and not even able to pay social insurance contributions, they have been, in majority of cases, living in poverty today. In both administrative procedure[132] and administrative court procedure,[133] remedies

[119]The foregoing questions are governed by the Law of the C.P.P. of 6 June 1997, J. of L. 1997, No. 89, item 555, as amended (http://isap.sejm.gov.pl (visited:10.02.2020) 18 September 2017) and in some instances—by special laws invoked accordingly. See more e.g. Waltoś and Hofmański (2016), Kulesza and Starzyński (2017).

[120]Art. 459–467, C.C.P.

[121]Art. 444–458, C.C.P.

[122]Art. 506, C.C.P.

[123]Art. 479, C.C.P.

[124]Art. 286, C.C.P.

[125]Art. 126, C.C.P.

[126]Art. 373, C.C.P.

[127]Art. 512 (1), C.C.P.

[128]Art. 518–539, C.C.P.

[129]Art. 539a–539f, C.C.P.

[130]Art. 540–548, C.C.P.

[131]Act of 23.02.1991 on the recognition of invalidity of rulings issued against persons persecuted for their activity towards an independent existence of Poland, J. of L. 1991, No. 31, item 149.

[132]Proceeding before public administration authorities.

[133]Proceeding before administrative courts, i.e. regional administrative courts and Supreme Administrative Court governed by the Act of 30.08.2002 on proceedings before administrative courts (PPSA), J. of L. 2002 No. 153, item 1270, as amended, http://isap.sejm.gov.pl (visited:10.02.2020). See more e.g. Borkowski and Adamiak (2017), Adamiak (2017), Gołaszewski (2017).

are subject to analogous division criteria.[134] Correspondingly, the administrative procedure distinguishes the following ordinary remedies: appeal,[135] interlocutory appeal,[136] motion for rehearing.[137] Extraordinary remedies encompass: application for reopening of proceedings,[138] motion to set aside decision.[139] In the administrative court proceedings, ordinary remedies comprise: cassation,[140] interlocutory appeal,[141] whereas extraordinary remedies divide into: application for reopening of a proceedings[142] and plea of illegality of a non-appealable ruling.[143]

The Act of 17.06.2004 on the complaint for an infringement of the right to have a case examined in pretrial proceedings, run or supervised by a prosecutor, and in court proceedings without undue delay[144] presents itself as a regulation that is evidently an aftermath of a frequently found in Polish cases disregard for the right to fair and public hearing pursuant to Art. 6 (1) of the European Convention. Therefore, the foregoing statute may be applied to any case pertinent to combating poverty and the right to development only when a prior pending lawsuit has satisfied the European Convention standards.

The protection of economic, social and cultural rights may be pursued through a constitutional complaint.[145] The right to file a constitutional complaint accrues to a person, whose constitutional rights and freedoms have been infringed.[146] Constitutional complaint may be lodged, once a judicial procedure has been exhausted and as long as such a route is provided for, within three months of the day the complainant was served with a final and binding judgement, decision or other final determination. Constitutional complaint may pertain to statute or other legislative act, by virtue of which a court or a public administration institution finally adjudicated on rights,

---

[134] Questions provided for by the Code of Administrative Procedure (C.A.P.) of 14.06.1960, J. of L. 1960, No. 30, item 168 as amended, http://isap.sejm.gov.pl (visited:18.02.2020). See more e.g. Gajewski (2017), Przybysz (2017).

[135] Art. 127 (1), C.A.P.

[136] Art. 141, C.A.P.

[137] Art. 127 (3), C.A.P.

[138] Art. 145, C.A.P.

[139] Art. 154–163a, C.A.P. Extraordinary remedies include also prosecutor's objection. However, since the party has no influence on its lodging, no discussion has been undertaken herein, http://en.frankbold.org/sites/default/files/publikacje/srodki_zaskarzenia_w_postepowaniu_administracyjnym_frank_bold.pdf (visited:28.02.2020).

[140] Art. 173, PPSA.

[141] Art. 194, PPSA.

[142] Art. 270–285, PPSA.

[143] Art. 285a–285l, PPSA.

[144] J. of L. 2004, No. 179, item 1843, as amended.

[145] Art. 79 (1), the Constitution.

[146] Principles of filing a constitutional complaint are provided for under the Act on 30 November 2016 on the organization and mode of procedure before the Constitutional Court, J. of L. 2016, item 2072. See more e.g. L. Bagińska (2010).

freedoms or obligations set forth in the Constitution.[147] Statutory provisions, executive act or international law act provisions are not to be made a review standard in the constitutional complaint.

Such institutions as the Ombudsman for Citizens' Rights,[148] the Ombudsman for Children's Rights[149] or the Ombudsman for Patients' Rights[150] may intervene *ex officio* or upon a request of the concerned party in cases related to the protection from poverty or the right to development.

Amongst the foregoing remedies that serve the protection from poverty, or alternatively, the entrenchment of the right to development, it is only the remedies canvassed within the scope of civil, penal and administrative procedures that are recognised in the international law as domestic remedies in their second meaning. More specifically, their exhaustion is a classic requirement that allows substantive assessment of an individual petition by the international review authorities. Filing of a constitutional complaint and launching other forms of action by the concerned party for the protection of its rights before the Ombudsman for Citizens' Rights, the Ombudsman for Children's Rights and the Ombudsman for Patients' Rights or before other relevant institutions, albeit taken into account in international proceedings, are not necessary for the commencement of such international proceedings.

The available case-law of general courts, the Supreme Court and the Constitutional Court, does not contain any rulings on the implementation of social rights in accordance with the guidelines following from Art. 2 (1) of the ICESC, which clearly results from a stance taken in this respect in the Constitution.

Domestic Constitutional or Legal Innovations

In the Polish Constitution, which is the supreme law established to permanently guarantee citizens their rights, and to ensure diligence and efficiency in the work of public authorities—all people are called upon 'to apply the Constitution by paying respect to an inherent dignity of a person, his or her right to freedom and an obligation of solidarity with others, and to recognise deference to said principles as the unshakable foundation of the Republic of Poland.[151] Human dignity has become thereby a constitutional cornerstone of social rights in Poland.[152] An

[147] http://trybunal.gov.pl/podstawowe-informacje/skarga-konstytucyjna/ (visited: 27.02.2020).

[148] Art. 80, the Constitution and the Act on the Ombudsman for Citizens' Rights of 15.07.1987, J. of L. 1987, No. 21, item 123, as amended, http://isap.sejm.gov.pl (visited:18.02.2020).

[149] Art. 72 (4), the Constitution and the Act on the Ombudsman for Childrens' Rights of 6.01.2000, J. of L. 2000 No. 6, item 69, as amended, http://isap.sejm.gov.pl (visited:10.02.2020).

[150] The Act of 6 November 2008 on patients' rights and on the Ombudsman for Patients' Rights, J. of L. 2009, No. 52, item 417, http://isap.sejm.gov.pl (visited:18.02.2020).

[151] Fragment of a preamble.

[152] G. Szpor (in:) Szpor (2009), p. 18.

inherent and inalienable human dignity is a source of personal and citizens' rights and freedoms. It is inviolable and its deference and protection belong to public authorities' duties.[153] The understanding of the question of social rights protection, i.e. the fight against poverty and for the right to development, is parallel to the angle adopted in the international law acts binding Poland with regard to human rights in general terms and more precisely with regard to economic, social and cultural rights.

It is likewise with a catalogue of social rights. In its very essence it corresponds to the resolutions passed by all the countries or devised by expert or local organizations. Neither has the right to development been identified within this group, nor the problem of fighting poverty has been referred to. Nonetheless, failure to entrench any of the social rights contemplated by the basic law will affect both the level of poverty among people and possibility of social and individual development. The right to work and related rights,[154] the right to social security,[155] the right to health protection,[156] the right to education,[157] or a freedom to enjoy products of culture[158] are from an individual's perspective fundamental tools protecting against poverty and enhancing development.

With reference to the human rights category, noteworthy is the fact that unlike international agreements providing social rights, the Constitution of the Republic of Poland establishes an express obligation of public authorities to ensure ecological security,[159] which is already deemed an action of solidarity.

Except for establishing an individual's and citizens' social rights, the Constitution also designs the foundations, framework and mechanisms of a system of specific administrations and their implementation, with ordinary statutes specifying their regime. The specificity and innovativeness of Polish law may very well be illustrated by, inter alia, the Social Security Administration. The Act of 4 September 1997 on government administration departments may be viewed here as the basis of such delimitation (UAR).[160] The Social Security Administration comprises sections that focus their work on: social insurance and social provision; pension funds; social welfare and benefits for individuals and households in difficult financial and social situation; prevention of pathologies; government welfare programmes, in particular for individuals and households in difficult financial and social situation, as well as for groups endangered with social exclusion; social benefits, employment, social and vocational rehabilitation for the disabled, veterans and repressed persons; social security system coordination, with the exception of healthcare in-kind benefits; public benefit activity, in its supervision of the public benefit organizations work;

[153] Art. 30, the Constitution.
[154] Art. 65–66, the Constitution.
[155] Art. 67, the Constitution.
[156] Art. 68, the Constitution.
[157] Art. 70, the Constitution.
[158] Art. 73, the Constitution.
[159] Art. 74, the Constitution.
[160] J. of L. 1997, No. 141, item 943, as amended; http://isap.sejm.gov.pl (visited: 06.02.2020).

coordination and organization of cooperation of public administration agencies, of entities operating in the public benefit field, including non-governmental organizations.[161]

The Government Social Security Administration is supervised by the Minister of Labour, Family and Social Policy.[162] The Minister is obliged to initiate and devise the policy of the Council of Ministers with regard to the department he/she is in charge of and to submit initiatives, projects of agenda, draft bills or draft normative acts to the sittings of the Council of Ministers—upon principles and in the mode stipulated in the code of procedure of the Council of Ministers. Within the department the Minister heads, he/she pursues the Council's policy and coordinates the work performed by agencies, offices and organizational units answerable, accountable to him/her or supervised by him/her as, for instance, the Social Insurance Board.[163]

For the objectives to be pursued, the Minister who heads the social security administration cooperates with other members of the Council of Ministers, other government administration agencies and public organizational units, self-government bodies as well as economic and professional bodies, trade unions and employers' associations and other social organizations, vocational and creative art institutions on principles and in the mode stipulated in separate provisions, and within the scope following from the needs of a given department.[164] In respect of said department, the Minister, who is in charge of the Social Security Administration, undertakes acts of international cooperation together with the Minister for Foreign Affairs, while with regard to the membership of the Republic of Poland in the European Union—the Minister remains in cooperation with the Minister for the membership of the Republic of Poland in the European Union.[165]

Pursuant to the Act of 23 January 2009 on the Voivode and government administration in the Voivodeship (UWAR),[166] the Voivode represents the Council of Ministers in the voivodeship.[167] The objectives of government administration are also pursued in the voivodeship by the government administration bodies integrated in the voivodeship, including heads of integrated services, inspection and guards, and by non-integrated government administration institutions.[168] Under the statute or agreement, tasks and objectives within the scope of social security are also carried

[161] Art. 31, the Act of 4 September on government administration (UAR).

[162] Regulation by the Council of Ministers of 3 December 2015 amending the Regulation on establishing the Ministry of Labour and Social Policy and abolishing the Ministry of Social Affairs, J. of L. 2015, item 2056; http://isap.sejm.gov.pl (visited:10.02.2020).

[163] Art. 34 (1) in connection with Art. 32a UAR.

[164] Art. 38 (1), UAR.

[165] Art. 38 (2), UAR.

[166] J. of L. 2009, No. 31, item 206, http://isap.sejm.gov.pl (visited:16.02.2020).

[167] Art. 2 (1), UWAR.

[168] Art. 2 (2) and (3), UWAR.

out by the self-government bodies.[169] Primarily, they have, in fact, their own objectives pertinent to social security, which they pursue in their own name and on their own responsibility in reliance upon separate statutes that shape self-government regime. Social welfare is specified there as the mission for the municipal, district/poviat and provincial/voivodeship self-governments, while the assistance to disabled persons is denoted as a separate scheme on the level of a district/poviat. However, the insurance tasks[170] have not been identified. Each municipality or commune may boast social welfare centres that perform a number of social security programmes.[171]

More comprehensive definition of specific public administration bodies would require a detailed review of relevant provisions of law. What is, nonetheless, worth underlining is the cooperation and joint action of government and non-government administration bodies within the framework of social security and an attendant multistage division of tasks between definite administration bodies. Not only does such structure enable more balanced a division of duties in pursuing the aims of social security, but it also ensures a sustainable public finance management in this domain.

[169] Art. 2 (4) and (5), UWAR.

[170] The Act of 5 June 1998 on the voivodeship self-government, J. of L. 1998, No. 91, item 576 as amended; Art. 14 (1)(4), http://isap.sejm.gov.pl (visited:10.02.2020); the Act of 5 June 1998 on the county self-government, J. of L. 1998, No. 91, item 578 as amended, http://isap.sejm.gov.pl (visited:10.02.2020); Art. 4 (1)(3), http://isap.sejm.gov.pl (visited:10.02.2020); the Act of 8 March 1990 on the municipal self-government, Art. 7 (1)(6), J. of L. 2016, item 446, as amended, http://isap.sejm.gov.pl (visited:10.02.2020). See also: G. Szpor (in:) Szpor (2009), pp. 21–22.

[171] The Act of 12 March 2004 on social welfare, J. of L. 2004, No. 64, item 593 as amended; the Act of 27 August 1997 on the vocational and social rehabilitation and the employment of disabled persons, J. of L. 1997, No. 123, item 776 as amended; the Act on 21 June 2001 on housing subsidies, J. of L. 2001, No. 71, item 734 as amended; the Act of 28 November 2003 on family benefits, J. of L. 2003, No. 228, item 2255 as amended; the Act of 7 September 2007 on the assistance to persons entitled to maintenance payments, J. of L. 2007, No. 192, item 1378 as amended; the Act of 1 February 2016 on state aid in raising children, J. of L. 2016, item 195 as amended; the Act of 21 November 1967 on universal obligation to defend the Republic of Poland, J. of L. 2015, item 827 as amended; the Act of 7 September 1991 on the system of education, J. of L. 2015, item 2156 as amended; the Act of 12 December 2013 on foreign nationals, J. of L. 2013, item1650 as amended; the Act of 27 August 2004 on health care benefits financed from public funds, J. of L. 2004, No. 210, item 2135 as amended; the Act of 19 August 1994 on protection of mental health, J. of L. 1994, No. 111, item 535 as amended; the Act of 5 December 2014 on the Charter of a Large Family, J. of L. 2014, item 1863 as amended; the Act of 27 August 2009 on public finance, J. of L. 2009, No. 157, item 1240 as amended. All the documents can be found at http://isap.sejm.gov.pl (visited:10.02.2020).

Policy Monitoring and/or Accountability Mechanisms

Polish authorities have been undertaking a variety of social initiatives that fit and fall within the pursuance of the Sustainable Development Goals (SDG) in compliance with the Millennium Development Goals perspective. Only selected instances of such activities have been presented herein below. What transpires from the devised projects is that their realisation results from a major contribution on the part of central and local government bodies, local government at all levels, with an active participation of a citizens, in particular non-governmental organizations, obviously, pursuant to the profile of their operation. The Act of 24 April 2003 on the public benefit activity and voluntary service enshrines provisions that prescribe forms of cooperation between the sector of non-governmental organizations and administration.

Cross-sectoral cooperation assumes in particular the forms of:

(1) commissioning public tasks performance;
(2) mutual informing of planned activity directions;
(3) consulting with non-governmental organizations and entities set forth in Art. 3 (3)[172] drafts of normative acts in the fields of the organizations' registered activity;
(4) consulting drafts of normative acts on public tasks with the public benefit works councils if such have been established by competent self-government bodies;
(5) establishing joint consulting and initiative-driven teams;
(6) agreement to implement a local initiative;
(7) partnership agreements.[173]

The foregoing cooperation is held on the principles of: subsidiarity, parties' autonomy, partnership, cost-effectiveness, fair competition and transparency. The law imposes on local self-government bodies an obligation to devise programmes of cooperation with the non-governmental organizations.[174] The Social Dialogue Council perfectly illustrates an influence of the non-governmental organizations on a broadly understood social policy.[175]

Family 500+ (Plus) Programme

Family 500+ Programme is a tax-free PLN 500 monthly payment for every second and subsequent child, such payment being subject to no conditions whatsoever. Families with a low income receive support also for the first or the only child. Yearly

[172] E.g. social co-operatives.

[173] J. of L. 2010, No. 234, item 1536, http://isap.sejm.gov.pl.

[174] https://www.mpips.gov.pl/spoleczenstwo-obywatelskie/wspolpraca-organizacji-pozarzadowych-z-administracja/.

[175] The institution, where the government and social partners regularly meet.

net amount of child benefit amounts even up to PLN 6000. Parental benefit is a long-term support. The Family 500+ programme is a systemic support for Polish families.[176] In July 2017, the governmental 'Family 500+' programme embraced more than 3992m children up to18 years of age. It is only since the beginning of 2017 that a sum of PLN 13.9 bn has reached Polish families. Across Poland, almost 57.9% of all children up to 18 years of age have been included in the 'Family 500+' programme. Parental benefit reaches 2617m families, in it 381 thousand are large families. Said benefit is received by over 726 thousand families with one 18-year-old child. There are over 1509m two-children families, 306 thousand of three-children, 56 thousand of four-children, 13 thousand of five-children and 6 thousand of six-children families that have access to said benefit. Amongst all of the families that receive parental benefit for the first child, as many as 116 thousand disabled-child families are covered by the underlying support. Approximately 60% of families receive parental benefit conditional upon an income criterion per the first or the only child—that is above 1564m, with 7257 thousand one-child families. Since the commencement of the programme, more than PLN 31.2 bn have gone to families, including PLN 30.8 bn of parental benefit, and PLN 378m of 500+ benefit to foster families. The 'Family 500+' programme started on 1 April 2016 to spread across Poland. Parents will be afforded a parental benefit of PLN 500 irrespective of an income for the second child and subsequent children up to the 18 years of age. In respect of families with a net income of PLN 800 a person (or net PLN 1200 where a disabled child is raised), such support may be accessed also for the first or the only child.[177]

Supported Accommodation

Supported accommodation may be accorded to a person who due to his/her difficult living conditions, age, disability or disease needs an assistance/support on a daily basis, but does not require services as rendered by a 24-hour care unit, in particular services provided to a person with mental disorders, to a person leaving foster care, within the meaning of the provisions on family support and foster care system, youth care centres, juvenile detention centres, as well as services rendered to a foreign national who has obtained a refugee status or supplementary protection in the Republic of Poland. Such form of social aid, which the supported accommodation obviously is, prepares the persons that residing there and are under the care of specialists to lead their independent lives, or replaces their stay in a 24-hour care unit. The supported accommodation secures conditions to function independently

[176] https://www.mpips.gov.pl/wsparcie-dla-rodzin-zdziecmi/rodzina-500-plus.

[177] https://www.mpips.gov.pl/aktualnosci-wszystkie/rodzina-500-plus/art,9089,ponad-3-99-mln-dzieci-objetych-rodzina-500.html.

and to integrate with a local community. Moreover, said accommodation may be run by any social welfare entity or public benefit organization.[178]

Aid for Economic Emancipation

For economic emancipation any individual or family may be provided by the municipality or commune with a monetary or in-kind assistance. Monetary aid may be granted as either a one-off designated/aim-specific benefit or an interest-free loan. An agreement with the municipality shall stipulate terms and conditions of a loan provision, repayment and security. Said loan may be forgiven in part or in whole if it is conducive to a more expeditious pursuance of social welfare objectives. Alternatively, an in-kind assistance, in the context of economic emancipation, assumes a form of sharing not only work tools and machinery that may facilitate establishing one's own workplace, but also devices that may help the disabled persons in their work. Sharing work tools and machinery is carried out under the lending for use agreement. In respect of a monetary or in-kind assistance for the purpose of economic emancipation the municipality cooperates with the district/poviat employment agency.[179]

Minimum Wage

Since 1 January 2016, a minimum wage of a person employed on a monthly full-time basis cannot be lower than PLN 1850 gross. In comparison with a minimum wage in 2015 (PLN 1750), there has been a rise of PLN 100, i.e. 5.7%. A sum of PLN 1850 was stipulated in the Regulation by the Council of Ministers of 11 September 2015 on the minimum wage for work in 2016 (J. of L., item 1385). Under Art. 6 (2) of the Act of 10 October 2002 on the minimum wage for work (J. of L. No. 200, item 1679, as amended), an employee's remuneration in the first year of work cannot be less than 80% of a minimum wage for work, i.e. in the year 2016, it must at least amount to a gross pay of PLN 1480.

The Food Aid Operational Programme 2014–2020

The Food Aid Operational Programme provides support to people and families in difficult situations. It consists in providing food aid in the form of parcels or meals. For the implementation of the Programme in the years 2014–2020, a budget of almost PLN 2.5 billion has been planned, mostly from the EU funds.

---

[178] https://www.mpips.gov.pl/pomoc-spoleczna/formy-udzielanej-pomocy/mieszkanie-chronione/.

[179] https://www.mpips.gov.pl/pomoc-spoleczna/formy-udzielanej-pomocy/pomoc-na-ekonomiczne-usamodzielnienie/.

From 1 August 2016 till 30 June 2017, circa PLN 297m worth of food in parcels and meals reached more than 1,300,000 people most in need of support. Amidst this group are families with the lowest income, elderly, disabled or homeless people.[180]

The number of municipalities committed to the pursuance of said Programme is on the rise, which translates into the fact that the assistance reaches a still growing number of eligible recipients. With the commencement of the Programme in 2014, its geographic range has been gradually extending to embrace 90% of municipalities across Poland today.

Every year, the value of a parcel is also increased: if in the year 2014 the value of a parcel sent to one recipient was PLN 40, in 2015—PLN 170, then in the year 2016—the value climbed to PLN 228. In the 2017 sub-programme, the value of a parcel sent to one recipient amounts to PLN 269. The number of products has also grown: from 5 on the start of the Programme, to 19 in 2017. Worth noting is also the fact that among the most committed and active parties are non-governmental organizations, including Food Banks.[181]

75+ (Plus) Programme

The project is addressed to all the patients who on the date the prescription for medicines is issued reach the age of 75, with their disease falling within the scope of recommendations for reimbursements. The list provides medicines, which under the reimbursement notice in force, are dispensed to the patients against a flat-rate or 30% payment.

In the applicable since 1 September 2017 catalogue of reimbursable medicines, foods for particular nutritional uses or medical devices, a list of complimentary medications for seniors contains as many as 1530 items (692 preparations), 113 of which are active substances. In the year 2015, the patients over the age of 75 expended approximately PLN 860m on reimbursable medicines. Once the law has become effective the bills of seniors over the age of 75 for reimbursable medicines will decrease to 40% in 2016 to reach over 60% in subsequent years.[182]

Housing+ (Plus) Programme

Housing+ Programme is a fundamental package of solutions that implements a new housing policy predicated on three pillars, with the aim being to facilitate designing a housing offer addressed to any and all households. The three pillars are:

---

[180] https://www.mpips.gov.pl/pomoc-spoleczna/programy/program-operacyjny-pomoc-zywnosciowa-2014–2020-popz/aktualnosci/html.

[181] https://www.mpips.gov.pl/aktualnosci-wszystkie/pomoc-spoleczna/art,9053,wiecej-gmin-z-pomoca-zywnosciowa.html.

[182] http://75plus.mz.gov.pl/.

- affordable rental housing on the State Treasury land;
- social rental housing;
- incentive for systematic saving for housing purposes.

Housing+ is primarily a new programme of building apartments affordable to families on a rental basis with a final ownership option, implemented through market financing and the national housing operator. Its novelty lies, inter alia, in the fact that:

- the State Treasury will tap into its immovables;
- market instruments, in particular a formula of a closed investment fund will play a major role;
- by its impact on the whole market, the programme will generate extra pressure to lower housing prices.

Housing+ is an initiative pursued in cooperation with local authorities and, in the long term, also with other entities, including the State Treasury.[183]

Unilateral/Bilateral Initiatives or Agreements

Poland has been committed to a variety of initiatives pertinent to social development and combating poverty through devising its own above discussed solutions and implementing the ones that result from its participation in the life of an international community.

In the first place, it is necessary to bring up bilateral agreements concluded with the countries, the relationships with which have not hitherto provided for the concepts of the right to development or to combat poverty. Such agreements usually fail to offer any novel or unique legal initiatives,[184] unless this becomes indispensable by reason of the specificity of relations between the interested parties,[185] and unless their enforcement and observance fall within the scope of treaty law rules.

Poland and other EU member states have decided to join their efforts to counteract poverty and social exclusion by earmarking adequate funds within the scope of a new financial perspective (2014–2020). The member states have committed to designing strategies to reduce and avert poverty, to engaging competent

[183]http://mib.gov.pl/2-NPM.htm.

[184]E.g. the Agreement of 2016 between the Government of the Republic of Poland and the Government of Israel on cooperation in the field of health and medicine, Official Gazette (Monitor Polski) 2010, No 36, item 505, http://isap.sejm.gov.pl (visited:05.02.2020).

[185]E.g. the Agreement between the Republic of Poland and the Federal Republic of Germany on special benefits export for entitled persons residing in the territory of the Republic of Poland, J. of L. 2015, item 714. Under this agreement German social security pensions for work in ghettos shall be transferred to entitled persons residing in the territory of the Republic of Poland, https://www.mpips.gov.pl/koordynacja-systemow-zabezpieczenia-spolecznego/umowy-miedzynarodowe-o-zabezpieczeniu-spolecznym/.

Table 9.1 Percentage of people receiving social aid and the poverty lines[a]

No	List	Year			
		2012	2013	2014	2015
1	People below minimum subsistence (%)	6.8	7.4	7.4	6.5
2	People below min. standard of living (%)	43.4	44.7	43.4	42.7

[a]https://www.mpips.gov.pl/aktualnosci-wszystkie/pomoc-spoleczna/art,8320,przeciwdzialanie-ubostwu-w-polsce.html; https://www.mpips.gov.pl/koordynacja-systemow-zabezpieczenia-spolecznego/umowy-miedzynarodowe-o-zabezpieczeniu-spolecznym/

stakeholders, and subsequently to monitoring progress, in particular with regard to living conditions. The work over the foregoing strategy in Poland has pivoted on two coordinates, i.e.: minimum subsistence and minimum standard of living.

Minimum subsistence level—a basket of goods necessary to maintain human life functions, mental and physical health. It factors in only such needs whose satisfaction cannot be delayed in time, since consumption at a lower level may result in emaciation and life loss risk. In the year 2015, the minimum subsistence of a single person with an earning capacity reached an amount of PLN 546.76, of a single retired person PLN 518, of a working five-person family (two adults plus minor plus two majors) PLN 477.82.

Minimum standard of living—an indicator defining household maintenance costs against a basket of goods necessary to satisfy socio-economic needs on a low but a fair and decent level. Not only do the adopted basket ingredients suffice for subsistence (compare: minimum subsistence), but also to have and raise children, as well as to maintain minimum social well-being. In the year 2015, the minimum standard of living for a single person with an earning capacity stood at the level of PLN 1079.53, of a single retired person PLN 1080.20, of a family with three minors—PLN 4198.12 (PLN 839.63 per one person in a family).

In 2015, social aid, irrespective of its form and sources of financing, reached 7.4% of Polish residents. Almost 4.6% of citizens received assistance in the form of a benefit granted upon a decision. In contrast to the year 2012 when a previous income criteria review had taken place, the values of both indicators went down by 1.0% and 0.4% respectively (Table 9.1).

Extreme poverty indicators in 2015 changed to the advantage of Polish residents—from 7.4% to 6.5% (with a decrease in number of 0.9% of Polish residents). Similarly, a favourable shift was noticed in respect of a relative poverty line—from 16.2% to 15.5% of Polish residents. Concurrently, a statutory poverty indicator stayed at the same level, that is 12.8%. Positive trends have been confirmed by the change of a "minimum standard of living"—it altered from 43.4% to 42.7%. It may be concluded that a long-term social policy to avert poverty consequences has been bringing an improvement in the socio-economic situation of a society in recent years.

Majority, almost 85% of families, under social aid through benefits programme, is also covered by support in the form of a social work—a special form of assistance consisting in a work with the whole family to help overcome hardships related not only to poverty, but also unemployment, educational problems, inability to run a household or other causes.

Social Aid Initiatives to Reduce Poverty

(a) monetary/cash benefits—permanent benefit, periodic benefit, designated benefit and special designated benefit, benefit and loan for economic emancipation, aid for emancipation and education continuation, monetary benefit for maintenance and to cover expenses of Polish language learning for foreign nationals who have received refugee status or a supplementary protection, or a temporary stay permit by reason of circumstances set forth in Art. 159(1)(1)(c) or (d) of the Act of 12 December 2013 on foreigners, compensation due to caregivers for care supplied awarded by court;
(b) in-kind benefits—social work, credit ticket, health insurance premiums, social insurance premiums, in-kind aid, in it for economic emancipation, for funeral arrangement, specialist counselling, crisis intervention, shelter, meal, indispensable clothing, care services at the place of residence, in support centres or family aid institutions, specialist nursing services at the place of residence and in support centres, supported accommodation, stay and services in welfare institutions, assistance in obtaining adequate living and residential conditions also in supported accommodation, assistance in employment, in-kind aid extended to emancipated persons for household development and management;
(c) income criteria in social welfare—since 1 October 2015, in compliance with the Ordinance of 14 July 2015 by the Council of Ministers on reviewed income criteria and social welfare benefit payments (Journal of Laws item 1058), such income criteria have been in force as below:

  - for a single and only person in his/her household—PLN 634 (PLN 542—so far),
  - for one person in a family—PLN 514 (PLN 456—so far).

Concurrently, it was established that:

- a maximum permanent benefit would amount to PLN 604 (PLN 529—so far);
- benefit for foreigners (with a refugee status and supplementary protection) would equal—PLN 1335 (PLN 1260—so far),
- hourly monthly income—PLN 288 (PLN 250—so far).

The foregoing income thresholds are so called 'statutory poverty line', which is applicable under the Act on social services.[186]

[186] J. of L. 2016, item 2174, http://isap.sejm.gov.pl/ (visited:10.02.2020).

Supportive Actions

(a) implementation of a long-term 'State aided food and nutrition service' programme. It is an initiative of financial assistance to municipalities in their realisation of food and nutrition service with a view to reducing malnutrition among children and youth in families with low incomes or experiencing a difficult situation. It is also intended for adult persons, in particular the elderly and people living alone. In general terms, the state has budgeted as much as PLN 550 on a yearly basis. In 2015, the Programme embraced as many as 2,042,054 people, including:

   – 286,074 children before starting education in a primary school;
   – 622,590 students till their completion of a high school/secondary school;
   – 810,896 other persons, specifically elderly, disabled and single persons.

   The aggregate sum earmarked for the "State-aided food and nutrition service" programme was up to PLN 811,469,097 (funds from the state budget and municipalities) in the year 2015. The same year, a number of meals served reached 103,594,519.

(b) implementation of the Operational Programme for Food Assistance 2014–2020 (OPFA)—the programme co-financed by the Fund for European Aid to the Most Deprived. Under the foregoing Programme food is distributed by non-governmental organizations on three: national, regional and local levels, with the aim being to provide food to the most needy and deprived in the form of parcels and/or meals, and to pursue actions attendant and supportive to the social inclusion of the food aid recipients. Within the scope of a Sub-programme 2015 (implemented from May 2015 till the end of June 2016), food aid went to a total number of 1,999,000 people. 7,663,483 parcels and 913,626 meals were served. Partner organizations pursued as many as 7251 attendant actions, in which almost 122,617 most deprived persons took part.

Furthermore, the Ministry of Family, Labour and Social Policy has been promoting and supporting local authorities in the implementation of their own initiatives through ministerial programmes addressed to the groups specifically endangered with social exclusion. Such programmes are addressed to:

- homeless people (the programme termed "Support Programme for the Social Re-Integration of the Homeless"—PLN 5.8m in 2016);
- persons suffering from violence (programme entitled "Support for Self-Government in the Establishment of a System for the Prevention of Family Violence"—PLN 3m in 2016);
- persons with mental disorders (programme entitled "Social Support for People with Mental Illnesses"—PLN 3m in 2016);

- socially excluded persons and activation programmes—"Active Forms of Counteracting Social Exclusion – a new dimension 2020"—PLN 3.6m in 2016).[187]

So devised a policy clearly exhibits an innovative contribution of Poland to combating poverty and promoting social inclusion in Europe. Compared to the solutions of other countries, such strategy may not only exemplify a specific approach adopted, but it may also develop from and on the basis of experiences that other EU member states or European countries tend to share. The social policy of an EU member state is subject to review and revision pursuant to EU law.

Aided with European funds, various government departments have been implementing programmes of combating poverty and social exclusion.[188] Accordingly, the Department of Implementing the European Social Fund in the Ministry of Family, Labour and Social Policy has announced a competition for the implementation of initiatives within the ambit of II priority axis—Effective public policies for the labour market, economy and education—of the Operational Programme Knowledge Education Development 2014–2020 (OP KED)—Activity 2.6, high quality policy in favour of employment and social inclusion of disabled persons.[189] An implementation of the foregoing projects started in 2014 and will last till 2020. An agreement with Nest Bank has been concluded within the scope of EU Programme for Employment and Social Innovation for the years 2014–2020 in reliance upon the resources of the European Fund for Strategic Investment which is a central element of the Investment Plan for Europe (so called Juncker Plan). Thanks to financial support of the European Commission, the European Investment Fund secures a guarantee that enables bank to afford loans on favourable terms of up to an aggregate sum of PLN 40m, which means a decrease in a profit margin, resignation from commission and the absence of a requirement to produce 'hard' guarantees.[190]

The foregoing examples attest to the fact that while the initiative came from EU, a concrete implementation idea transpired from the actions undertaken by the Republic of Poland. The characteristics of such actions shall both determine and reflect the commitment and contribution of the concerned groups of citizens. The adequacy and effectiveness of said projects are scrutinized and appraised pursuant to EU law criteria of European funds appropriation and application. Report and its assessment shall be accessible to all member states which may see this as a very good point of reference for their own initiatives.

Furthermore, it was on the initiative of OECD that Poland amongst 17 countries participated in a Thematic Review of Adult Learning (TRAL) 1999–2004. The

[187] https://www.mpips.gov.pl/aktualnosci-wszystkie/pomoc-spoleczna/art,8320,przeciwdzialanie-ubostwu-w-polsce.html.

[188] https://www.mr.gov.pl/media/27996/wytyczne_CT9_24.pdf.

[189] https://www.mpips.gov.pl/aktualnosci-wszystkie/fundusze-europejskie/art,9006,konkurs-w-ramach-dzialania-2-6-po-wer-.html.

[190] https://www.mpips.gov.pl/aktualnosci-wszystkie/fundusze-europejskie/art,8628,rusza-nowy-unijny-instrument-dla-polskich-mikroprzedsiebiorcow.html.

research and review resulted in two comparative reports, the first report of 2003—"Beyond Rhetoric: Adult Learning Policies and Practices," and published in 2005 "Promoting Adult Learning" report.[191] Voluntary nature notwithstanding, participation in such programmes entails given country's specific operations and financial contribution. Performance or results may always be perceived as valuable and as such they may emphasize the necessity to adjust a given country's conduct, to receive support from international community or, in a broader sense, to influence the direction of operations a given organization has taken.

Conclusions

The foregoing perspective of combating poverty and an implementation of the right to development fit into a broad context of human rights protection which, in turn, is a result of interests and expectations that countries, nations, communities and individuals exhibit. Legislation, international or domestic, is an expression of a palette of directions, measures and dimensions taken to ensure specific rights. In Poland, the tradition of shaping and implementing human rights, not precluding social rights, is deeply embedded in an international law, parallel to the experience, participation and achievements in the life of an international community. Alternatively, what is noticeable is the influence domestic law regimes have on the direction of international law development. Legal solutions in the underlying area tend to permeate and overlap, absorb or supplement one another. The current profile of social rights protection with an attendant fight against poverty, as well as commitment towards social and individual development has emerged, inter alia, from rejection of an approach related to communist regime, from economic transformation, political changes, aspirations of Poles for self-realization and of Poland for genuine and pure self-determination. Concurrently, for the foregoing reasons, an internal and external situation of the country was undergoing sudden changes, which triggered as many positive as negative phenomena. Massive bankruptcy of companies, huge unemployment, drastically rising poverty level generated a need to ensure at least a minimum social protection, since it was no longer plausible to return to social security limits established in the times of a nation of working people coming from towns and villages. All the above phenomena have been undoubtedly familiar to all the countries, albeit in different dimension, from another perspective or matching other social background. Under such circumstances every country will seek solutions in the experience of other countries, adjusting the whole process to its own specific nature and enriching it with their own concepts, methods and measures. Poland's achievement in the field of initiative implementation lies undoubtedly in its legislation designed to protect social rights, which is expressly manifested by the commitment that the country's structures, institutions and authorities exhibit to the

[191]http://www.oecd.org/edu/adultlearning.

development and enforcement of said rights. Such an approach may very well become a potential point of reference for other international law entities, in particular countries which are still for the same reasons in an epoch of removing the traces of deservedly foregone political and economic systems and establishing their new position in an international community.

References

Adamiak B (2017) Skarga i skarga kasacyjna w postępowaniu administracyjnym. Komentarz, Complaint and plea in cassation in administrative procedure. Commentary, Warszawa

Bagińska L (2010) Skarga konstytucyjna, Constitutional Complaint, Warszawa

Banaszak B (2017) Prawo konstytucyjne, Constitutional Law, Warszawa

Barcik J, Srogosz T (2014) Prawo międzynarodowe publiczne, Public international law, Warszawa

Borkowski J, Adamiak B (2017) Prawo administracyjne i sądowoadministracyjne, Administrative and administrative court law, Warszawa

Czapliński W, Wyrozumska A (2014) Prawo międzynarodowe publiczne. Zagadnienia systemowe, Public international law. Problems of system, Warszawa

Czarny P (2013) "Konstytucyjny status jednostki w prawie polskim" (w:) Prawo konstytucyjne RP, 'Individual's constitutional status in Polish law' In: Sarnecki P (ed) Constitutional law of the Republic of Poland, Warszawa

Fik P, Nartowski D, Staszczyk P (2013) Postępowanie cywilne. Repetytorium, Civil Procedure, Compendium, Warszawa

Florek L (1997) "Zgodność przepisów prawa pracy z Konstytucją", Compliance of the labour law provisions with the Constitution, Praca i Zabezpieczenie Społeczne, No. 11

Gajewski S (2017) Kodeks postępowania administracyjnego. Nowe instytucje, The Code of Administrative Procedure. New Institutions, Warszawa

Gierach E (2015) "Zgromadzenie Narodowe – wybrane zagadnienia", 'The National Assembly – selected aspects' INFOS, No 14 (197)

Gołaszewski P (2017) Sporządzanie środków zaskarżenia w postępowaniu administracyjnym i sądowoadministracyjnym. Drafting complaints in administrative and administrative court procedures, Warszawa

Iriye A (2000) Global community: the role of international organizations in the making of the contemporary world, Berkeley

Kulesza C, Starzyński P (2017) Postępowanie karne, Penal procedure, Warszawa

Masternak-Kubiak M (1997) Umowa międzynarodowa w prawie konstytucyjnym, International agreement under Constitutional law, Warszawa

Office of the Committee for European Integration (2009) Wytyczne polityki legislacyjnej i techniki prawodawczej. Zapewnienie efektywności prawu Unii Europejskiej w polskim prawie krajowym, Legislative policy and mechanism guidelines. Ensuring EU law efficacy in Polish law, Warszawa

Oniszczuk J (1993) Orzecznictwo Trybunału Konstytucyjnego w latach 1989–1993, The Constitutional Court case law in the years 1986–1993, Warszawa

Oniszczuk J (2005) Wolności i prawa socjalne oraz orzecznictwo konstytucyjne, Social rights and freedoms and constitutional case-law, Warszawa

Przybysz P (2017) Kodeks postępowania administracyjnego. Komentarz, The Code of Administrative Procedure. Commentary, Warszawa

Salitra D (2003) "Zasady przyzwoitej legislacji orzecznictwa Trybunału Konstytucyjnego", 'Principles of decent legislation in the case-law of the Constitutional Court', Przegląd Sejmowy, 4 (57)

Szpor G (w:; in:) Szpor G (ed) (2009) System ubezpieczeń społecznych. Zagadnienia podstawowe, Social insurance system. Elementary issues. Warszawa

Waltoś S, Hofmański P (2016) Proces karny. Zarys systemu, Penal proceedings, System synopsis, Warszawa

Wiśniewski T (2016) Przebieg procesu cywilnego. Komentarz praktyczny dla sędziów i pełnomocników procesowych, Civil procedure profile. Commentary practical for judges and litigators, Warszawa

Chapter 10
The Fight Against Poverty and the Right to Development in Taiwan

Li-Ju Lee

Abstract This report conducts a survey on the development of the socio-economic rights and the legal measures adopted to fight against poverty in Taiwan. The first part of this national report examines Taiwan's constitutional protection of the socio-economic rights and various legal instruments to realize these rights. The second part discusses Taiwan's effort to keep in line with the international human rights law despite its struggle to gain access to international organizations and receive global recognition.

Instruction

The social and economic rights are protected by the Constitution in Taiwan. However, in the authoritarian era, these constitutional mandates and guidance were mostly ignored, except for mandatory education to all school-age children and social insurance to limited groups (i.e., government employees, military personnel, school teachers) to advance state interests: pursuing economic growth and maintaining political stability. Meanwhile, it was the traditional family system that played the role of social welfare programs. Such top-down welfare policy has changed since Taiwan's transition to democracy in the 1990s. The rising demand for social justices, human rights and welfare services have contributed to a significant increase of welfare legislation and a series of Constitutional Court rulings. The first part of this report examines Taiwan's Constitutional protection of socio-economic rights and the legislations to fight against poverty as well as to realize the right to development. The second part focuses on Taiwan's effort to keep in line with the international human rights law. Despite the difficulties of formally entering international agreements, Taiwan has voluntarily abided by several major international

L.-J. Lee (✉)
Law School, Chung Yuan Christian University, Taoyuan, Taiwan
e-mail: lijulee@cycu.edu.tw

M. Andenas et al. (eds.), *The Fight Against Poverty and the Right to Development*, Ius Comparatum - Global Studies in Comparative Law 52,
https://doi.org/10.1007/978-3-030-57324-9_10

human rights conventions and developed a review mechanism involving international law experts, the government agencies, local NGOs and judicial review to discuss and improve the protection of human rights.

Domestic Law and Remedies

Constitutional Protection

The Right of Existence and an Adequate Standard of Living

According to Article 15 of the Constitution, "[t]he right of existence, the right of work and the right of property shall be guaranteed to the people". The "right of existence", a rather broad and vague claim, is commonly understood as "the right to an adequate standard of living" and subject to judicial review conducted by the Grand Justices of the Constitutional Court.

The guaranteed "right to an adequate standard of living", according to the Grand Justices, is not a fixed standard hoping to fit all individuals and/or families. Rather, it should be a standard aiming to accommodate an individual's (and their families) basic needs and conditions. In other word, such standard should be decided on a case-by-case basis.[1] The Justices clarified the concept of "an adequate standard of living" in a case concerning "the Act Governing the Reduction of Farm Rent [Rate] to 37.5 Percent", a legislation aiming to protect tenant farmers from landlords' exploitation, preventing the landlord from terminating the lease if the termination would result in the tenant farmer's "economic hardship" to support his family. The "economic hardship" happened, according to the administrative rule issued by the Ministry of Interior, when the income of tenant farmer's family fell under the minimum living expense standard announced by the local governments. However, in *JY Interpretation No. 422*, the Constitutional Court struck down this administrative rule, rejecting the use of a Minimum Living Expense Standard Table to estimate the annual living expense for the tenant farmer and his family, for "it is neither realistic nor reasonable to apply fixed amounts to estimate the family living expense for individual tenant farmers without considering the actual family livelihood of the tenant farmer on a case-by-case basis and the difficulties a particular tenant farmer may encounter".[2]

[1]But see Chang (2011), pp. 168–174.
[2]JY Interpretation No. 422 (1997).

Social, Economic and Cultural Rights

Article 15 of Taiwan's Constitution guarantees the right to work. In practice, the right-to-work claim is often used by the individuals who seek challenge laws or regulations depriving their "right to choose a profession". In 2017 the Justices issued *JY Interpretation No. 749*. Citing the Constitutional guarantee of the right to work, The Court struck down a law authorizing to revoke the taxi drivers' license if the drivers have a criminal record of fraud, grand larceny and other specified crimes.[3] Moreover, the right-to-work clause was invoked to challenge the constitutionality of labor laws and regulations.[4]

The right to education is mentioned in several provisions of the Constitution. According to Article 21, the Constitution guarantees that all citizens shall receive primary education. The Grand Justices further recognized the right to receive higher education as an unremunerated right protected by Article 22.[5] To prevent discrimination against the disadvantaged groups, the framers added Article 159, providing that all citizens shall have an equal opportunity to receive education. In *JY Interpretation No. 626*, the Justices struck down a policy to deny admissions for color-blindness of the Central Police Academy for it violated the guarantee of the citizens' equal opportunity to receive higher education.[6]

The right to housing is not mentioned in the Constitution. The Grand Justices nevertheless have ruled on the issue in several occasions. In *JY Interpretation No. 485* (issued in 1999), the Justices upheld a statue that provides subsidy for the reconstruction of military family housing. Although the Court recognized housing benefit as "welfare resources" and therefore deferred to legislative discretion on the distribution of welfare resources, the Justices urged the legislature to consider "the economic and financial conditions of the state, the principle of resource utilization", and "the equity between beneficiaries and other people" to make appropriate allocation of welfare resources.[7] In 2013, the Court invoked the freedom of residence (Article 10 of the Constitution) and the "adequate standard of living" proscribed in Article 11(1) of the International Covenant on Economic, Social and Cultural Rights in a case involving the constitutionality of the Urban Renewal Act. Balancing the right to property (Article 15) and the freedom of residence (Article 10) with the state interest of promoting urban renewal, the Justices announced several provisions of the Act unconstitutional. In this case, the Court explained that the freedom of residence guarantees people "the freedom to choose their residence and to enjoy

[3] JY Interpretation No. 749 (2017).

[4] For example, please see JY Interpretation No. 750 (2017) (upholding a rule requiring those who received dental education from foreign institutes to complete a clinical training program in Taiwan before they could take the written examination). JY Interpretation No. 711 (2013) (striking down a law limiting the practice of pharmacists to one location or setting).

[5] JY Interpretation No. 382 (1995).

[6] JY Interpretation No. 626 (2007).

[7] JY Interpretation No. 485 (1999).

their life in privacy without intrusion", while the "adequate standard of living" was cited by the Justices as a rationale to support the government program of urban planning and renewal for improving housing condition and safety.[8]

In addition to the fundamental rights mentioned above, Chapter XIII of the Constitution, entitled "Fundamental National Policies", requires the state to promote national economy (Section 3), social security (Section 4), and education and culture (Section 5) by providing or establishing the following services or social systems: to establish financial institutions for providing unemployment relief (Article 150);[9] to provide job opportunities to those who are capable to work (Article 152);[10] to improve the livelihood of laborers and farmers (Article 153);[11] to establish social insurance system to promote social security and welfare (Article 155);[12] to have the equal opportunity of education (Article 159)[13] and receive free primary education (Article 160);[14] to provide relief and social welfare services and to promote universal health insurance.[15] Nevertheless, these "Fundamental National Policies" Clauses do not guarantee fundamental rights to these services or resources. Although the Grand Justices considered these policies as Constitutional mandates, the individuals may not bring suits against the state when it fails to carry out these obligations.

It is worth noted that according to Article 155, 157 and Article 10 of the Amendment of the Constitution, the state is required to establish a system of universal health care and medical insurance. Despite the fact that these Clauses do not equal to the "fundamental rights" guarantees, the Court has considered these "fundamental policies of the state" as the state's primary obligation. This promise was fulfilled in 1994, when the *National Health Insurance Act* was passed by the Congress (the Legislative Yuan). In 1999, the Constitutional Court issued *JY*

[8]JY Interpretation No. 709 (2013).

[9]Article 150 of the Constitution: "The State shall extensively establish financial institutions for the common people, with a view to relieving unemployment."

[10]Article 152 of the Constitution: "The State shall provide suitable opportunity for work to people who are able to work."

[11]Article 153 of the Constitution: "(1) The State, in order to improve the livelihood of laborers and farmers and to improve their productive skill, shall enact laws and carry out policies for their protection. (2) Women and children engaged in labor shall, according to their age and physical condition, be accorded special protection."

[12]Article 155 of the Constitution: "The State, in order to promote social welfare, shall establish a social insurance system. To the aged and the infirm who are unable to earn a living, and to victims of unusual calamities, the State shall give appropriate assistance and relief."

[13]Article 159 of the Constitution: "All citizens shall have equal opportunity to receive an education."

[14]Article 160 of the Constitution: "(1) All children of school age from six to 12 years shall receive free primary education. Those from poor families shall be supplied with books by the Government. (2) All citizens above school age who have not received primary education shall receive supplementary education free of charge and shall also be supplied with books by the Government."

[15]Article 10 of the Amendment of the Constitution (section 5): "The State shall promote universal health insurance and promote the research and development of both modern and traditional medicines."

Interpretation No. 472, upholding the mandatory converge (and therefore people are compelled to pay the premium) required by "*the National Health Insurance Act*".[16] The Justices called the law a "realization of the aforesaid provisions of the Constitution". The Court also advised that "to those who cannot afford to pay the premium, the state shall give appropriate assistance and relief and shall not refuse to pay benefits, in order to fulfill the Constitution's [mandate] of promoting national health insurance, protecting senior citizens, the infirm and the financially disadvantaged".[17]

The Legal Instruments to Realize the Social, Economic, and Cultural Rights

Workers' Rights

The Labor Standards Act, enacted in 1984, proscribes minimum standards for working conditions to protect workers' rights. The Act ensures the minimum wage (150 NT dollars per hour since 2019) and regulates the working hours, minimum rest periods, annual holidays and a maximum working hours per week. It prohibits sex discrimination and requires equal pay for equal work. To protect workers against occupational accidents, the Congress enacted *the Occupational Safety and Health Act,* requiring the employers to provide safety and health facilities and measures to workers.

The Right to Social Security and Social Protection/The Right to an Adequate Standard of Living

Enacted in 1958, *the Labor Insurance Act* has played a crucial role in protecting workers' adequate livelihood and promoting social security. According to the Act, two types of insurance are available: (1) ordinary insurance, which pays benefits for childbirth, injuries, illnesses, medical care, disabilities and death, and (2) occupational accident insurance, which pays benefits for injuries, illnesses, medical care, disabilities and death.

Although the Constitution dedicates a whole chapter to national economic and social policies as mentioned above, the government had not been paying much attention to social welfare and the social security system had not developed until the democratization in the 1990s. *The Public Assistance Act*, after the 1997 and 2000 overhaul, has become the key measure of Taiwan's social welfare system. It aims to help the households, rather than the individuals, in need of economic relief. In other

[16]National Health Insurance Act was passed on July 19, 1994 and took effect on March 1, 1995 by the Congress. Legislative Yuan Gazette 83:54, 73–76 (1994).

[17]JY Interpretation No. 472 (1999).

words, the Act continues to rely on family as the primary safety net for Taiwanese people and the state-constructed social security system is built on the basis of the family system. According to the Public Assistance Act, the low-income and lower middle-income households may apply for public assistance such as cash assistance, medical subsidies, and emergency/disaster aid.

In addition to provide public assistance to the households with economic difficulties, the Congress, urged by various social groups and activists, has passed laws to protect rights and interests of the disadvantaged groups as follows:

(a) *The Protection of Children and Youths Welfare and Rights Act*[18] is to protect children and youths' rights and welfare, especially their right to development. The Act mandates the local governments to establish integrated services and encourage private sector to provide welfare services to children and youth, such as a reporting system and service network for premature babies and children with developmental delays; parental education and family consultation services; cash and/or medical benefits to the children and youths whose parents are unable to support them or those who were born premature, or are suffered from rare diseases, serious illness, or developmental delays; shelters and care for children and youths without parents or guardians or unable to support themselves due to pregnancy or child birth.
(b) *The Senior Citizens Welfare Act*, enacted in 1980, is to maintain dignity, improve health, keep an adequate standard of living, and to protect rights and welfare of the elderly. According to the Act, life subsidies, cash and medical benefits, and pension payments should be provided to the elderly in order to ensure that senior citizens, especially those who are on low-income or lower middle-income, may maintain an adequate standard of living.
(c) *The People with Disabilities Rights Protection Act*[19] is to protect rights and interests of the people with disabilities, ensure their equal opportunity to participate in social, political, economic and cultural activities, achieve independence and their right to development. According to the act, the local governments are to provide people with disabilities, according to their needs, with subsidies for maintaining adequate standard of living, medical care, assistive divorce, day care or housing. In order to protect the right to work of the people with disabilities, the Act requires government agencies, public schools, services and state-owned enterprises (the public sector) with 34 or more employees to hire people with disabilities to at least 3 percent of all employees. Moreover, for private schools,

[18]The Child Welfare Act was first promulgated in 1973 to govern the affairs of children under 12, but it was at most just a gesture of the authoritarian government. It was until the 1990s, the Child Welfare Act was amended to meet the actual needs of children and their families. In 2003, the Act was combined with the Youth Welfare Act, governing the affairs of children between 12 and 18, to become the Child and Youth Welfare Act. The new law was later amended in 2011 and renamed as the Protection of Children and Youths Welfare and Rights Act.

[19]In 1980, the Disabled People's Welfare Act was enacted. It was overhauled and renamed as the Disabled Citizens Protection Act in 1997. In 2007, the Act was again amended and renamed as the People with Disabilities Rights Protection Act.

institutions, and businesses (the private sector) with 67 or more employees, at least 1 percent of their employees should be people with disabilities. Those who fail to meet such requirement are obligated to contribute to the Disabled Employment Fund. The government is also obligated to provide job training services, supportive employment services, and necessary accommodation in the workplace.

(d) *The Indigenous Peoples Basic Law* was promulgated in 2005 to protect the fundamental rights, especially their right to development, of the indigenous people of Taiwan. According to the Act, the government shall protect indigenous people's rights to education, right to work, maintain indigenous culture (article 10), be attended to their housing needs, promote economic empowerment projects, such as community savings and credit cooperatives and other financial cooperatives, and tax credits should be provided to such cooperatives.

The Support to the Family

According to Taiwan Tax rules, tax credits are available to the families with children and dependents. For low-income and lower middle-income families, the social welfare program offers cash benefits and subsidies. In addition, the legislature passed *the Act of Assistance for Family in Hardship*[20] to pay special attention to the family headed by single parent, domestic violence victim, or grandparents. The Act provides subsidies, medical benefits, children nursery allowance, children education allowance, and even subsidies for litigation, as well as loan for career development or business venture. The purpose of this Act is to assist these families to maintain an adequate living standard and to protect children's well-being.

The Right to Health

As stated above, according to *The National Health Insurance Act,* a universal and compulsory health care system has been established. Benefits shall be provided during the insured term under the provisions of this Act, in case of illness, injury or maternity occurred to the insured citizen.

---

[20] In 2000, the Act of Assistance for Woman in Hardship was enacted to help poor single mother households, especially to those single mothers who had suffered from domestic violence or the loss of their spouses. In 2009, the legislature decided to extend such assistance to all single parent households encountered with economic difficulties and promulgated the Act of Assistance for Family in Hardship in 2009.

The Right to Education

According to *the Primary and Junior High School Act,* children between 6 and 15 years of age (the school-age children) shall receive free and compulsory primary and junior high school education. The parents who fail to send their school-age children to school will be fined.[21] In addition, the Act requires the government to provide fellowship and scholarship to children of low-income families. Citizens older than school age who have not received primary and junior high school education shall be provided an opportunity to receive supplementary education. Since 2016, when the Congress passed *the Senior High School Education Act*,[22] senior high school education has become free and compulsory as well. For students with disabilities, local governments and private sectors are encouraged to establish special education schools to meet their needs and protect their right to development.

The "New Poor" Problem and the Legal Responses in Taiwan's Fight Against Poverty

The Social Welfare System

In Taiwan, the "low-income" families are the primary target of most social welfare benefits and services. Households (not individuals) are classified as "low-income" if the family members' combined average monthly income (and property values) does not reach a threshold (estimated monthly minimum) set by each local government (city or county). As the official record shows, only less than 2 percent of Taiwanese people are defined as "poor". However, it has been criticized that the government-set threshold was too low to reflect the needs and reality of the society.[23] In 2011, the government raised the poverty line and allowed another 600,000 people to become eligible for cash benefits. In 2017, several major cities have raised the line again. Since most social assistance and benefits are only available to low-income families, other individuals or families, especially those who are striving to keep themselves above the poverty line, are not getting much public assistance and services. For such struggling-to-get-by individuals and families, any unexpected expenses, traffic accidents or even bad investment could make them tumble into poverty immediately. On the other hand, any extra income or property often worries low-income families for they could lose their eligibility of the public benefits which are so desperately needed. In recent years, Taiwan's long standing "all or nothing" social welfare system, and its underpinning residual welfare ideology, are facing serious challenges. The government is pressured to overhaul this current welfare system to

[21]In recent years, homeschooling has also been legally recognized.

[22]Legislative Yuan Gazette 102:46 (2013).

[23]Tsai (2018), pp. 205–210.

better identify individuals and families in need and to assist people and families of working poor from falling into poverty.

The "New Poor" Problem

In recent years, the emergence of the "new poor" problem has caused great concerns to the society and challenged the conventional concept of poverty defined by the current social welfare system. The "new poor" refers to people who are not usually recognized as disadvantaged and their household income or assets may be above the official poverty line, but in fact they are not earning a decent level of living and often feel insecure or deprived. Although many have not enough cash income to maintain their livings, they are not eligible to public assistance since they are not quality as the low-income or middle lower-income families.

Many people found themselves becomes "new poor" or near poor because they are unemployed or work part-time. Taiwan's economy is driven by exports and under great influence of global market. Since the 1990s, many Taiwanese businesses and factories have relocated to China or south-east Asia countries in response to globalization and Taiwan's difficulties in entering reginal trade agreements. Low-skilled workers have become obvious victims of such transition for they were often the ones left unemployed. Many workers and their families could not bear the economic burden and found themselves tumbling into poverty.[24] Meanwhile, some young adults, even college graduates, were trapped in low paying or part-time jobs. Many of them have to count on family support to stay afloat. Many scholars and activists have concerned about the increase of new poor, working poor, and the growing social/economic inequality in society.[25]

Until recently, Taiwan's welfare system has been relied heavily on the close-knit family system while the state welfare programs played a supplementary role in Taiwan's social security network.[26] However, with the increase of divorce rate, the decline in birth rate, and the population aging, Taiwanese family system is changing fast and this once reliable private safety net has stretched too thin to take on its traditional mission. For example, since the population continues to grow older, the middle-aged people are now financially responsible for their aging parents for a much longer period of time, even with the help of the universal healthcare coverage. For those elderly who are incapable of taking care of themselves, family members have to shoulder the care-taking responsibility. Many of them even have to quit their jobs to take care of their parent(s) full time. It often results in financial difficulty, among other problems, for those families with incompetent elders or patients in needs of long-term care.[27]

---

[24]Li (2007), pp. 198–201.

[25]Lin (2015), pp. 49–50, 62.

[26]Wu (2009), p. 166.

[27]Lin (2010), pp. 148–162.

The credit card debt is another reason why many Taiwanese people went into financial troubles. In the late 1990s, several new banks tried to pursue new customers by aggressively selling credit cards and cash cards. As Taiwan's economy had turned sluggish by then, many people with limited income and resources soon found themselves unable to reimburse their loans and sinking deeper and deeper into debt. Up to 2006, more than half a million people were considered "credit card slaves", referring to those who could hardly pay the minimum balance on their credit card debt every month with no hope to dig themselves out of debt. Unable to pay for living expenses, some debtors became homeless and some even committed suicide. The credit card debt has push many people into poverty and resulted in serious social problems.[28]

Legal Responses

Responding to rapid change and social demands, the legislature reformed *the Public Assistance Act* in 2015. As mentioned above, this Act was based on the assumption that the extended family members would and should take care of their own. Consequently, the social welfare system was designed to assist the household, rather than the individual. However, along with the industrialization and urbanization, the size of Taiwanese family has been shrinking fast and the ties between family members have been not as close-knit as they were in the old days. In other words, for many Taiwanese, the "family safety net" is in crisis. Dealing with the new social reality, the 2015 amendment significantly relax the requirement for applying public assistance and benefits. Although the family/household–centered welfare system remains, the "household" is now much more narrowly defined and the new Act hinted a sign of moving toward individual-based public relief system.

Unemployment has become the major reason contributing for Taiwan's poverty problem. The legislature passed an amendment to *the Employment Insurance Act* in 2015 to order better job training to be provided. More importantly, the Act guarantees that the insured worker is eligible for unemployment benefits in a 6–12 months period, early reemployment incentives, and vocational training living allowance (should the unemployed worker registered with a public employment agency for job placement and full-time vocational training), as well as health insurance premium subsidies for the insured worker and his/her dependents. To implement the law, the Ministry of Labor issued an administrative rule requiring public employment agencies to offer employment counseling, job placement and vocational training.

In order to help the increasing single parent (especially single mother) households, the legislature passed a statute "*the Act of Assistance for Family in Hardship*" offering cash benefits and services to these families under stress. Besides, several local governments set up several fight-against-poverty programs tailored to the needs

[28]Yang (2007), pp. 148–149.

of single parent families. The programs provide various benefits, child care subsidies, job training, extended learning, living expenses, special loans to single mothers with low interest or free interest to start their own business. Moreover, some programs are initiated to help these families to organize savings and credit cooperatives or provide financial empowerment services.[29]

In 2017, the central government launched a pilot program to help the children of low-income or lower middle-income households to receive higher education and better job training for the future. For each child participating in the program, the government deposits 10,000 NT dollars to her account. Encouraging parents to contribute to the account, the government promises to match 100% of the money the parent saves in their child's account up to a maximum of 15,000 NT dollars per year for each child. The interests generated from this saving account is tax free (up to 1000 NT dollars per year). In addition, the money in this account is not considered as the family property so it won't hurt their chance to receive low-income family benefits. Well-received and welcomed by the society, the program was later signed into law titled "*the Act Governing Savings Accounts for Future Education and Development of Children and Youth*".

To deal with the credit card debt crisis, the government issued administrative orders and regulations to order banks to change their practice in selling credit cards and cash cards, including raising the income and job requirements, prohibiting improper and harsh compound interest and debt collecting tactics. In 2006, the bankers' association came to an agreement to establish a Public Asset Management Cooperation to help low-income debtors to restructure and solve their debt. Later in 2007, the legislature passed *the Individual Debtors Repayment Act,* offering the debtors a chance to have a financial fresh start. Under the supervision of the courts, the debtors and banks could work together to settle the debt. Two most important measures of the Act are to prevent debtors from losing their homes during the debt remonstrating period and to allow the debtors to keep basic living expenses.[30] Four years later, the legislature further relaxed the requirements. Since then, more requests have been filed for debt restructure and repayment.[31]

[29]For example, from 2013 to 2019, the New Taipei City initiated "The program for the single-parent vulnerable family development account to fight-against-poverty". To encourage the participant families to save for education or their own business, the government matches every dollar the participants deposit in the account up to a certain amount.

[30]Shyuu (2008), pp. 180–181, 190–194, 200–207.

[31]Judicial Statistics, Statistical table 7 of the Individual Debtors Repayment Act, https://www.judicial.gov.tw/juds/ (last visited Feb. 12, 2019).

Taiwan's Unique Status and International Laws

The Republic of China (ROC) had been a charter member of the United Nations and one of the five permanent members of the Security Council until 1971. On October 1971, according to General Assembly Resolution 2758, People's Republic of China (PRC) was recognized as the sole representation of China. As a result, the Republic of China, Taiwan (hereinafter Taiwan) was no longer recognized as the member of United Nations and thus lost its membership in all the intergovernmental organizations related to the United Nations. Taiwan has been struggling to be officially recognized as in the global community ever since.

Two international instruments on the right to development were signed and ratified before 1971, when ROC still held membership of the UN: *The Charter of the United Nations* and *The International Convention on the Elimination of All Forms of Racial Discrimination.* The former was ratified on September 28 and the latter was ratified on November 14, 1970.

Another two important United Nations human rights instruments on the right of development: *The International Covenant on Civil and Political Rights* and *the International Covenant on Economic, Social and Cultural Rights* were signed on October 5, 1967, but did not complete the ratification process until March 31 2009, when Taiwan was no longer recognized by the UN. Despite the fact that the UN did not accept the deposit of Taiwan's ratification of the two Covenants, Taiwanese government decided to comply with the two Covenants with good faith. The legislature soon passed "*the Act to Implement the International Covenant on Civil and Political Rights and the International Covenant on Economic, Social and Cultural Rights*" on April 22, 2009. The law took effect on December 10, 2009.[32]

In 2007, *the Convention on the Elimination of All Forms of Discrimination against Women* (CEDAW) was ratified on January 5. On May 20, 2011, "*the Enforcement Act of Convention on the Elimination of All Forms of Discrimination against Women*" was enacted to implement CEDAW.[33]

Moreover, although the process of ratification has not yet completed, the *Convention on the Rights of the Child* (CRC) has been recognized by the lawmakers. "*The Implementation Act of the Convention on the Rights of the Child*" was passed on May 20 2014, and took effect on November 20, 2014. The legislature also promulgated "*the Act to Implement the Convention on the Rights of Persons with Disabilities*" in 2014 to implement *The Convention on the Rights of Persons with Disabilities* (CRPD).

Taiwan has now ratified several important international human rights instruments related to the right to development and the fight against poverty, such as ICCPR, ICESCR, CEDAW and CRC. However, after 1971, Taiwan is no longer a member of UN and unable to become an official party state of the above international human right instruments ever since. Unfortunately, it also means that the review

[32]Liao (2010), pp. 96–99, 101–102.

[33]Legislative Yuan Gazette 96:10, 33–35 (2007). Legislative Yuan Gazette 100:42, 60–61 (2011).

mechanisms provided by some treaties, such as ICCPR or CEDAW, are thus not available for Taiwanese individuals.

Nevertheless, Taiwan are willing to comply with human rights treaties and has passed laws to implement ICCPR, ICESCR, CEDAW, CRC and CRPD as stated above. All these implementing domestic laws require the government to render state reports following the guidelines issued by the UN treaty bodies. Moreover, these state reports were reviewed by a group of international human rights experts invited by the government to issue concluding observations and recommendations.[34] The review processes were also fully in line with the UN's practices. Taiwan's initial report on the ICCPR & ICESCR was published in 2012 and reviewed by international human rights experts in 2013. The second state report was published in 2016 and the review was completed in 2017. The local NGOs were invited to participate in the drafting and reviewing procedure of the Taiwanese state report required by ICCPR and ICESCR, as well as CRC, CEDAW and CRPD. Some NGOs provided critical information to the government agencies and give formal comments to the government's state reports. Others even filed their own shadow reports to the reviewers. It is worth noting that the reviewers not only considered information provided by state agencies and the NGOs, they also paid special attention to the court decisions regarding human right issues to monitor how these international conventions were interpreted and implemented in real cases.[35] In the past few years, Taiwan's self-implemented review mechanism has created a platform for dialogues among the reviewers (international human rights law experts), government agencies, local NGOs and the courts, working to further clarify and realize the human rights, including the right to development, in national practice.

References

Chang T-J (2011) On the constitutional right to minimum subsistence guarantee (in Chinese). Chengchi Law Rev 123:121–191

Chen J-h (2011) Taiwan's initial country report of CEDAW and monitoring mechanism for human rights-- a unique case (in Chinese). Taiwan Int Law Q 8(2):53–93

Judicial Statistics, Statistical table 7 of the Individual Debtors Repayment Act, https://www.judicial.gov.tw/juds/ (last visited Feb. 12, 2019)

JY Interpretation No. 382 (1995)

JY Interpretation No. 422 (1997)

JY Interpretation No. 472 (1999)

JY Interpretation No. 485 (1999)

JY Interpretation No. 626 (2007)

JY Interpretation No. 709 (2013)

JY Interpretation No. 711 (2013)

JY Interpretation No. 749 (2017)

[34] Chen (2011), pp. 71–74, 80–84.

[35] Weng (2017), pp. 1119–1120, 1163–1165.

JY Interpretation No. 750 (2017)
Legislative Yuan Gazette 100:42 (2011)
Legislative Yuan Gazette 102:46 (2013)
Legislative Yuan Gazette 83:54 (1994)
Legislative Yuan Gazette 96:10 (2007)
Li S-J (2007) New poverty in Taiwan: the phenomenon and policies (in Chinese). Soochow J Soc Work 17:193–219
Liao FF-T (2010) Local government and domesticalization of international human rights treaties (in Chinese). Taiwan Int Law Q 7(2):75–116
Lin W-I (2010) The coming of an aged society in Taiwan: issues and policies. Asian Soc Work Policy Rev 4(3):148–162
Lin T-H (2015) Causes and consequences of increasing class inequality in Taiwan (in Chinese). Taiwan Econ Forecast Policy 45(2):45–68
Shyuu S-H (2008) The new revolution of the consumer debt clearance system (in Chinese). Natl Taiwan Univ Law J 37(4):179–251
Tsai W-I (2018) The practice of the social assistance to low income families and the policy suggestions in Taiwan (in Chinese). Taiwan Law Rev 277:200–210
Weng VY-C (2017) Dialogue and bargain: mapping the international human rights law to understand the implementation of universal human rights conventions in Taiwan (in Chinese). Natl Taiwan Univ Law J 46(Special Issue):1115–1201
Wu J-N (2009) A study of the amendments to the social assistance act-- supplemental principles (in Chinese). Tunghai Univ Law Rev 30:161–198
Yang S-W (2007) Failure performance of customer loans (credit card and loan card) (in Chinese). Chengchi Law Rev 98:143–182

Chapter 11
Poverty and the Right to Development in the United States of America

Jörg Fedtke

Abstract In Mai 2020, some time after completion of this chapter, America seems to be coming apart at the seams. Fear of SARS-CoV-2 and the countermeasures introduced across the country have left much of the economy in tatters and produced well over 40 million newly unemployed. Many existences, difficult even before this global crisis, have become untenable. Pictures of long lines in front of food banks made international headlines. America, one of the richest societies in the world, is in deep trouble. With economic pain comes civil unrest. Demonstrations, often violent, are paralysing cities across the nation. Triggered by the death of George Floyd in a police incident on the streets of Minneapolis, citizens are expressing deep frustration with not only unequal treatment by law enforcement but also the deteriorating socio-economic situation of many communities. The income gap in America is one of the most pronounced among OECD nations; areas like Los Angeles are experiencing unprecedented numbers of homeless people; staggering differences in the quality of health care are having a measurable impact on the life expectancy of citizens; and spending cuts for public education are coming under judicial scrutiny and putting courts at loggerheads with the executive and legislative branches of government in states like Kansas or Kentucky. This contribution describes the constitutional parameters that shape these dramatic developments and define economic existence in the United States of America. It highlights the very limited protection provided for the essential core of human life (food, water, housing and health care), education or other socio-economic entitlements under both the federal and state constitutions, and contrasts these findings with the elaborate system of statutory social welfare programs that many Americans believe should determine the country's identity but are today under siege in light of budgetary constraints and an increasingly partisan political landscape. The challenges of allocating dwindling public resources to

J. Fedtke (✉)
University of Passau, Passau, Germany

Tulane Law School, New Orleans, LA, USA
e-mail: joerg.fedtke@uni-passau.de

M. Andenas et al. (eds.), *The Fight Against Poverty and the Right to Development*, Ius Comparatum - Global Studies in Comparative Law 52,
https://doi.org/10.1007/978-3-030-57324-9_11

competing needs, problems created by the internal migration of citizens seeking a better future in other parts of the country, tensions caused by significant economic differences between the component parts of a federal system, and America's strained relationship with the international community and global approaches to poverty and development are related themes that feature in this analysis. America, so the conclusion, lacks constitutional consensus about what society must provide in terms of individual socio-economic security. Leaving this decision to the ebb and flow of political majorities is likely to further increase wealth disparity, put considerable pressure on the country's democratic institutions, waste valuable human potential and risk alienating citizens that have lost trust in the ability of the system to provide sufficient opportunity for personal development.

Introduction

The dream of making it from rags to riches is still very much alive in America—as it is, viewed from afar, in the minds of many outside observers. Reality is different. Life in the lower socio-economic strata of contemporary American society is increasingly tough, with fewer success stories to keep alive what must remain a mirage for most.[1] Increasing pressures to introduce or increase minimum wages across the country—despite comparatively low unemployment rates—and bleak data concerning the cost of education, the quality of housing, the level of health care and even life expectancy reflect the dwindling chances, slim in the first place, of leapfrogging upwards individually or, from one generation to the next, as a family. Social mobility is low and income inequality on the rise.[2] The political system is adapting to this development. The field of Democratic hopefuls looking toward the 2020 race for the White House has created a sharply divided political landscape—even by American standards—not just on immigration and the environment but also on a host of broad socio-economic issues including (again) health insurance, education and childcare support.[3] The legal system may be slower to respond. This contribution seeks to summarize the contemporary narrative on poverty and the right to development inside America; sets out what constitutional footholds there are at the federal and state levels to invoke socio-economic entitlements; and analyses critically the limited influence international instruments or doctrines have on this part of

[1]See e.g., the New York Times of 19 November 2018 (*The American Dream is Alive. In China.*).

[2]See Organization for Economic Cooperation and Development (OECD), United States, at https://data.oecd.org/united-states.htm (last accessed 28 February 2019).

[3]See, e.g., reports in the New York Times of 26 August 2018 (*The New Socialists*), 24 January 2019 (*Young Voters Keep Moving to the Left on Social Issues, Republicans Included*), 9 February 2019 (*For Democrats Aiming Taxes at the Superrich, 'the Moment Belongs to the Bold'*), 17 February 2019 (*How Much Will Americans Sacrifice For Good Health Care?*), 19 February 2019 (*Elizabeth Warren proposes Universal Child Care*) and 22 February 2019 (*Democrats for Family Values*).

American law. The final section offers some thoughts about the significance of comparative constitutional experience in the field.

Domestic Law and International Standards

The United States is reluctant to join regional or international legal regimes outside the areas of trade and defence. The keys to understanding this position are manifold. Economic or strategic considerations that *require* the country to engage with the world outside rarely have an equivalent in the realm of human rights. Data protection, an area closely intertwined with commercial interests, is perhaps the only exception.[4] The importance of national sovereignty and a general—and often openly articulated—sense of superiority and exceptionalism among many influential American actors provide additional insight. President Donald Trump's 'America First' (a slogan actually going back to a movement opposing the country's involvement in World War II) is only the most recent expression of a wide spread sentiment, found across the entire political spectrum, that America has little to learn from other nations or international initiatives and—more importantly—will not subject its own national interests, representatives, companies, citizens or, more generally, its legal system to (apparently lesser) external standards. It is therefore hardly a surprise that international expectations regarding socio-economic entitlements have just as little—and likely even less—impact on domestic law as foreign expectations in other policy areas. National law and policy approaches, so the predominant view, are best able to protect the interests, socio-economic or otherwise, of American citizens.

A closer look at particular international and regional instruments confirms this broad assessment. The United States, as explained in the introductory chapter of this volume, is reluctant to ratify international or regional instruments relating to human rights protection generally or the fight against poverty and the right to development in particular. The country signed the American Convention on Human Rights and the International Covenant on Economic, Social and Cultural Rights in 1977 as well as the International Convention on the Rights of the Child in 1995 but did not ratify any of these instruments. The United States is also critical towards the recognition of a *right* to development. It has, however, developed a *national* approach (the Millennium Challenge Account, MCA), which is administered by the Millennium Challenge Corporation (MCC), an independent federal agency created by Congress in 2004, and endorses the United Nations Sustainable Development Goals (SDGs) of 2015.[5]

---

[4]See the cooperation with Switzerland and the European Union with respect to personal data (Privacy Shield).

[5]See the statement on U.S. policy towards the SDGs on the website of USAID at https://www.usaid.gov/GlobalGoals (last accessed on 28 February 2019).

Adequate Living Conditions

The U.S. Constitution of 1789 does not recognize a general right to an adequate standard of living. Obligations to care for the poor—if not the right to an adequate standard of living—are, however, found in some constitutions at the state level. The New York State Constitution declares that 'the aid, care and support of the needy are public concerns and shall be provided by the state and by such of its subdivisions (...) as the legislature may (...) determine.'[6] This amounts to a guiding principle of (state) policy and may be the reason for the steady stream of socio-economic initiatives generated by legislators across the State. Issues covered most recently include paid vacation for private sector workers and minimum wage requirements in New York City. The Constitution of Alabama requires counties 'to make adequate provisions for the maintenance of the poor.'[7]

Specific and Justiciable Socio-Economic Entitlements

The U.S. Constitution does not recognize justiciable socio-economic entitlements. The drafters of the document were primarily concerned with the abuse of government power and left the enjoyment of rights to work, health, education, housing, food or water to be determined by statute. The same is true for guiding principles of state policy, found in systems like India, or the articulation of positive government obligations. The only tangential exception in this context is the—negative—protection of property. A measure of—albeit indirect—protection is offered by equality considerations.

This bleak assessment should be qualified by three observations. First, there has always been *political* concern about socio-economic rights. President Theodore Roosevelt famously articulated their importance, alongside civil and political rights, in his State of the Union Address of 1941:

> The basic things expected by our people of their political and economic systems are simple. They are: equality of opportunity for youth and for others; jobs for those who can work; security for those who need it; the ending of special privilege for the few; the preservation of civil liberties for all; the enjoyment of the fruits of scientific progress in a wider and constantly rising standard of living. These are the simple, the basic things that must never be lost sight of in the turmoil and unbelievable complexity of our modern world. The inner and abiding strength of our economic and political systems is dependent upon the degree to which they fulfil these expectations.[8]

Roosevelt's legislative agenda was driven, inter alia, by the need to create jobs and improve working conditions; the desire to secure a pay that provides for

[6]New York State Constitution (1938), Article XVII.

[7]Constitution of Alabama (1901), Section 88.

[8]F. D. Roosevelt, *The Four Freedoms*—speech delivered on 6 January 1941.

adequate food, clothing and recreation; the wish to ensure decent homes for families; the concern about adequate medical care and the opportunity to achieve and enjoy good health; the right to adequate protection from the economic fears of old age, sickness, accident and unemployment; and the right to a good education.[9] Presidents Lyndon B. Johnson and Richard Nixon took Roosevelt's legacy forward by putting in place significant social programs. The success of these political efforts is mixed. More than seven decades since Roosevelt, and despite much progress in a number of these areas, large parts of his progressive agenda remain unfulfilled. Contemporary conflicts over health care, the enforcement of minimum wage requirements or living conditions in inner city areas show, however, that the country remains deeply engaged in the debate over socio-economic entitlements. The financial resources dedicated to health care, housing or education (both by government at various levels of the system and philanthropy) are substantial. There is, without doubt, a 'constituent commitment'[10] to socio-economic policy in the sense that American society will expect a certain level of action by governments at all levels of the system with respect to meeting the core needs of its citizens regardless of specific duties enshrined in constitutional law.[11]

A second point to make is that at least *some* socio-economic entitlements have for *some time* entered the bloodstream of federal constitutional law—despite their continued absence from the *text* of the U.S. Constitution—via decisions of the U.S. Supreme Court (USSC). The support of Roosevelt's administration for socio-economic rights generally translated into wider national (congressional) power in the area. Connections between interstate commerce and labour practices,[12] equality and education (concerning racially segregated public school systems),[13] poverty and criminal law (free legal representation on their first appeal of a criminal conviction),[14] the right to free movement and the receipt of social welfare benefits (waiting period for new residents in California),[15] and the constitutional protection of property and social welfare entitlements (property interest in social security)[16] were acknowledged by the USSC between the late 1930s and mid-1970s. An increasingly restrictive approach of the Court, following judicial appointments by President Nixon and starting with *Dundridge v. Williams*, brought this jurisprudence to a halt. In *Dundridge*, the USSC confirmed that the U.S. Constitution contains no affirmative state obligation to care for the poor.[17] The decision was followed by

[9]F. D. Roosevelt, State of the Union Message to Congress of 11 January 1944.

[10]Sunstein (2004), p. 62.

[11]Michelman (2008), pp. 664–666.

[12]*National Labor Relations Board v. Jones & Laughlin Steel Corporation*, 301 U.S. 1 (1937).

[13]*Brown v. Board of Education*, 347 U.S. 483 (1954).

[14]*Douglas v. California*, 372 U.S. 353 (1963).

[15]*Shapiro v. Thompson*, 394 U.S. 618 (1969).

[16]*Mathews v. Eldridge*, 424 U.S. 319 (1975).

[17]*Dundridge v. Williams*, 397 U.S. 471 (1970).

restrictive rulings concerning housing (eviction proceedings)[18] and the right to education.[19] This trend has continued in recent years.[20]

Some socio-economic entitlements, finally, can be found at state level. This is true for the right to education, which is mentioned in state constitutions across the country and has been litigated successfully not only in the context of *equal access* claims but also with respect to *adequate (substantive) levels of education*.[21] A particularly striking decision in terms of the right to adequate education is *Gannon v. Kansas*, which displays the increasing willingness of state judges to inquire into the levels of public financing as well as the substantive quality of public school curricula.[22] Other areas sometimes addressed in state constitutions are welfare assistance,[23] housing[24] and health care.[25] Some of these provisions have provided individual entitlements such as the right to emergency shelter for homeless persons in New York[26] while others merely place obligations on states to expand access via legislative programs and funding. The latter is largely true for the provision of health care.

Remedies

Individual remedies related to the fight against poverty or the right to development, widely defined, depend very much on the system engaged (federal or state) and the entitlement involved. Actions aimed at judicial review offer the best chances of success; in many of the cases cited in this chapter, individual relief was provided simply by invalidating unconstitutional state legislation that restricted access to a particular entitlement. Decisions that are more exceptional have required public authorities to actively provide relief. State courts have thus crafted remedies that oblige public authorities to offer a sufficient number of beds and prescribe in some

---

[18] *Lindsay v. Normet*, 405 U.S. 56 (1972).

[19] *San Antonio Independent School District v. Rodriguez*, 411 U.S. 1 (1973).

[20] See, e.g., *Department of Housing and Urban Development v. Rucker*, 535 U.S. 125 (2002) concerning the eviction of residents from public housing units in cases of drug-related activities by a household member or guest and *Kelo v. City of New London*, Connecticut, 125 S. Ct. 2655 concerning the confiscation of property on the basis of eminent domain power for the purpose of economic development.

[21] See, e.g., *Edgewood Independent School District v. Kirby*, 777 S.W.2d 391 (Texas 1989); *Rose v. Council for Better Education*, 790 S.W.2d 186 (Kentucky 1989) and *Campaign for Fiscal Equality v. The State of New York*, 719 N.Y.S.2d 475 (New York 2001).

[22] *Gannon v. State of Kansas*, P.3d 1196 (Kansas 2014).

[23] New York State Constitution (1938), Article XVII.

[24] Ibid. Article XVIII.

[25] Alaska, Hawaii, Michigan, Mississippi, North Carolina, New York, South Carolina and Wyoming.

[26] *Callahan v. Carey, New York County Supreme Court*, Index No. 42582/79.

detail the spatial and sanitary arrangements that have to be made for individuals in need of emergency shelter.[27] In the large majority of instances, however, courts have refrained from ordering specific remedies and left it to the executive and legislative branches of government to address perceived shortcomings—for example with respect to the financing of schools, curricular standards, the training of school teachers or the physical infrastructure of educational facilities (desks, chairs and textbooks)—in ways deemed most appropriate in light of competing policy considerations. Courts take a similar position when it comes to the constitutional duty of states to provide health care. This speaks to the cautious approach that American judges take with regard to disputes that raise separation of powers issues.

National Claims and International Review Mechanisms

The link between the enforcement of socio-economic entitlements at the national level and regional and/or international review mechanisms is tenuous at best. As pointed out above, there is considerable reluctance in the United States to subject its own national interests, representatives, companies, citizens or, more generally, its legal system to external standards or control by outside courts, tribunals or commissions. U.S. courts often display considerable reluctance to engage with foreign ideas or principles of international law. This is particularly true for the area of human rights protection. The comparative argument as well as references to international instruments are nevertheless advocated as a strategy to engage with the world outside on matters of mutual concern[28] and, in particular, to move state courts towards a more progressive stance in the interpretation of state constitutions.[29]

Essential Core and Progressive Realization in U.S. Law

The 'essential core' approach or strategies attempting to achieve the protection of socio-economic entitlements progressively or as a function of growing economic government capacity do not have a clear domestic parallel in U.S. legislation or case law. Emergency medical treatment is free of charge and must be offered to the needy regardless of their health insurance status; and the provision of emergency shelter has been identified as a core obligation under state constitutional law. These 'entitlements' arguably reflect essential core thinking. Limited resources and competing public needs, factors closely linked to the debate surrounding the realization

[27] *Callahan Consent Decree: Establishing a Legal Right to Shelter for Homeless Individuals in New York City* (August 1981).

[28] Jackson (2007), p. 7 ff.

[29] Albisa and Schultz (2009), p. 248.

of socio-economic rights in light of finite capacities, feature in the national conversation surrounding health care, housing, or food stamps. Courts tend to see limited government resources as a reason to limit judicial intervention in cases involving socio-economic claims and have not established a link between (potentially) growing public budgets and a corresponding realization of socio-economic entitlements. There is currently very little expectation that this is set to change in the years to come. This is especially true in times of shrinking public budgets.

The U.S. Contribution to International Developments in the Field

The U.S. Constitution—very much a product of a different age—does not address the fight against poverty or a right to development beyond the country's borders. Scepticism, in particular, towards the recognition of a right to development played out in the United Nations on occasion of the vote on the 1986 General Assembly Declaration on the Right to Development; the United States was the only country to oppose the Declaration.[30] Subsequent initiatives by the United Nations have received negative responses from Washington for decades.[31] A shift in this position occurred under the administration of President Barack Obama—the United States does endorse the United Nations Sustainable Development Goals of 2015.[32] It should be noted, however, that the granting of foreign aid has for a long time been institutionally linked to and regarded as part of foreign policy and, more specifically, as an integral component of national security considerations. Diplomacy and international development efforts complement military capacity as key instruments in shaping the country's national security strategy. Federal spending on development has been considerable in the past, regardless of the wider political outlook of the White House, and it is only under President Trump that serious budget cuts have been suggested in this area.

More importantly, there have always been striking similarities between the international approach to development and its functional equivalents in the United States. This suggests that opposition to an international model of development is more political in nature than a question of substance. Much of the dispute stems from the American insistence that the provision of development aid remain a sovereign political decision of donor countries rather than a binding obligation under international law. Other reasons include the country's own experience with development (based on self-reliance, entrepreneurship and economic liberty); insistence on the promotion of civil and political rights as a key ingredient of a successful development strategy; the belief that the right to development is aspirational and progressive

[30]Resolution 128/41 was passed with a vote of 146:1 with eight abstentions.

[31]For a summary of the position of the U.S. see Marks (2004), pp. 141–152.

[32]Resolution A/70/1 of 25 September 2015.

in character rather than a fundamental and enforceable entitlement; and jurisdictional concerns with respect to adjacent areas of international law (in particular international trade) that should not be conflated with—and possibly compromised by—human rights considerations. The United States again raised these issues in the context of the United Nations Sustainable Development Goals. The U.S. were happy to see a strong recognition of the need to eradicate extreme poverty (Goal 1) but issued critical statements with respect to potential ripple effects on related policy areas (in particular trade); the decisions, processes, actions, and governance of autonomous institutions such as the World Trade Organization (WTO); the integrity TRIPS;[33] and the voluntary nature of any technology transfer.[34] The right to development was again singled out as a 'non-binding and non-consensus document' that should not be specifically referenced in the Post-2015 Development Agenda.[35] This general policy outlook is unlikely to change for some time should Republicans retain their hold on national politics after November 2020.

The U.S. approach to development at the international level—despite the country's criticism of many initiatives pursued by the United Nations in past decades—nevertheless features many conceptual similarities with the right to development as set out in the 1986 Declaration. A rough comparison between the Declaration and what is perhaps the closest U.S. equivalent, the Millennium Challenge Account, shows that both recognise a duty of developed nations to share their wealth by committing substantial resources to the task; a need for accountability and good governance on the side of recipient nations; a focus on health, education and food; active cooperation (partnership) with respect to specific projects; and economic growth as a key to development.[36] The U.S. approach may, however, place more emphasis on what are regarded sound economic policies that foster enterprise and entrepreneurship including, inter alia, open markets, sustainable budget policies, and initiatives of the private sector.[37] Another difference lies in the choice of the performance indicators that determine the eligibility of projects for funding. The MCA focuses less on human rights considerations and more on government effectiveness, the control of corruption, the rule of law, macro-economic factors (such as a country's credit rating, inflation rate or budget deficit), and an empowerment of the private sector. Development through economic growth, finally, is perhaps the third element which distinguishes the U.S. approach (albeit in a nuanced fashion) from the right to development as endorsed by the majority of countries. Free market principles, increased productivity and the creation of jobs play a decisive role here.

---

[33] WTO Agreement on Trade-Related Aspects of Intellectual Property Rights of 1995.

[34] *Closing statement and explanation of position by Ambassador Elizabeth Cousens, U.S. Representative to the Economic and Social Council, at the Open Working Group on Sustainable Development Goals*, New York (19 July 2014).

[35] *U.S. Statement on July 30 Draft, Post-2015 Intergovernmental Negotiations* (30 July 2015).

[36] On the Millennium Challenge Corporation generally see Tarnoff (2018).

[37] USAID, *Millennium Challenge Account* (Press Release of 3 June 2002).

The International Right to Development from a U.S. Perspective

The United States, as indicated above, formally endorses the Sustainable Development Goals; the key national agency in the area, the U.S. Agency for International Development (USAID), subscribes to the SDGs. That said, there are serious doubts about the level of engagement in future years. The Joint Strategy Plan of the U.S. State Department and USAID for 2018–2022 clearly focuses on the strategic interests of the United States and harnesses the potential of USAID for the benefit of the country's global political reach and national economic development.[38] Goal 2.2 of the Joint Strategy Plan thus states that the U.S. will 'promote healthy, educated and productive populations in partner countries to drive inclusive and sustainable development, *open new markets and support U.S. prosperity and security objectives*.'[39] The document does not at any point mention the international right to development model or the United Nations Sustainable Development Goals. The website of the Department of State provides only a mere link to the SDGs.[40] This suggests that engagement of the United States in the global conversation and the 2015 consensus on the right to development is waning.

The Sustainable Development Goals in the U.S.

The United States does have a policy framework in place that is in large part compatible with the Sustainable Development Goals, including SDG 1 (end poverty in all its forms everywhere), and is administered by agencies like USAID and the Millennium Challenge Corporation. USAID's mission statement, a key component of the agency's development policy,[41] currently states:

> On behalf of the American people, we promote and demonstrate democratic values abroad, and advance a free, peaceful, and prosperous world. In support of America's foreign policy, the U.S. Agency for International Development leads the U.S. Government's international development and disaster assistance through partnerships and investments that save lives, reduce poverty, strengthen democratic governance, and help people emerge from humanitarian crises and progress beyond assistance.
>
> Our objective is to support partners to become self-reliant and capable of leading their own development journeys. We make progress toward this by reducing the reach of conflict, preventing the spread of pandemic disease, and counteracting the drivers of violence, instability, transnational crime and other security threats. We promote American prosperity

[38] U.S. Department of State and U.S. Agency for International Development, Joint Strategic Plan FY 2018–2022 (February 2018), 3 (Goals 1–4).

[39] Ibid. Goal 2.2. (emphasis provided by the author).

[40] See https://www.state.gov/globalgoals/ (last accessed on 28 February 2019).

[41] See USAID, ADS Chapter 200, Development Policy, at 200.3.3.1.

> through investments that expand markets for U.S. exports; create a level playing field for U.S. businesses; and support more stable, resilient, and democratic societies. We stand with people when disaster strikes or crisis emerges as the world leader in humanitarian assistance.[42]

There are a few marked and a number of more nuanced differences between the U.S. model of international development and its United Nations counterpart, but while these seemed to have mattered less in practice under the administration of President Obama the gap has again widened considerably under his successor. The Joint Strategy Plan of the U.S. Department of State and USAID, published only very recently, defines the country's development policy through the prism of U.S. security and economic interests. International cooperation aimed at combatting poverty as a global challenge *regardless* of immediate national interests is not part of this strategy. This is not to say that future U.S.-funded development initiatives will completely disengage from the Sustainable Development Goals of 2015. Paired with the expected long-term budget cuts for both diplomacy and development cooperation, the right to development as conceptualised by the U.N. General Assembly will, however, very likely receive less support from the United States.

The Role of Civil Society in U.S. Development Policy

USAID, which administers by far the largest share of U.S. funding, maintains elaborate programming policy guidelines that are transparent but largely driven by the organization itself and coordinated with the Department of State. This programming framework is described as evidence-based, inclusive, sustainable and coherent.[43] In particular, USAID declares that development policies be

> inclusive by ensuring practices and approaches are grounded in participation, non-discrimination, and accountability. All groups of people should be able to participate in development programs, share the benefits of such efforts, and participate in decision-making processes.[44]

The ability of individuals or NGOs to engage with U.S. development or anti-poverty policy is nevertheless limited. The most significant way of interacting with USAID is at the level of specific development projects. The private sector is encouraged to participate in common initiatives but these are based on the development goals already set by USAID rather than a collaborative process leading up to a common definition of what should be achieved in conceptual terms.

[42] See https://www.usaid.gov/who-we-are/mission-vision-values.

[43] USAID, ADS Chapter 200, Development Policy, at 200.3.1.

[44] Ibid. at 200.3.2.1.

International Agreements

The United States, as pointed out above, is reluctant to enter into binding international policy agreements concerning the fight against poverty or the right to development. The main obstacle to bi- or multilateral agreements in this policy area is the fear that they could compromise national sovereignty with respect to the aims pursued and resources deployed. While the United States does engage with other players, both public and private, at the level of specific development projects (both USAID and the Millennium Challenge Account interact with a large number of partner countries in executing U.S. development policy), it is not a system that would provide much guidance with respect to the creation and implementation of legal mechanisms that could be adopted at the regional or global levels.

The most visible engagement of the United States with the fight against poverty or the right to development in recent years is the Millennium Challenge Account, together with the Millennium Challenge Corporation, which was created by U.S. Congress in 2004 to emulate unilaterally at the national level the 1986 General Assembly Declaration on the Right to Development. The initiative is focused on good governance and development through economic growth. The budget allocated to it is far smaller than initially planned but not insubstantial. In conceptual terms, the initiative is geared towards a competitive process that rewards countries for past actions measured by objective performance indicators. It seeks to reduce poverty mainly through economic growth; focuses its resources on countries that feature broad-based civil society involvement; requires recipient countries to create similar development funds, agencies and programs (known as 'compacts'); and places much emphasis on accountability and public transparency.[45] Candidate countries must fall below the threshold of upper-middle income nations established by the World Bank. The limit for 2017 was a Gross National Income (GNI) per capita of $3955. Local sustainability, effective measures to curb corruption, and local ownership of the envisaged development effort—including substantial stakeholder participation—are further indicators for support.[46] Measurable results are critical.[47] Congress is, however, debating substantial budget cuts in this area; resources available to the Account could be reduced by as much as 11% in the mid-term.

[45]Tarnoff (2018), 1/2.

[46]See MCC, Compact Development Guidance, at https://www.mcc.gov/resources/pub-pdf/guidance-compact-development-guidance.

[47]For a summary of MCC's mission see MCC, *NEXT: A Strategy for MCC's Future*, available at https://www.mcc.gov/resources/doc/next.

Comparative Constitutional Law

Constitutional transition and reform—including socio-economic rights, the distribution of resources within a country, and challenges of multi-level governance—have been key issues in many regions over the past decade. Questions of development, including constitutional mechanisms that help establish and secure even levels of social and economic opportunity across a given territory, are often discussed but rarely given sufficient attention in the drafting of new constitutional arrangements.

The constitutional framework of a country can support or stifle development. Three points deserve emphasis. Systems like South Africa display—sometimes quite dramatically[48]—the limits of constitutionally protected socio-economic rights in light of limited government resources. Despite these challenges, these systems also seem to offer some potential for long-term success given that the constitutional framework creates powerful incentives for gradual but sustained, transparent and accountable legislative and administrative efforts with respect to key areas such as health care, food, water, housing and education. The United States, conversely, also displays quite dramatic shortcomings in just these areas despite comparatively vast resources but very limited constitutional socio-economic entitlements. This suggests that development efforts at the national, regional or global level should also take into account constitutional mechanisms that can help address poverty and inequality. Constitutional and non-constitutional tools need to be combined.

Another observation concerns the distribution of development efforts within a country. Experience from Germany (in the years following reunification of West Germany and the German Democratic Republic in 1990) or the United Kingdom (growing economic disparity between Greater London and the rest of the country) indicates that uneven levels of access to socio-economic opportunities can undermine the political stability of a system and lead to internal migration—and in the worst case displacement—with additional and long-term consequences for the provision of populations with adequate housing, health care, education or economic opportunities. Constitutional safeguards such as specific rules on the distribution of resources between different levels of government via mechanisms of financial equalization, rights to local or regional socio-economic development or—more generally—a paradigm of constitutionally encouraged cooperation between political adversaries, different tiers of government or historically distinct parts of a country (cooperative forms of governance) can help limit the risk of uneven development. Federalism in the United States, by contrast, is characterized by a highly competitive approach to the distribution of resources that relies more on political deals involving the exercise of federal authority to spend for the general welfare[49] than constitutionally defined mechanisms that might foster even development across the country. The

[48]See the difficult choices that had to be made by the Constitutional Court of South Africa in *Soobramoney v Minister of Health* (Case CCT 32/97) and *Government of the Republic of South Africa and Others v Grootboom and Others* (Case CCT 11/00).

[49]Art. 1, Section 8 U.S. Constitution.

economic disparity between states—often a result of geographic coincidence rather than political acumen—is as pronounced as their varying ability to provide for their citizens. This leads to considerable interstate migration and all the negative consequences that come with it for both the regions left behind and those attracting large numbers of incoming migrants seeking jobs, housing or schools. The bicentennial census and corresponding adjustment of congressional districts makes this process very visible as far as the representation of states in the House of Representatives is concerned.

Constitutional engineering, finally, is not limited to the area of socio-economic rights or even specific development efforts within a country. Reforms of the Constitution of Egypt in 2014 attempted to tie specific shares of the national GDP to socio-economic efforts such as the improvement of health care[50] or the education system.[51] It is not clear whether these mechanisms will achieve the desired effect especially in light of the considerable uncertainties concerning their legal (rather than political) enforcement. Developments in Egypt since the overthrow of the Muslim Brotherhood and the constitutional reforms of 2014 cast considerable doubt on the effectiveness of this approach. The Egyptian case shows, however, that a range of different constitutional tools can foster development and that a more creative use of the discipline may bear more fruit in the future.[52]

Legal frameworks support development. This is particularly true with respect to constitutional law. Substantive entitlements, administrative procedures, development as an obligation of the state or a right of particular regions, the distribution of resources or the dedication of shares of the national GDP to specific socio-economic needs are good examples of how constitutional engineering can not only raise awareness for but also offer mechanisms to resolve conflicts surrounding poverty and the lack of development. Human rights protection more generally and safeguards against corruption provide further examples.

Conclusion

America has many lessons to offer when it comes to the choice between addressing socio-economic needs through constitutional law or (ordinary) social legislation. The U.S. Constitution was drafted at a time when much emphasis was placed on the protection of rights and freedoms from undue government interference; it is a system that focusses on the defensive dimension of human rights protection. The need for socio-economic safeguards has since been acknowledged by many observers but never developed sufficient momentum to overcome the considerable hurdles

[50] Constitution of Egypt (2014), Article 18.

[51] Ibid. Article 19.

[52] On constitutional transition in Egypt see Carter Center, Pre-Referendum Statement of January 6, 2014.

connected to formal constitutional amendment. Such change is not likely to happen in the near future either, which means that statutory reforms of the social security system—widely defined—will continue to determine the political agenda especially in election times. Disputes in distinct areas like education may also invite the courts to play a more active role in the protection of socio-economic entitlements. The internal pressure to provide more opportunities to disadvantaged individuals and communities is, in any case, very likely to increase. Will these developments translate into a different outlook with respect to America's engagement with the outside world? The picture that emerges from this analysis suggests that the differences between the United States and the international community with respect to combatting poverty and fostering development may be too large to overcome anytime soon. Recent decisions of the Trump administration, for example its stance on the World Health Organization, indicate that the gap is more likely to widen. A change in the country's leadership would probably soften this position but America's approach to most of the issues discussed in this chapter has followed a clear trajectory for decades regardless of the general political outlook of changing majorities in Washington. This trajectory is not likely to change.

References

Albisa C, Schultz J (2009) The United States. In: Langford M (ed) Social rights jurisprudence. CUP, p 230

Jackson V (2007) Transnational challenges to constitutional law: convergence, resistance, engagement. Fed Law Rev 7

Marks S (2004) The human right to development: between rhetoric and reality. Harv Hum Rights J 137

Michelman FI (2008) Socioeconomic rights in constitutional law: explaining America away. ICON 6:663

Sunstein CR (2004) The Second American Revolution: FDR's unfinished revolution and why we need it more than ever. Basic Books

Tarnoff C (April 2018) (Congressional Research Service), Millennium Challenge Corporation

Chapter 12
The International Dimensions of the Right to Development: Enabling Poverty-Reduction in Domestic Legal Orders by a Reformed International Legal Order

Olivier De Schutter

Abstract The right to development can only be fully realized if we take into account the interdependency of States, and if we take seriously the duty to reshape the global environment in which they operate. Such international obligations include both extraterritorial obligations imposed on States as regards their unilateral actions or omissions, insofar as such actions or omissions can affect people or situations outside their territories and/or jurisdiction; and global obligations, which concern States acting collectively in global and regional partnerships. This report clarifies the normative content of these international obligations. It first lists a number of areas directly relevant to the realization of the right to development in which, in recent years, States have achieved a broad consensus, and it notes the advances achieved in general international law to improve the coherence of global governance, by building bridges between the different regimes. It then provides a conceptual framework, emphasizing in particular the status of the obligation of States to cooperate with one another with a view to adopting new international agreements. It then then applies the conceptual framework to six key areas in which the international environment should be improved in order to enable domestic poverty-reduction efforts at domestic level: the management of the foreign debt, which requires in particular that loans take into account the impact of adjustment programmes on the right to development and that States act against vulture funds; the elimination of illicit financial flows, by strengthening the fight against tax evasion and transfer pricing within multinational

This contribution is based on the study prepared by the author for the United Nations Working Group on the Right to Development, "The international dimensions of the right to development: a fresh start towards improving accountability" (UN doc. A/HRC/WG.2/19/CRP.1).

O. De Schutter (✉)
Centre for Philosophy of Law (CPDR), Institute for Interdisciplinary Research in Legal Sciences (JUR-I), University of Louvain (UCL), Ottignies-Louvain-la-Neuve, Belgium
e-mail: olivier.deschutter@uclouvain.be

M. Andenas et al. (eds.), *The Fight Against Poverty and the Right to Development*, Ius Comparatum - Global Studies in Comparative Law 52,
https://doi.org/10.1007/978-3-030-57324-9_12

groups; the improvement of the effectiveness of development cooperation policies; the design of trade and investment policies so as to further the realization of the right to development; and the establishment of universal social protection floors. The report closes, finally, with a proposal to build on the mechanisms established to ensure policy coherence for sustainable development in order to institutionalize the assessment of the extraterritorial human rights impacts of measures adopted by States, as well as of the positions they take in international negotiations.

Introduction

When it adopted the Declaration on the Right to Development on 4 December 1986, the General Assembly of the United Nations defined the right to development as "an inalienable human right by virtue of which every human person and all peoples are entitled to participate in, contribute to, and enjoy economic, social, cultural and political development, in which all human rights and fundamental freedoms can be fully realized".[1] Although the Declaration is not, as such, binding international law, many of its provisions are anchored in binding legal instruments, including the Charter of the United Nations[2] and human rights treaties: as such, the Declaration can be seen as making explicit and bringing together a number of obligations already well recognized in international law, to highlight their contribution to a human-centered form of development, and to the establishment of a social and international order in which all the rights of the Universal Declaration of Human Rights can be realized.[3]

The right to development however shall only be achieved if States accept corresponding duties, and if such duties are effectively monitored. This requires strengthening the consensus on the normative components of the right, as well as on appropriate indicators to measure compliance. Such a consensus has proven particularly difficult to achieve as regards the international dimensions of the right to development, i.e., the dimensions that go beyond the adoption by States of measures that affect only people on their national territories and/or subject to their jurisdiction. The objective of this report is to help to overcome the obstacles to such a consensus.

[1] A/RES/41/128 (4 Dec. 1986), art. 1. The Declaration was adopted by 146 votes to 1, with 8 abstentions. Neither the definition of the right to development nor the Declaration in its entirety refer to sustainable development, particularly in its environmental dimension. This dimension was added with the Rio Principles adopted at the United Nations Conference on Environment and Development of 3–14 June 1992 (A/CONF.151/26). The Vienna Declaration and Programme of Action, adopted by the World Conference on Human Rights on 25 June 1993 and endorsed by General Assembly resolution 48/121 of 20 December 1993, proclaimed that "The right to development should be fulfilled so as to meet equitably the developmental and environmental needs of present and future generations" (para. 11). This was reaffirmed most prominently in the 2030 Development Agenda.

[2] Charter of the United Nations (June 26, 1945), 59 Stat. 1031, *entered into force* Oct. 24, 1945.

[3] GA Res. 217, UN GAOR, 3d sess., UN Doc. A/810 (1948) (Art. 28).

In order to achieve this, it builds on recent advances of international human rights law, in order to illustrate how such advances can breathe new life into the international dimensions of the right to development. Since it was first enunciated in 1986, and especially since the launch of the first attempts to define criteria which could be used to measure progress in its realization,[4] the right to development has been lost in debates on criteria and operational sub-criteria, partly due to disagreement over the concept and its normative content. Far from facilitating the achievement of a consensus, the proposals made so far have proven both divisive politically, and—because the proposals that were made came to diverge from the methodology designed to measure compliance with other human rights, and used in other parts of the UN human rights system—difficult to incorporate in human rights monitoring. The result is that, more than 30 years after its proclamation, the right to development remains contested and has not been utilized as a human right enshrining obligations for which States can be held accountable. It continues to be the subject of academic interest and political rhetoric and debate, but its significance is largely confined to intergovernmental debates.

This report proposes a new start. It identifies a number of reasons why the time has come to further strengthen the international dimensions of the right to development. It then recalls the three levels of obligations that correspond to the right to development—national, extraterritorial, and global—each of which poses specific challenges. Next, focusing on the so-called "international" dimensions of the right to development, which include the extraterritorial and the global obligations of States, it seeks to identify the key normative components of the right. It proceeds in two steps. It first offers a conceptual framework. It then applies that framework to six key areas in which the international environment should be improved in order to enable efforts at implementing poverty-reduction strategies at domestic level that can contribute to realizing the right to development. For the realization of the right to development, priority attention should be given to managing the debt burden; addressing illicit financial flows; improving the design of development cooperation policies; directing trade and channelling foreign direct investment towards the realization of the right to development; and supporting the establishment of social protection floors.

Finally, the report closes with a proposal to build on the mechanisms established to ensure policy coherence for sustainable development in order to institutionalize the assessment of the extraterritorial human rights impacts of measures adopted by States, as well as of the positions they take in international negotiations (VI).

[4]The search for such criteria was initiated by para. 171 of the Report prepared by the Secretary-General pursuant to Commission on Human Rights resolution 1989/45 (E/CN.4/1990/9/Rev.1) (26 Sept. 1990), where it was noted that: "The formulation of criteria for measuring progress in the realization of the right to development will be essential for the success of future efforts to implement that right. Such criteria must address the process of development as well as its results; quality as well as quantity; the individual as well as social dimension of human needs; and material as well as intellectual and cultural needs. Both objective and subjective measurements must be included in any analysis".

Although the study does include an examination of the duties of States to control transnational corporations and to ensure that international organisations of which they are members comply with the right to development, its focus is exclusively on States. It seeks to clarify the duties that are imposed on States by the Declaration on the Right to Development and the normative instruments in which the Declaration is grounded, in order to contribute to making the right to development operational in the United Nations human rights machinery. This is not to deny, of course, the important role of non-State actors (including transnational corporations and international intergovernmental and non-governmental organizations) in the realization of the right to development;[5] but that would be the topic of another study.

Three Opportunities

Victories of Multilateralism

The present context provides a number of opportunities. First, a number of international agreements or consensus documents have been adopted in recent years, on which the interpretation of the Declaration on the Right to Development can build. They include in particular the Rio Declaration on Environment and Development, adopted in 1992,[6] and the outcome document "The Future We Want" adopted at the United Nations Conference on Sustainable Development convened in Rio de Janeiro from 20 to 22 June 2012;[7] the Addis Ababa Action Agenda of the Third International

---

[5]See for instance, on the roles of the World Bank and the International Monetary Fund, the reports by the Independent Expert on the promotion of a democratic and equitable international order (in particular the report submitted to 36th session of the Human Rights Council (A/HRC/36/40) and to the 72nd session of the General Assembly (A/72/187), respectively on the World Bank and on the impact of the conditionality of loans from the International Monetary Fund on development and human rights); and the report of the Special Rapporteur on extreme poverty and human rights on the World Bank and human rights, submitted to the 70th session of the General Assembly (A/70/274). As regards the role of transnational corporations, the Committee on Economic, Social and Cultural Rights observes that "In certain jurisdictions, individuals enjoy direct recourse against business entities for violations of economic, social and cultural rights, whether in order to impose on such private entities (negative) duties to refrain from certain courses of conduct or to impose (positive) duties to adopt certain measures or to contribute to the fulfilment of such rights" (General Comment No. 24 on State obligations under the International Covenant on Economic, Social and Cultural Rights in the context of business activities (E/C.12/GC/24), para. 4 (citing Constitutional Court of South Africa, *Daniels v. Scribante and others*, case CCT 50/16, judgment of 11 May 2017, paras. 37–39 (leading judgment by J. Madlanga) (positive duties imposed on the owner to ensure the right to security of tenure in conditions that comply with the requirements of human dignity)). Indeed, the idea that corporations may be imposed to comply with human rights, including with economic, social and cultural rights, is increasingly accepted: see, e.g., International Centre for Settlement of Investment Disputes case No. ARB/07/26, *Urbaser S.A. and others v. Argentina* (award of 8 December 2016), paras. 1194 and 1195.

[6]A/CONF.151/26.

[7]Endorsed by General Assembly resolution 66/288, adopted on 11 September 2012.

Conference on Financing for Development, adopted in 2015,[8] which builds on the 2002 Monterrey Consensus and the 2008 Doha Declaration on Financing for Development; the 2030 Agenda for Sustainable Development,[9] as summarized in the Sustainable Development Goals, adopted in 2015; and the Paris Agreement, adopted on 13 December 2015 under the United Nations Framework Convention on Climate Change, and in force since 4 November 2016.[10] Standard-setting has also made progress within the Human Rights Council, in a number of areas directly related to the implementation of the right to development. Major achievements include the endorsement of the Guiding Principles on Business and Human Rights[11] by the Human Rights Council in resolution 17/4; of the Guiding Principles on Foreign Debt and Human Rights,[12] by resolution 20/10; and of the Guiding Principles on Extreme Poverty and Human Rights,[13] by resolution 21/11. In the areas covered by the International Labour Organisation, the adoption by the International Labour Conference of the 2012 Recommendation (No. 202) concerning National Floors of Social Protection[14] and of the 2016 Resolution concerning decent work in global supply chains[15] are significant advances.

This list of achievements is striking by its heterogeneity, whether we consider the status of these various documents or their subject-matter. It is also very incomplete. It does illustrate, however, the ability of the international community to achieve consensus on certain issues essential for the realization of the right to development, where the right conditions are present. The further implementation of the right to development should build on this consensus, rather than seek to develop in isolation. Considering the full implications that can be drawn from these instruments and consensus documents, significant progress could be achieved in clarifying the content of the international dimensions of the right to development. Moreover, as this report will illustrate, the interpretation of international human rights law has developed significantly in recent years, particularly as regards the extraterritorial and global dimensions of States' obligations under the human rights treaties they have

[8]Adopted at the Third International Conference on Financing for Development (Addis Ababa, Ethiopia, 13–16 July 2015) and endorsed by the General Assembly in its resolution 69/313 of 27 July 2015.

[9]A/RES/70/1.

[10]FCCC/CP/2015/10/Add.1.

[11]A/HRC/17/31.

[12]Guiding principles on foreign debt and human rights. Report of the Independent Expert on the effects of foreign debt and other related international financial obligations of States on the full enjoyment of all human rights, particularly economic, social and cultural rights, Cephas Lumina, to the 20th session of the Human Rights Council (10 April 2011) (A/HRC/20/23).

[13]A/HRC/21/39.

[14]Adopted by the 101st session of the General Conference of the International Labour Organisation, on 14 June 2012.

[15]Adopted by the 105th session of the General Conference of the International Labour Organisation, on 10 June 2016.

ratified. The right to development can be further strengthened by aligning its reading on the current understanding of human rights law.

Bridges Across Different International Regimes

Second, significant efforts have been made recently to move beyond the fragmentation of international law and the existing division of labor in global governance. Due to the increasingly technical and complex nature of the topics that are the subject of international cooperation, specific instruments have established separate arrangements in areas such as international trade, the environment, technology transfers and intellectual property rights, or human rights. Each of these areas of international cooperation has specific negotiation fora and means of enforcement, including dispute settlement mechanisms. As a result, international law is divided into a number of self-contained regimes, each with their own norms and dispute-settlement mechanisms, and relatively autonomous both vis-à-vis each other and vis-à-vis general international law.[16] While the tendency towards regime-specialization can provide benefits, including a greater effectiveness in problem-solving with the assistance of technical expertise provided by international agencies, it also may lead to inconsistencies. And, unless we manage to bridge different regimes, we may fail to identify potential synergies, by identifying mechanisms in which one regime can serve to support the achievement of objectives that are the primary goal of other regimes.

In addition to the adoption by the international community of global development goals, such as the Millennium Development Goals and the Sustainable Development Goals, and beyond the role of Article 103 of the Charter of the United Nations—which implies that, in case of conflict between human rights obligations and commitments under other instruments, the former should prevail[17]—various mechanisms have been resorted to in order to overcome the negative effects of fragmentation. Increasingly, with a view to ensuring greater consistency, international agreements refer to values or objectives pursued in other international agreements. Human rights may be referred to in climate change agreements, for instance;[18] the

[16]Report of the Study Group of the International Law Commission, *Fragmentation of international law: difficulties arising from the diversification and expansion of international law*, A/CN.4/L.702, 18 July 2006, para 8. See also, *inter alia*, Simma (1985), pp. 111–136; Abi-Saab (1999), pp. 919–933; Pauwelyn (2004), pp. 903–917; Simma and Pulkowski (2006), pp. 483–529.

[17]Charter of the United Nations, cited above (article 103, combined with article 56).

[18]Thus, the 2015 Paris Agreement adopted at the 21st Conference of Parties to the United Nations Framework Convention on Climate Change states in its Preamble, "[a]cknowledging that climate change is a common concern of humankind", that the Parties "should, when taking action to address climate change, respect, promote and consider their respective obligations on human rights, the right to health, the rights of indigenous peoples, local communities, migrants, children, persons with

reference to sustainable development may appear in trade agreements;[19] or investment agreements may refer to health, labour rights and environmental objectives as legitimate reasons to restrict investors' rights.[20] The preparation of impact assessments prior to the conclusion of international agreements constitutes another tool: one of their objectives is to ensure that issues not explicitly addressed in the agreements under discussion, but that the implementation of such agreements could affect, shall be taken into consideration.[21] Attempts are now emerging to systematize the use of human rights impact assessments in trade and investment agreements,[22] as well as in the negotiation of loan agreements,[23] as recommended by

---

disabilities and people in vulnerable situations and the right to development, as well as gender equality, empowerment of women and intergenerational equity".

[19]Thus, the preamble of the Agreement establishing the World Trade Organization (WTO) states that Members' relations "should be conducted with a view to raising standards of living, ensuring full employment and a large and steadily growing volume of real income and effective demand, and expanding the production of and trade in goods and services, *while allowing for the optimal use of the world's resources in accordance with the objective of sustainable development*, seeking both to protect and preserve the environment and to enhance the means for doing so in a manner consistent with their respective needs and concerns at different levels of economic development" (emphasis added). Similarly, it has become routine in bilateral and regional free trade agreements to include references to sustainable development.

[20]For instance, para. 4, b) of Annex B to the 2012 Model Bilateral Investment Treaty proposed by the United States of America, in which the notion of "expropriation" is further clarified, provides that: "Except in rare circumstances, non-discriminatory regulatory actions by a Party that are designed and applied to protect legitimate public welfare objectives, such as public health, safety, and the environment, do not constitute indirect expropriations".

[21]For instance, in the Declaration concerning the aims and purposes of the International Labour Organization (Declaration of Philadelphia) adopted on 10 May 1944, and integrated to the Constitution of the ILO, the International Labour Conference reaffirmed the need to ensure that the growth of trade should not be at the expense of workers' rights (paras. I(a) and (c)) and it stated that "all national and international policies and measures, in particular those of an economic and financial character, should be judged in this light and accepted only in so far as they may be held to promote and not to hinder the achievement of this fundamental objective [of ensuring that all human beings, irrespective of race, creed or sex, have the right to pursue both their material well-being and their spiritual development in conditions of freedom and dignity, of economic security and equal opportunity]" (para II(c)). These principles were reaffirmed in the ILO Declaration on Social Justice for a Fair Globalization adopted statement of principles and policies adopted unanimously on 10 June 2008 by the International Labour Conference at its 97th session. The Declaration builds on principles recognized in the Constitution of the International Labour Organization, including the Declaration concerning the Aims and Purposes of the ILO of 1944 and the Declaration on Fundamental Principles and Rights at Work of 1998.

[22]See Guiding Principles on human rights impact assessments of trade and investment agreements, Addendum to the Report of the Special Rapporteur on the right to food, Report of the Special Rapporteur on the right to food to the 19th session of the Human Rights Council (A/HRC/19/59, Add.5) (2012).

[23]See in this regard the work currently undertaken by the Independent Expert on foreign debt and human rights, following the request expressed in Human Rights Council resolution 34/3 that he develop in consultation with States, international financial institutions and other relevant stakeholders Guiding Principles for human right impact assessments of economic reform policies. In its Statement of 24 June 2016 on "Public debt, austerity measures and the International Covenant on

various human rights treaty bodies.[24] A third tool is to impose policy coherence for sustainable development. Under Sustainable Development Goal 17, one target is to "enhance policy coherence for sustainable development", and the associated indicator is the number of countries with mechanisms in place to this effect.[25] Finally, at the level of implementation, a fourth tool consists in encouraging an interpretation of international treaties in the light of other relevant rules of international law applicable between the Parties.[26]

These various mechanisms are the functional equivalent of bridges, that link different international regimes to one another, reducing the risk of inconsistencies—or even worse, of conflicting obligations being imposed on States—and encouraging the search for synergies between the different objectives pursued through global partnerships. These bridges too present opportunities for the further realization of the right to development. In the face of the increased fragmentation of international law, a virtuous cycle might emerge, in which the right to development

Economic, Social and Cultural Rights" (E/C.12/2016/1), the Committee on Economic, Social and Cultural Rights considers that both Lenders and States seeking loans should carry out a human rights impact assessment prior to the provision of the loan concerned, in order to ensure that any conditionalities attached shall not disproportionately affect economic, social and cultural rights (para. 11).

[24]See, e.g., Committee on the Rights of the Child, Concluding Observations: El Salvador, 30 June 2004, CRC/C/15/Add.232 at para. 48; Committee on the Elimination of Discrimination against Women, Concluding Observations: Colombia, 2 February 2007, CEDAW/C/COL/CO/6, at para. 29; Committee on the Elimination of Discrimination Against Women, Concluding Observations: Philippines, 25 October 2006, CEDAW/C/PHI/CO/6 at para. 26; Committee on the Elimination of Discrimination Against Women, Concluding Observations: Guatemala, 2 June 2006, CEDAW/C/GUA/CO/6 at para. 32. The Committee on Economic, Social and Cultural Rights highlighted in particular the contribution such impact assessments could make to the right to development. "The conclusion of [trade or investment] treaties", the Committee writes, "should [. . .] be preceded by human rights impact assessments, taking into account both the positive and negative human rights impacts of trade and investment treaties, including their contribution to the realization of the right to development" (Committee on Economic, Social and Cultural Rights, General Comment No. 24 on State Obligations under the International Covenant on Economic, Social and Cultural Rights in the context of Business Activities (E/C.12/GC/24) (24 June 2016), para. 13).

[25]Revised list of global Sustainable Development Goal indicators (E/CN/3/2017/2), target 17.14 and indicator 17.14.1.

[26]Article 31.3(c) of the Vienna Convention on the Law of Treaties provides that, in the interpretation of treaties, "[t]here shall be taken into account together with the context . . . any relevant rules of international law applicable in the relations between the parties" (Vienna Convention on the Law of Treaties, opened for signature on 23 May 1969, entered into force on 27 January 1980, 1155 UNTS 331, 8 ILM 679). Occasionally, international agreements refer to the rules of interpretation set out in the Vienna Convention on the Law of Treaties (see, e.g., Article 3(2) of the Dispute Settlement Understanding included among the WTO agreements (Agreement establishing the World Trade Organization, Marrakesh, 15 April 1994, entered into force on 1 January 1995 (33 ILM 1125 (1994)), stating that WTO agreements must be interpreted 'in the light of customary rules of interpretation'). However, even absent such a reference, it is generally recognized that the Vienna Convention has acquired the status of customary international law: see, e.g., International Court of Justice, *Territorial Dispute Case (Libyan Arab Jamahiriya v. Chad)*, (1994), I.C.J. Reports p. 6.

supports greater coherence across regimes, while benefiting in turn from this search for coherence.

Advances of International Law

Third, international law itself, and international human rights law in particular, have been evolving in recent years in ways that can strengthen the international dimensions of the right to development. The most significant advances concern the understanding of the responsibility of States as members of international organisations, and the rise of extraterritorial obligations in the area of human rights, and of economic, social and cultural rights in particular.

The International Law Commission, after literally decades during which it was unable to arrive at a consensus on this issue,[27] has now made it clear that "A State member of an international organization incurs international responsibility if, by taking advantage of the fact that the organization has competence in relation to the subject-matter of one of the State's international obligations, it circumvents that obligation by causing the organization to commit an act that, if committed by the State, would have constituted a breach of the obligation".[28] In other terms, where a State seeks to avoid compliance with an international obligation by transferring powers to an international organisation and allowing it to take measures that run counter to such international obligations, it engages its responsibility under international law.

This provides a helpful clarification to the scope of States' duties as members of international organisations. It imposes on States that, prior to transferring powers to an international organization, they act with due diligence to ensure that such powers shall only be exercised in conformity with their pre-existing human rights obliga-

[27]See International Law Commission, *Draft Articles on the Responsibility of States for Internationally Wrongful Acts* (Report of the International Law Commission on the work of its 53rd session, *Official Records of the General Assembly*, 56th session, Supplement No. 10 and corrigendum (A/56/10 and Corr. 1), chap. IV, sect. E.1; annex to General Assembly resolution 56/83 of 12 December 2001, and corrected by document A/56/49 (Vol. I)/Corr.4)). When it discussed the *Draft Articles on the Responsibility of States for Internationally Wrongful Acts*, the International Law Commission ended up agreeing simply on a 'non-prejudice' clause on the highly contentious topic of the responsibility of States for the acts adopted by the international organizations of which they are members. Under the slightly misleading title of 'Responsibility of an international organization', article 57 of the *Draft Articles* reads: 'These articles [listed in the text adopted by the ILC in August 2001] are without prejudice to any question of the responsibility under international law of an international organization, or of any State for the conduct of an international organization'.

[28]Art. 61 of the Draft Articles on the Responsibility of International Organizations, adopted by the International Law Commission at its 63rd session, in 2011 (A/66/10, para. 87), welcomed by the UN General Assembly in Res. 66/100 of 9 December 2011.

tions.[29] More generally, the Draft Articles on the Responsibility of International Organizations adopted by the International Law Commission prohibit the use by its member States of the channel of an international organisation in order to commit acts that would be a violation of those States' obligations if they were to be committed by those States acting alone.[30] This is similar to the view long adopted by human rights treaty bodies, which consider that States "cannot ignore their human rights obligations when acting in their capacity as members of these organisations".[31] In the framework of the International Covenant on Economic, Social and Cultural Rights, the Committee on Economic, Social and Cultural Rights has expressed its view on a number of occasions that States parties to the Covenant would be acting in violation of their obligations if they were to delegate powers to international agencies and to allow such powers to be exercised without ensuring that they do not infringe on human rights, or if they were to exercise their voting rights within such agencies without taking such rights into account.[32]

In parallel, the extraterritorial dimensions of the duties of States under international human rights law have become increasingly prominent and widely accepted. The Members of the United Nations have pledged "to take joint and separate action in cooperation with the Organization..." to achieve the purposes set out in Article 55 of the Charter, including: "... universal respect for, and observance of, human rights and fundamental freedoms for all without distinction as to race, sex, language,

[29]The International Law Commission remarked that: "the existence of an intention to avoid compliance is implied in the use of the term 'circumvention'. International responsibility will not arise when the act of the international organization, which would constitute a breach of an international obligation if done by the State, has to be regarded as the unintended result of the member State's conduct. On the other hand, the present article does not refer only to cases in which the member State may be said to be abusing its rights". However, a result cannot be said to be 'unintended' if it is the consequence of the deliberate choice by a State not to ensure that its pre-existing international obligations shall be taken into account in the activities of the organisation, where the State knew or should have known that such would be the result of transferring powers to the organisation in the field concerned. Bearing witness, perhaps, to the difficulty of defining with sufficient clarity the scope of the due diligence obligation that States must accept when they transfer powers to an international organisation, the commentary to article 25 in an earlier draft, the equivalent of article 61 in the final text of the Articles, tended to impose on the State a slightly higher burden if it wished to avoid responsibility: it was explained then that "the existence of a specific intention of circumvention is not required and responsibility cannot be avoided by showing the absence of an intention to circumvent the international obligation" (Report of the International Law Commission on the work of its 58th session, 1 May-9 June and 3 July-11 August 2006, I.L.C. Report, A/61/10 (2006), chap. VI, paras. 77–91).

[30]For instance, a State would be engaging its international responsibility if it were providing aid or assistance to an international organisation for the commission of an act that would be internationally wrongful if committed by that State (Article 58. Aid or assistance by a State in the commission of an internationally wrongful act by an international organization).

[31]Committee on Economic, Social and Cultural Rights, Public Debt, Austerity Measures and the International Covenant on Economic, Social and Cultural Rights (24 June 2016) (E/C.12/2016/1), para. 9.

[32]General Comment No. 14 (2000), The right to the highest attainable standard of health (article 12 of the International Covenant on Economic, Social and Cultural Rights), E/C.12/2000/4, para. 39.

or religion."[33] This duty is expressed without any territorial limitation, and should be taken into account when addressing the scope of States' obligations under human rights treaties. Also in line with the Charter, the International Court of Justice has acknowledged the extraterritorial scope of core human rights treaties, focusing on their object and purpose, legislative history and the lack of territorial limitation provisions in the text.[34] Customary international law also prohibits a State from allowing its territory to be used to cause damage on the territory of another State, a requirement that has gained particular relevance in international environmental law.[35] The Human Rights Council has confirmed that such prohibition extends to human rights law, when it endorsed the Guiding Principles on Extreme Poverty and Human Rights in resolution 21/11.[36]

Human rights treaty bodies have long recognized the extraterritorial implications of the instruments that they are tasked to supervise. Thus for instance, in its 2011 Statement on the obligations of States Parties regarding the corporate sector and economic, social and cultural rights, the Committee on Economic, Social and Cultural Rights reiterated that States Parties' obligations under the Covenant do not stop at their territorial borders, and that States Parties are required to take necessary steps to prevent human rights violations abroad by corporations which they can control, without infringing the sovereignty or diminishing the obligations of the host States under the Covenant.[37] The Committee has also addressed specific extraterritorial obligations of States Parties concerning business activities in General

[33]Charter of the United Nations, cited above note 2, article 56.

[34]*Legal Consequences of the Construction of a Wall in the Occupied Palestinian Territory*, Advisory Opinion, 2004 I.C.J. 136 (9 July), paras. 109–112.

[35]*See* Trail Smelter Case (United States v. Canada), 3 R.I.A.A. 1905 (1941), pg. 1965; *Corfu Channel Case (United Kingdom v. Albania) (Merits)* 1949 I.C.J. 4 (9 Apr.), para. 22; and *Legality of the Threat or Use of Nuclear Weapons*, Advisory Opinion, 1996 I.C.J. 226 (8 July), para. 29. See also International Law Commission, *Draft Principles on the Allocation of Loss in the Case of Transboundary Harm Arising out of Hazardous Activities*, adopted at the 58th session of the International Law Commission (A/61/10) (2006) (in particular Principle 4, stipulating that "Each State should take all necessary measures to ensure that prompt and adequate compensation is available for victims of transboundary damage caused by hazardous activities located within its territory or otherwise under its jurisdiction or control"). The Maastricht Principles on the Extraterritorial Obligations of States in the Area of Economic, Social and Cultural Rights, adopted by a range of academics, research institutes and human rights non-governmental organizations in 2011, provide a restatement of the current state of international human rights law on this topic, contributing to its progressive development.

[36]The *Guiding Principles on Extreme Poverty and Human Rights submitted by the Special Rapporteur on extreme poverty and human rights* (A/HRC/21/39) provide that "as part of international cooperation and assistance, States have an obligation to respect and protect the enjoyment of human rights, which involves avoiding conduct that would create a foreseeable risk of impairing the enjoyment of human rights by persons living in poverty beyond their borders, and conducting assessments of the extraterritorial impacts of laws, policies and practices" (para. 92).

[37]Statement on the obligations of States parties regarding the corporate sector and economic, social and cultural rights (E/C.12/2011/1), paras. 5–6.

Comments relating to the right to water,[38] the right to work,[39] the right to social security[40] or the right to just and favourable conditions of work,[41] and in its General Comment No. 24 on State obligations under the International Covenant on Economic, Social and Cultural Rights in the context of business activities.[42] Similar positions have been adopted by the Committee on the Rights of the Child,[43] as well as by other human rights treaty bodies.[44]

This is, therefore, a time of opportunities. The advances summarized above can guide the identification of the normative components (or attributes) of the international dimensions of the right to development, as articulated in the Declaration on the Right to Development, thus placing the right at the confluence of these efforts to build an international economic and legal order that is conducive to the full realization of all human rights. This shall firmly anchor the right to development as part of international human rights law and contribute to the acceptance of this right, enabling human rights mechanisms—including the Universal Periodic Review and the Special Procedures of the Human Rights Council, including the Special Rapporteur on the right to development—to monitor its implementation.[45] It shall also encourage reforming the international legal order, as required by Article 28 of the Universal Declaration of Human Rights, to support poverty-reduction strategies anchored in human rights at the domestic level. It is to this effort that this report seeks to contribute.

The National and International Obligations Corresponding to the Right to Development

As noted by the 1993 Vienna Declaration and Programme of Action: “Lasting progress towards the implementation of the right to development requires effective development policies at the national level, as well as equitable economic relations

---

[38]General Comment No. 15 (2002): The right to water (arts. 11 and 12) (E/C.12/2002/11), paras. 31, 33.

[39]General Comment No. 18 (2006): The right to work (art. 6) (E/C.12/GC/18), para. 52.

[40]General Comment No. 19 (2008): The right to social security (art. 9) (E/C.12/GC/19), para. 54.

[41]General Comment No. 23 (2016): The right to just and favourable conditions of work (E/C.1/GC/23), para. 70.

[42]E/C.12/GC/24, paras. 25–37.

[43]General Comment No. 16 (2013) on State obligations regarding the impact of the business sector on children’s rights (CRC/C/GC/16), paras. 43–44.

[44]For example, Committee on the Elimination of Racial Discrimination, Concluding Observations: Norway (2011) (CERD/C/NOR/CO/19–90), para. 17; Human Rights Committee, Concluding Observations: Germany (2012) (CCPR/C/DEU/CO/6), para. 16.

[45]Appointed in accordance with United Nations Human Rights Council resolution 33/14, adopted on 29 September 2016.

and a favourable economic environment at the international level".[46] Indeed, the Declaration on the Right to Development defines corresponding States' obligations both at the national and at the international levels: in adopting the Declaration, States have accepted "the primary responsibility for the creation of *national and international* conditions favourable to the realization of the right to development";[47] and they have acknowledged that "Steps should be taken to ensure the full exercise and progressive enhancement of the right to development, including the formulation, adoption and implementation of policy, legislative and other measures *at the national and international levels*".[48] The High-Level Task Force on the implementation of the right to development also noted that the right to development implied three levels of States' responsibility, including (1) States acting collectively in global and regional partnerships; (2) States acting individually as they adopt and implement policies that affect persons not strictly within their jurisdiction; and (3) States acting individually as they formulate national development policies and programmes affecting persons within their jurisdiction.[49]

National, Extraterritorial and Global Obligations

Three levels of obligations ought therefore to be distinguished. First, States have *national-level* obligations. These are obligations that concern the relationship between the State and individuals and groups on its territory or subject to its jurisdiction. In particular, States have "the right and the duty to formulate appropriate national development policies that aim at the constant improvement of the well-being of the entire population and of all individuals, on the basis of their active, free and meaningful participation in development and in the fair distribution of the benefits resulting therefrom".[50] Article 8 of the Declaration clarifies further the scope of this obligation, which has also been clarified by case-law.[51]

---

[46] Adopted by the World Conference on Human Rights on 25 June 1993 and endorsed by General Assembly resolution 48/121 of 20 December 1993, para. 10.

[47] Art. 3(1).

[48] Art. 10.

[49] High-Level Task Force on the implementation of the right to development, right to development criteria and operational sub-criteria, A/HRC/15/WG.2/TF/2/Add.2 (8 March 2010), Annex.

[50] Art. 2(3).

[51] Article 22 of the African Charter on Human and People's Rights provides that "All peoples shall have the right to their economic, social and cultural development with due regard to their freedom and identity and in the equal enjoyment of the common heritage of mankind", and imposes on States a duty, "individually or collectively, to ensure the exercise of the right to development". For examples of how this provision is interpreted, see in particular African Commission on Human and Peoples' Rights, Compl. No. 276/03, *Centre for Minority Rights Development (Kenya) and Minority Rights Group (on behalf of Endorois Welfare Council) v. Kenya*, decision adopted at the 46th Ordinary Session of the African Commission on Human and Peoples' Rights held from 11–25 November 2009; or African Court of Human Rights, *African Commission on Human and*

Second, States have *extraterritorial* obligations. States' actions and omissions may have impacts on persons or situations outside the States' territory or jurisdiction, including human rights impacts, that they cannot ignore. The Declaration on the Right to Development is relatively vague on this point, however it does recognize the duty of each State to adopt international development policies not only collectively, but also *individually*. This acknowledges the impacts that measures adopted unilaterally by one State can have on the ability of populations under the territorial jurisdiction of another State to benefit from the right to development.[52]

Third, States have *global* obligations: as actors in international relations, they should contribute to the establishment of bilateral, regional and global cooperation agreements, including for the setting up of international agencies, and they should exercise their rights within intergovernmental organizations, in accordance with the requirements of the right to development. Article 3(3) of the Declaration on the Right to Development provides in this regard that "States have the duty to co-operate with each other in ensuring development and eliminating obstacles to development. States should realize their rights and fulfil their duties in such a manner as to promote a new international economic order based on sovereign equality, interdependence, mutual interest and co-operation among all States, as well as to encourage the observance and realization of human rights". This is further clarified in Article 4, which stipulates a duty of all States "to take steps, individually *and collectively*, to formulate international development policies with a view to facilitating the full realization of the right to development", with "sustained action [being] required to promote more rapid development of developing countries". The Vienna Declaration and Programme of Action further confirm that "States should cooperate with each other in ensuring development and eliminating obstacles to development. The international community should promote effective international cooperation for the realization of the right to development and the elimination of obstacles to development".[53]

The Interaction Between the Levels

A careful reading of the Declaration on the Right to Development suggests the existence of a hierarchy, expressed in terms of subsidiarity, between the different levels. The design by each State, at domestic level, of national development policies, as defined in article 2(3) of the Declaration, comes first: provided such policies are

Peoples' Rights v. Kenya (in the case of the Ogiek Community of the Mau Forest), Appl. No. 006/2012, Judgment of 26 May 2017, paras. 207–211.

[52]See art. 4(1): "States have the duty to take steps, individually and collectively, to formulate international development policies with a view to facilitating the full realization of the right to development".

[53]Vienna Declaration and Programme of Action, cited above note 46, para. 10.

defined "on the basis of [the] active, free and meaningful participation" of the population, as they must be in accordance with the same provision, they may be seen as the result of the exercise of the right of peoples to self-determination which, referring to article 1 of the International Covenant on Economic, Social and Cultural Rights and of the International Covenant on Civil and Political Rights, article 1(2) of the Declaration reaffirms. For such a right to self-determination to be effectively exercised however, an enabling international environment should be established, consistent with article 28 of the Universal Declaration of Human Rights.[54] This imposes obligations on States, both as they act unilaterally (extraterritorial obligations) and as they act jointly (global obligations).

Importantly however, the duty to contribute to the establishment of an enabling international environment does not authorize States to act unilaterally in order to enforce the duty of another State to adopt measures at domestic level that support the right to development, for instance by the adoption of discriminatory trade measures or of other forms of economic sanctions. Indeed, the Declaration on the Right to Development emphasizes that the realization of the right to development "requires full respect for the principles of international law concerning friendly relations and co-operation among States in accordance with the Charter of the United Nations".[55] The Declaration of Principles of International Law Concerning Friendly Relations and Co-operation among States in accordance with the Charter of the United Nations (approved by General Assembly resolution 2625(XXV) of 24 October 1970), commits of each State to "refrain in its international relations from the threat or use of force against the territorial integrity or political independence of any State, or in any other manner inconsistent with the purposes of the United Nations", and not to "use or encourage the use of economic, political or any other type of measures to coerce another State in order to obtain from it the subordination of the exercise of its sovereign rights and to secure from it advantages of any kind", consistent with the "inalienable right" of each State "to choose its political, economic, social and cultural systems, without interference in any form by another State".[56]

---

[54] The Declaration on the right to development speaks in this regard of "international conditions favourable to the realization of the right to development" (Art. 3(1)) or of "international development policies . . . facilitating the full realization of the right to development" (Art. 4(1)). The Addis Ababa Action Agenda (cited above, note 8) also notes that "national development efforts need to be supported by an enabling international economic environment, including coherent and mutually supporting world trade, monetary and financial systems, and strengthened and enhanced global economic governance" (para. 9); and it includes a commitment to "pursuing policy coherence and an enabling environment for sustainable development at all levels and by all actors" (id.; see also para. 20).

[55] Art. 3(2).

[56] See also Guiding Principles on foreign debt and human rights, cited above note 13, paras. 25–26 (referring in the context of States borrowing from foreign lenders, to "the sovereign and inalienable right [of States] to implement a process of national development independently and free from pressure, influence or interference from external actors, including other States and international financial institutions").

The right to development therefore does not justify the adoption of unilateral measures as a means to obtain from a State that it changes its course of conduct. In particular, threatening a State with the denial of certain advantages in order to force the State to conclude an international agreement would constitute coercion in the meaning of article 52 of the Vienna Convention on the Law of Treaties.[57] Indeed, the Declaration of Principles of International Law Concerning Friendly Relations and Co-operation among States in accordance with the Charter of the United Nations recalls that "States have the duty to co-operate with one another, irrespective of the differences in their political, economic and social systems, in the various spheres of international relations, in order to maintain international peace and security and to promote international economic stability and progress, the general welfare of nations and international co-operation free from discrimination based on such differences". This in turn has inspired articles 3(3) and 4 of the Declaration on the Right to Development, already referred to above. Article 6(1) provides that "All States should co-operate with a view to promoting, encouraging and strengthening universal respect for and observance of all human rights and fundamental freedoms for all without any distinction as to race, sex, language or religion".

Such duties to cooperate have been reiterated on many occasions since, both in consensus documents[58] and in various international human rights instruments.

It may therefore be concluded that, under the Declaration on the Right to Development, (1) States should adopt national policies that ensure that every human person is "entitled to participate in, contribute to, and enjoy economic, social, cultural and political development, in which all human rights and fundamental freedoms can be fully realized" (Art. 1); (2) States should abstain from taking measures that might obstruct the efforts towards realizing the right to development in other countries, and instead should adopt policies supportive of such efforts; and (3) in order to create an international environment conducive to the full realization of the right to development, States should cooperate with one another. These are the three levels of obligations corresponding to the right to development. This report seeks to clarify the implications of the two latter, "international" obligations. This first requires a definition of the normative components of these obligations, or what might be called the attributes of the right to development, in its international dimensions.

---

[57] See the Declaration on the prohibition of military, political or economic coercion in the conclusion of treaties, Annex to the Final Act of the United Nations Conference on the Law of Treaties (First and Second sessions, 26 March—24 May 1968 and 9 April—22 May 1969) (A/CONF.39/26), p. 285 (which "condemns the threat or use of pressure in any form, whether military, political, or economic, by any State in order to coerce another State to perform any act relating to the conclusion of a treaty in violation of the principles of the sovereign equality of States and freedom of consent").

[58] See, e.g., Millennium Declaration, General Assembly Resolution 55/2 (8 September 2000), para. 2 (in which the Heads of States and Governments recognized unanimously that: ". . . in addition to our separate responsibilities to our individual societies, we have a collective responsibility to uphold the principles of human dignity, equality and equity at the global level").

The International Dimensions of the Right to Development: A Conceptual Framework

In order to clarify the normative content of human rights, it has become increasingly common to distinguish between three categories of duties imposed on States: States must respect human rights, by abstaining from interfering with existing levels of enjoyment of human rights unless this is justified as necessary for the pursuance of a legitimate public welfare objective; they must protect human rights from interference by private actors, which the State must therefore control, adopting to that effect all measures that can reasonably be taken in order to avoid such interference from occurring; finally, they must fulfil human rights, by putting in place regulatory and policy frameworks that shall be conducive to the full realization of the right in question. This typology of State obligations is appropriate for the discussion both of the domestic and of the international dimensions of human rights obligations of States. At the same time however, both categories of international obligations outlined above present special characteristics that distinguish them from domestic human rights obligations.

Extraterritorial Human Rights Obligations

Extraterritorial human rights obligations encounter what we might call the "paradox of the many hands": the larger the number of States involved in a situation that creates obstacles to the ability of any one State to fulfill its human rights obligations, the more difficult it will be to assert a responsibility of any individual State in that situation. This problem is well known in the area of climate change.[59] But it is equally relevant here, where the question is whether any State may be held responsible for a situation—resulting in the lack of realization of the right to development in another State—for which not the conduct of the former State alone, but that conduct *in combination with that of a large number of other States*, has contributed to this result.[60]

In international law, it is accepted that the responsibility of the State may be engaged even though the adoption by that State of a different conduct may not have led to a different result: if a particular conduct of the State is illegal, responsibility is not conditional upon the likelihood that the outcome, in terms of prejudice suffered by the victims, would have been different. In the *Bosnian Genocide Case*, the International Court of Justice noted that, in order to find Serbia responsible for not having prevented acts of genocide: "...it is irrelevant whether the State whose responsibility is in issue claims, or even proves, that even if it had employed all

[59]Voigt (2008), pp. 1–22.

[60]See in particular Salomon (2007).

means reasonably at its disposal, they would not have sufficed to prevent the commission of genocide. As well as being generally difficult to prove, this is irrelevant to the breach of the obligation of conduct in question, the more so since the possibility remains that the combined efforts of several States, each complying with its obligation to prevent, might have achieved the result — averting the commission of genocide — which the efforts of only one State were insufficient to produce".[61] According to the Court, how much the adoption by the State of a different conduct could have altered the outcome would only be relevant to the question of damages to be awarded.[62]

This is consistent with the position adopted by the International Law Commission in the 2001 *Draft Articles on the Responsibility of States for Internationally Wrongful Acts*, which stipulates that "Where several States are responsible for the same internationally wrongful act, the responsibility of each State may be invoked in relation to that act".[63] Such a responsibility exists even though, if the State had refrained from the action or omission that constitutes a violation of its international obligations, the result could have been no different. As the International Law Commission remarked when it addressed the issues of foreseeability and causality—the link between conduct and result—in its Commentary to Principle 4 of its 2006 *Draft Principles on the Allocation of Loss in the Case of Transboundary Harm Arising out of Hazardous Activities*: "The principle of causation is linked to questions of foreseeability and proximity or direct loss. Courts in different jurisdictions have applied the principles and notions of proximate cause, adequate causation, foreseeability and remoteness of the damage. This is a highly discretionary and unpredictable branch of law. Different jurisdictions have applied these concepts with different results. It may be mentioned that the test of proximity seems to have been gradually eased in modern tort law. Developments have moved from strict *condicio sine qua non* theory over the foreseeability ('adequacy') test to a less stringent causation test requiring only the "reasonable imputation" of damage".[64]

Thus for instance, a particular violation of economic, social and cultural rights may be attributed to the conduct of one State, even if other, intervening causes, or the conduct adopted by a number of other States, have also played a role in the violation. The problem nevertheless remains that alleging the responsibility of one State in a situation for which other States also bear some responsibility (potentially to an even larger degree) may be politically difficult to justify. This is especially the case where the argument made is that the State in question should have done more to support the

[61] International Court of Justice, *Case concerning Application of the Convention on the Prevention and Punishment of the Crime of Genocide (Bosnia and Herzegovina v. Serbia and Montenegro)* (Judgment of 26 February 2007), *ICJ Reports*, para. 430.

[62] Id., para. 461.

[63] International Law Commission, *Draft Articles on the Responsibility of States for Internationally Wrongful Acts*, cited above note 27, article 47 (Plurality of responsible States).

[64] International Law Commission, *Draft Principles on the Allocation of Loss in the Case of Transboundary Harm Arising out of Hazardous Activities*, adopted at the 58th session of the International Law Commission (A/61/10) (2006).

realization of the right to development and economic and social rights in another State, not only by the adoption of certain unilateral measures, for instance by increasing the level of development aid or by facilitating access of that State to international finance, but also by contributing to reshaping the international economic order by the conclusion of agreements involving other States. It is one thing for a State to be found responsible for implementing trade policies that destroy local producers' ability in another State to compete on their own domestic markets;[65] it is quite another to seek to engage the responsibility of the former State for not ensuring that the multilateral trading system works for the benefit of the State which, due to its poor trade balance, finds it difficult to make progress on development indicators. The first situation may be addressed by relying on classic understandings of causality and attribution: if the conduct attributable to one State negatively impacts human rights in another State and is in breach of the duties of the former State, the responsibility of that State may be engaged.[66] The second situation raises the question of whether a State may be responsible for what is, in essence, a failure not of that State alone, but of a plurality of States (or the "international community" as a whole), to establish an international environment that enables the realization of the right to development. This is the specific challenge raised by the emergence of global obligations.

Global Obligations

Global obligations are the duties of States as actors in international relations. With a view to facilitating accountability in the implementation of the right to development by clarifying the legal regime of the range of duties implicated, this report proposes to distinguish three categories of global obligations: duties to seek to conclude *new* agreements (bilateral or multilateral, including regional), which may or may not lead to the establishment of a new international organisation with a separate international legal personality;[67] duties to cooperate internationally by taking part in *existing* fora, by participating in decision-making bodies of international organisations (as such organisations have become a major source of normative development of

[65]See, for instance, Committee on Economic, Social and Cultural Rights, Concluding Observations: Germany (E/C.12/DEU/CO/5 (2011)), para. 9.

[66]International Law Commission, *Draft Articles on the Responsibility of States for Internationally Wrongful Acts*, cited above note 27, article 2 (Elements of an internationally wrongful act of a State).

[67]The notion of 'international organizations' is understood here, as under Article 2(1)(i) of the Vienna Convention on the Law of Treaties (United Nations, *Treaty Series*, vol. 1155, p. 331) or under Article 2(1)(i) of the Vienna Convention on the Law of Treaties between States and International Organizations or between International Organizations of 21 March 1986 (A/CONF.129/15), as organizations set up by States in order to favor intergovernmental cooperation. In principle, the members of such international organizations are States, who conclude among themselves a treaty in order to establish the organization. However, the discussion in this report would not be significantly affected if such organisations included non-State actors as members.

international law[68]); and finally, duties to comply with obligations already stipulated under *existing* international agreements, or to implement decisions or recommendations emanating from bilateral, regional or global partnerships. From the point of view of international law, each of these categories of global obligations poses specific questions. Each therefore deserves a specific treatment.

A Duty of States to Seek to Conclude New Bilateral or Multilateral Agreements

The first category of duty is to seek a solution at bilateral or multilateral level in order to address an issue that presents a transnational dimension and thus calls for international cooperation, by cooperating with other States. It is common for human rights treaties to refer to a duty of international cooperation, and to include in the definition of such a duty the duty to seek to conclude agreements with other States. A duty to cooperate for the full realization of human rights is included, for instance, in the Convention against Torture and Other Cruel, Inhuman or Degrading Treatment or Punishment, which requires States Parties to provide each other "the greatest measure of assistance in connection with criminal proceedings" relating to torture including "the supply of all evidence at their disposal necessary for the proceedings."[69] A comparable commitment is contained in the International Convention for the Protection of all Persons from Enforced Disappearance.[70] Similarly, the Convention on the Rights of Persons with Disabilities,[71] "recogniz[ing] the importance of international cooperation and its promotion, in support of national efforts for the realization of the purpose and objectives of the present Convention", commits States parties to "undertake appropriate and effective measures in this regard, between and among States and, as appropriate, in partnership with relevant international and regional organizations and civil society, in particular organizations of persons with disabilities".[72] The Convention on the Rights of Child also provides that States Parties shall take measures for the implementation of the economic, social

[68]See also Alvarez (2005), pp. 601–608 (suggesting that, due to the large representation within modern international organizations of both states and non-state actors, treaties may be negotiated within that framework which are "intended to codify, but that also progressively develop, the fundamental constitutive rules of the international system – such as the rules governing treaties, the way states ought to conduct their diplomatic relations, or those governing the global commons", such "legislative treaties" in addition having the capacity to influence the formation of customary rules of general applicability).

[69]Art. 9 (1).

[70]Article 15 provides that "States Parties shall cooperate with each other and shall afford one another the greatest measure of mutual assistance with a view to assisting victims of enforced disappearance, and in searching for, locating and releasing disappeared persons and, in the event of death, in exhuming and identifying them and returning their remains."

[71]United Nations, *Treaty Series*, vol. 2515, p. 3 (opened for signature on 13 December 2006 by resolution 61/106 of the General Assembly (A/RES/61/106)).

[72]Article 32(1).

and cultural rights of the child, "where needed, within the framework of international co-operation",[73] leading the Committee on the Rights of the Child to note that "When States ratify the Convention, they take upon themselves obligations not only to implement it within their jurisdiction, but also to contribute, through international cooperation, to global implementation."[74]

While some instruments refer simply to a duty of international assistance and cooperation without referring explicitly to the conclusion of new international agreements, others do provide such an explicit reference, where the conclusion of such agreements is seen as essential for the fulfilment of the aims of the convention. Thus for instance, the Optional Protocol to the Convention on the Rights of the Child on the Sale of Children, Child Prostitution and Child Pornography,[75] provides that "States Parties shall take all necessary steps to strengthen international cooperation by multilateral, regional and bilateral arrangements for the prevention, detection, investigation, prosecution and punishment of those responsible for acts involving the sale of children, child prostitution, child pornography and child sex tourism. (...)".[76]

The duty of international assistance and cooperation is given a particular emphasis in the International Covenant on Economic, Social and Cultural Rights, which is the most relevant human rights instrument in the fight against poverty. Article 2(1) of the Covenant provides that the States parties to the Covenant undertake to "take steps, individually *and through international assistance and co-operation*, especially economic and technical", to the maximum of their available resources, "with a view to achieving progressively the full realization of the rights" recognized in the Covenant. The notion of international co-operation also is mentioned in relation to the right to an adequate standard of living in article 11(1) of the Covenant, according to which "States Parties will take appropriate steps to ensure the realization of this right, recognizing to this effect the essential importance of international co-operation based on free consent". Under Part IV of the Covenant, which relates to the measures of implementation, two provisions relate to international assistance and

[73]Convention on the Rights of the Child (United Nations, *Treaty Series*, vol. 1577, p. 3; opened for signature on 20 November 1989 by resolution 44/49 of the General Assembly (A/RES/44/49)), art. 4. Article 45 of the Convention refers to the relations that may develop between the Committee on the Rights of the Child and the specialized agencies of the United Nations, the United Nations Children Fund (Unicef), and other United Nations organs.

[74]Committee on the Rights of the Child, General Comment No. 5: General Measures of Implementation for the Convention on the Rights of the Child (CRC/GC/2003/5), para. 5.

[75]Adopted and opened for signature, ratification and accession by General Assembly resolution A/RES/54/263 of 25 May 2000.

[76]Art. 10(1). The Optional Protocol to the Convention on the Rights of the Child on the involvement of children in armed conflict, also adopted by General Assembly resolution A/RES/54/263 of 25 May 2000, provides for a duty of States parties to "cooperate in the implementation of the ... Protocol, including in the prevention of any activity contrary thereto and in the rehabilitation and social reintegration of persons who are victims of acts contrary thereto, including through technical cooperation and financial assistance. Such assistance and cooperation will be undertaken in consultation with the States Parties concerned and the relevant international organizations" (art. 7 (1)). It is less explicit, however, on the conclusion of new agreements to that effect.

co-operation. Article 22 states that the Economic and Social Council may bring to the attention of other UN bodies and agencies concerned with furnishing technical assistance any information arising out of the reports submitted by States under the Covenant which "may assist such bodies in deciding, each within its field of competence, on the advisability of international measures likely to contribute to the effective progressive implementation of the present Covenant". Article 23 specifies the different forms international action for the achievement of the rights recognized in the Covenant may take: such international action

> includes such methods as the conclusion of conventions, the adoption of recommendations, the furnishing of technical assistance and the holding of regional meetings and technical meetings for the purpose of consultation and study organized in conjunction with the Governments concerned.[77]

Imposing an obligation on a State to enter into any form of international agreement or to negotiate such an agreement may seem both odd and impractical, since it can hardly be reconciled with the principle of State sovereignty—one of the implications of which is that States cannot be forced to enter into agreements against their will. In fact however, it is not unusual for international law to impose a duty to *seek, in good faith, to conclude an international agreement.*[78] In general international law, an obligation to negotiate emerges in particular in situations where States are recognized to have conflicting rights, which can only be reconciled through a process of negotiation clarifying the respective rights and duties.[79] A duty to

---

[77]The implication is that, for instance, in order to comply with the right to food, "States parties should, in international agreements whenever relevant, ensure that the right to adequate food is given due attention *and consider the development of further international legal instruments to that end*" (Committee on Economic, Social and Cultural Rights, General Comment No. 12 (1999): The right to adequate food (art. 11) (E/C.12/1999/5) (1999), para. 36 (emphasis added)).

[78]A classic example is Article VI of the Treaty on the Non-Proliferation of Nuclear Weapons, which was opened for signature on 1 July 1968 (*United Nations Treaty Series*, vol. 729, p. 161): "Each of the Parties to the Treaty undertakes to pursue negotiations in good faith on effective measures relating to cessation of the nuclear arms race at an early date and to nuclear disarmament, and on a treaty on general and complete disarmament under strict and effective international control".

[79]International Court of Justice, *Fisheries Jurisdiction Case*, 1974 I.C.J., p. 31 (negotiations are required between Iceland and Great Britain who both have legitimate fishing rights in certain maritime areas). A most authoritative voice has dismissed as purely hortatory, rather than binding, provisions in international treaties that call on parties to negotiate further agreements. Such provisions, it has been written, "are *pacta de contrahendo*, which cannot be enforced if the parties do not reach agreement. There is no way in which an agreement can be forced upon them and there is likewise no way in which they can be compelled to negotiate. The assertion that the duty to negotiate or to conclude an agreement implies a duty to negotiate in good faith is an empty one. Unless appropriate machinery has been set up, no court or other agency can determine whether a State has or has not negotiated in good faith and what the duty to negotiate in good faith requires. In the relations of States, a complaint that negotiations have not been carried on in good faith is mere rhetoric" (Baxter 1980, pp. 549–566 at p. 552). This however conflates a duty to *negotiate in good faith*, with the duty to *reach an agreement*; yet, the former may be imposed without the latter necessarily following: the Permanent Court of International Justice established this distinction long ago (Advisory Opinion No. 42, *Railway Traffic Between Lithuania and Poland*, 1931 P.C.I.J. (ser.

negotiate in good faith may also be derived from situations where, in the absence of a negotiation, States would have to resort to unilateral measures. It has been noted above that, by referring in article 3(2) to the Principles of International Law Concerning Friendly Relations and Co-operation among States in accordance with the Charter of the United Nations, the Declaration on the Right to Development expresses a preference for multilateralism, and cautions against the adoption of unilateral measures by States to impose compliance with the right to development.[80] In its various resolutions on unilateral coercive measures, the Human Rights Council has emphasized the threat to human rights, including the right to development, that could result from the adoption of such measures, as well as the risk that multilateralism be circumvented by the most powerful States, who are best placed to impose their views by resorting to unilateral measures.[81] But there is a positive obligation implied in this condemnation of unilateral coercive measures: it is to cooperate in good faith in the search of solutions through multilateralism.

Such a duty to enter into negotiations in order to find solutions through multilateralism has been regularly affirmed in the new area of sustainable development. Principle 12 of the 1992 Rio Declaration on Environment and Development[82] expresses a strong encouragement for the search for solutions at the multilateral level:

> Unilateral actions to deal with environmental challenges outside the jurisdiction of the importing country should be avoided. Environmental measures addressing transboundary or global environmental problems should, as far as possible, be based on international consensus.

Similarly, paragraph 2.22(i) of Agenda 21, also adopted at the 1992 Earth Summit, provides:

A/B) No. 42, at p. 116 (about the duties following from a resolution of the Council of the League of Nations recommending that "the two governments [Polish and Lithuanian]... enter into direct negotiations as soon as possible" concerning the railway connections between the two countries); see also Rogoff (1994), pp. 141–185 at p. 148 (emphasizing the importance of distinguishing the obligation to negotiate from the obligation to conclude an agreement)). Moreover, here—as regards a duty to enter negotiations for the conclusion of international agreements in support of the right to development—we do have "appropriate machinery" which could assess whether the efforts of the State are genuine, or the negotiation conducted "in good faith": the Special Rapporteur on the right to development and, in their respective fields of competence, human rights treaty bodies, may perform such a role. Indeed, this report proposes criteria which, in so doing, they may seek inspiration from.

[80] See above, text corresponding to notes 55–57.

[81] See, for instance, Resolution 34/13, Human rights and unilateral coercive measures (adopted on 24 March 2017 by a recorded vote of 32 to 14, with no abstentions); and Resolution 21/27, Human rights and unilateral coercive meaasures (adopted on 26 September 2014 by a recorded vote of 32 to 14, with two abstentions) (establishing the mandate of the Special Rapporteur on the negative impact of unilateral coercive measures on human rights).

[82] Adopted at the United Nations Conference on Environment and Development, Rio de Janeiro (Brazil), 3–14 June 1992 (A/CONF.151/26).

> Governments should encourage GATT, UNCTAD and other relevant international and regional economic institutions to examine, in accordance with their respective mandates and competences, the following propositions and principles: . . .
>
> (i) Avoid unilateral action to deal with environmental challenges outside the jurisdiction of the importing country. Environmental measures addressing transborder problems should, as far as possible, be based on an international consensus.

A similar duty to enter into bilateral or multilateral agreements can be identified for the realization of the right to development. Such a duty should be treated as an obligation of means: the State should deploy its best efforts to cooperate internationally with a view to finding such agreement. The responsibility of the State cannot be engaged merely due to its failure to arrive at an agreement. A State may however be accountable for its failure to seek, in good faith, to conclude new partnerships. Indeed, the precedents cited above in the field of sustainable development were referred to by the Appellate Body of the World Trade Organisation when, in the *Shrimp/Turtle* dispute, it took the view that the requirement of non-discrimination under article XI:1 of the 1994 General Agreement on Tariffs and Trade prohibited the adoption of unilateral measures, unless such measures have been preceded by good faith attempts to reach an agreement with the trading partners on the adoption of common standards achieving the desired objective. The Appellate Body could of course not require that such agreement be reached: unilateral measures remain available to the WTO Members, as a last resort, should multilateralism fail. In its view however, it would not be acceptable for a Member to impose on other Members compliance with certain standards, without giving at least a fair chance for a joint approach to succeed.[83]

[83] *United States — Import Prohibition of Certain Shrimp and Shrimp Products*, WT/DS58/AB/R, 12 October 1998 (Report of the Appellate Body), paras 161 to 165, 171, 172. At issue in this case was Section 609 of Public Law 101–162, adopted by the United States in 1989. This provision required the imposition of an import ban on imports from countries where shrimp were harvested with technology that could adversely affect certain sea turtles, unless the countries concerned were certified by the President, on an annual basis, as having a regulatory programme governing the incidental taking of sea turtles in the course of harvesting comparable to that of the United States, or having an average rate of incidental taking of sea turtles comparable to that by United States vessels using turtle-excluding devices, or having a fishing environment such that there exists no threat of incidental taking of sea turtles in the course of such harvesting. Faced with this unilateral measure adopted by the United States, the Appellate Body noted: "...the failure of the United States to engage the appellees, as well as other Members exporting shrimp to the United States, in *serious, across-the-board negotiations with the objective of concluding bilateral or multilateral agreements for the protection and conservation of sea turtles*, before enforcing the import prohibition against the shrimp exports of those other Members" (emphasis added) (para. 166). The resort to unilateral trade measures is condemned in the following terms: "... an alternative course of action was reasonably open to the United States for securing the legitimate policy goal of its measure, a course of action other than the unilateral and non-consensual procedures of the import prohibition under Section 609. It is relevant to observe that an import prohibition is, ordinarily, the heaviest "weapon" in a Member's armoury of trade measures. The record does not, however, show that serious efforts were made by the United States to negotiate similar agreements with any other country or group of countries before (and, as far as the record shows, after) Section 609 was enforced on a world-wide basis on 1 May 1996. Finally, the record also does not show that the appellant, the United States,

The case illustrates that it is possible, in such a quasi-judicial context, to assess the "seriousness" of the efforts of a country to search for a negotiated solution to the issue at hand, by examining for instance the time and energy that went into searching for such a solution, the reasonableness of the offers made to the other parties, and so forth. For the understanding of global obligations corresponding to the realization of the right to development, this can be essential, since the right to development is, *inter alia*, about the duty to contribute to design solutions through bilateral or multilateral partnerships, including partnerships at regional level, that can lead towards shaping an international environment enabling development efforts deployed at domestic level.

In order to assess whether States have sought, in good faith, to conclude an international agreement in order to contribute to the realization of the right to development, it shall be required to consider: first, whether they have put forward proposals, with a view to strengthening international cooperation, that are sufficiently concrete; and second, whether such proposals have a reasonable chance of attracting support. The first requirement is of a procedural kind. It is that States do not remain passive, but make concrete steps towards reaching an international agreement. Under the International Covenant on Economic, Social and Cultural Rights, States are expected to take steps towards the progressive realization of the rights recognized in the Covenant that are "deliberate, concrete and targeted as clearly as possible towards meeting the obligations recognized in the Covenant".[84] A similar requirement could be imposed, at the level of global obligations, as regards the duty to put forward proposals that could move towards an international environment supporting efforts at domestic level at achieving the right to development. Thus, though this obligation is procedural in nature, it is not simply a *pro forma* obligation to be open to discussions: rather, to borrow from the language of the *Graeco-German* Arbitration, the engagement should be "meaningful".[85]

The second requirement concerns the substance of the negotiation position taken. It is a requirement that the proposals States put forward in negotiation fora be *reasonable*. Though there exists no clear consensus on precise benchmarks in this regard, it may be suggested that this requires assessing the potential impacts of the proposals put forward in order to examine:

---

attempted to have recourse to such international mechanisms as exist to achieve cooperative efforts to protect and conserve sea turtles before imposing the import ban" (emphasis added) (para. 171).

[84]Committee on Economic, Social and Cultural Rights, General Comment No 3 (1990): The Nature of States Parties' Obligations (art. 2(1)) (E/1991/23), para 2.

[85]In this case, in which Greece argued that Germany was under an obligation under Article 19 of the 1953 Agreement on German External Debts (333 United Nations, *Treaty Series*, p. 3) to enter into negotiations to settle certain outstanding claims, the Arbitral Tribunal explained that "To be meaningful, negotiations have to be entered into with a view to arriving at an agreement. Though ... an agreement to negotiate does not necessarily imply an obligation to reach an agreement, it does imply that serious efforts towards that end will be made" (Graeco-German Arbitration (1972), 91 R. I.A.A., p. 57). The duty, the Tribunal stated, is to "negotiate, bargain, and in good faith attempt to reach a result acceptable to both parties" (id., p. 56).

(a) whether such proposals shall enable the States to whom such proposals are addressed to respect, protect and fulfil human rights, consistent with their international obligations;
(b) whether they shall benefit, as a matter of priority, the most marginalized groups within the States concerned; and
(c) whether, in the distribution of the burdens and benefits, such proposals take into account the principle of common but differentiated responsibilities and respective capabilities.

Thus, the reasonableness of a proposal for a new international agreement may be assessed on the basis of three criteria. The first criterion is that the agreement should not make it more difficult, or impossible, for the States concerned to comply with their duties to respect, protect and fulfil human rights. This follows from the principle of *pacta sunt servanda*,[86] as well as from the axiomatic rule according to which States may not escape preexisting treaty-based commitments by the conclusion, with other parties, of another treaty covering the same subject, whose provisions would in some way conflict with the earlier treaty: the posterior treaty could not be invoked against the parties to the earlier treaty, for whom it is a *res inter alios acta*.[87] Indeed, even if it were suggested that all States parties to a human rights treaty be involved in negotiations on a new agreement reducing these pre-existing obligations, the status of human rights norms as norms that cannot be derogated from by mutual agreement because of their peremptory character would in most cases prohibit such an agreement from entering into force;[88] if it were to be signed and

[86]Vienna Convention on the Law of Treaties of 23 May 1969 (cited above note 26), art. 26.

[87]Vienna Convention on the Law of Treaties, cited above note 26, art. 30 ('Application of successive treaties relating to the same subject-matter') (see, specifically, Article 30 § 4, b)). As explained by Special Rapporteur Fitzmaurice: "Since anything that some of the parties to a treaty do *inter se* under another treaty is clearly *res inter alios acta*, it cannot in law result in any formal diminution of the obligation of these parties under the earlier treaty, or affect juridically the rights or position of the other parties, which remain legally intact and subsisting" (Fitzmaurice 1958, p. 43). For further discussions of the rule, see in particular Rousseau (1932), pp. 133–192; Vierdag (1988), pp. 92–111; Czaplinski and Danilenko (1990), pp. 12–28; Mus (1998), pp. 208–232.

[88]Vienna Convention on the Law of Treaties, cited above note 26, art. 53 (defining a peremptory norm of international law as "a norm accepted and recognized by the international community of States as a whole as a norm from which no derogation is permitted and which can be modified only by a subsequent norm of general international law having the same character"). Disagreements persist as to whether the full list of human rights recognized in the International Bill of Rights have the status of *jus cogens*, however (see, for instance, de Wet and Vidmar 2012). The debate is not new: 50 years ago, Judge Tanaka was already suggesting in his dissenting opinion in the *South West Africa* case that human rights law belonged to the *jus cogens*, which is imperative, as opposed to the *jus dispositivum*, that States could freely dispose of: 'If we can introduce in the international field a category of law, namely jus cogens, recently examined by the International Law Commission, a kind of imperative law which constitutes the contrast to jus dispositivum, capable of being changed by way of agreement between States, surely the law concerning the protection of human rights may be considered to belong to the jus cogens' (Judge Tanaka, dissenting opinion in the *South West Africa* Case (*Ethiopia v. South Africa; Liberia v. South Africa*), Second Phase, Judgment [1966] ICJ Rep 298). The issue of peremptory norms of general international law (*jus cogens*) is currently

ratified by the States concerned, it would have to considered as null and void.[89] Such an agreement, in any event, would have to be treated as incompatible with Article 103 of the UN Charter, and thus inapplicable.[90]

The second criterion on the basis of which the reasonableness of a proposal may be assessed is by asking whether, if accepted, the proposal would contribute to the reduction of inequalities.

The prohibition of discrimination is a core obligation of States both under the UN Charter and under international human rights law. Discrimination constitutes any distinction, exclusion, restriction or preference or other differential treatment that is based on any ground such as race, colour, sex, language, religion, political or other opinion, national or social origin, property, birth or other status, and which has the purpose or effect of nullifying or impairing the recognition, enjoyment or exercise by all persons, on an equal footing, of all rights and freedoms. Any proposal for an international agreement that would entail discrimination thus defined would not pass the reasonableness test. But human rights law goes further. It also prohibits any action or omission that disproportionately affects members of a particular group, in the absence of a reasonable and objective justification, thus constituting *de facto* discrimination.[91] Thus, proposed international agreements should be assessed in order to ensure that they shall not have such impacts. Such agreements may, however, provide for differential treatment benefiting certain categories of the population facing systemic disadvantage. Indeed, in order to eliminate *de facto* discrimination, States may be under an obligation to adopt special measures to attenuate or suppress conditions that perpetuate discrimination. Such measures are legitimate to the extent that they represent reasonable, objective and proportionate means to redress *de facto* discrimination and are discontinued when substantive equality has been sustainably achieved.

The third criterion is that the agreement put forward takes into account the principle of common but differentiated responsibilities and respective capabilities. This principle originally emerged in international economic law to justify positive discrimination in favor of developing countries: as an illustration, the Second

under examination within the International Law Commission, with a view to contributing to the codification and progressive development of the topic.

[89]Vienna Convention on the Law of Treaties, cited above note 26, art. 64.

[90]Whereas a treaty found to be in violation of a *jus cogens* norm is void and must be considered to have never existed, a treaty incompatible with obligations flowing from membership in the United Nations does not disappear; however, as a result of article 103 of the UN Charter, it shall not be applied to the extent of such an incompatibility: see Dupuy (2002), p. 305; and see also the Report of the Study Group of the International Law Commission, *Fragmentation of international law: difficulties arising from the diversification and expansion of international law*, cited above note 16, para. 41: '(*a*) A rule conflicting with a norm of *jus cogens* becomes thereby *ipso facto* void; (*b*) A rule conflicting with Article 103 of the United Nations Charter becomes inapplicable as a result of such conflict and to the extent of such conflict'. Comp. Combacau (1991), pp. 195–203.

[91]Human Rights Committee, General Comment No. 18: Non-discrimination (37th session, 1989); Committee on Economic, Social and Cultural Rights, General Comment No. 20: Non-Discrimination in Economic, Social and Cultural Rights (art. 2, para. 2) (E/C.12/GC/20).

UNCTAD conference, convened in 1968, expressed itself in favour of "the early establishment of a mutually acceptable system of generalized, non-reciprocal and non-discriminatory preferences beneficial to the developing countries in order to increase the export earnings, to promote the industrialization, and to accelerate the rates of economic growth of these countries".[92] The principle of differentiation then penetrated international environmental law, inspiring the 1987 Montréal Protocol on Substances that Deplete the Ozone Layer to the 1985 Vienna Convention for the Protection of the Ozone Layer.[93] Principle 7 of the Rio Declaration describes it as follows:

> States should co-operate in a spirit of global partnership to conserve, protect and restore the health and integrity of the Earth's ecosystem. In view of the different contributions to global environmental degradation, States have common but differentiated responsibilities. The developed countries acknowledge the responsibility that they bear in the international pursuit of sustainable development in view of the pressures their societies place on the global environment and of the technologies and financial resources they command.

As illustrated by the United Nations Framework Convention on Climate Change and the Convention on Biological Diversity, the first examples of the implementation of the principle of common but differentiated responsibilities agreed on in Rio,[94] this principle requires that the allocation of responsibilities between States should

---

[92]Resolution 21 (ii) adopted at the Second United Nations Conference on Trade and Development (1968). This commitment resulted, in particular, in the adoption of decisions granting waivers from the most-favored nation principle under the General Agreement on Tariffs and Trade, allowing for General Systems of Preferences to be set up in order to accelerate the integration of developing countries in international trade: see Decision relating to the establishment of generalized, non-reciprocal and non-discriminatory preferences beneficial to the developing countries, Decision L/3545 (25 June 1971) GATT B.I.S.D. (18th Supp) at 24 (1972); Decision on Differential and More Favourable Treatment, Reciprocity and Fuller Participation of Developing Countries, Decision L/4903 (28 November 1979) GATT B.I.S.D. (26th Supp) at 203 (1980) (providing that "contracting parties may accord differential and more favourable treatment to developing countries, without according such treatment to other contracting parties").

[93]United Nations, *Treaty Series*, vol. 1522, p. 3, in force since 1 Jan. 1989. In the Preamble of the Montréal Protocol, the Parties acknowledge that "special provision is required to meet the needs of developing countries, including the provision of additional financial resources and access to relevant technologies, bearing in mind that the magnitude of funds necessary is predictable, and the funds can be expected to make a substantial difference in the world's ability to address the scientifically established problem of ozone depletion and its harmful effects"; see also art. 5 (providing for specific treatment of developing countries).

[94]United Nations Framework Convention on Climate Change (1992, in force on 21 March 1994 (*United Nations Treaty Series*, vol. 1771, p. 107; 31 ILM 851 (1992)), Art. 3 (States parties should act "on the basis of equity and in accordance with their common but differentiated responsibilities and respective capabilities"); Convention on Biological Diversity (1992, in force on 29 December 1993 (*United Nations Treaty Series*, vol. 1760, p. 79)), Art. 20(4) ("The extent to which developing country Parties will effectively implement their commitments under this Convention will depend on the effective implementation by developed country Parties of their commitments under this Convention related to financial resources and transfer of technology and will take fully into account the fact that economic and social development and eradication of poverty are the first and overriding priorities of the developing country Parties"). The principle of common but differentiated

take into account both each State's contribution to the issue to be addressed through international cooperation,[95] and each State's ability to contribute to addressing that issue (capabilities, as measures by financial resources and technologies).[96] In its New Delhi Declaration of Principles of International Law relating to Sustainable Development, adopted at the 70th Conference of the International Law Association (ILA) held in New Delhi on 2–6 April 2002, the ILA described the principle thus:

> 3.1. States and other relevant actors have common but differentiated responsibilities. All States are under a duty to co-operate in the achievement of global sustainable development and the protection of the environment. International organizations, corporations (including in particular transnational corporations), non-governmental organizations and civil society should co-operate in and contribute to this global partnership. Corporations have also responsibilities pursuant to the polluter-pays principle.
>
> 3.2. Differentiation of responsibilities, whilst principally based on the contribution that a State has made to the emergence of environmental problems, must also take into account the economic and developmental situation of the State, in accordance with paragraph 3.3.
>
> 3.3. The special needs and interests of developing countries and of countries with economies in transition, with particular regard to least developed countries and those affected adversely by environmental, social and developmental considerations, should be recognized.
>
> 3.4. Developed countries bear a special burden of responsibility in reducing and eliminating unsustainable patterns of production and consumption and in contributing to capacity-building in developing countries, inter alia by providing financial assistance and access to environmentally sound technology. In particular, developed countries should play a leading role and assume primary responsibility in matters of relevance to sustainable development.

At the World Summit on Sustainable Development held in Johannesburg in August–September 2002, at which the implementation of the Agenda 21 and the Rio Declaration on Environment and Development was discussed, Heads of State and governments pledged to take "concrete actions and measures at all levels and to enhancing international cooperation, taking into account the Rio principles, including, inter alia, the principle of common but differentiated responsibilities as set out in principle 7 of the Rio Declaration on Environment and Development".[97] The

---

responsibilities has now grown into a general principle of international environmental law: see Cullet (2003), Rajamani (2006), and Honkonen (2009).

[95]In international environmental law, this may be seen as a manifestation of the polluter-pays principle. See the International Law Association New Delhi Declaration on Principles of International Law relating to Sustainable Development, adopted at the seventieth conference of the International Law Association (ILA resolution 3/2002, annex as published in UN doc. A/57/329), principle 3.

[96]These two dimensions, which are respectively looking backward and looking forward, shall often converge: an inequitable trading system, for instance, shall often be the result of past unfair trading practices, and the partner having benefited most shall have greater capacities to remedy the resulting imbalances.

[97]See paragraphs 2 and 81 of the 2002 Plan of Implementation adopted at the Johannesburg Summit.

principle of common but differentiated responsibilities also appears in the 2030 Development Agenda, particularly in targets 10.a and 12.1 of the Sustainable Development Goals, and in the Addis Ababa Action Agenda of the Third International Conference on Finance for Development.[98]

One obstacle to the implementation of the principle of common but differentiated responsibilities and respective capabilities is that there exists no unanimous agreement on how countries should be classified in order to operationalize the principle. The category of "developing countries"—leaving aside even its implicit but highly contestable suggestion that there would exists a single pathway to development, one "script" that all countries should follow—is hardly helpful to identify the countries' differentiated responsibilities. Today, the group of 159 "developing countries", categorized as such by the United Nations, is widely heterogenous: they include countries whose situations, trajectories and prospects differ widely, leading the World Bank to reject the use of this category since the 2016 edition of its *World Development Report*.

Other classifications are barely more helpful, however. The World Bank classifies countries as "low-income", "lower middle income", "upper middle income" and "high-income", on the basis of their GNI per capita, using a 3 year average exchange rate to avoid the classification being influenced by short-term changes in currency values.[99] However, though for most countries there is a strong correlation between GNI per capita and social indicators,[100] GNI per capita remains a crude proxy to assess the level of development of a country. It does not, for instance, take into account adequately the activity in the informal sector or the non-monetary segments of the economy. Nor does it reflect fully the nature of the challenges certain countries may be facing: small island developing States and landlocked developing countries, for instance, face specific constraints due to their geography, which may have to be taken into account, although such constraints may not be reflected in their position on a GNI per capita ranking; similarly, poor countries with a high level of debt face challenges of their own, which were recognized when a separate category of "heavily indebted poor countries" eligible for special assistance from the International Monetary Fund and the World Bank was defined when the HIPC initiative was launched in 1996. Finally, a separate classification is based on the list of Least-Developed Countries (LDCs). This list is decided upon by the United Nations Economic and Social Council and, ultimately, by the General Assembly, on the basis of recommendations made by the Committee for Development Policy, using a

[98]See in particular paragraph 59.

[99]The classification is published on http://data.worldbank.org and is revised once a year on July 1st, at the start of the World Bank fiscal year. For instance, for the current 2018 fiscal year, low-income economies are those with a GNI per capita of $1005 or less in 2016; lower middle-income economies are those with a GNI per capita between $1006 and $3955; upper middle-income economies are those with a GNI per capita between $3956 and $12,235; high-income economies are those with a GNI per capita of $12,236 or more. See https://datahelpdesk.worldbank.org/knowledgebase/articles/906519.

[100]See Fantom and Serajuddin (2016).

set of criteria including per capita GNI, a human assets index and an economic vulnerability index.[101]

These various approaches were each designed for specific purposes and in specific institutional settings, and they are more or less well suited to those ends. But they appear insufficient to capture the full spectrum of conditions that countries face. Classifying countries in "groups", separated by more or less arbitrarily defined boundaries, may not be the most justifiable approach. Instead, taking into account the principle of common but differentiated responsibilities and respective capabilities for the implementation of the right to development may require to identify for each country (1) the contribution that it has made in the past to the emergence of environmental problems, (2) the capacity of each country to contribute to the right to development, based on the resources (natural, financial, technological and human) that it could mobilize to that effect, and (3) the constraints (including geographical constraints, the debt burden and the lack of diversification of the economy) the country faces. The classification of countries on the basis of these criteria could be regularly updated, ideally on an annual basis, in order to arrive at a shared understanding of which efforts can be expected from each State, where the burden of realizing the right to development should be shared between countries. Proposals to improve the international social and economic order should be assessed on the basis of whether they take account the respective responsibilities of countries, on the basis of this set of criteria.

To summarize, the global obligations of States derived from the right to development include a duty to seek to conclude new agreements (bilateral, regional or multilateral) in order address issues of a transnational nature that call for collective action by States. That duty has until now remained highly theoretical and abstract. It could be made more concrete, however, once agreement is found on certain core attributes. This report suggests that the duty is of a procedural nature: it is a requirement to enter in good faith in negotiations, and not to conclude an agreement. It suggests, further, that such a duty can be effectively monitored, provided it is understood as a duty to make concrete proposals that are reasonable, enabling partner countries to better respect, protect and fulfil human rights; that contribute to the reduction of inequalities both within and between countries, as supported by the 2030 Agenda for Sustainable Development;[102] and that are consistent with the principle of common but differentiated responsibilities and respective capabilities. Human rights monitoring bodies could gradually build on these principles to assess whether a State has sought, in good faith, to contribute to an international legal order supporting the realization of internationally recognized human rights, by constructively entering into negotiations to that effect.

[101]See United Nations (2008).

[102]Target 10.1 of the Sustainable Development Goals provides that States should "progressively achieve and sustain income growth of the bottom 40 per cent of the population at a rate higher than the national average".

A Duty of the State to Take the Right to Development into Consideration as a Member of International Organisations

The second category of obligation raises the question of whether the State has exercised its rights as a member of the organisation (particularly, its voting rights), taking into account its human rights obligations and the right to development. In addressing the impact of structural adjustment programmes on the enjoyment of economic, social and cultural rights, the Committee on Economic, Social and Cultural Rights took the view in 1990 that "States parties to the Covenant, as well as the relevant United Nations agencies, should [. . .] *make a particular effort to ensure* that [the protection of the most basic economic, social and cultural rights] is, to the maximum extent possible, built-in to programmes and policies designed to promote adjustment".[103] The implication is that States parties to the Covenant have obligations, *as member States* of the international financial institutions, insofar as such institutions impose on indebted States certain austerity programmes as a condition for access to the international financial markets. In the General Comment on the right to the highest attainable standard of health, which it adopted in 2000,[104] the Committee on Economic, Social and Cultural Rights uses an even stronger formulation, moving from the affirmation of an obligation of means to an obligation of result. It notes that "States parties have an *obligation to ensure* that their actions as members of international organizations take due account of the right to health. Accordingly, States parties which are members of international financial institutions, notably the International Monetary Fund, the World Bank, and regional development banks, should pay greater attention to the protection of the right to health in influencing the lending policies, credit agreements and international measures of these institutions".[105] A very similar formulation appears in the General Comment on the right to water.[106]

Nor is the duty of States to take their human rights obligations into account as members of international organisations limited to international financial institutions; it is relevant also, for instance, to the conduct of trade negotiations. The Committee

---

[103]Committee on Economic, Social and Cultural Rights, General Comment No. 2 (1990): International technical assistance measures (art. 22) (E/1990/23), para. 9.

[104]Committee on Economic, Social and Cultural Rights, General Comment No. 14 (2000): The right to the highest attainable standard of health (art. 12) (E/C.12/2000/4) (2000), para. 39 ("In relation to the conclusion of other international agreements, States parties should take steps to ensure that these instruments do not adversely impact upon the right to health").

[105]Id.

[106]See Committee on Economic, Social and Cultural Rights, General Comment No. 15 (2002): The right to water (arts. 11 and 12 of the International Covenant on Economic, Social and Cultural Rights) (E/C.12/2002/11) (26 November 2002), para. 36: "States parties should ensure that their actions as members of international organizations take due account of the right to water. Accordingly, States parties that are members of international financial institutions, notably the International Monetary Fund, the World Bank, and regional development banks, should take steps to ensure that the right to water is taken into account in their lending policies, credit agreements and other international measures".

on Economic, Social and Cultural Rights takes the view, for instance, that "the right to water [should be] given due attention in international agreements and, to that end, should consider the development of further legal instruments. With regard to the conclusion and implementation of other international and regional agreements, States parties should take steps to ensure that these instruments do not adversely impact upon the right to water. Agreements concerning trade liberalization should not curtail or inhibit a country's capacity to ensure the full realization of the right to water".[107]

This is not a new requirement. In its 1997 General Comment on the relationship between economic sanctions and respect for economic, social and cultural rights,[108] the Committee on Economic, Social and Cultural Rights already took the view that States imposing sanctions should not, in doing so, jeopardize the economic, social and cultural rights of the population in the targeted State. In other terms, a State may engage its responsibility under the International Covenant on Economic, Social and Cultural Rights by voting in favor of economic sanctions, for instance as a member of the UN Security Council. The Committee stated the following:

> While this obligation of every State is derived from the commitment in the UN Charter to promote respect for all human rights, it should also be recalled that every permanent member of the Security Council has signed the Covenant, although two (China and the United States) have yet to ratify it [[109]]. Most of the non-permanent members at any given time are parties. Each of these States has undertaken, in conformity with article 2, paragraph 1, of the Covenant to 'take steps, individually and through international assistance and cooperation, especially economic and technical, to the maximum of its available resources, with a view to achieving progressively the full realization of the rights recognized in the present Covenant by all appropriate means ...'. When the affected State is also a State party, it is doubly incumbent upon other States to respect and take account of the relevant obligations. To the extent that sanctions are imposed on States which are not parties to the Covenant, the same principles would in any event apply, given the status of the economic, social and cultural rights of vulnerable groups as part of general international law, as evidenced, for example,

[107]Committee on Economic, Social and Cultural Rights, General Comment No. 15 (2002), The right to water (arts. 11 and 12 of the International Covenant on Economic, Social and Cultural Rights), cited above note 106, paras. 31 and 35–36. See also, e.g., Statement of the Committee on Economic, Social and Cultural Rights to the Third Ministerial Conference of the World Trade Organization, Seattle, 30 November–3 December 1999 (E/C.12/1999/9); Committee on Economic, Social and Cultural Rights, General Comment No. 12 (1999), *The right to adequate food (art. 11)* (E/C.12/1999/5), at paras. 19 and 36 ("States parties should, in international agreements whenever relevant, ensure that the right to adequate food is given due attention"); Committee on Economic, Social and Cultural Rights, General Comment No. 14 (2000), The right to the highest attainable standard of health (article 12 of the International Covenant on Economic, Social and Cultural Rights), cited above note 104, para. 39 ("In relation to the conclusion of other international agreements, States parties should take steps to ensure that these instruments do not adversely impact upon the right to health").

[108]Committee on Economic, Social and Cultural Rights, General Comment No. 8 (1997): The relationship between economic sanctions and respect for economic, social and cultural rights (E/1998/22).

[109]China ratified the International Covenant on Economic, Social and Cultural Rights in 2001, after the date at which this General Comment was adopted.

by the near-universal ratification of the Convention on the Rights of the Child and the status of the Universal Declaration of Human Rights.[110]

The notion of an obligation that is "doubly incumbent" on a State refers to the fact that, while a State party to the International Covenant on Economic, Social and Cultural Rights would violate its obligations under this instrument if it were to contribute to the adoption of sanctions that violate the economic, social and cultural rights of populations in the country targeted by the sanctions, it is prohibited, in addition, to coerce another State into violating its own obligations under international human rights law. It matters not, according to the Committee on Economic, Social and Cultural Rights, that a State imposes such sanctions unilaterally, or that it imposes such sanctions by exercising its voting rights within an organisation (such as the United Nations, acting through the Security Council) so as produce the same effect. As summarized most recently by the Committee in its Statement of 24 June 2016 on public debt, austerity measures and the International Covenant on Economic, Social and Cultural Rights:

> States parties to the Covenant would be acting in violation of their obligations if they were to delegate powers to the IMF or to other agencies and to allow such powers to be exercised without ensuring that they do not infringe on human rights. Similarly, they would be acting in breach of their obligations if they were to exercise their voting rights within such agencies without taking such rights into account. The same duties apply to States that are not parties to the Covenant, under human rights law as part of general international law. Their responsibility would not be absolved even where a State party, in its capacity of a member State of an international organisation, would be acting fully in accordance with the rules of the organisation.[111]

This is noteworthy, since under general international law, a member State of an international organisation can only exceptionally be considered to engage its responsibility simply as a result of exercising its rights within the organisation. In article 58 (Aid or assistance by a State in the commission of an internationally wrongful act by an international organization) of its Draft Articles on the Responsibility of International Organizations, the International Law Commission does provide that a State may be responsible for aiding or assisting an international organisation in the commission of an internationally wrongful act by the latter "if (a) the State does so with knowledge of the circumstances of the internationally wrongful act; and (b) the act would be internationally wrongful if committed by that State".[112] Such a responsibility however would not in principle arise where a State does no more than exercise its rights in accordance with the constitutive rules of the organisation:

[110]Committee on Economic, Social and Cultural Rights, General Comment No. 8 (1997) (E/1998/22), para. 51.

[111]E/C.12/2016/1, para. 9.

[112]Article 58, para. 1.

> An act by a State member of an international organization done in accordance with the rules of the organization does not as such engage the international responsibility of that State under the terms of this article.[113]

The commentary to article 58 states in part that where the State is a member of the international organisation concerned, "the possibility that aid or assistance could result from conduct taken by the State within the framework of the organization cannot be totally excluded. However, as specified in paragraph 2 [quoted above], an act by a member State which is done in accordance with the rules of the organization does not as such engage the international responsibility of that State for aid or assistance. These criteria could entail some difficulties in ascertaining whether aid or assistance has taken place in borderline cases. The factual context such as the size of membership and the nature of the involvement will probably be decisive."[114]

General international law therefore appears to impose stricter conditions on the engagement of the responsibility of States for the acts adopted in accordance with the rules of the organisation of which it is a member, than does international human rights law;[115] even under general international law, however, such a responsibility cannot be excluded. Thus, a State could engage its responsibility if it were to exercise its powers as a member of an international organisation, so as to lead the organisation to take measures that do not comply with the right to development.

A Duty of States to Faithfully Implement Decisions and Recommendations Emanating from International Organisations, Where This Supports the Right to Development

The third category of global obligations consists in implementing, in good faith, decisions and recommendations emanating from international organisations of which the State concerned is a member, where such decisions and recommendations contribute to the realization of the right to development. This goes beyond the duty to comply, in good faith, with the treaties which the State is a party to.[116] It includes the expectation that States involved in regional or global partnerships which contribute to the right to development shall treat as binding the decisions and recommendations adopted in such settings, and accept to be held accountable for implementation. The requirements of the right to development, in other terms, are gradually clarified by such decisions and recommendations, insofar as they are

[113] Id., para. 2.

[114] Report of the International Law Commission on the work of its 58th session, 1 May-9 June and 3 July-11 August 2006, I.L.C. Report, A/61/10 (2006), chap. VI, paras. 77–91.

[115] The Guiding Principles on foreign debt and human rights (cited above, note 13) define the duty of international assistance and cooperation as including a requirement that States, "*individually or through membership of international institutions*, do not adopt or engage in policies that undermine the enjoyment of human rights or further engender disparities between and within States" (para. 22 (emphasis added)).

[116] Vienna Convention on the Law of Treaties, cited above note 26, art. 26.

Table 12.1 Conceptual framework: typology of obligations and associated legal regimes

Extraterritorial obligations	
Respect	1. Duty of each State not to take measures that have negative impacts on the right to development outside the State's national territory
Protect	2. Duty of each State to take measures that ensure that actors over which it can exercise control/authority shall not infringe on the right to development outside the State's national territory
Fulfil	3. Duty of each State, commensurate with its abilities, to contribute to the realization of the right to development in other States by supporting their efforts
Global obligations	
Establish new forms of international cooperation	4. Duty to seek, in good faith, to conclude new partnerships with a view to shaping an international environment enabling development efforts deployed at domestic level, by putting forward proposals for international agreements that (1) enable all States to respect, protect and fulfil human rights; (2) shall benefit, as a matter of priority, the most marginalized groups within the States concerned; and (3) take into account the principle of common but differentiated responsibilities and respective capabilities
Operate within international negotiation fora	5. Duty of each State to join existing partnerships that contribute to the realization of right to development and, as member of such partnerships, to exercise its rights within them with a view to supporting the right to development
Implement existing partnerships	6. Duty of each State to implement decisions and recommendations adopted within international organisations that contribute to the realization of the right to development

supportive of the right. The criteria on the basis of which such decisions and recommendations should be identified, however, remain unclear. One of the objectives of this report is to help make progress towards such identification.

Summary

The conceptual framework presented here may be summarized in the form of Table 12.1, linking each category of obligations to a specific legal regime:

The International Dimensions of the Right to Development: Attributes and Indicators

The attributes of the international dimensions of the right to development are defined here in six areas, which are central to enable poverty-reduction strategies at domestic level: these are the alleviation of the burden of the foreign debt; the tackling of illicit financial flows; the management of international development cooperation; the direction of trade towards sustainable development; the channelling of foreign direct investment towards development needs; and the universalisation of social protection floors. For each of these areas, this report recalls the current understanding of the requirements of international human rights law; and it seeks to relate such understanding to the various categories of extraterritorial and global obligations defined in the conceptual framework described above.

Alleviating the Burden of Foreign Debt: Attributes Related to the Alleviation of the Foreign Debt

In reviewing the human rights records of States parties to the various United Nations human rights treaties, expert human rights treaty bodies have regularly been confronted with the argument that the burden of the foreign debt or the macroeconomic adjustment programmes imposed by international financial institutions as a condition for the continued receipt of loans constituted a major obstacle to the ability of States to comply with their human rights obligations, particularly as regards the realization of economic, social and cultural rights.[117] Conversely, some countries

[117]See, for example, the reports submitted to the Committee on the Rights of the Child, in chronological order, by the Central African Republic (CRC/C/11/Add.18 (1998)), by Honduras (CRC/C/65/Add.2 (1998), paras. 35–36 and 124 ("the economic contraction resulting from reforms of the economic system and the payment of a crushing external debt, considerably reduces the possibilities for priority attention to human development")), by Suriname (CRC/C/28/Add.11 (1998)), by Mozambique (CRC/C/41/Add.11 (2001), para. 8 ("a heavy foreign debt service burden, which has delayed much-needed investment in the social area to provide the majority of Mozambicans"), by Madagascar (CRC/C/70/Add.18 (2003), para. 67), by Zambia (CRC/C/11/Add.25 (2002), para. 16 ("The burden of servicing a huge external debt has taken a heavy toll on the national budget, and severely shrunk resources available for development")), by Sri Lanka (CRC/C/70/Add.17 (2002), paras. 128 and 144), by Nepal (CRC/C/65/Add.30 (2004), paras. 36 and 37 ("Debt servicing already claims about 14 per cent of the total budget and its impact adversely affects public investments and expenditure in the social sector, and, in particular, the provision of basic social services")), by Ecuador (CRC/C/65/Add.28 (2004), para. 53), by Kenya (CRC/C/KEN/2 (2006), para. 30 ("large allocations for debt servicing, salaries and other recurrent costs in the Government budget have crowded out spending on social services")); the reports submitted to the Committee on Economic, Social and Cultural Rights by Soudan ((E/1990/5/Add.41)(1998), para. 64), by Morocco ((E/1990/6/Add.20) (1999), para. 209), by Algeria ((E/1990/6/Add.26) (2000), paras. 59–61), by Benin ((E/1990/5/Add.48), para. 35), by Ecuador (E/1990/6/Add.36) (2002),

reported an improvement after they managed to reimburse their debt[118] or benefited from debt relief measures, for instance under the Heavily Indebted Poor Countries initiative, allowing them to increase the budgets dedicated to social sectors.[119]

This has led the Committee on Economic, Social and Cultural Rights to express the view that, while "adjustment programmes [imposed on indebted countries as a condition for receiving further loans] will often be unavoidable and that these will frequently involve a major element of austerity", where such programmes are adopted,

> ... endeavours to protect the most basic economic, social and cultural rights become more, rather than less, urgent. States parties to the Covenant, as well as the relevant United Nations agencies, should thus make a particular effort to ensure that such protection is, to the maximum extent possible, built-in to programmes and policies designed to promote adjustment. Such an approach, which is sometimes referred to as "adjustment with a human face" or as promoting "the human dimension of development" requires that the goal of protecting the rights of the poor and vulnerable should become a basic objective of economic adjustment. Similarly, international measures to deal with the debt crisis should take full account of the need to protect economic, social and cultural rights through, *inter alia*, international cooperation. In many situations, this might point to the need for major debt relief initiatives.[120]

The Committee on Economic, Social and Cultural Rights, as well as other human rights treaty bodies, have regularly noted that the burden of the reimbursement of the foreign debt, as well as the implementation of structural adjustment programmes (or poverty reduction strategy papers premised on similar macro-economic considerations), might seriously impede the ability of the States concerned to realize economic, social and cultural rights.[121] In a typical formulation, the Committee on

---

para. 309 ("The constraints imposed by the adjustment policies implemented by Governments in order to achieve a balanced budget have had an impact on the lowest income groups. In recent years, they have accelerated demographic changes in Ecuador in the shape of migration from the countryside to the cities, resulting in extremely fast growth of marginal urban areas forming belts of poverty,. . .")); or by Kenya ((E/C.12/KEN/1)(2007), para. 90 ("Although the structural adjustment programmes were presented as the panacea to underdevelopment and poverty in the country, the cut in public expenditure in key social sectors have had a devastating effect on the enjoyment of socio-economic rights in general and the right to adequate standard of living in particular")).

[118] See, for instance, the report submitted by Egypt to the Committee on Economic, Social and Cultural Rights (E/1990/5/Add.38) (1998), para. 8.

[119] See, for instance, the combined third to fifth reports of States parties due in 2012 submitted by the Democratic Republic of Congo in 2016 (CRC/C/COD/3–5) (24 June 2016), para. 25 ("In 2010, external debt relief for the Democratic Republic of the Congo was approved to the level of US$ 13 billion, that is to say approximately 90 per cent; this has made it possible to redirect the resources earmarked for debt payment to social welfare measures and stabilization of the macroeconomic framework").

[120] Committee on Economic, Social and Cultural Rights, General Comment No. 2: International technical assistance measures (art. 22 of the Covenant) (E/1990/23 (2 Feb. 1990)), para. 9.

[121] See, for instance, the Concluding Observations adopted by the Committee on the Rights of the Child on Tanzania in 2001 ((CRC/C/15/Add.156) (2001), para. 9 (noting "the impact of the structural adjustment programme, high external debt payments, and increasing levels of unemployment and poverty within the State party")), on Niger in 2002 ((CRC/C/15/Add.179) (2002), para.

Economic, Social and Cultural Rights noted that the efforts of Honduras to comply with its obligations under the International Covenant on Economic, Social and Cultural Rights "are impeded by the fact that it is classified as a highly indebted poor country and that up to 40 per cent of its annual national budget is allocated to foreign debt servicing", and it acknowledged that "the structural adjustment policies in the State party have negatively affected the enjoyment of economic, social and cultural rights by the population, especially the vulnerable and marginalized groups of society".[122]

On 24 June 2016, the Committee on Economic, Social and Cultural Rights adopted a Statement titled "Public Debt, Austerity Measures and the International Covenant on Economic, Social and Cultural Rights".[123] The statement examines in particular the duties under the Covenant of States parties as lenders. The Committee remarked that "States parties to the Covenant would be acting in violation of their obligations if they were to delegate powers to [international organisations providing loans] and to allow such powers to be exercised without ensuring that they do not infringe on human rights. Similarly, they would be acting in breach of their obligations if they were to exercise their voting rights within such agencies without taking such rights into account".[124] When States provide bilateral loans, they should keep in mind the prohibition imposed under international law of "coercing other States into violating their own obligations under either the Covenant or under other rules of international law."[125] Therefore, the Committee concluded: "Both as Lenders in bilateral loans and as members of international organisations providing financial assistance, all States should [...] ensure that they do not impose on borrowing States

8 (recommending that Niger "ensure the effective implementation of the Poverty Reduction Strategy Paper, paying special attention to the possible negative short-term impact of structural adjustment on the social rights of children")), or on Burkina Faso in 2002 ((CRC/C/15/Add.193) (2002), para. 16 (recommending that Burkina Faso "Undertake a study on the impact of structural adjustment programmes on the right of children to social services")); or the Concluding Observations adopted by the Committee on Economic, Social and Cultural Rights on Zambia in 2005 ((E/C.12/1/Add.106) (2005), para. 48); CRC/C/Add.207 (Sri Lanka); CRC/C/15/Add.197 (Republic of Korea); CRC/C/15/Add.193 (Burkina Faso); CRC/C/15/Add.190 (Sudan); CRC/C/15/Add.186 (Netherlands/Netherlands Antilles); CRC/C/15/Add.179 (Niger); CRC/C/15/Add.174 (Malawi); CRC/C/15/Add.172 (Mozambique); CRC/C/15/Add.160 (Kenya); CRC/C/15/Add.152 (Turkey); CRC/C/15/Add.138 (Central African Republic); CRC/C/15/Add.130 (Suriname); CRC/C/Add.124 (Georgia); and CRC/C/15/Add.115 (India). See also Human Rights Council, Consolidation of findings of the high-level task force on the implementation of the right to development, 25 March 2010, A/HRC/15/WG.2/TF/2/Add.1, para. 54.

[122]E/C.12/1/Add.57 (2001), paras. 9–10.

[123]Committee on Economic, Social and Cultural Rights, Public Debt, Austerity Measures and the International Covenant on Economic, Social and Cultural Rights (24 June 2016) (E/C.12/2016/1).

[124]Id., para. 9.

[125]Id., para. 11 (referring to International Law Commission, *Draft Articles on the Responsibility of States for Internationally Wrongful Acts*, cited above note 27, art. 18; and to Committee on Economic, Social and Cultural Rights, General Comment No. 8 (1997): The relationship between economic sanctions and respect for economic, social and cultural rights, E/1998/22, para. 51).

obligations that would lead the latter to adopt retrogressive measures in violation of their obligations under the Covenant."[126]

The Vienna Declaration and Programme of Action adopted on 25 June 1993 by the World Conference on Human Rights calls upon the international community to "make all efforts to help alleviate the external debt burden of developing countries, in order to supplement the efforts of the Governments of such countries to attain the full realization of the economic, social and cultural rights of their people".[127] In 2000, the Millennium Declaration also included a call on industrialized countries to "implement the enhanced programme of debt relief for the heavily indebted poor countries without further delay and to agree to cancel all official bilateral debts of those countries in return for their making demonstrable commitments to poverty reduction",[128] and it included a pledge to "deal comprehensively and effectively with the debt problems of low- and middle-income developing countries, through various national and international measures designed to make their debt sustainable in the long term".[129] Building on the 2002 Monterrey Consensus[130] and the 2008 Doha Declaration, the Addis Ababa Action Agenda recognizes "the need to assist developing countries in attaining long-term debt sustainability through coordinated policies aimed at fostering debt financing, debt relief, debt restructuring and sound debt management, as appropriate", and includes a pledge to "continue to support the remaining HIPC-eligible countries that are working to complete the HIPC process" and, "on a case-by-case basis" to "explore initiatives to support non-HIPC countries with sound economic policies to enable them to address the issue of debt sustainability". It acknowledges that, while "maintaining sustainable debt levels is the responsibility of the borrowing countries", "lenders also have a responsibility to lend in a way that does not undermine a country's debt sustainability".[131]

[126]Id., para. 11. The position expressed by the Committee in this recent statement was largely foreshadowed in earlier statements by the same body, in particular in the General Comment No. 18: The right to work (E/C.12/GC/186 (2005)), where it had already made it clear that "To comply with their international obligations in relation to article 6, States parties should endeavour to promote the right to work in other countries as well as in bilateral and multilateral negotiations. In negotiations with international financial institutions, States parties should ensure protection of the right to work of their population. States parties that are members of international financial institutions, in particular the International Monetary Fund, the World Bank and regional development banks, should pay greater attention to the protection of the right to work in influencing the lending policies, credit agreements, structural adjustment programmes and international measures of these institutions. The strategies, programmes and policies adopted by States parties under structural adjustment programmes should not interfere with their core obligations in relation to the right to work and impact negatively on the right to work of women, young persons and the disadvantaged and marginalized individuals and groups" (para. 30).

[127]Vienna Declaration and Programme of Action, cited above note 46, para. 12.

[128]Millennium Declaration, adopted by Res. 55/2 of the General Assembly, para. 15.

[129]Id., para. 16.

[130]Report of the International Conference on Financing for Development, Monterrey, Mexico, 18–22 March 2002 (A/CONF.198/11), chapter 1, resolution 1, annex, paras. 47–51.

[131]Addis Ababa Action Agenda, cited above note 8, para. 97.

The Addis Ababa Action Agenda also notes "the importance of debt restructurings being timely, orderly, effective, fair and negotiated in good faith", and that "successful debt restructurings enhance the ability of countries to achieve sustainable development and the sustainable development goals."[132] However, in a clear reference to so-called "vulture funds", it expresses its concern at "the ability of non-cooperative minority bondholders to disrupt the will of the large majority of bondholders who accept a restructuring of a debt-crisis country's obligations", and encourages Governments to adopt legislation to counter such actions.[133]

Fortunately, the international community has made progress on both issues. On 10 September 2015, the UN General Assembly adopted resolution 69/319, declaring that sovereign debt restructuring processes should be guided by nine Basic Principles, including the right to sovereign debt restructuring, good faith, transparency, equitable treatment, sovereign immunity, legitimacy, sustainability and the principle of majority restructuring. The resolution was adopted by a vote of 136 in favour and 6 against, with 41 abstentions. The Independent Expert on the effects of foreign debt and human rights expressed the view that the nine Basic Principles "reflect customary law and general principles of international law to a large extent and, as such, are legally binding".[134]

In parallel, some creditor States, including the EU Member States and the Members of the Club of Paris, pledged not to sell their claims on highly-indebted poor countries (HIPCs) to creditors unwilling to provide debt relief, and two countries (the United Kingdom and Belgium) adopted legislation specifically aimed to combating the abusive practices of vulture funds.[135] The Advisory Committee of the Human Rights Council, in a report requested by resolution 27/30 of the Human Rights Council, recommends that States enact legislation aimed at curtailing the predatory activities of vulture funds within their jurisdiction, (1) covering both HIPCs and other countries; (2) applying to commercial creditors that refuse to negotiate any restructuring of the debt; (3) prohibiting the filing of claims that are manifestly disproportionate to the amount initially paid to purchase the sovereign debt.[136] It also recommends that States refuse to "give effect to foreign judgments or conduct enforcement procedures in favour of vulture funds that are pursuing a disproportionate profit", i.e., granting claims that are in excess of the discounted price originally paid for the bonds.[137] This is consistent with, and clarifies the implications of, the call included in Human Rights Council resolution 27/30, that

---

[132] Addis Ababa Action Agenda, cited above note 8, para. 98.

[133] Addis Ababa Action Agenda, cited above note 8, para. 100.

[134] "Restructuring of sovereign debt: UN expert stresses GA Principles are binding", press release, New York, 10 September 2015.

[135] See Report of the Human Rights Council Advisory Committee on the activities of vulture funds and the impact on human rights (A/HRC/33/54) (20 July 2016).

[136] Id., para. 87(a).

[137] Id., para. 87(b).

States "consider implementing legal frameworks to curtail predatory vulture fund activities within their jurisdictions" (Table 12.2).[138]

Eliminating Illicit Financial Flows: Attributes Related to the Elimination of Illicit Financial Flows

Tax evasion and avoidance as well as other illicit money flows represent a huge loss to countries, and it is of particular consequence (as a percentage of their public budgets) in low- and middle-income countries.[139] In 2008, Global Financial Integrity estimated that, during the 2002–2006 period, illicit financial flows represented an average of between US$859 billion and US$1.06 trillion on a yearly basis.[140] For Africa alone, a conservative estimate is that illicit financial flows have amounted to a total of US$854 billion for the period 1970–2008.[141] These outflows have been steadily growing throughout the period at an average rate of 12.1% per year (with peaks reached in oil-producing countries such as Nigeria and Sudan linked to increases in the price of oil). The impacts are considerable: by the end of 2008, the same study notes, the cumulative impact of these outflows meant that each African woman, man or child lost US$989 to illicit financial outflows.[142] In fact, the total financial flows for 1970–2008 represent a sum far in excess of the external debt of all African countries (US$279 billion in 2008): in other terms, taking into account illicit financial flows, Africa is a net creditor to the world, and by tackling such illicit financial flows, about US$600 billion could have been mobilized for the fight against poverty on the continent.[143] Although the situation in Africa is particularly troubling, the continent is not alone in this regard. For instance, according to the Inter-American Development Bank, evasion rates of personal and corporate income taxes

[138] A/RES/37/30, para. 2. The resolution was adopted by a recorded vote of 33 to 5, with 9 abstentions.

[139] For a useful assessment, see OECD, *Development Co-Operation Report 2014. Mobilising Resources for Sustainable Development* (OECD Publishing, Paris, 2014), chapter II.13. See also the Final study on illicit financial flows, human rights and the 2030 Agenda for Sustainable Development of the Independent Expert on the effects of foreign debt and other related international financial obligations of States on the full enjoyment of all human rights, particularly economic, social and cultural rights, Juan Pablo Bohoslavsky (A/HRC/31/61) (15 January 2016), paras. 10–11 (recalling estimates concerning the levels of wealth, mostly undeclared, sheltered in tax havens, and noting that these amounts have significantly increased in recent years).

[140] Kar and Cartwright-Smith (2008).

[141] Kar and Cartwright-Smith (2010).

[142] Kar and Cartwright-Smith (2010), p. 12.

[143] This was also the conclusion reached by Ndikumana and Boyce (2008).

Table 12.2 Alleviating the burden of debt (A)—typology of obligations and associated implementation measures

Extraterritorial obligations	
Respect	(A1.1) Lender States should design foreign debt strategies so as to avoid hampering the improvement of conditions guaranteeing the enjoyment of human rights and so as to ensure, *inter alia*, that "debtor States achieve an adequate level of growth to meet their social and economic needs and their development requirements, as well as fulfilment of their human rights obligations"[a]
	(A1.2) Lender States should also "perform due diligence on the credit-worthiness and ability to repay of the borrower"; "refrain from providing a loan in circumstances where the lender is aware that the funds will be used for non-public purposes or for a non-viable project";[b] and ensure that the loan "will not be wasted through official corruption, economic mismanagement or other unproductive uses in the Borrower State",[c] and that it shall not "increase the Borrower State's external debt stock to an unsustainable level that will make debt repayment difficult and impede the creation of conditions for the realization of human rights"[d]
	(A1.3) Borrower and Lender States should prepare human rights impact assessments prior to negotiating structural adjustment programmes with creditors[e]
Protect	(A2.1) Adoption of legislation against vulture funds, prohibiting commercial creditors that refuse to negotiate any restructuring of the debt from filing claims that are manifestly disproportionate to the amount initially paid to purchase the sovereign debt, and refusing the execution of foreign judgments in favour of vulture funds that are pursuing a disproportionate profit[f]
Fulfil	
Global obligations	
Establish new partnerships	(A4.1) Borrower and Lender States should enter into renegotiation and restructuring of the foreign debt in good faith where servicing the debts compromises the Borrower State's capacity to fulfil its international human rights obligations,[g] or when a moratorium on repayment would be justified following a change in circumstances beyond the control of the Borrower State[h]
Operate within partnerships	(A5.1) As members of international financial institutions, States should ensure any economic, financial or technical advice, instruction guidance or similar recommendation by such institutions, which are meant to address the problems occasioned by external indebtedness, must respect the debtor State's independent process of national development[i]
Implement partnerships	

[a]Guiding Principles on foreign debt and human rights, cited in note 13, para. 8
[b]Id., para. 23
[c]Id., paras. 38
[d]Id., para. 39
[e]Id., para. 12: "States should analyse policies and programmes, including those relating to external debt, macroeconomic stability, structural reform and investment, with respect to their impact on poverty and inequality, social development and the enjoyment of human rights, as well as their gender implications, and adjust them as appropriate, to promote a more equitable and

(continued)

non-discriminatory distribution of the benefits of growth and services"; see also Id., para. 40–41 (clarifying the content of such human rights impact assessments)
[f]Report of the Human Rights Council Advisory Committee on the activities of vulture funds and the impact on human rights (A/HRC/33/54) (20 July 2016), para. 87. See also UNCTAD's Principles on Promoting Responsible Sovereign Lending and Borrowing (2012), Principle 7 (Debt Restructurings) ("A creditor that acquires a debt instrument of a sovereign in financial distress with the intent of forcing a preferential settlement of the claim outside of a consensual workout process is acting abusively")
[g]Guiding Principles on foreign debt and human rights, cited in note 13, paras. 52–54
[h]Id., para. 58. See also UNCTAD's Principles on Promoting Responsible Sovereign Lending and Borrowing (2012), Principle 7 (Debt Restructurings); and General Assembly resolution 69/319, basic principle 2
[i]Guiding Principles on foreign debt and human rights, cited in note 13, para. 75

average 50% in 10 representative Latin American countries, with Guatemala topping the league with an evasion rate of 70%.[144]

This is now described to be a priority in various international outcome documents. In the Addis Ababa Action Agenda, the Heads of State and Government and High Representatives recognize the need to curb illicit financial flows.[145] Specifically, governments have committed to "redouble efforts to substantially reduce illicit financial flows by 2030, with a view to eventually eliminating them, including by combating tax evasion and corruption through strengthened national regulation and increased international cooperation"; and to "reduce opportunities for tax avoidance". The means to achieve this which are relevant to understanding the international dimensions of the right to development include (1) "inserting anti-abuse clauses in all tax treaties"; (2) "enhanc[ing] disclosure practices and transparency in both source and destination countries, including by seeking to ensure transparency in all financial transactions between Governments and companies to relevant tax authorities"; (3) ensuring that "all companies, including multinationals, pay taxes to the Governments of countries where economic activity occurs and value is created, in accordance with national and international laws and policies";[146] (4) implementing the "Financial Action Task Force standards on anti-money-laundering/counter-terrorism financing";[147] (5) "making the [United Nations Convention against Corruption] an effective instrument to deter, detect, prevent and counter corruption and

---

[144]Corbacho et al. (2013), p. 121 (Fig. 7.4). These estimates are based on data from the period 2003–2010, with different years for the different countries (for Guatemala for instance, the reference year in 2006). They should therefore be treated with caution as a source of cross-country comparisons. They do provide, however, an idea of the magnitude of the problem.

[145]Addis Ababa Action Agenda, cited above note 8, para. 18.

[146]Id., para. 23.

[147]Id., paras. 23–24. The Financial Action Task Force (FATF), an independent intergovernmental body established in 1989 to support the fight against money laundering, adopted a set of recommendations addressed to its Member States. Known as the *International Standards on Combating Money Laundering and the Financing of Terrorism and Proliferation* (AML/CFT standards) the recommendations were initially drawn up in 1990; they were most recently updated in 2012, and have been endorsed by 180 countries. See for the text of the recommendations: http://www.fatf-gafi.

bribery, prosecute those involved in corrupt activities, and recover and return stolen assets to their country of origin"; and (6) "eliminat[ing] safe havens that create incentives for transfer abroad of stolen assets and illicit financial flows".[148] While, in 2000, the Millennium Development Goals had remained silent on the issue, States have now pledged to significantly reduce by 2030 illicit financial flows and strengthen the recovery and return of stolen assets in the Sustainable Development Agenda 2030 (target 16.4). Though the commitments contained in the Addis Ababa Action Agenda and, especially, in the Sustainable Development Goals, remain too vague to be truly enforceable, they nevertheless send a strong political signal.

The Special Rapporteur on Extreme Poverty and Human Rights recalled that: "Individual countries, in particular low-income countries, are severely constrained in the measures that they alone can take against tax abuse. Illicit financial flows are international in nature and therefore beyond the capacity of one State alone to tackle. The availability of offshore financial centres (tax havens) that offer low or no taxes and secrecy is a major factor."[149] The Addis Ababa Action Agenda explicitly acknowledges the need for enhanced international tax cooperation on these issues,[150] beyond the more classic forms of international cooperation in the form of "aid for tax" strategies.[151] As noted by the Independent Expert on the effects of foreign debt and other related international financial obligations of States on the full enjoyment of all human rights, entering into such forms of cooperation to contribute to fight illicit financial flows, including both tax evasion and tax avoidance, is an obligation for States parties to human rights instruments such as the International Covenant on Economic, Social and Cultural Rights: "While the Covenant refers in particular to economic and technical assistance and cooperation, international assistance may comprise other measures, including provision of information to people in other countries or cooperation with their State, for example, to trace stolen public funds".[152]

---

org/media/fatf/documents/recommendations/pdfs/FATF_Recommendations.pdf (last consulted on 28 Feb. 2016).

[148]Id., para. 25.

[149]Report of the Special Rapporteur on extreme poverty and human rights, Magdalena Sepulveda Carmona, presented at the 26th session of the Human Rights Council (A/HRC/26/28) (22 May 2014), para. 61.

[150]Id., para. 27.

[151]These consist in supporting local institutions in charge of tax collection: see in this regard OECD, *Tax and Development: Aid Modalities for Strengthening Tax Systems* (OECD Publishing, Paris, 2013). As part of the Third International Conference on Financing for Development, Tax Inspectors Without Borders was launched as an OECD/UNDP joint initiative to help developing counties bolster domestic revenues by strengthening their tax audit capacities.

[152]Final study on illicit financial flows, human rights and the 2030 Agenda for Sustainable Development of the Independent Expert on the effects of foreign debt and other related international financial obligations of States on the full enjoyment of all human rights, particularly economic, social and cultural rights, Juan Pablo Bohoslavsky (A/HRC/31/61) (15 January 2016), para. 42.

Stepping up efforts against illicit financial flows is thus clearly a human rights issue, and has clear implications for the realization of the right to development.[153] Indeed, recognizing that "illicit capital flight undermines the capacity of State Parties to implement the African Charter on Human and Peoples' Rights and to attain the Millennium Development Goals", the African Commission on Human and Peoples' Rights has called upon States parties to the African Charter on Human and Peoples' Rights "to examine their national tax laws and policies towards preventing illicit capital flight in Africa".[154] That these efforts are essential for the fulfilment of human rights is made increasingly explicit by United Nations human rights treaty bodies. The Committee on Economic, Social and Cultural Rights noted in concluding observations related to the United Kingdom that "financial secrecy legislation [allowing its Overseas Territories and Crown Dependencies to prosper as tax havens] and permissive rules on corporate tax are affecting the ability of the State party, as well other States, to meet their obligation to mobilize the maximum available resources for the implementation of economic, social and cultural rights", and it recommended that it "intensify its efforts, in coordination with its Overseas Territories and Crown Dependencies, to address global tax abuse".[155] The Committee on the Elimination of Discrimination against Women also recently recommended that Switzerland "Undertake independent, participatory and periodic impact assessments of the extraterritorial effects of its financial secrecy and corporate tax policies on women's rights and substantive equality, and ensure that such assessments are conducted in an impartial manner with public disclosure of the methodology and finding".[156]

Importantly, the Addis Ababa Action Agenda includes a reference to the risks entailed in the use of tax incentives to attract investment, which may lead to a race to the bottom and, ultimately, to a reduced ability of all States to mobilize the domestic resources required to finance their sustainable development strategies.[157] This is particularly the case where corporations operating across different jurisdictions are allowed to resort with impunity to profit-shifting, taking advantage of differences between tax rates by artificially shifting profits across borders. This is done by

[153] See, e.g., Research-based study on the impact of flow of funds of illicit origin and the non-repatriation thereof to the countries of origin on the enjoyment of human rights, including economic, social and cultural rights—Progress report of the Advisory Committee of the Human Rights Council (A/HRC/36/52) (9 August 2017).

[154] Resolution adopted by the Commission at its 53rd ordinary session, 23 April 2013.

[155] Committee on Economic, Social and Cultural Rights, Concluding Observations on the sixth periodic report of the United Kingdom of Great Britain and Northern Ireland (E/C.12/GBR/CO/6, 14 July 2016), paras. 16–17.

[156] Committee on the Elimination of Discrimination against Women, Concluding Observations on the combined fourth and fifth reports of Switzerland (CEDAW/C/CHE/CO/4–5) (18 November 2016), para. 41.

[157] The Addis Ababa Action Agenda (cited above note 8) states in this regard that: "Tax incentives can be an appropriate policy tool. However, to end harmful tax practices, countries can engage in voluntary discussions on tax incentives in regional and international forums" (para. 27).

declaring profits in tax havens where they may have no staff or productive activities or only minimal activities, rather than declaring such profits (and paying the corresponding taxes) where their activities take place, thus leading to eroding the tax base allowing States to finance public policies and the provision of social services essential to the enjoyment of human rights.[158] Transfer pricing between different companies of a multinational group is one technique that allows to achieve this, in general, without violating the law. And it plays an increasingly important role: intra-group trade is currently estimated to represent 30% of global trade.[159] This is why instruments such as the United Nations Model Double Taxation Convention between Developed and Developing Countries[160] or the Organisation for Economic Co-operation and Development (OECD) Model Tax Convention on Income and on Capital[161] encourage countries to adopt the "arm's length standard", according to which (following the wording of article 9 of the UN Model Double Taxation Convention) they should prohibit mispricing between different parts of the multinational group, which is deemed to occur where such relations between related enterprises "differ from those which would be made between independent enterprises".

The international consensus on the issues above has been strengthening significantly during the past decade. In 2010, the Convention on Mutual Administrative Assistance in Tax Matters, initially the result of a joint effort of the OECD and the Council of Europe in 1988, was amended in order to allow for the participation of developing countries. The new text was opened for signature on 1 June 2011. It now covers 109 jurisdictions, including 15 jurisdictions covered by extension.[162] It provides for various forms of administrative cooperation between States in the assessment and collection of taxes, facilitating the exchange of information and the recovery of foreign tax claims with a view to supporting States' efforts to combat tax avoidance and evasion. At the same time, the G20 has identified base erosion and profit shifting (BEPS) as a major concern for tax justice worldwide, and the OECD

---

[158]Final study on illicit financial flows, human rights and the 2030 Agenda for Sustainable Development of the Independent Expert on the effects of foreign debt and other related international financial obligations of States on the full enjoyment of all human rights, particularly economic, social and cultural rights, Juan Pablo Bohoslavsky (A/HRC/31/61) (15 January 2016), para. 18.

[159]*United Nations Practical Manual on Transfer Pricing for Developing Countries*, UN Department of Economic and Social Affairs (ST/ESA/347) (United Nations, New York, 2013), para. 1.1.3. Estimates of the volume of intra-group trade (trade between different enterprises related to a same multinational group) are however notoriously difficult to arrive at: see Lanz and Miroudot (2011).

[160]The United Nations Model Double Taxation Convention between Developed and Developing Countries was initially adopted in 1980, and revised subsequently in 1999 and in 2011.

[161]The OECD Model Tax Convention on Income and on Capital has been regularly updated. The current version dates from 2014, but it is undergoing a revision at the time of writing.

[162]Thus, Anguilla, Bermuda, the British Virgin Islands, the Cayman Islands, Gibraltar, Guernsey, the Isle of Man, Jersey, Montserrat and the Turk and Caicos Islands are covered by extension from the United Kingdom; Aruba, Curaçao and Sint Maarten, the latter two formerly part of the Netherlands Antilles, are covered by extension from the Netherlands; the Faroe Islands are covered by extension of Denmark.

adopted a 15-point action plan in 2013 in order to address this, to be progressively implemented in the next few years ("OECD/G20 BEPS package").[163] Finally, on 7 June 2017, 68 jurisdictions signed the Multilateral Convention to Implement Tax Treaty Related Measures to Prevent Base Erosion and Profit Shifting (MLI), and nine other jurisdictions pledged to join. The MLI amends the large number of bilateral tax treaties concluded to eliminate double taxation between the parties; and it contains provisions aimed at combating tax abuse (Table 12.3).

Supporting the Right to Development Through Official Development Assistance: Attributes of the Duty to Provide International Assistance

An international consensus exists on the commitment of rich countries to contribute 0.7% of their gross national income (GNI) to official development assistance (ODA). The benchmark originated from the UNCTAD II conference, held in New Delhi in February and March 1968, as part of a broader objective that 1% of the wealth created in "economically advanced" countries (gross national product (GNP)) be transferred to developing countries as a combination of both official and private financial flows. UNCTAD II took note of the fact that some developed countries declared their willingness, within the framework of the 1% target for total flows, to provide a minimum of 0.75% of their GNP in net flows of official resources.[164] The 1% target of total flows was supported the following year by the Commission on International Development (headed by Lester B. Pearson, and established at the request of the President of the World Bank Robert McNamara), which in addition recognized "a special need for official development assistance on concessional terms, that is, [for aid] in the form of grants or loans on soft terms. [...] On the assumption that increases in aid can be more closely linked to efficient use and performance than hitherto, we recommend a substantial increase in official aid flows. Specifically, official development assistance should be raised to 0.70 percent of donor GDP by 1975, and in no case later than 1980".[165] This target was endorsed by

[163] OECD, *Development Co-Operation Report 2014. Mobilising Resources for Sustainable Development*, cited above (note 11), at 167–176.

[164] Decision on the aid volume target, adopted on 28 March 1968 at the 79th plenary meeting, Proceedings of the United Nations Conference on Trade and Development, Second Session, New Delhi, 1 Feb.-29 March 1968, vol. I: Report and Annexes, pp. 38–39. The decision was adopted by 69 votes to none, with 8 abstentions.

[165] *Partners in Development. Report of the Commission on International Development* (New York: Praeger Publ., 1969), p. 18. Indeed, the decision on the desirable volumes of aid endorsed at UNCTAD II included as part of official financial flows: "official cash grants and grants in kind including grants for technical assistance but excluding grants for defence purposes; sales of commodities against local currencies exclusive of utilization of such currencies by the donor country for its own purposes; government lending for periods exceeding 1 year net of repayments

Table 12.3 Eliminating illicit financial flows (B)—typology of obligations and associated implementation measures

Extraterritorial obligations	
Respect	(B1.1) Refrain from competitive taxation strategies as a means of attracting investors[a]
Protect	(B2.1) Require corporations whose activities are transnational to report publicly on a country-by-country basis, in order to expose major misalignments between the distribution of profit and the location of real economic activity[b]
Fulfil	(B3.1) Close tax havens which, thanks to bank secrecy laws, allow undeclared or illegally acquired assets or revenues to escape taxation, thus undermining the ability of all countries to broaden the tax base allowing for the collection of public revenue[c]
	(B3.2) Strengthen tax administrations, by a targeted use of ODA[d]
Global obligations	
Establish new partnerships	(B4.1) Ensure that any future tax convention incorporates the "arm's length principle" as a means to avoid tax avoidance through transfer pricing, taking into account the United Nations Model Double Taxation Convention between Developed and Developing Countries, and initiate negotiations towards a multilateral convention to combat abusive tax practices, a consolidation and apportionment system for taxing global corporate profits, leading to treat transnational corporations as single and unified firms[e]
Operate within partnerships	(B5.1) Accede to the OECD Convention on Mutual Administrative Assistance in Tax Matters
	(B5.2) Accede to the Multilateral Convention to Implement Tax Treaty Related Measures to Prevent Base Erosion and Profit Shifting (MLI)
Implement partnerships	(B6.1) Implement the Financial Action Task Force standards on anti-money-laundering/counter-terrorism financing[f]

[a]Addis Ababa Action Agenda, cited in note 8, para. 27

[b]Final study on illicit financial flows, human rights and the 2030 Agenda for Sustainable Development of the Independent Expert on the effects of foreign debt and other related international financial obligations of States on the full enjoyment of all human rights, particularly economic, social and cultural rights, Juan Pablo Bohoslavsky (A/HRC/31/61) (15 January 2016), para. 81

[c]E/C.12/GBR/CO/6, paras. 16–17; CEDAW/C/CHE/CO/4–5, para. 41

[d]Final study on illicit financial flows, human rights and the 2030 Agenda for Sustainable Development of the Independent Expert on the effects of foreign debt and other related international financial obligations of States on the full enjoyment of all human rights, particularly economic, social and cultural rights, Juan Pablo Bohoslavsky (A/HRC/31/61) (15 January 2016), para. 85

[e]Final study on illicit financial flows, human rights and the 2030 Agenda for Sustainable Development of the Independent Expert on the effects of foreign debt and other related international financial obligations of States on the full enjoyment of all human rights, particularly economic, social and cultural rights, Juan Pablo Bohoslavsky (A/HRC/31/61) (15 January 2016), para. 88. This proposal is inspired by the Independent Commission for the Reform of International Corporate Taxation, which suggested in the set of recommendations it presented in 2015 that: "Multinational corporations act – and therefore should likewise be taxed – as single firms doing business across international borders. This is essential because multinational corporations often structure transfer pricing and other financial arrangements to allocate profits to shell operations in low tax jurisdictions" (para. 3 of the Statement of Principles)

[f]Such implementation requires both that legislative/regulatory reforms be undertaken where there are lacunae, and that the legislative/regulatory framework is effectively implemented. The Financial Action Task Force (FATF) supports mutual evaluations between members, ensuring that both these dimensions are taken into account

the United Nations General Assembly in Resolution 2626 (XXV) on the International Development Strategy for the Second United Nations Development Decade adopted on 24 October 1970, which stated that:

> Each economically advanced country will progressively increase its official development assistance to the developing countries and will exert its best efforts to reach a minimum net amount of 0.7% of its gross national product at market prices by the middle of the Decade.

The target has been refined since it was initially affirmed in 1970, in order to ensure that the LDCs would be given priority in ODA. Most developed countries have pledged to achieve the target of 0.7% of ODA/GNI and 0.15–0.20% of ODA/GNI to least developed countries, and the UN human rights treaty bodies have regularly emphasized that delivering on this promise forms part of their duty of international cooperation.[166] Yet, as noted in the Addis Ababa Action Agenda, this commitment appears to be honoured more in the breach than in the observance.[167] Meanwhile, there is a growing consensus that aid as usual (quite apart from the levels of aid provided) is inadequate to address the real causes of poverty, which are more structural in nature.

The critique has two layers. Some authors, such as Erik Reinert, have questioned the Millennium Development Goals for their failure to encourage the diversification of economies in the global South: the MDGs, he states, "are far too biased towards palliative economics rather than structural change, towards treating the symptoms of poverty rather than its causes"; in his view, unless the productive capacities of poor countries are improved, the MDGs shall amount to little else than "a system where nations producing under increasing returns (industrialized nations) pay annual compensation to nations producing under constant or diminishing returns (raw material producers) for their losses".[168] This argument is that advocates of higher levels of development aid are proponents of "palliative economics" (in Reinert's phrase), and that they fail to question existing obstacles to development that result from the established international division of labour. Aid, in other terms, should not become a substitute (a palliative) for the restructuring of the international economic

---

of principal; grants and capital subscriptions to multilateral aid agencies, and net purchases of bonds, loans and participation from those agencies." No distinction was made therefore, in the 0.75% target for official flows, between concessional and non-concessional financing.

[166] See, for instance, Committee on Economic, Social and Cultural Rights, Concluding Observations: Germany (E/C.12/DEU/CO/5 (2011), para. 33); Committee on Economic, Social and Cultural Rights, Concluding Observations: Finland (E/C.12/FIN/CO/6 (2014), para. 8); Committee on the Rights of the Child, Concluding Observations: Germany (CRC/C/DEU/CO/3–4 (2014), para. 21); Committee on the Rights of the Child, Concluding Observations: Finland (CRC/C/FIN/CO/4 (2011), para. 22). This practice appears not to be followed by the Committee on the Rights of Persons with Disabilities, however. Article 32 of the Convention on the Rights of Persons with Disabilities does include a detailed set of prescriptions on international cooperation, laying the emphasis however on the need to support specifically the rights of persons with disabilities through international cooperation; it is this more targeted approach that the CRPD Committee has retained.

[167] Addis Ababa Action Agenda, cited above note 8, para. 51.

[168] Reinert (2007), pp. 262 and 265. See also Chang (2005).

order in order for it to be made more "fair"—less biased in favor of the countries that are currently most industrialized and who own the technologies on which the most advanced sectors of the economy depend. Another critique is more radical, however, since it denounces the perverse incentives of aid itself. Angus Deaton, the 2015 Laureate of the Nobel Prize in Economics, notes that foreign aid can lead to a lack of accountability of governments in receiving countries: the aid received allows these governments to maintain in place a system favorable to their interests without having to collect revenues from the population, and the population therefore has fewer incentives to control how the money is spent.[169] This argument against foreign aid as a development tool already figured prominently in the pamphlets of William Easterly[170] and Dambisa Moyo,[171] published respectively in 2006 and 2009.

These critiques tend to ignore that development aid too can be made more transparent and accountable to the population.[172] Yet, both the denunciation of foreign aid as purely "palliative" and the questions that have been raised as to how it affects the bonds between the governments in developing countries and their populations, explain the efforts in recent years to strengthen aid effectiveness.[173] It remains vital to maintain (and in many cases to increase) levels of official development assistance, and to ensure that how ODA levels are calculated is consistent with the promise of rich countries to dedicate 0.7% of their GNI to ODA (and 0.15–0.20% to least developed countries). But, in addition, indicators should be developed to assess aid effectiveness.

Official Development Assistance, as monitored by the OECD's Development Assistance Committee (DAC), includes financial support provided by OECD-DAC member countries to developing countries in the form either of grants or of "concessional" loans to developing countries, to support sectors such as health, sanitation, education, infrastructure, and strengthening tax systems and administrative

[169]Deaton (2013), p. 121. See also Saiz (2013), pp. 77–104 at p. 83.

[170]Easterly (2006), pp. 15–17 ("Feedback and Accountability").

[171]Moyo (2010), p. 58 ("In most functioning and healthy economies, the middle class pays taxes in return for government accountability. Foreign aid short-circuits this link. Because the government's financial dependence on its citizens has been reduced, it owes its people nothing.").

[172]See Report of the Special Rapporteur on the right to food, Olivier De Schutter, to the 10th session of the Human Rights Council, The role of development cooperation and food aid in realizing the right to adequate food: moving from charity to obligation (A/HRC/10/5) (11 February 2009), para. 26 ("A human rights framework requires that we deepen the principles of ownership, alignment and mutual accountability, by shifting our attention to the role of national parliaments, civil society organizations, and the ultimate beneficiaries of aid - the rights-holders - in the implementation and evaluation of foreign aid. It is this triangulation, away from a purely bilateral relationship between Governments, which the adoption of a human rights framework requires").

[173]These critiques also explain the demand that donor countries better align their policies in other areas that may impact on developing countries with their professed aim to support development efforts: the claim for "policy coherence for development" (now reframed as "policy coherence for sustainable development") emerged from that preoccupation. It is dealt with separately in this report.

capacity, among others.[174] For monitoring purposes, an official definition of ODA has been approved, which refers to financial assistance, channelled bilaterally or through multilateral agencies, which is:

1. provided by official agencies, including state and local governments, or by their executive agencies; and
2. each transaction of which:
   (a) is administered with the promotion of the economic development and welfare of developing countries as its main objective; and
   (b) is concessional in character and conveys a grant element of at least 25% (calculated at a rate of discount of 10%).

Neither military aid nor contribution to peacekeeping operations are included in ODA, with the exception of certain aspects of peacekeeping under a UN mandate. Support to civilian police can be included, except for certain aspects that relate to the paramilitary role of the police in controlling insurgencies or to intelligence work for counter-terrorism. Perhaps more controversially, in addition to assistance to refugees in developing countries, the temporary assistance (up to 12 months) provided to refugees from developing countries arriving in donor countries is reportable as ODA, and all costs associated with eventual repatriation to the developing country of origin are also reportable. How ODA is calculated of course has major impacts on how the 0.7% of GNI is assessed. For instance, due to the large inflow of refugees in the EU in 2015, some EU Member States were reported to have increased ODA in significant proportions (Greece by 39%, Germany by 26% and Hungary by 25%), but this has been discounted as "inflated aid" by non-governmental organizations, as it corresponds to the disbursements linked to the arrival or refugees in these countries, and does not contribute to meeting development needs in the countries of origin of these migrants. Indeed, one estimate is that for the year 2015, 17% of the aid from the EU countries "did not reflect a real transfer of resources to developing countries, because it went to "in-donor" refugee spending, debt relief, student costs, tied aid and interest payments".[175]

Moreover, industrialized countries pledged to mobilize jointly $100 billion a year by 2020 for climate mitigation and adaptation strategies in developing countries. The commitment was initially made at the December 2009 Copenhagen 15th session of the Conference of Parties (CoP) to the UN Framework Convention on Climate Change,[176] and it was reiterated at the 21st session of the CoP held in Paris in

[174]This definition is slightly adapted from the OECD DAC definition as it appears on: http://www.oecd.org/dac/financing-sustainable-development/development-finance-standards/ (last consulted on 1 Oct. 2017).

[175]Concord (European NGO confederation for relief and development), *Aidwatch Report 2016*, p. 6.

[176]See para. 8 of the Copenhagen Accord of 18 December 2009, agreed at the 15th conference of parties to the UN Framework Convention on Climate Change held in Copenhagen from 7 to 19 December 2009 (FCCC/CP/2009/11/Add.1) ("In the context of meaningful mitigation actions

December 2015.[177] The roadmap presented in October 2016 by developed countries offered estimates from the OECD that the aggregate volume of public and private climate finance mobilised by developed countries for developing countries reached US$62 billion in 2014, up from US$52 billion in 2013.[178] However, even apart from the important controversies about how such calculations are made (what "counts" as climate finance), it would be a source of concern if this funding were ODA repackaged, and diverted from the assistance provided to other sectors such as health, education or rural development. Nothing in the decisions made by the Parties to the UNFCCC appears to prevent that risk.

Finally, neither nominal flows of ODA nor levels of ODA as a proportion of GNI provide indications as to the quality of aid that is provided, and in particular, as to whether aid is predictable over a number of years[179] and untied, thus allowing receiving countries to plan long-term strategies and ensuring national ownership. The Paris Declaration on Aid Effectiveness, adopted in 2005, put forward the five key principles of ownership (developing countries set their own strategies for poverty reduction, improve their institutions and tackle corruption), alignment (donor countries align behind these objectives and use local systems), harmonisation (donor countries coordinate, simplify procedures and share information to avoid duplication), results (developing countries and donors shift focus to development results and results get measured) and mutual accountability (donors and partners are accountable for development results), in order to improve the quality of aid. Consistent with the 2001 DAC Recommendation on Untying Official Development Assistance to the Least Developed Countries, the commitments adopted in the Paris Declaration on Aid Effectiveness included untying aid, as a means to "reduce transaction costs for partner countries and improving country ownership and alignment".[180] Indeed, tied aid (linking the aid provided to the purchase of goods and

and transparency on implementation, developed countries commit to a goal of mobilizing jointly USD 100 billion dollars a year by 2020 to address the needs of developing countries. This funding will come from a wide variety of sources, public and private, bilateral and multilateral, including alternative sources of finance").

177 See para. 114 of Decision 1/CP.21, Adoption of the Paris Agreement (CCC/CP/2015/10/Add.1) (the Conference of Parties "strongly urges developed country Parties to scale up their level of financial support, with a concrete road map to achieve the goal of jointly providing USD 100 billion annually by 2020 for mitigation and adaptation while significantly increasing adaptation finance from current levels and to further provide appropriate technology and capacity-building support"). The figure itself does not appear, however, under the corresponding clause (Article 9) of the Paris Agreement, which states that "Developed country Parties shall provide financial resources to assist developing country Parties with respect to both mitigation and adaptation in continuation of their existing obligations under the Convention" (art. 9.1).

178 *Roadmap to US$100 billion*, October 2016.

179 The 2005 Paris Declaration on Aid Effectiveness included a commitment to "provide more predictable and multi-year commitments on aid flows to committed partner countries" (para. 4, ii).

180 Id., para. 31. See also the 2008 Accra Agenda for Action (adopted at the Third High-Level Forum on Aid Effectiveness, Accra, 2–4 September 2008), which includes a pledge by donors to "elaborate individual plans to further untie their aid to the maximum extent", to "promote the use of

services from the donor country) not only makes the purchases of beneficiary countries more expensive; it also undermines national ownership and makes it more difficult for aid finance to contribute to local economic development, despite the multiplier effects that could result from buying from local service providers and manufacturers and generating local jobs. Similarly, the need to make aid more predictable was emphasized both in the 2005 Paris Declaration on Aid Effectiveness, and in the 2008 Accra Agenda for Action, in which donors pledged, in particular, to "provide developing countries with regular and timely information on their rolling three- to five-year forward expenditure and/or implementation plans, with at least indicative resource allocations that developing countries can integrate in their medium-term planning and macroeconomic frameworks".[181]

The Addis-Ababa Action Agenda reiterated these earlier pledges to "improve the quality, impact and effectiveness of development cooperation and other international efforts in public finance", reaffirming governments' "adherence to agreed development cooperation effectiveness principles". It stated:

> We will align activities with national priorities, including by reducing fragmentation, accelerating the untying of aid, particularly for least developed countries and countries most in need. We will promote country ownership and results orientation and strengthen country systems, use programme-based approaches where appropriate, strengthen partnerships for development, reduce transaction costs, and increase transparency and mutual accountability. We will make development more effective and predictable by providing developing countries with regular and timely indicative information on planned support in the medium term.[182]

The Global Partnership for Effective Development Co-operation was established following the 2011 Busan High Level Forum to sustain political momentum and accountability for implementing Busan commitments. It supports a monitoring of progress towards aid effectiveness by a regular reporting process, based on a set of 10 indicators based on the 2005 Paris Declaration on Aid Effectiveness and on the additional dimensions introduced by the 2012 Busan Partnership agreement, at the request of developing countries. These indicators are mentioned in Table 12.4.

A relatively new trend in development finance concerns the role of blended finance, defined as "the strategic use of public or private investment with a development objective, including concessional tools, to mobilise additional finance with a commercial motivation for SDG-aligned investments in developing countries".[183] Consistent with the new paradigm, originating in the 2002 Monterrey Consensus and confirmed in the subsequent Financing for Development conferences, according to which development finance should span a much larger set of tools than ODA alone,

---

local and regional procurement by ensuring that their procurement procedures are transparent and allow local and regional firms to compete", and to "build on examples of good practice to help improve local firms' capacity to compete successfully for aid-funded procurement" (para. 18).

[181] Accra Agenda for Action, para. 26.

[182] Addis-Ababa Action Agenda, cited above note 8, para. 58.

[183] OECD Development Action Committee, Blended Finance for Sustainable Development: moving the agenda forward (OECD, DCD/DAC(2017)9), 24 February 2017, para. 15.

Table 12.4 Aid effectiveness—indicators such as included in Busan Partnership Agreement on Development Cooperation monitoring process

Indicator	Description
Indicator 1 Development co-operation is focused on results that meet developing countries' priorities	Extent of use of country results frameworks by cooperation providers
Indicator 2 Civil society operates within an environment which maximises its engagement in and contribution to development	A preliminary assessment of CSO Enabling Environment building on qualitative, multi-stakeholder information
Indicator 3 Engagement and contribution of the private sector to development	A three-dimensional index providing a measure of the quality of public-private dialogue
Indicator 4 Transparency: information on development co-operation is publicly available	Measure of state of implementation of the common standard by co-operation providers
Indicator 5(a) Development co-operation is more predictable—Annual Predictability	Proportion of development co-operation funding disbursed within the fiscal year within which it was scheduled by co-operation providers; and Halve the gap—halve the proportion of aid not disbursed within the fiscal year for which it was scheduled (baseline year 2010)
Indicator 5(b) Development co-operation is more predictable—Medium-term Predictability	Proportion of development cooperation funding covered by indicative forward spending plans provided at country level
Indicator 6 Aid is on budgets which are subject to parliamentary scrutiny	% of development co-operation funding scheduled for disbursement that is recorded in the annual budgets approved by the legislatures of developing countries
Indicator 7 Mutual accountability among development co-operation actors is strengthened through inclusive reviews	% of countries that undertake inclusive mutual assessments of progress in implementing agreed commitments
Indicator 8 Gender equality and women's empowerment	% of countries with systems that track and make public allocations for gender equality and women's empowerment
Indicator 9(a) Effective institutions: country systems are strengthened	Quality of developing country public financial management systems
Indicator 9(b) Effective institutions: developing country systems are used	Use of country public financial management and procurement systems
Indicator 10 Aid is untied	% of aid that is fully untied

blended finance refers to the catalytic use of ODA in order to stimulate the mobilization of other sources of financing to achieve development objectives: its objective is "to generate additional funds and finance through crowding-in commercial finance, that does not have a development mandate, into projects or programmes that are development priorities – i.e., to make development (more) investable".[184] Blending finance therefore aims to reduce the risk of private investment in certain areas related to development, or to provide concessional funding to maximize the contribution of private investment to a development objective, in order to harness the potential of private investment to serve sustainable development objectives.[185] Until now, blended finance has primarily focused on the financial sector and infrastructures, and climate action represents a significant proportion of the facilities (about one in five) relying on blended finance.[186]

The Addis-Ababa Action Agenda identified both opportunities and risks in the reliance on blended finance:

> For harnessing the potential of blended finance instruments for sustainable development, careful consideration should be given to the appropriate structure and use of blended finance instruments. Projects involving blended finance, including public-private partnerships, should share risks and reward fairly, include clear accountability mechanisms and meet social and environmental standards.[187]

Indeed, while blended finance are often described as a necessity in a context in which the fulfilment of development goals shall require considerable financial contributions that ODA alone shall not be able to provide,[188] it also involves certain challenges. Such challenges include: (1) agreeing on a clear definition of blending and how ODA's role in support of blended finance should be reported, in order to ensure that ODA commitments are not circumvented by the "double accounting" of ODA when combined with private finance; (2) ensuring that the contribution of concessional funding is not simply a way to compensate for poor project design by private financiers or investors; (3) ensuring that blending operations do not crowd out private investment, especially local investors; (4) ensuring that blending does not distort the targeting of ODA towards LDCs and social sectors, insofar as blending is better suited to middle-income countries and to the productive sectors, and thus could ultimately divert ODA support from where it is most urgently needed; (5) ensuring that blending does not result in tying aid—in violation of the commitments reiterated in the Addis-Ababa Action Agenda[189]—by linking aid to support to

---

[184] Id., para. 16.

[185] See Pereira (2017), p. 5.

[186] Id., para. 3.

[187] Addis Ababa Action Agenda, cited above note 8, para. 48.

[188] The financing gap in developing countries to achieve the SDGs is estimated to be about US$2.5 trillion (UN Conference on Trade and Development (UNCTAD), *World Investment Report 2014: Investing in the SDGs: An Action Plan* (Geneva: UNCTAD, 2014)); this compares with US$142.6 billion in ODA for the year 2016 (OECD, *Blended finance. Mobilising resources for sustainable development and climate action in developing countries. Policy perspectives* (Paris: OECD, 2017)).

[189] Addis Ababa Action Agenda, cited above note 8, para. 58 (in which countries pledge to "align activities with national priorities, including by reducing fragmentation, accelerating the untying of aid, particularly for least developed countries and countries most in need"). The percentage of untied aid is indicator 10 of the Global Partnership monitoring framework, referred to above.

economic actors from the donor country; (6) ensuring that blending remains consistent with the principles guiding aid effectiveness, including in particular country ownership and mutual accountability.

The Financing for Development follow-up process could set for itself, as a priority in the next few years, to achieve a consensus on these various items, in order to maximize the potential of blended finance while avoiding that such risks associated with the growth of blending materialize. OECD's Development Action Committee is currently considering a set of *Principles on Blended Finance*, in order to guide OECD Member States in their use of these new financing tools. This could provide a useful starting point for a multilateral approach to this issue.

Indicators should be developed to ensure that developed countries keep their promise to dedicate 0.7% of their GNI to ODA (and 0.15–0.20% to least developed countries), and to improve the effectiveness of aid. This should mean agreeing with receiving countries how ODA levels are to be calculated (and the extent to which, in particular, expenses in the donor country can be included); ensuring that new pledges linked specifically to climate finance are not included in ODA count (so that the pledge to finance climate mitigation and adaptation in developing countries up to US$100 billion by 2020 is additional to, not a substitute for, the earlier ODA pledges in support of economic development); and further strengthen the monitoring the effectiveness of aid, particularly to ensure that the principles of country ownership, predictability and mutual accountability are complied with, building on the work of the Global Partnership for Effective Development Co-operation. The increased use of blended finance deserves special attention in this regard, since—given the financing gap that ODA in itself shall not be sufficient to fill—it is bound to increase in the future. Taking into account the significant misunderstandings that persist about blending finance for development and the risks of aid diversion, moving development assistance away from commitments made since the 2005 Paris Declaration on Aid Effectiveness, it is urgent to improve transparency and discipline in its use. At a minimum, countries relying on blended finance by supporting private sector-driven projects should ensure that, consistent with the UN Guiding Principles on Business and Human Rights,[190] the private actors they support fully respect human rights and act with due diligence to seek information about the human rights impacts of their activities, including the impacts on the right to development, and mitigate any negative impacts identified (Table 12.5).

[190]See Principle 4 of the Guiding Principles on Business and Human Rights (A/HRC/17/31), providing that, in addition to their general duty to protect human rights, "States should take additional steps to protect against human rights abuses by business enterprises that are owned or controlled by the State, or that receive substantial support and services from State agencies such as export credit agencies and official investment insurance or guarantee agencies, including, where appropriate, by requiring human rights due diligence".

Table 12.5 Supporting the right to development through official development assistance (C): typology of obligations and associated implementation measures

Extraterritorial obligations	
Respect	(C1.1) All countries should ensure that the transboundary impacts of the measures they adopt are assessed, where such measures could have an impact on the right to development through channels such as finance, trade or investment. This could be achieved by relying on the existing tools that have been established to ensure policy coherence for sustainable development (PCSD)
Protect	(C2.1) Donor countries should ensure that any private actor (whether for-profit or non-profit) supported through ODA or through other (non-concessional) forms of support comply with the UN Guiding Principles on Business and Human Rights
Fulfil	(C3.1) Rich countries should deliver on their commitment to dedicate 0.7% of their GNI to ODA (and 0.15–0.20% to least developed countries), and to improve the effectiveness of aid
Global obligations	
Establish new partnerships	(C4.1) Agree on a multilateral framework to guide the use of blended finance to support the achievement of SDGs
Operate within partnerships	
Implement partnerships	(C6.1) Cooperate with the Global Partnership for Effective Development Co-operation and further strengthen its ability to ensure that progress is accelerated towards aid effectiveness

Putting Trade in the Service of the Right to Development: Attributes of the Duty to Support the Right to Development Through Trade

Ensuring Trade Agreements Do Not Impede the Realization of the Right to Development

The conclusion of trade agreements can have an impact on the right to development through various channels. Insofar as such agreements lower barriers to trade, they can affect livelihoods, where they lead some sectors of the economy of one State to face new forms of competition, especially when such competition is "unfair", due to the various forms of support that foreign competitors receive from their own governments.[191] The new generation of trade agreements moreover addresses

[191]For instance, in Concluding Observations addressed to Germany in 2011, the Committee on Economic, Social and Cultural Rights expressed its concern at "the impact of the State party's agriculture and trade policies, which promote the export of subsidized agricultural products to developing countries, on the enjoyment of the right to an adequate standard of living and particularly on the right to food in the receiving countries", and it therefore urged the State party to "fully apply a human rights-based approach to its international trade and agriculture policies, including by

non-tariff barriers (obstacles to trade that result from States adopting different regulatory approaches), which may lower the standards of protection of the health of consumers or affect the right to life or the right to health of the general population by lowering environmental requirements. Such agreements also routinely include chapters on intellectual property protection, which may result in obstacles to the dissemination of technologies and reduce access to medicines or to new plant varieties, with impacts on the right to health or on the right to food. Finally, many free trade agreements now include investment chapters that protect the rights of the investors of the other Party, and ensure that they have access to arbitral tribunals in order to complain about any restrictions to such rights, which may make it more difficult for the host State to effectively regulate these actors.

For all these reasons, as noted above, human rights treaty bodies and Special Procedures established by the Human Rights Council have insisted that the negotiation and conclusion of trade agreements should be preceded by human rights impact assessments—assessments which, it has been stated, should be conducted independently according to a transparent and participatory methodology, and relying on the normative content of human rights.[192]

In addition, in its General Comment No. 24 on State obligations under the International Covenant on Economic, Social and Cultural Rights in the context of business activities, the Committee on Economic, Social and Cultural Rights recommended that trade and investment agreements include a specific provision about the primacy of human rights obligations:

> The interpretation of trade and investment treaties currently in force should take into account the human rights obligations of the State, consistent with Article 103 of the Charter of the United Nations and with the specific nature of human rights obligations. (Inter-American Court of Human Rights, *Sawhoyamaxa Indigenous Community v. Paraguay* (judgment of 29 March 2006, Series C No. 146), para. 140). States parties cannot derogate from the obligations under the Covenant in trade and investment treaties that they may conclude. They are encouraged to insert, in future treaties, a provision explicitly referring to their human rights obligations, and to ensure that mechanisms for the settlement of investor-State disputes take human rights into account in the interpretation of investment treaties or of investment chapters in trade agreements.[193]

The inclusion of a reference to the primacy of human rights and the preparation of human rights impact assessments of trade agreements are important safeguards. But they remain *defensive* in nature. They seek to ensure that the conclusion of trade agreements shall not negatively affect human rights, including the right to development; but they generally do not inquire as to how such agreements, if properly designed, could make a positive contribution to the realization of human rights. Moreover, human rights impact assessments of trade *agreements* are not a substitute for the need to ensure that trade *policies* States implement comply with human

reviewing the impact of subsidies on the enjoyment of economic, social and cultural rights in importing countries" (E/C.12/DEU/CO/5, para. 9).

[192] See above, text corresponding to notes 21–24.

[193] At para. 13.

rights, and support efforts towards their progressive realization. In order to ensure that trade contributes to the right to development, it is therefore important to move beyond assessing the human rights impacts of trade agreements per se, and to ask how trade can become a tool to that effect.

Ensuring Trade Agreements Contribute to the Right to Development

The growth of trade opportunities, by the lowering of barriers to trade (both tariff and non-tariff), presents a dual relationship to the realization of the right to development. On the one hand, it can provide an opportunity for growth and it allows countries to have access to foreign currencies, which in turn allows them to import consumer items and technologies to favor the diversification of the economy. On the other hand, however, export-led growth may lock countries into certain lines of production that are not sustainable, either because they are highly labour-intensive and require that competitiveness be based on low wages and poor conditions of work (especially in the manufacturing sector, for countries that are latecomers to globalization), or because they rely on the exploitation of natural resources, that are used (and potentially depleted) to serve not the needs of the local population, but those of industries in more developed countries or the affluent lifestyles of rich countries' consumers.

What is needed is to shape trade in order to ensure that it contributes to the right to development. The choice is not between unregulated liberalization of trade, in which labour rights, environmental standards and human rights are eroded in order to improve the competitiveness of the export sector and in which regulatory standards are gradually lowered or removed in order to avoid the accusation of protectionism, and mercantilist policies in which restrictions to imports are seen as a means to protect local producers; the choice is, rather, between trade governed by rules set with a view exclusively to maximize wealth creation by efficiency gains, and trade governed by rules that serve the right to development—supporting diversified economies, inclusive societies, and sustainable forms of growth. Trade can be a tool for development, provided countries use the flexibilities allowed under the multilateral trade regime, and provided they remain guided, in their reliance on such flexibilities, by the universally agreed human rights norms.

Unfortunately, the guidance provided by the SDGs is woefully inadequate in this regard. The SDGs propose to "promote a universal, rules-based, open, non-discriminatory and equitable multilateral trading system under the World Trade Organization, including through the conclusion of negotiations under its Doha Development Agenda" (Target 17.10, associated with an indicator referring to the lowering of the worldwide weighted tariff-average (17.10.1)); to "significantly increase the exports of developing countries, in particular with a view to doubling the least developed countries' share of global exports by 2020" (Target 17.11, associated with an indicator referring to the share of global exports of developing countries and LDCs (17.11.1)); and to "realize timely implementation of duty-free and quota-free market access on a lasting basis for all least developed countries, consistent with World Trade Organization decisions, including by ensuring that preferential rules of origin applicable to imports from least developed countries are transparent and simple, and contribute to facilitating market access" (Target 17.12, associated with an indicator referring to the lowering of the average tariffs faced by developing countries, LDCs and small island developing States (17.12.1)). These targets provide a blueprint for trade liberalization, and for increasing exports of developing countries; they are entirely silent, however, about the type of development that would result from the deepening of the international division of labour under current conditions. They do not even allude to the risk that export-oriented growth will result in a lack of diversification of economies (although diversification is both a condition for development and a source of resilience against economic shocks, such as exchange rate variations and fluctuations of commodity prices), and they say nothing about how the gains and losses from specialization should be spread. It is as if the increase of trade volumes were an end in itself. But trade is just an instrument for sustainable development, as emphasized in the Preamble of the Marrakesh Agreement itself.[194]

The inadequacy of the current trade regime as a tool for sustainable development is most obvious once one considers its relationship to climate change. First, international competition may be a disincentive for the adoption of regulatory standards that, though motivated by the will to mitigate climate change, may raise costs to the enterprises operating from within the State seeking to adopt such standards. It is arguable at least that the more economies are characterized by a high degree of openness to trade—depending more on exports to be able to important more in order to satisfy their needs—the more difficult it will be to justify the adoption of measures imposing constraints on companies, in the form of stronger environmental requirements, that are perceived as reducing the competitiveness on global markets.[195]

[194]Agreement establishing the World Trade Organization, Marrakesh, 15 April 1994, entered into force on 1 January 1995 (33 ILM 1125 (1994)). The preamble of the Agreement establishing the World Trade Organization (WTO) states that Members' "relations in the field of trade and economic endeavour should be conducted with a view to raising standards of living, ensuring full employment and a large and steadily growing volume of real income and effective demand, and expanding the production of and trade in goods and services, while allowing for the optimal use of the world's resources in accordance with the objective of sustainable development, seeking both to protect and preserve the environment and to enhance the means for doing so in a manner consistent with their respective needs and concerns at different levels of economic development".

[195]Of course, the relationship between constraints imposed on companies based on environmental concerns, leading for instance to a higher price of energy or to obliging a company to acquire allowances for greenhouse gas emissions, and the competitiveness of companies, understood as their ability to maintain sufficient profit margins, is not a direct one, and depends on a range of factors, including the trade openness of the sector concerned and the ability for the companies concerned to pass on the increases in production costs to the consumer: see, for a detailed discussion of this point, *Trade and Climate Change. A Report by the United Nations Environment Program and the World Trade Organization*, World Trade Organization, Geneva, 2009, at p. 99 (finding that "the effects on competitiveness of environmental regulations, including climate change policies, are relatively small, or are likely for only a small number of sectors, because the costs of compliance with a regulation are a relatively minor component of a firm's overall costs", yet acknowledging at

Moreover, the expansion of trade as such affects the volume of greenhouse gas emissions. International trade favours increased economic growth and higher levels of consumption. It therefore frees up resources from their less productive uses to be reinvested or spent elsewhere. This 'scale effect' of trade is built into the very idea of trade contributing to improved allocative efficiency, and thus to increased levels of outputs and reduced prices for the end consumer. But it opens up the question under which conditions it is compatible with SDG 12, which refers to the need to ensure sustainable consumption and production patterns.

This is not to deny, of course, that trade may also make a positive contribution to the mitigation of climate change. Trade may support sustainable production patterns, especially in agriculture and in production that is intensive in the use of natural resources, if each country specializes into lines of production in which it has a comparative advantage, increasing allocative efficiency. Moreover, trade favours in many cases the diffusion of cleaner technologies which, once taken up, can lead to less carbon-intensive types of growth in the importing country.[196] This 'technology effect' occurs through a variety of channels, including by the importation of innovations embodied in intermediate goods (products used in further production processes) and capital goods (machinery and equipment); the transfer of knowledge about new production processes; and increased learning opportunities from international economic relations, accelerating the ability for developing countries to develop cleaner technologies.[197]

On the whole, however, the trade agenda is poorly aligned with the climate change agenda. In the absence of special incentives rewarding countries or exporters that rely on the cleanest technologies available and use the least polluting methods of production by improved market access, export-led policies result in a regulatory chill: regulators fear to increase environmental standards, in particular related to greenhouse gas emissions, if this could put certain of their industries at a disadvantage. And various studies show that the 'scale effects' of increased trade volumes significantly outweigh the more benevolent 'technology effects': the paradox is that, while we seek to encourage more sustainable consumption patterns, trade presents consumers with a cornucopia of goods that are cheap, disposable, and have an

---

the same time that environmental regulations impact the competitiveness of "a few energy-intensive manufacturing industries" and that "the carbon constraint in some emission trading schemes . . . is expected to be increasingly stringent, with fewer free allowances, which will therefore increase the potential impact on the competitiveness of a number of sectors").

[196] WTO Members have pledged to accelerate this diffusion by prioritizing the liberalization of trade of environmental goods and services. See Doha Ministerial Declaration, WTO doc. WT/MIN(01)/DEC/1, para. 31 (iii) (committing to negotiate "the reduction or, as appropriate, elimination of tariff and non-tariff barriers to environmental goods and services").

[197] See, describing these various channels, *Trade and Climate Change. A Report by the United Nations Environment Program and the World Trade Organization*, World Trade Organization, Geneva, 2009, at p. 61 (and referring, in particular, to Eaton and Kortum 2001, pp. 1195–1235; and Helpman 1997).

increasingly short life span—in other terms, the increased consumption of which cannot be reconciled with sustainability goals.[198]

Labour rights provide another example. With the progress of trade liberalization, particularly since the finalization of the Uruguay round of trade negotiations which led to the establishment of the World Trade Organization, concerns have increased about the dangers of regulatory competition between States. The fear is that in labour-intensive industries (in which labour costs represent a significant proportion of the total costs of production), States that do not raise labour standards, particularly as regards minimum wage, health and safety at work, or freedom of association and collective bargaining, would be gaining an "unfair advantage" in global competition, and would thereby be able to attract investors in increasingly segmented global production chains.

The evidence is mixed. Econometric studies tend to show that the countries with the most open trade policies have witnessed improvements in working conditions, at faster rates than countries with closed trade policies.[199] But that does not prove that fears of social dumping are without foundation. First, correlation does not imply causality. The improvement in labour conditions may be attributable to a range of other factors than trade per se. Among such factors, we may include the role of foreign investment and the arrival of multinational corporations in the country concerned, general progress in the standard of living (i.e. that trade may or may not have accelerated, depending on the position of the country in the international division of labour and the evolution of the terms of trade) or, perhaps most importantly, the level of organization of workers and the strength of their bargaining position. Secondly, a generally positive correlation between trade openness and working conditions does not provide information about the counter-factual: although trade openness may be correlated to improvements in working conditions, this does not exclude that if a country had resorted to more protectionist policies, shielding certain sectors from competition, working conditions would have improved even further.

It is equally difficult to arrive at definitive conclusions concerning the relationship between trade openness and the evolution of labour regulations in any particular country. How the regulatory framework evolves depends, first and foremost, on the balance of political forces in a country at any point in time, as well as on the respective bargaining power of employers and workers' unions. Trade openness is one among many factors that influences the respective positions of the different social and political actors in the country. It implies, for instance, that the employers

---

[198]See Heil and Selden (2001), pp. 35–49; Cole and Elliott (2003), pp. 363–383. For an overview, see *Climate and Trade. Why climate change calls for fundamental reforms in world trade policies*, report authored by Santarius (2009).

[199]See, eg, providing a systematic empirical analysis, Flanagan (2006). Flanagan concludes that fears of 'social dumping' are largely ill-founded. However, even he does note one exception: 'If trade threatens working conditions, the threat is strongest for some workers in the richest countries, not the poorest countries. The evidence suggests that trade has a small negative impact on the wages of unskilled workers in industrialized countries' (p. 85).

may with some plausibility threaten to relocate production plants if the workers demand too much, or if the labour legislation imposes excessive costs on them: such a threat becomes realistic once it appears that they could easily produce goods in another location, or provide services from elsewhere, without losing access to the consumers in the home country. How much weight this argument will have, however, will depend on the particular context of the country concerned, and this again is only one of the inputs in a political system that shall receive many others.

Arguments about the empirical relationship between trade and the evolution of labour standards are therefore difficult to assess. Establishing a stronger linkage between trade and labour rights may be justified, however, even in the absence of a consensus that trade openness will result in a deterioration of working conditions or a dismantling of labour regulations, all in the name of ensuring competitiveness on global markets. 'Trade openness' can be designed in a number of ways, and forms of trade liberalization that include a protection against the risks of global competition leading to a worsening of working conditions may be seen to be preferable to forms of trade liberalization that simply ignore that there may be any such link. Improving the linkages between trade and labour standards seeks to ensure that trade will not be used as an opportunity to lower labour standards or as a pretext to refuse to improve the protection of workers or to raise their wages as labour productivity improves. It is precisely because the risks of abuse are difficult to ascertain that taking out such an insurance policy makes sense.

Various attempts have been made to define a trade regime that would serve sustainable development and, thus, contribute to full realization of the right to development.[200] Though the details may differ, the general approach is that trade can, and should, be shaped in order to serve development objectives. It is wrong to think of trade and development in sequential terms, as if trade could be conceived of simply as an engine for economic growth, to then be complemented by policies that serve development needs. Instead, because trade influences production and consumption patterns, the bargaining powers of social partners, regulatory choices and how resources are allocated, how trade is designed should from the start take into account the need to serve development.

Even taking into account the disciplines they imposed under the WTO framework, WTO Members can use a number of flexibilities to that effect. The most obvious option is to impose higher import tariffs on goods or services that are not produced according to certain environmental standards (or that do not use the cleanest technologies available), or that do not ensure full compliance with labour rights in the supply chain.[201]

---

[200] See, *inter alia*, De Schutter (2015), Bürgi Bonanomi (2015), Stiglitz (2006), and Stiglitz and Charlton (2005).

[201] Other options include border tax adjustments, which aim to compensate for differences between the respective taxation systems of the exporting and the importing countries (Article II:2(a) of the General Agreement allows WTO Members to apply a charge on imports equivalent to an internal tax provided that such a charge complies with the national treatment principle, in other terms, provided the charge is not 'in excess of those applied ... to like domestic products'); state-

The WTO Dispute-Settlement Bodies have generally treated regulatory requirements that concern *production or process methods* (PPMs) (as opposed to requirements that concern the *physical characteristics* of the product), when extended to foreign goods, as a quantitative measure, comparable to a quota or an import ban. Since Article XI GATT forbids quantitative restrictions without allowing for measures that take that form to be justified (leaving aside the narrow exceptions of Article XI:2), restrictions of that category can only be allowed by the successful invocation of the General Exception Clause of Article XX GATT, which contains a closed set of admissible justifications to otherwise prohibited measures. This Clause could justify the reliance on environmental conditions to restrict access to markets of certain products (as a means to ensure the 'conservation of exhaustible natural resources' (Article XX(g), GATT)). It could also justify imposing similar restrictions on goods or services that do not comply with labour rights: such conditions could be considered 'necessary to protect public morals', a wording which appears in both Article XX(a) GATT and Article XIV(a) GATS, provided at least that the restriction is justified by the need to protect internationally recognized labour rights (such as those that appear in the 1998 ILO Declaration on Fundamental Principles and Rights at Work), and is neither discriminatory nor resulting in a disguised restriction on international trade.

The more a WTO Member resorts to trade policy measures that are unilateral to encourage positive development outcomes, however, the more it will be important to do so by referring to objectives that are shared by the international community as a whole, and by coupling any restrictions to trade with appropriate burden-sharing towards developing countries. The right to development may serve as a useful reference in this regard, especially if combined with a reference to the common but differentiated responsibilities and respective capabilities of different States. The significance of such a reference is that trade policy measures should provide positive incentives, rewarding jurisdictions that achieve the most to ensure the realization of the right to development, and that the other jurisdictions should be supported in their efforts to improve further in this regard. Such trade policy measures should not turn into a sanctioning mechanism: they should rather be a mechanism encouraging countries to move in the right direction.[202]

As already noted, the right to development therefore does not justify the adoption of unilateral measures as a means to obtain from a State that it changes its course of conduct.[203] Therefore, in order to dispel any risk that such incentives would be abused to serve protectionist objectives, and a means to deprive developing countries

---

sponsored labelling schemes, that fall to be examined under the Agreement on Technical Barriers to Trade (TBT Agreement); or the use of public procurement schemes, since the Government Procurement Agreement (GPA) now allows the inclusion of considerations that are not purely economic in public tenders (Target 12.7 of the SDGs is to "Promote public procurement practices that are sustainable, in accordance with national policies and priorities"). These various options cannot be explored in detail here.

[202]See Khor et al. (2017).

[203]See above, text corresponding to notes 55–57.

of what they may see as their comparative advantage, confidence-building measures could be adopted, such as (1) reference to universally recognized standards, rather than standards imposed unilaterally by the importing jurisdiction; (2) assessment of compliance with these standards by independent monitoring bodies, rather than by the importing jurisdiction alone; (3) a phased application of the measures, leaving time for consultations and for improvements to be made in the exporting country concerned, before any disadvantages are imposed; (4) a use of any funds collected as a result of an increase in import tariffs aiming to encourage compliance with the standards, for the benefit of programmes supporting reforms in developing countries, including through the transfer of technologies and capacity-building, or by financing the establishing of standing social protection schemes.

Trade can be made fair. The inclusion in trade policies of conditions based on universally agreed standards derived from the right to development can contribute to reconciling trade with the development agenda of the international community. But such unilateral measures should only be seen as a solution if they are not a pretext for protectionist policies, and if they fit within a broader set of policies, that include strong support to the development objectives of poor countries.[204] In contrast to the current fragmentation, linking access to markets to the right to development can encourage all countries to step up efforts towards the realization of this right. WTO law generally allows for such linkages to be established. This would ensure a greater consistency between the right to development and the trade agendas. It would support the least well organized and weakest segments of the workforce in all countries to obtain a better share of the benefits of whatever growth trade may serve to stimulate, and it encourage civil society globally that seeks to defend and promote the right to development (Table 12.6).

Channeling Foreign Direct Investment Towards Development Needs: Attributes of the Duty to Ensure Foreign Direct Investment Supports the Right to Development

Already in 2006, referring to MDG8 on a global partnership for development, the Working Group on the right to development stated that the right to development "implies that foreign direct investment (FDI) should contribute to local and national development in a responsible manner, that is, in ways that are conducive to social development, protect the environment, and respect the rule of law and fiscal obligations in the host countries. The principles underlying the right to development, . . ., further imply that all parties involved, i.e. investors and recipient countries, have

[204]For a detailed attempt to identify the institutional conditions that could ensure that the linkage of trade policies to labour standards will benefit the poorer countries, by increasing the rewards for improving such standards, and the most disadvantaged groups, by increasing the incentives for their governments to design policies that will benefit them, see Barry and Reddy (2008).

Table 12.6 Putting trade in the service of the right to development: (D): typology of obligations and associated implementation measures

Extraterritorial obligations	
Respect	(D1.1) Prepare human rights impact assessments both prior to the conclusion of trade or investment agreements and at regular intervals following the entry into force of such agreements, to ensure that the agreement shall not create obstacles to the ability for each of the States concerned to respect, protect and fulfil human rights, including the right to development
	(D1.2) Refrain from measures that seek to achieve a competitive advantage in global trade by the lowering of standards that contribute to the realization of the right to development, conceived as a right to enjoy a form of development "in which all human rights and fundamental freedoms can be fully realized" (art. 1(1) of the Declaration on the right to development)
Protect	(D2.1) By effectively regulating corporations domiciled in the territory and/or jurisdiction of the State, ensuring that such corporations shall not encourage regulatory competition between States in areas that relate to the realization of the right to development
Fulfil	(D3.1) Design trade policies that reward countries and/or supply chains that have the best track record in contributing to the full realization of the right to development
Global obligations	
Establish new partnerships	(D4.1) Gradually move towards a common understanding, agreed upon at multilateral level, as to the best practices that States could rely on in order ensure an appropriate linkage between trade and the realization of the right to development
Operate within partnerships	(D5.1) Within the WTO framework, encourage an interpretation of the flexibilities available to countries that allows to better link trade to the right to development
Implement partnerships	

responsibilities to ensure that profit considerations do not result in crowding out human rights protection. The impact of FDI should, therefore, be taken into account when evaluating progress in Goal 8 in the context of the right to development".[205]

Two human rights norms are of particular relevance concerning the regime of international investment law. The Declaration on the Right to Development makes direct reference, as one of its key components, to the right to self-determination of peoples and, specifically, the right of all peoples freely to dispose of their natural wealth and resources. as stipulated under article 1 of both 1966 Covenants implementing the Universal Declaration of Human Rights.[206] The right to

[205] Report of the Working Group on the right to development. 7th session (conclusions) (E/CN.4/2006/26), para. 59.

[206] International Covenant on Economic, Social and Cultural Rights (adopted on 16 December 1966, G.A. Res. 2200(XXII), U.N. GAOR, 21st sess., Supp. No. 16, U.S. Doc. A/6316 (1966)

self-determination is one of the most under-rated and under-utilized norms in the international human rights system of protection. If taken seriously, self-determination means that the peoples, not governments alone, should be making the fundamental choices as to how the resources available should be used: in essence, it is a norm about participatory democracy, particularly in the context of the use, exploitation and allocation of natural resources.

The norm has been invoked, for instance, in order to protect indigenous communities or traditional groups from being deprived of equitable access to the resources on which they depend for their livelihoods. In *Apirana Mahuika et al. v. New Zealand*, the Human Rights Committee reads Article 1(2) of the International Covenant on Civil and Political Rights—in conjunction with Article 27 of the Covenant, that recognizes the rights of minorities—as allowing an arrangement about the management of fishing resources, noting that the Maori people "were given access to a great percentage of the quota, and thus effective possession of fisheries was returned to them", and that the new control structure put in place ensures not only a role for the Maori in safeguarding their interests in fisheries but, in addition, their "effective control".[207] The implication would appear to be that these provisions would be violated should any people be deprived of the use they make traditionally of the land and resources on which they rely.[208]

This component of the right to self-determination should not benefit indigenous peoples alone. The requirements applicable to indigenous peoples are now extended to at least certain traditional communities that entertain a similarly "profound and all-encompassing relationship to their ancestral lands" centered on "the community as a whole" rather than on the individual: this, the Inter-American Court of Human Rights noted, applies for instance to the Maroon communities living in Suriname,

(993 UNTS 3); and International Covenant on Civil and Political Rights (A/RES/21/2200A, 16 December 1966) (999 UNTS 171).

[207]Human Rights Committee, *Apirana Mahuika et al. v. New Zealand*, Communication No. 547/1993, CCPR/C/70/D/547/1993 (2000), para. 9.7. The Human Rights Committee observed that "minorities shall not be denied the right, in community with the other members of their group, to enjoy their own culture[, which] may consist in a way of life which is closely associated with territory and use of its resources. This may particularly be true of members of indigenous communities constituting a minority": General Comment No. 23: The rights of minorities (Art. 27) (50th session, 1994), (CCPR/C/21Rev.1/Add.5) (4 August 1994), paras. 1 and 3.2.

[208]A similar conclusion has been derived by the Committee on the Elimination of Racial Discrimination from Article 5(d)(v) of the International Convention on the Elimination of All Forms of Racial Discrimination, which protects the right to property: this requires from States parties that they "recognize and protect the rights of all indigenous communities to own, develop and control the lands which they traditionally occupy, including water and subsoil resources" (Committee on the Elimination of Racial Discrimination, Concluding Observations: Guyana (CERD/C/GUY/CO/14), 4 April 2006, para. 16).

which are not indigenous to the region, but are tribal communities of former slaves that settled in Suriname in the seventeenth and eighteenth century.[209]

Indeed, under Article 1 of the Covenants on Civil and Political Rights and on Economic, Social and Cultural Rights, which the Declaration on the Right to Development refers to, the right to self-determination is recognized to all "peoples", and its enjoyment is not made conditional on these peoples being "indigenous". Indeed, the clearest illustration of how this relates to the regulation of foreign investors is provided by a case that did not relate, strictly speaking, to indigenous peoples. In Nigeria, local Ogoni communities complained that they were not protected from the negative impacts of the presence of foreign oil companies exploiting the subsoil of the Niger delta in disregard of the consequences on the surroundings. On the basis of a provision of the 1981 African Charter on Human and Peoples' Rights worded in terms very similar to those of Article 1(2) of the 1966 Covenants—which recognizes the right of all peoples to "freely dispose of their natural wealth and resources" and prohibits depriving any people from its own means of subsistence[210]—the African Commission on Human and Peoples' Rights affirmed a State violates its duties under the Charter if it allows private actors, including foreign companies, to "devastatingly affect the well-being" of the peoples under its its jurisdiction.[211]

---

[209] *Case of the Moiwana Community v. Suriname. Preliminary Objections, Merits, Reparations and Costs*, Judgment of June 15, 2005. Series C No. 124, paras. 132–133. See also *Saramaka People. v. Suriname,* Judgment of 28 November 2007, para. 86 (finding that "the Court's jurisprudence regarding indigenous peoples' right to property is also applicable to tribal peoples because both share distinct social, cultural, and economic characteristics, including a special relationship with their ancestral territories, that require special measures under international human rights law in order to guarantee their physical and cultural survival").

[210] Article 21 of the African Charter on Human and Peoples' Rights (adopted June 27, 1981, OAU Doc. CAB/LEG/67/3 rev. 5, 21 I.L.M. 58 (1982), entered into force Oct. 21, 1986), provides that: "1. All peoples shall freely dispose of their wealth and natural resources. This right shall be exercised in the exclusive interest of the people. In no case shall a people be deprived of it. 2. In case of spoliation the dispossessed people shall have the right to the lawful recovery of its property as well as to an adequate compensation. 3. The free disposal of wealth and natural resources shall be exercised without prejudice to the obligation of promoting international economic co-operation based on mutual respect, equitable exchange and the principles of international law. 4. States parties to the present Charter shall individually and collectively exercise the right to free disposal of their wealth and natural resources with a view to strengthening African unity and solidarity. 5. States Parties to the present Charter shall undertake to eliminate all forms of foreign economic exploitation particularly that practised by international monopolies so as to enable their peoples to fully benefit from the advantages derived from their national resources".

[211] *The Social and Economic Rights Action Center and the Center for Economic and Social Rights v. Nigeria*, African Commission on Human and Peoples' Rights, Comm. No. 155/96 (2001), para. 58. The Commission was explicit on the contribution that Article 21 of the African Charter on Human and Peoples' Rights was expected to make in getting rid of the remnants of colonialism. The origins of that provision, it recalled, "may be traced to colonialism, during which the human and material resources of Africa were largely exploited for the benefit of outside powers, creating tragedy for Africans themselves, depriving them of their birthright and alienating them from the land. The aftermath of colonial exploitation has left Africa's precious resources and people still

The second norm relevant to the definition of international investment law regimes is derived from the extraterritorial duties of States under existing human rights instruments. Human rights treaty bodies have regularly found that human rights treaties impose duties on States also outside their national territories. One of the implications is that States should control private actors over which they can exercise control, consistent with general international law, in order to prevent such actors from infringing on human rights in foreign territories.[212] The Committee on Economic, Social and Cultural Rights has addressed the duty of States to control transnational corporations in its General Comments relating to the right to water,[213] the right to work,[214] the right to social security[215] and the right to just and favourable conditions of work.[216] Its most systematic treatment of the topic appears in General Comment No. 24 on the Obligations of States under the International Covenant on Economic, Social and Cultural Rights in the Context of Business Activities, adopted in 2017. Consistent with the Resolution concerning decent work in global supply chains adopted in 2016 by the International Labour Conference,[217] the Committee took the view that States should "regulate corporations that are domiciled in their territory and/or jurisdiction: this includes corporations incorporated under their laws, or which have their statutory seat, central administration or principal place of business on their national territory".[218] This position is similar to that of other human rights treaty bodies.[219] For instance, in the general comment it adopted in

vulnerable to foreign misappropriation. [In adopting Article 21,] the drafters of the Charter obviously wanted to remind African governments of the continent's painful legacy and restore co-operative economic development to its traditional place at the heart of African Society" (id., para. 56).

[212]Statement on the obligations of States parties regarding the corporate sector and economic, social and cultural rights (E/C.12/2011/1), paras. 5–6.

[213]General Comment No. 15 (2002): The right to water (arts. 11 and 12) (E/C.12/2002/11), paras. 31, 33.

[214]General Comment No. 18 (2006): The right to work (art. 6) (E/C.12/GC/18), para. 52.

[215]General Comment No. 19 (2008): The right to social security (art. 9) (E/C.12/GC/19), para. 54.

[216]General Comment No. 23 (2016): The right to just and favorable conditions of work (art. 7) (E/C.12/GC/23), para. 70.

[217]Conclusions attached to the Resolution concerning decent work in global supply chains, adopted by the 105th session of the General Conference of the International Labour Organisation (2016), para. 16, i).

[218]Committee on Economic, Social and Cultural Rights, General Comment No. 24: State obligations under the International Covenant on Economic, Social and Cultural Rights in the context of business activities (E/C.12/GC/24), para. 31.

[219]The Committee on the Elimination of Racial Discrimination considers that State parties should also protect human rights by preventing their own citizens and companies, or national entities from violating rights in other countries (Committee on the Elimination of Racial Discrimination, Concluding Observations: Canada (CERD/C/CAN/CO/18), para. 17; Concluding Observations: United States (CERD/C/USA/CO/6), para. 30). The Human Rights Committee, operating under the International Covenant on Civil and Political Rights, encourages States to "set out clearly the expectation that all business enterprises domiciled in its territory and/or its jurisdiction respect human rights standards in accordance with the Covenant throughout their operations" and to "take

2013 on State obligations regarding the impact of the business sector on children's rights, the Committee on the Rights of the Child takes the view that:

> Home States also have obligations, arising under the Convention and the Optional Protocols thereto, to respect, protect and fulfil children's rights in the context of businesses' extraterritorial activities and operations, provided that there is a reasonable link between the State and the conduct concerned. A reasonable link exists when a business enterprise has its centre of activity, is registered or domiciled or has its main place of business or substantial business activities in the State concerned.[220]

In practice, and in order to avoid any controversy concerning the legitimate scope of extraterritorial jurisdiction of States, this means imposing on corporations that are domiciled under the State's jurisdiction (whether they are incorporated within the State, or whether they have located their statutory seat or their principal place of business within the territory of that State) not only that they respect human rights, but also that they act with due diligence to ensure that their subsidiaries or business partners (suppliers and franchisees) comply. Far from interfering with the sovereignty of the State under the jurisdiction of which such subsidiaries are established or on the territory of which these business partners operate, the home State discharging thus its obligation to protect human rights would strengthen the ability for the host State to effectively enforce the regulatory measures adopted by that State in the name of public health, a healthy environment, workers' rights, or the rights of local communities.

Victims of business-related human rights abuses should therefore have access to effective remedies also in a transnational context. A number of obstacles remain in this regard, however: they relate, for instance, to the existence of collective redress mechanisms in mass tort litigation; to the admissibility of evidence collected abroad; to the availability of legal aid; or, unless parent-company direct liability is organized, to the restrictive conditions under which the corporate veil may be lifted. A number of recommendations were made for the removal of such obstacles in the report of the United Nations High Commissioner for Human Rights on improving accountability and access to remedy for victims of business-related human rights abuse.[221] By facilitating access to justice for victims of transnational corporate human rights

---

appropriate measures to strengthen the remedies provided to protect people who have been victims of activities of such business enterprises operating abroad" (CCPR/C/DEU/CO/6, par. 16). See also Human Rights Committee, comm. n°2285/2013, *Yassin et al. v. Canada*, Views of 26 July 2017, para. 6.5 ("While the human rights obligations of a State on its own territory cannot be equated in all respects with its obligations outside its territory, the Committee considers that there are situations where a State party has an obligation to ensure that rights under the Covenant are not impaired by extraterritorial activities conducted by enterprises under its jurisdiction").

[220] General comment No. 16 (2013) on State obligations regarding the impact of the business sector on children's rights (CRC/C/GC/16), para. 43. This goes further than the position adopted by the Committee on Economic, Social and Cultural Rights, since it refers to a duty of the State to control any extraterritorial impacts of the activities not only of corporations that are domiciled under its jurisdiction, but also that have "substantial business activities" on the State's territory.

[221] A/HRC/32/19 and Add.1. The Human Rights Council welcomed the report at its 32nd session (2016), A/HRC/RES/32/10, OP 1.

abuses, States would be facilitating the efforts of the host State to regulate the activities of business enterprises which may affect the enjoyment of human rights, and thus to ensure that the arrival of foreign direct investment supports the right to development.

Ensuring that transnational corporations respect human rights in the States in which they operate, thus ensuring that they shall not create obstacles to the realization of the right to development in the State concerned, can be achieved primarily by States operating unilaterally: both the territorially competent State (where the corporation operates) and the home State (where the corporation is domiciled) have duties in this regard. Further international cooperation may be required, however, for such measures to be fully effective. Global obligations emerge in two areas:

Firstly, as noted by the Committee on Economic, Social and Cultural Rights, the adoption of international instruments could strengthen the duty of States to cooperate in order to improve accountability and access to remedies for victims of violations of Covenant rights in transnational cases: "Improved international cooperation should reduce the risks of positive and negative conflicts of jurisdiction, which may result in legal uncertainty and in forum-shopping by litigants, or in the inability for victims to obtain redress".[222] The Working Group on the issue of human rights and transnational corporations and other business enterprises has also dedicated a study on best practices and on how to improve on the effectiveness of cross-border cooperation between States with respect to law enforcement on the issue of business and human rights.[223] Specifically, agreements providing for mutual legal assistance might include provisions related to the collection of evidence; to the freezing or seizure of assets; to the execution of judgments; or to the sharing of information between law enforcement authorities. Such forms of cooperation would ensure that the transnational nature of the corporation's activity shall not result in a form of impunity. In a resolution on "Business and human rights: improving accountability and access to remedy", adopted at its 32nd session in June 2016, the Human Rights Council expressed its concern at the "legal and practical barriers to remedies for victims of business-related human rights abuses, which may leave those aggrieved without opportunity for effective remedy, including through judicial and non-judicial avenues".[224] Referring to the above-mentioned report of the United Nations High Commissioner for Human Rights on improving accountability and access to remedy for victims of business-related human rights abuse, the resolution further

> *[E]ncourages* States to take steps to improve the effectiveness of international cooperation between State agencies and judicial bodies with respect to law enforcement of domestic legal regimes to address business-related human rights abuses;

[222]General Comment No. 24, para. 35.

[223]A/HRC/35/33.

[224]Preamble, para. 5.

> *Invites* regional and international bodies responsible for promoting and facilitating international cooperation with respect to cross-border investigation, legal assistance and enforcement of judicial decisions to take steps to improve the speed and effectiveness of such cooperation in cross-border cases of business-related human rights abuses through legal, practical and capacity-building means.[225]

Therefore, any progress towards improved cooperation between States for the enforcement of human rights duties in the context of transnational corporate human rights abuses should be seen as a contribution towards the establishment of an international legal order in which human rights can be fully realized, as required under article 28 of the Universal Declaration of Human Rights[226] and the right to development.

Secondly, international cooperation may be required to ensure that human rights obligations are given priority over investors' rights, whenever a risk of conflict occurs. States have routinely concluded bilateral or multilateral trade or investment agreements including provisions protecting investors' rights, in order to attract foreign direct investment. In general, these treaties pertain to admission of investment (defining the conditions of entry of FDI into the country); they protect investors from various forms of expropriation, both direct and indirect (the latter often under the requirement of a "fair and equitable treatment"); they include guarantees of "national treatment" (according to which investors enjoy a treatment similar to that enjoyed by the nationals of the host State) and "most-favored nation" (according to which they enjoy treatment similar to the best treatment accorded to investors from any other country), as well as provisions allowing the transfer and repatriation of profits (capital transfer provisions); and they have dispute settlement clauses allowing investors to challenge measures taken by the host State before international arbitral tribunals designated as competent to settle disputes between the investors covered by the treaty and the host State, established under the rules of the 1965 International Convention on the Settlement of Disputes between States and the nationals of other Parties (ICSID)[227] or under the UNCITRAL Arbitral Rules.[228]

Because investment treaties (or provisions on investors' rights in trade agreements) protect investors from the adoption of regulations that amount to indirect expropriation, situations may arise in which the rights of investors are pitted against those of the individuals or communities whose rights are negatively affected by the investment—which is why the Guiding Principles on Business and Human Rights insist that "States should maintain adequate domestic policy space to meet their human rights obligations when pursuing business-related policy objectives with other States or business enterprises, for instance through investment treaties or

---

[225]OP 5 and 6.

[226]Cited above (note 3).

[227]575 U.N.T.S. 159.

[228]The Arbitral Rules adopted by the United Nations Commission on International Trade Law (UNCITRAL) were adopted initially on 28 April 1976; they were revised in 2010.

contracts".[229] The Special Representative of the UN Secretary-General on the issue of human rights and transnational corporations and other business enterprises notes in his commentary to the Guiding Principles that:

> Economic agreements concluded by States, either with other States or with business enterprises – such as bilateral investment treaties, free-trade agreements or contracts for investment projects – create economic opportunities for States. But they can also affect the domestic policy space of governments. For example, the terms of international investment agreements may constrain States from fully implementing new human rights legislation, or put them at risk of binding international arbitration if they do so. Therefore, States should ensure that they retain adequate policy and regulatory ability to protect human rights under the terms of such agreements, while providing the necessary investor protection.[230]

In order to avoid the risk that investment treaties result in obstacles to the right to development, for instance by chilling a State from adopting certain measures that the investor of the other Party may seek to challenge as discriminatory or as imposing a disproportionate cost, investment treaties (or investment chapters in free trade agreements) may have to include specific references to the human rights obligations of the host State. Where investment agreements are insufficiently explicit about the right of the State to regulate foreign investors in order to ensure full compliance with the State's human rights obligations, as such obligations may evolve from time to time in the name of progressive realization, there is a need to ensure that these human rights obligations are fully taken into account in investor-State dispute settlement proceedings (Table 12.7).[231]

Establishing Universal Social Protection Floors: Attributes of the Duty to Support Universal Social Protection Floors

In June 2012, the General Conference of the International Labour Organisation adopted Recommendation (No. 202) Concerning National Floors of Social Protection, referred to as Social Protection Floors Recommendation, 2012. An overwhelming majority of delegates from the ILO's 185 member States, including government, employer and worker delegates, supported the initiative, with 453 votes in favour of adopting the Recommendation and one abstention. Social protection and, in particular, universal social protection, figure prominently among the set of SDGs: Goal 1.3 is to "Implement nationally appropriate social protection systems and measures for

---

[229] A/HRC/17/31, Principle 9.

[230] Id.

[231] See Committee on Economic, Social and Cultural Rights, General Comment No. 24 (cited above, note 25), para. 13 (encouraging States parties to "insert a provision explicitly referring to their human rights obligations in future [trade or investment agreements], and to ensure that mechanisms for the settlement of investor-State disputes take human rights into account in the interpretation of investment treaties or of investment chapters in trade agreements").

Table 12.7 Foreign Direct Investment (E): typology of obligations and associated implementation measures

Extraterritorial obligations	
Respect	
Protect	(E1.1) Adequately monitoring investments that negatively impact human rights and the right to development in the host country, or that foreseeably create such a risk, in the absence of appropriate safeguards; in particular, where land-related investments are concerned, ensure that the investment does not result in a violation of the right to self-determination of peoples, as an element of the right to development
Fulfil	
Global obligations	
Establish new partnerships	(E4.1) Seeking to conclude international agreements providing for judicial cooperation/mutual legal assistance, in support of the prosecution or litigation of transnational cases
	(E4.2) In future investment treaties, insert a clause referring specifically to the primacy of human rights and to the requirement that the protection of investors' rights should not interfere with the right to development
Operate within partnerships	(E5.1) Encouraging arbitral tribunals established under existing investment treaties to interpret general clauses concerning public welfare, public health or the environment, in line with the requirements of international human rights law, including the right to development
Implement partnerships	

all, including floors, and by 2030 achieve substantial coverage of the poor and vulnerable".

Recommendation No. 202 defines social protection floors as "nationally defined sets of basic social security guarantees which secure protection aimed at preventing or alleviating poverty, vulnerability and social exclusion."[232] The Recommendation calls on ILO member States, "in accordance with national circumstances", to "establish as quickly as possible and maintain their social protection floors comprising basic social security guarantees."[233] Social protection floors as envisaged in Recommendation No. 202 should include at least four basic social security guarantees: (a) access to a nationally defined set of goods and services, constituting essential health care, including maternity care, that meets the criteria of availability, accessibility, acceptability and quality; (b) basic income security for children providing access to nutrition, education, care and any other necessary goods and services, at a nationally defined minimum level; (c) basic income security, at least at a nationally defined minimum level, for persons in active age who are unable to earn sufficient income, in particular in cases of sickness, unemployment, maternity

[232]International Labour Organisation, Text of the Recommendation Concerning National Floors of Social Protection, para. 2 (2012).

[233]ILO, Recommendation Concerning National Floors, at para. 4.

and disability; and (d) basic income security, at least at a nationally defined minimum level, for older persons.[234]

Since it was initially articulated, the concept of the social protection floor has been gaining international recognition and support.[235] The United Nations Chief Executive Board adopted the Social Protection Floor Initiative in April 2009 as one of the nine UN joint initiative multilateral actions to address the global crises of 2008 (food, financial and economic). The social protection floor approach was again endorsed by the United Nations Chief Executives Board and by the Heads of State and Government in the 2010 Millennium Development Summit, where it was part of an integrated set of "social policies designed to guarantee income security and access to essential social services for all, paying particular attention to vulnerable grounds and protecting and empowering people across the life cycle."[236] Following the publication of the ILO's Advisory Group's Report in 2011 and only days after the adoption of Recommendation No. 202, the leaders of the G-20 meeting in Los Cabos on 18–19 June 2012 released a declaration in which they offered support for the promotion and adoption of social protection systems.[237] Similar messages have also been put forward, for instance, in the High Level Segment Ministerial Declaration of the United Nations Economic and Social Council.[238]

The international dimensions related to the universal establishment of social protection floors has been comparatively neglected. That dimension, however, was present from the outset. Recommendation No. 202 was inspired by the report presented on 27 October 2011 by the Social Protection Floor Initiative's advisory group convened by the ILO with the collaboration of the World Health Organization (WHO).[239] The report includes recommendations for coherence and coordination

[234] *Id.* at para. 5.

[235] For a list of endorsements of the Social Protection Floor, see International Labour Organisation, Social Protection Floor Advisory Group: International Endorsement, http://www.ilo.org/public/english/protection/spfag/endorsement/index.htm.

[236] Advisory Report, at xxii.

[237] G-20, Leaders Declaration, at para. 22 (Mexico, 2012). The Declarations supports this by stating "Recognizing the impact of the continuing crisis on developing countries, particularly low income countries, we will intensify our efforts to create a more conducive environment for development, including supporting infrastructure investment. Our policy actions will improve living conditions across the globe and protect the most vulnerable. In particular, by stabilizing global markets and promoting stronger growth, we will generate significant positive effects on development and poverty reduction across the globe." *Id.* at para. 9.

[238] *See* High Level Segment of the United Nations Econ. & Soc. Council, Draft Ministerial Declaration of the 2012 High-Level Segment para. 10, E/2012/L.10 (July, 2012) ("We stress the need to provide social protection to all members of society, fostering growth, resilience, social justice, and cohesion, including those who are not employed in the formal economy. In this regard, we strongly encourage national and local initiatives aimed at providing social protection floors for all citizens. We support global dialogue on best practices for social protection programmes that takes into account the three dimensions of sustainable development and, in this regard, we note the International Labour Organization Recommendation 202 concerning National Floors of Social Protection.").

[239] Advisory Group, *Report of the Advisory Group: Social Protection Floor for a Fair and Inclusive Globalization* (International Labour Organisation, Geneva, 2011).

among international organizations and calls for innovative solutions to address economic shocks, structural changes and sustainability as well as for finding creative sources for financing social protection.[240] It stresses the importance of linking the social protection floor initiative to other strategies on the international level, noting that adopting social protection could be a major step towards achieving the UN Millennium Development Goals in 2015, in particular to eradicate extreme poverty and hunger, reduce child mortality rates, improve maternal health and combat HIV/AIDS, malaria and other diseases.[241] Perhaps in response, Recommendation No. 202 provides that, while "national social protection floors should be financed by national resources", "Members whose economic and fiscal capacities are insufficient to implement the guarantees may seek international cooperation and support that complement their own efforts".[242]

The international dimension of the effort to establish national social protection floors remains conspicuously absent, however, from the Concept Note presenting the Global Partnership for universal social protection to achieve the Sustainable Development Goals, presented jointly by the ILO and the World Bank Group on 21 September 2016, which refers instead to the "sustainable domestic financing" of national social protection floors, and does not refer to international assistance among the sources of financing—although it does mention "using reductions of debt or debt servicing" to that effect.[243] This is particularly disappointing, since Goal 1.6 of the Sustainable Development Goals is to "Ensure significant mobilization of resources from a variety of sources, including through enhanced development cooperation, in order to provide adequate and predictable means for developing countries, in particular least developed countries, to implement programmes and policies to end poverty in all its dimensions".

International obligations are key, however, to the realization of right to social security, and thus to the achievement of SDG 1 and to the right to development. A number of proposals have been made in this regard. In 2002, the Independent Expert on the right to development argued in favor of the conclusion of development compacts between developing countries adopting a development programme through participatory means (setting out the sequence of measures to be adopted) and donors (who would accept a responsibility to support the programme), adequately supervised by a monitoring mechanism to ensure each party complies with its commitments.[244] In October 2012, the Special Rapporteur on the right to food and

---

[240] Advisory Report, at xi-xii, 71–75, 82–83.

[241] Advisory Report, at 39–41, 96.

[242] ILO, Recommendation Concerning National Floors, at para. 12.

[243] Concept Note, p. 3.

[244] Thus conceived, development compacts are "a mechanism for ensuring that all stakeholders recognize the mutuality of obligations, so that the obligations of developing countries to carry out rights-based programmes are matched by reciprocal obligations of the international community to co-operate to enable the implementation of the programmes. The purpose of development compacts is to assure the developing countries that if they fulfil their obligations, the programme for realizing the right to development will not be disrupted owing to lack of financing" (*Fifth Report of the*

the Special Rapporteur on extreme poverty and human rights jointly proposed the establishment of a new fund, called the Global Fund for Social Protection, which, they suggested, could provide two services: (1) to respond to "structural," or endemic, poverty by providing support for States to meet basic social protection floors; and (2) to serve as a reinsurance provider offering protection to the State against unexpected shocks to their social insurance systems, thus allowing LDCs, whose economies are typically less diversified and more susceptible to shocks due to weather-related events or to sudden commodity price variations, to cede the relevant risks and sustainably operate social protection systems.[245] The proposal was referred to (though not explicitly endorsed) by the High-Level Panel of Eminent Persons on the Post-2015 Development Agenda in the Report they submitted in May 2013 to the Secretary-General.[246] The Committee on Economic, Social and Cultural Rights saw it as "an important step in the right direction [that] could support initial investment in sustainable public social protection systems", in the Statement on social protection floors it adopted in March 2015.[247]

Various contributions presented to the Third International Conference on Financing for Development referred to this proposal and suggested various modes of implementing it.[248] The Addis Ababa Action Agenda includes a call to establish "fiscally sustainable and nationally appropriate social protection systems and measures for all, including floors, with a focus on those furthest below the poverty line and the vulnerable, persons with disabilities, indigenous persons, children, youth and older persons".[249] It remains vague, however, on the international dimension,

Independent Expert on the Right to Development, E/CN.4/2002/WG.18/6, para. 14). Such development compacts thus clarify, by mutual agreement, the content of the obligations that correspond to the right to development, both for developing countries and for developed countries that are in a position to assist (see also Sengupta 2002, pp. 837–889).

[245] Special Rapporteur on the right to food and Special Rapporteur on extreme poverty and human rights, De Schutter and Sepuvelda (2012).

[246] *A New Global Partnership: Eradicate Poverty and Transform Economies through Sustainable Development*, Report of the High-Level Panel of Eminent Persons on the Post-2015 Development Agenda (May 2013), p. 60.

[247] Committee on Economic, Social and Cultural Rights, Statement on social protection floors: an essential element of the right to social security and of sustainable development goals (E/C.12/54/3), para. 15.

[248] In particular, the Global Coalition for Social Protection Floors proposed the setting up of Global Fund for Social Protection Floors (GFSPFs), to "provide technical support for national efforts to plan and design national SPFs and the training of national planning and administrative staff", and to "co-finance of SPF transfers in exceptional cases" (*Global Coalition Paper: A Global Fund for Social Protection: A proposal for the Conference on Financing for Development* (April 2015), see: http://www.socialprotectionfloorscoalition.org/wp-content/uploads/2015/05/FfD_GFSP14April2015final.pdf). The proposal also received support from the International Labour Office.

[249] Addis Ababa Action Agenda, cited above note 8, para. 12.

Table 12.8 Establishing universal social protection floors (F)—typology of obligations and associated implementation measures

Extraterritorial obligations	
Respect	
Protect	
Fulfil	(G3.1) Support the establishment of social protection floors through ODA
Global obligations	
Establish new partnerships	(G4.1) Launch a negotiation on a new international mechanism for the financing of the establishment of social protection floors in low-income countries (countries with a gross national income per capita of less than US$1215)
Operate within partnerships	(G5.1) As members of international financial institutions, ensuring that structural adjustment programmes imposed on Borrowers include social safeguards ensuring that priority shall not go to reducing public deficits at the cost of the right to social security
Implement partnerships	

although the Heads of State and Government and High Representatives do pledge to provide "strong international support for these efforts".[250]

Nor does the Addis Ababa Action Agenda take into consideration the impact of structural adjustment programmes (now generally referred to as poverty reduction strategy documents), the adoption of which has been imposed by international financial institutions in exchange for loans, on the ability of countries to finance social protection schemes. However, such programmes have major impacts in low-income countries.[251] Strongly diverging views exist as to whether these programmes have included sufficient social safeguards in the past: for instance, whereas an IMF Staff Policy Paper argued, in May 2017, that two thirds of IMF-supported programmes included targets for social spending or other priority spending, on sectors such as health and education,[252] researchers have reviewed the data presented and have challenged the effectiveness of the social safeguards, which have been routinely ignored as priority has been given to cuts in social spending to maintain budget balance, criticizing the methodology followed by the Fund in its study.[253] Moreover, the IMF advocates greater targeting of social spending, in the name of the improved effectiveness of social programmes, whereas many fear that targeting create a risk of exclusion, particular of the most marginalized groups of the population (Table 12.8).

---

[250] Id.

[251] See, e.g., Kentikelenis (2017); Kentikelenis et al. (2016), pp. 543–582.

[252] IMF, Social safeguards and program design in PRGT and PSI-supported programs, 21 April 2017, available at: http://www.imf.org/en/Publications/Policy-Papers/Issues/2017/06/01/pp042117social-safeguards-and-program-design-in-prgt-and-psi. PRGT refers to the concessional financial granted through the Funds' Poverty Reduction and Growth Trust; PSI refers to Policy Support Instrument provided by the Fund.

[253] Stubbs and Kentikelenis (2017).

Operationalizing the International Dimensions of the Right to Development at Domestic Level: Institutional and Policy Frameworks

In order to discharge their international obligations in support of the right to development, States should establish appropriate institutional mechanisms ensuring that their extraterritorial and global obligations are complied with. The tools developed to ensure policy coherence for sustainable development, insofar as they aim to ensure synergies across different policy areas with a view to supporting sustainable development in its transboundary (and intergenerational) dimensions, may be built on in this regard, where such tools already exist.

Target 17.14 of the Sustainable Development Goals refers to the need to enhance policy coherence for sustainable development (PCSD), and the associated indicator is the number of countries with mechanisms in place to enhance policy coherence of sustainable development (17.14.1). Policy coherence for development (as it was initially referred to) aims to ensure that the policies developed countries design and implement in areas that may have an impact on developing countries (such as trade, investment, technology transfer and intellectual property, or international cooperation in the area of taxation and in the fight against illicit financial flows) shall support, and not undermine, development efforts. The OECD refers to eight "building blocks" which contribute to PCSD. These are mentioned in Table 12.9.

Figure 12.1 developed by the OECD PCD Unit provides a useful summary of the various "building blocks" that can ensure policy coherence for sustainable development.

Table 12.9 Building blocks contributing to Policy Coherence for Sustainable Development—OECD

Political commitment and leadership	PCSD requires a whole-of-government approach ensuring that the SDGs are translated into concrete and coherent actions at international, national and local levels
Integrated approaches to implementation	Implementation measures should consider the linkages between economic, social and environmental policy areas before their adoption
Intergenerational timeframe	Prior to the adoption of decisions, the long-term impacts (and impacts on future generations) should be considered
Analysis and assessments of potential policy effects	The potential impacts, both positive and negative, of decisions on the well-being of people in other countries, should be assessed prior to the adoption of a decision
Policy and institutional coordination	Conflicts of interests or inconsistencies between different priorities and policies should be addressed
Local and regional involvement	Different levels of government should be assigned responsibilities in the implementation of the SDGs
Stakeholder participation	In order to ensure that SDGs are owned by people, actions should be taken to mobilize knowledge and resources about the Goals
Monitoring and reporting	Assess where progress has been achieved and where it has been lacking, in order to take corrective measures and accelerate learning

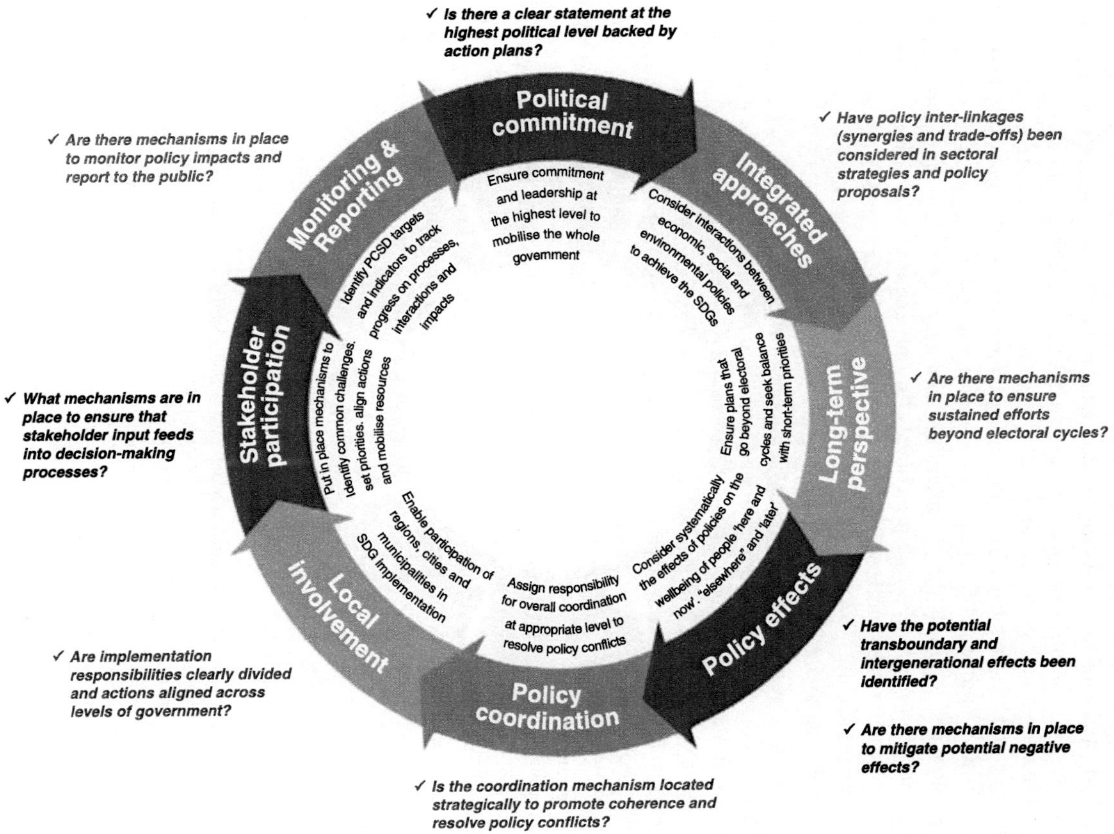

Fig. 12.1 Developed by the OECD PCD Unit. Source: OECD PCD Unit, in *Policy Coherence for Sustainable Development 2017: Eradicating Poverty and Promoting Prosperity* (Paris: OECD, 2017), chap. 2, p. 5

Although the concrete institutional tools that States have established in order to deliver on PCSD differ from State to State, such tools typically include the following: (1) an inter-ministerial taskforce or an office located under the prime minister in order both to demonstrate political commitment at the highest level and to ensure coordination across policy areas; (2) a strategic framework or action plan, regularly updated in line with the evolving international political commitments, to set the general direction, to ensure consistent approaches across different levels of government (national, regional, local) and to better take into account intergenerational timeframes and the need to preserve and enhance stocks of capital (economic, natural, human and social); (3) tools to assess the long-term impacts of measures adopted now and to assess the potential transboundary effects, i.e., how production and consumption, as well as policy choices, in one country, may affect the well-being of populations elsewhere (in particular, through finance, trade, migration and knowledge transfers);[254] (4) platforms or fora allowing for a broad participation of various parts of society, including the private sector and civil society (ensuring a "whole-of-society" approach and thus facilitating ownership),[255] whether within or outside parliament, in order to increase accountability, to help addressing trade-offs between different components of the 2030 Agenda for Sustainable Development, and to identify the social and technological innovations that can support changes in production patterns and in lifestyles within the population; (5) robust monitoring and reporting tools to ensure that the strategies in place are regularly adjusted in the light of their results, and to increase accountability and transparency in their implementation.

The institutional frameworks that have been set up since the Rio Earth Summit of 1992 in support of sustainable development, and that have been gradually established in OECD countries since the mid-1990s in support of policy coherence for development, are now merging into mechanisms for policy coherence for sustainable development. They aim to ensure both a "whole-of-government"

[254]For instance, production and consumption patterns in one country may affect the use of natural resources in other countries, making it more difficult for those other countries to ensure a sustainable use of such resources; the international division of labour encouraged by trade relations may be an obstacle to the diversification of the economies of raw materials exporting countries; migration policies may lead to "brain-drain" at the risk of creating obstacles to the development of countries from where trained professional emigrate.

[255]Target 16.7 of the Sustainable Development Goals is to ensure "responsive, inclusive, participatory and representative decision-making at all levels". Target 17.16 of the Sustainable Development Goals includes the establishment of "multi-stakeholder partnerships that mobilize and share knowledge, expertise, technologya and financial resources, to support the achievement of the Sustainable Development Goals in all countries, particularly developing countries"; the associated indicator (17.16.1) is the number of countries reporting progress in the establishment of multi-stakeholder development effectiveness monitoring frameworks that support achievement of the SDGs.

approach and a "whole-of-society" approach; to integrate both an intergenerational perspective and a transboundary perspective on policy choices; and to ensure adequate monitoring, accountability and feedback.

The growing preoccupation with the establishment of institutional and policy frameworks to ensure Policy Coherence for Sustainable Development (PCSD) presents an opportunity for the implementation of the right to development, not only in its national dimension, but also as regards its extraterritorial and global dimensions. Such frameworks aim to assess the transboundary impacts of production and consumption patterns and policy choices. They therefore could be adjusted to serve the implementation of the right to development, by relying on indicators guiding impact assessments that are informed by the normative content of human rights. This would give such indicators a strong legitimacy, and allow them to serve as a bridge between sustainable development and human rights.

Conclusion

The right to development has a crucial role in guiding poverty-reduction efforts at domestic level. It was also conceived, however, as having to guide reforms of the international legal order, to enable States to make progress under their jurisdiction. The international dimensions of the right to development, until now, have been largely neglected, perhaps because of their suspicious resemblance to the New International Economic Order of the 1970s, the agenda of which many governments, particularly among rich countries, were deeply suspicious about, if not overtly hostile.

It is now time that we rescue these international dimensions of the right to development. This can be achieved by building on the recent advances both of general international law and of international human rights, and by making progress towards identifying the normative components (the attributes, in UN jargon) of the extraterritorial and global duties associated with these dimensions. The building blocks are there. Human rights monitoring bodies can contribute to fill in the gaps that remain. Only then shall the promise of Article 28 of the Universal Declaration of Human Rights, to establish an international legal order in which all the rights of the Declaration may be realized, be kept.

Annex: List of Official Documents

UN General Assembly: Resolutions and Treaties

- 1945—Charter of the United Nations (June 26, 45), 59 Stat. 1031—(entered into force Oct. 24, 1945) https://treaties.un.org/pages/ViewDetails.aspx?src=TREATY&mtdsg_no=I-1&chapter=1&clang=_en

- 1948—GA Res. 21—UN GAOR, 3d sess., UN Doc. A/810 (1948) (Art. 28). Universal Declaration of Human Rights
- 1953—Agreement on external German Debt (16 September) United Nations Treaty series UNTS 333 p. 3 https://treaties.un.org/Pages/showDetails.aspx?objid=080000028013dc13
- 1966—A/RES/21/2200—International Covenant on Economic, Social and Cultural Rights (adopted on 16 December 1966 U.N. GAOR, 21st sess., Supp. No. 16, U.S. Doc. A/6316) (1966). United Nations Treaty series UNTS 993 p. 3
- 1966—A/RES/21/2200A—International Covenant on Civil and Political Rights—16 December 1966. UNTS United Nations Treaty series 999 p. 171
- 1969—Vienna Convention of the Law of Treaties 23 May. United Nations Treaty Series *1155* p. 331
- 1966—A/RES/21/2205 (XXI) of 17 December 1966 UNICITRAL United Nations Convention on International Trade law
- 1968—Treaty on the Non-Proliferation of Nuclear Weapons, opened for signature 1 July 1968. United Nations Treaty Series UNTS, 729, p. 161
- 1970—A/RES/25/2625—The Declaration of Principles of International Law Concerning Friendly Relations and Co-operation among States in accordance with the Charter of the United Nations. 24 October. https://www.un.org/documents/ga/res/25/ares25.htm
- 1976—A/RES/31/98 Arbitration Rules of the United Nations Commission on International Trade Law. 15 December
- 1984—A/RES/39/46 Convention against Torture and Other Cruel, Inhuman or Degrading Treatment or Punishment of 10 December 1984 (entry into force 26 June 1987, in accordance with article 27 (1)) United Nations Treaty series UNTS, vol. 1465, p. 85
- 1986—Vienna Convention on the Law of Treaties between States and International Organizations or between International Organizations
- 1986—A/RES/41/128—Declaration on the Right to Development (4 Dec. 1986)
- 1989—Montreal Protocol on Substances that Deplete the Ozone Layer (with annex). Concluded at Montreal on 16 September. United Nations Treaty Series UNTS vol. 1522 p. 3
- 1989—A/RES/44/49—Convention for the right of the child. United Nations Treaty Series UNTS vol. 1577, p. 3; depositary notifications C.N.147.1993. TREATIES-5 of 15 May 1993 [amendments to article 43 (2)]1; and C. N.322.1995.TREATIES-7 of 7 November 1995 [amendment to article 43 (2)]. https://treaties.un.org/Pages/ViewDetails.aspx?src=IND&mtdsg_no=IV-11&chapter=4&lang=en
- 1992—Convention on Biological Diversity, in force on 29 December 1993—United Nations Treaty Series UNTS vol. 1760, p. 79, Art. 20(4)
- 1992—United Nations Framework Convention on Climate Change (1992, in force on 21 March
- 1994 (United Nations Treaty Series, vol. 1771, p. 107; 31 ILM 851 (1992)), Art. 3
- 1993—A/RES/48//121(20 Dec. 1993) World Conference on Human Rights https://www.un.org/documents/ga/res/48/a48r121.htm

- 2000—A/RES/54/263 (May 25 2000) Optional Protocols to the Convention on the Rights of the Child on the Sale of Children, Child Prostitution and Child Pornography—adopted 16 March 2001 https://undocs.org/en/A/RES/54/263
- 2000—A/RES/55/2—Millennium Declaration, General Assembly Resolution (8 September 2000)—https://www.un.org/millennium/declaration/ares552e.htm
- 2001—Annex to A/RES/56/83 A/56/49 (vol. 1)/Corr.4—Responsibility of States for Internationally wrongful Acts December on 2001 International Law Commission I.L.C. *Draft Articles on the Responsibility of States for Internationally Wrongful Acts* (Report of the International Law Commission on the work of its 53rd session)
- 2006—A/RES/61/106—Convention on the Rights Persons with Disabilities 13 December 2006 (entering into force 3 May 2008, in accordance with article 45(1). United Nations, Treaty Series UNTS vol. 2515, p. 3
- 2006—A/RES/61/177—International Convention for the Protection of All Persons from Enforced Disappearance—20 December—United Nations Treaty Series UNTS vol. 2716, p. 3
- 2011—A/RES/66/100 of 9 December 2011 on Art. 61 of the Draft Articles on the Responsibility of International Organizations, adopted by the International Law Commission at its 63rd session, in 2011 (A/66/10, para. 87)
- 2011—A/RES 66/100—The Responsibility of International Organizations. December 9—Vienna Convention on the Law of Treaties opened for signature on 23 May 1969, A/CONF.39/11/Add.2. Entered into force on 27 January 1980, 1155 United Nations Treaty Series UNTS 331, 8 ILM (International Legal Materials) 679
- 2012—A/RES/66/288—The Future We Want. 11 September
- 2015—A/RES/69/313 (27 July 2015)—Agenda—the 3rd Conference on Financing for Development—Addis Ababa Agenda General, basic principle 2
- 2015—A/RES/70/1—Sustainable Development Goals on 2030—Agenda for Sustainable Development

UN General Assembly: Reports

- 2001—A/56/10 and Corr.1. International Law Commission—I.L.C.—*Draft Articles on the Responsibility of States for Internationally Wrongful Acts* (Report of the International Law Commission on the work of its 53rd session) August 2001 see annex to A/RES/56/83 and A/56/49 (vol. 1)/Corr.4
- 2006—A/61/10 I.L.C. Report on its report 58th session
- 2010—The Millennium Development Goals Report. https://www.un.org/en/mdg/summit2010/pdf/MDG%20Report%202010%20En%20r15%20-low%20res%2020100615%20-.pdf
- 2011—A/66/10, para. 87—International Law Commission—I.L.C.—*Draft Articles on the Responsibility of International Organizations* at its 63rd session

- 2013—Report SDGs—Sustainable development Goals. A New Global Partnership: Eradicate Poverty and Transform Economies through Sustainable Development. High-Level Panel of Eminent Persons on the Post-2015 Development Agenda (May)
- 2015—A/70/274 Report of the Special Rapporteur on extreme poverty and human rights August 4
- 2017—A/72/187 Promotion of a democratic and equitable international order—Note by the Secretary-General—21 July—the sixth report of the Independent Expert on the promotion of a democratic and equitable international order, Alfred-Maurice de Zayas, submitted in accordance with Assembly resolution A/RES/71/190

UN General Assembly: Conferences

- 1969—A/CONF.39/26—Declaration on the prohibition of military, political or economic coercion in the conclusion of treaties, Annex to the Final Act of the United Nations Conference on the Law of Treaties (First and Second sessions, 26 March—24 May 1968 and 9 April—22 May 1969)
- 1980—A/CONF.39/11/Add.2. Vienna declaration and programme of Action—Vienna Convention on the Law of Treaties, opened for signature on 23 May 1969, Entered into force on 27 January 1980, 1155 UNTS 331, 8 ILM (International Legal Materials) 679
- 1986—A/CONF.129/15—21 March—United Nations Conference on the Law of Treaties between States and International Organizations or between International Organizations. United Nations Treaty Series UNTS vol. 1155:331
- 1992—A/CONF.151/26—Rio Declaration on Environment and Development 3–4 June 1992—(the United Nations Conference on Environment and Development of 3–14 June 1992)
- 2002—A/CONF.198/11—Report of the International Conference on Financing for Development, Monterrey, Mexico, 18–22 March 2002), chapter 1, resolution 1, annex, paras. 47–51
- 2002—A/CONF.199/20 World Summit on Sustainable Development-Johannesburg in August-September 2002—the implementation of the Agenda 21

United Nations Framework Convention on Climate Change

- 2009—FCCC/CP/2009/11/Add.1—Report of the Conference of the Parties. The Copenhagen Accord of 18 December 2009. Decisions at the 15th conference of parties to the UN Framework Convention on Climate Change held 7 to 19 December 2009 (March 2010)

- 2015—FCCC/CP/2015/10/Add.1para. 114 of Decision 1/CP.21, Adoption of the Paris Agreement (January 2016)
- 2016—FCCC/CP/2015/10/Add.1. Paris Agreement 13 Dec. 2015—entered into force November 2016

United Nations Department of Economic and Social Affairs

- 2013—ST/ESA/347—UN Department of Economic and Social Affairs. U*nited Nations Practical Manual on Transfer Pricing for Developing Countries*. United Nations, New York, 2013: see Rainer Lanz and Sébastien Miroudot, "Intra-Firm Trade: Patterns, Determinants and Policy Implications"

International Law Commission

- 2001—A/56/10 and Corr. 1—*Draft articles on* Responsibility of States for internationally wrongful Acts Official Records of the General Assembly, 2001 December 12 Annex to General Assembly resolution A/RES/56/83 of 12 December 2001, and corrected by document A/56/49 (Vol. I)/Corr.4
- 2006—A/61/10 (2006 Report of the International Law Commission on the work of its 58th session, 1 May–9 June and 3 July–11 August 2006, I.L.C. Report), chap. VI, paras. 77–91
- 2006—A/CN.4/L.702 I.L.C. Report on its report 58th session Report of the Study Group of the International Law Commission, Fragmentation of international law: difficulties arising from the diversification and expansion of international law, July 18
- 2011—A/66/10 draft articles International Responsibility of Organizations—A/RES/66/100—December 9

UN Human Rights Council: Resolutions

- 2011—A/HRC/RES/17/4/Protect, Respect and Remedy—Human rights and transnational corporations and other business enterprises (6 July)
- 2012—A/HRC/RES/20/10—The effects of foreign debt and other related international financial obligations of States on the full enjoyment of all human rights, particularly economic, social and cultural rights (18 July)
- 2012—A/HCR/RES/21/11—Guiding principles on Extreme Poverty and Human Rights (18 October)
- 2014—A/HCR/RES/21/27—Human rights and unilateral coercive measures (26 September)

- 2016—A/HRC/RES/33/14—29-09-2016 The right to development (05/10/2016)
- 2016—A/HRC/RES/32/10—The Human Rights Council OP 1. Business and human rights: improving accountability and access to remedy
- 2017—A/HRC/RES/34/3—Guiding Principles for human right impact assessments of economic reform policies by Independent expert on Foreign debts and Human rights (April)
- 2017—A/HRC/RES/34/13—Human rights and unilateral coercive measures (24 March)

UN Human Rights Council: Reports

- 2001—A/HRC/17/31—Guiding Principles on Business and Human Rights
- 2009—A/HRC/10/5 February 11—Report of the Special Rapporteur on the right to food, Olivier De Schutter. The role of development cooperation and food aid in realizing the right to adequate food: moving from charity to obligation
- 2011—A/HRC/20/23 April 10—Guiding principles on Foreign Debt and Human Rights—A/HRC/RES/20/10
- 2011—A/HRC/36/40—Guiding principles on Extreme Poverty and Human Rights
- 2012—A/HRC/19/59, Add.5 Guiding Principles on human rights impact assessments of trade and investment agreements, Addendum to the Report of the Special Rapporteur on the right to food, Report of the Special Rapporteur on the right to food to the 19th session of the Human Rights Council
- 2012—A/HRC/21/39—The Guiding Principles on Extreme Poverty and Human Rights submitted by the Special Rapporteur on extreme poverty and human right. July 18 2012
- 2014—A/HRC/26/28—Report of the Special Rapporteur on extreme poverty and human rights, Magdalena Sepulveda Carmona. May 22 2014
- 2016—A/HRC/31/61—the Final study on illicit financial flows, human rights and the 2030 Agenda for Sustainable Development of the Independent Expert—Juan Pablo Bohoslavsky—on the effects of foreign debt and other related international financial obligations of States on the full enjoyment of all human rights, particularly economic, social and cultural rights (15 January 2016), paras. 10–11
- 2016—A/HRC/32/19 and Add.1—Explanatory notes on guidance to improve accountability and access to remedy for victims of business-related human rights abuse—Addendum to report of the United Nations High Commissioner for Human Rights
- 2016—A/HRC/33/54—Report of the Human Rights Council Advisory Committee on the activities of vulture funds and the impact on human rights (20 July 2016)
- 2017—A/HRC/35/33—Best practices and how to improve on the effectiveness of cross-border cooperation between States with respect to law enforcement on the issue of business and human rights: Study of the Working Group on the issue

of human rights and transnational corporations and other business enterprise June 2017 (24 April)

- 2017—A/HRC/36/52 (Research-based study on the impact of flow of funds of illicit origin and the non-repatriation thereof to the countries of origin on the enjoyment of human rights, including economic, social and cultural rights—Progress report of the Advisory Committee of the Human Rights Council (9 August))

UN Human Rights Council: Working Groups

- 2010—A/HCR/WG/15.2/TF/2/Add.2—Annex, High-Level Task Force on the implementation of the right to development, right to development criteria and operational sub-criteria (8 March)
- 2010—A/HRC/15/WG.2/TF/2/Add.1—Human Rights Council, Consolidation of findings of the high-level task force on the implementation of the right to development (25 March)
- 2018—A/HRC/WG.2/19/CRP.1. The international dimensions of the right to development: a fresh start towards improving accountability—United Nations Working Group on the Right to Development (26 March)

Human Rights Committee

- 1993—CCPR/C/70/D/547/1993—Human Rights Committee, *Apirana Mahuika et al. v. New Zealand*, Communication No. 547/1993, (2000), para. 9.7
- 1994—CCPR/C/21Rev.1/Add.5—Human Rights Committee—General Comment No. 23: The rights of minorities (Art. 27), 50th session (4 August 1994), paras. 1 and 3.2
- 2012—CCPR/C/DEU/CO/6—Human Rights Committee, Concluding Observations: Germany para. 16
- 2013—CCPR/C/120/D/2285/2013—Human Rights Committee, comm. n°2285/2013, *Yassin et al. v. Canada*, Views of 26 July 2017, para. 6.5—View Adopted: 2017.07.26

Economic, Social and Cultural Rights Committee: Reports

- 1990—E/1990/5/Add.41—Committee on Economic, Social and Cultural Rights. Report submitted by Soudan (1998)
- 1990—E/1990/5/Add.38—Committee on Economic, Social and Cultural Rights. Report submitted by Egypt (1998)

- 1990—E/1990/6/Add.20—Committee on Economic, Social and Cultural Rights. Report submitted by Morocco (1999)
- 1990—E/1990/6/Add.26—Committee on Economic, Social and Cultural Rights. Report submitted by Algeria (2000) 35/33
- 1990—E/1990/5/Add.48—Committee on Economic, Social and Cultural Rights. Report submitted b by Benin (2001)
- 1990—E/1990/6/Add.36—Committee on Economic, Social and Cultural Rights. Report submitted b by Ecuador (2002)
- 2007—E/C.12/KEN/1—Committee on Economic, Social and Cultural Rights. Report submitted by Kenya

Economic, Social and Cultural Rights Committee: General Comment

- 1989—E/C.12/GC/20—Committee on Economic, Social and Cultural Rights. General Comment No. 18: Non-discrimination (37th session, 1989)
- 1990—E/1990/23—Committee on Economic, Social and Cultural Rights. General Comment No. 2: International technical assistance measures (art. 22), para. 9
- 1991—E/1991/23—Committee on Economic, Social and Cultural Rights. General Comment No 3: The Nature of States Parties' Obligations
- 1998—E/1998/22—Committee on Economic, Social and Cultural Rights, General Comment No. 8 (1997): The relationship between economic sanctions and respect for economic, social and cultural rights
- 1999—E/C.12/1999/5—Committee on Economic, Social and Cultural Rights. General Comment N°12. The right to adequate food (art. 11) paras 19 and 36 (emphasis added))
- 1999—(E/C.12/1999/9); Committee on Economic, Social and Cultural Rights, General Comment No. 12
- 2000—E/C.12/2000/4—Committee on Economic, Social and Cultural Rights. General Comment No. 14. April 14. The right to the highest attainable standard of health (art. 12) para. 39
- 2002—E/C.12/2002/11—Committee on Economic, Social and Cultural Rights. General Comment No. 15: The right to water (arts. 11 and 12) paras. 31, 33—26 November 2002, para. 36
- 2006—E/C.12/GC/18 Committee on Economic, Social and Cultural Rights. General Comment No. 18: The right to work (art. 6), para. 52
- 2008—E/C.12/GC/19 Committee on Economic, Social and Cultural Rights. General Comment No. 19 (2008): The right to social security (art. 9), para. 54
- 2016—E/C.12/GC/23—Committee on Economic, Social and Cultural Rights General Comment No. 23: The right to just and favourable conditions of work, para. 70

- 2016—E/C.12/GC/24—Committee on Economic, Social and Cultural Rights—General Comment No. 24 on State obligations under the International Covenant on Economic, Social and Cultural Rights in the context of Business Activities June 24

Economic, Social and Cultural Rights Committee: Concluding Observations

- 2001—E/C.12/1/Add.57—Committee on Economic, Social and Cultural Rights. Concluding Observations on Honduras
- 2005—E/C.12/1/Add.106—Committee on Economic, Social and Cultural Rights. Concluding Observations on Zambia
- 2011—E/C.12/DEU/CO/5 Committee on Economic, Social and Cultural Rights. Concluding Observations: Germany
- 2014—E/C.12/FIN/CO/6—Committee on Economic, Social and Cultural Rights. Concluding Observations: Finland
- 2016—E/C.12/GBR/CO/6—Committee on Economic, Social and Cultural Rights. Concluding Observations on the sixth periodic report of the United Kingdom of Great Britain and Northern Ireland 14 July 2016

Economic, Social and Cultural Rights Committee: Statements

- 2011—E/C.12/2011/1 S—Committee on Economic, Social and Cultural Rights. Statement on the obligations of States parties regarding the corporate sector and economic, social and cultural rights July 12
- 2015—E/C.12/54/3—Committee on Economic, Social and Cultural Rights, Statement on social protection floors: an essential element of the right to social security and of sustainable development goals para. 15. March 6
- 2016—E/C.12/2016/1—Committee on Economic, Social and Cultural Rights. Statement on Public debt, austerity measures and the International Covenant on Economic, Social and Cultural Rights June 24

Rights of Child Committee CRC: Reports

- 1998—CRC/C/11/Add.18—Committee on the Rights of the Child—Report submitted by the Central African Republic
- 1998—CRC/C/65/Add.2—Committee on the Rights of the Child—Report submitted by Honduras-

- 1998—CRC/C/28/Add.11—Committee on the Rights of the Child—Report submitted by Suriname
- 2001—CRC/C/41/Add.11—Committee on the Rights of the Child—Report submitted by Mozambique
- 2003—CRC/C/70/Add.18—Committee on the Rights of the Child—Report submitted by Madagascar
- 2002—CRC/C/11/Add.25—Committee on the Rights of the Child—Report submitted by Zambia
- 2002—CRC/C/70/Add.17—Committee on the Rights of the Child—Report submitted Sri Lanka
- 2004—CRC/C/65/Add.30—Committee on the Rights of the Child—Report submitted by Nepal
- 2004—CRC/C/65/Add.28—Committee on the Rights of the Child—Report submitted by Ecuador
- 2006—CRC/C/KEN/2—Committee on the Rights of the Child—Report submitted by Kenya

Rights of Child Committee CRC: Concluding Observations

- 2000—CRC/C/15/Add.115—Committee on the Rights of the Child. Concluding Observations on India
- 2000—CRC/C/Add.124—Committee on the Rights of the Child. Concluding Observations on Georgia
- 2000—CRC/C/15/Add.130—Committee on the Rights of the Child. Concluding Observations on Suriname
- 2000—CRC/C/15/Add.138—Committee on the Rights of the Child. Concluding Observations on Central African Republic
- 2001—CRC/C/15/Add.152—Committee on the Rights of the Child. Concluding Observations on Turkey
- 2001—CRC/C/15/Add.156—Committee on the Rights of the Child. Concluding Observations on Tanzania in 2001
- 2001—CRC/C/15/Add.160—Committee on the Rights of the Child. Concluding Observations on Kenya
- 2002—CRC/C/15/Add.172—Committee on the Rights of the Child. Concluding Observations on Mozambique
- 2002—CRC/C/15/Add.174—Committee on the Rights of the Child. Concluding Observations on Malawi
- 2002—CRC/C/15/Add.179—Committee on the Rights of the Child. Concluding Observations on Niger
- 2002—CRC/C/15/Add.186—Committee on the Rights of the Child. Concluding Observations on the Netherlands/Netherlands Antilles
- 2002—CRC/C/15/Add.190—Committee on the Rights of the Child. Concluding Observations on Sudan

- 2002—CRC/C/15/Add.193—Committee on the Rights of the Child. Concluding Observations on Burkina Faso
- 2003—CRC/C/15/Add.197—Committee on the Rights of the Child. Concluding Observations on the Republic of Korea
- 2003—CRC/C/15/Add.207—Committee on the Rights of the Child. Concluding Observations on Sri Lanka
- 2004—CRC/C/15/Add.232—Committee on the Rights of the Child—Concluding Observations: El Salvador, 30 June
- 2011—CRC/C/FIN/CO/4—Committee on the Rights of the Child, Concluding Observations: Finland

Rights of Child Committee CRC: General Comments

- 2003 CRC/GC/2003/5—Committee on the Rights of the Child—General Comment: General Measures of Implementation for the Convention on the Rights of the Child
- 2013—CRC/C/GC/16—Committee on the Rights of the Child—General Comment No. 16 on State obligations regarding the impact of the business sector on children's rights
- 2014—CRC/C/DEU/CO/3-4—Committee on the Rights of the Child. Concluding Observations: Germany
- 2016—CRC/C/COD/3-5—Committee on the Rights of the Child. Report (third to fifth reports of States parties due in 2012) submitted by the Democratic Republic of Congo. 24 June 2016

Committee on the Elimination of Discrimination Against Women, CEDWA

- 2006—CEDAW/C/PHI/CO/6—Committee on the Elimination of Discrimination against Women Concluding Observations: Philippines, October 25
- 2006—CEDAW/C/GUA/CO/6—Committee on the Elimination of Discrimination against Women Concluding Observations: Guatemala, June 2
- 2007—CEDAW/C/COL/CO/6—Committee on the Elimination of Discrimination against Women Concluding Observations: Colombia, February 2
- 2016—CEDAW/C/CHE/CO/4-5—Committee on the Elimination of Discrimination against Women. Concluding Observations on the combined fourth and fifth reports of Switzerland 18 November

Committee on the Elimination of Racial Discrimination, CERD

- 2006—CERD/C/GUY/CO/14—Committee on the Elimination of Racial Discrimination. Concluding Observations: Guyana (4 April 2006, para. 16)
- 2008—CERD/C/USA/CO/6—Committee on the Elimination of Racial Discrimination. Concluding Observations: United States, para. 30
- 2009—CERD/C/CAN/CO/18—Committee on the Elimination of Racial Discrimination. Concluding Observations: Canada para. 17
- 2011—CERD/C/NOR/CO/19–90—Committee on the Elimination of Racial Discrimination. Concluding Observations: Norway

Economic and Social Council

- 1990—E/CN.4/1990/9/Rev.1—(26 Sept. 1990)—Economic and Social Council. Report by Secretary-General on Global pursuant to Commission on Human Rights resolution 1989/45
- 2002—E/CN.4/2002/WG.18/6—Economic and Social Council. Fifth Report of the Independent Expert on the Right to Development, para. 14
- 2006—E/CN.4/2006/26—Economic and Social Council. Report of the Working Group on the right to development. 7th session (conclusions). Para. 59
- 2012—E/2012/L.10—Economic and Social Council. Draft Ministerial Declaration of the 2012. High-Level Segment para. 10 (July, 2012)
- 2017—E/CN.3/2017/2—Economic and Social Council. Report on the interagency Expert group on Sustainable Development Goal indicators March

International Court of Justice

- 1966—Judge Tanaka, dissenting opinion in the *South West Africa* Case (*Ethiopia v. South Africa; Liberia v. South Africa*), Second Phase, Judgment ICJ Rep 298
- 1974—Fisheries *Jurisdiction Case*, 1974 I.C.J., p. 31
- 1994—*Territorial Dispute Case (Libyan Arab Jamahiriya v. Chad) I.C.J. Reports p. 6*
- 2004—*Legal Consequences of the Construction of a Wall in the Occupied Palestinian Territory*, Advisory Opinion, 2004 I.C.J. 136 (9 July), paras. 109–112
- 2007—*Case concerning Application of the Convention on the Prevention and Punishment of the Crime of Genocide (Bosnia Herzegovinia V. Serbia Montenegro).* I.C.J. Judgement (26 February 2007)—I.C.J. Reports para. 430 and 461

Permanent Court of International Justice

- 1931 P.C.I.J—Advisory Opinion No. 42, *Railway Traffic Between Lithuania and Poland.* (ser. A/B) No. 42, at p. 116

UN International Arbitral Awards: Reports R.I.A.A.

- 1972—Graeco-German Arbitration (1972), 91 R.I.A.A., p. 57

ILO International Labour Organization

- ILO—Social protection Floor—Social Protection Floor Advisory Group: International Endorsement http://www.ilo.org/public/english/protection/spfag/endorsement/index.htm; https://www.ilo.org/secsoc/areas-of-work/legal-advice/WCMS_205341/lang%2D%2Den/index.htm
- 1944—ILO—Declaration of Philadelphia May 10—https://www.ilo.org/dyn/normlex/en/f?p=1000:62:0::NO:62:P62_LIST_ENTRIE_ID:2453907:NO#declaration
- 1998—ILO—Declaration on Fundamental Principles and Rights at Work https://www.ilo.org/declaration/thedeclaration/textdeclaration/lang%2D%2Den/index.htm
- 2008—ILO Declaration on Social Justice for a Fair Globalization adopted statement of principles and policies adopted unanimously on 10 June 2008 https://www.ilo.org/global/about-the-ilo/mission-and-objectives/WCMS_371208/lang%2D%2Den/index.htm
- 2011—ILO—Advisory group report. Social protection floor for a fair and inclusive globalization. in collaboration with the WHO—ILO Geneva 2011 http://www.ilo.org/wcmsp5/groups/public/@dgreports/@dcomm/@publ/documents/publication/wcms_165750.pdf
- 2012—ILO—R202—Social Protection Floors Recommendation 2012 14 June https://www.ilo.org/dyn/normlex/en/f?p=NORMLEXPUB:12100:0::NO::P12100_ILO_CODE:R202
- 2015—ILO—Global Coalition for Social Protection Floors—Global Coalition Paper: A Global Fund for Social Protection: A proposal for the Conference on Financing for Development (April 2015), see: http://www.socialprotectionfloorscoalition.org/wp-content/uploads/2015/05/FfD_GFSP14April2015final.pdf
- 2016—ILO—Resolution decent work in global supply chains. 10 June https://www.ilo.org/jakarta/WCMS_555927/lang%2D%2Den/index.htm

- 2016—ILO—Concept Note presenting the Global Partnership for universal social protection to achieve the Sustainable Development Goals, with the World Bank Group on 21 September 2016, https://www.ilo.org/global/topics/social-security/WCMS_378991/lang%2D%2Den/index.htm

International Monetary Fund, IMF

- 2017—IMF—Social safeguards and program design in PRGT and PSI-supported programs, 21 April: http://www.imf.org/en/Publications/Policy-Papers/Issues/2017/06/01/pp042117social-safeguards-and-program-design-in-prgt-and-psi.

UNCTAD

- 1968—Proceedings of the United Nations Conference on Trade and Development, Second Session, New Delhi, 1 Feb.-29 March 1968, vol. I: Report and Annexes, pp. 38–39
- 1971—Decision L/3545 (25 June 1971) GATT B.I.S.D. (18th Supp) at 24 (1972) Decision relating to the establishment of generalized, non-reciprocal and non-discriminatory preferences beneficial to the developing countries
- 1979—Decision L/4903 (28 November 1979) GATT B.I.S.D. (26th Supp) at 203 (1980) Decision on Differential and More Favourable Treatment, Reciprocity and Fuller Participation of Developing Countries
- 2012—UNCTAD. Principles on Promoting Responsible Sovereign Lending and Borrowing, Principle 7: Debt Restructurings. https://unctad.org/en/Pages/GDS/Sovereign-Debt-Portal/Sovereign-Lending-and-Borrowing.aspx
- 2014—UNCTAD—World Investment Report 2014: Investing in the SDGs: An Action Plan (Geneva: UNCTAD, 2014)

World Bank

- World bank development classification—http://data.worldbank.org; https://datahelpdesk.worldbank.org/knowledgebase/articles/906519
- 1969—the Commission on International Development—Partners in Development: Report of *Report of the Commission on International Development* New York: Praeger, 1969. 400 pp

ICSID, International Centre for Settlement of Investment Disputes

- 1965—1965 International Convention on the Settlement of Disputes between States and the nationals of other Parties (ICSID). 575 U.N.T.S. 159
- 2016—Case N° ARB/07/26 (8 Dec. 2016)

World Trade Organization

- 1994—WTO—World trade Agreement establishing the WTO—1994 April 15—Marrakesh—entered into force January 95 1—33 ILM 1125 https://www.wto.org/english/docs_e/legal_e/04-wto_e.htm
- 1998—WT/DS58/AB/R, *United States — Import Prohibition of Certain Shrimp and Shrimp Products*, 12 October (Report of the Appellate Body), paras 161 to 165, 171, 172
- 2001—WT/MIN(01)/DEC/1. 20 November 2001 (01-5859)
- 2008—Doha Declaration on Financing and Development
- 2009—WTO—*Trade and Climate Change. A Report by the United Nations Environment Program and the World Trade Organization*, World Trade Organization, Geneva, 2009

African Commission on Human and Peoples' Rights

- 1982—African Charter of Human and peoples' Rights 1981, OAU Doc. CAB/LEG/67/3 rev. 5, 21 I.L.M. 58 (1982), entered into force Oct. 21, 1986
- 2001—*The Social and Economic Rights Action Center and the Center for Economic and Social Rights v. Nigeria.* African Commission on Human and Peoples' Rights, (2001), Comm. No. 155/96 para. 58
- 2005—African Charter of Human and Peoples' rights—ACHPR—http://www.achpr.org/instruments/achpr/
- 2009 Compl. No. 276/03, *Centre for Minority Rights Development (Kenya) and Minority Rights Group (on behalf of Endorois Welfare Council) v. Kenya*, decision adopted at the 46th Ordinary Session of the African Commission on Human and Peoples' Rights held from 11–25 November 2009; http://caselaw.ihrda.org/doc/276.03/
- 2013—African Commission on Human and Peoples' Rights—ACHPR—Resolution adopted by the Commission at its 53rd ordinary session, 23 April 2013. http://www.achpr.org/sessions/53rd/info/communique53/

African Court of Human Rights

- 2017 *African Commission on Human and Peoples' Rights v. Kenya (in the case of the Ogiek Community of the Mau Forest)*, Appl. No. 006/2012, Judgment of 26 May 2017, paras. 207–211. http://en.african-court.org/index.php/55-finalised-cases-details/864-app-no-006-2012-african-commission-on-human-and-peoples-rights-v-republic-of-kenya-details

Inter-American Court of Human Rights

- 2006—*Sawhoyamaxa Indigenous Community v. Paraguay* (judgment of 29 March 2006, Series C No. 146), para. 140
- *2007—The Moiwana Community v. Suriname. Preliminary Objections, Merits, Reparations and Costs*, Judgment of June 15, 2005. Series C No. 124, paras. 132–133
- 2007—*Saramaka People. v. Suriname,* Judgment of 28 November 2007, para. 86

FATF Financial Action Task Force

- The *International Standards on Combating Money Laundering and the Financing of Terrorism and Proliferation* (AML/CFT standards)-http://www.fatf-gafi.org/publications/fatfrecommendations/?hf=10&b=0&s=desc(fatf_releasedate) (last consulted on 12 April 2019)

International Law Association, ILA

- 2002—International Law Association ILA resolution 3/2002, New Delhi Declaration on Principles of International Law relating to Sustainable Development April 2–6 2002, annex as published in UN doc. A/57/329, principle 3

OECD

- 2005—OECD—High Level Forums on Aid Effectiveness—Paris Declaration on Aid Effectiveness http://www.oecd.org/dac/effectiveness/parisdeclarationandaccraagendaforaction.htm

- 2008—OECD—High Level Forum on Aid Effectiveness—AAA—Accra Agenda for Action http://www.oecd.org/dac/effectiveness/parisdeclarationandaccraagendaforaction.htm
- 2011—OECD—High Level Forum on Aid Effectiveness—Busan—Partnership Agreement http://www.oecd.org/development/effectiveness/busanpartnership.htm
- 2014—OECD—*Development Co-Operation Report 2014. Mobilising Resources for Sustainable Development.* (OECD Publishing, Paris, 2014, chapter II.13
- 2013—OECD—*Tax and Development: Aid Modalities for Strengthening Tax Systems* (OECD Publishing, Paris, 2013)
- 2017—OECD—*Blended finance. Mobilising resources for sustainable development and climate action in developing countries. Policy perspectives* (Paris: OECD, 2017))
- 2016—OECD—*Roadmap to US$100 billion*, October 2016
- 2017—OECD—DCD/DAC(2017)9—Development Action Committee, Blended Finance for Sustainable Development: moving the agenda forward (OECD,), 24 February 2017, para. 15
- 2017—OECD—PCD Unit, *Policy Coherence for Sustainable Development 2017: Eradicating Poverty and Promoting Prosperity* (Paris: OECD, 2017), chap. 2, p. 5

References

Abi-Saab G (1999) Fragmentation or unification: some concluding remarks. N Y Univ J Int Law Polit 31(4):919–933

Alvarez JE (2005) International organizations as law-makers. Oxford University Press, Oxford, pp 601–608

Barry C, Reddy SG (2008) International trade and labor standards. a proposal for linkage. Columbia University Press, New York

Baxter RR (1980) International law 'In Her Infinite Variety'. Int Comp Law Q 29(4):549–566

Bürgi Bonanomi E (2015) Sustainable development in international law making and trade. Edward Elgar, Cheltenham

Chang H-J (2005) Kicking away the ladder. Development strategy in historical perspective. Anthem Press, London

Cole M, Elliott R (2003) Determining the trade-environment composition effect: the role of capital, labor and environmental regulations. J Environ Econ Manag 46(3):363–383

Combacau J (1991) In: Virally MM (ed) Logique de la validité contre logique d'opposabilité dans la Convention de Vienne sur le droit des traités. Pedone, Paris, pp 195–203

Concord (European NGO confederation for relief and development), Aidwatch Report 2016, p 6

Corbacho A, Cibils VF, Lora E, Inter-American Development Bank (eds) (2013) More than revenue: taxation as a development tool. Palgrave Macmillan

Cullet P (2003) Differential treatment in international environmental law. Ashgate, Aldershot

Czaplinski W, Danilenko GM (1990) Conflict of norms in international law. Netherlands Int Law Rev 21:12–28

De Schutter O (2015) Trade in the service of sustainable development. Linking trade to labour rights and environmental standards. Hart, Oxford

De Schutter O, Sepuvelda M (2012) Underwriting the poor. A global fund for social protection. https://www.ohchr.org/Documents/Issues/Food/20121009_GFSP_en.pdf

de Wet E, Vidmar J (2012) Hierarchy in international law: the place of human rights. Oxford University Press, Oxford

Deaton A (2013) The great escape. Health, wealth, and the origins of inequality. Princeton University Press, Princeton

Dupuy P M (2002) L'unité de l'ordre juridique international. Cours général de droit international public. Recueil des cours - Académie de Droit International de La Haye 0169-5436 297:305

Easterly W (2006) The White Man's burden. Why the west's efforts to aid the rest have done so much ill and so little good. Penguin Books

Eaton J, Kortum S (2001) Trade in capital goods. Eur Econ Rev 45(7):1195–1235

Fantom N, Serajuddin U (2016) The World Bank's classification of countries by income. Policy Research Working Paper WPS7528. World Bank, Washington, D.C. http://documents.worldbank.org/curated/en/408581467988942234/pdf/WPS7528.pdf

Fitzmaurice G (1958) Third report ILC yearbook, vol II, p 43

Flanagan RJ (2006) Globalization and labor conditions. Working conditions and worker rights in a global economy. Oxford University Press, Oxford

Heil M, Selden T (2001) International trade intensity and carbon emissions: a cross-country econometric analysis. J Environ Dev 10(1):35–49

Helpman E (1997) R&D and productivity: the international connection. National Bureau of Economic Research (NBER) Working Paper 6101, Cambridge

Honkonen T (2009) The common but differentiated responsibility principle in multilateral environmental agreements. Kluwer Law International

Kar D, Cartwright-Smith D (2008) Illicit financial flows from developing countries: 2002–2006. Global Financial Integrity, Washington DC, December 2008

Kar D, Cartwright-Smith D (2010) Illicit financial flows from Africa: hidden resource for development. Global Financial Integrity, Washington DC

Kentikelenis A (2017) Structural adjustment and health: a conceptual framework and evidence on pathways. Soc Sci Med. https://doi.org/10.1016/j.socscimed.2017.02.021

Kentikelenis A, Stubbs T, King L (2016) IMF conditionality and development policy space, 1985–2014. Rev Int Polit Econ 23:543–582. https://doi.org/10.1080/09692290.2016.1174953

Khor M, Montes M F, Williams M, Yu III V P B (2017) Promoting sustainable development by addressing the impacts of climate change response measures on developing countries. South Centre Research Paper No. 81, October 2017

Lanz R, Miroudot S (2011) Intra-firm trade: patterns, determinants and policy implications. OECD Trade Policy Papers N° 114, OECD Publishing Papers, Paris

Moyo D (2010) Dead Aid. Why aid is not working and how there is another way for Africa. Penguin Books (reprint)

Mus JB (1998) Conflicts between treaties in international Law. Netherlands Int Law Rev 29:208–232

Ndikumana L, Boyce K J (2008) New estimates of capital flight from sub-Saharan African countries: linkages with external borrowing and policy options. University of Massachusetts, Amherst

Pauwelyn J (2004) Bridging fragmentation and unity: international law as a universe of inter-connected islands. Mich J Int Law 25:903–917

Pereira J (2017) Blended finance for development. Background paper prepared in support of the first session of the Intergovernmental Group of Experts on Financing for Development, Geneva, 8–10 November 2017

Rajamani L (2006) Differential treatment in international environmental law. Oxford University Press, New York

Reinert ES (2007) How rich countries got rich... and why poor countries stay poor. Constable, London

Rogoff MA (1994) The obligation to negotiate in international law: rules and realities. Mich J Int Law 16:141–185
Rousseau C (1932) De la compatibilité des norms juridiques contracdictoires dans l'ordre international. Revue générale de droit international public
Saiz I (2013) Resourcing rights: combating tax injustice from a human rights perspective. In: Nolan A, O'Connell R, Harvey C (eds) Human rights and public finance: budgets and the promotion of economic and social rights. Hart Publishing, Oxford
Salomon ME (2007) Global responsibility for human rights: world poverty and the development of international law. Oxford University Press, Oxford
Santarius T (2009) Climate and trade. Why climate change calls for fundamental reforms in world trade policies. Report authored by for the German NGO Forum on Environment and Development and Heinrich Böll Foundation
Sengupta A (2002) On the theory and practice of the right to development. Hum Rights Q 24 (4):837–889
Simma B (1985) Self-contained regimes. Netherlands Yearb Int Law 16:111–136
Simma B, Pulkowski D (2006) Of planets and the universe: self-contained regimes in international law. Eur J Int Law 17(3):483–529
Stiglitz JE (2006) Making globalization work. W.W. Norton & Co, New York
Stiglitz JE, Charlton A (2005) Fair trade for all. How trade can promote development. Oxford University Press
Stubbs T, Kentikelenis A (2017) Targeted social safeguards in the age of universal social protection: the IMF and health systems of low-income countries. Crit Public Health. doi.org/10.1080/09581596.2017.1340589
United Nations (2008) Handbook on the least developed country category: inclusion, graduation and special support measures. United Nations publication, Sales No. E.07.II.A.9. http://www.un.org/esa/analysis/devplan/cdppublications/2008cdphandbook.pdf
Vierdag EW (1988) The time of the conclusion of a multilateral treaty: Article 30 of the Vienna Convention on the law of treaties and related provisions. Br Yearb Int Law 59:92–111
Voigt C (2008) State responsibility for climate change damages. Nordic J Int Law 77:1–22